P9-APA-983

INTERNATIONAL
ECONOMICS

The Addison-Wesley Series in Economics

INTERNATIONAL ECONOMICS

Fifth Edition

Steven Husted
University of Pittsburgh

Michael Melvin
Arizona State University

Boston San Francisco New York
London Toronto Sydney Tokyo Singapore Madrid
Mexico City Munich Paris Cape Town Hong Kong Montreal

TO MARIE AND BETTINA

Acquisitions Editor: Victoria Warneck
Senior Production Supervisor: Juliet Silveri
Marketing Manager: Dara Lanier
Manufacturing Supervisor: Hugh Crawford
Cover and Text Designer: Regina Hagen
Publishing Services: Lachina Publishing Services

Cover photographs © Digital Vision/PictureQuest

Library of Congress Cataloging-in-Publication Data

Husted, Steven L.
    International economics / Steven Husted, Michael Melvin.--5th ed.
        p. cm.
    Includes bibliographical references and index.
    ISBN 0-321-07746-6
        1. International economic relations. 2. Commercial policy. 3. International finance.
4. United States--Commercial policy. I. Melvin, Michael, 1948–. II. Title.

HF1359. H87 2000
337--dc21   00-041631

2 3 4 5 6 7 8 9 10—MA—03 02 01 00

CONTENTS

PREFACE

At the beginning of the twenty-first century, international trade plays a larger role in the world economy than at any other time in history. We live at a time when many corporations are truly global and consumers have access to a wide variety of goods produced all over the world. Indeed, during the 1990s, trade in manufactures grew four times faster than overall world production. In addition, trade in services has also expanded considerably. Part of this growth is because many developing countries are adopting more market-based, outward-looking development strategies. Many countries in transition from centrally planned economies have chosen to follow similar policies. Another factor is the continued reduction in world trade barriers. New reductions are underway as signatory countries implement Uruguay Round commitments. Overseeing this process is the World Trade Organization (WTO) that began operations in 1995. The WTO administers existing trade agreements, settles trade disputes between member countries, and provides a forum for future trade negotiations. It has quickly become an effective institution in settling trade disputes. As such the WTO has become very controversial, especially with those opposed to the rapid globalization of commercial activity.

Recent years have also seen a number of changes in international financial arrangements. The foreign-exchange market continued to grow at record pace, with trading activity occurring around the clock and trading volume exceeding $1.5 trillion per day! Perhaps because the market grew so large, countries found it increasingly difficult to influence its behavior. Major bank mergers have eliminated some of the famous names of the past (Chemical Bank) and created mega-banks that are truly global giants. International investment continues to grow and now it is common for individual households to own mutual funds specializing in foreign markets so that a middle-income household may have an internationally-diversified portfolio. National economies are now more closely linked than ever, and developing an understanding of these links is crucial to interpreting domestic and foreign social, political, and economic developments.

As we have stated in previous editions of this book, our goal in writing this text is simple: We hope to provide the student with a guide to the study of international economics that is accessible, comprehensive, relevant, and up to date. Judging by the many favorable reviews we have received from students and professors who have used this book, we feel that we have been generally successful in accomplishing our goal. Our purpose remains unchanged. To that end, we have substantially revised this edition in order to cover all of the material discussed above as well as many other topics, such as the effect of trade on the quality and quantity of U.S. jobs, that have recently been the subject of substantial debate.

LEVEL OF PRESENTATION

We have sought to write a text that covers current developments in international economics but at the same time is accessible to students who may have had only one or two courses in the principles of economics. To that end, we have minimized mathematics and relegated more difficult extensions to appendixes. The book contains a wide range of helpful learning aids, including a marginal glossary that defines new concepts, boxed items and case studies that present "real-world" counterparts to the ideas being developed in the main text, and a set of exercises at the end of each chapter. Going beyond the text presentation, we have incorporated interesting and timely material from Internet Web sites into exercises that build upon chapter material. At the end of each chapter a WWW icon in the margin will identify a reference to the *International Economics* Web site, where Internet exercises may be found. The exercises allow a dynamic relevancy not possible in standard textbook approaches. In addition to these features, a *Study Guide* is available to accompany the book. This guide offers a variety of problems and questions aimed at helping the student explore and learn the text material.

COVERAGE AND EMPHASIS

To give the student a better feel for the issues discussed in the text, we have incorporated an extensive amount of data from the real world. For instance, Chapter 1 is devoted almost entirely to describing national economies and the patterns and directions of international trade. Other tables appear throughout the book. To every extent possible, we have sought to provide the most up-to-date statistics currently available.

Chapter 2 is one of the more unusual chapters to be found in a textbook on international economics. Its purpose is to provide a review of basic general equilibrium analysis, and, in particular, to introduce students to the logic and method of economic model building. The chapter begins with a straightforward analysis of the general equilibrium of a closed economy, using simple production possibility frontier diagrams. It then proceeds to the first description of what it means for an economy to engage in international trade. The next two chapters of the text detail the classical and Heckscher-Ohlin models of trade, using production possibility frontiers as the chief analytical tool. New to Chapter 4 is a presentation of the specific factors model.

Chapter 5 is devoted to empirical tests of the classical and HO trade models. It then goes on to deal briefly with new trade theories, including models involving imperfect competition and increasing returns to scale. Chapter 6 introduces a five chapter sequence of material on commercial policy with a discussion of tariffs. Strategic trade policy and protection of the environment as justifications for trade protection are discussed in Chapter 7. Chapter 8 provides considerable detail on U.S. trade policy, including trade policy case studies that deal with environmental issues, the enforcement of U.S. dumping laws, and a recent trade dispute with the European Union (EU) over bananas. Also in this chapter is an extended discussion of the Uruguay Round agreement and the WTO.

Chapter 9 is devoted entirely to the economics of regional trade agreements. The chapter begins with a standard discussion of the costs and benefits of such arrangements. It then turns to consider both NAFTA and the EU. Chapter 10 completes this section of the book with a treatment of trade and growth and international flows of factors of production.

Chapter 11 provides an introduction to international finance and introduces important concepts along with data. Chapter 12 covers the balance of payments and uses the national income accounts to illustrate the links between national saving, investment, and the current account. The description of the foreign exchange market in Chapter 13 goes well beyond the traditional detail found in other texts. A descripton of the 24-hour nature of the market, including local trading times and trading volumes, is included. Chapters 14 and 15 provide solid grounding in the fundamentals with links between prices and exchange rates and interest rates and exchange rates discussed in the context of current examples and data. The Chapter 16 discussion of international investment has been expanded in this edition to include a detailed analysis of international financial crises. Chapter 17 presents balance of payments theories. Theories of the exchange rate are presented in Chapter 18. Chapter 19 presents a history and current analysis of international monetary standards, including exchange rate target zones and currency boards. International banking and country risk analysis are covered in Chapter 20. The text concludes with Chapter 21 on open-economy macroeconomics. Throughout the text, examples and applications have been updated to current high-interest issues that engage the reader in real-world controversies.

ALTERNATIVE COURSE EMPHASES

The text is designed to provide sufficient flexibility to be used for a one-term survey of international economics or two separate terms devoted to a more comprehensive study of international trade and international finance. Realizing that individual instructors may have unique preferences regarding material to be presented, we offer the following suggestions:

- For a one-term overview of international economics: Chapters 1–4, 6–8, 11–15, and 19–20
- For a one-term course in international trade theory: Chapters 1–10
- For a one-term course in international finance: Chapters 11–21

An *Instructor's Manual* is available to accompany the text. It includes suggested answers to the end-of-chapter questions.

ACKNOWLEDGMENTS

No textbook can be written without imposing on friends and colleagues for comments, criticism, and ideas. We owe considerable debts to a number of people: Arsene Aka, Jim Cassing, Passcal Gauthier, John K. Hill, Ked Hogan, Douglas Irwin,

Ali Kutan, Jacquie Pomeroy, and Roy Ruffin. Special mention should go to Marie Connolly, Bettina Peiers, and Eugenio Dante Suarez, who read, edited, and proof-read a considerable portion of the text, and to Lawrence Officer, whose ideas about content and level of presentation were utilized heavily in the first part of the text.

Throughout the course of writing this text, we benefitted from the comments of external readers. Help with this edition was provided by Bassam Harik, Magnus Johansson, Byunglak Lee, Michael A. McPherson, David A. Riker, Daniel Ryan, Bansi L. Sawhey, John A. Shaw, Edward Tower, and Michael Veseth. The preparation of earlier additions was aided by the thoughtful comments of Richard V. Adkisson, Mohsen Bahmani-Oskooee, Lloyd B. Brown, Phillip J. Bryson, James H. Cassing, Steven Skeet Chang, Robert V. Cherneff, Addington Coppin, Satya P. Das, Zane Dennick-Ream, Lewis R. Gale, Panos Hatzipanayotou, Thu-Mai Ho-Kim, Bang Nam Jeon, Susan K. Jones, Yoonbai Kim, Denise Eby Konan, Kishore Kulkarni, William E. Laird, Chyi-Ing Lin, Joseph A. McKinney, Richard Milam, Michael H. Moffett, William E. Morgan, Douglas Nelson, John Neral, Walter G. Park, Susan Pozo, Andreas Savvides, Garry Brooks Stone, Harold R. Williams, Darrel Young, and Allan H. Zeman. We were not always able to incorporate all of their excellent suggestions, but they have added greatly to the final product. The editorial staff at Addison Wesley Longman, including Denise Clinton, Deb Lally, and Victoria Warneck, have made our task as pleasant as possible.

Finally, we owe a debt of gratitude to our families for supporting our efforts and to many former students in international economics classes who helped to shape our ideas regarding the appropriate methods and topics for both our classes and this text.

Steven Husted
Michael Melvin

ABOUT THE AUTHORS

Michael Melvin

Professor of Economics and Dean's Council Distinguished Scholar, Arizona State University. Co-editor, *Journal of International Money and Finance.* Ph.D., UCLA. Past experience includes Visiting Scholar: Federal Reserve Board and International Monetary Fund; and Visiting Professor: Kellogg Graduate School of Management, Northwestern University; Anderson Graduate School of Management, UCLA; Department of Economics, U.C. San Diego, and Pacific Asian Management Institute, University of Hawaii. Professor Melvin's research interests are in international finance, and he has published scholarly articles in *American Economic Review, Journal of Finance,* and other major journals.

Steven Husted

Professor of Economics and Associate Dean, Graduate Studies & Research, University of Pittsburgh. Ph.D., Michigan State University. Past experience includes Senior Staff Economist: Council of Economic Advisers; Visiting Scholar: International Monetary Fund; and Visiting Professor: Department of Economics and Research School of the Social Sciences, Australian National University; and Department of Economics, University of Strathclyde. Professor Husted's research interests are in international trade policy and international finance, and he has published scholarly articles in *Journal of Political Economy, Review of Economics and Statistics,* and other major journals.

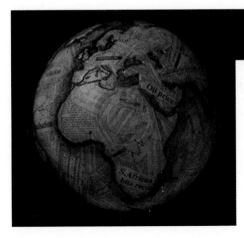

CHAPTER 1

An Introduction to

International Trade

TOPICS TO BE COVERED

National Production
Magnitude of International Trade
Trading Partners
Patterns of Trade Flows

KEY WORDS

Gross national product (GNP)
Gross domestic product (GDP)
Exports
Imports

Index of openness
Trade deficits
Trade surpluses

I nternational economists study fascinating questions. Does growing reliance on international trade lead to a loss of "good" jobs for Americans? Can U.S. firms compete against firms in low wage countries? What influence does the World Trade Organization (WTO) have over U.S. policy? Why does the United States have such a large trade deficit, and is this deficit harmful to the economy? What is the appropriate value of the dollar? In other words, international economists are concerned with a variety of real-world topics that appear in the evening news reports almost every day.

This book provides a comprehensive introduction to international economics. We discuss all of the issues just mentioned. We show you how economists go about investigating these issues. We provide you with a large amount of information on the extent and nature of international commercial transactions. Along the way we attempt to relate the many issues and concepts we encounter to real-world events. Finally, and most important, we attempt to provide you with a simple analytical tool kit that will allow you to study issues such as those mentioned in the preceding paragraph and to weigh future events as they occur.

Recall that when you took Principles of Economics, the course material was divided into two main parts: microeconomics and macroeconomics. In international economics in general, and in this book in particular, there is a similar division of material. The first ten chapters of this book deal with the theory of international trade (international microeconomics). Of central importance in these chapters is the international exchange of goods and services. Questions of particular interest include the following: Why do nations engage in international trade? What goods do nations trade? How does international trade affect the amount and distribution of jobs and the level of earnings in the economy? Should international trade be regulated by tariffs, quotas, or other barriers, and, if so, to what extent should the regulation occur? And how are countries affected by international flows of labor and capital? In addition to these questions, this part of the book discusses how trade policies are formulated in the United States and elsewhere and describes the various currently existing forms of trading arrangements between countries.

Chapters 11 through 21 are concerned with international finance (or international macroeconomics). The subject matter in these chapters tends to focus on the international exchange of financial assets. Issues that are studied include the balance of payments; the determination of exchange rates; the relationship between exchange rates, prices, and interest rates; international banking, debt, and risk; and the interaction of macroeconomic policies between various nations. Also discussed in these chapters are the evolution of the world's international monetary system and the role of international organizations, such as the International Monetary Fund, in today's international economy.*

The purpose of economics is to develop an explanation for the patterns of commercial transactions that we observe in the real world. International economics focuses its analysis on the commercial interactions between the countries of the

---

*For an extended introduction to international finance, see Chapter 11.

world. The goal of international economics is to fashion a theoretical framework that is sufficiently general to allow one to offer explanations of phenomena and to make predictions about the likely outcome of changes in the international environment. Thus, much of the discussion in this book is devoted to developing theories about economic behavior. But theorizing should not be done in a vacuum. It is important to know the facts before we begin. How important is international trade to the nations of the world? Which countries trade with which other countries? What goods do countries trade? The remainder of this chapter is devoted to presenting the factual answers to questions such as these.

CHARACTERISTICS OF NATIONAL ECONOMIES

There are over 190 countries in the world today. They come in all shapes and sizes. There are large countries with large populations (China, India) and large countries with small populations (Australia, Canada). There are small countries with large populations (Japan) and small countries with small populations (Jamaica, Singapore). No matter what their size, however, there are certain characteristics that are common to all. In each, for instance, there is economic activity. Goods and services are produced, exchanged, and consumed.

The extent of economic activity in a country can be measured in many ways. The two most common measures are the **gross national product (GNP)** and the **gross domestic product (GDP)** of a country. Both GNP and GDP provide estimates of the total value of sales of final goods and services for a given country. And, because sales of goods and services constitute income to those selling these products, GNP and GDP can also be thought of as indicators of total national income. The difference between GNP and GDP has to do with who is producing the goods, and where. Gross domestic product refers to production within a country, no matter whether the factors of production (e.g., labor and capital) are domestic or foreign. Gross national product refers to production by domestic factors, no matter where they are located. Thus, goods produced by Canadians working in factories in the United States would count as part of U.S. GDP and would also be part of Canadian GNP. For most countries there are only very small differences between GNP and GDP. That there is any difference at all is because some factors of production (labor, capital, etc.) are internationally mobile. In Chapter 10 we discuss some of the economic implications of international factor mobility.

A crude measure of the standard of living in a country is obtained by the ratio of that country's GNP (or GDP) to its population. This measure is known as the country's *income per capita,* or *per capita GNP (GDP).* In essence, it tells us how much each resident of a country would have if the value of a country's production were equally divided among all members of society. By this standard, some countries are low or middle income (even though some residents may be rich) while other countries are high income (even though some residents may be poor). In this book poorer countries are referred to as *developing countries.* Richer countries are identified as *developed* or *industrialized.*

Gross national product (GNP)
The value of final goods and services produced by domestic factors of production.

Gross domestic product (GDP)
The value of final goods and services produced within a country.

Exports
Goods sold by economic agents located in one country to economic agents located in another.

Imports
Goods purchased by economic agents located in one country from economic agents located in another.

Index of openness
A measure of the importance of international trade to an economy, calculated as the ratio of exports over total domestic production.

All countries participate in international trade. That is, some goods and services produced within every country are sold to economic agents (individuals, firms, governments) in other countries; these products are known as **exports.** Some goods and services consumed within a country have been purchased from economic agents in other countries; these goods are known as **imports.**

Countries differ in how much they participate in international trade. A measure of this participation (again, a very crude measure) is given by the ratio of exports to GDP (or GNP) multiplied by 100. This measure is known as the **index of openness**. In general, this number will vary between 0 and 100, although values greater than 100 are possible.* Countries with high values of this index trade a lot with the rest of the world and are said to be relatively *open.* Countries with low values of the index are said to be relatively *closed,* because international trade is only a small part of their economic activity.

To understand better the concepts we have presented so far, let's consider some numbers from the real world. In Table 1.1 we display data for a large set of countries. Information is presented on country size in terms of population and area. Also shown are data on GNP per capita (measured in two ways), indices of openness (exports of goods and services as a percentage of GDP) for 1980 and 1998, and merchandise trade figures (imports and exports for 1997).

Let's explore some of the facts contained in the table. First, note that for each country category, the data are arranged by ascending order of GNP per capita. The poorest countries of the world tend to be located in Africa and Asia. The richest countries tend to be the industrialized countries of Western Europe, North America, and the Pacific Rim. Except for China and India, physical size (land area) and population size appear to have little role in explaining income per capita.

According to the numbers in column 3 of the table, most of the low- and middle-income countries are desperately poor. GNP per capita in these countries is often less than $500, compared with an average GNP per capita in excess of $23,000 in the high-income countries. In China, for instance, per capita GNP was calculated to be $750 in 1998. You may wonder how anyone could survive for one year with such a low income level. Part of the answer to this question lies in the fact that differences in productivity levels and government policies mean that individuals in these countries pay much lower prices for many of the goods and services they consume than people pay in the United States or other developed countries. For example, in the mid-1980s residents of Shanghai, China, could rent a one-bedroom apartment for $3 per month. Hence, standard GNP numbers are not directly comparable across

---

*A value greater than 100 means that the country's exports are bigger than its overall level of production (GDP or GNP). Such a situation could occur if much of the economic activity of the country in question involved the assembly and export of final products made from imported raw or partially assembled materials. The value in excess of 100 comes about from the fact that output is (always) measured in terms of value added—the value of capital and labor services devoted in this case to the assembly of goods—while exports are measured in terms of the total value of goods—including the value of the imported parts. Clearly, in such circumstances it is quite likely for exports to be greater than value added.

TABLE 1.1   Basic Characteristics of Selected Countries

	1998 Population (millions)	Area (1000 sq. km.)	GNP per Capita 1998 ($)	GNP per Capita PPP estimate ($)	GNP per Capita Avg. Yearly % Growth 1990–98	Index of Openness 1980	Index of Openness 1998	Goods & Services Exports 1997 (million $)	Goods & Services Imports 1997 (million $)
Low-income economies									
Ethiopia	61	1,104	100	500	2.3	11	16	1,017	1,683
Burundi	7	28	140	620	−5.9	9	6	96	139
Sierra Leone	5	72	140	390	−7.5	18	22	91	160
Niger	10	1,267	190	830	−2.0	25	16	300	441
Malawi	11	118	200	730	0.8	25	33	672	1,269
Nepal	23	147	210	1,090	2.0	12	23	1,295	1,855
Mozambique	17	802	210	850	3.1	11	12	500	1,005
Tanzania	32	945	210	490	−0.4	n.a.	16	1,200	1,961
Chad	7	1,284	230	n.a.	1.1	17	17	271	563
Rwanda	8	26	230	690	−5.5	14	5	152	488
Burkina Faso	11	274	240	1,020	0.8	10	14	298	654
Mali	11	1,240	250	720	0.5	15	24	642	896
Madagascar	15	587	260	900	−1.9	13	21	755	1,032
Central African Republic	3	623	300	1,290	−0.9	25	16	171	241
Nigeria	121	924	300	820	−0.7	29	23	15,994	14,213
Uganda	21	241	320	1,170	3.9	19	10	825	1,651
Togo	4	57	330	1,390	−1.1	51	34	709	836
Kenya	29	580	330	1,130	−0.9	28	26	2,994	3,771
Bangladesh	126	144	350	1,100	2.9	4	14	5,096	7,677
Benin	6	113	380	1,250	1.3	23	24	524	673
Ghana	18	239	390	1,610	1.1	8	27	1,655	2,640
Haiti	8	28	410	1,250	−4.9	22	8	218	810
Mauritania	3	1,026	410	1,660	1.0	37	40	407	414
India	980	3,288	430	1,700	4.1	6	12	44,102	59,236
Pakistan	132	796	480	1,560	1.3	12	16	9,956	14,677
Senegal	9	197	530	1,710	0.0	27	32	1,281	1,557
Guinea	7	246	540	1,760	2.0	n.a.	22	741	834
Cameroon	14	475	610	1,810	−2.6	28	27	2,443	2,041
Zimbabwe	12	391	610	2,150	−0.6	23	45	3,059	3,692
Indonesia	204	1,905	680	2,790	3.9	34	28	63,238	62,830
Congo, Rep.	3	342	690	1,430	−2.2	60	63	1,800	1,368
Cote d'Ivoire	14	322	700	1,730	0.4	35	43	4,927	3,693
Honduras	6	112	730	2,140	0.3	36	42	2,191	2,511
China	1,239	9,597	750	3,220	9.9	6	22	207,251	166,754
GROUP AVERAGE			379	1,279	0.2	22	24	11,084	10,714
Middle-income economies									
Sri Lanka	19	66	810	n.a.	3.9	32	36	5,514	6,569
Papua New Guinea	5	463	890	2,700	3.1	43	56	2,557	2,407
Bolivia	8	1,099	1,000	2,820	1.5	25	15	1,362	2,049
Philippines	75	300	1,050	3,540	0.7	24	56	40,365	50,477
Bulgaria	8	111	1,230	n.a.	−2.5	36	61	6,277	5,730

(Continued)

TABLE 1.1   *Basic Characteristics of Selected Countries* (Continued)

	1998 Population (millions)	Area (1000 sq. km.)	GNP per Capita			Index of Openness		Goods & Services	
			1998 ($)	PPP estimate ($)	Avg. Yearly % Growth 1990–98	1980	1998	Exports 1997	Imports 1997 (million $)
Middle-income economies (*continued*)									
Morocco	28	447	1,250	3,120	0.0	17	28	9,510	10,627
Egypt	61	1,001	1,290	3,130	1.9	31	17	16,171	18,296
Romania	22	238	1,390	3,970	−0.1	35	24	9,853	12,448
Jordan	5	89	1,520	3,230	0.2	40	50	3,572	5,186
Ecuador	12	284	1,530	4,630	0.5	25	25	6,000	5,787
Algeria	30	2,382	1,550	4,380	−1.4	34	29	14,779	8,568
Guatemala	11	109	1,640	4,070	1.2	22	17	3,187	4,193
Jamaica	3	11	1,680	3,210	−0.9	51	49	3,192	4,005
Paraguay	5	407	1,760	3,650	−0.2	15	45	4,343	4,960
Dominican Republic	8	49	1,770	4,700	3.4	19	32	7,060	7,780
El Salvador	6	21	1,850	2,850	2.9	34	24	2,706	3,885
Tunisia	9	164	2,050	5,160	2.4	40	42	8,081	8,644
Thailand	61	513	2,200	5,840	6.0	24	47	72,415	72,437
Russia	147	17,075	2,300	3,950	−6.9	n.a.	27	102,196	90,065
Peru	25	1,285	2,460	n.a.	3.9	22	12	8,356	10,842
Colombia	41	1,139	2,600	7,500	2.0	16	17	15,861	18,784
Costa Rica	4	51	2,780	6,620	1.6	26	43	4,478	4,666
South Africa	41	1,221	2,880	6,990	−0.7	36	29	35,440	34,626
Panama	3	76	3,080	6,940	2.3	51	36	8,316	8,649
Turkey	63	775	3,160	n.a.	2.3	5	25	52,004	56,536
Venezuela	23	912	3,500	8,190	−0.5	29	17	25,120	18,282
Malaysia	22	330	3,600	6,990	4.9	58	118	92,897	91,521
Slovak Republic	5	49	3,700	n.a.	0.3	n.a.	56	10,959	12,367
Poland	39	323	3,900	6,740	4.3	28	25	39,717	46,367
Mexico	96	1,958	3,970	8,190	0.5	11	31	121,831	122,424
Hungary	10	93	4,510	n.a.	0.1	39	45	24,514	25,067
Brazil	166	8,547	4,570	6,160	1.7	9	7	60,256	79,817
Chile	15	757	4,810	12,890	6.1	23	25	20,608	22,218
Czech Republic	10	79	5,040	n.a.	−0.1	n.a.	58	29,868	32,713
Uruguay	3	177	6,180	9,480	3.1	15	22	4,256	4,450
Hong Kong	7	1	6,755	22,000	2.1	90	125	228,877	231,485
Korea	46	99	7,970	12,270	5.1	34	38	164,920	171,300
Argentina	36	2,780	8,970	10,200	3.8	5	9	29,382	34,968
GROUP AVERAGE			2,979	5,161	1.5	30	37	34,126	35,558
High-income economies									
Portugal	10	92	10,690	14,380	2.2	25	31	32,339	40,684
Greece	11	132	11,650	13,010	1.5	16	15	14,863	25,601
Spain	39	506	14,080	16,060	1.7	16	26	148,357	142,478
New Zealand	4	271	14,700	15,840	1.5	30	29	18,224	18,269
Israel	6	21	15,940	17,310	1.9	44	32	30,320	38,810
Ireland	4	70	18,340	18,340	6.8	48	76	61,447	51,711
Canada	31	9,971	20,020	24,050	0.8	28	41	247,438	236,225
Italy	58	301	20,250	20,200	1.0	22	27	310,550	261,884

	1998 Population (millions)	Area (1000 sq. km.)	GNP per Capita		Avg. Yearly % Growth 1990–98	Index of Openness		Goods & Services	
			1998 ($)	PPP estimate ($)		1980	1998	Exports 1997	Imports 1997
								(million $)	
High-income economies (*continued*)									
Australia	19	7,741	20,300	20,130	2.3	19	21	83,703	81,891
United Kingdom	59	245	21,400	20,640	1.8	27	29	375,033	375,128
Finland	5	338	24,110	20,270	1.5	33	40	48,228	37,976
Netherlands	16	41	24,760	21,620	1.9	51	56	216,530	193,107
France	59	552	24,940	22,320	1.0	22	24	365,342	319,781
Belgium	10	33	25,380	23,480	1.3	57	73	185,415	173,865
Sweden	9	450	25,620	19,480	0.7	29	44	100,989	84,779
Germany	82	357	25,850	20,810	1.1	n.a.	27	590,984	558,835
Austria	8	84	26,850	22,740	1.3	36	42	88,266	91,446
United States	270	9,364	29,340	29,340	1.8	10	12	937,434	1,043,473
Singapore	3	1	30,060	28,620	5.8	215	187	156,252	144,168
Japan	126	378	32,380	23,180	1.0	14	9	478,542	431,094
Denmark	5	43	33,260	23,830	2.4	33	34	63,680	57,971
Norway	4	324	34,330	24,290	3.3	43	41	63,213	52,286
Switzerland	7	41	40,080	26,620	−0.4	35	40	120,696	107,187
GROUP AVERAGE			22,962	21,190	1.9	39	42	206,947	200,006

NOTE: n.a. = not available

SOURCE: World Bank, *World Development Report 1999/2000,* various tables (New York: Oxford University Press, 1999).

countries. That is, when national GNP numbers are converted to U.S. dollars using market exchange rates, they do not provide a true picture of the standard of living in that country. Recently, several international agencies have begun publishing new measures of standards of living that take into account international differences in prices paid for goods and services. In essence what these numbers do is answer the question, How many dollars would it take in the United States to buy what the average citizen of a country can buy in his or her country at prevailing local prices? At the heart of these measures is an exchange rate concept known as purchasing power parity (PPP); 1998 values of per capita GNP based on PPP exchange rates appear in column 4.* Notice that for the poorest countries in the table, the numbers in column 4 tend to be substantially larger than those in column 3. This indicates that international differences in average standards of living, while still quite large, are not as extreme as the column 3 numbers would seem to indicate. For instance, the conventional measure of China's per capita GNP is $750 per year. Using the PPP measure, the standard of living of the typical Chinese citizen is $3,220.

---

*For more on the concept of purchasing power parity, see Chapter 14. For more on the process of calculating GNP measures using purchasing power parity exchange rates, see Samuel Brittan, "Some Common Sense on US and China," *Financial Times,* January 10, 1994, 12.

Economic Growth

For some of the countries in Table 1.1, the 1990s represented an era of deteriorating standards of living. This was especially true for the low-income and middle-income countries in Africa and several middle-income countries in Eastern Europe. In several of these countries, per capita GNP fell by more than 5 percent per year (see column 5).* However, not all developing countries saw their incomes fall over this period. Growth experience was uneven. In the poorest countries, growth rates varied considerably, with both large negative average annual rates (as low as −7.5 percent in Sierra Leone) and large positive rates (almost 10 percent in China). Indeed, the most highly populated of the low-income countries (China, India, Indonesia, Pakistan, and Bangladesh) all experienced positive growth over the decade.

Among the low-income economies, the most severe negative growth rates between 1990 and 1998 occurred in Sierra Leone, Burundi, Rwanda, Haiti, Cameroon, the Congo, and Niger, where per capita GNP fell at rates of 2 percent or more per year. Middle-income countries with similar problems were two transition economies, Bulgaria and Russia. Negative growth in per capita income means that, on average, each individual in society has less income than he or she had in the previous year. A variety of factors can produce sustained periods of declining standards of living. In some countries falling per capita GNP is brought on by war (or civil war) in which factories and economic infrastructure (e.g., harbors, public utilities, railroads, airports) are destroyed. In other countries, it may result from prolonged falls in the prices of commodities (e.g., coffee, copper, cocoa, sugar, petroleum) upon which these economies depend; these price falls may be coupled with misguided government policies aimed at encouraging rapid industrialization. In some countries, negative growth may simply reflect a stagnant economy combined with high population growth. Finally, in the case of the economies of Eastern Europe, negative growth is the result of the dismantling of various inefficient industries and consequent large-scale unemployment as these countries undertake the transition of their economies into market-based economies. No matter the cause, negative growth, especially over long periods, is symptomatic of terrible economic distress.

In contrast, other countries have exhibited strong growth over the same period. Several of these are located along the Pacific Rim. They are China, Indonesia, Malaysia, Thailand, and two of the newly industrialized countries (NICs), Korea and

---

*Column 5 reports percentage changes in the ratio of GNP to population. Throughout this text, we will use the notation "^" to denote the percentage change in a variable. So that, for instance, $\hat{x}$ denotes the percentage change in x. If x equals the ratio of two numbers, such as per capita GNP ($x = y/z$ where $y =$ GNP and $z =$ population), there is a simple approximation rule that allows one to determine the rate of growth of x. The rule is $\hat{x} = \hat{y} - \hat{z}$. We will make use of this approximation from time to time. In this particular circumstance, the formula states that growth in per capita GNP depends positively on GNP growth but negatively on population growth. If, for instance, GNP is constant but population is growing at 3 percent then per capita GNP will be falling at 3 percent.

Singapore.* Other countries with strong growth (in excess of 3.5 percent per year) over this period include Uganda, India, Argentina, Sri Lanka, Peru, Chile, Poland, and Ireland. In addition to Singapore and Ireland, the economies of other high-income countries also did quite well over the period 1990–1998, with per capita GNP growing at an average annual rate of 1.9 percent.

Why is there a difference in growth rates both within various country groups and between low-income developing economies and high-income developed economies? Economies grow over time because their endowments of factors of production (e.g., labor, capital, and technology) grow, not only in number but in quality. A recent study argues that the main engine of growth is the accumulation of knowledge and skills by workers.[†] This growth in human capital takes place in schools, in laboratories, and on the job. Investment in plant and equipment that increases physical capital is also important. But, what appears to be crucial is that workers function in an environment that requires them to face new challenges and thus to acquire new skills. Such an environment is provided in countries where exports represent a large share of output. The twin challenges of producing goods that will be desired in the global market and competing with producers from other countries for this market places a premium on growth in inventiveness and the continuing acquisition of entrepreneurial, managerial, and technical skills. Without the pressure from outside competitive forces, acquisition of human capital, and thus overall economic growth, may be slow. Hence, it is no surprise that the faster growing countries in Table 1.1 tend, on average, to be more open.

International Trade

The importance of international trade for the countries of the world differs considerably. In columns 6 and 7, we present values of the index of openness for the years 1980 and 1998. Let's consider the values for 1980 first. For most countries, the ratio of exports to GDP was between 10 and 40. In other words, for most countries exports accounted for between 10 and 40 percent of GDP. The average for all of the countries reported was 29.

The most open country of all was Singapore, with a value of 215 (i.e., exports were more than double its GDP!). Other highly open economies included Hong Kong (index of openness = 90), the Congo (60), Malaysia (58), Belgium (57), Togo (51), Jamaica (51), Panama (51), and the Netherlands (51). The most closed economies included Brazil (9), China (6), India (6), and the United States (10). This pattern of behavior for the index of openness points out the fact that larger economies (as measured by area and population) tend to be more closed, while

---

*The reader should note that even though China, Indonesia, Malaysia, Thailand, Korea, and Singapore had strong growth in GNP per capita over the period 1990–1998, each was adversely affected by the Asian financial crisis that began in 1997. In several, especially Indonesia, Thailand, and Korea, GNP per capita fell sharply in 1997 and 1998. For more on the financial crisis that hit these economies, see Chapter 20.

†The argument presented in the remainder of this paragraph is developed more completely in Robert E. Lucas, Jr., "Making a Miracle," *Econometrica* (1993).

smaller economies tend to be more open. The commonsense explanation of this fact is that smaller economies tend not to be able to produce the many types of products that people want to consume. Thus, there is a need for exports, which can be sold to other countries in exchange for goods not available domestically. Larger countries are better able to diversify their production, especially if these countries possess a wide variety of resources and large endowments of various factors of production.

Between 1980 and 1998, most countries became more open. The average value of the index of openness rose from 29 to 33. As with economic growth, however, changes in openness differed considerably across income groups. On average, low-income economies remained the most closed.

Singapore (187), Hong Kong (125), and Malaysia (118) remained among the most open. Other countries with export levels at least 50 percent of GDP included several in Europe—the Slovak Republic (56), Belgium (73), Ireland (76), Bulgaria (61), the Czech Republic (58), and the Netherlands (56)—and several African and Asian economies—Jordan (50), the Congo (63), the Philippines (56), and Papua New Guinea (56).

In general, countries that were closed in 1980 tended to be much more open in 1998. China's index rose from 6 to 22, Paraguay's from 15 to 45; and Turkey's from 5 to 25. By contrast, India (12), Brazil (7), Japan (9), and the United States (12) remained relatively closed. It is interesting to note that even though the United States and Japan were two of the most closed economies according to the index of openness, they ranked first and third in the value of their exports in 1997 (see column 8). This illustrates the massive size of these two economies relative to other countries in the world. Even though the United States and Japan sell enormous amounts of goods and services on world markets, their exports are small relative to overall economic activity, and hence their indices of openness are very low.

The growth in the average level of openness is indicative of the fact that international trade has become increasingly important for the world economy. Consider Figure 1.1. There we plot total exports and commodity output (world GDP), measured in real (volume) terms, between 1950 and 1997. In order to preserve space, each series of levels has been converted into an index number that equals 100 in 1950. As the plot shows, output and exports expanded at roughly the same rates between 1950 and 1960. Beginning in the early 1960s, world exports began to rise much more rapidly than output. In 1973 world exports had risen 500 percent over their level in 1950, while world output was about 200 percent higher. By 1989 world exports were 1,000 percent higher than in 1950, while world output had risen more than 400 percent.* As the figure shows, world trade exploded in the 1990s. From 1990 to 1997, world exports rose by almost 60 percent. During the same period, world output rose by 14 percent.

What has caused this explosion of world trade? There is no simple answer to the question. One factor that has certainly played an important role has been the reduction in barriers to international trade that has occurred during this period. Barriers

---

* Not included in the export statistics are levels of international trade in commercial services.

FIGURE 1.1   *World exports and output in real terms, 1950–1997.*

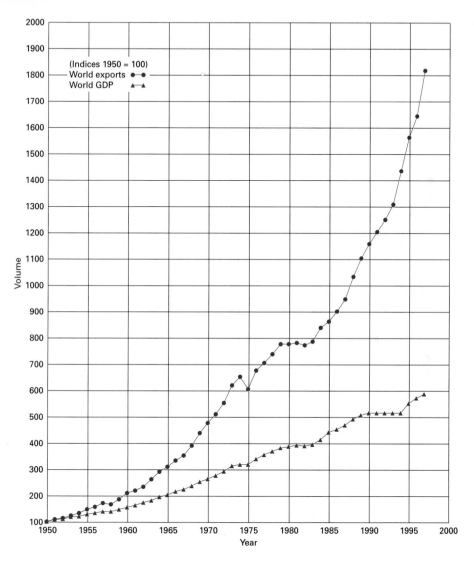

SOURCE: GATT, International Trade (various volumes).

to trade include transportation and communication costs. With improvements in technology in these areas, such as container ships, supertankers, and satellite telecommunications networks, it is now much easier for sellers in one country to contact consumers in another and to deliver goods to them in a timely fashion.

Barriers to trade also include government-imposed limits on trade, including tariffs and quotas on imports and exports. During the past 40 years, governments around the world, especially in industrialized economies, have entered into a series of multilateral agreements to lower government-imposed barriers to trade. Some of these agreements have been between small groups of countries, such as the formation in 1957 of what is now called the European Union (EU), which has brought virtual free trade in manufactured goods to Western Europe. Other agreements, such as the tariff reduction agreements that were reached in the Kennedy Round talks held in the 1960s and the Tokyo Round talks held in the 1970s, have been between a much broader set of countries. These agreements resulted in two successive cuts of over 30 percent in tariff levels of the major industrialized countries. In Chapters 6 and 7 we discuss how tariffs and other policies affect international trade. In Chapters 8 and 9 we describe this movement to lower trade barriers as well as the creation of several other regional trade agreements and current U.S. trade policy measures.*

Columns 8 and 9 of Table 1.1 provide data on exports and imports of the various countries listed in the table. A quick comparison of the group averages of the two columns suggests that *on average* there is a rough equality between exports and imports. That is, for some countries (during some years) exports are higher than imports, and vice versa in the remaining cases. However, looking over broader groups of countries for one year or the average trade flows of a typical country over several years (this is not shown in the table), exports and imports have a tendency to balance out. This rough equality between exports and imports is no accident. It illustrates that the revenue earned from selling exports is the primary means countries have for purchasing imports. Without sufficient export sales, imports can be purchased by borrowing. And just as individuals cannot borrow indefinitely, neither can countries. Thus, in some years countries will have to export more than they import in order to repay past debts or to build up assets that can be used in future years to purchase imports.

Trade deficits and surpluses

A country has a trade deficit (surplus) if its imports (exports) exceed its exports (imports).

Countries whose imports exceed exports are said to run **trade deficits**. The magnitude of the deficit provides an approximation of the amount of borrowing that a country has undertaken in order to purchase its imports. Countries with higher levels of exports than imports are said to run **trade surpluses**. The size of a country's trade surplus offers a measure of the amount by which that country has reduced its debt to foreigners or expanded its asset holdings. The trade balance is one measure of a country's balance of payments. In Chapter 12, we will discuss measures of the balance of payments in more detail.

As previously noted, in 1997 the United States was the world's largest exporter. It was also the world's largest importer and had the world's largest trade deficit. In 1997, Japan had the world's largest trade surplus, although only a few years earlier, in 1980, it had experienced a trade deficit. In 1997, Japan was the world's third largest exporter, following the United States and Germany. The remainder of the top ten exporters in 1997 were the United Kingdom, France, Italy, Canada, Hong Kong, the Netherlands, and Belgium.

---

*For a statistical analysis of some of the factors that have caused trade to rise faster than output, see Andrew Rose, "Why Has Trade Grown Faster than Income?" *International Finance Discussion Papers* (Washington, D.C.: Board of Governors of the Federal Reserve System, November 1990).

THE DIRECTION OF INTERNATIONAL TRADE

We have established that international trade is on the rise. Has trade expanded for all countries at an equal rate? Which countries trade with each other? Have these patterns changed over time? We turn now to addressing these questions. Figure 1.2 provides data on the geographic distribution of international trade by region for 1965 and 1997 as well as the overall size of export flows in these two years. Trade is measured in billions of U.S. dollars. Exports from six regions are shown in the figure. These regions include both groups of industrialized countries (e.g., the United States and Canada and the EU) and groups of developing countries (e.g., Latin America, Africa, and the Middle East). Asia includes three traditional industrialized countries—Japan, Australia, and New Zealand, several newly industrialized countries—Hong Kong, Korea, and Singapore, and a number of developing countries, including China, India, Indonesia, and Pakistan.

The data in the figure offer a number of stylized facts about trade patterns.* First, they confirm that industrialized countries account for the bulk of world trade. In 1965, the United States, Canada, and the 15 countries of the EU produced 63 percent of world exports. If we include the exports of Australia, Japan, and New Zealand, industrialized country exports made up 70 percent of world exports during that year.† In 1997, the exports of these 20 countries constituted 63 percent of the world total.

Not only are industrialized countries the largest exporters in the world, but the data indicate they are also the largest importers. The United States, Canada, and the EU served as primary markets for the exports of all regions in both years.

A remarkable feature of the figure is the growth in importance of Asia as a producer of exports. The value of world exports was 34 times higher in 1997 than it was in 1965, but exports from Asia in 1997 were 77 times greater in value terms than they had been in 1965. The share of Asian exports in total world trade rose from 12 percent to 28 percent in 32 years. As noted previously, the countries chiefly responsible for this phenomenal growth were China, Japan, and the NICs.

While Asia was growing in importance as a producer of exports, Latin America and Africa saw their positions erode. Latin America's share of world exports declined from 7 percent to 5 percent. Africa's share fell from almost 5 percent to about 2 percent. North America's export share also fell over this period, from more than 20 percent to about 16 percent.

Table 1.2 lists the major trading partners of a selected set of countries for the year 1997. For each country, its top 10 trading partners in terms of merchandise exports are presented. The table reveals several common patterns. First, the United

---

*A stylized fact (or empirical regularity) is a pattern that is observed in real-world data on a regular basis. For instance, the regular occurrence that young and old people tend to spend more than they earn while middle-aged people save is a stylized fact of consumption behavior.
†The export levels for these three countries are included in the exports of Asia. In 1965, they totaled $12.5 billion, of which Japan's share was $8 billion. In 1997, the exports of these countries totaled $498 billion; Japan's share that year was $421 billion.

FIGURE 1.2 *Geographic pattern of merchandise trade: 1965 and 1997.*

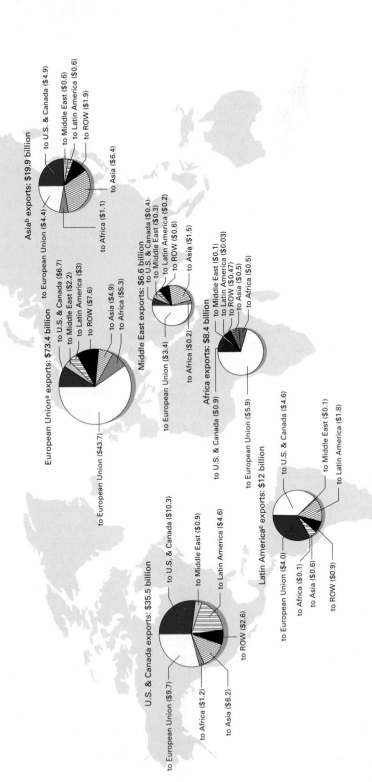

1965 World exports: $162.2 billion

Asia[b] exports: $19.9 billion
to U.S. & Canada ($4.9)
to Middle East ($0.6)
to Latin America ($0.6)
to ROW ($1.9)
to European Union ($4.4)
to Africa ($1.1)
to Asia ($6.4)

European Union[a] exports: $73.4 billion
to U.S. & Canada ($6.7)
to Middle East ($2.2)
to Latin America ($3)
to ROW ($7.6)
to Asia ($4.9)
to Africa ($5.3)
to European Union ($43.7)

Middle East exports: $6.6 billion
to U.S. & Canada ($0.4)
to Middle East ($0.3)
to Latin America ($0.2)
to ROW ($0.6)
to Asia ($1.5)
to European Union ($3.4)
to Africa ($0.2)

Africa exports: $8.4 billion
to Middle East ($0.1)
to Latin America ($0.03)
to ROW ($0.47)
to Asia ($0.5)
to Africa ($0.5)
to U.S. & Canada ($0.9)
to European Union ($5.9)

U.S. & Canada exports: $35.5 billion
to U.S. & Canada ($10.3)
to Middle East ($0.9)
to Latin America ($4.6)
to ROW ($2.6)
to Asia ($6.2)
to Africa ($1.2)
to European Union ($9.7)

Latin America[c] exports: $12 billion
to U.S. & Canada ($4.6)
to Middle East ($0.1)
to Latin America ($1.8)
to ROW ($0.9)
to Asia ($0.6)
to Africa ($0.1)
to European Union ($4.0)

ROW exports: $6.4 billion [d]

[a]European Union: Austria, Belgium, Denmark, Finland, France, Germany, Greece, Ireland, Italy, Luxembourg, Netherlands, Portugal, Spain, Sweden, United Kingdom.
[b]Asia includes Australia and New Zealand.
[c]Latin America includes Mexico.
[d] ROW: Rest of World.

FIGURE 1.2 Geographic pattern of merchandise trade (Continued)

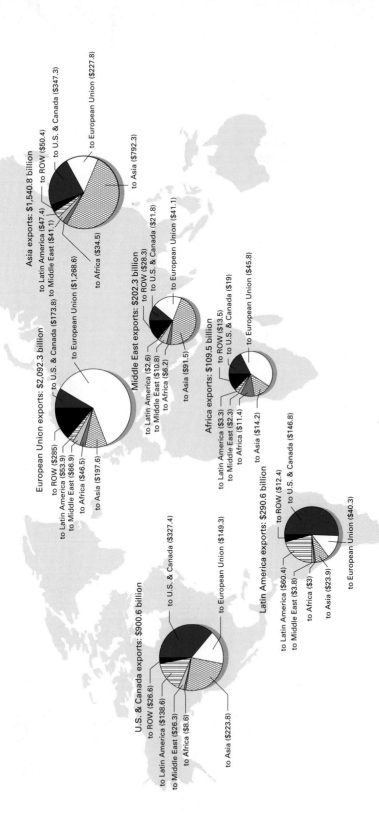

1997 World exports: $5,527.9 billion

Asia exports: $1,540.8 billion
to Latin America ($47.4) — to ROW ($50.4)
to U.S. & Canada ($173.8) to Middle East ($41.1) — to U.S. & Canada ($347.3)
to European Union ($1,268.6) — to European Union ($227.8)
to Africa ($34.5) to Asia ($792.3)

European Union exports: $2,092.3 billion
to ROW ($285)
to Latin America ($53.9)
to Middle East ($66.9)
to Africa ($46.5)
to Asia ($197.6)

Middle East exports: $202.3 billion
to Latin America ($2.6) — to ROW ($28.3)
to Middle East ($10.8) — to U.S. & Canada ($21.8)
to Africa ($6.2) — to European Union ($41.1)
to Asia ($91.5)

Africa exports: $109.5 billion
to Latin America ($3.3) — to ROW ($13.5)
to Middle East ($2.3) — to U.S. & Canada ($19)
to Africa ($11.4) — to European Union ($45.8)
to Asia ($14.2)

U.S. & Canada exports: $900.6 billion
to U.S. & Canada ($327.4)
to ROW ($26.6)
to Latin America ($138.6)
to Middle East ($26.3)
to Africa ($8.6)
to Asia ($223.8)
to European Union ($149.3)

Latin America exports: $290.6 billion
to Latin America ($60.4) — to ROW ($12.4)
to Middle East ($3.8) — to U.S. & Canada ($146.8)
to Africa ($3)
to Asia ($23.9)
to European Union ($40.3)

ROW exports: $391.8 billion [a]

[a]ROW: Rest of World

SOURCE: *International Monetary Fund, Direction of Trade Statistics Yearbook* (Washington, D.C.: International Monetary Fund, Bureau of Statistics).

TABLE 1.2	*Top Ten Trading Partners of Selected Countries, 1997*

(PERCENTAGE OF TOTAL MERCHANDISE EXPORTS)

United States		United Kingdom		France	
Canada	21.83	United States	12.55	Germany	15.49
Mexico	10.38	Germany	10.90	United Kingdom	9.87
Japan	9.55	France	8.68	Italy	9.07
United Kingdom	5.29	Netherlands	7.39	Belgium-Luxembourg	7.86
Korea	3.65	Ireland	5.02	Spain	7.83
Germany	3.56	Italy	4.38	United States	6.35
Taiwan	2.97	Belgium-Luxembourg	4.34	Netherlands	4.59
Netherlands	2.88	Spain	3.59	Switzerland	3.45
Singapore	2.57	Japan	2.47	Japan	1.69
France	2.41	Sweden	2.33	Portugal	1.38

Germany		Japan		Canada	
France	10.66	United States	28.12	United States	83.24
United States	8.63	Taiwan	6.55	Japan	3.43
United Kingdom	8.45	Hong Kong	6.49	United Kingdom	1.27
Italy	7.37	Korea	6.20	Korea	0.94
Netherlands	7.00	P.R. of China	5.15	Germany	0.89
Belgium-Luxembourg	5.83	Singapore	4.82	P.R. of China	0.75
Austria	5.18	Germany	4.27	Netherlands	0.56
Switzerland	4.54	Thailand	3.47	Hong Kong	0.56
Spain	3.74	Malaysia	3.44	France	0.52
Poland	2.33	United Kingdom	3.28	Italy	0.52

Mexico		Brazil		India	
United States	85.60	United States	17.44	United States	19.22
Canada	1.99	Argentina	13.54	United Kingdom	6.01
Japan	1.09	Netherlands	7.42	Hong Kong	5.71
Spain	0.82	Japan	5.75	Japan	5.41
Chile	0.72	Germany	4.82	Germany	5.11
Germany	0.63	Belgium-Luxembourg	2.78	United Arab Emirates	4.20
United Kingdom	0.63	Paraguay	2.60	Belgium-Luxembourg	3.30
Brazil	0.63	United Kingdom	2.41	Italy	3.00
Venezuela	0.63	Chile	2.23	Singapore	2.70
Argentina	0.45	France	2.23	Netherlands	2.40

Singapore		Egypt		Russia	
United States	18.44	United States	11.54	Ukraine	8.55
Malaysia	17.48	Italy	11.28	Germany	7.72
Hong Kong	8.86	Israel	7.95	United States	5.94
Japan	7.02	Germany	6.92	Belarus	5.46
Thailand	4.63	Netherlands	6.67	Netherlands	5.46
Taiwan	4.47	Greece	4.62	P.R. of China	4.75
Korea	3.67	France	3.85	Switzerland	4.39
United Kingdom	3.35	Singapore	3.85	Italy	4.28
P.R. of China	3.27	Saudi Arabia	3.59	United Kingdom	3.33
Germany	2.87	Turkey	2.56	Finland	3.33

SOURCE: *International Monetary Fund, Direction of Trade Statistics Yearbook* (Washington, D.C.: International Monetary Fund, Bureau of Statistics, 1996).

States is the major trading partner for many countries. This reflects the size of the U.S. economy and the high income levels found in America relative to other markets in the world. Second, there is considerable evidence that distance plays a role in trade patterns. Canada and the United States are each other's largest trading partners. The United Kingdom, France, and Germany all trade extensively with each other and with Western European countries in general. Mexico trades largely with the United States; Singapore, with countries in the Western Pacific; and Russia, with countries of Eastern Europe.

Summarizing the trade patterns described in this section, we have shown that industrialized countries account for the bulk of world exports and world imports. In particular, the largest amount of trade occurs between industrialized countries. Asian countries have seen their share in world trade double over the past 30 years, with Asia the second largest source of exports after the EU as well as a significant customer for exporters from other parts of the world.

In terms of national trading patterns, countries tend to trade extensively with their neighbors. Nowhere is this more apparent than in North America, where Canada, the United States, and, increasingly, Mexico are major markets for each other's goods. In addition, the United States is an important market for the exports of many other countries.

WHAT GOODS DO COUNTRIES TRADE?

Up to this point we have established that trade is a relatively small (on average slightly more than 30 percent of GDP) but rapidly growing part of the world economy. We have also described a series of stylized facts about aggregate trade patterns. In this section we present some information on the individual goods that countries trade. Before we consider major exports and imports of individual countries, let's examine which goods are most likely to be traded.

Consider Table 1.3. There, goods are ranked according to their share (by value) in world trade in 1996.* Office machines, computers, and parts were the largest single traded item (by value) in 1996. This category of goods has risen in rank and value in each of the previous years detailed in the table. Automobiles were the second most traded product in terms of value in 1996, while petroleum ranked third. Petroleum had ranked number one in 1979 and 1985. Chemicals, transistors, clothing, plastics, and iron and steel rounded out the top eight traded commodity categories. Many Americans might have been able to guess that these goods would

---

*Industries are identified in the left-hand column of this table according to the Standard International Trade Classification (SITC) code. This code divides industries into ten very broad groups numbered 0 to 9. Within each broad category, industries are further divided according to the specific type of production that occurs. These industry groupings are given two-digit identification numbers, with the first of these digits being the same as the major industry group. For instance, road vehicles are identified as industry 78 within group 7 (machines and transport equipment). Even more detail can be found by considering three-digit industries. Thus, passenger motorcars are classified as industry 781.

TABLE 1.3 *World Trade Major Products: 1979, 1985, 1991, 1996*
(RANK, VALUE IN BILLIONS OF $, PERCENT SHARE)

SITC code	Product	1979			1985			1991			1996		
		Rank	Value	Share	Rank	Value	Share	Rank	Value	Share	Rank	Value	Share
751+752+759	Office machines, computers, parts	16	22.2	1.4	5	54.9	2.9	2	142.9	4.2	1	249.2	4.8
781	Passenger motor cars	4	55.1	3.4	2	83.5	4.3	1	171.6	5.0	2	245.6	4.8
333	Crude petroleum	1	211.2	12.9	1	170.0	8.8	8	98.7	2.9	3	239.8	4.7
51	Organic chemicals	10	30.1	1.8	10	37.4	1.9	12	73.8	2.2	4	223.5	4.3
776	Transistors, valves, etc.	30	12.2	0.7	17	24.6	1.3	13	71.2	2.1	5	184.1	3.6
84	Clothing	6	33.9	2.1	7	47.0	2.4	4	109.0	3.2	6	171.2	3.3
58+893	Artificial resins, plastics	9	30.2	1.8	9	38.0	2.0	6	100.4	3.0	7	153.8	3.0
67	Iron and steel	3	57.3	3.5	4	55.2	2.9	5	107.3	3.2	8	146.7	2.8
65	Textiles	5	46.3	2.8	6	50.0	2.6	3	109.9	3.2	9	142	2.8
63+64	Wood manufactures, paper	8	31.1	1.9	11	36.2	1.9	10	84.2	2.5	10	135.2	2.6
764	Telecom equipment and parts	26	13.2	0.8	16	25.3	1.3	14	65.1	1.9	11	123.7	2.4
784	Motor vehicle parts	7	33.2	2.0	8	43.8	2.3	9	85.6	2.5	12	122.2	2.4
334	Petroleum products	2	66.1	4.0	3	82.1	4.3	7	98.7	2.9	13	105.9	2.1
792	Aircraft	21	14.8	0.9	18	22.6	1.2	11	80.9	2.4	14	79.4	1.5
541	Medicinal & pharmaceutical prods.	29	12.4	0.8	29	16.3	0.8	18	41.3	1.2	15	76.7	1.5
03+08142	Fish and preparations	22	14.6	0.9	27	17.3	0.9	17	41.5	1.2	16	73.9	1.4
05	Fruit and vegetables	12	25.7	1.6	14	28.1	1.5	15	54.4	1.6	17	71	1.4
772	Electrical parts for circuits	14	24.3	1.5	32	14.7	0.8	19	39.5	1.2	18	65.8	1.3
04	Cereals and preparations	11	28.1	1.7	13	28.6	1.5	27	33.7	1.0	19	65.5	1.3
2873+684	Bauxite, alumina, aluminum	18	17.7	1.1	31	15.6	0.8	26	34.2	1.0	20	63.3	1.2
749	Nonelectric machinery parts	23	14.5	0.9	30	15.8	0.8	22	37.7	1.1	21	59.1	1.1
713	Piston engines	25	13.2	0.8	22	18.9	1.0	24	36.4	1.1	22	57	1.1
874	Measuring instruments	34	11.3	0.7	23	18.0	0.9	21	39.1	1.2	23	56.1	1.1
782	Lorries, special vehicles	17	19.1	1.2	20	21.1	1.1	20	39.2	1.2	24	49.4	1.0
821	Furniture	19	17.5	1.1	35	12.6	0.7	30	31.8	0.9	25	48.8	0.9

		R	V	S	R	V	S	R	V	S	R	V	S
341	Gas, natural and manufactured	24	14.3	0.9	12	34.9	1.8	16	45.4	1.3	26	47.4	0.9
01	Meat and preparations	35	11.0	0.7	26	17.4	0.9	25	36.2	1.1	27	46	0.9
667	Pearls & precious stones	20	15.4	0.9	33	14.6	0.8	31	31.5	0.9	28	44.4	0.9
851	Footwear	39	10.3	0.6	34	13.7	0.7	33	29.6	0.9	29	43.6	0.8
894	Toys, sporting goods	33	11.3	0.7	43	10.2	0.5	35	27.2	0.8	30	41	0.8
2871+288+682	Copper, copper ore, scrap	46	7.2	0.4	36	12.2	0.6	28	32.5	1.0	31	40.8	0.8
741	Heating and cooling equip.	47	4.9	0.3	47	8.9	0.5	37	25.1	0.7	32	39.9	0.8
62	Rubber articles	15	23.5	1.4	37	12.0	0.6	36	25.5	0.8	33	39.5	0.8
24	Cork and wood	41	9.5	0.6	28	16.9	0.9	32	30.2	0.9	34	38.2	0.7
793	Ships and boats	27	12.9	0.8	21	19.7	1.0	29	32.1	0.9	35	36.2	0.7
22+42+081	Oilseeds, veg. oils, oil cakes	13	24.5	1.5	15	25.6	1.3	23	37.0	1.1	36	34.2	0.7
52	Inorganic chemicals	40	10.2	0.6	25	17.6	0.9	34	27.9	0.8	37	33.3	0.6
07	Coffee, tea, cocoa, spices	42	8.9	0.5	19	21.7	1.1	43	20.8	0.6	38	31.7	0.6
881+882+883	Photo apparatus and supplies	45	7.9	0.5	40	11.0	0.6	42	21.8	0.6	39	31.7	0.6
736	Metal working machine tools	43	8.8	0.5	46	9.1	0.5	39	23.1	0.7	40	30.4	0.6
02	Milk and products, eggs	44	8.3	0.5	39	11.4	0.6	41	22.0	0.6	41	30	0.6
714	Engines and motors, n.e.s.[1]	38	10.5	0.6	44	9.9	0.5	38	23.8	0.7	42	29.8	0.6
112	Alcoholic beverages	28	12.9	0.8	45	9.3	0.5	44	20.0	0.6	43	28.3	0.5
723	Civil engineering equip.	32	11.5	0.7	38	12.0	0.6	45	18.3	0.5	44	24	0.5
32	Coal	37	10.5	0.6	24	17.8	0.9	40	22.4	0.7	45	22.3	0.4
26-266-267	Natural textile fibers	36	10.5	0.6	42	10.6	0.6	46	17.0	0.5	46	22	0.4
281+282	Iron ore and scrap	31	11.5	0.7	41	11.0	0.6	47	12.7	0.4	47	16.5	0.3
	TOTAL OF ABOVE IN $ BILLIONS		1,111.6	67.7		1,305.1	67.9		2,410.2	70.9		3,760.1	73.0
	TOTAL WORLD MERCHANDISE TRADE IN $ BILLIONS		1,635.0			1,931.0			3,398.7			5,149.9	

[1] n.e.s = Not elsewhere specified

SOURCES: United Nations, *1996 International Trade Statistics Yearbook* (New York: United Nations Department of International Economic and Social Affairs, 1997), and GATT, *International Trade* (Geneva: GATT, various years).

appear at the top of the world imports list. Over the past several decades, Americans have become familiar with news stories about oil imports from the Mideast; steel mills closing down in Pittsburgh, Gary (Indiana), and elsewhere; unemployed autoworkers moving from Michigan to Texas; and apparel makers urging Americans to look for the *Made in America* logo. In short, because the United States imports more products than any other country in the world, it should not be surprising that the goods most commonly traded are some of America's major import items.

Table 1.3 goes on to list other products commonly traded in world markets. These products include wood products and paper, petroleum products, telecommunications equipment, and aircraft. Many of these products are exports of the United States.

Note that, with rare exceptions, the most commonly traded goods tend to be agricultural products, raw materials, semimanufactured goods, or capital goods (e.g., petroleum, iron and steel, textiles, office equipment, cereal grains, automobile parts, natural gas, plastics, chemicals, wood, fruits and vegetables, oilseeds, aircraft, and telecommunications equipment). Very few imports appear to compete directly in world markets for the types of goods purchased by consumers.* Rather, a relatively common pattern seems to be that countries import raw materials or partially manufactured products and then complete the manufacturing process before marketing a good.

Not included in Table 1.3 is any information regarding international trade services. Trade in services is a growing part of world commerce. In 1996, world trade in services totaled $1.27 trillion, accounting for about 19 percent of all international trade. There are three main categories of services that are traded internationally: transportation services, travel services, and other. Trade in transportation services involves the hiring by residents of one country of another country's boats, airlines, or motor vehicles to move goods or people from one place to another. For instance, it is often the case that American firms hire ships from other countries, such as Panama, to move goods to foreign ports. The amounts paid for the use of these vessels represents an American import of transportation services. In 1996 transportation services accounted for about 25 percent of all services trade.

Travel services include purchases of certain items by residents of one country when they travel to another country. These purchases include such items as lodging, food, tours, etc. Travel services represented almost a third of international services exports in 1996. Many countries that are highly regarded as vacation sites, such as the Bahamas and Jamaica, depend heavily on the export of travel services.

Examples of other service trade include banking, medicine, consulting, insurance, and education. For example, when foreign students enroll at an American university, that is an American export of education. Other services represented slightly more than 40 percent of world trade in services in 1996.

As it is with merchandise, the United States is the world's largest exporter and importer of services. In 1997, the United States exported $229.9 billion in services

---

*Exceptions, of course, are passenger motorcars, home computers, clothing, and toys.

and imported $150.1 billion. The United Kingdom was the second most important services exporter ($85.5 billion) followed by France ($80.3 billion), Germany ($75.4 billion), and Italy ($71.1 billion). Japan was the world's second largest importer of services ($122.1 billion), followed by Germany ($120.1 billion), Italy ($70.1 billion), and the United Kingdom ($68.6 billion).*

Table 1.4 provides some detail on the merchandise exports from selected countries for the year 1996.[†] Consider exports of the United States (column 1). Almost 50 percent of these goods were machines and transportation equipment. Within this group, motor vehicles (mostly exports of autos to Canada) accounted for 8 percent of all U.S. exports. Aircraft represented over 5 percent of exports, and office machines (including computers) accounted for another 7 percent. Other major U.S. export sectors included food—the bulk of that category was exports of cereal grains (e.g., wheat)—crude materials (including paper and pulp wood), chemicals, and basic manufactures.

Almost all of Japan's exports (see column 5) came from basic manufactures (11.1 percent) and machines and transport equipment (69.4 percent). Iron and steel exports made up more than one-third of the exports of basic manufactures. Motor vehicles accounted for about 25 percent of machines and transport equipment exports.

Let's compare for a moment the differences between U.S. and Japanese export patterns. The United States exports a wide variety of products, with significant amounts from all major industry categories except beverages and tobacco and animal and vegetable fats. Japan's exports are concentrated in only two industry categories. What could explain this difference?

One answer has to do with the availability of resources. The United States is an enormous country with vast tracts of farm and forest lands. It also has a large and skilled work force and abundant capital. Thus, it has the resources to be able to produce a wide variety of goods. Japan is a very small country with virtually no natural resources. Farmland is extremely scarce. On the other hand, Japan has a large and skilled work force. Over time, its firms have invested in new plants and equipment. Thus, Japan has the resources needed to produce manufactured goods, but not those required to produce enough food or crude (raw) materials to feed its population or supply its factories.

We have presented some possible reasons for differences between U.S. and Japanese export patterns. The types of goods each country imports provide additional (but not complete) support to the explanation given above. Consider Table 1.5. Almost 10 percent of U.S. imports in 1996 comprised mineral fuels. This reflects the fact that U.S. petroleum supplies are not plentiful enough to accommodate needs. Another 4 percent of U.S. imports was in the food category. About 16 percent of these were coffee, tea, and cocoa, items not grown in significant quantities in the United States. Other major import categories for the United States included manufactured goods—

---

*The World Trade Organization (WTO) has recently begun efforts to provide information on services trade and its importance relative to trade in merchandise. For more, see the *WTO Annual Report* (Geneva: World Trade Organization).
[†]This table also uses SITC codes to identify industries.

TABLE 1.4 Broad Categories of Exports of Selected Countries, 1996 (PERCENTAGE OF TOTAL EXPORTS)

SITC Code	Product	United States	United Kingdom	France	Germany	Japan	Canada	Mexico	Brazil	Singapore	Egypt
0	Food and live animals	7.35	4.13	10.57	4.08	0.38	6.28	6.85	22.49	1.81	11.43
04	Cereal grains	2.95	1.00	2.68	0.74	0.00	2.18	0.00	0.00	0.00	2.86
07	Coffee, tea, cocoa, spices	0.00	0.42	0.60	0.51	0.00	0.00	1.10	5.15	0.46	0.29
1	Beverages and tobacco	1.28	2.62	2.96	0.68	0.00	0.49	0.74	3.43	1.49	0.00
12	Tobacco products	1.08	0.00	0.00	0.31	0.00	0.03	0.00	3.17	1.03	0.00
2	Crude materials	5.19	1.50	2.15	1.60	0.74	10.74	2.54	12.44	1.13	5.71
24	Cork and wood	0.88	0.00	0.28	0.00	0.00	4.80	0.21	0.91	0.12	0.00
27	Fertilizer	0.26	0.31	0.00	0.00	0.00	0.43	0.36	0.30	0.00	0.57
3	Mineral fuels	2.01	6.63	2.61	1.37	0.53	10.18	10.26	0.90	7.88	48.57
32	Coal and coke	0.63	0.00	0.00	0.00	0.00	0.86	0.00	0.00	0.00	1.43
33	Petroleum products	1.25	6.25	1.16	0.80	0.46	5.47	9.97	0.89	7.72	45.71
4	Fats and oils	0.27	0.00	0.00	0.00	0.00	0.00	0.00	1.84	0.29	0.00
5	Chemicals	9.83	13.07	14.16	12.72	6.80	5.52	4.94	6.55	5.49	5.71
6	Basic manufactures	9.15	14.04	16.10	15.62	11.13	16.27	11.36	23.63	5.75	22.86
65	Textiles	0.96	2.08	2.68	2.69	1.69	0.82	1.62	2.14	1.08	11.43
67	Iron and steel	0.92	2.55	3.63	3.04	3.72	1.59	3.17	8.85	0.68	2.00
68	Nonferrous metals	1.16	1.62	1.62	1.68	0.91	3.92	1.71	3.43	1.36	5.71
7	Machines and transport equip.	49.08	44.12	40.61	49.56	69.38	39.01	52.26	19.91	65.88	0.57
75	Office machines and computers	7.35	7.33	3.45	2.36	8.53	2.57	3.68	0.74	26.45	0.00
763	Sound recorders, phonographs	0.00	0.39	0.00	0.00	1.15	0.00	0.67	0.00	1.43	0.00
78	Motor vehicles	8.30	8.68	11.13	16.46	17.83	21.32	15.28	6.13	1.03	0.00
792	Aircraft	5.22	2.85	4.65	1.56	0.00	1.73	0.43	0.96	0.43	0.00
8	Misc. manufactures	10.89	12.53	9.93	10.22	8.41	5.56	10.65	6.24	7.51	8.57
84	Clothing	1.20	1.89	1.94	1.44	0.00	0.62	3.43	0.52	1.12	5.71
851	Footwear	0.00	0.00	0.35	0.00	0.00	0.00	0.24	3.28	0.00	0.29
88	Photographic equip.	0.85	1.16	0.81	0.94	2.86	0.00	0.46	0.49	1.63	0.00
9	Other goods	4.93	1.23	0.67	3.92	2.53	5.68	0.34	2.57	2.77	0.00

SOURCE: United Nations, 1996 International Trade Statistics Yearbook (New York: United Nations Department of International Economic and Social Affairs, 1997).

TABLE 1.5   *Broad Categories of Imports of Selected Countries, 1996*

(PERCENTAGE OF TOTAL IMPORTS)

SITC Code	Product	United States	United Kingdom	France	Germany	Japan	Canada	Mexico	Brazil	Singapore	Egypt
0	Food and live animals	3.80	7.85	8.58	8.06	13.20	5.04	4.27	8.92	2.78	23.85
04	Cereal grains	0.00	0.70	0.80	0.59	1.98	0.55	1.56	3.59	0.33	13.08
07	Coffee, tea, cocoa, spices	0.60	0.70	0.98	0.90	0.59	0.56	0.00	0.32	0.26	0.77
1	Beverages and tobacco	0.86	1.59	1.24	0.95	1.28	0.48	0.19	0.66	1.29	1.54
12	Tobacco products	0.00	0.35	0.62	0.29	0.72	0.00	0.00	0.00	0.73	1.54
2	Crude materials	2.80	3.38	3.16	3.85	9.05	3.24	4.19	4.65	1.02	8.46
24	Cork and wood	0.97	0.67	0.40	0.41	3.34	0.51	0.24	0.00	0.00	3.85
27	Fertilizer	0.00	0.21	0.29	0.29	0.53	0.00	0.36	0.40	0.00	0.54
3	Mineral fuels	9.43	3.87	8.33	7.92	17.45	4.39	2.13	12.13	9.38	1.54
32	Coal and coke	0.00	0.39	0.40	0.00	2.01	0.30	0.00	1.75	0.00	0.77
33	Petroleum products	8.45	3.17	6.44	5.47	11.94	3.95	1.45	9.57	9.37	0.46
4	Fats and oils	0.00	0.39	0.40	0.29	0.00	0.00	0.76	0.74	0.28	3.85
5	Chemicals	5.60	9.79	11.97	8.62	6.46	8.19	9.25	14.97	5.76	12.31
6	Basic manufactures	11.85	15.89	15.64	15.26	10.90	12.62	16.60	11.48	9.91	20.00
65	Textiles	1.31	2.78	2.58	2.61	1.87	1.95	2.44	2.55	1.46	2.31
67	Iron and steel	2.04	2.01	2.91	2.72	1.30	2.00	2.67	0.94	2.08	7.69
68	Nonferrous metals	1.70	2.08	2.11	2.05	2.60	1.33	1.42	1.85	1.48	0.77
7	Machines and transport equip.	45.13	42.27	36.23	34.34	24.36	50.98	43.13	39.12	57.82	25.38
75	Office machines and computers	0.83	0.56	0.69	0.59	5.58	5.37	2.61	3.13	11.65	0.62
763	Sound recorders, phonographs	0.91	0.53	0.36	0.38	0.33	0.29	1.03	0.00	0.74	0.00
78	Motor vehicles	12.90	11.34	10.37	10.22	3.73	17.74	5.29	10.76	1.95	4.62
792	Aircraft	0.94	1.90	1.82	1.82	0.72	1.40	0.12	0.50	2.29	0.00
8	Misc. manufactures	16.71	13.98	14.11	14.92	15.24	11.03	12.56	7.30	10.55	1.54
84	Clothing	5.32	3.38	3.97	5.42	5.64	1.50	2.64	0.69	1.32	0.00
851	Footwear	1.57	0.88	0.91	1.04	0.89	0.45	0.12	0.00	0.00	0.00
88	Photographic equip.	1.25	1.23	1.05	1.04	1.19	0.74	0.70	0.99	1.81	0.31
9	Other goods	3.62	0.92	0.36	5.83	1.83	3.87	6.93	0.00	1.21	0.00

SOURCE: United Nations, *1996 International Trade Statistics Yearbook* (New York: United Nations Department of International Economic and Social Affairs, 1997).

trade that is not necessarily consistent with the lack of domestic resources needed to manufacture such items.

Similar to its export pattern, Japanese imports were much more concentrated. Mineral fuels were the second largest import category, accounting for about 17 percent of total imports. Raw materials and food made up another 22 percent of total imports. That is, almost 40 percent of Japanese imports can be explained by the fact that Japan has very limited natural resources.

Thus, the following trade patterns emerge for these two countries: Japan exports manufactured products to the rest of the world in exchange for food, raw materials, and fuel. The United States exports manufactured goods, but also raw materials and food. It imports fuel, tropical products, and many kinds of manufactured products.

Trying to explain U.S.–Japanese trade patterns is an illustration of the analysis of the commodity composition of trade. Such analysis seeks to answer the question, Which countries trade what to whom? Because there are so many goods and countries in the world and such a wide variety of economic activity, it is extremely difficult to describe, much less to understand, all that is going on. As a result, international economists have sought to build economic theories—models of international commerce that make certain simplifying assumptions so that fundamental patterns of activity can be understood. In the chapters to come we set out to build several such theories. For instance, the theory that countries export goods based on the quantities of resources and factors of production that are locally available is known as the Heckscher-Ohlin theory of comparative advantage. This theory is discussed in detail in Chapter 4. Other theories of international trade are discussed in Chapters 3 and 5. First, however, in Chapter 2 we discuss the general approach economists take in building their models of economic activity.

SUMMARY

1. International trade is a small but growing part of world economic activity. Over the past four decades international trade has expanded by more than 1700 percent in volume terms.

2. Industrialized countries are the major participants in world trade today. They account for more than 60 percent of total world exports. Much of their trade is with each other. They are also the largest markets for the products of developing countries.

3. The United States is the largest single participant in international trade (measured by the sum of imports and exports). It is a major trading partner for many other countries.

4. Most countries tend to trade extensively with their neighbors.

5. Although automobiles rank second in world exports (in value terms), most of the goods that enter international trade are agricultural products, raw materials, semimanufactured goods, or capital goods.

EXERCISES

1. Explain why neighboring countries tend to trade extensively with each other.

2. Use the information in Tables 1.4 and 1.5 and your knowledge of the Mexican economy to summarize and explain the trade pattern of Mexico.

3. Find five interesting facts in Table 1.1.

4. Find five interesting facts in Tables 1.4 and 1.5.

5. Compare the export rankings of the top ten leading exports of 1979 with the rankings of the top ten leading exports in 1996 (see Table 1.3). Discuss some of the reasons why these rankings have changed so dramatically.

6. Use Table 1.1 to find the five most open economies in 1996. How does the growth performance of these countries compare with the growth of the average country listed in the table?

7. Use Table 1.4 to compare the structure of U.S. and Canadian exports. Comment on similarities and differences. Are there any obvious reasons for the patterns you observe?

8. According to Figure 1.2, intra–European Union trade is a huge fraction of EU trade. What factor or factors might account for this fact?

9. According to Figure 1.2, the EU is a major customer of exports from Africa and the Middle East. What types of products do you think these areas produce for export, and why do you think the EU is their best customer?

10. Use Table 1.5 to compare and contrast the import patterns of France and Germany.

INTERNET APPLICATIONS

Please visit our Web site at www.awl.com/husted_melvin for more exercises and readings.

CHAPTER 2

Tools of Analysis for International Trade Models

TOPICS TO BE COVERED

Methodology of Economics
General Equilibrium Models
National Supply
National Demand
Price Determination

KEY WORDS

Positive analysis
Normative analysis
General equilibrium
Money illusion
Relative price
Nominal price
Production possibility frontier (PPF)

Opportunity (or social) cost
Indifference curve
Community indifference curve (CIC)
Autarky
National supply
National demand

One of the messages of the last chapter is that the international economy is extremely complex. All countries of the world take part. Some trade extensively, others very little. Each country is different in terms of its endowment of productive resources and level of economic development. Most countries have many trading partners. Thousands of different types of goods are exchanged. How can all of this activity be understood and explained?

In this chapter and the chapters that follow we seek to answer that question. In particular, in this chapter we begin to build an economic model of a nation that engages in international trade. Once the model, or theory, is constructed, it will be used to answer a number of important questions. For instance, *why does international trade occur*? What are the benefits that are gained, and what are the costs that are incurred? It would seem obvious that there are gains from trade, or else people would not participate. It seems equally obvious that not everyone within a country gains equally from trade, or else trade would not be the contentious issue it is today.

There are a number of questions related to the characteristics of countries engaged in international trade that we would like our theory to answer. For instance, *what goods will a country import, and what will it export*? This is one of the oldest questions in the theory of international economic relations. And, as we shall see, there are a number of alternative answers. In addition, *what will be the volume of trade*? Is trade likely to be large or small relative to the overall size of the economy? And *what will be the prices at which trade occurs*? One measure of international prices is known as the terms of trade. This measure is defined as the price of a country's exports divided by the price of its imports. As we shall see, changes in a country's terms of trade are closely related to gains from international trade for that country.

Finally, we would like our theory to be able to explain *the effect of trade on payments to various factors of production*. That is, how does international trade affect the level of wages paid to labor or rents paid to owners of capital goods? This is perhaps the most important question we can ask regarding international trade; and yet, at first glance, it would seem that trade has little effect on wages or rents. As groups such as the United Steelworkers of America are quick to remind us, however, trade can have a profound effect. For instance, competition from foreign steel producers has helped lead to large-scale reductions in domestic steel employment and to wage concessions from the union to the domestic industry. And, of course, it is situations such as this that produce opposition to free international trade and call for protection from foreign competition. Hence, we would also like our theory to be able to explain how government can regulate the volume of international trade and what the effects of such regulation might be.

We proceed in our development of the theory of international trade as follows: In this chapter we concentrate on the basic elements of economic model building. Our attention will be focused on the economy of a country that lives in isolation from the rest of the world. We study such an economy to understand how prices and outputs are determined in the absence of international trade, so that we can compare these prices and outputs with those that prevail once trade is allowed. In the next two chapters we introduce this country to a world of international trade under differing assumptions about the production characteristics of the country.

Beginning with Chapter 6 we show how to incorporate government-imposed restraints on trade into the model and how to analyze the effects of these restraints.

SOME METHODOLOGICAL PRELIMINARIES

An economy is a collection of agents (including individuals and firms) that interact with each other in the exchange of goods and services. In international economics, economies are separated from each other by national boundaries, and countries are treated as economic agents as well. International economics is interested in explaining the interaction of countries in the exchange of goods and services.

Economists often build economic models to help them understand the pattern of economic behavior. An *economic model* is a theoretical description of this behavior. An economic model can take a variety of forms. It can be a purely verbal statement about economic behavior. Verbal models are the most important of all, because it is through these that economists can pass along their understanding of economic phenomena to the general public. Because the audience is the general public, verbal models are usually very simple. But to be truly useful, a model must be capable of application to a variety of circumstances. Thus, the challenge of building a good verbal model is to ensure that underlying the model is a formal structure that is consistent in its internal logic. And since mathematics is the formal language of logic, we often find that economists use this tool in formulating their theories.

Mathematical expressions of economic theories can take two forms. They can be geometric, which is the case with most of the models found in this book. The advantages of a geometric model are that it is a formal mathematical statement, it is relatively simple for most people to understand, and it can be readily manipulated to analyze many different phenomena. A disadvantage of a geometric model is that it is necessarily limited to no more than three dimensions. This restricts the number of variables that can be studied or manipulated at any one time.

Models can also be algebraic. An algebraic model is useful for several reasons. First, it is not hampered by dimensionality limitations. Second, it can be used in conjunction with a computer to conduct a statistical evaluation of economic data or to simulate an economic behavior.

Despite differences in their degree of formality, all economic theories have certain common characteristics. Models are abstractions from reality; that is, they employ assumptions about the environment to be studied or the behavior of the agents that allow the economist to make the most precise predictions the theory allows. Theories are necessarily simpler than the real world; and not surprisingly, therefore, they are not always correct in their explanation of or predictions about behavior. A Nobel Prize–winning economist, Milton Friedman, has argued that a test of the validity of a theory is not to question the plausibility of the assumptions employed but rather to compare the predictions of the theory with experience.*

---

*Milton Friedman, "The Methodology of Positive Economics," in *Essays in Positive Economics* (Chicago: University of Chicago Press, 1953), 3–43.

Theories can be rejected if their predictions are frequently contradicted, or if they are correct less often than the predictions of alternative theories. This is a methodology that is common to all sciences. However, it is particularly difficult to apply in economics—because economists can rarely carry out controlled experiments.

Consider the following example: From introductory microeconomics we know that (under the usual assumptions about demand and supply) the effect of the imposition of a tax on a product is to raise its price. Suppose a tax is imposed on the sale of cigarettes, and shortly thereafter the price of cigarettes falls. Is economic theory wrong? According to a naive interpretation of the criterion for judging economic theories discussed above, the answer would seem to be yes. However, it is simple to show that if, at the same time the tax is imposed, the demand for cigarettes is falling (due perhaps to an announcement by the surgeon general regarding the health effects of smoking), cigarette prices could fall. Ideally, then, we would like our theory to be a complete enough picture of the world so that we can distinguish between the effects of various and possibly conflicting forces at work on the economy. Once these forces have been identified, the theory is stated in terms of the effect a variable has on the economy, holding all other variables constant. Going back to our example, the correct way to express our theory is that, all else constant, a tax on cigarettes will lead to an increase in their price.

As we shall see in the coming chapters, real-world phenomena do not always square well with the predictions made by our theories regarding international trade. In some cases, this lack of agreement will cause us to search for factors we have not properly taken into account. In other cases, it will cause us to develop new theories.

A second common feature of all theories in economics is that they can be used to conduct both **positive** and **normative analysis**. Positive analysis refers to the attempt to answer descriptive questions, such as the effect of a tax on cigarettes on the amount of cigarettes produced or consumed. In normative analysis, the effort is to answer questions that are more prescriptive in nature, such as, Should the government impose a tax on cigarettes? The answers to the first type of question are usually noncontroversial, especially among economists. Any two economists working with the same model should reach the same conclusions (although different models may give very different answers). Answers to normative questions depend much more on value judgments and could differ strongly from one economist to the next. In this book we try to point out where and when our own value judgments enter into the analysis presented. We shall also try to give an evenhanded account of opposing viewpoints on the optimality of various government policies related to the international economy.

Positive analysis
Analysis that studies economic behavior without making recommendations about what is or ought to be.

Normative analysis
Economic analysis that makes value judgments regarding what is or should be.

THE BASIC MODEL: ASSUMPTIONS

General equilibrium
Simultaneous equilibrium in all the markets of an economy.

We begin now to build a basic model of an economy that engages in international trade. The model we build is known as a **general equilibrium** model. By *general equilibrium* we mean that production, consumption, prices, and (eventually) international trade are all determined simultaneously for all goods produced and consumed in the country.

There are many advantages to a general equilibrium model. The principal benefit is that such a model allows us to keep track of what is happening to all sectors of an economy as it engages in trade. A chief drawback of general equilibrium models is that if we were truly interested in exploring simultaneous changes in the production and the consumption and the prices of *all* goods that could potentially be produced or consumed in any economy, we would quickly find that our model is too large and complicated to be studied effectively. Thus, we are forced to make some simplifying assumptions. We begin by making seven.

ASSUMPTION 1 All economic agents, in particular firms and consumers, exhibit rational behavior.

Economic agents are goal oriented. Firms make production decisions in an attempt to maximize profits. Consumers maximize utility (satisfaction) through their consumption decisions. This is a fundamental tenet in economics. If this assumption does not hold, then economic behavior would be random and hence inexplicable.

ASSUMPTION 2 There are only *two countries* in the world, America (denoted by the letter *A*) and Britain (denoted by the letter *B*). There are also only *two goods* in the world, soybeans (denoted by the letter *S*) and textiles (denoted by the letter *T*). Each good is identical in its characteristics in the two countries, and some of each is always consumed in each country.

Both parts of this assumption are made for geometric convenience. As it turns out, general equilibrium models can be expressed algebraically, wherein both the number of countries and the number of goods can exceed two by any arbitrary amount. All the conclusions of this chapter carry through in these more general models. However, in some cases the results in chapters to come do not carry through when the number of goods or countries is greater than two. We shall try to indicate where this is true.

ASSUMPTION 3 There is *no* **money illusion**.

Money illusion
A situation where individuals make decisions based on changes in some prices without taking into account changes in others.

That is, we assume that when firms make their production decisions and when consumers make their consumption choices, they take into account the behavior of all prices rather than only a few. Thus, they are not fooled into changing their behavior when nothing "real" in the economy has changed. To make the implications of this assumption more clear, consider the following example:

Suppose a farmer is trying to decide which crop to plant in a given year. He has two choices (say, corn and wheat), each of which he can grow in equal amounts with equal effort.* Suppose that, initially, each product sells for the same price. Under these situations, the farmer is indifferent to planting either of these commodities and decides, perhaps by flipping a coin, to grow wheat. Now, just before planting, the

---

*For those of you who are familiar with farming, we realize this is a rather contrived and implausible example, but bear with us.

farmer learns that the price of corn has doubled. Should he plant corn? The answer is, Not necessarily. First, he should examine what has happened to the price of wheat. He should plant corn instead of wheat if the price of corn has risen by more than the price of wheat. If wheat prices have also doubled, then he is no better off by switching to corn production. If wheat prices have more than doubled, he is worse off by switching to corn. The farmer who looks only at changes in one price without considering changes in others suffers from money illusion.

Consider another example. Suppose that from one year to the next an individual is given a 10 percent increase in his or her salary. An individual with money illusion would think that simply because his or her income had increased in nominal (money) terms, his or her buying power (real income) had also increased. Clearly, this is not necessarily so, since the prices of the goods this person buys could have risen by more than 10 percent.

How can we represent the assumption that firms and individuals do not suffer from money illusion when they operate in the economy? The answer is to require that all economic decisions (i.e., decisions to produce or to consume) are based on **relative** rather than **nominal prices**. Nominal prices refer to money prices, such as the dollar price of soybeans, denoted as P_S, or the dollar price of textiles, P_T. A relative price refers to a price ratio, say P_S/P_T. To understand how relative prices work, consider the following important rule:

Relative price
A ratio of two product prices.

Nominal price
A price expressed in terms of money.

$$\text{If } P_S/P_T = k, \text{ then 1 unit of } S = k \text{ units of } T \text{ (in value)}$$

or

$$1 \text{ unit of } T = 1/k \text{ units of } S \text{ (in value)}$$

For example, suppose that 1 bushel of soybeans costs $10, and 1 yard of textiles costs $5. The relative price of soybeans in terms of textiles, P_S/P_T, would be 2. That is, 1 bushel of soybeans could be sold in the market to yield enough cash to purchase 2 yards of textiles. Note further that this would still be true if both prices doubled or changed by any other proportionate factor.

We can also illustrate the notion of relative prices graphically. Consider Figure 2.1. On the vertical axis we measure textiles in physical units. On the horizontal axis we measure units of good S, soybeans. Suppose that P_S/P_T equals 2. Suppose further that a farmer produces 10 units of soybeans and sells them all in the market. What is the maximum amount of textiles that could be purchased with the proceeds from this sale? Since soybeans are twice as expensive as textiles, the answer is 20 units. We show this relation on the graph by drawing a line between 20 units of T and 10 units of S. This line is known as the price (or terms of trade) line. The price line shows us (for a given relative price) all the possible combinations of the two goods that can be purchased with a fixed amount of money.

The most important feature of the price line is that the slope of the line (in absolute value) tells us the relative price P_S/P_T. Consider the graph again. If the farmer sells 1 unit of S, we know that the resulting revenue can be exchanged for 2 units of

---

| FIGURE 2.1 | *Example of a price line.* |

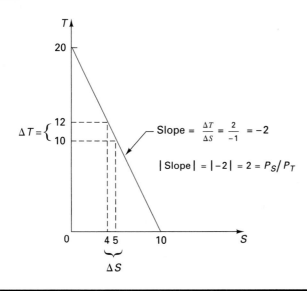

T. Thus, movements along the line reflect trades of equal value—the only type of uncoerced exchange one should be willing to make.

Note that the end points of the line tell us something about the income level of the person making the trade. That is, we began this example by assuming that the farmer produced 10 units of S. Suppose he had produced 1,000 units and then taken this amount to the market to sell. What would be the maximum amount of T he could purchase? The answer is, of course, 2,000 units. Hence, the end points of the price line would be 1,000 on the S axis and 2,000 on the T axis, and the slope of the line connecting these points would again be 2 (in absolute value)—the relative price of S. Thus, for any given level of S (or T) the price line tells us at what rate that good could be exchanged in the market for the other.

Finally, suppose that P_S/P_T rises from 2 to 3. What will be the effect on the price line? It will get steeper. What does this imply? It means that the same amount of S now trades for 3 units of textiles rather than 2 units. That is, T has become relatively cheaper, or, equivalently, S has become relatively more expensive. Hence, graphically, price lines that are steep denote the fact that S is relatively expensive compared with T, while price lines that are flat denote the opposite.

ASSUMPTION 4 In each country factor endowments are fixed and the set of technologies available to each country is constant.

If these conditions hold, then we can illustrate the supply conditions of a country by a **production possibility frontier (PPF)**. A production possibility frontier tells us the maximum amount of output of one type of good, say T, that can be

Production possibility frontier (PPF)
A diagram that shows the maximum amount of one type of good that can be produced in an economy, given the production of the other.

produced in a country, given the technology of that country, that country's factors of production (land, labor, capital, etc.), and the level of output of the other good, S. Figure 2.2 illustrates two possible shapes for a country's PPF. In part a of the figure, we provide the diagram familiar from most textbooks. Given the country's resources, production can occur anywhere along or inside the curve DE. If the output point of the country is on the frontier, say, for instance, at point G, then resources are fully employed and production is said to be efficient. This is because it is not possible to increase the output of one good without lowering the output of the other. If production occurs in the interior of the PPF, say at point I, then there is inefficiency in production, since the output of one or both goods can be increased without increasing the resource base of the country. And it is assumed that production cannot occur at a point outside the frontier (e.g., point H), because this would require resources or technology not available to the country.

Recall that when resources are being efficiently utilized, it is not possible to increase the production of any one good without decreasing the production of the other. We define the **opportunity (or social) cost** of producing one more unit of S (T) as the amount of T (S) that must be sacrificed in order to use resources to produce S (T) rather than T (S). Now, note that the PPF in Figure 2.2a has a bowed (concave to the origin) shape. This shape signifies the assumption that production of the two goods in the country is subject to *increasing opportunity costs*. That is, beginning from point E (where the economy is producing only good T), as the economy moves toward producing more and more S (i.e., as the economy moves down its PPF), the cost in terms of foregone production of T increases. More simply, as Figure 2.2a indicates, for each additional unit of S produced in the economy, the amount of T produced falls by an increasing amount. Mathematically, we can define

Opportunity (or social) cost
The amount of production of one type of good that must be sacrificed to produce one more unit of the other.

FIGURE 2.2   *Examples of production possibility frontiers: (a) increasing opportunity costs; (b) constant opportunity costs.*

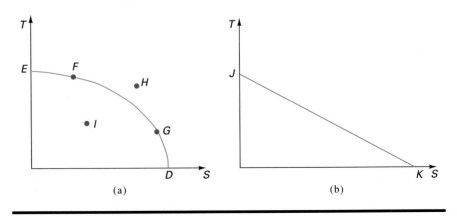

the cost of producing an additional unit of S as minus the slope of the PPF at the initial production point, that is, $-\Delta T/\Delta S$.*

What could cause opportunity costs to be increasing? One possibility is that the two industries, S and T, use factors of production in different combinations in the production process. For instance, textiles might require large amounts of labor to produce, while soybeans need only small amounts; likewise, soybeans might require vast tracts of land, while textile production could be concentrated in a very small area. Now consider point E in the diagram. At that point all of the country's resources are concentrated in the T industry. To move away from that point, the T industry must release factors to industry S. Given that T needs large amounts of labor but only a little land, while S requires just the opposite, an efficient reallocation of resources would prompt T as it contracts to release initially to S more land than labor. As a result, the output of T would fall by only a small amount, while the production of S would rise by a large amount. However, this process cannot go on indefinitely. If the output of S is to continue to expand, eventually more and more labor relative to land will be released from T. As this begins to happen, the output of T will fall by larger and larger amounts.

Part b of Figure 2.2 illustrates an alternative assumption, namely, *constant opportunity costs*. In this case, as the production of S expands, the output of T falls, but at a constant rate. A condition that would produce this situation would be one where factors of production are used in fixed proportions identical with each other in both industries. For example, suppose that both industries always employ 100 workers per acre of land. Then, as one industry contracts, it will always release factors at this rate, and output will fall by a fixed amount. Meanwhile, the expanding industry will want to absorb resources at this rate, and its output will rise by a fixed amount.

In the models that follow, we have occasion to assume that the economy is subject to either constant or increasing opportunity costs. While both situations are possible in the real world, most economists agree that the assumption of increasing opportunity costs offers a better approximation of reality. On the other hand, the assumption of constant opportunity costs is sometimes very useful, since it is somewhat easier to work with and leads to powerful predictions about the effect of international trade on various characteristics of the economy.

ASSUMPTION 5 Perfect competition prevails in both industries in both countries. In addition, there are no externalities in production.

Recall that the opportunity cost (i.e., social cost) of producing one more unit of good S is the amount of output of good T foregone in the process. Assumption 5 guarantees that market prices reflect the true social (opportunity) costs of production. From basic principles of microeconomics we know that a competitive firm maximizes its profits by producing at the point where price equals marginal cost (i.e., the

---

*Because the slope of the PPF is negative, we include a minus sign in the definition of opportunity cost so that cost is measured in terms of positive numbers. Alternatively, we can define the cost as the absolute value of the slope of the PPF at the initial production point.

cost of the last unit produced). If there are no externalities in production (e.g., if no pollution is created as the good is manufactured), then the marginal cost of producing one more unit of S is precisely the value of the resources (including normal profit) used in the production of this good. The alternative to using these resources for the production of S would be to employ them to produce T, so that there is complete correspondence between production and opportunity costs in this case.

Two points deserve further mention. First, this assumption offers a convenient graphical counterpart. Perfect competition requires that price equals marginal cost. In our example, the price of S in terms of T must equal the cost of producing S in terms of T. Or, equivalently, the absolute value of the slope of the PPF at the production point, $|\Delta T/\Delta S|$, must equal the relative market price ratio P_S/P_T. This is illustrated graphically in Figure 2.3.

Second, the assumption of perfect competition extends to factor markets as well. This means that labor unions and the like, which in the real world could lead to factor payments higher than those observed in competitive factor markets, are assumed not to exist.

> ASSUMPTION 6 Factors of production are *perfectly mobile* between the two industries within each country.

The implication of this assumption is that factors of production will move between the industries in response to any potential differences in factor payments. This guarantees, then, that factors (e.g., labor) earn the same factor payments (i.e., wages) in both industries within a country.

Assumptions 4 through 6 describe the supply side of the economy we shall study. The next assumption, Assumption 7, has to do with demand. However, before we spell out the last assumption, it is necessary to digress for a moment to review the theory of individual consumer choice.

FIGURE 2.3   *Relationship between price line and production point.*

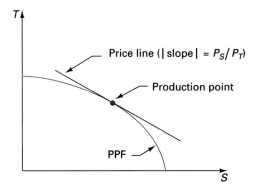

Whenever an individual goes to a market, he or she is faced with a number of choices. What determines the final choices of the consumer? Economists believe that how much of each type of item a consumer buys depends upon the prices to be paid for each of the many items being considered, the total amount to be spent, and established preferences (or tastes) for these items. In particular, based on prices, budget, and preferences, it is assumed that the consumer will choose the bundle of goods that yields the highest possible level of satisfaction (or utility).

How can this process of utility maximization for the individual consumer be illustrated? Consider a simplified example. Suppose that Ms. Jones is offered the choice between two different bundles of goods, each containing some S and some T. These bundles are illustrated in Figure 2.4a by the points 0 and 1. Bundle 0 contains S_0 units of S and T_0 units of T, while bundle 1 contains S_1 units of S and T_1 units of T. Suppose further that Ms. Jones is not allowed to sell or give away any of the goods contained in the bundle she chooses. Ms. Jones has only three options. She could

FIGURE 2.4   *Indifference curves and individual utility maximization.*

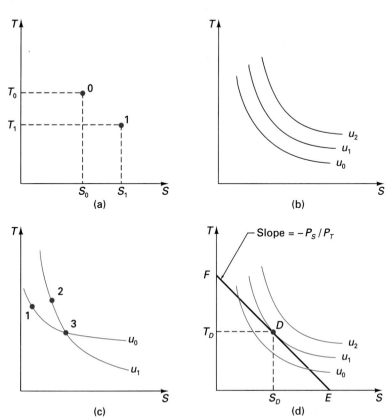

Indifference curve
A diagram that
expresses the
consumption
preferences of an
individual consumer.

prefer bundle 0 to bundle 1; she could prefer bundle 1 to bundle 0; or she could be equally happy to receive either of the two bundles, in which case she is said to be indifferent (or equally satisfied). Economists define an **indifference curve** as a locus of bundles of goods that each yield the same level of satisfaction to an individual consumer.

Indifference curves have a number of important properties. We use Figure 2.4b to illustrate some of these. First, they are individual specific. That is, everything about their location and shape depends upon the tastes of the individual in question. Second, they are downward sloping. This simply reflects that both goods are truly "goods" to the consumer, so that if one bundle has less T, it must have more S for it to be equally pleasing to the consumer. Third, indifference curves are convex to the origin. This reflects the common belief that people like variety, so that the more they have of one type of good, the less they want still more of it. Note, however, that some people may have a particular preference for bundles with large amounts of one type of good, say T, relative to the other. In this case, their indifference curves would have the shape depicted in Figure 2.4b but would lie closer to the T axis.

Fourth, since, hypothetically at least, consumers should be able to describe their feelings regarding any conceivable consumption bundles, there are infinitely many indifference curves, each lying above the other. We have illustrated three such curves in the diagram. It is important to note that higher indifference curves reflect higher levels of satisfaction. Finally, indifference curves cannot intersect. This guarantees that preference rankings are always consistent.

To understand the importance of this last property, suppose that, as drawn in Figure 2.4c, two indifference curves did intersect. Bundles 1 through 3 lie on these two indifference curves. For the individual represented in this diagram, 2 (which contains more of both goods) is on a higher curve than 1, and thus he or she prefers 2 to 1. Since 3 is on the same curve as 2, this individual should also prefer 3 to 1. But in the diagram, 3 is also on the same indifference curve as 1, indicating that these two bundles provide equal satisfaction. Here is the logical contradiction. If a person's tastes are consistent, he or she cannot prefer 3 to 1 *and* be indifferent to the choice between 3 and 1.

Now that we have established the important properties of indifference curves, we can use these to show the solution to Ms. Jones's problem of finding that bundle that maximizes her satisfaction. Suppose that Ms. Jones plans to spend M dollars on goods S and T. When she goes to the market she must pay P_S for each unit of S and P_T for each unit of T. If she spends all M dollars on the two goods, then her expenditure must satisfy the equation

$$P_S \times S_j + P_T \times T_j = M \tag{2.1}$$

where S_j and T_j represent the number of units of S and T purchased by Ms. Jones. Equation 2.1 is an example of something we have already studied, a price line (see Assumption 3). Consider Figure 2.4d. The graph of the price line is, as before, a straight line with slope equaling P_S/P_T in absolute value. The end points of the price line correspond to the maximum amounts of *S* (point *E*) and *T* (point *F*) this person could buy, given that she only wants to spend *M* dollars on the two goods. Thus, the line represents all of the various combinations of *S* and *T* she could buy with *M* dollars. The bundle that yields the highest level of satisfaction for this consumer is found by the point of tangency of the price line to the consumer's indifference curves (point *D*). Any other bundle on the price line is associated with lower indifference curves and hence lower levels of satisfaction. Higher indifference curves pass through bundles that could not be purchased with the amount budgeted for these goods.

Now, reflect for a moment. You have visited stores on thousands of occasions to make purchases. Were you even aware that you have indifference curves (or that economists think that you do)? The answer is probably no. Doesn't that fact invalidate all of the previous discussion? Again, the answer is no. What is important (and what the analysis is trying to reflect) is that, given various constraints you might face, such as the amount of money you have to spend and the prices you must pay, what you choose to buy is that combination of goods that gives you the most satisfaction. Figure 2.4d simply illustrates that process.

We turn now from the analysis of a single individual and the choices he or she makes to the analysis of a group of individuals (e.g., a community or a country) and the choices it makes. To do so, we make the following assumption:

> ASSUMPTION 7 Community preferences in consumption can be represented by a consistent set of community indifference curves.

That is, we assume that there is a set of **community indifference curves (CICs)** that expresses the preferences of the community over the consumption of various bundles of goods in exactly the same manner as a set of indifference curves expresses the preferences of an individual. If these curves are consistent, they possess all of the properties of individual indifference curves, which we just described.

As it turns out, Assumption 7 is very strong. What it says, in effect, is that various individuals can be grouped together and asked to rank their preferences over all possible consumption bundles. But in the real world, this is harder than it might at first seem. How do groups make preference decisions? One way is to have an election. The decision that is made then reflects the preferences of the majority of voters. As the following example illustrates, in such elections, if people are very different but consistent in their individual preferences, as a group they may not be consistent.

Consider a three-person economy and three bundles of goods, *A, B,* and *C.* Table 2.1 illustrates the preference rankings by each of the individuals for these bundles. Now, let there be an election to decide how the community would rank these bundles. If the group were to rate *A* against *B, A* would win two votes to one, as both Moe and Curly prefer *A* over *B.* If the group then decided between *B* and *C, B* would win because in this case Moe and Larry would prefer *B* to *C.* Hence, it would seem that if the group likes *A* better than *B* and *B* better than *C,* the group must prefer *A* to *C.* Yet, as the table clearly shows, the group would vote two to one

Community indifference curve (CIC)
A diagram that expresses the preferences of all the consumers of a country.

TABLE 2.1	*Illustration of Condorcet's Voting Paradox*		
Order of Preference	Moe	Larry	Curly
1	A	B	C
2	B	C	A
3	C	A	B

that *C* is better. Here is the obvious problem. Even though the individuals are consistent in their preferences, the group is not.* This result should not be surprising. Anyone familiar with group activities knows how difficult it is to get a group to decide on anything.

What will it take to ensure that Assumption 7 holds? There are a variety of circumstances where group decisions can be guaranteed to be consistent. One situation is a one-person, Robinson Crusoe–type (before Friday) economy. Here, the tastes of the individual and the community are obviously identical. A second situation where our assumption holds is in a strict one-person dictatorship, where the tastes of the dictator determine entirely the consumption choices of the populace. Finally, if every person in an economy has identical tastes and identical incomes, then the community's indifference curves would look exactly like the indifference curve of any of the (identical) members of the population. These community indifference curves would have *all* the properties of individual indifference curves. For the time being, we shall assume that this last situation holds true.[†]

THE BASIC MODEL: SOLUTIONS

Now that the assumptions are in place, it is straightforward to solve the model for its general equilibrium solution. In particular, we shall combine the elements of supply and demand to find production, consumption, and prices. Before doing so, however, we note that the solution we shall obtain is the **autarky** solution. Autarky means self-sufficiency. A self-sufficient country is one that abstains from international trade. Such an economy is said to be closed. Thus, the autarky solution we find is the general equilibrium solution for a closed economy.

Autarky
A situation where a country does not take part in international trade.

Figure 2.5 illustrates this solution under the assumption of constant opportunity costs. The line *EF* is the economy's production possibility frontier. The lines CIC_0, CIC_1, and CIC_2 denote several of the economy's community indifference curves. How do the forces of supply and demand interact in this model? Recall that Assumption 1 states that all economic agents act in rational fashion. Hence, consumers will

---

*This paradox was originally explained by the French mathematician Marquis de Condorcet (1743–1794). For more on the problems of constructing community indifference curves, see Kenneth J. Arrow, *Social Choice and Individual Values* (New York: John Wiley and Sons, 1951).
†For more on the interpretation and geometry of community indifference curves, see Edward Tower, "The Geometry of Community Indifference Curves," *Weltwirtschaftliches Archiv* (1979).

FIGURE 2.5 *General equilibrium for a closed economy; constant opportunity costs.*

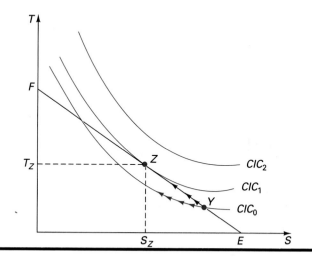

seek to purchase that combination of goods that maximizes their satisfaction. Suppliers, through their production decisions, will attempt to meet consumers' demands. From the diagram, it is easy to see that consumers maximize their collective utility at point Z, the point of tangency of their community indifference curves with the economy's production possibility frontier. Thus, point Z is the ideal consumption point for the economy. Since this economy exists in isolation, point Z is also the ideal production point—that is, producers maximize their profits by producing goods in the combinations desired by society. The conclusion, then, is that, in isolation, this country will produce and consume a bundle of goods that contains S_Z units of soybeans and T_Z units of textiles.

We have now established the levels of production and consumption for both goods. What will be their relative price? From Assumption 5, we know that the price ratio is determined by the slope of the PPF at the production point. Hence, the price ratio in this case corresponds to the slope of the line segment *EF*. This is an interesting result because it says that so long as some of both goods are produced—if production occurs under the condition of constant opportunity costs—then demand plays no role in determining relative prices. The only role for demand in such a world is in picking out the precise combination of outputs of the two goods.

How does demand interact with supply to guarantee that the economy ends up at point Z? Consider what would happen if producers guess wrong and produce a bundle of goods other than Z, say bundle Y. If the economy is initially at Y, more S (less T) is being produced than is desired by consumers. Consumers would be happy with this bundle of goods only if the relative price of S were to fall to a level equal to the slope of the *CIC*-intersecting point Y. That is, the price consumers have to pay for S—the market-relative price—is higher than the price they want to pay. Given this, there will be a tendency for the consumption of S to fall, generating a short-run excess supply of S in the market, which in turn will lead to a reduction in the production of S (i.e., there is a short-run tendency for production to move inside the PPF). As factors become unemployed in the S industry, they are reemployed in the T industry. And as the factors become reemployed and the production of T expands, the economy moves back to its PPF and toward point Z.

Demand has a more interesting role in the case of an economy with increasing opportunity costs. This is illustrated in Figure 2.6. Again, we show supply conditions via a production possibility frontier (curve GH in the diagram) and demand conditions by representative community indifference curves (the CIC curves). As before, the optimum consumption and production point is determined by the tangency of the PPF with the community indifference curves. This point is denoted by point X. The relative price of good S is found by the slope of the PPF at point X.

If producers were to produce a bundle other than at point X, how would the economy respond? Consider what would happen at point U. There, T production exceeds (S production falls short of) the general equilibrium level. At point U, consumers are willing to pay a higher price for S (given by the slope of the CIC curve at that point) than the prevailing market price (given by the slope of the PPF at that point). Pressure from consumer demand will tend to drive the relative price of S up, encouraging S producers to expand their production levels and encouraging T producers to contract their production. The combination of these effects on national output will move the economy to point X, where the price consumers are willing to pay exactly equals the market price—the price they have to pay.

We have established the economy's consumption and production levels for the two goods and the relative price at which they are traded in the market. How long

FIGURE 2.6   *General equilibrium for a closed economy; increasing opportunity costs.*

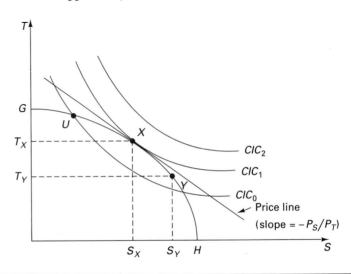

will this continue to be the solution to the model? The answer is that X will remain optimal so long as nothing changes. What could change? Production conditions could change due to a technical innovation in either or both industries. In such circumstances, the PPF would change shape, and the tangency would occur at some new and probably higher point. Without more information, it is impossible to predict the effect on relative prices.

Tastes could change. Suppose that for some reason consumers as a group increased their preference for S relative to T. Their community indifference curve map would move, rotating toward the S axis (not shown in Figure 2.6). This would imply a new optimal consumption point, such as point Y. Under such circumstances, how would production and prices behave? Clearly, at point Y the demand for good S has risen (from S_X to S_Y), while the demand for good T has fallen (from T_X to T_Y). How can producers be encouraged to change their output levels to match this change in demand? The answer lies in prices. As the demand for S rises in the economy, so too does its price. Meanwhile, falling demand for T causes its price to fall. Thus, the relative price of S, P_S/P_T, rises. This provides an incentive to producers to shift resources from textiles to soybeans. An example of a situation where producers respond to changes in relative prices is given in Item 2.1.

ITEM 2.1   Relative Prices in Saudi Arabia*

Saudi Arabia is a desert country in the Middle East and one of the world's major oil producers. As a leading member of the Organization of Petroleum Exporting Countries (OPEC), it has feared for some time that wheat exporters might retaliate against it for the oil shortages of the 1970s. Consequently, the government established a program to try to encourage the domestic production of wheat. It offered potential farmers free land plus grants and low-interest loans for machinery. Most importantly, it offered a very high relative price of wheat.

In 1985, for instance, the Saudi government offered to pay $26 per bushel. This price was roughly equal to the world price of a barrel of petroleum. So, measured in terms of barrels of oil, the relative price of wheat in Saudi Arabia in 1985 was 1. The world (free-market) price of wheat in dollars in 1985 was about $3.50. In terms of barrels of oil, wheat cost about one-eighth of a barrel ($3.50/$26.00). The Saudi policy meant that it paid one barrel of oil to buy a bushel of wheat from its own farmers, almost certainly the highest price of wheat anywhere in the world. If it had bought the wheat in world markets, it could have purchased eight bushels with one barrel of oil!

Not surprisingly, the farmers who received this high price were elated and responded by increasing their production of wheat. Even city dwellers began part-time wheat farming in plots outside of towns. The Saudis produced bumper crops of wheat, twice what was being consumed in the country. In some parts of the country farmers had to wait for up to seven months after harvest to deliver their grain to the government silos because there was no room to store the excess supplies.

---

*For more details, see B. Rosewicz, "Saudi Arabia Battles a Glut, but It Isn't the One You Think," *Wall Street Journal*, April 2, 1986.

MEASURING NATIONAL WELFARE

One of the important goals of economics is to be able, whenever possible, to illustrate the economic benefits of various types of economic activity. For instance, economists would like to be able to demonstrate whether perfect competition is preferred to monopoly under most economic situations. Recall from our preceding discussion that judgments such as these are part of the realm of normative economics. One of the normative questions we would like to answer in this text relates to the preferability of free international trade to other trading arrangements. For this purpose, we need to develop a measure of economic welfare (or well-being), which can then be applied to different trading scenarios.

We have already established one possible measure of economic welfare for a country, the community indifference curve. However, we know that the use of *CIC* analysis requires strict assumptions about group preferences, assumptions that are very unlikely to hold in the real world. Furthermore, even if these assumptions were to hold, how would we know what a country's level of satisfaction is, since there is neither a precise measure of satisfaction nor a spokesperson for the economy to tell us how well the country is doing? Fortunately, there is a simple and straightforward way around this problem. In this section, we shall show the relationship between community satisfaction and a more common measure of national well-being, gross domestic product (GDP).

Recall from our preceding discussion that each *CIC* is associated with a fixed level of satisfaction and that higher curves are associated with higher levels of satisfaction. How can we measure these levels of satisfaction? The answer is that we can't, at least not directly. The reason for this is obvious. Satisfaction is something that cannot be observed except subjectively, and furthermore, it can't be compared between individuals. Students who are familiar with the television show *American Bandstand* should be aware of this problem. On that show several people were asked to listen to a new record and then rate it on a scale of 1 to 100. If person *A* gave a particular record a score of 80, while person *B* gave the same record a 68, would we really know whether the first person liked it better than the second? The answer is no. What we need is some criterion that can provide us with a less ambiguous measure of satisfaction. The criterion used in the case of *CICs* is real gross domestic product.

Recall from Chapter 1 that gross domestic product is defined as the level of output of new goods and services produced by an economy during a certain period of time (usually one year) and valued at market prices. In our simple model, where only two goods are produced, the formula for GDP is given by Equation 2.2:

$$GDP = P_S \times S + P_T \times T \qquad (2.2)$$

This equation states that at any point in time, a country's GDP is equal to the value of that country's production of soybeans and textiles (remember that in the real world, GDP measures would include the value of many other items as well as these from our model). As the formula also shows, GDP can change for at least two reasons. Either production levels are altered (i.e., *S* or *T* changes) or prices change.

Clearly, there are different implications from these two types of changes. In the first case, a rise in GDP means that there are more goods available for consumption. This is said to be an increase in *real* GDP. If, instead, rising GDP merely comes about because of an increase in prices, then *nominal* GDP is said to rise, but real GDP is constant.

To maintain the distinction between these two types of changes, suppose that we divide both sides of Equation 2.2 by P_T. This has the effect of changing our units of measure of GDP from money terms to real (units of T) terms. To verify this, consider Equation 2.3:

$$GDP/P_T = (P_S/P_T) \times S + T \qquad (2.3)$$

From our discussion of price lines we know that P_S/P_T represents the price of S measured in terms of T, so that the first term on the right-hand side of Equation 2.3 is the value of S production measured in units of T. The second part of that side of the equation is simply the amount of T production. Thus, when these two terms are combined in this fashion, we have a measure of real GDP. And by measuring GDP in this fashion, any change in GDP reflects real (output) changes rather than nominal (price) changes.

Now consider Figure 2.7. There we graph a number of GDP lines identical with Equation 2.3. The slope of each is the same and equal in absolute value to a given relative price. The height of each line is determined by the value of GDP. Higher lines represent higher GDP levels. The important point is that for a given value of

FIGURE 2.7   *Determination of real GDP level.*

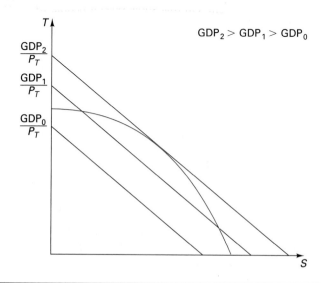

$$GDP_2 > GDP_1 > GDP_0$$

P_S/P_T, production on the production possibility frontier leads to the highest possible GDP. Similarly, so long as consumers are maximizing their collective utility, increases (decreases) in real GDP may imply increases (decreases) in the community standard of living.

We use the word *may* for several reasons. First, a country's population may also be growing over time (recall that Assumption 4 rules this out in our model). Hence, even if a country's real output is growing, if population grows faster, then, on average, there are fewer goods and services available to each individual for consumption. Consequently, a better measure of standard of living is per capita real GDP. Even this measure is not perfect, however, since it implicitly assumes that all individuals are able to share in the growing standard of living. Also, as calculated in the real world, this statistic ignores quite a bit of economic activity (housework, illegal trade, etc.) and leaves unmeasured other factors that contribute to the quality of life, such as leisure time. Item 2.2 provides information on measuring real GDP as well as some information on the level of real GDP in the United States and elsewhere.

NATIONAL SUPPLY AND DEMAND

We conclude this chapter with an extension of our analysis of the general equilibrium model. First, we show how the geometric tools we have developed can be used to derive national demand and supply curves for the two commodities. These curves provide an alternative (but equivalent) way of illustrating how production, consumption, and prices are determined in an economy. Then, we use these curves to show the incentives that could induce international trade between countries.

From principles of economics, we know that the firm's supply curve of a particular product is a schedule of amounts of output the firm would produce at various market prices. We define the **national supply** curve for a product, say S, as the amount of S produced in the nation at various (relative) prices of S. Such a curve can be derived quite simply.

National supply
The amount of national output of a particular good at various relative prices for that good.

Consider Figure 2.8a. In the top diagram, we have reproduced the production possibility frontier for country A. We have also imposed three different price lines on the diagram, reflecting three possible prices that might exist. These prices are 1/2, 1, and 2. Recall that the production point in the economy is determined by the relative price level. In particular, as the price of S begins to rise, producers respond by producing more S. This is reflected in the top diagram by the rightward movement of the tangency points.

This process is shown in a different fashion in the lower diagram. There, we transfer the information from the top diagram to a graph where the relative price of S appears on the vertical axis and output on the horizontal axis, and we plot output levels of S that correspond to the different prices. The resulting curve is A's national-supply-of-S curve. We label it NS_S. Note that this curve has the familiar upward slope to it. This is because of our assumption, in this case, of increasing opportunity costs. In fact, as we move down A's PPF, the underlying national supply curve

ITEM 2.2	Measurement of Real Income

In our illustration of the measurement of real income, we divided the GDP equation by the nominal price of T, P_T (see Equation 2.3). Hence, we measured real GDP in units of T. Because of this, T is known as the *numeraire* good. In the real world there are hundreds of thousands of goods produced in any economy, and seldom if ever is any one good singled out as a numeraire good. Rather, a common practice is first to define a basket of goods and then to divide nominal GDP by the price of this basket. The resulting number reflects the value of GDP measured in terms of that basket of goods. In the United States, the prices that are most often used to calculate real GDP numbers are the *consumer price index (CPI)* and the *GDP deflator*. The CPI is the cost of a large collection of goods representing the items that an average U.S. consumer purchases relative to the cost of the same basket of goods in the base year. The GDP deflator represents the value of all goods produced in the United States in a particular year relative to the value of goods produced in the base year. Other countries use different but nonetheless similar measures. For this reason, it is not strictly legitimate to compare the level and changes in per capita real GDP across countries, since we are not using the same basket of goods as numeraire.

With this warning in mind, consider the following table. There, we present per capita real GDP figures for a number of countries over several years. All figures are measured in constant value (1990) U.S. dollars. Note that for most countries listed in the table, per capita real GDP rose for the 30 years from 1960 to 1990. For many countries, real per capita GDP more than doubled during these 30 years. Japan and Korea grew much faster, with per capita real GDP quintupling over this period. For many of the countries in this table, growth slowed during the 1980s. This is especially true for Brazil and Mexico, where real per capita GDP growth was negative.

Per Capita Real GDP: Selected Countries, 1960–1990 (1990 dollars)

Country	1960	1970	1980	1990
United States	12,115	15,487	18,393	21,826
Canada	8,358	11,624	15,905	19,498
Japan	3,445	8,429	11,864	17,113
Sweden	7,973	11,750	13,747	16,212
France	6,234	9,675	13,048	15,489
United Kingdom	7,947	9,980	11,837	14,953
Germany	5,568	8,044	10,466	12,846
Brazil	1,199	1,545	2,596	2,544
Egypt	340	387	585	695
India	167	195	215	298
Mexico	1,425	2,053	2,951	2,655
Republic of Korea	935	1,612	3,097	5,561

SOURCE: Central Intelligence Agency, *Handbook of Economic Statistics,* 1991.

FIGURE 2.8   *Derivation of national supply and demand curves.*

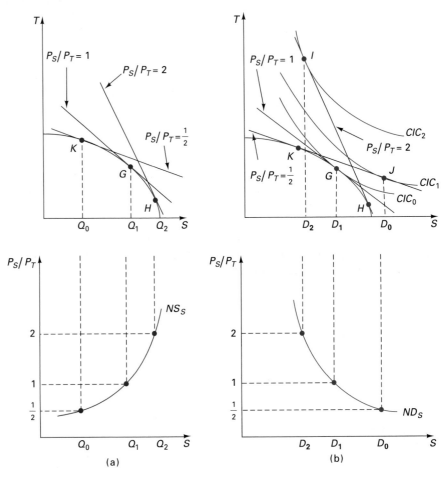

(a)   (b)

becomes increasingly steep. This simply reflects the fact that to encourage additional production of S requires greater and greater price increases to compensate producers for the greater and greater costs they incur.

In panel b of the diagram, we show how to derive A's national demand curve for S. The **national demand** curve for a product tells us how much a country would want to consume of a product at various relative prices. In the top diagram of the panel, we show A's production possibility frontier as well as several *CICs* and market prices. Recall that in order to maximize satisfaction, consumers would choose that bundle of goods located along the price line at the point of tangency with the

National demand
The amount of national consumption of a particular good at various relative prices.

highest *CIC*. From the diagram we see that when P_S/P_T equals 1, the desired level of consumption is D_1 (directly below point *G*). Now, let the price rise to 2. Clearly, consumers will no longer want to consume D_1 units of *S*. Instead, and if they could, they would prefer D_2 units (directly below point *I*, where the new price line is just tangent to a *CIC*). Similarly, if the price was to fall to 1/2, *A*'s consumers would like to expand their consumption of *S* to D_0 (below point *J*). Of course, in autarky, neither points *I* nor *J* can be reached, since they lie outside of the country's PPF.

In the lower part of panel b, information on desired consumption levels of *S* is recorded on a graph with P_S/P_T on the vertical axis and units of *S* on the horizontal. The curve that is produced is the nation's demand-for-*S* curve, labeled ND_S. As drawn, it has the familiar downward slope (although this does not have to be the case). Its position and slope depend, in part, on the location of the country's *CIC*s. They also depend on the location of the economy's production point.

In Figure 2.9 we reproduce only the country's national demand and supply curves to provide an alternative depiction of the determination of the autarky equilibrium point. Note that in this example, when the price equals 1, demand equals national supply. At prices above 1, say 2, consumers prefer less *S* (bundle *I* in Figure 2.8b, top diagram), while producers want to produce more (bundle *H* in Figure 2.8b, top diagram). In other words, there is excess supply of good *S*.

Now, let's bring country *B* into the analysis. In Figure 2.10 we illustrate, without deriving, national supply and demand curves for country *B* (and for country *A*). Unless country *B* is identical in both production capacity and tastes with country *A*, its demand and supply curves will have a different position and shape from those of *A* and will be likely to intersect at a different autarky price. As we have drawn them, they intersect at a price of 2.

FIGURE 2.9   *Alternative derivation of the autarky price ratio.*

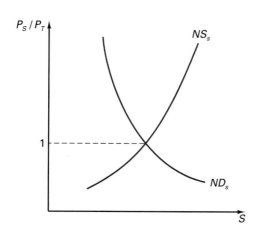

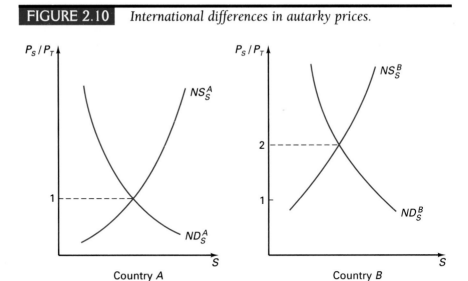

FIGURE 2.10   *International differences in autarky prices.*

Country A   Country B

Suppose now that we consider what might happen if trade were allowed to occur between these two countries. Beginning at a point of autarky equilibrium prices in the two countries, consumers in country B would want to buy S from producers in country A, where it is cheaper. This additional demand would drive up the price of S in A (not shown in the diagram). Suppliers of S in A would expand their production, thus generating goods for export to B. Similarly, because B begins with a lower relative price of T, consumers in A would want to import T from B so that the demand for T would rise in B, driving up the relative price and leading to an excess supply, which could be sold to consumers in country A (not shown in the diagram).

Because country A has a lower autarky (relative) price of S, it is said to have a comparative advantage in S and a comparative disadvantage in T. By identical logic, country B has a comparative advantage in T and a comparative disadvantage in S. As we have seen from the diagram, incentives exist for trade to develop along the lines of comparative advantage. That is, each country exports its comparative advantage good and imports its comparative disadvantage good.

How do countries achieve comparative advantage in certain goods? According to the diagrams we have just studied, the answer must lie with international differences in demand or supply. For well over 200 years, economists have attempted to address this question in a more complete fashion. Most of their work has concentrated on international differences in supply, although some analysis has also been devoted to demand. In the next several chapters we review this effort to explain comparative advantage, following the general historical development of our modern-day understanding of this important topic.

SUMMARY

1. Economists build economic models to help them understand the interaction of various economic forces. Assumptions are employed in these models in order to simplify the analysis and to sharpen the predictive power of the analysis.

2. This chapter builds a general equilibrium model of a closed economy. A general equilibrium model is one in which all goods are analyzed simultaneously in terms of production, consumption, prices, and (eventually) international trade.

3. The solution of our model predicts that in autarky, production and consumption will occur at the same point on the country's production possibility frontier. This result guarantees that, given the autarky prices, people enjoy the highest standard of living possible.

4. Finally, we showed that if people in this economy were allowed to take advantage of international trade, then trade would tend to take place along the lines of comparative advantage.

EXERCISES

1. Suppose that an economy produces three goods—raisins (R), soybeans (S), and textiles (T). What would its PPF look like under conditions of constant opportunity costs? What would it look like with increasing opportunity costs?

2. Using the following data, calculate the country's nominal and real GDP levels:

Case	P_S	S	P_T	T
a	$ 5	20	$1	15
b	$10	20	$2	15
c	$ 4	40	$8	12
d	$ 4	60	$8	18

3. Using your calculations from Exercise 2, compare changes in nominal and real GDP between cases a and b. Explain your result.

4. Suppose an economy is characterized by constant opportunity costs so that P_S/P_T equals 1.5. Derive the economy's national supply curve. How does it differ from the one derived in Figure 2.8? Explain.

5. Suppose that in world markets the relative price of S is lower than country A's autarky price. Would A be a net exporter or importer of S? What would be the case for good T in country A in this situation?

6. Derive country A's national supply and demand curves for good T. Be careful how you label the axes!

7. If a country is at a point on its PPF where the slope of the PPF is flatter than the slope of the *CIC* touching that same point, then the standard of living would rise if outputs of the two goods would change so as to move down the PPF. True or false? Demonstrate and explain.

8. Suppose that country *A* produces two goods under conditions of constant opportunity costs. Given its resources, the maximum *S* that it can make is 500 units and the opportunity cost of making *T* is 2. What is the maximum amount of *T* that it can produce? Draw a graph and explain.

9. Suppose that a country produces two goods, *X* and *Y*, with two factors of production, *K* and *L*. The production of good *X* always requires more *K* per unit than the production of good *Y* does. What does this imply for the shape of the country's PPF? Explain carefully.

10. Why are relative prices more important for decisions about consumption and production than nominal prices are? Provide an example to illustrate your answer.

11. Suppose that a small, tropical country produces mangoes for domestic consumption and possibly for export. The national demand and supply curves for mangoes in this country are given by the following:

$$P = 50 - M \qquad \text{(national demand)}$$

$$P = 25 + M \qquad \text{(national supply)}$$

where *P* denotes the relative price of mangoes and *M* denotes the quantity of mangoes (in metric tons).
   a. Illustrate these relationships geometrically.
   b. What are the autarky price and the quantity exchanged?
   c. Suppose that the world price of mangoes is 45. Will this small country export mangoes? If so, how many tons?

INTERNET APPLICATIONS

Please visit our Web site at www.awl.com/husted_melvin for more exercises and readings.

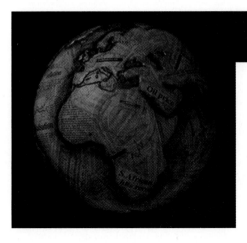

CHAPTER 3

The Classical Model
of International Trade

TOPICS TO BE COVERED

International Division of Labor
Labor Theory of Value
Absolute Advantage
Prices in International Trade
Comparative Advantage
Specialization in Production
International Trade Equilibrium
Gains from International Trade
Relative Wage Determination

KEY WORDS

International division of labor
Mercantilism
Constant returns to scale
Absolute advantage
Comparative advantage
Terms of trade

Consumption possibility frontier
Trade triangle
Walras Law
Reciprocal demand
Importance of being unimportant

W̶e now have all the tools necessary to develop a theory of how and why nations engage in international trade. We begin that task in this chapter by presenting the *classical theory of international trade.* This theory was first developed by Adam Smith in his famous book *The Wealth of Nations,* published in 1776. Many other economists of that and subsequent decades made important contributions to this theory. These economists include David Ricardo, Robert Torrens, and John Stuart Mill. Ricardo's contributions to international trade theory have been deemed so important, in fact, that the classical theory is sometimes also referred to as *Ricardian theory.*

Ricardo published his ideas on international trade in Chapter 7 of his book *On the Principles of Political Economy,* in 1819. Included in this chapter is a discussion of the concept of comparative advantage, the principle that most economists believe determines fundamental trade patterns. Although Ricardo is often credited with discovering the law of comparative advantage, students of the history of economic thought are likely to criticize this practice, because there is substantial evidence that Robert Torrens, a less well-known English economist of the time, developed the notion of comparative advantage years earlier, in 1808.

Whether Ricardo knew of Torrens's work and borrowed this idea or whether he developed the concept separately we shall never know. The principle of comparative advantage is so important that it alone justifies our discussion of a theory first laid out over 200 years ago. There are other reasons for studying the classical theory. First, the assumptions of the model are suggestive of certain real-world situations that exist today. In particular, they help us to understand the basis for a mutually beneficial trading relationship that can occur between a developed and a developing country. Second, this theory explains how wages can be high in a country like the United States and yet American goods can still compete in world markets. Finally, it illustrates, perhaps better than any other theory, the gains from the international specialization of production.

ABSOLUTE ADVANTAGE AS A BASIS FOR TRADE: ADAM SMITH'S MODEL*

If you were to build a model of international trade, where would you start? An obvious place to begin is to look at the world around you. Perhaps the economic behavior that you observe can be generalized to explain the interaction of nations. This is what Adam Smith, a Scottish professor, did prior to writing *The Wealth of Nations.* What he saw was a world where factories were becoming important tools of production. The chief advantage of factories, in Smith's eyes, was that each worker specialized in a certain task. As a result of specialization, the output of the factory far

---

*For a more mathematical development of the classical model, see Akira Takayama, *International Trade* (New York: Holt, Rinehart and Winston, 1972); or Miltiades Chacholiades, *International Trade Theory and Policy* (New York: McGraw-Hill, 1978).

exceeded the sum of what each worker could produce by working on his or her own. Smith illustrated this idea by describing the operation of a pin factory:

> [A] workman not educated in this business [pin making], nor acquainted with the use of the machinery employed in it . . . could scarce, perhaps, with his utmost industry, make one pin in a day, and certainly not twenty. But in the way in which this business is now carried on, . . . it is divided into a number of branches. . . . One man draws out the wire, another straights it, a third cuts it, a fourth points it, a fifth grinds it at the top for receiving the head; to make the head requires two or three distinct operations . . . ; it is even a trade by itself to put them into the paper; and the important business of making a pin is . . . divided into about eighteen distinct operations. . . . I have seen a small manufactory of this kind where ten men only were employed. . . . [T]hey could . . . make among them about twelve pounds [48,000 pins] in a day. . . . Each person . . . might be considered as making four thousand eight hundred pins a day.*

Smith dubbed this process the division of labor, and his example illustrates the dramatic advantages that can be obtained through such a division.

Now, let's take this example one step further, just as Smith did. Suppose we think of the world as a factory that is capable of producing a large variety of goods. How much production would occur in the world if each country remained in autarky? This would be similar to the production of a number of individuals each making pins all by themselves. Consider instead how much more production there would be if countries specialized in the production of only a few goods, just as workers in a factory specialize in a few tasks. An **international division of labor** similar to the division found in factories could lead to a level of world production that would far exceed the sum of autarky production levels. The surplus produced in this situation could then be divided between countries through international trade so that all would have more than they would without trade.

This was Smith's recommendation for how world production should be patterned. But as Smith looked around his world, he saw a set of institutions, laws, and regulations that had been put into place by various governments to restrict international trade and hence the international division of labor. This system of government practices to restrict international trade was known as **mercantilism**. The mercantilist system of the eighteenth century, which prevailed in England and throughout most of Europe and elsewhere, included such practices as taxes on imported goods, bans on the importation of other goods, and special laws and taxes designed to favor certain industries at the expense of others. A goal of the mercantilist system was to encourage exports and to discourage imports.† Smith argued that discouraging the availability of foreign goods and encouraging the export of domestic goods, mercantilism served to lower the wealth, or standard of living, of a country. Smith used his book to attack the mercantilist system and to promote free international trade.

International division of labor
Specialization by nations in the production of only a few goods.

Mercantilism
A system of government policies and institutions aimed at increasing exports and decreasing imports.

---

*See Adam Smith, *The Wealth of Nations* (New York: Modern Library, 1937), 4–5.
†For a description and analysis of British mercantilist thought, see Douglas Irwin, *Against the Tide* (Princeton: Princeton University Press, 1996), Chapter 2.

How would free trade accomplish the goal of achieving the correct international division of labor? In particular, how would it be determined who should produce what? Furthermore, what should be the exact distribution of the goods once they are produced? To provide answers to these questions and others that you may be considering, we must develop a model of an economy engaged in international trade. Remember that, in so doing, the first thing we should do is to spell out our assumptions. We shall retain the seven we described in Chapter 2 and add five more:

ASSUMPTION 8   Factors of production cannot move between countries.

This assumption simply guarantees that a nation's production possibilities frontier does not change shape or location once international trade begins. It does imply, however, that some of the real-world phenomena we observe daily, such as immigration (both legal and illegal) and multinational corporations, are not allowed in this model. In Chapter 10 we take up the question of international factor mobility. Note a second implication of this assumption. If, for instance, labor is not allowed to migrate between countries, then there is no reason to expect wage rates, when measured in the same currency, to be equal between countries even after trade begins.

ASSUMPTION 9   There are no barriers to trade in goods.

That is, we are assuming free trade in all goods. This means that we rule out, for the time being at least, the existence of tariffs, quotas, and even transport costs. A complete discussion of the extent and importance of trade barriers is given in Chapters 6 through 8. An important implication of Assumption 9 is that once trade begins, prices for the same good must be identical worldwide.

ASSUMPTION 10   Exports must pay for imports.

In other words, trade must be balanced. This assumption rules out the net flows of money between countries. What it says is that to obtain the goods a country wants from foreigners, it must pay for these goods with goods of equivalent value rather than money. In the long run, it is unlikely that foreigners would prefer any country's money to that country's goods. This is simply because the value of a country's money is very closely related to the things that the money will buy. And money loses value— that is, it commands fewer goods—as prices in an economy rise over time. Thus, when exporters earn foreign money through their sales of goods to foreigners, they are not likely to hold on to it for very long. Instead, they will typically sell it to their local bank; and that bank will, in turn, sell the foreign money to a local importer who needs it to purchase foreign goods. In this way, the foreign money is repatriated. But if foreign money is completely repatriated, then, in essence, goods have paid for goods. Assumption 10 merely guarantees that this holds true in our model.

How well does Assumption 10 hold in the real world? In Chapter 1 we have already seen that in any given year there is a rough equality between exports and imports for most countries. This was especially true for the average trade flows of countries from each of the income groups in Table 1.1. However, it is also the case that some countries, notably the United States and Japan, have recently experienced large trade imbalances.

The last three assumptions were related to the behavior of countries engaged in free trade. We continue to retain these assumptions throughout this and the next chapter. The following two assumptions relate only to the classical model and will be dropped at the end of this chapter:

> ASSUMPTION 11 Labor is the only relevant factor of production in terms of productivity analysis or costs of production.

This may seem to be a rather odd assumption to make. However, it is more plausible than it may initially appear. Another way to express this assumption is to state that while *both* labor and capital are required for production of either soybeans (*S*) or textiles (*T*), these factors are always used in the same ratio in either industry (e.g., one worker/one shovel). Furthermore, the assumption implies that workers bring their tools with them when they report to the workplace (think of carpenters or possibly mechanics). Note that while we are assuming an identical labor and capital mix within a country, we are *not* assuming that the capital-to-worker mix is identical across countries or that workers in different countries use the same kind of tools.

Assumption 11 is a modern way of expressing a very old idea. Classical economists believed in a theory of price determination known as *the labor theory of value*. This theory states that for countries in autarky, the price of a good is determined by the amount of labor it took to produce it. This would seem to be an easy theory to disprove. One can think of many goods whose prices are identical but that obviously involve much different quantities of labor in their direct production. The classical economists saw this as a much more difficult process, however, because they assumed that in counting the amount of labor used in production, one should also include the labor to produce the physical capital employed in the production process.

Many economists have believed for some time that the labor theory of value is not a very good approximation of reality. For it to hold true, one would have to make a number of very restrictive additional assumptions. Fortunately for us, our assumption is somewhat more general than the labor theory of value. Furthermore, even Assumption 11 is much more restrictive than is necessary for the theory to hold. On the other hand, this assumption allows us to illustrate results that are universal, in the simplest possible manner.

> ASSUMPTION 12 Production exhibits **constant returns to scale** between labor and output.

Constant returns to scale
A technological relationship such that proportionate changes in inputs lead to proportionate changes in output.

By *constant returns to scale* we mean a technological relationship such that proportionate changes in all inputs lead to proportionate changes in output. For instance, doubling all factors of production in a particular industry leads to double the original output level. In the classical model there is only one relevant factor of production, labor. So, in this case, the assumption of constant returns to scale implies a fixed ratio between the quantity of labor employed in the production process and the amount of output produced. Furthermore, this fixed ratio, which may be determined by the technology available in the country, by the country's climate, or by the quality of its soil, holds true for all levels of output. For example, if it takes 8 hours to make 1 yard of textiles in country *A*, it takes 16 hours to make 2 yards and 80 hours to make 10 yards. This assumption is another extreme simplification that allows us to illustrate in the most dramatic fashion the implications for domestic production of the opening of a country to international trade.

Now that we have our new assumptions in place, let's consider how our model fits together. Suppose the fixed input/output ratios for the two industries S and T in countries A and B are given by the values in Table 3.1. In particular, the numbers in the table reflect the hours it takes to make 1 unit of output of a certain good in a certain country. For instance, it takes 3 hours to produce one more unit of S in country A; and, because of Assumption 12, this relationship holds true no matter what amount of S is currently being produced.

Consider Table 3.1 carefully; much can be learned from it. First, we see that workers in country A can produce S in less time than workers in B, while workers in B have an edge in the ability to produce T. Because country A's workers can produce S in less time than country B's workers, A is said to have an **absolute advantage** in the production of S. By analogous reasoning, in this example B has an absolute advantage in the production of T.

Absolute advantage
The ability of a country to produce a good using fewer productive inputs than is possible anywhere else in the world.

Adam Smith argued that the proper international division of labor would be one where countries specialized in the production of goods in which they have an absolute advantage. In this case, rather than producing both goods, as they would do in autarky, country A should concentrate on the production of S, and country B on the production of T.

Consider what would happen if each country followed this principle. The results of such a process are illustrated in Table 3.2. Suppose the output of textiles (T) is reduced by 1 unit in country A. This would free up 6 hours of labor. Let that worker move to soybean (S) production. With 6 more hours of labor, the output of soybeans will rise by 2 units. In similar fashion, let the output of S in country B fall by 1 unit. In this case, 12 hours of labor are released to the T industry. With 12 more hours of labor, 3 additional units of textiles can be produced.

Now, let's total the results. In A, a transfer of 6 hours of labor from textiles to soybeans leads to a reduction of T output by 1 unit and to an increase in S output by 2 units. In B, when the output of S falls by 1 unit, the output of T rises by 3 units. For the world as a whole, the output of S rises by 1 unit and the output of T rises by 2 units. Thus, we see the benefits of an international division of labor. Without using any new resources, total world output has risen! This rise has come about by

TABLE 3.1	*Absolute Advantage as a Basis for Trade*[1]	
	Country	
	A	B
Soybeans	3	12
Textiles	6	4

[1]Numbers in the table denote labor required to produce one unit.

TABLE 3.2	*Per Unit Gains from Specialization When Country* A *Moves to Specialize in Soybeans* (S), *and Country* B *in Textiles* (T)

	Per Unit Gain	
	In Production of *S*	In Production of *T*
In *A*	+2	−1
In *B*	−1	+3
In world	+1	+2

following the simple rule that each country should concentrate on the production of those goods it produces most efficiently.

The problem still remains as to what is required to persuade workers in each country to concentrate their efforts along the lines of absolute advantage. As Smith saw it, the solution to this problem was simple. Market forces would guarantee that this will happen. Recall that the labor theory of value states that pretrade prices of goods are determined by their labor content. Given the existence of perfect competition in each industry (Assumption 5), we can easily establish that the price of a good in autarky is simply equal to the cost of the labor inputs used in its production, which, in turn, equals W_i, the wage rate in country i, times the amount of labor input.

From Table 3.1 we can determine, then, the pretrade ratio P_S/P_T for each country. In particular, in country A,

$$P_S = W_A \times \text{hours}_{SA} = W_A \times 3$$

$$P_T = W_A \times \text{hours}_{TA} = W_A \times 6$$

Hence,

$$P_S/P_T \text{ in } A = (W_A \times 3)/(W_A \times 6) = 3/6 = 1/2$$

Likewise,

$$P_S/P_T \text{ in } B = (W_B \times 12)/(W_B \times 4) = 12/4 = 3$$

What these calculation tell us is that in autarky, S costs 1/2 units of T in A but 3 units of T in B. Once trade is allowed, consumers in B will want to buy their soybeans from A's producers rather than from their own because A's price is lower. Thus, the demand for A's soybeans will rise. How can production rise to meet this demand? The resources must come from the textile industry. Will they? Again, market forces will see that this happens. In particular, country *A*'s autarky price of textiles is 2 units of soybeans, while *B*'s price is only 1/3 unit. Hence, once the opportunity exists for *A*'s consumers to buy from *B*, their demand for textiles produced in their own country will fall. Falling demand in *A*'s textile industry leads to layoffs. Workers leave that industry for the expanding soybean industry. Of course, exactly the opposite process occurs in *B*, where rising demand for textiles leads to an expansion of that industry, while the soybean industry shrinks.

Let's take a moment to summarize our results so far. Adam Smith's model of international trade included the following points:*

1. For a variety of reasons, including differences in technology and climate, countries of the world differ in their ability to produce various goods.

2. World output could be expanded if, rather than closing borders through mercantilist practices, countries would specialize in the production of goods in which they enjoy absolute advantage.

3. Such a situation is easy to achieve because it is the natural outcome of market forces combined with free international trade. This is because each good is cheapest in the country that has an absolute advantage in its production.

COMPARATIVE ADVANTAGE AS A BASIS FOR TRADE: DAVID RICARDO'S MODEL

A number of questions may still be bothering you. First, what if one country has absolute advantage in *both* goods? This question worried many people who first read Adam Smith's book. The answer, as Torrens and Ricardo first pointed out, is that in this case, countries should specialize where they have their *greatest absolute advantage* (if they have absolute advantage in both goods) or in their *least absolute disadvantage* (if they have an absolute advantage in neither good). This rule is known as the law of **comparative advantage.**

Comparative advantage
A country has comparative advantage in a good if the product has a lower pretrade relative price than is found elsewhere in the world.

Consider the example in Table 3.3. As in the earlier input–output table, the numbers indicate the amount of labor time required to produce 1 unit of output of a particular good in a particular country. Note the one major difference in this example from the example we saw earlier: Here, country *A* has an absolute advantage in both goods! However, the strength of these absolute advantages is not identical for the two industries. In particular, note that country *A* is 4 times more efficient in the production of good *S* relative to country *B* (compare 3 hours with 12 hours). However, *A* is only 4/3 more efficient in the production of *T* relative to country *B* (compare 6 hours with 8 hours). Because *A*'s greatest absolute advantage is in the production of *S*, it is said to have a comparative advantage in *S*. Likewise, because *B*'s

---

*For additional discussion of Smith's views on trade, see Douglas Irwin, op. cit, Chapter 6.

TABLE 3.3	*Comparative Advantage as a Basis for Trade*[1]	
		Country
	A	B
Soybeans	3	12
Textiles	6	8

[1] Numbers in the table denote labor hours per unit of output.

TABLE 3.4	*Per Unit Gains from Specialization According to Comparative Advantage as A Produces More S, and B Produces More T*	
	Per Unit Gain	
	In Production of *S*	In Production of *T*
In *A*	+2	−1
In *B*	−1	+1.5
In world	+1	+0.5

least absolute disadvantage is in the production of *T, B* is said to have a comparative advantage in *T*.

According to the law of comparative advantage, once trade is allowed between the two countries, each country should move to specialize in the production of its comparative-advantage good and then export the excess of the production of that good to the other country in exchange for the other good. What will be the result of this procedure? Suppose there is a very modest move in the direction of comparative advantage. Such a move is illustrated in Table 3.4.

If country *A* expands production in the direction of comparative advantage, its output of *S* will rise. The resources for this expansion must come from the *T* industry. In other words, the output of *T* must fall. Suppose it falls by 1 unit. This frees up 6 hours of labor time. This labor can be employed in the *S* industry, and the result will be an expansion of output of *S* by 2 units. In *B*, let the output of *S* fall by 1 unit. This frees up 12 hours of labor. That much labor working in the textile industry could be used to produce 1.5 additional units of textiles. As you can see from Table 3.4, in this example we have the remarkable result that even though there are no new resources in the world *and* even though country *A* has an absolute advantage in both goods, the output of both goods rises by following the law of comparative advantage. It is possible to construct examples where following the law of comparative advantage will not lead to an increase in the production of all goods. However, even in that case, all countries are better off by specializing in this fashion. This is because each country is producing more goods that it will sell in world markets and getting a higher price for every unit sold.

THE GENERAL EQUILIBRIUM SOLUTION
OF THE CLASSICAL MODEL

So far, our discussion of the classical model has followed very closely the train of logic and the mode of presentation found in the writings of the classical economists. It is time now to illustrate the classical model in a somewhat more formal fashion using the tools of analysis that we developed in the last chapter.

We continue to assume that the technology illustrated in Table 3.3 holds for our two countries. First, note that we can derive the production possibility frontiers for the two countries directly from knowledge of the values in the table. For instance, suppose that country A was endowed with enough workers so that in a given year, total hours worked would equal 12,000 hours. What would be the maximum amount of S that could be produced? The answer, of course, is 4,000 units (12,000 hours/3 hours per unit). The maximum amount of T that could be produced equals 2,000 units (12,000 hours/6 hours per unit). Country A's PPF is found by plotting these output levels on the S and T axes, respectively, and connecting the two points. This is done in Figure 3.1a.

Why is the PPF a straight line? The answer has to do with the assumption of fixed input-output technology for all levels of output of the two goods. For example, beginning at an output of 2,000 units of T and no production of S, if we were to reduce the output of T by 1,000 units, this would free up 6,000 hours of labor, which could then be employed in the S industry. For every additional 3 hours of labor employed in S, one new unit of output is produced. An increase in employment in the S industry of 6,000 hours would then imply 2,000 additional units of output of S. An implication of this example is that the opportunity cost of S in terms

---

FIGURE 3.1   *Production possibility frontiers: (a) country A;
(b) country B*

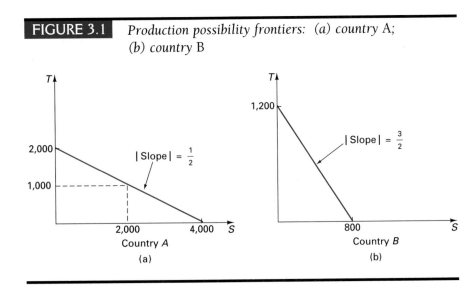

of T in country A is equal to 1/2. That is, for every additional unit of S produced in country A, the output of T must fall by 1/2 unit. We should know this result, of course, because the slope of A's PPF is 1/2 in absolute value; and from the discussion in Chapter 2, we should know that the slope of the PPF tells us the country's pretrade relative price P_S/P_T.

We can repeat the same analysis for country B. Suppose it also has 9,600 hours of available labor. In this country the maximum amount of S that could be produced would be 800 (9,600/12) units, while the maximum amount of T that could be produced is 1,200 (9,600/8) units. The opportunity cost of S in country B (and therefore B's autarky relative price) is 3/2 (1,200/800).

Summarizing what we have established so far in the example we are considering, the autarky price of S is 1/2 unit of T in A but 3/2 units of T in B. We found this out by graphing the PPFs for each country, using the labor requirements for the production of each commodity in the two countries and information on the size of each country's workforce. Note that we could have easily calculated the autarky prices by simply forming ratios of the data in the columns of Table 3.3.

If both countries live in autarky, competitive behavior will lead to general equilibrium solutions somewhere along each country's production possibility frontier. These points are determined by the tangency of the PPF with the country's set of community indifference curves. Examples of such equilibrium points are indicated in Figures 3.2a and 3.2b by points K and L, respectively.

What would happen to the general equilibrium solution for each country if the two were allowed to trade internationally? Let's consider the forces at work. We know that the autarky price of S is lower in A than in B, while the autarky price of T is lower in B than in A. Can these price differentials continue to exist after we allow for trade? Given our assumptions, the answer is no. In particular, because there are

FIGURE 3.2   *Pretrade equilibriums: (a) country A; (b) country B.*

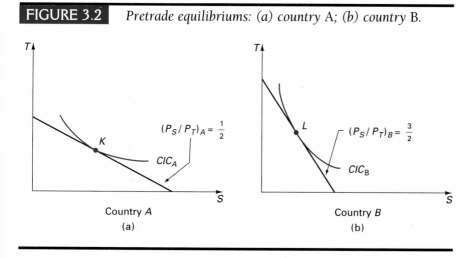

Terms of trade
The relative price at
which trade occurs
between countries.

no barriers to trade, the demand for S will rise in *A* and fall in *B*. As this happens, the relative price of *S* will begin to rise in *A* and fall in *B*. (By identical reasoning, demand for *T,* and therefore its relative price—P_T/P_S—will fall in *A* and rise in *B*.) Thus, P_S/P_T will continue to move until a new equilibrium is reached. This new equilibrium is known as the *international trade equilibrium.*

What are the characteristics of this equilibrium? First, instead of two autarky prices, there will be only one world price. This price is known as the **terms of trade**. In a moment we'll take up the process by which the world price is determined. We know now, however, that the world price will be between 1/2 (*A*'s autarky price) and 3/2 (*B*'s autarky price). This is because *A*'s producers would never sell *S* on the world market at a price below what they could receive in autarky (1/2), and *B*'s consumers would never pay more than what they would pay for *S* in autarky (3/2). Consider what would happen in each country if the terms of trade become, say, 3/4.

In *A*, producers of *S* who had received the equivalent of 1/2 unit of *T* for their output can now sell their product on the world market to consumers from both countries for the equivalent of 3/4 units of *T*. Because of this change in opportunities, country *A*'s soybean producers will want to expand their production levels. On the other hand, *A*'s textile producers, seeing the price of their product fall from the equivalent of 2 units of soybeans to only 4/3 units, will begin to contract output. Since they were a competitive industry in autarky, they were making only normal profits at the old prices. Now, with the fall in price of *T,* they are incurring losses and will be forced out of business. As the *T* industry closes down in *A,* labor becomes available for the expansion of the *S* industry. When will this process stop? Given our assumption of constant opportunity costs, the answer must be that in the new equilibrium, *A* will completely specialize in the production of *S*. And, of course, since an analogous process is occurring in *B,* it will completely specialize in the production of *T.*

Note, then, a *very important result.* Under the preceding conditions, free international trade leads each country to specialize completely in the production of its comparative-advantage good. That is, production of the good with the lower autarky price expands, and, by definition, the country with a *lower autarky price* of a product has *comparative advantage* in that product. Therefore, production and trade follow the line of comparative advantage.

How do we illustrate the process of complete specialization graphically? Consider the graphs in Figure 3.3. As before, part a denotes the situation in country *A,* while part b describes the situation in country *B*; and, as before, points *K* and *L* represent the autarky equilibrium points for the two countries, respectively. In each part of the figure, we have added a new line. This line, labeled *TOT,* has two important features. First, its slope is equal (in absolute value) to the terms of trade, which we have continued to assume to be equal to 3/4. Second, the line is connected to each country's PPF at the international trade production point for that country. Hence, it starts at point *J* in Figure 3.3a and at point *M* in Figure 3.3b. As we just explained, the opportunity for country *A* to trade internationally in this example will result in an expansion in the production of *S* and a contraction of *T.* The arrows along *A*'s PPF indicate this process, although this is not likely to be the actual path the economy takes in reaching point *J*. Similar arrows in Figure 3.3b denote the expansion of *T* and contraction of *S* in country B.

The *TOT* line represents the **consumption possibility frontier** for a country that engages in international trade. A country's consumption possibility frontier tells us the various combinations of goods (consumption bundles) a country can obtain for itself by taking advantage of international trade. Consider country A again. With international trade, it is completely specialized in the production of *S* and could, if its residents wanted, close off its borders to trade. Of course, then only *S* would be available for consumption. Alternatively, for every unit of *S* that producers in A put on the world market at price 3/4, they receive 3/4 unit of *T*.

What will be A's consumption choice? At an international price of 3/4, country A's preferred consumption bundle is given by the tangency point of A's community indifference curves with the *TOT* line. In Figure 3.3a this point is point *I*. How can country A get to point *I*? Again, consider the diagram. At point *J*, country A is producing *OJ* units of *S* and no units of *T*. Its preferred consumption bundle, point *I*, contains *OH* units of *S* and *HI* units of *T*. Thus, A is producing *HJ* units more of *S* than its residents would like to consume. The difference becomes exports. Likewise, its residents would like to consume *HI* units more of *T* than country A produces. These must be imports.

The triangle *HIJ* is country A's **trade triangle**. A trade triangle tells us how much the residents of a country want to trade at a given world price. In particular, the sides of the triangle tell us the desired exports and imports for a given term of trade, which, in turn, is defined by the absolute value of the slope of the hypotenuse of the triangle.

If we turn now to part b of Figure 3.3, we can derive country B's trade triangle in an identical fashion. For that country, production becomes specialized in the output of *T* at point *M*. Desired consumption at a price of 3/4 would occur along the

Consumption possibility frontier
The various bundles of goods that a country can obtain by taking advantage of international trade.

Trade triangle
A geometric device that tells us the amounts a country is willing to trade at a particular world price.

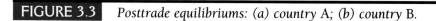

FIGURE 3.3   *Posttrade equilibriums: (a) country A; (b) country B.*

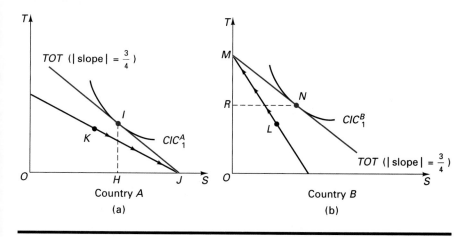

TOT line at point *N*. Therefore, *B*'s trade triangle is given by the triangle *MRN*. Country *B*'s exports are given by *MR,* and its imports by *RN*.

What can we say about the trade triangles of the two countries? First, recall from geometry that similar triangles have the same shape but not necessarily the same size (i.e., they share the same internal angles). From our derivation of trade triangles, then, it should be clear that they are always (geometrically) similar. How do we know this? Recall that the slope of the hypotenuse (the side of the triangle opposite the right angle) is the same for each, because it reflects the world price. Now, note that both triangles have a right angle. Thus, we see that the two triangles always share the same internal angles. Second, in international trade equilibrium, the two triangles must not only be similar but also congruent. (This means that the two triangles are identical.) This is because of our assumption that goods must pay for goods. In equilibrium, *A*'s desired exports of *S* (in this example, the base of *A*'s triangle) must equal *B*'s desired imports of *S* (the base of *B*'s triangle). Since we are measuring goods in physical units on the axes, equilibrium requires the two lengths to be identical. In the same fashion, we argue that equilibrium requires the heights of the two triangles to be the same.

Interestingly, it is a property of both the laws of geometry and the laws of economics that if the bases of the two similar triangles are equal in length (i.e., if *A*'s desired exports of *S* equal *B*'s desired imports of *S*), then the heights of the two triangles will also be equal (i.e., *A*'s desired imports of *T* will be equal to *B*'s desired exports of that product). More formally, the economics version of this law is known as **Walras Law**. This law states that if there are *n* markets in the world and any $n - 1$ of these markets are in equilibrium, so too will be the *n*th market. For our purposes, this law is especially handy, since we have only two markets. In this model, if one market is in equilibrium, so is the other.

Suppose the two trade triangles are not congruent but only similar. It must be the case geometrically, then, that one triangle has both a larger side and a larger base than the other. In terms of economics, residents of the country with the larger triangle want to trade more than their foreign counterparts. In this case, how can a trading equilibrium be attained? The geometric answer to this question is simple. The smaller triangle must become larger and the larger triangle must become smaller. Is there an economic process that would bring this about? The answer is yes. The process is known as **reciprocal demand.**

Reciprocal demand refers to the interaction of international demand and supply. It works in a fashion that is similar to demand and supply in other markets. If demand does not equal supply in world markets, the international price will change to bring about equality. As the price changes in the world market, the shapes of the two triangles also change. In particular, desired consumption of the two goods will change in each country (convince yourself of this fact by rotating a ruler up and down in Figure 3.3a but keeping it attached to point *J*). So long as a country remains completely specialized in the production of its exportables, the production point will stay fixed. Thus, with changing consumption but constant production levels in each country, desired amounts of trade for each country change as the international price changes. That is, the trade triangles change shape with changes in the international price.

Walras Law
In a world with *n* markets, if $n - 1$ are in equilibrium, so is the *n*th.

Reciprocal demand
The process of international interaction of demand and supply necessary to produce an equilibrium international price.

To achieve international equilibrium, the price of the imports of the country with the larger trade triangle must rise so that its residents will demand less, while the price of the imports of the country with the smaller trade triangle must fall so that its citizens will want to trade more. In other words, in the market where there is excess demand, the price must rise. In the market where there is excess supply, the price must fall. This is nothing more than the usual price adjustment pattern we expect to see in markets. As the prices change, the trade triangles begin to converge in size. When the process is fully carried out, the result is international trade equilibrium (congruent trade triangles).

Let us summarize what we have learned from our model so far:

1. It is not necessary for a country to possess absolute advantage in the production of any product for that country to be able to participate in international trade. What is required is for a country to possess comparative advantage in the production of one or more goods. In a two-good, two-country world, a country has comparative advantage in the product that has a lower pretrade relative price than in the other country.

2. International trade will occur along the lines of comparative advantage. Countries will export their comparative-advantage good in exchange for their comparative-disadvantage good. This is because the comparative-advantage good of each country will initially sell at a lower price than in other countries, hence establishing the desired pattern of trade.

3. The international trade equilibrium is characterized by the following conditions: There will be one world price—the terms of trade. This price will lie somewhere between the autarky prices of the two countries. It is established through the forces of international supply and demand, known as reciprocal demand. In particular, the international price moves to ensure that there is balanced trade in all markets.

THE GAINS FROM INTERNATIONAL TRADE

We have already established that free international trade leads to a specialization of production in each country's comparative-advantage good and in many cases to an increase in total world output. Who benefits from international trade? Do both countries gain from trade, or is one made better off at the expense of the other? It would seem that residents of both countries must be better off than in autarky, or else trade would not take place. In this section we spell out the answers to these and other questions regarding the gains from trade.

Consider Figure 3.4. This diagram reproduces the graph of the trade equilibrium for country *A*. The effect of international trade for *A* is to move from the autarky equilibrium at point *K* to specialize in the production of *S* at point *J* but to consume the bundle denoted by point *I*. Recall that *A* reaches point *I* by exporting *HJ* units of

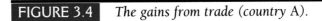

FIGURE 3.4   *The gains from trade (country A).*

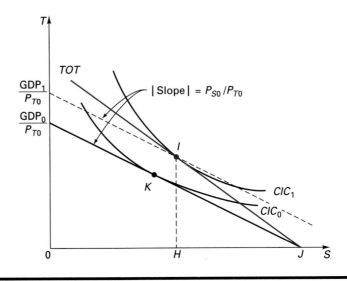

S in exchange for *HI* units of *T*. Are residents of *A* better off than they would be at point *K*? The answer is yes. How do we know? There are a variety of arguments that can be employed to prove this proposition.

First, note that point *I* is above and to the right of point *K*. This implies that this consumption bundle has more of both goods in it than would be available in bundle *K*. And since we have assumed no change in population for the country, it would be easily feasible in the new equilibrium to distribute to the population of *A* equal amounts of the additional goods made available through international trade. Thus, at least potentially, everyone in *A* is better off than in autarky.

Note, however, that residents of a country need not choose an international trade consumption point that contains more of both goods. In particular, they can choose any bundle found on the *TOT* line. Is there a more general way to determine what has happened to economic welfare? Based on our assumption in the previous chapter regarding the existence and meaning of community indifference curves, we know that *A*'s residents are better off with international trade. This is because point *I* lies on a higher community indifference curve than point *K*. If higher *CICs* connote higher levels of community well-being, then welfare has risen in country *A*. Recall, however, the very restrictive assumptions we had to make to justify the existence of community indifference curves. The restrictiveness of these assumptions suggests that we might want an even more straightforward proof that *A* is better off with trade. Fortunately, such a criterion exists.

The rule we shall follow is the one described in the last chapter, the criterion of real GDP. In particular, if measured using autarky prices, *A*'s real GDP while in autarky is given by GDP_0/P_{T0}. Now, consider the dashed line drawn through point

I (the international trade consumption point) with slope equal to the pretrade value of P_{S0}/P_{T0}. The fact that the intercepts of this second line lie outside the intercepts of A's PPF implies that when measured in terms of either good, the value of A's consumption at point I exceeds the value at point K. In other words, A's standard of living has risen. Alternatively, while living in autarky, the population of A could not have afforded the bundle of goods it consumes with international trade.

What are the sources of the gains from trade for A? There are two. First, there are consumption gains from trade. These come about because, by being exposed to international markets, A's consumers are now able to purchase goods more cheaply. The second source of gain is called the production gain from trade. This comes about because international trade causes production to be centered in those sectors where A's labor is relatively more efficient. The greater output that results means that A's real GDP has risen, enabling its citizens to expand their consumption of goods and thereby increase their collective standard of living. How substantial are these gains? As we shall discuss next, the answer is that they differ from one country to the next and depend on how much the terms of trade differ from the pretrade price ratio. The gains can be quite large. Consider, for instance, Item 3.1. There, we discuss what happened to Japan when it opened its markets to world trade in the nineteenth century.

The gains from trade are intimately related to the terms of trade. In our two-country, two-good example, the closer the terms of trade are to one country's pretrade price ratio, the greater the gains for the other country. Recall our example. The pretrade price ratio was 1/2 in A and 3/2 in B. For A to gain from trade, there must exist an international price ratio greater than 1/2. Since A sells S in world markets

---

ITEM 3.1 | Japan's Gains from Entry into World Trade in 1858

Until 1858, Japan was almost entirely isolated from world trade. In that year, the Japanese government ended self-imposed trade restrictions and began trading with the rest of the world. Richard Huber has published a fascinating study of the effects on the economy of Japan of this change in policy.*

Once trade opened, Japan specialized in two major exports, silk and tea. In autarky the prices of these products had been very low. Once trade began, they rose dramatically. Silk prices in Japan rose 26 percent in real terms. Tea prices rose more than 50 percent. Prices of Japanese imports fell equally dramatically, on average by

39 percent in real terms. Japanese producers and consumers responded to this sharp improvement in the Japanese terms of trade. Within 12 years after markets were opened, foreign trade had increased by 7,000 percent. Professor Huber calculates that the combination of improved terms of trade as well as the gains from adopting improved technology from abroad may have accounted for as much as a 65 percent rise in real national income.

---

*See J. Richard Huber, "Effect on Prices of Japan's Entry into World Commerce after 1858," *Journal of Political Economy* (1971).

for *T*, its residents are better off the higher the relative price of *S* (and therefore the lower the relative price of *T*). For residents of B to benefit from trade, there must exist a terms of trade less than 3/2. If the international price ends up between the two autarky price ratios, *both* countries gain relative to autarky. Clearly, *A*'s residents gain more and *B*'s gain less from trade if the international price ends up being at or very near 3/2. Alternatively, *A*'s residents gain less and *B*'s gain more if the international price ends up at or near 1/2. Is there anything more that can be said about how the international price is determined, and therefore about which country will gain relatively more from international trade?

As we noted previously, the international price is determined through the process of reciprocal demand. It settles down at that level where trade flows are balanced. As it turns out, the degree to which the international price moves from its autarky level for each country depends upon the strength of foreign demand and supply factors. If there is a large increase in demand for a product in a country due to the presence of foreign demand, then the price may rise a lot. If foreign demand is small relative to domestic consumption, then there may be little or no effect on the price.

This analysis suggests the following general rule: If two countries of approximately equal size and with similar patterns of taste engage in international trade, the gains from trade will be divided about equally between them. On the other hand, the larger one country is relative to the other, the fewer gains from trade accrue to the larger country. In fact, in cases where countries are very dissimilar in size, it is more likely that the large country will continue to produce its comparative-disadvantage good, because the small country will not be able to supply all of the worldwide demand for this product. If this turns out to be the case, the small country gets *all* the gains from trade. This situation is known as the **importance of being unimportant**.

Importance of being unimportant
When small countries trade with big countries, the small are likely to enjoy most of the mutual gains from trade.

THE RELATIONSHIP BETWEEN TRADE AND WAGES

What does the classical theory have to say about the relationship between international trade and factor payments? To get a handle on this question, recall our earlier discussion about the determination of money prices in the two economies. We have assumed that both industries are everywhere perfectly competitive and that labor is the only factor of production that receives payment for its services, so it must be that in pretrade equilibrium the following set of relationships holds:

$$P_{SA} = W_A \times \text{hours}_{SA} = W_A \times 3$$

$$P_{TA} = W_A \times \text{hours}_{TA} = W_A \times 6$$

$$P_{SB} = W_B \times \text{hours}_{SB} = W_B \times 12$$

$$P_{TB} = W_B \times \text{hours}_{TB} = W_B \times 8$$

(3.1)

where the prices and wage rates are in terms of local currency and reflect pretrade levels. If trade is to occur along the lines of comparative advantage once it is allowed, it must be that when measured *in the same currency,* the pretrade money price of a country's comparative-advantage good is less than or equal to the pretrade price of that good abroad. And, for any incentive to trade at all, there must be at least one good that is priced lower. Suppose, for simplicity of exposition, that strict inequalities hold for both prices. Then, for trade to occur along the lines of comparative advantage in our example, the following conditions must hold simultaneously:

$$P_{SA} < E \times P_{SB}$$

and $\qquad\qquad$ (3.2)

$$P_{TA} > E \times P_{TB}$$

where E is an exchange rate that translates units of B's currency into units of A's. (If we assume that A stands for America and B for Great Britain, then $E = \$2$ implies that 2 dollars buys 1 pound sterling.) Now, using the information in Equation 3.1, we can convert the inequalities in Equation 3.2 as follows:

$$W_A \times 3 < E \times W_B \times 12$$

and $\qquad\qquad$ (3.3)

$$W_A \times 6 > E \times W_B \times 8$$

The system of inequalities can be solved simultaneously. The procedure is simple. In the first inequality, divide both sides by $E \times W_B$. Then, divide both sides by 3. This moves all the algebraic terms to the left-hand side of the inequality and all of the pure numbers to the right, but it does not change the truthfulness of the expression. Now, follow a similar procedure in the second inequality. The results of these operations are

$$W_A/(E \times W_B) < 4$$

and $\qquad\qquad$ (3.4)

$$W_A/(E \times W_B) > 4/3$$

or, after combining terms,

$$4/3 < W_A/(E \times W_B) < 4 \qquad\qquad (3.5)$$

Study Equation 3.5 very carefully. The term in the center of the expression, $W_A/(E \times W_B)$, is known as the *relative wage ratio.* That is, it is the value of the wage rate in country A divided by the value of the wage rate in country B (measured in terms of A's currency). What Equation 3.5 says, then, is that for trade to occur along the lines of comparative advantage, workers in A must earn more than workers in B. In particular, they must earn no more than 4 times the wages and no less than 4/3 the wages paid to workers in B. How do we explain this result?

The answer has to do with differences in labor productivity in the two countries. Recall again the data found in Table 3.3. In that example, A's workers are more productive than B's workers in both industries (i.e., A has absolute advantage in both soybeans and textiles). The message of Equation 3.5 is that because A's workers can produce more output than B's workers in the same amount of time, A's workers should earn higher wages than B's workers. How much higher? In A's comparative-advantage industry, soybeans, A's workers are 4 times as productive as B's workers. Thus, A's wage rate should be no more than 4 times B's wage rate. In A's comparative-disadvantage industry, textiles, A's workers are only 4/3 more productive than B's workers. Hence, A's wages should be no less than 4/3 greater than B's wages.

We have established that money prices in the two countries in pretrade are intimately related to each country's wage rate. In particular, as wage rates rise, so will prices. Suppose that wages in either A or B get out of line with productivity. What will be the effect on international trade? Let's consider country A. Suppose that wages in A rise to 5 times the wages in country B; that is,

$$W_A = 5 \times E \times W_B.$$

What will be the pattern of pretrade prices in the two countries?

$$P_{SA} = W_A \times 3 = (5 \times E \times W_B) \times 3 = E \times W_B \times 15$$

$$P_{TA} = W_A \times 6 = (5 \times E \times W_B) \times 6 = E \times W_B \times 30$$

(3.6)

Now, recall the level of pretrade prices in country B measured in terms of A's currency. These prices are

$$E \times P_{SB} = E \times W_B \times 12$$

$$E \times P_{TB} = E \times W_B \times 8$$

(3.7)

Compare the prices in the two countries, given by Equations 3.6 and 3.7. Clearly, the pretrade prices of both goods are higher in country A than they are in country B. This is because the wage differential between the two countries exceeds the maximum productivity differential.

In a case such as the example we have just described, country B has an incentive to sell both goods to country A. Country A, on the other hand, has nothing to sell to country B. In such cases in the real world, country B will run a balance-of-trade surplus with country A. That is, country B's exports will exceed its imports, and vice versa for country A, which will run a balance-of-trade deficit.

This example offers two valuable lessons. First, for two-way trade to occur between countries with different productivity levels, wages must be higher in one country than in the other. In particular, if differences in technology confer higher productivity levels, then the technologically advanced country must have a higher wage rate. This simple example explains how U.S. workers can enjoy relatively high wages, especially when compared with the wages paid in developing countries, and still compete in world markets. Item 3.2 applies this type of analysis to make predictions about the direction of comparative advantage between the United States and Mexico.

ITEM 3.2	Wage and Productivity Comparisons for the United States and Mexico

In a recent study of the potential trade effects of the North American Free Trade Agreement (NAFTA), Andrew Solocha undertakes an analysis similar to our discussion of the relationship between trade and wages.[†] Using data from the early 1990s for the United States, Canada, and Mexico on wages and labor productivity in various industries, Professor Solocha tries to determine patterns of comparative advantage based on whether or not wages in a particular industry in a given country are out of line with labor productivity.

The approach undertaken by Professor Solocha is more complicated than the simplified model we discuss in the text. This is because there are many industries rather than two in each country and, more importantly, wages within any one country differ across industries.[‡] Nonetheless, the basic story is very similar to our presentation. Let a_j represent labor hours necessary to produce a unit of good j in the home

country (e.g., 3 hours to make a unit of S in A) and a_j^* be the comparable number for the foreign country (e.g., 12 hours in country B). We saw above that A loses its comparative advantage in good S if $W_A/E \times W_B$ is greater than a_j^*/a_j (i.e., 12/3). In his study, Andrew Solocha provides calculations of similar ratios. The main differences between his study and our presentation is that his wage ratios are industry specific (i.e., $W_{Aj}/E \times W_{Bj}$) and he weights each ratio by average ratios for all of manufacturing in a particular country (i.e., wages and productivity in industry j are measured relative to average wages and productivity levels for each country). Professor Solocha argues that if the wage ratio for a particular industry is less than (exceeds) the productivity ratio for that industry, then the United States (Mexico) has comparative advantage in that industry. His calculations are presented in the following table.

U.S.–Mexican Relative Wage and Productivity Data

Industry	Relative Wages	Relative Productivity
Food Products	.979	1.624
Beverages	1.212	1.345
Tobacco	1.052	.755
Textiles	.756	1.049
Wearing apparel	.699	1.306
Footwear	.673	.865

[†]See Andrew Solocha, "Implications of Comparative Cost Advantages for the NAFTA," *The International Trade Journal*, 1994.
[‡]Recall we assume only two industries and that wages are equal in both.

(Continued)

ITEM 3.2	Wage and Productivity Comparisons for the United States and Mexico (Continued)

Industry	Relative Wages	Relative Productivity
Wood products	.940	1.553
Furniture	.952	.961
Paper and products	1.034	1.376
Pulp, paper	1.256	1.915
Printing, publishing	.819	1.175
Industrial chemicals	1.038	1.088
Basic excl. fertilizers	.932	.730
Synthetic resins	1.115	1.105
Other chemicals	.850	2.043
Drugs and medicines	.901	2.686
Petroleum, coal products	1.255	.683
Rubber products	.585	.727
Plastic products	.853	1.242
Pottery, china	1.008	1.157
Glass and products	.784	1.004
Nonmetal products	.747	.909
Iron and steel	1.316	.597
Nonferrous metals	.924	.375
Metal products	.973	1.114
Machinery	.905	.780
Office, computing	.888	.606
Electrical machinery	1.152	1.170
Radio, television	1.339	1.159
Transport equipment	1.187	.521
Motor vehicles	1.182	.512
Professional goods	.848	1.580
Other industries	.339	.940

To better understand these numbers, suppose that wages paid in Mexico were equal in all industries and that Mexican workers are equally productive no matter where they work. *Under this special assumption,* consider the iron and steel industry entry. The value 1.316 means that U.S. workers are paid about 30 percent more than the average U.S. manufacturing wage. This is probably not too far from the true relation. The value .597 would imply that U.S. iron and steel industry workers are only about 60 percent as productive as the average U.S. manufacturing worker. This is probably very far off the mark. Rather it is more likely that U.S. workers are very productive but that Mexican workers in this industry are much more productive in this sector than they are in general. In any event, because 1.316 is considerably greater than .597, Professor Solocha's calculations suggest that Mexico has a comparative cost advantage in this industry. In addition, Mexico appears to have clear comparative cost advantage in the nonferrous metals, transport, and petroleum product industries. The United States appears to have a comparative cost advantage over Mexico in food products, wood products, paper, pharmaceuticals, plastics, and professional goods. Surprisingly the analysis also suggests that the United States has a comparative labor cost advantage in wearing apparel and textiles.

Second, the example illustrates that a country can lose its comparative advantage, which is due to the productivity of its workers, if wages get out of line with productivity. In particular, in the last example we considered, we assumed that $W_A = 5 \times E \times W_B$. For workers in A to be internationally competitive, W_A should be no higher than $4 \times E \times W_B$. What can be done in country A about this situation? There are two possible solutions. Either wages in A must fall relative to wages in B (i.e., they must fall to a ratio of 4 or less times country B's), or B's wages, when measured in terms of A's currency, must rise in value relative to A's wages. This can happen if the value of E rises. When E rises, B's currency becomes more expensive in terms of A's.

To what extent do either of these changes tend to occur naturally in the international economy? This is one of the many questions we address in the latter part of this text. For the time being, we assume away the question by requiring that wages be in line with productivity.

AN EVALUATION OF THE CLASSICAL MODEL

As we noted at the beginning of this chapter, many of the basic building blocks of the classical model have been a standard part of the economics repertoire for over 200 years. The test of time suggests that there are many good things to be learned from this model. What are they?

Clearly, one of the most important is the notion that trade occurs along the lines of comparative advantage. What this teaches us is that international trade is a phenomenon that aids in increasing the productive capacity of our planet. It is also a phenomenon that leads to a higher standard of living for the countries involved. Furthermore, it is something that occurs as a direct consequence of free-market activity.

There are problems with the classical model. The model is seriously incomplete in many ways; that is, while the model bases trade on differences in productivity levels between countries, nowhere does it explain why these differences exist. The model also makes extreme predictions that are not borne out in the real world. It predicts that countries will completely specialize in production of exportables and entirely get out of the business of producing import-competing goods. In the real world, however, it seems apparent that countries often continue to produce import-competing products; for instance, the United States imports and produces steel. Finally, the model seems to suggest that the greatest gains from trade come about when the countries involved are very dissimilar in their technologies. Yet, as we showed in Chapter 1, the vast majority of international trade is between the various industrialized countries—countries with similar standards of living and technology.

Is the classical theory only a teaching device and no longer useful to explain trading phenomena? The answer is no. It shows us, for instance, the motives for trade to occur between developed and developing countries. It also explains in a very intuitive fashion why high-wage countries can continue to trade profitably even when faced with low-wage competing countries. In the next chapter we investigate a more modern theory of international trade. This theory attempts to address some of the problems with the classical model that we have noted.

SUMMARY

1. The classical model of international trade was developed over 200 years ago by Adam Smith. He believed that different countries possessed unique advantages in the production of certain goods. He then showed that world output would rise if countries traded freely along the lines of their productive advantages.

2. Torrens and Ricardo expanded on this theory by showing that even if a country did not have an absolute advantage in *any* good, it and all other countries would still benefit from international trade. This would be the case if countries specialized in the production of those goods with which they had the greatest absolute advantage or the least absolute disadvantage. This is known as the law of comparative advantage.

3. Pretrade relative prices determine the direction of comparative advantage and therefore the direction of trade. A country has a comparative advantage in that good with the *lower* pretrade price, relative to the other good and the other country.

4. The international price will lie somewhere between the pretrade relative prices of the two countries. The closer the international price is to one country's pretrade relative price, the greater the gains from trade for the other country.

5. Labor productivity is higher in technologically advanced countries, and therefore wages should also be higher in these countries. So long as wages are related to productivity, high-wage countries retain their comparative advantage.

EXERCISES

1. For each of the following cases determine the following: (a) the pretrade relative prices; (b) the direction of comparative advantage; and (c) the limits to the relative wage rate.

Hours of Labor Required to Produce S or T

Case 1	A	B		Case 2	A	B
S	6	15		S	10	5
T	2	12		T	4	5

Case 3	A	B
S	10	8
T	20	4

Case 4	A	B
S	4	9
T	2	3

2. Show that if country A has absolute advantage in S while country B has absolute advantage in T, A has comparative advantage in S, and B has comparative advantage in T.

3. Show that if a country has comparative advantage in good S, it has comparative disadvantage in good T.

4. Using the data from Table 3.3, show the effect on world output if each country moved toward specialization in the production of its comparative-*disadvantage* good.

5. Suppose there are 20,000 hours of labor available in country A. Five hours of labor are required to produce 1 unit of S, while 4 hours are required to produce 1 unit of T. Find the shape and dimensions of A's PPF.

6. Use the information in Exercise 5 plus the following additional data to graph A's trade triangle: world relative price = 2; A's imports = 2,000; A's exports = ?

7. Evaluate the following statements:
   a. Developed countries have nothing to gain by trading with developing countries.
   b. Developed countries get all the gains from trade when they trade with developing countries because they can dictate their prices to these countries.
   c. The United States can no longer compete in world markets because American wages are too high.

8. Show that less than complete specialization in production leads to a lower level of welfare than complete specialization.

9. Suppose that the technologies available to A and B are given by the following table:

	A	B
S	4	8
T	2	4

Are there any incentives for trade in this example? Explain.

10. For case 2 in Exercise 1, which country would prefer a term of trade of 1.1 rather than an international price of 2? Explain.

11. Consider two countries, A and B, with the technologies given by case 4 in Exercise 1. Suppose that the wage rate in A, W_A, equals $10 per hour and the wage rate in B, when measured in dollars, $E \times W_B$, equals $5 per hour. Calculate the pretrade price of S and T in both A and B. Is there a basis for mutually beneficial trade? Why or why not? Suppose that W_A rises to $12 per hour. Everything else held constant, what would happen to trade patterns? Why? What options would be available to A to resolve this situation?

12. Consider two countries, A and B, with the technologies given by case 3 in Exercise 1. Suppose that the wage rate in A, W_A, equals $10 per hour; then, for mutually beneficial trade to occur, the wage rate in B, when measured in dollars, $E \times W_B$, must lie in a range from $X to $Y. Calculate X and Y and explain your answer.

13. The classical model predicts that countries will completely specialize in the production of their comparative-advantage good. Explain why the opportunity to engage in international trade would lead to this result.

14. Suppose that country A has 10,000 worker-hours available for production and that it initially has the technology given by case 3 of Exercise 1. Derive its PPF and determine its exact dimensions. Now, suppose that scientists in A develop a technology that doubles labor productivity in both industries. What would happen to A's PPF? Derive and explain. What would happen to the pattern of comparative advantage? Derive and explain.

15. Suppose that country A has 40,000 worker-hours available for production and that it initially has the technology given by case 4 of Exercise 1. Derive its PPF and determine its exact dimensions. Now, suppose that scientists in A develop a technology that doubles labor productivity in producing good S. What would happen to A's PPF? Derive and explain. What would happen to the pattern of comparative advantage? Derive and explain.

INTERNET APPLICATIONS

Please visit our Web site at www.awl.com/husted_melvin for more exercises and readings.

APPENDIX 3.1

THE CLASSICAL MODEL WITH MANY GOODS*

It is straightforward to extend the classical model to a case where there are two countries and many goods. The main result from such an extension is that the countries will tend to specialize in the production of one or more goods after trade opens and to trade for the remainder of the goods in their consumption basket.

Suppose we assume that instead of two goods in the world, S and T, there are five, S, T, X, Y, and Z. Suppose further that all the other assumptions of the classical model hold. In particular, production in all five industries and in both countries is characterized by fixed labor-output ratios. Let those labor-output ratios be given by the numbers in Table A3.1. If we examine the data in the table, we see that in this particular example, country B is the technologically advanced country. Country B's greatest technical advantage, and therefore its greatest comparative advantage, lies with good T, where B's workers are three times as efficient as A's. Country A's greatest technical advantage, and therefore its greatest comparative advantage, lies in the production of good Y, where its workers are as efficient as B's workers.

From our earlier analysis in this chapter, we now know two things. First, if there were only two goods, once trade begins, country A will move to specialize in its comparative-advantage good Y and begin to export it, while B will move to specialize in and export some T. That statement is true here as well. What about the remaining three goods? Where will they be produced? The answer depends upon the relative wage ratio.

In particular, remember another lesson from this chapter: For trade to occur along the lines of comparative advantage, the relative wage ratio must lie between the extremes of the differences in relative productivity. Hence, wages in A, the

TABLE A3.1	*Labor Requirements by Industry and Country*				
	Industry				
	S	T	X	Y	Z
Country A	4	9	10	2	5
Country B	2	3	4	2	3

*For additional results in a classical model with many goods, see Rudiger Dornbusch, Stanley Fischer, and Paul Samuelson, "Comparative Advantage, Trade, and Payments in a Ricardian Model with a Continuum of Goods," *American Economic Review* 67 (1977): 823–39; and Charles Wilson, "On the General Structure of Ricardian Models with a Continuum of Goods: Applications to Growth, Tariff Theory, and Technical Change," *Econometrica* 48 (1980): 1675–1702.

TABLE A3.2	Ratio of Labor Hours in Country B to Labor Hours in Country A by Industry

	Industry				
	T	X	S	Z	Y
Ratio	0.33	0.4	0.5	0.6	1

technologically backward country, must be no more than wages in B—when measured in the same currency—but no less than 1/3 B's wages. Or, in terms of the relative wage formula developed in the chapter,

$$1/3 < W_A/(E \times W_B) < 1 \qquad (A3.1)$$

Let's go back to the information in Table A3.1 and rearrange goods from left to right in the order of A's comparative advantage. In particular, on the left we'll have A's (B's) least (greatest) comparative-advantage good. We develop this ordering by simply dividing B's labor hours by A's labor hours, so that the numbers in the table will become fractions listed in ascending order. See Table A3.2. This rank ordering is known as the *chain of comparative advantage*. The value of the relative wage rate that prevails between the two countries determines the final trade pattern. In particular, suppose that the relative wage ratio equaled 0.66. This would imply that workers in A earn 2/3 of B's wages (when measured in the same currency). Now consider Table A3.2. We know the relative wage rate must lie between the differences in productivity. A value of the relative wage of 0.66 is smaller than 1 but is bigger than all other relative productivity levels. In that case, B would be able to undersell A in all goods except Y. Hence, the trade pattern that would emerge here would be for A to concentrate production only in good Y and attempt to trade this product for a bundle containing some or all other goods in the model. If the relative wage was lower, say 0.45, then A could also profitably sell goods S and Z. Consequently, the value of the relative wage rate determines where the chain of comparative advantage is divided into groups of goods that A will export and that B will export.

APPENDIX 3.2

OFFER CURVES AND THE TERMS OF TRADE

In the chapter we discussed the process by which the terms of trade are determined. Recall that we dubbed this process *reciprocal demand*. In this appendix we develop an alternative geometric device to illustrate the process of reciprocal demand. This device is known as the *offer curve*.

Consider Figure A3.1. There we show the PPF for country A as well as its desired consumption point if the terms of trade equal TOT_1. Note that in this equilibrium, country A would like to export EH units of good S and import HF units of good T. Now, let us consider the interesting question of what happens to A's desired trade levels as the terms of trade change. This is pictured in Figure A3.2.

In Figure A3.2 we illustrate A's desired trade points for three different values of the terms of trade. As the TOT line gets steeper, we see that A's desired level of imports rises (from T_0 to T_3), while, in this example, its desired level of exports also rises (from S_0 to S_3). The curve $GFJK$ denotes the set of desired consumption bundles for A at different world prices. This line segment is known as A's price-consumption curve.

Now, consider a diagram where units of S and T *traded internationally* are measured on the horizontal and vertical diagrams, respectively. Let us graph in this

---

FIGURE A3.1   *Country A's trading equilibrium.*

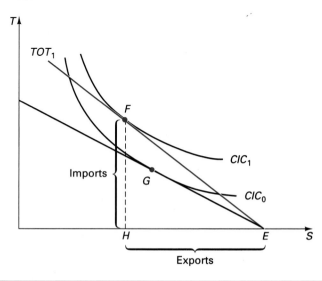

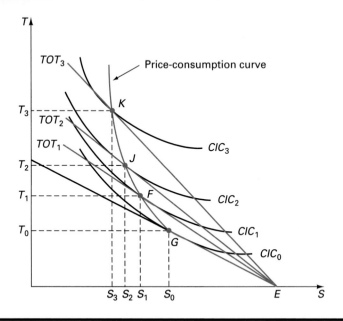

FIGURE A3.2   *Country A's price-consumption curve.*

space *A*'s desired trades at various prices. As we have developed this information already, such a graph is easy to derive. In particular, attach the line segment *EG* to *A*'s price-consumption curve and rotate the resulting line so that *E* becomes the point at the origin. The new curve is given in Figure A3.3. This curve is known as *A*'s offer curve.

Consider the figure very carefully. The axes are labeled world trade in *S* and *T*, respectively; and for each, the units of measure are physical quantities (e.g., bushels of soybeans, yards of cloth). To understand various points on *A*'s offer curve, recall again the information contained in Figure A3.2. First, we note that if after trade began, the price of *S* remained at 1/2, then country A would have a variety of options with regard to world trade, any one of which would leave it as well off as in autarky. For instance, *A* could choose not to trade at all. Or, it could move to specialize completely in the production of *S*, trading ES_0 units for S_0G ($= T_0$) units of *T*. Or, it could choose to produce somewhere along its PPF between points *E* and *G* and then trade at a world price of 1/2 units of *S* to be able to consume at point *G*, the welfare-maximizing consumption point. Thus, when the world price is 1/2, *A* would be willing to export any amount of *S* from 0 (at point *E*) up to a maximum of S_0 units. To illustrate this graphically, *A*'s offer curve is drawn as a straight line with slope 1/2 from the origin to point *G* (above S_0 units).

Again referring to Figure A3.2, we know that for *A* to want to engage in additional amounts of trade, the price of *S* must rise. For instance, as the price rises to

FIGURE A3.3   *Derivation of country A's offer curve.*

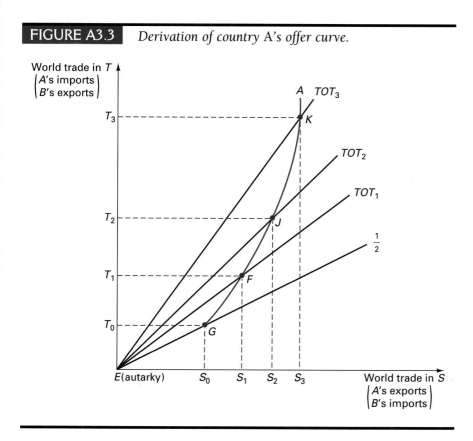

TOT_1, A's desired exports rise to the amount represented by the distance from E to S_1 units. And, of course, when the world price is TOT_1, A's desired level of imports is given by the height of this country's offer curve above point S_1 (i.e., T_1 units of T). Thus, depending upon which axis we are referring to, A's offer curve tells us *both* its desired exports and its desired imports.

Now, let's repeat the process just detailed for country B. (We leave it to you to carry out this derivation.) In Figure A3.4 we show this curve, labeled EB, as well as repeat our depiction of A's offer curve. Several things are important to note. Since A's offer curve tells us A's desired trades at different prices, and B's offer curve tells us the same information for B, international equilibrium must occur where the two offer curves intersect. Only at such an intersection point are desired trades identical. Such an intersection is illustrated in the diagram by point J. Point S_J on the S axis directly below point J represents A's desired exports of S and B's desired imports of S. Obviously, since these points are identical there must be equilibrium in the world market for S. Note also that since the two curves have the same height at their intersection, there must be equilibrium in the trade of T. This is a simple reaffirmation of Walras Law.

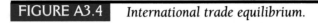

FIGURE A3.4   *International trade equilibrium.*

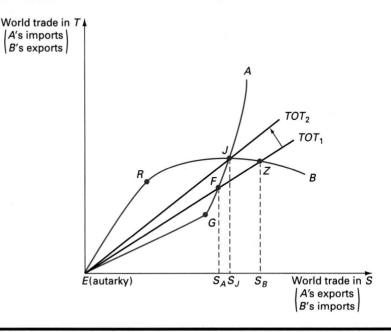

The slope of the line segment from the origin (point E) to the intersection point determines the terms of trade, here denoted by TOT_2. We can illustrate the process of reciprocal demand, which causes this price to obtain in world markets in a very straightforward fashion. Suppose that the price was TOT_1. At that price, country A wants to be at point F (exporting S_A units of S), while B wants to be at point Z (importing S_B units of S). Clearly, B's demand for S in world markets exceeds A's supply. The price must rise to clear the market. This is shown by the arrow in the diagram.

Finally, note that since both A and B are on their price-consumption paths at point J, the CICs of the two countries *at that point* must be tangent to each other. Hence, the allocation of goods between the two countries must lie on a contract curve in international trade equilibrium. Note that this is not the case at the autarky consumption points G and R. This represents a graphical depiction of a result that we have already seen in the tables of the chapter. Free international trade is more efficient than autarky.

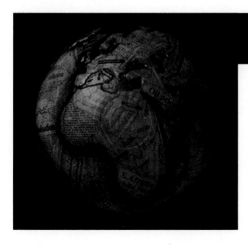

CHAPTER 4

The Heckscher–Ohlin Theory

KEY WORDS

Factor endowments
Labor intensive
Capital intensive
Labor abundant

Capital abundant
Incomplete specialization
Factor price equalization (FPE)

Economists, like all other scientists, are not happy until they think they have things right. As we showed in the last chapter, the classical theory of international trade has a number of serious defects. In particular, it offers several extreme predictions that are not borne out in real-world trade patterns. This inconsistency between reality and theoretical predictions provided economists in the nineteenth and twentieth centuries with the motivation to explore further the causes and consequences of international trade.

At first, economists sought to increase their understanding of international trade by relaxing some of the strict assumptions of the classical model. For instance, the assumption of constant opportunity costs was abandoned, and instead, economists assumed that production was characterized by increasing opportunity costs. This modification removed from the theory the stark and often-violated prediction that trade would lead countries to abandon completely the production of import-competing goods. But problems with the classical theory still remained. It was built on the notion that trade arose due to differences in productivity levels between countries, yet it was incapable of explaining why these differences might exist. Furthermore, contrary to the theory's prediction, trade seemed to prosper between the nations of Europe and between Europe and the United States, countries with similar levels of economic development.

Some economists chose to abandon the classical theory altogether in search of an alternative explanation of comparative advantage. In the early twentieth century an important new theory of international trade emerged. The Heckscher–Ohlin (HO) model of the patterns and determinants of international trade was developed by two Swedish economists, Eli Heckscher and Bertil Ohlin. Heckscher laid out the basic fundamentals of the model in a paper first published in 1919. This paper, however, was written in Swedish and was not translated into English for almost 30 years.* Consequently, the model received little attention. Heckscher's pupil, Ohlin, elaborated on these ideas in his 1924 doctoral dissertation (also in Swedish) and later in a book published in English by Harvard University in 1933.[†]

Heckscher and Ohlin built their theory around two basic characteristics of countries and products. Countries differ from each other according to the factors of production they possess. Goods differ from each other according to the factors that are required in their production. Given these features of the world, Heckscher and Ohlin argued that a country will be able to produce at lower cost (and therefore have comparative advantage in) those products whose production requires relatively large amounts of the factors of production (also known as **factor endowments**, e.g., labor, land, capital, natural resources) with which that country is relatively well endowed. For instance, countries with relatively large amounts of land relative to

Factor endowments
The quantities of factors of production (e.g., labor and machines) possessed by a country.

---

*An English translation of this paper, entitled "The Effect of Foreign Trade on the Distribution of Income," appears in Howard S. Ellis and Lloyd A. Metzler, eds., *Readings in International Trade* (Philadelphia: The Blakiston Co., 1949).
[†]Ohlin's book is titled *Interregional and International Trade* (Boston: Harvard University Press, 1933).

other factors (e.g., Australia) will have a comparative advantage in producing goods that require relatively large amounts of land for efficient production (e.g., wheat).

Following the publication of Ohlin's book, the ideas of Heckscher and Ohlin quickly gained adherents among economists around the world. The appeal of the model was its fundamental simplicity, its logical completeness, and the ease with which it could be manipulated to understand the causes and effects of international trade. As economists studied the model, they found that it was capable of providing important insights into such issues as the effect of international trade on wages and other factor prices, and the impact of economic growth on the pattern of international trade. It also provides an explanation for the political behavior of various interest groups in an economy.

In the remainder of this chapter, we examine the HO model. We begin, as we have in the previous two chapters, by spelling out the assumptions behind the model. Then, we turn our attention to a number of important extensions to the model. Throughout, we compare and contrast the structure and predictions of the classical and HO theories.

THE HO MODEL: BASIC ASSUMPTIONS

By now, you should be familiar with the way economists construct a theory. First, they establish its framework by spelling out a series of assumptions. Then, once the assumptions are in place, the model can be solved, and experiments can be performed with it. That is the approach we shall take here. To demonstrate the workings of the HO model, we retain the first 10 assumptions described in Chapters 2 and 3. We *drop* the assumptions that labor is the only relevant factor of production (Assumption 11) and that the technology in each country can be completely described with knowledge of unit labor inputs (Assumption 12). These last two assumptions pertain only to the classical model. Instead, we add five new assumptions.

ASSUMPTION 13 There are two factors of production: labor (L) and capital (K). Furthermore, owners of capital are paid a rental payment (R) for the services of their assets. Labor receives a wage payment (W).

This assumption relaxes one of the strict assumptions of the classical model. Recall from the last chapter that we had assumed that the only relevant factor of production was labor. This was because labor was assumed to *always* use the same (fixed) amount of machinery in the production process of either good. In the HO model the number of machines that workers use in production becomes an important factor in determining trade patterns and may change with changes in relative factor prices.

ASSUMPTION 14 The technology sets available to each country are identical.

This assumption is one of the most crucial in the HO model. It says that for any good, say textiles, producers in both countries have ready access to the same choices of production techniques. That is, various methods exist for the production of most goods; these methods typically involve the use of various quantities of labor versus capital inputs. The actual choice of production technique made by producers in each country will depend upon factor prices in those countries. That is, if labor is relatively cheap compared with capital in *A* versus *B*, then textile producers in *A* will tend to use more labor-intensive technologies than textile producers in *B*. *However, if factor prices are identical in the two countries, then exactly the same production processes for any given industry will be employed in both.* Note that the effect of this assumption is to *rule out the classical basis for international trade.* Thus, the HO model represents a clear departure from classical theorizing.

> ASSUMPTION 15 In both countries, the production of textiles (good *T*) always requires more labor per machine than the production of soybeans (good *S*). The production of both goods in both countries is subject to constant returns to scale.

Labor (capital) intensive
A good is labor (capital) intensive relative to another good if its production requires more (less) labor per machine than the other good requires in its production.

The first part of this assumption simply says that *T* is more **labor intensive** than *S*, or, equivalently, that *S* is more **capital intensive** than *T*. Thus, for any level of production and in either country, the amount of labor used per machine is higher in the *T* industry than in the *S* industry. Mathematically, the following relationship always holds true:

$$L_T/K_T > L_S/K_S$$

or, equivalently,

$$K_T/L_T < K_S/L_S$$

where L_j is the amount of labor employed in the *j* industry ($j = S$ or T), and K_j is the amount of capital employed in the *j* industry.

The reader should keep two things in mind when thinking about this assumption. First, the choice of *T* as the relatively labor-intensive commodity is purely arbitrary. Second, in defining labor (or, equivalently, capital) intensity, we emphasize the notion of *relative* labor intensity. That is, what is crucial here is that one of the two goods must utilize more workers *per machine* than the other and not simply more workers. Thus, an industry does not become labor intensive simply by being larger than another industry and therefore employing more labor. Differences in the capital/labor ratio K_j/L_j determine relative factor intensities. That such differences exist in the real world would seem to be rather obvious. However, to confirm the general validity of this assumption, Item 4.1 provides detail on the capital/labor ratios in various U.S. industries.

The second part of Assumption 15 says that proportionate changes in the use of capital and labor lead to equiproportionate changes in output. For example, one way to double the current output of textiles would be to double the amount of labor and capital employed in the textile industry.

ITEM 4.1 | Capital/Labor Ratios of Selected U.S. Industries

One of the crucial elements of the Heckscher–Ohlin theory is that different goods display different factor intensities in their production. In this item, we illustrate some examples of factor intensities for a variety of U.S. industries. Consider the following table. A number of interesting points emerge as we study the results in the table. First, there is considerable variation in the capital/labor ratio across industries. In 1960, values for this ratio ranged from a low in the apparel industry of $1,500 of capital per worker to a high in the petroleum- and coal-products industry of $93,800 of capital per worker. In 1980, these industries also represented the extremes in capital per worker, with the ratio in the apparel industry being $3,200 and the coal- and oil-products ratio being $161,200 per worker.

A second thing to note is that over time, the capital/labor ratio has risen in all industries. This result reflects the fact that, for many years, the capital stock of the United States has risen more rapidly than the labor force. Third, the ranking by industry has shown no dramatic changes over the twenty-year period shown in the study.

Capital/Labor Ratios: U.S. Industries, Selected Years (thousands of 1972 dollars)

Industry	1960	1980
Food and kindred products	12.2	22.5
Tobacco manufactures	9.0	31.9
Textiles	8.4	14.3
Apparel	1.5	3.2
Lumber	9.6	16.0
Furniture	4.6	7.6
Paper products	20.2	38.4
Printing and publishing	10.2	11.9
Chemicals	30.4	58.9
Petroleum and coal	93.8	161.2
Rubber and plastics	10.3	18.8
Leather products	2.3	4.3
Stone, clay, glass products	16.2	26.7
Primary metals	26.5	37.1
Fabricated metals	8.7	13.2
Nonelectrical machines	9.0	14.6
Electrical machines	6.4	13.0
Transportation equipment	10.5	20.3
Instruments and related products	6.5	13.3
Miscellaneous manufacturing	4.1	9.7
AVERAGE	15.0	26.8

SOURCE: E.R. Berndt and D.O. Wood, "Energy Price Stocks and Productivity Growth: A Survey," working paper (Cambridge, Mass.: MIT, 1985).

ASSUMPTION 16 Countries differ in their endowments of factors of production, L and K. In our presentation we will assume that A is relatively capital abundant, while B is relatively labor abundant.

Labor (capital) abundant
A country is labor (capital) abundant relative to another country if it has more (less) workers per machine than the other country.

What does it mean for a country to be relatively **labor (or capital) abundant**? The definition we will use says that a country is relatively labor abundant if the total workforce relative to the total capital stock is greater there than in the other country.* Mathematically, then, country A would be relatively capital abundant if

$$K_A/L_A > K_B/L_B$$

where L_k is the size of the total workforce in country k ($k = A$ or B), while K_k is the total amount of machines available in country k. As with the discussion of factor intensity in the production of the two goods, relative differences matter here.† Thus, a country cannot be labor abundant simply by having a larger population. The size of that country's capital stock must also be taken into account. More simply, ratios are important, not levels. Item 4.2 provides some detail on capital/labor ratios in various countries. In addition, we will assume that countries that are labor abundant (i.e., that have labor forces that are large relative to their capital stocks) will have low wages relative to rental payments, and vice versa for capital-abundant countries.‡

Combining the implications of Assumptions 15 and 16 allows us to develop graphically the shapes of the production possibility frontiers for the two countries. First, because the two goods differ in factor intensity in both countries, the PPFs of each country will exhibit increasing opportunity costs. To understand this point better, consider the following experiment: Suppose that in country B we begin with all of B's capital and labor working in the S industry. This would establish one point on

---

*The definition of factor abundance we employ is known as the *quantity definition*. There is an alternative (and not necessarily consistent) definition. The *price definition* of relative factor abundance says that a country is relatively labor abundant if the wage-to-rental payment in its country is lower than the wage-to-rental payment in the other country. Thus, according to Assumption 16 and the price definition, the following relationship obtains:

$$W_A/R_A > W_B/R_B$$

where W_k is the wage rate in country k ($k = A$ or B) and R_k is the rental rate in country k. In the text we assume that both definitions hold simultaneously. However, there is no law in economics that guarantees this to be true.
†The astute reader will note that in describing the technology of producing goods we refer to T as the labor-intensive product, while in referring to countries we describe B as the labor-abundant country. It has become common practice in the literature on the HO model to refer to the factor intensity of production and the factor abundance of countries. We will continue to employ this terminology throughout.
‡This is known as Samuelson's strong factor abundance assumption.

ITEM 4.2	Capital/Labor Ratios of Selected Countries

A group of economists at the University of Pennsylvania has constructed a data set on various characteristics of the economies of the world. Included in this data set are demographic characteristics and estimates of capital stocks. These capital stocks are measured in international prices, a common unit of account created by the authors, so that expenditures in different countries can be meaningfully compared. In essence, the authors have carefully examined data from different countries and remeasured prices in such a fashion that the same good costs the same in each country. In so doing, international differences in capital stocks reflect quantity differences rather than price differences.

As the table shows, the most capital-abundant countries of the world are Switzerland and Germany, each with more than 50,000 in capital per worker in 1990. The United States has a capital/labor ratio of 34,705, less than half than that found in Switzerland. Not surprisingly, there seems to be a clear correlation between economic development and capital per worker. The poorest countries in the table are all from Africa and have the lowest capital/labor ratios. Several of these are less than 10 percent of the ratio found in Switzerland.

The table provides several other interesting facts. First, the 1980s was a time of falling capital/labor ratios in the poorer countries of the table, but in richer countries the ratios tended to grow. The largest growth in percentage terms was in Taiwan and Korea, where capital per worker doubled during the decade. Finally, note the strong regional pattern in these statistics.

Capital Stock Per Worker: Selected Countries, 1980, 1990

(1985 INTERNATIONAL PRICES)

Country	1980	1990
Switzerland	57,061	73,459
Germany	43,739	50,116
Norway	41,244	48,135
Finland	33,564	45,767
Canada	28,910	42,745
Sweden	28,773	39,409
Australia	31,080	37,854
Belgium	31,324	36,646
Japan	22,085	36,480
France	29,104	35,600
United States	27,551	34,705
Austria	25,486	34,562
Denmark	28,223	33,125
New Zealand	28,190	33,080
Netherlands	28,922	32,380
Italy	25,391	31,640
Spain	19,428	27,300
Taiwan	13,664	25,722
Greece	19,891	23,476

(Continued)

Capital Stock Per Worker: Selected Countries, 1980, 1990 *(Continued)*

Country	1980	1990
Ireland	17,585	21,660
Israel	21,578	21,453
United Kingdom	16,563	21,179
Venezuela	21,827	18,271
Republic of Korea	9,759	17,995
Mexico	14,047	12,900
Hong Kong	12,189	12,762
Colombia	11,800	12,650
Portugal	8,111	11,819
Argentina	11,663	11,244
Chile	6,997	9,543
Peru	8,969	8,796
Dominican Republic	4,837	6,022
Bolivia	7,752	5,721
Botswana	3,222	5,345
Thailand	3,359	4,912
Honduras	5,660	4,133
Mauritius	2,628	3,845
Zimbabwe	6,197	3,823
Philippines	3,698	3,698
Guatemala	4,118	3,647
Swaziland	4,558	3,523
Jamaica	4,636	3,471
Morocco	2,669	1,991
India	1,514	1,946
Madagascar	1,848	1,738
Zambia	2,373	1,349
Cote d'Ivoire	1,086	1,029
Kenya	1,224	907
Nigeria	991	702
Malawi	508	428
Sierra Leone	178	223

SOURCE: Penn World Tables 5.6

B's PPF, the point on the *S* axis. (See point *Z* on Figure 4.1.) Now, imagine that the managers of the *S* industry are asked to cut back their production by 1 unit of output. The *S* industry now has excess factors of production, which can be used to produce some of good *T*.

How is *S* likely to contract its output? It would seem that the industry would try to retain as much capital as possible, since the production of *S* requires relatively more capital. Thus, as it reduces output, this industry is likely to release, at first, mostly labor, since *S* requires relatively less of that factor. So initially, at least, it is

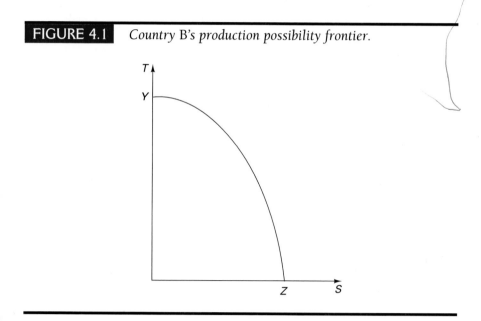

FIGURE 4.1   *Country B's production possibility frontier.*

likely that as S contracts, relatively more labor than capital is laid off and therefore becomes available to industry T. But T happens to utilize relatively more labor than capital in its production. Consequently, the release of factors by S to T occurs in precisely the fashion required for T to expand most readily. Hence, initially, as we move away from point Z in the figure, the output of T increases greatly, while the output of S contracts only a little.

Why does B's PPF become flatter as we near point Y? Think again about the process of expansion and contraction of the two industries. As we near point Y, the output of S is nearing zero. We would expect that, as output has fallen, the S industry has tried to retain as much capital per remaining worker as possible. However, it should be clear that the closer output S comes to zero, the greater are the amounts of capital being idled by that industry. When the T industry absorbs greater and greater amounts of capital relative to labor, it is able to expand by smaller and smaller amounts. This again is due to our assumptions about the underlying technology required to produce T.

Thus, we have established that country B has a PPF that exhibits increasing opportunity costs. Because technology is identical in the two countries, A will also have a PPF that exhibits increasing opportunity costs. Although both PPFs will be nonlinear, they will not have the same shapes. Because country B is assumed to be relatively labor abundant and good T is assumed to be relatively labor intensive, we would expect B's PPF to lie primarily along the T axis (see Figure 4.1). That is, given its resources and the technology for making the two goods, country B should be able to make relatively more T than S. By identical reasoning, we would expect A's PPF to lie mainly along the S axis.

We have now laid out the supply side of the economies of both countries. We turn now to demand.

ASSUMPTION 17   Tastes in the two countries are identical.

This assumption simply states that the community indifference curves for the two countries are identical. Consequently, if faced with the same relative price ratio and the same level of GDP, each country would consume exactly the same amounts of the two goods. As we shall establish in more detail in the next section, the purpose of this assumption is to guarantee that comparative advantage, and therefore the direction of trade, is determined by supply conditions in the two economies rather than demand factors.

THE HO THEOREM

As we just discussed, the HO model holds that the direction of international trade flows between two countries is determined by the endowment of productive factors in the two countries and the factor content of the goods involved. In the two-good case, the theory can be stated more precisely in the form of a theorem known as the HO theorem.

THE HO THEOREM   A country will have comparative advantage in, and therefore will export, that good whose production is relatively intensive in the factor with which that country is relatively well endowed.

Put more simply, the theorem states that the country that is relatively capital abundant compared with the other country will have a comparative advantage in the good that requires more capital per worker to produce. With regard to our assumptions, we would expect that country B (A) will have a comparative advantage in textiles (soybeans), since we have assumed that B (A) is relatively labor (capital) abundant and that textiles (soybeans) production is relatively labor (capital) intensive.

Let's try to prove the HO theorem graphically.* Consider Figure 4.2. In discussing the assumptions of the model, we have already determined that the PPFs of the two countries will exhibit increasing opportunity costs and will have different shapes. This is illustrated in panels (a) and (b) in Figure 4.2, where we show country A and B, respectively. Our goal is to find the autarky (pretrade) price ratios for the two countries to determine the direction of comparative advantage. To do that, we need to bring demand factors into the story. Recall that we have assumed that tastes in the two countries are identical. In terms of our diagrams, this means that the *CIC*s for the two countries should have the same shape and should lie in the same general location in the two graphs. The *CIC*s we have drawn have this property and, to emphasize the point that they represent the same preferences, are both

---

*This proof is based essentially on the quantity definition of factor abundance. In Appendix 4.1 we sketch out a proof of the theorem using the price definition of abundance.

FIGURE 4.2 *Proof of the HO theorem.*

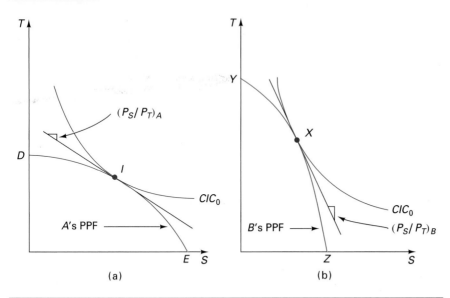

(a)

(b)

labeled CIC_0.* Consider now the autarky equilibrium production and consumption points for the two countries. These occur at point I for A and point X for B.

As we learned in Chapter 2, the slope of the PPFs at the production point defines the price ratio for that country. Consequently, we have drawn in the price lines tangent to the PPFs at the production points and labeled them $(P_S/P_T)_A$ and $(P_S/P_T)_B$. From the diagram, it is clear that

$$(P_S/P_T)_A < (P_S/P_T)_B$$

This establishes that country A (B) has a comparative advantage in the production of good S (T).[†] Now, let's go back to our assumptions. Recall that S was assumed to be the capital-intensive good and that A was assumed to be the capital-abundant country. This proves the theorem. Before you read on, however, you should convince yourself that we haven't only proved the theorem for country A, but we have established that it is true for country B as well.

---

*Note carefully that even though both *CICs* have the same label, this does not mean that the two countries experience equal levels of satisfaction (or real GDP) in autarky. If the two countries are not at the same levels of satisfaction, we must also assume that the *CICs* are sufficiently well behaved so that their shape does not change radically as one moves to lower or higher levels of community satisfaction. A sufficient condition for our proof to hold is that as real GDP grows at constant relative prices, consumers continue to buy more of both goods in the same proportions.
[†]Recall that a country has a comparative advantage in a good if the good has a lower autarky relative price in that country.

So far, we have shown how comparative advantage is determined in the HO model. How do we know that trade will flow in the direction of comparative advantage? The answer to this question is the same as that found in Chapter 3. Namely, in a competitive environment, trade flows are determined by profit-seeking activities of economic agents. If a product is relatively cheap in one country, it will tend to be exported to those places where it is relatively expensive. Consequently, we would expect to see country A export good S. Likewise, exporters in B should want to export T to A, where it is (at first) relatively more expensive.

EQUILIBRIUM IN THE HO MODEL

Let us now consider the effect of the introduction of international trade on the production and consumption decisions of a single country. After we analyze this effect, we turn to an examination of the world trade equilibrium in the HO model. Again, we know from previous chapters that once trade is allowed between two countries, differences in relative prices will not persist. Consequently, the price of S will begin to rise in A (where it was initially low) and fall in B (where it was initially high). For the time being, let's focus our attention on country A.

Consider Figure 4.3. Once trade begins, the price of S will start to rise in A. This is illustrated by the terms of trade lines $(P_S/P_T)_0$, $(P_S/P_T)_1$, and $(P_S/P_T)_2$. The flattest

---

FIGURE 4.3　　*The effect of rising world prices of good S on country A's trade.*

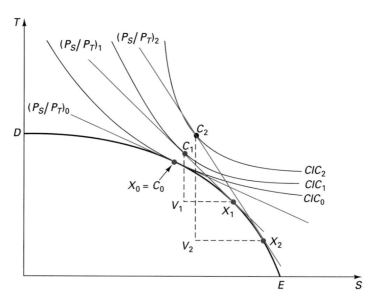

price line, $(P_S/P_T)_0$, is tangent to A's PPF at the autarky point $X_0 (= C_0)$. As the terms of trade rise to $(P_S/P_T)_1$, the production of T declines, and factors are released to the S industry, allowing A's production point to move to point X_1. At that point, the supply of S exceeds the local demand for it, and some can be exported to country B in exchange for T. This allows consumption to move off A's PPF to point C_1. How much is traded at price $(P_S/P_T)_1$? This is given in the figure by the triangle $V_1C_1X_1$. Triangle $V_1C_1X_1$ is A's trade triangle when the price is $(P_S/P_T)_1$. The base of the triangle, V_1X_1, represents exports, while the side, V_1C_1, is A's desired imports.

If the terms of trade were to continue to rise, say to $(P_S/P_T)_2$, then the production point would continue to move down A's PPF, this time to X_2. At this point, A is almost completely specialized in the production of soybeans. Country A's consumption point moves from C_1 to C_2. Thus, it relies more and more on country B for the textiles it consumes. As the figure clearly shows, A's trade triangle has grown in size to $V_2C_2X_2$.

The figure we have just been discussing is slightly misleading. The reader should note carefully that at any point in time, only one price will prevail in the market. What will be that price, and how is it determined? Again, the answer is the same as with the Ricardian model. The terms of trade that will prevail once trade begins are determined by international forces of demand and supply known as *reciprocal demand*.* These forces seek a price that can prevail simultaneously in *both* countries so that desired trade flows are balanced. After all, if desired trade flows are not balanced, then, by definition, one country wants to trade more than the other, and this will cause the terms of trade to change.

Diagrammatically, the condition for international equilibrium is that the trade triangles of the two countries be congruent. This is the same equilibrium condition as before. Recall that the sides of these triangles represent desired trade amounts for a given international price, which, in turn, is represented in the trade triangles by the slope of the hypotenuse.

An example of an international trade equilibrium is given in Figure 4.4. In panel (a), we illustrate Country A's trade triangle. In particular, after trade begins and equilibrium is reached, production in A occurs at point X_A, while consumption occurs at point C_A. Country A's exports are given by the distance V_AX_A, and its imports are given by the distance V_AC_A. Panel (b) illustrates equilibrium for B. There, production occurs at point X_B, and consumption occurs at C_B. Country B's exports are denoted by the distance X_BV_B, and its imports by V_BC_B.

How do we know that this diagram illustrates an international trade *equilibrium*? The answer is that the trade triangles of the two countries have the congruency property just described. That is, the distance V_AX_A—country A's desired exports when the international price is $(P_S/P_T)_1$—is equal in quantity terms to country B's desired imports—denoted by the distance V_BC_B—at the same international price. In terms of simple geometry, the bases of the two triangles have the same length. And, as we

---

*Recall that we defined and discussed the concept of reciprocal demand in Chapter 3.

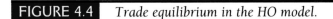

FIGURE 4.4   *Trade equilibrium in the HO model.*

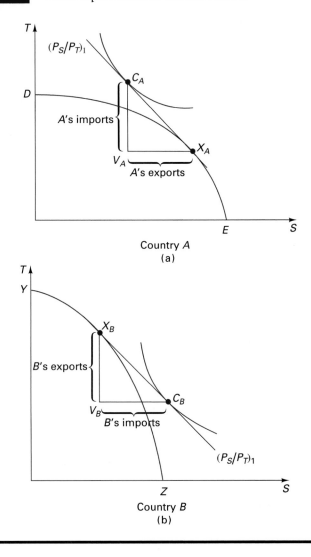

Country A
(a)

Country B
(b)

**Incomplete
specialization**
A country is
incompletely
specialized in
production if, after
trade begins, it
continues to produce
some of the good it
imports.

have seen several times now, if the international market is in equilibrium for product S, we know that it is also in equilibrium for product T. Hence, we know that the sides of the two triangles are also equal in length.

What are some of the other characteristics of this equilibrium, and how do they compare with those we have studied in our analysis of the classical model? Note first that neither country completely specializes in the production of its comparative-advantage good. **Incomplete specialization** in production is a straightforward result of the presence of increasing opportunity costs. That is, as the introduction of international trade leads to an increase in the relative price of a country's exportable good, there is an incentive to produce more of that good. Production will continue to expand so long as the relative cost of expanding production is less than or just equal to the relative price. However, as production expands in this model, so do relative costs. Consequently, there will tend to be a point beyond which relative costs exceed the relative price. This point represents the barrier to further expansion of production, unless the price were to rise still more.

Is complete specialization likely in the HO model? No, but it can't be ruled out. As we noted earlier, the production point depends upon the relative price of exportables. It remains a possibility that the price could rise so much that all of the economy's resources could be attracted to the export industry. A second factor that would make complete specialization more likely would be if the two goods were relatively similar in their use of factor inputs. The more similar the techniques used in producing the two goods, the less additional output of one good is lost as factors are increasingly attracted to the other industry. In other words, as goods become more similar in production, the less bowed out are the PPFs, and the PPFs begin to look more like the straight-line, constant-cost PPFs found in the classical model—where complete specialization always tends to occur.

A second and closely related difference between the HO model and the classical model has to do with the manner in which the process of reciprocal demand leads to an equilibrium terms of trade. Recall that in the classical model, once trade begins, the production point is fixed at the point of complete specialization. This means that equilibrium levels of exports and imports are achieved solely through changes in demand in the two countries. In the HO model, reciprocal demand leads to an equilibrium price by inducing changes in *both* demand and supply. This point is established in Figure 4.5.

In the top part of the figure, we present the national demand and supply curves that are implied by the assumptions of the classical model. In the bottom part of the diagram, we illustrate the national demand and supply curves for the two countries under HO assumptions. The major difference between these two diagrams is the shape of the national supply curves. The classical national supply curves are horizontal up to a certain point, reflecting the underlying assumption of constant opportunity costs. Afterward, these curves become vertical, illustrating that once complete specialization is reached, no more can be produced in the economy regardless of how high the price becomes. The HO national supply curves are also vertical at the point of complete specialization. However, before that point is reached, they are upward sloping, reflecting the existence of increasing opportunity costs.

Let us now consider the differences between the two models in the process of reciprocal demand. For ease of exposition, we let the Greek letter ρ (rho) denote the relative price P_S/P_T. Consider first the situation under the classical model. Figures 4.5a and 4.5b show how the autarky prices of S are determined in the two countries. These prices are, respectively, ρ_A and ρ_B. At these prices the autarky production levels are Q_{AA} and Q_{BA}, respectively.

Because ρ_A is less than ρ_B, country A has a comparative advantage in S and will export it to B. We know that once international trade begins, there can be only one world price. Suppose that price is ρ_0. In A, the production of S will rise to Q_M units,

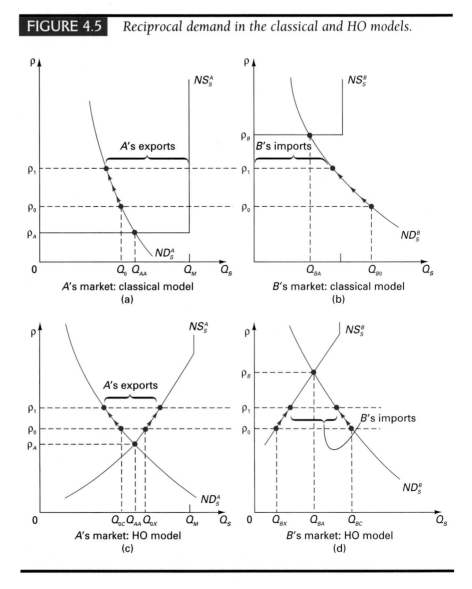

FIGURE 4.5   *Reciprocal demand in the classical and HO models.*

while consumption of S will fall to Q_0 units. The difference between these two amounts reflects A's desired exports to B.

In country B, if the price falls from ρ_B to ρ_0, local production will fall to zero, while consumption rises to Q_{B0}. The difference between these two amounts represents B's desired imports of S. Casual inspection of the diagram indicates that at ρ_0, B's desired imports exceeds A's desired exports. In other words, there is excess demand in the market for traded goods; to close this imbalance, the world price must rise above ρ_0. As the price rises, the excess demand begins to fall, but in a special way. Note from the diagram that total world supply remains constant at Q_M units, the amount produced in country A. On the other hand, as the price rises, consumption of S in *both* countries falls (note the pattern of the arrows in the diagram). Finally, as ρ rises, total world consumption falls enough so that world markets are in equilibrium. In the diagram this occurs at ρ_1.

In the lower part of Figure 4.5, the mechanism of reciprocal demand using HO assumptions is illustrated. As before, the autarky prices and outputs for the two countries are given by ρ_A, ρ_B, Q_{AA}, and Q_{BA}, respectively. Again, we are assuming that A has the lower autarky price of S and therefore has comparative advantage in that good. Once trade opens, the price of S will rise in A and fall in B, generating an incentive for S to flow from A to B. If the price settles first at ρ_0, then A's desired exports would be the difference between the amount produced and consumed at that price, $Q_{0X} - Q_{0C}$. Country B's desired imports at price ρ_0 would be given by the amount $Q_{BC} - Q_{BX}$. Again, by inspection we can see that there is initially an excess demand. How is this excess demand eliminated? The price must rise. But note the difference in this model. As ρ rises, consumption falls in both countries (as was the case before), but supply also rises in both countries. In other words, the higher the world price in the exporting country, the more that country exports—for two reasons. First, its own citizens will demand less; and second, its producers will want to produce more. In the importing country, the higher the world price, the less it imports, for precisely the same reasons: Its consumers purchase less, and its domestic producers produce more.

A second major difference between the HO model and the classical model has to do with the importance of assumptions made about demand. The classical model places no restrictions on assumptions about consumer tastes in the two countries, except that consumers be sufficiently cosmopolitan so that some of both goods be consumed before and after trade opens. The reason so little attention is paid to demand is that the autarky prices in that model are determined solely by supply conditions (see again the top part of Figure 4.5). On the other hand, the HO model assumes that tastes be identical. Why is this assumption made?

In Figure 4.6 we replicate the demand and supply curves from the lower part of Figure 4.5. Consider the following thought experiment: Suppose that instead of the demand and supply curves as they are drawn, we change the assumptions of the model so that tastes in each country are very different. In particular, suppose that citizens of country A strongly prefer good S, while citizens of country B abhor this product. Under these alternative conditions, the supply curves would not change, but the demand curves would shift from those initially drawn to $ND_S^{A'}$ and $ND_S^{B'}$, respectively. Autarky prices would be given by ρ_A' and ρ_B', and because ρ_B' is lower than ρ_A', the direction of comparative advantage shifts so that B would have comparative advantage in good S. Note that this would be true even though, for any corresponding level of output, A's supply curve is lower, indicating that A has a natural comparative advantage in terms of lower costs of production. Thus, we see the importance of assumptions. By ruling out differences in tastes, we prevent tastes from overturning the predictions of the HO model.

FIGURE 4.6   *The importance of assuming identical tastes.*

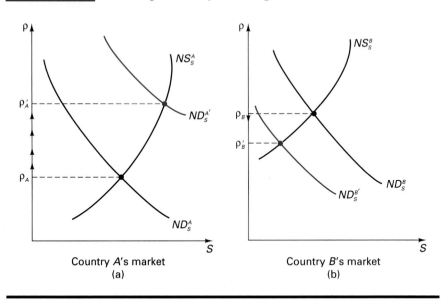

Country A's market
(a)

Country B's market
(b)

SOME NEW HO THEOREMS

In addition to the HO theorem, which predicts the direction of comparative advantage, the HO model offers several other important theorems about economic behavior in an economy engaged in international trade. These theorems refer to issues such as the effect of economic growth on trade and the impact trade has on the distribution of income in a society. The first of these is known as the Rybczynski theorem.*

> **THE RYBCZYNSKI THEOREM** At constant world prices, if a country experiences an increase in the supply of one factor, it will produce more of the product intensive in that factor and less of the other.

Accordingly, if country A were to increase its capital stock above its initial endowment, everything else held constant, it would produce more S than before and less T. This example is illustrated in Figure 4.7. Growth in A's capital stock leads to an outward shift in its PPF. Most of this shift occurs along the S axis, because S is in the capital-intensive industry. The new production point (after growth has occurred) is given by point X_1, the point on the new PPF where its slope is equal to the (fixed) world price ρ.

---

*This theorem was originally developed in T.M. Rybczynski, "Factor Endowments and Relative Commodity Prices," *Economica* (1955).

| FIGURE 4.7 | *The effect of an increase in A's capital stock.* |

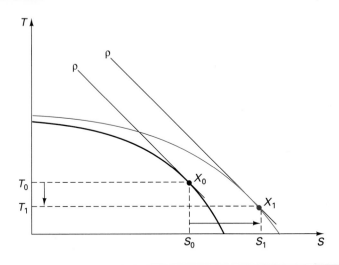

Because S is A's export good, an increase in the size of A's capital stock would lead producers in A to try to expand their exports. Conversely, if A's labor force were to increase, holding all other things constant, including world prices and the size of A's capital stock, A would want to produce more T relative to S and trade less.

A proof of the Rybczynski theorem is left for Appendix 4.1. However, the intuition behind this theorem is straightforward. It basically says that the way in which a country grows has an impact on the production and trade mixes of that country. Countries with low savings rates that invest little in new plants and equipment will tend to produce and trade goods with high labor content. Countries with high savings and investment rates will tend to produce and trade more capital-intensive goods.*

Perhaps the most controversial theorem of the HO model is concerned with the effect of international trade on factor prices. This theorem is known as the **factor price equalization (FPE) theorem.**[†]

> THE FACTOR PRICE EQUALIZATION THEOREM Given all the assumptions of the HO model, free international trade will lead to the international equalization of individual factor prices.

Factor price equalization (FPE) Factor price equalization occurs if all individual factor prices (e.g., wages, rental payments) are identical when measured in the same currency.

---

*See Chapter 10 for an expanded discussion of the relationship between economic growth and international trade.

[†]That international trade might lead to factor price equalization was first suggested by Heckscher in his article. Ohlin felt that there would be only a tendency toward factor price equalization. Samuelson proved that trade would lead to factor price equalization in his article "International Trade and the Equalization of Factor Prices," *Economic Journal* (1948). Interestingly, shortly after Samuelson's article appeared, he learned that another economist, Abba Lerner, while a student in England in 1933, had written a term paper that also proved the theorem.

In other words, in countries that have high wages before trade begins, there will be a tendency for wages to fall. In countries with initially low wages, trade will produce a tendency for wages to rise. Under the strict assumptions of the HO model, these tendencies will continue until the equalization of wages is achieved. The same will be true for rental rates on capital.

To understand this theorem better, let's try to prove that it is true. Recall our assumptions. Country *A* is assumed to be abundant in capital and scarce in labor. This would suggest that, initially, wages are high in *A*, while rents are low. In *B*, where capital is scarce and labor plentiful, we would expect just the opposite situation initially. Now, let trade occur. In *A* there will be a tendency for the output of *S* to increase and for the output of *T* to contract. The *S* industry employs relatively more capital per worker than the *T* industry does. Consequently, there will be an initial mismatch between industry *S*'s increased demand for factors and the factors that actually become available to the *S* industry as the *T* industry contracts. In particular, we would expect that *T* would idle more labor and less capital than *S* initially desires. Hence, in the factor markets there are an excess supply of labor at the initial wage and an excess demand for capital at the existing rental rate. For equilibrium to return, we would expect that wages would fall in *A*, while rents would rise.

In country *B*, trade leads to an expansion in the output of *T*. The resources required to facilitate this expansion must come from *S*. Industry *S* uses relatively more capital per worker than *T*; hence, as it cuts back production, industry *S* releases to *T* relatively more capital per worker than *T* would like to hire at the existing factor prices. What is required for equilibrium here? Rents must fall and wages must rise.

We see from this discussion that there is a tendency for wages (rents) to fall when they are initially high and to rise when they are initially low. How do we know that they will equalize? The answer is simple. International trade leads to a common (product) price worldwide. We have assumed that markets are competitive and that technology is identical. Since each country will continue to produce some of both goods, and these goods will be produced at the same price using the same technology, it is straightforward to conclude that factor prices will equalize.

It is important to note how strict the conditions are for factor price equalization to occur. In particular, all of the assumptions of the HO model must hold perfectly. Two of the most important of these are the assumptions of no barriers to trade and of access to identical technology. If workers everywhere have the same productivity, then free trade guarantees that they earn the same wage. However, if there are restrictions on the ability to trade, then some workers may earn more than their equally productive foreign counterparts. Since neither assumption is perfectly satisfied in the real world, we should not expect complete factor price equalization.

There is some support, however, for the main predictions of the theorem. A recent study by Dan Ben-David has looked to see how lowering trade barriers between countries has affected income levels in different countries.* His analysis

---

*See Dan Ben-David, "Equalizing Exchange: A Study of the Effects of Trade Liberalization," *Quarterly Journal of Economics* (1993).

focused on the effect of lowering trade barriers in Western Europe following the formation of the European Union. He shows in his study that trade liberalization leads to a marked reduction in the dispersion of incomes across countries. Since the technologies available to each of the countries in the study are quite similar, Ben-David's findings are in line with the model.

The factor price equalization theorem predicts that some factor payments will rise and others fall with the introduction of trade. The next HO theorem spells out in more detail the winners and losers from trade.

THE STOLPER–SAMUELSON THEOREM Free international trade benefits the abundant factor and harms the scarce factor.*

To understand the implications of this theorem, let's return to our proof of the FPE theorem. There, we showed that wages fall in *A*, the labor-scarce country, and rise in *B*, the labor-abundant country. Also, we concluded that rents will rise in *A*, the capital-abundant country, and fall in *B*, the capital-scarce country. This, in fact, proves the theorem.[†]

The abundant factor enjoys an increase in its payment for productive efforts, while the scarce factor loses. The intuition behind this result is straightforward. Why are wages initially high in *A*? The answer is, Because labor is relatively scarce and hence can exploit its scarcity power in the factor markets. The introduction of international trade means that manufacturers using scarce labor in *A* must now compete with manufacturers using more abundant labor in *B*. International competitive pressures tend to force down wages in *A*. Thus, even though labor is immobile between countries, its price is equalized through competitive bidding for its services, embodied in the production of goods.

What are the implications of the Stolper–Samuelson theorem? First, we now have established a reason for some groups in a society to oppose international trade. In the classical model, international trade benefits everyone. This is because no adjustment in wages is required to guarantee full employment as workers are displaced from import-competing industries toward expanding export industries. In the HO model, scarce factors must agree to a cut in their compensation in order to remain employed (in either industry). Item 4.3 discusses an empirical study of the U.S. economy that explores various implications of the HO model, including the Stolper-Samuelson theorem.

The Stolper–Samuelson theorem provides insights into why governments may impose barriers to trade. Clearly, workers who expect their wages to fall because of trade should be opposed to trade. Similarly, so should capitalists in capital-scarce countries. Consequently, we would expect that scarce factors lobby their respective

---

*This theorem was first spelled out in Wolfgang Stolper and Paul Samuelson, "Protection and Real Wages," *Review of Economic Studies* (1941).
[†]However, a more formal proof of this theorem is provided in Appendix 4.1.

ITEM 4.3 | Trade, Wages, and Jobs in the U.S. Economy

One of the features of the international trade experience of the United States over the past two decades is the rising importance of manufactured goods imported from Asian and certain Latin American countries. Most prominent among these are the Asian NICs (Hong Kong, the Republic of Korea, Singapore, and Taiwan) as well as China, Brazil, Malaysia, Mexico, and Thailand.* At the same time, there have been several important changes in the U.S. labor market that many view with concern. These include (1) a sharp reduction in employment in manufacturing, especially in low-skill sectors such as textiles and footwear and (2) a significant widening in the gap between wages paid to high skilled workers and low-skilled workers. Some observers of these two phenomena, including economist Adrian Wood and politicians Ross Perot and Patrick Buchanan, view them as closely linked. They argue that trade with low-wage countries is destroying the U.S. manufacturing base and the process of factor price equalization predicted by the HO model is causing low-skilled wages to fall toward wage rates paid in developing countries. Others, including economists Paul Krugman and Robert Lawrence and the Clinton administration, maintain that trade has little to do with these trends. They argue that rapid technological change has caused firms to reduce their demand for low-skilled workers, leading to reduced wages and employment levels.[†]

In an important study, Jeffrey Sachs and Howard Shatz have tried to evaluate the degree to which international trade has contributed to the reduction of blue-collar employment and wages in the U.S. economy.[‡] Sachs and Shatz use a modified version of the HO model to organize their analysis. They assume that there are two factors of production, skilled labor and unskilled labor, and that goods vary according to the amount of skilled labor required in their manufacture. In such a world, the United States is assumed to be abundant in skilled labor and therefore to have comparative advantage in skilled-labor intensive goods. In such a model, it is straightforward to see that expanded trade with developing economies would produce a reduction in the output of unskilled-labor-intensive goods and a fall in the wages paid to unskilled labor. It is these patterns that Sachs and Shatz look for in the data.

To conduct their analysis, the economists divide U.S. manufacturing industries into 10 categories based on their skilled-labor intensities. They then perform a hypothetical experiment wherein they try to determine the level of employment in each of these ten sectors that would have existed in 1990 if there had not been the increase in net imports over the period 1978–1990, holding final demand for these goods constant. In other words, they try to measure the effects of increased trade on manufacturing employment. Their findings are reproduced in the following table.

The numbers in the table represent percentage changes in employment of workers in a particular industry that Sachs and Shatz estimate might be due to expanded trade with particular types of countries during the 1980s. These numbers point to a number of interesting findings. First, the economists calculate that manufacturing job losses due to expanded trade largely

*These nine countries accounted for 79 percent of the increase in U.S. trade with all developing countries between 1978 and 1990.
[†]For more on these differing views, see Adrian Wood, *North-South Trade, Employment and Inequality: Changing Fortunes in a Skill-Driven World* (Oxford: Clarendon Press, 1994), Paul Krugman and Robert Lawrence, "Trade, Jobs and Wages," *Scientific American* (1994), and Gary Burtless, "International Trade and the Rise of Earnings Inequality," *Journal of Economic Literature* (1995).
[‡]See Jeffrey Sachs and Howard Shatz, "Trade and Jobs in U.S. Manufacturing," *Brookings Papers on Economic Activity* (1994).

occurred in unskilled-labor-intensive industries (i.e., levels 6 and higher). Indeed, in the highest skill levels Sachs and Shatz estimate that expanded trade might have led to expanded employment in manufacturing. They go on to estimate the effect of expanded trade on all manufacturing employment by skill category and find that expanded trade with developed countries had almost no overall effect (i.e., a reduction of 0.2 percent), while expanded trade with developing countries has led to a 5.7 percent fall in manufacturing employment. They conclude that expanded trade during the 1980s may have been responsible for a decline of 1.2 million manufacturing jobs. They argue that this is about 40 percent of the decline in manufacturing employment that occurred over this period relative to historical trends. Thus, they cannot rule out the claim that technological change has also played a major role in reducing manufacturing employment.

In evaluating the size of the Sachs and Shatz estimates, one should keep in mind several additional statistics. First, total employment in the United States grew from about 100 million workers in 1978 to almost 118 million in 1990.

So, even though these economists report evidence of certain types of job losses due to trade in this period, overall jobs were increasing. Moreover, 1.5 million jobs is a small fraction of the overall total. Finally, the Sachs and Shatz estimates assume that labor productivity in these industries remained constant throughout the sample period. This means that one should interpret their estimates as being on the high side of the true effects of trade. Nonetheless, their study suggests that both trade and technology have played major roles in establishing recent trends in U.S. labor market experience.

In the latter part of their study, Sachs and Shatz go on to determine the effects of trade on wages over this period. There is no direct way to determine this effect. What these economists attempt to find is whether, after controlling for productivity changes, trade has led to reductions in the price of a product. In such cases, according to the Stolper–Samuelson theorem, the payment to the intensive factor in that industry would have to fall. Sachs and Shatz find weak evidence that this has occurred. Prices tended to fall as unskilled-labor intensity rose. Overall, these results help to explain recent labor market experience and are broadly consistent with the predictions of the HO model.

Trade Effects on U.S. Employment in Manufacturing

Industry Skill Level	Developing Country Trade	Developed Country Trade	All Trade
1	0.2	12.2	12.3
2	−0.9	0.9	0.0
3	−2.8	−1.7	−4.4
4	−2.3	2.9	0.5
5	−2.0	−1.6	−3.6
6	−5.5	−2.4	−7.9
7	−5.2	−1.4	−6.6
8	−2.6	−2.1	−4.7
9	−3.4	−6.7	−10.1
10	−23.5	−3.6	−27.1
All Manufacturing	−5.7	−0.2	−5.9
Unskilled Workers	−6.2	−1.0	−7.2
Skilled Workers	−4.3	2.2	−2.1

governments for measures to restrict the amount of international trade that could occur. On the other hand, abundant factors are apt to lobby for free-trade policies.*

Finally, it is important to remember that even though some in society lose from international trade, the country overall gains from international trade relative to autarky. To convince yourself of this fact, go back and reexamine Figure 4.4. Clearly, after trade is established, each country consumes a bundle of goods that would have been unattainable in autarky. This implies a higher standard of living for each economy as a whole. Put more simply, the gainers gain from trade more than the losers lose.[†] This is an interesting result that has a potential policy implication. It should be possible for a system of taxation and transfers to be developed that could compensate the losers for their loss while leaving the gainers better off than they would be in autarky. Such a system has never been implemented, but attempts at such programs (albeit highly imperfect) have been made in the United States and elsewhere. In Chapter 8 we briefly discuss the U.S. program known as trade adjustment assistance, put into place after World War II.

SOME FINAL OBSERVATIONS

This chapter has sought to spell out the simple Heckscher–Ohlin model of the commodity composition of international trade. For about twenty years, from about 1933 to 1953, this model was perhaps the most revered general equilibrium theory in all of economics. Economists marveled at its logical tightness, its seeming explanation for many of the phenomena found in real-world trade patterns, and the degree to which the model could be manipulated to study issues such as the effect of trade on the distribution of income. For these reasons, even today most trade economists prefer to work with this model.

As we shall see in the next chapter, problems have emerged with the model. Much as with the problems encountered with the classical model, these revolve around difficulties economists have had in squaring the many predictions of the model with reality. This, in turn, has led some economists to try to expand the model, most notably by adding *additional* factors and goods to the analysis. These efforts require the use of mathematical tools, such as linear algebra, to illustrate and are generally not amenable to geometry. Consequently, we forgo their discussion in this text. Suffice it to say, however, that some of the more interesting and clear-cut

---

*In an interesting and highly readable paper, Stephen Magee tests this proposition. He finds that in nineteen of twenty cases, industry and labor groups take identical positions with respect to protectionist policies. One explanation of these findings is that in the short run, capital is not mobile between sectors. For more on this point, see Appendix 4.2. The reference is Stephen Magee, "Three Simple Tests of the Stolper–Samuelson Theorem," in *Current Issues in World Trade and Payments*, ed. P. Oppenheimer (London: Routledge & Kegan Paul, 1980).

[†]An elegant proof of this statement can be found in Avinash Dixit and Victor Norman, *Theory of International Trade* (Cambridge, England: Cambridge University Press, 1980).

predictions of the simple HO model, such as factor price equalization, hold less well under more general specifications of the model.*

Other economists, prompted by the apparent shortcomings of the HO model, have sought to develop new theories of international trade patterns. Several of these new theories are discussed in the next chapter. However, none of these theories is as complete in its structure as the HO model. Thus, despite its shortcomings, the HO model is likely to retain an important place in international trade theory for some time to come.

SUMMARY

1. The Heckscher–Ohlin (HO) model of comparative advantage is a complete model of the workings of an economy as it engages in international trade. This model holds that comparative advantage is determined by the underlying factor endowments of a country relative to endowments in the rest of the world.

2. The HO theorem states that a country has a comparative advantage in those goods whose production is intensive in the factors with which that country is relatively well endowed.

3. Unlike the classical model, the HO model predicts that in equilibrium each country will continue to produce some of both goods.

4. Also unlike the classical model, the HO model requires that strict assumptions be made about the nature of tastes in each country, or else the predictions of the theory could be overturned.

5. The HO theory also includes several other important theorems: the Rybczynski theorem, the factor price equalization theorem, and the Stolper–Samuelson theorem.

6. The Rybczynski theorem predicts that if a country's endowment of a factor increases (at constant prices), there will be a tendency for that country to

---

*A clear and concise presentation of the HO model with many goods and factors can be found in Edward Leamer, *Sources of Comparative Advantage: Theory and Evidence* (Boston: MIT Press, 1984). See especially Chapter 1, which also contains a very interesting discussion of the effects on the predictions of the model when its various underlying assumptions are violated. Other contributions to the literature on the multifactor, multigood HO model include Alan Deardorff, "Weak Links in the Law of Comparative Advantage," *Journal of International Economics* (1979); Wilfred Ethier, "Some of the Theorems of International Trade with Many Goods and Factors," *Journal of International Economics* (1974); Ronald Jones and José Scheinkman, "The Relevance of the Two-Sector Production Model in Trade Theory," *Journal of Political Economy* (1977); Jaroslav Vanek, "The Factor Proportions Theory: The N-Factor Case," *Kyklos* (1968); and James Williams, "The Factor Proportions Theorem: The Case of *m* Commodities and *n* Factors," *Canadian Journal of Economics* (1977). These and many other important papers on this topic are surveyed in Wilfred Ethier, "Higher Dimensional Issues in Trade Theory," in *Handbook of International Economics*, vol. 1, eds. Ronald Jones and Peter Kenen (Amsterdam: North-Holland, 1984).

produce more of the product whose production is intensive in the growing factor and less of the other.

7. The factor price equalization theorem predicts that under the strict assumptions of the HO model, free trade will lead to an international equalization of individual factor payments.

8. The Stolper–Samuelson theorem predicts that trade benefits the abundant factors of a country and harms the scarce factors. This result differs from the classical model, which predicts that all individuals gain from international trade.

9. Despite the implications of the Stolper–Samuelson theorem, it is still true that trade benefits both countries, because the gainers outweigh the losers.

EXERCISES

1. Use a general equilibrium depiction of trade equilibrium in the HO model (e.g., either graph in Figure 4.4) to prove that complete specialization in the production of exports will, in general, lower the standard of living of an economy relative to incomplete specialization.

2. Some have argued that the factor price equalization theorem implies that American wages must fall to the level of those found in the least developed countries of the world. Comment on the validity of this statement.

3. Consider the following data on the factor endowments of two countries, A and B:

Factor Endowments	Countries	
	A	B
Labor force (in millions of workers)	45	20
Capital stock (in thousands of machines)	15	10

   a. Which country is relatively capital abundant?
   b. Which country is relatively labor abundant?
   c. Supposing that good S is capital intensive relative to good T, which country will have comparative advantage in the production of S? Explain.

4. Compare and contrast the classical and HO theories of the commodity composition of trade. Discuss differences in assumptions, posttrade production points, and the effects of trade on the distribution of income.

5. Australia is land abundant, India is labor abundant. Wheat is land intensive relative to textiles. Graphically demonstrate the pretrade and posttrade equilibria between these two countries. Find and label the trade triangles for each. Which factors gain and which factors lose when trade arises between these two countries? Explain carefully.

6. One of the important changes in the world economy over the past three decades has been the rapid increase in capital investment in the countries of the Pacific Basin (notably Japan and Korea). What are the implications of this investment for the commodity patterns of trade of these two countries, say, with respect to the United States? Explain carefully. (Hint: Think about the Rybczynski theorem.)

7. Explain carefully why the assumption of identical technology worldwide eliminates the classical basis for international trade.

8. Use the Rybczynski theorem to prove that the more dissimilar countries become in their factor endowments, the more likely it is for complete specialization to occur once trade begins.

9. Answer the questions in Exercise 3 using the following data on factor endowments of countries *C* and *D*:

	Countries	
Factor Endowments	*C*	*D*
Labor force (in millions of workers)	12	30
Capital stock (in thousands of machines)	48	60

10. Based on the information in Item 4.2 and your knowledge of the HO model, what types of goods would you expect Kenya or India to have comparative advantage in? What about Norway or Japan?

11. Suppose that country *A* is labor abundant. It can produce two goods, *X* and *Y*. Good *X* is capital intensive relative to good *Y*. Derive *A*'s PPF and determine the pretrade relative price of *X* in terms of *Y*. Now, suppose that there is technological innovation that makes capital more productive in the *X* industry, but not in making *Y*. In a separate diagram, illustrate what would happen to *A*'s PPF and explain your result. Show as well what would happen to the pretrade relative price of *X* in *A*. How might this affect *A*'s trade patterns? Explain.

12. The assumption of identical tastes in the HO model increases the likelihood that comparative advantage will be determined by international differences in factor endowments. True or false? Explain.

INTERNET APPLICATIONS

Please visit our Web site at www.awl.com/husted_melvin for more exercises and readings.

APPENDIX 4.1

ALTERNATE PROOFS OF SELECTED HO THEOREMS

In this appendix we provide rigorous proofs of the HO theorem and some of its basic corollaries. The principal geometric tool we use is the *production isoquant*. A production isoquant describes the various combinations of labor and capital required to produce a fixed quantity of a given product. For example, suppose good S is produced using labor (L) and capital (K). Figure A4.1 illustrates a possible isoquant map for that industry. On the axes we are measuring units of factor inputs, K and L. Along each of the curves the level of S output is constant. This is illustrated on the diagram by output levels S_0, S_1, and S_2. Note, in particular, that output increases as the isoquants lie farther and farther from the origin. This reflects the fact that more input leads to more output.

The curvature of the isoquants represents the ease with which labor can be substituted for capital and still maintain constant production. While this figure shows isoquants as they are most frequently drawn, economic theory does not limit them to having this shape. In particular, they may take the form of right angles. If this is the underlying technology, then factors are said not to be substitutable for each other. They are always used in fixed proportion, with additional amounts of any one factor useless toward the production of more output. At the other extreme, isoquants could be straight (negatively sloped) lines, indicating that factors are perfect substitutes for each other. Let us demonstrate how knowledge of these isoquants can be used to prove the various theorems.

FIGURE A4.1   *Isoquant map for the S industry.*

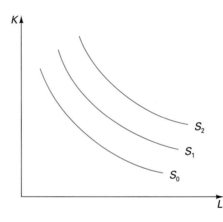

The Heckscher–Ohlin Theorem (Price Definition)

The HO theorem states that a country that is relatively abundant in a certain factor will have a comparative advantage in producing the good whose production is relatively intensive in that factor. How do we translate this theorem about factor endowments and intensities into a diagram?

In our example from the main part of this chapter, we illustrated the theorem by assuming that country A (B) was relatively abundant in K (L), and that good S (T) was relatively K (L) intensive in its production. Therefore, A (B) should have a comparative advantage in the production of good S (T).

Consider Figure A4.2. There, we superimpose a single isoquant from the isoquant maps for good S and good T onto a single diagram. Each isoquant represents the various technologies required to produce *exactly 1 unit* of the relevant product.

Before proceeding with the proof, let us note several things about the diagram. First, the S isoquant is shown as being closer (than the T isoquant is) to the K axis. This reflects our underlying assumption that S is more capital intensive than T. Second, we have illustrated only one isoquant for each product. The assumption of constant returns to scale production functions in each industry means that isoquants are regularly spaced and identical with each other as output levels increase. Thus, if we can establish that a particular theorem holds for one combination of output levels, it will apply to all levels, since to increase or decrease output requires only to

---

FIGURE A4.2   *Proof of the HO theorem (price definition).*

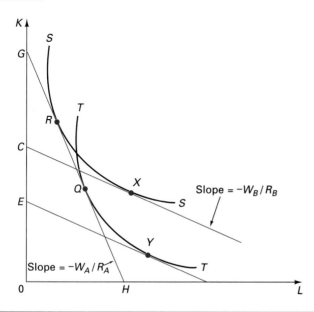

increase or decrease factors by equiproportionate changes. The assumption of constant returns to scale (and no fixed costs) also implies that average cost and marginal cost are constant and equal to each other for all levels of production.

Third, the assumption of identical technology in both countries means that these isoquants apply equally well to the production situations faced in country A or B. Hence, we can use one diagram to compare costs between countries. Finally, recall that a firm chooses its input combinations by finding the least costly input combination that will allow it to produce a desired level of output. In the diagram, such a combination occurs at the tangency of an *isocost* line (such as GH) with the isoquant, such as point R for industry S or point Q for industry T.

We turn now to a proof about comparative advantage. What is it that we want to show? In particular, we would like to demonstrate that when the autarky wage/rental ratio is higher in A than in B, the autarky relative price of T (S) is higher in A (B) than in B (A). Suppose that the autarky price of S, P_S/P_T, in A equals 1; that is, in money terms, S and T have the same price. If that is so, then the line segment GH must refer to the pretrade cost constraint facing A's firms. Why? Since this line is tangent to both the S and T isoquants, the cost of producing 1 unit of each must be identical. This follows directly from the fact that GH is an isocost line; that is, it represents all of the combinations of K and L that can be hired with a given amount of money for the going rental and wage rates. Relying on the facts that (a) the total cost of producing 1 unit is also the marginal cost of that unit and (b), in perfect competition, price is set equal to marginal cost (MC), point G can also be described by the following ratio:

$$(MC_{SA} = P_{SA} = MC_{TA} = P_{TA})/R_A$$

By analogy, point H can be described by the ratio

$$(MC_{SA} = P_{SA} = MC_{TA} = P_{TA})/W_A$$

This implies, of course, that the slope of the line connecting points G and H is, in absolute value, equal to W_A/R_A, the autarky wage/rental ratio in A.

Let's turn our attention to country B. Because B is assumed to be more labor abundant than A, its wage/rental ratio must be lower than A's. Hence, by construction, the line segment GH *cannot apply* to country B. Instead, it must be the case that two separate but parallel isocost lines are required to illustrate B's optimal input choices for 1 unit of each good. These combinations are illustrated by points X and Y in Figure A4.2. Now, note that because the isocost line to produce 1 unit of S in B is higher than the isocost line to produce 1 unit of T in B, it must be the case that the marginal cost of a unit of S in B is greater than the marginal cost of a unit of T. That is, $MC_{SB} > MC_{TB}$. But, again, since price equals marginal cost, the condition above implies that $P_{SB} > P_{TB}$. This is exactly what we wanted to show. Since the relative price of S equals 1 in A but is greater than 1 in B, we have shown that A has a comparative advantage in S, while B has a comparative advantage in T.

The Rybczynski Theorem

The Rybczynski theorem states that if a country experiences an increase in its endowment of any one factor, say labor, then, holding all other things constant (including factor and product prices), the output of the good that uses the factor intensively will rise, and the output of the other good will fall. To prove this theorem, we again rely on the isoquant map.

Consider Figure A4.3. There, we show two isoquants, one each for S and T. The isoquants we illustrate refer to an output of $1 worth of each good. Suppose that the relative price of S is equal to 1. As we have seen from the discussion above, this must imply that there is an isocost line that is just tangent to the two isoquants, just as drawn in the diagram. Furthermore, we know that the vertical and horizontal intercepts of this isocost line must equal $1/R$ and $1/W$, respectively. The tangency points F and D determine the optimal input combinations to produce $1 of S output and $1 of T output. And, if wages and rental rates are held fixed, the assumption of constant returns to scale guarantees that the slope of the rays from the origin passing through points F and D determines the optimal capital/labor use ratios for the two industries, given those factor prices.

How does the economy divide up its output between the two products? This depends upon the overall supply of available factors of production. Suppose that the

---

FIGURE A4.3   *Proof of the Rybczynski theorem.*

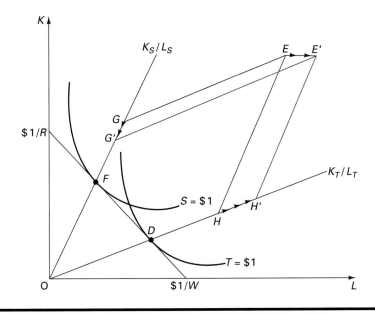

economy is initially endowed with a set of factors defined by point E. To find the optimal production of S and T, complete the parallelogram from point E to the two rays emanating from the origin. This defines points G and H on the two rays. These points represent optimal production levels of S and T, given the prices prevailing in the economy. How do we know that this is true? First, we know that output must occur on the rays. Second, we want to use all available resources. If, for instance, we add the factor combination represented by the line OG to point H, we reach the total endowment level E. Similarly, if we add OH to G, we also reach point E.

Now we are in position to prove the theorem. Suppose that the country's endowment of labor rises, but capital and prices do not change. This pulls the country's endowment point horizontally away from E to, say, E'. By completing the parallelogram with points E' and O at the corners, we see that the optimal production levels of S and T have changed from their old levels. In particular, the output of S has fallen (to G'), while that of T has risen (to H'). This proves the theorem.

The Stolper–Samuelson Theorem

The Stolper–Samuelson theorem states that the factor that is used intensively in the product whose relative price has risen gains from this price rise, while the other factor loses. In the context of the HO model, this theorem translates into the simple statement that the abundant factor gains from trade, while the scarce factor loses. To see that this is true, consider Figure A4.4.

As in the preceding discussion, we illustrate two isoquants representing $1 of output of both S and T. Let the economy produce some of both goods. At initial prices and values of W and R, the optimal input allocation for $1 of output of each good is given by points F and D. Now, let the price of T rise, say, due to the opening of international trade. At a higher price for T, $1 worth of this product would lie on a lower isoquant (remember that isoquants refer to physical units). Thus, the T = $1 isoquant would become the isoquant labeled T'. If some of both goods are still to be produced, the $1 isocost line must rotate to maintain tangency with the two isoquants S and T'. How can this be accomplished? Wages and rents must change. The new isocost line has intercepts $1/R' and $1/W'. Since the numerators of these fractions are the same as before, we can deduce what has happened to rents and wages by simply comparing 1/R with 1/R' and 1/W with 1/W'. In the first case, the fraction has risen. This could occur only if R' < R, that is, if rents have fallen. On the other hand, a comparison of horizontal intercepts shows that W has risen.

These changes in W and R are nominal changes. What has happened to the purchasing power of capitalists and labor? For capitalists, the answer is straightforward. We have assumed that the price of S has stayed fixed while the price of T has risen. A fall in R, therefore, means that capitalists have lost purchasing power in terms of either product—they are definitely worse off when the price of the labor-intensive good T rises relative to the price of the capital-intensive good S.

What about labor? The rise in W definitely means that labor can afford to purchase more S, because its price has been assumed to remain constant. However, the

FIGURE A4.4   *Proof of the Stolper–Samuelson theorem.*

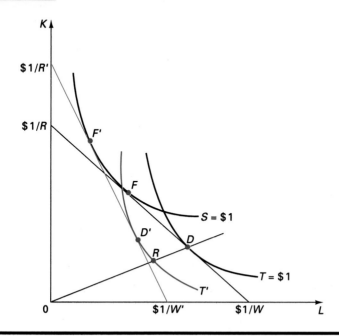

price of *T* has risen. Can labor buy more or less of this product? The answer is more. How do we know? Graphically, the increase in wages can be found by comparing the proportion (1/*W*)/(1/*W′*). This increase is greater than the proportionate increase in the price of *T*, which can be found by the ratio of the line segments *OD/OR*. This proves the theorem.

APPENDIX 4.2

THE SPECIFIC FACTORS MODEL

The Heckscher–Ohlin model takes a long-run view of the world. By that we mean that in comparing one equilibrium point to another enough time is assumed to have elapsed to allow capital equipment to be shifted from one industry to another. In the real world, machines tend to have very specific uses, and shifting capital resources across industries can take considerable time. As it turns out, if factors cannot move quickly between sectors then the short-run impacts of international trade may be somewhat different than the long-run impacts. In this appendix, we present a brief discussion of the specific factors, or Ricardo–Viner, model. This model is very useful in helping us to understand the short-run impact of international trade on an economy.

The specific factors model maintains all of the assumptions and structure of the HO model with one exception: In this model, one of the factors is immobile between industries. Here we will assume that the immobile factor is capital, so that the machinery used in the S industry is distinct from the machinery used in the T industry. Moreover, these two types of machines cannot be substituted for each other in the production process. Since the two types of machines are completely distinct, there is no guarantee that the owners of these machines receive the same rental payments. On the other hand, labor is assumed to be perfectly mobile, ensuring that the wage rate is the same in both industries.

Figure A4.5 shows the pretrade equilibrium situation in Country A's labor market. The figure is somewhat different than others we have presented, so some explanation is required. The length of the horizontal axis measures the total amount of labor in A, with units of labor in the S industry measured off to the right from point O_S and labor in T measured to the left from O_T. The two vertical axes both measure the wage rate in A. The VMP_S curve represents the S industry's demand for labor. The height of this demand curve at a particular level of employment equals the value marginal product of labor, $P_S \times MP_{LS}$. This amount of money is the revenue that firms in S receive by selling what the last worker hired has produced. Clearly, firms will want to hire workers only so long as the cost of the last worker hired does not exceed the value of that worker's marginal product. In other words, the S industry will hire workers until $W = P_S \times MP_{LS}$.

The VMP_T curve is the T industry's demand for labor. It points in the opposite direction because we measure labor working in T starting at point O_T and increasing as we move left in the figure. As was the case with industry S, the T industry will also hire workers until $W = P_T \times MP_{LT}$.

Labor market equilibrium occurs at the intersection of the two curves. The height of the intersection point determines the wage paid workers, no matter where

FIGURE A4.5   *Equilibrium in the specific factors model.*

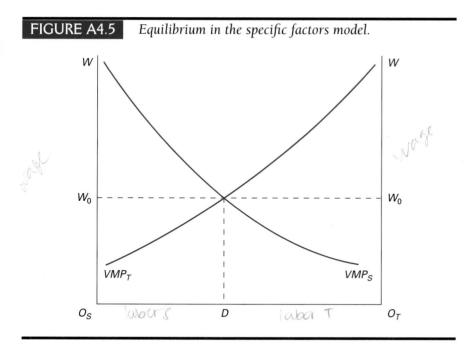

they are employed. At that point, and at no other in the diagram, $W = P_S \times MP_{LS}$ and $W = P_T \times MP_{LT}$. In equilibrium, $O_S D$ workers are employed in the S industry and DO_T workers in industry T. The wage paid workers in both industries is W_0.

Let's use the specific factors model to consider the effect on wages and rental rates if Country A opens up to international trade. We have already established that A has comparative advantage in good S and that once trade opens P_S/P_T will rise in A. It is easiest to illustrate what will happen in A's labor market if we suppose that the relative price rises because P_S rises while P_T remains constant. Under this assumption, the demand for labor will rise in industry S by the amount of the increase in P_S while the demand for labor in industry T will remain constant. We show this in Figure A4.6.

How have things changed in the new equilibrium? Employment has risen in S, from $O_S D$ workers to $O_S G$ workers, while employment in T has fallen by the same amount. As the diagram illustrates, international trade causes a redistribution of jobs. In this case, the money wage paid to all workers rises, from W_0 to W_1. Are workers better off? Not necessarily, because the price of S has gone up too and by more than the rise in W. If workers consume large amounts of S and only little T, they are worse off.

What about owners of capital? In industry S, capital owners are better off in real terms. The same number of machines produce more because there are more work-

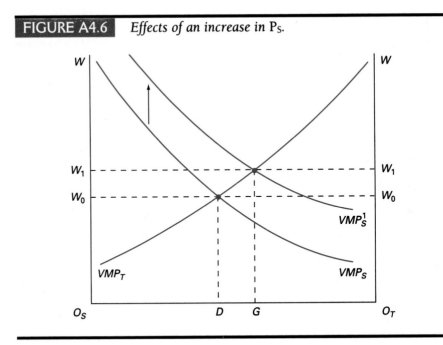

FIGURE A4.6   *Effects of an increase in* P_S*.*

ers and the goods are sold at a higher price. Thus, rental payments must rise. In contrast, owners of capital used in T must be worse off. Their machines produce less, because employment has declined and the price of T has not changed. Thus rental payments earned in T must fall. Given this, it is easy to imagine why capital and labor in certain industries might oppose the expansion of international trade.

CHAPTER 5

Tests of Trade Models

The Leontief Paradox

and Its Aftermath

TOPICS TO BE COVERED

KEY WORDS

Input-output table   Intraindustry trade
Leontief paradox   Increasing returns to scale
Product life cycle

I n this chapter we discuss attempts at testing the validity of the models of comparative advantage we have studied up to this point. How do economists go about testing theories? The answer is that they locate economic data related to the theory they want to test and examine these data to see if the facts conform to predictions of the model. For almost 50 years, various economists have followed these procedures in developing tests of both the classical and the Heckscher–Ohlin (HO) models. As we shall see, the results of these tests have been at best inconclusive and often controversial.

Largely because the tests we are about to describe have failed to resolve the question of the general validity of either the classical or the HO model, some economists have begun to explore new ideas about the determinants of international trade. These new models differ from the models we have already studied in that they usually focus on trade in only a limited number of product categories and are often only partial equilibrium in nature. Despite those limitations, several of these new models have gained many adherents. And, recent empirical analysis finds considerable support for some of the predictions of these models. Therefore, in this chapter we also discuss in detail some of these new theories of international trade.

TESTS OF THE CLASSICAL MODEL

We consider first a well-known test of the classical model. The test was developed by an economist named G.D.A. MacDougall, who published his results in 1951.* MacDougall had data on the exports (by industry) of both the United States and the United Kingdom to the rest of the world for the year 1937.[†] He also had data on overall outputs and labor inputs for the production of these goods in each country. In all, 25 different industries were included in the study.

The test MacDougall devised was straightforward. The classical model predicts that a country will have comparative advantage in those goods in which that country's labor is relatively more efficient than in other goods and other countries. What MacDougall proposed to do was to compare labor productivity and export performance on an industry-by-industry basis across the two countries. His hypothesis was that in those industries in which (after adjusting for differences in wages) labor productivity in the United States was high relative to that in the United Kingdom, U.S. exports should be high relative to U.K. exports.

How did MacDougall carry out his experiment? First, by dividing industry output by industry labor input, MacDougall obtained a measure of labor productivity (the average product of labor, APL) for each industry in each country. Then, to find a measure of relative labor productivity, he formed the ratio of U.S. APL to U.K. APL

---

*See G.D.A. MacDougall, "British and American Exports: A Study Suggested by the Theory of Comparative Costs," *Economic Journal* 61 (1951).
[†]Trade between the two countries was negligible in 1937, owing in part to high tariffs, especially in the United States.

for each industry in the study. For example, if the resulting number for industry Z equaled 3.5, then, on average, an American worker in the Z industry produced 3.5 times more output than his or her British counterpart.

At the time of his study, wages in the United States were about twice the wages in the United Kingdom. Thus, according to the classical model, the United States should have had comparative advantage in those industries in which U.S. workers were more than twice as productive as U.K. workers—in other words, where MacDougall's measure of productivity exceeded 2. MacDougall chose as his measure of relative comparative advantage the ratio of U.S. exports from a particular industry to U.K. exports from the same industry.

Table 5.1, taken from MacDougall's paper, presents some of the results from MacDougall's experiment. As the table illustrates, there does appear to be support for the classical model. Out of 25 products, 20 obey the general hypothesis that U.S. exports will be greater than U.K. exports if U.S. productivity is more than twice U.K. productivity. Furthermore, in industries where U.S. workers are less than twice as productive, U.K. exports tend to exceed U.S. exports.

TABLE 5.1	*Results from MacDougall's Test of the Classical Model*	
Industries[1]	U.S. Output per Worker / U.K. Output per Worker	U.S. Exports / U.K. Exports
Radios	More than 2	8
Pig iron		5
Glass containers		4
Tin cans		3.5
Machinery		1.5
Paper	More than 2	1
Cigarettes	1.4–2	0.5
Linoleum		0.33
Hosiery		0.33
Leather footwear		0.33
Coke		0.2
Rayon weaving		0.2
Cotton goods		0.11
Rayon making		0.09
Beer	1.4–2	0.06
Cement	Less than 1.4	0.09
Men's woolens		0.04
Margarine		0.03
Woolen and worsted	Less than 1.4	0.004

[1]Exceptions (U.S. output per worker more than twice U.K. output per worker but U.S. exports less than U.K. exports): electric lamps, rubber tires, soap, biscuits, and matches.

SOURCE: MacDougall, "British and American Exports," Table I.

What do we conclude from the results of this test?* First, we should accept it as evidence of a relationship between export performance and labor productivity. However, this need not be evidence of the general validity of the classical model—for three reasons. First, the classical model seeks to explain trade between two countries and not trade from two countries to third countries (the type of trade studied by MacDougall). Strictly speaking, if the classical model is correct, then either the United States or the United Kingdom should export the product, but not both.

Second, the results reported by MacDougall do not completely rule out other models. For instance, it is possible to show that under certain relatively common conditions, the HO model would also predict the pattern of trade observed by MacDougall.[†] Finally, note that MacDougall's procedure allows one to compare only the relationship between relative export levels and relative labor productivity levels. It does not control for the influence of other factors, such as transport costs, product differentiation, and discriminatory trade barriers, which might explain the trade patterns observed by MacDougall.

TESTS OF THE HO MODEL

Perhaps the most famous test in the history of economics is a test of the HO theory conducted by Wassily Leontief in the early 1950s.[‡] At the time of this test, Leontief was a member of the faculty at Harvard. He was already a world-famous economist, noted especially for his empirical modeling of general equilibrium systems. The chief tool used in his analyses was an input-output table, a formulation so important that it would win for him a Nobel Prize in economics in 1973.

Input-output table
A table that details the sales of each industry to all other industries in an economy.

An **input-output table** describes the flows of goods and services between every sector of the economy. Each industry in an economy depends upon other industries for much of its raw materials and intermediate inputs. For instance, computer production requires steel, plastics, semiconductors, paper (for packaging), and even computer services (for design and the like). Similarly, production in virtually every industry requires the use of computers. Thus, the computer industry buys products from other industries and also sells products to these same industries.

---

*MacDougall's results for the United States and the United Kingdom have been reconfirmed in several other studies. See especially G.D.A. MacDougall, Monica Dowley, Pauline Fox, and Senta Pugh, "British and American Productivity, Prices, and Exports: An Addendum," and Robert Stern, "British and American Productivity and Comparative Costs in International Trade," both in *Oxford Economic Papers* (1962). For contradictory evidence, see Mordechai Kreinin, "The Theory of Comparative Cost—Further Empirical Evidence," *Economic Internazionale* (1969); and James McGilvray and David Simpson, "The Commodity Structure of Anglo-Irish Trade," *Review of Economics and Statistics* (1973).

[†]The proof of this statement is somewhat beyond the scope of this book. The advanced reader may want to consult J. Ford, "On the Equivalence of the Classical and Factor Models in Explaining International Trade Patterns," *The Manchester School* (1967); and Rodney Falvey, "Comparative Advantage in a Multi-factor World," *International Economic Review* (1981).

[‡]The results of this test were reported in a paper entitled "Domestic Production and Foreign Trade: The American Capital Position Reconsidered," read before the American Philosophical Society in 1953. This article has been reprinted in part in Richard Caves and Harry Johnson, eds., *Readings in International Economics* (Homewood, Ill.: Richard D. Irwin, Inc., 1968).

Similar relationships between industries are found across every sector of an economy. An input-output table details these interindustry transactions that occur in the production process.

The best way to think of an input-output table is as a spreadsheet of columns and rows. Each industry in the economy appears once as a column entry and once as a row entry. Column entries refer to purchases made by a specific industry in a given year from all of the other industries in the economy. Thus, reading down the computer column, for instance, one can find out the value of steel required to produce that year's output of computers, the value of semiconductors that are required, the value of paper required, the value of plastics required, and so on. Row entries represent sales by a specific industry to all other industries in the economy. Reading across a row provides information as to which industries buy the outputs of a particular industry.

The great advantage of an input-output table is that it illustrates quite graphically how interrelated industries are. For instance, to produce more autos requires more steel, more glass, more paint, and the like. Thus, if events were to occur that would bring about an expansion of an industry such as autos, industries that supply inputs to the auto industry would also have to expand. And, as these other industries grew, expansion would occur in still others. Of course, it is not possible for industries to expand without the services of additional labor and capital. Hence, accompanying an input-output table is a set of information that details the labor and capital requirements for a fixed amount of output of a given industry.

While it is interesting to know on a purely scientific basis about these relationships between economic sectors, in some instances input-output tables have been or are being used for economic planning and policy. During wartime the information in the input-output table can be especially important. If, for instance, the government decides that more airplanes must be built, the table shows all the industries in the economy in which additional resources will be required.

Leontief built his input-output table using data from 200 different U.S. industries. In addition to the interindustry detail described in the table, the model detailed the labor and capital requirements of each of the 200 industries. During World War II, Leontief served as a consultant to the U.S. government, and the model was used extensively to plan production decisions for the economy. At the end of the war, however, economic planning by the government was no longer required. Consequently, Leontief turned his attention toward applying his model to new uses. One such use would be to test the general validity of the HO model.

At first, it might not seem very clear how one could use an input-output table to test the HO model. In fact, the procedure is relatively simple and straightforward. Leontief began with data on U.S. exports and imports for 1947. He then considered the following experiment: Suppose that U.S. exports were decreased proportionately by $1 million and U.S. imports were increased proportionately by $1 million. What would be the capital and labor requirements necessary to carry out this change in production levels?

Before we tell you the results of this test, let us consider what we might expect Leontief would find. Clearly, the United States in 1947 was the dominant economy in the world. The war had left the U.S. capital stock untouched, and the war effort had helped to rejuvenate the U.S. economy from the depression that had preceded the war. All of this would seem to imply that the United States, at least at that point in history, might well have been the most capital-abundant country in the world.* If so, the HO model predicts that the United States should export capital-intensive goods and import labor-intensive goods. In such a situation, Leontief's experiment would show that the amount of capital per worker idled by a hypothetical reduction in U.S. exports would exceed the amount of capital per worker needed to produce a hypothetical expansion of U.S. import-competing products. What Leontief found was exactly the opposite!

Using his input-output table with data for 1947, Leontief showed that to replace $1 million of U.S. imports by domestic output expansion would require 170 additional years per worker of labor and $3.1 million of capital.[†] Reducing U.S. exports by $1 million would provide 182.3 years per worker of labor and $2.6 million in capital. Thus, according to the experiment, U.S. exports tend to be labor intensive relative to U.S. imports. Because this finding was so unexpected, it has become known as the **Leontief paradox**.

Leontief paradox
The finding that U.S. exports tend to come from labor-intensive industries, while U.S. imports are produced using relatively capital-intensive techniques.

As its name suggests, the Leontief paradox was one of the most puzzling and troubling empirical findings ever uncovered by an economist. From its first theoretical development, the HO model had been regarded by most economists as "the" model to explain comparative advantage. The logical completeness of the model, its seeming agreement with casual observations about the trade flows, and the ease with which it could be manipulated to study the effects of trade on other aspects of the economy (e.g., factor payments) all served to enhance the model's reputation among economists. Then suddenly, the model appeared to be unable to explain trade patterns even in the presumably unambiguous case of the United States.

ATTEMPTED RECONCILIATIONS OF LEONTIEF'S FINDINGS

Not surprisingly, the immediate reaction among many economists was to attempt to resurrect the model by developing explanations for the Leontief paradox within the context of the model. Leontief was the first to try this. He argued that his results were

---

*Note carefully that at the time Leontief conducted his tests, there was no way to test this statement directly. Data on capital stocks did not exist on a national basis. Even today, the data we have on capital stocks are quite crude. This is because there are many types of capital goods. Screwdrivers, computers, and bulldozers are all capital goods, as are many other types of products. How do you add all these goods into a single measure of capital? The only available solution is to total the value of all these goods available at any point in time. But it should be clear that $100,000 worth of screwdrivers does not have the same implications for production possibilities in a country as does $100,000 worth of computers.
[†]Note that Leontief excluded from his study imports of products such as coffee and bananas, not produced in the United States.

due to the fact that the implicit assumption of the model that American workers were of equal productivity to their foreign counterparts was incorrect. He wrote:

> Let us . . . reject the simple but tenuous postulate of comparative technological parity and make the plausible alternative assumption that in any combination with a given quantity of capital, *one man year of American labor is equivalent to, say, three man years of foreign* [emphasis added]. Then in comparing the relative amounts of capital and labor possessed by the United States and the rest of the world . . . the total number of American workers must be multiplied by three.*

As the quotation indicates, Leontief's suggested reconciliation was to argue that because American workers were so productive relative to workers in the rest of the world, the United States should more properly be viewed as being relatively labor abundant. Under these alternative circumstances, then, Leontief's findings become consistent with the HO theory.

How does Leontief's reconciliation square with the facts? As the quotation hints, Leontief was clearly guessing about the relative superiority of American labor. He had made his claim based on a presumption that the production orientation of American society, with its emphasis on entrepreneurship and organization, as well as the general education system, would produce relatively more efficient workers. Considerable evidence has been accumulated since Leontief published his findings that his claim about the superiority of American labor is incorrect or at least overstated.†

Other reconciliations followed Leontief's. Jaraslav Vanek argued that tests based on a simple two-factor (capital and labor) model would be bound to produce the kinds of results found by Leontief. This is because an important third factor, natural resources, had been omitted from the analysis. Vanek's argument proceeds as follows: Suppose the United States is relatively scarce in natural resources but relatively abundant in labor and capital. Under these circumstances, the HO model would predict that the United States should import natural-resource-intensive products. But Leontief was not looking for this in his data. Furthermore, natural resources, such as minerals, tend to be produced using capital-intensive techniques (e.g., mining and smelting). In this fashion the paradox may be explained. On a two-factor basis, U.S. imports appeared to be relatively capital intensive. On a three-factor basis, in fact, these products were relatively natural-resource intensive. Some more

---

*Wassily Leontief, "Domestic Production and Foreign Trade," 523–24.

†See, for instance, Mordechai Kreinin, "Comparative Labor Effectiveness and the Leontief Scarce-Factor Paradox," *American Economic Review* (1955). In the paper, Kreinin showed, based on questionnaires submitted to American managers of multinational corporations, that these managers viewed American labor in the early 1950s to be only slightly superior to foreign labor. However, in a recent test of the HO model, Daniel Trefler finds strong support for its predictions provided that factor endowment measures are corrected for international differences in productivity. He concludes that Leontief had the right idea, but not necessarily the right numbers, in arguing that productivity adjustments are necessary in order to test the model correctly. See Daniel Trefler, "International Factor Price Differences: Leontief Was Right!" *Journal of Political Economy* (1993).

recent tests of the HO model have attempted to take into account Vanek's reconciliation by excluding from the data natural-resource-intensive imports and exports. In some cases, when this is done, the paradox disappears.*

W.P. Travis, writing in the early 1960s, argued that the Leontief paradox could be explained by the prevailing U.S. tariff structure.[†] Specifically, U.S. tariffs on labor-intensive products tended to be high, often exceeding 25 percent. Tariffs on capital-intensive items tended to be lower. This tariff structure, Travis claimed, could lead to a distortion in U.S. trade patterns away from natural comparative advantage, toward imports of relatively capital-intensive goods. While Travis's comments are correct, it is difficult to test his proposition conclusively, because such tests would necessarily involve what U.S. imports might have been in the absence of tariffs.

Another suggested reconciliation offered at the time was that Assumption 17—the international equality of tastes—is violated. Recall from Chapter 4 that the HO model assumes tastes are identical across countries. As we showed, if this were not the case, trade need not flow along the lines suggested by the HO model. One way to test the hypothesis that tastes are identical is to examine consumption patterns across countries. Only limited statistics are available. What data there are, however, seem to suggest that expenditure patterns differ. Consider, for instance, the information presented in Table 5.2. This table summarizes consumption data for the year 1975 collected and first published by the United Nations. More recently, these data have appeared in a study of the determinants of comparative advantage conducted by Edward Leamer.[‡]

The table illustrates the wide diversity of expenditure patterns that exist across countries. For instance, Indians spend almost 60 percent of their total consumption expenditures on food, while only about 14 percent of U.S. consumption is devoted to food. Similarly, the French and Dutch spend 11 percent of consumption on medical care, while the British spend only 1 percent. While some differences should be expected due to the fact that tariffs, transportation costs, and many government policies change relative prices from one country to the next, it is almost surely the case that Assumption 17 is violated. Are tastes sufficiently different to overturn the HO predictions? No one has been able to offer a convincing demonstration that they are.

Finally, we note one additional explanation of the paradox. In his tests, Leontief used the U.S. input-output table to construct the factor requirements for both U.S. exports and U.S. import-*competing* goods. The assumption he then made was that foreign goods would be produced using technologies identical with those found in

---

*Vanek's argument was first developed in his book *The Natural Resource Content of United States Foreign Trade* (Boston: MIT Press, 1963). See Table 4.1 (p. 484) in Alan Deardorff, "Testing Trade Theories," in *Handbook of International Economics*, vol. 1, eds. Ronald Jones and Peter Kenen (Amsterdam: North-Holland Publishers, 1984), for a comparison of results from several tests with and without natural-resource-intensive goods.
[†]See W.P. Travis, *The Theory of Trade and Production* (Boston: Harvard University Press, 1964).
[‡]The study is found in Leamer's *Sources of International Comparative Advantage: Theory and Evidence* (Boston: MIT Press, 1984). We have more to say about the results of this study in a later section. The consumption data summarized in Table 5.2 are detailed in Leamer's Table 1.6, found on page 40.

TABLE 5.2	*Extremes in Consumption Patterns across Countries*		

(PERCENTAGES OF TOTAL PRIVATE CONSUMPTION DEVOTED TO EACH CATEGORY)[1]

Category	High	Low	Average[2]
Food	India (59.7)	United States (14.4)	33.3
Beverages	Ireland (14.4)	Libya (1.1)	5.1
Tobacco	Sri Lanka (6.6)	France (0.9)	2.9
Clothing and shoes	Ghana (14.2)	Jamaica (4.3)	8.8
Rent, fuel, power	Israel (20.7)	Sri Lanka (6.8)	13.6
Furniture	Belgium (15.0)	Korea (3.2)	8.4
Medical care	Netherlands and France (11.2)	United Kingdom (1.0)	4.9
Transportation and communication	Cyprus (19.6)	Philippines (2.2)	11.2
Recreation	Singapore (12.3)	Sri Lanka (2.6)	6.8

[1]Data are based on information from national account statistics for 39 countries for the year 1975.

[2]Numbers are computed as simple averages for the individual levels of the 39 countries.

SOURCE: Compiled from information in Leamer, *Sources of International Comparative Advantage: Theory and Evidence* (Boston: MIT Press, 1984), Table 1.6, p. 40.

U.S. import-competing industries. While this assumption is consistent with the identical-technology assumption of the HO model (recall Assumption 14), it is true in the HO model only if factor prices are equalized internationally or if there is no possibility for industries in different countries to substitute between labor and capital in the production process as factor prices change. If these conditions fail to hold (which is certainly the case) and if labor is relatively more expensive in the United States than in the rest of the world (which was probably the case at the time of his study), then Leontief's procedure would estimate that U.S. imports are relatively more capital intensive than the techniques actually used to produce these goods in the rest of the world. This is because foreign producers, reacting to their relatively lower labor costs, use more labor-intensive production methods than are employed in the United States, where labor is relatively more expensive.

OTHER TESTS OF THE HO MODEL

Testing of the HO model did not end with Leontief's original study. Leontief himself repeated his experiment using data from 1951. He found that the paradox still remained. Robert Baldwin examined U.S. data for the year 1962 and also reported finding the paradox. Robert Stern and Keith Maskus studied U.S. trade data for 1972. In that year, the capital/labor ratio in the U.S. export sector exceeded that found in the U.S. import sector; since then, the paradox seems to have vanished (provided one still assumes that the United States is relatively capital abundant).*

Tests similar to those of Leontief have also been performed on data from other countries. Japanese trade was also shown to exhibit a paradox. Using data from the 1950s, when Japan would have been considered to be labor abundant, Japanese exports were found to be capital intensive and imports to be labor intensive. This paradox was explained by the fact that, at that time, Japan was relatively more industrialized than some of its trading partners and relatively less industrialized than others. Consequently, according to the HO theory, it should export capital-intensive goods to its less developed trading partners and labor-intensive goods to its industrialized trading partners. This was shown to be the case when only Japan–U.S. trade was considered.[†]

More examples of paradoxical results were uncovered in trade data from Canada—where exports (mostly to the United States) were shown to be capital intensive—and from India—where Indian exports to the United States were also shown to be more capital intensive than Indian imports from the United States. This latter study also showed, however, that overall Indian exports were relatively more labor intensive than Indian imports were, evidence that would seem to agree with HO predictions. Moreover, a recent test of the determinants of trade between various developing countries also reports strong support for the HO model.[‡]

Several studies have also examined trade patterns of Eastern European countries. Exports of the former East Germany were found to be relatively capital intensive. Given that much of East Germany's trade was with other Eastern European countries, this finding appears to be consistent with HO. In a study involving data over a 13-year span of the 1950s and 1960s, Steven Rosefielde has shown that the trade pattern of the former Soviet Union was strongly consistent with the HO theorem.[**]

RECENT TESTS OF THE HO MODEL

Since the beginning of the 1980s, there has been a resurgence of interest in tests of the Heckscher–Ohlin model. This interest has been based on at least two factors.

---

*For further details, see Wassily Leontief, "Factor Proportions and the Structure of American Trade: Further Theoretical and Empirical Analysis," *Review of Economics and Statistics* (1956); Robert Baldwin, "Determinants of the Commodity Structure of U.S. Trade," *American Economic Review* (1971); and Robert Stern and Keith Maskus, "Determinants of the Structure of U.S. Foreign Trade, 1958–76," *Journal of International Economics* (1981).

[†]For more details, see M. Tatemoto and S. Ichimura, "Factor Proportions and Foreign Trade: The Case of Japan," *Review of Economics and Statistics* (1959).

[‡]See D. Wahl, "Capital and Labour Requirements for Canada's Foreign Trade," *Canadian Journal of Economics and Political Science* (1961); R. Bharadwaj, "Factor Proportions and the Structure of Indo–U.S. Trade," *Indian Economic Journal* (1962); and Oli Havrylyshyn, "The Direction of Developing Country Trade: Empirical Evidence of Differences between South-South and South-North Trade," *Journal of Development Economics* (1985).

[**]See Wolfgang Stolper and Karl Roskamp, "Input-Output Table for East Germany with Applications to Foreign Trade," *Bulletin of the Oxford University Institute of Statistics* (1961); and Steven Rosefielde, "Factor Proportions and Economic Rationality in Soviet International Trade, 1955–1968," *American Economic Review* (1974).

First, economists have come to understand that the tests conducted by Leontief and others were necessarily incomplete because these tests looked at the factor intensity of trade without directly linking trade flows to the factor endowments of the countries involved in the test.* In part, this failure to test fully the HO model was due to a severe lack of data on national factor endowments. By the late 1970s, however, better data had become available. These offered economists a chance to test heretofore untested implications of the theory.

A second factor that helped to rekindle interest in tests of the theory was a theoretical observation by Edward Leamer based upon a multifactor (more than two-factor) version of the Heckscher–Ohlin model. Recall from the preceding discussion that Vanek had argued that U.S. imports were actually intensive in a third factor, natural resources. This could mean that U.S. exports might be relatively intensive in the other two factors, capital *and* labor. When the data were reexamined, this turned out to be true. In such circumstances, how would one be able to deduce whether the United States was more capital abundant or labor abundant, since the goods it exported contained relatively large amounts of both capital and labor services? Leamer showed that if the capital-to-labor input in the goods Americans exported exceeded the capital-to-labor input used to produce the goods Americans consumed, then the United States is revealed to be relatively capital abundant. And, again, when Leontief's data were reexamined, this turned out to be the case.[†]

Thus, based on a multifactor version of the HO model, Leamer had appeared to resolve the Leontief paradox. Leamer went on to test this version of the model in a series of important experiments. The results from one of these tests appeared in his book *Sources of Comparative Advantage,* published in 1984.[‡] There, Leamer undertook a careful study of data on the trade flows of 58 countries. What he did was to measure the endowments of 11 factors (capital, skilled labor, literate nonprofessional labor, illiterate labor, four types of land, coal, minerals, and oil) for each of the countries in the study. Then, he compared these endowments with the goods that countries trade. To keep his study under manageable proportions, he used a statistical technique to group various commodities into trade aggregates. The criterion Leamer used for grouping any two goods into the same category was that if countries tended to export one of the goods, they also exported the other. Beginning with information on 62 different products, he was able to lump these goods into 10 product groups based upon the similarity of their trade characteristics; for instance, fruit, sugar, coffee, beverages, and crude rubber were combined into a product group called *tropical products.* Then, Leamer compared trade in the various product groups with endowments of factors of production. He was able to show that the relative

---

*Recall that Leontief's results were considered to be paradoxical only because economists believed the United States must have been capital abundant relative to countries of the rest of the world. Leontief's reconciliation of his findings was that the United States was, in fact, labor abundant. No attempt was made to collect data to resolve this question.

[†]For more details, see Edward Leamer, "The Leontief Paradox, Reconsidered," *Journal of Political Economy* (1980).

[‡]See Edward Leamer, *Sources.* Much of this book is highly readable, even for undergraduates. The bar graphs found in Appendix D of the book, which compare trade flows and factor endowments, offer an easily interpreted summary of the main findings of the study.

availability of any given factor of production is important in explaining the goods a country exports. For instance, countries that are relatively well endowed with tropical farmland will tend to be net exporters of tropical products.

As with all of the other tests of the HO model discussed so far, the test just described is not a complete test of the model. This is because Leamer grouped his commodities together according to similarity of trade patterns rather than similarity of factor intensities. That is, Leamer showed that trade patterns and factor endowments were related to each other. Leontief and others had already shown that trade patterns and factor intensities were related to each other, albeit in a sometimes paradoxical fashion. The HO model would not be fully tested until the complete set of theoretical links between endowments *and* intensities to international trade could be established or rejected. This effort was undertaken in two separate studies by Keith Maskus and by Harry Bowen, Edward Leamer, and Leo Sveikauskas.*

Maskus looked at U.S. data on factor endowments. He also used the U.S. input-output table to calculate the factor intensities of the goods the United States trades. What he found was largely contradictory of the strictest predictions of the HO model. For instance, according to 1958 factor endowment data, the United States was most abundant in physical capital, with skilled labor next, and unskilled labor the scarcest factor. Data on factor intensities revealed, however, that exports were most intensive in unskilled labor, followed by skilled labor, and least intensive in physical capital. Similar results were obtained when 1972 data were examined.

The study by Bowen et al. also reached similar conclusions, but for a larger set of countries. These authors went on to examine the issue of why their tests may have failed to verify the HO model. They considered the possibilities that consumption patterns and/or technologies may differ across countries. They also considered the possibility that the data they were working with contained substantial errors in measurement. In the end, they concluded that the poor performance of the HO model in their tests may have been due to data problems as well as the apparent unrealistic assumption that U.S. input-output tables could be used to describe the technologies employed in other countries of the world.

In the past several years, empirical tests have shifted emphasis to explore modified versions of HO model that might be more consistent with real world experience. Daniel Trefler shows that if one allows for technological differences across countries, then there is considerable support for factor price equalization.† In a second paper, he finds that combining the assumption of technological differences with an assumption that preferences in each country are biased toward domestically produced goods resolves much of the discrepancies between real world trade flows and those predicted by the HO model.‡ In a similar vein, James Harrigan finds that a model that combines technological differences and factor endowments differences

---

*See Keith Maskus, "A Test of the Heckscher–Ohlin–Vanek Theorem: The Leontief Commonplace," *Journal of International Economics* (1985); and Harry Bowen, Edward Leamer, and Leo Sveikauskas, "Multicountry, Multifactor Tests of the Factor Abundance Theory," *American Economic Review* (1987).
†See Daniel Trefler, "International Factor Price Differences: Leontief Was Right!," *Journal of Political Economy* (1993).
‡See Trefler, "The Case of the Missing Trade and Other Mysteries," *American Economic Review* (1995).

does a good job of explaining specialization in production across countries.* Thus, a message of this work is that theoretical models that combine elements of the classical and HO models are supported by the data.

Despite these latest results, the disappointing performance of the HO model in empirical tests has led some economists to abandon it as an overriding explanation of international trade, choosing instead to develop alternative explanations of comparative advantage. We turn now to a brief discussion of these alternative theories.

ALTERNATIVE THEORIES OF COMPARATIVE ADVANTAGE

The alternative theories that have been developed since the publication of Leontief's findings fall into two main categories. Some have come about as one or more of the restrictive assumptions of the HO model is relaxed. In the remaining cases, the HO framework has been abandoned altogether. As the following discussion indicates, the new theories that have emerged are much less general than the HO model, usually aiming to explain trade in only a narrow class of products.

Human Skills Theory

One of the leading alternative theories was developed by Donald Keesing.[†] Of the alternative models, his ideas come closest to the HO model. The major difference is that instead of focusing on differences in capital and labor across countries and goods, Keesing argued that the emphasis should be on differences in endowments and intensities of skilled and unskilled workers. Specifically, some countries have more highly skilled labor forces than others. Some products require greater intensities of high-skilled labor inputs than others (think of computers vs. textiles). Countries with relatively large endowments of high-skilled labor will have comparative advantage in products that are relatively intensive in skilled labor.

Keesing's model provides a straightforward explanation of the Leontief paradox. Because the United States has a highly trained and educated workforce relative to many other countries, U.S. exports tend to be *skilled-labor intensive.*[‡] One strong bit of empirical evidence to support this theory has been provided by Irving Kravis, who

---

*See James Harrigan, "Technology, Factor Supplies and International Specialization: Testing the Neoclassical Model," *American Economic Review* (1997).

[†]For a more complete discussion of his theory and some tests of its predictions, see Donald Keesing, "Labor Skills and International Trade: Evaluating Many Trade Flows with a Single Measuring Device," *Review of Economics and Statistics* (August 1965); and "Labor Skills and Comparative Advantage," *American Economic Review* (May 1966).

[‡]Recall that Leontief made no attempt to distinguish between inputs of skilled and unskilled workers. Moreover, note carefully the distinction between this explanation of the paradox and Leontief's own reconciliation. Leontief argues, in effect, that *all* U.S. workers are relatively more efficient than their foreign counterparts, and hence the United States is really labor abundant. Keesing argues that the ratio of skilled to unskilled workers in the U.S. labor force is high relative to that found in other countries, so that the United States is relatively abundant in skilled workers.

showed that high-wage industries in the United States account for the bulk of U.S. exports, while U.S. imports tend to concentrate in products that are produced in lower-wage American industries.[*]

Product Life Cycle Theory

Product life cycle
The process by which a product is invented and then over time becomes more standardized as consumers and producers gain familiarity with its features.

Raymond Vernon has argued that, for many manufactured goods, comparative advantage may shift over time from one country to another.[†] This is because these goods go through a **product life cycle.** This life cycle involves a stage during which goods are invented and tested in the marketplace. During this period of time, the production of the good also undergoes considerable experimentation.

Later, when the product is successful and become firmly established in the marketplace, a standardization process occurs. During this period, competing products from different manufacturers take on an increasingly common appearance, and the manufacturing processes used to make the good also become more and more identical. At this point, the product has matured. It may be sold for many years in this stage, or it may be displaced over time by new inventions.

How does the product life cycle relate to comparative advantage? The answer is simple. Early in a product's life, the country that invents the product has comparative advantage. As the country exports the good to the rest of the world, and as the product becomes increasingly more standardized, it is possible for competing firms in other countries to begin to gain market share, if these firms have a cost advantage in large-scale manufacturing. In such instances, comparative advantage shifts from the inventing country to countries where manufacturing costs are lower.

Note how this model can be used to reconcile the Leontief paradox. Let us assume that the United States is an innovating country that produces many new products. The United States will have comparative advantage in recently invented manufactured goods. Because these goods have yet to become standardized, their production is apt to be quite labor intensive. Investment in fixed capital is likely to be postponed until it becomes certain what features are most popular with the public and how best to automate the production of the good. Thus, U.S. exports will tend to be labor intensive. And, because standardization involves the adoption of more capital-intensive production techniques, if later the United States loses comparative advantage in a good and begins to import it, this good will tend to be capital intensive.[‡]

---

[*]This result continues to hold today. For more details on the study by Kravis, see his article "Wages and Foreign Trade," *Review of Economics and Statistics* (1956).
[†]See Raymond Vernon, "International Investment and International Trade in the Product Cycle," *Quarterly Journal of Economics* (1966).
[‡]In an interesting paper, Richard Brecher and Eshan Choudhri show how the existence of newly invented products can be used to explain the Leontief paradox. In particular, they show that even if the United States were capital abundant, if its newly invented goods were labor intensive in their production, then U.S. trade patterns would tend to have the features detected by Leontief. See "New Products and the Factor Content of International Trade," *Journal of Political Economy* (1984).

The product life cycle model is a model that has limited applicability. It represents an attempt to explain trade in manufactured products that require some degree of technical sophistication in their invention, design, and development. In some cases, the theory seems to fit the facts. For instance, color television was invented in the United States, and in the early days of the product, the United States produced and exported this good. Then, over time, the production of color televisions has shifted almost entirely to countries such as Japan, Taiwan, Korea, and elsewhere.

For other sophisticated products, such as computers and aircraft, the model seems to do less well. The United States, which took the lead in the development of these goods, still retains substantial comparative advantage despite the fact that each is now a relatively mature product. These examples point to the fundamental weakness of the product life cycle model—its inability to generalize its predictions about the timing of changes in the location of comparative advantage.*

Similarity of Preferences Theory

All the theories we have discussed so far have one common theme: The source of comparative advantage is found on the supply side. That is, the country with the lowest autarky cost of production will export the product. The differences between the theories we have examined lie in what factors tend to explain why costs are lower in one country than in another. Stefan Linder has argued that an explanation for the direction of trade in differentiated manufactured products lies on the demand side rather than the supply side.† Consequently, for trade in manufactured goods, he would reject all the explanations we have considered, offering a novel alternative.

Linder's hypothesis can be described as follows: In each country, industries produce goods designed to please the tastes of the consumers in that country. However, not every consumer is alike. Some prefer alternative products, with slightly different characteristics. International trade provides a means to obtain these goods. The advantage of international trade, then, is that consumers benefit from a wider variety of goods.

Going further, Linder's hypothesis explains which types of countries are most likely to trade with each other. Countries with similar standards of living (per capita GDP) will tend to consume similar types of goods. Standards of living are determined in part by the factor endowments of countries. Countries with large amounts of capital per worker tend to be richer than countries with lower amounts of capital

---

*A recent study by Joseph Gagnon and Andrew Rose casts further doubt on the importance of the product life cycle in explaining trade flows. They looked at detailed data on U.S. and Japanese trade flows over the period from 1962 to 1988. They found that most goods that were net U.S. exports (imports) in 1962 were also net U.S. exports (imports) in 1988. Similar results held for Japan. This finding is inconsistent with the notion that the location of comparative advantage shifts over time, as is implied by the product life cycle model. See "Dynamic Persistence of Industry Trade Balances: How Pervasive Is the Product Cycle?" *Oxford Economic Papers* (1995).

†Linder presented his hypothesis in his book *An Essay on Trade and Transformation* (New York: John Wiley and Sons, 1961).

per worker. Thus, there should be a considerable volume of trade between countries with similar characteristics. Rich countries will tend to trade with other rich countries, and poor countries with other poor countries. This implication of Linder's hypothesis provides a sharp contrast to the predictions of the HO model, in which countries with dissimilar factor endowments would seem to have the greatest incentives to trade with each other, because they would exhibit the greatest disparity in pretrade relative prices. And the prediction that rich countries trade extensively with other rich countries is one of the trade patterns we noted in Chapter 1.

Several additional points bear noting. First, Linder's theory applies only to differentiated manufactured products. He tends to explain trade in raw materials or agricultural products by using an HO-type model. Second, since he rejects the HO explanation for trade in manufactured goods, he finds nothing paradoxical about the Leontief paradox. Rather, Leontief's findings might simply reflect a desire on the part of American consumers for capital-intensive goods.

Intraindustry trade
The simultaneous import and export of similar types of products by a country.

Third, Linder's model provides an explanation for an important phenomenon in international trade, **intraindustry trade**. This type of trade occurs when countries both export *and* import the same kinds of products. Simple models of comparative advantage would seem to rule out this type of trade behavior. However, if, as Linder suggests, trade takes place to satisfy the need for variety in consumption, then it should not be surprising that a country such as the Netherlands exports Heineken beer and imports Löwenbrau. Finally, we note that despite the appeal of Linder's hypothesis, early studies of the theory revealed little empirical support. Several recent studies, however, report evidence in favor of Linder's theory.* In addition, the growing importance of intraindustry trade has spurred the development of alternative theories of the supply side of the economy capable of explaining this phenomenon. We now turn to a discussion of these issues.

INTRAINDUSTRY TRADE

Examples of intraindustry trade are not hard to find in the real world. Computers made by IBM are exported to countries around the world at the same time that Americans import computers made by Hitachi, NEC, and other foreign companies. Similarly, while Boeing exports commercial aircraft, some American airline companies have purchased aircraft made by Airbus, a European manufacturer. Despite these examples, the extent to which intraindustry trade occurs is an open empirical question.

Some studies have argued that intraindustry trade is pervasive. Consider Table 5.3. There, we show estimates of the degree of intraindustry trade by country for the

---

*See Jerry and Marie Thursby, "Bilateral Trade Flows, the Linder Hypothesis, and Exchange Risk," *Review of Economics and Statistics* (1987); and Jeffrey Bergstrand, "The Heckscher–Ohlin–Samuelson Model, the Linder Hypothesis, and the Determinants of Bilateral Intra-Industry Trade," *Economic Journal* (1990).

TABLE 5.3	*Intraindustry Trade by Country, 1983*					
Rank	Country	IIT	Rank	Country	IIT	
1	United Kingdom	68.5	28	El Salvador	29.5	
2	Belgium-Luxembourg	67.2	29	Yemen	28.2	
3	France	63.9	30	Tunisia	26.4	
4	Austria	63.4	31	Greece	24.4	
5	Netherlands	61.4	32	Australia	22.4	
6	Singapore	59.5	33	Jordan	21.8	
7	Canada	55.2	34	Turkey	20.6	
8	Ireland	54.4	35	Japan	19.4	
9	Sweden	54.1	36	Brazil	19.3	
10	Denmark	53.0	37	Trinidad	19.2	
11	Switzerland	52.7	38	Ivory Coast	18.6	
12	Italy	47.9	39	New Zealand	18.1	
13	United States	47.5	40	Thailand	17.6	
14	Germany	46.7	41	Colombia	16.4	
15	Costa Rica	46.2	42	Indonesia	14.4	
16	Yugoslavia	44.5	43	Pakistan	12.8	
17	Hong Kong	43.0	44	Sri Lanka	12.8	
18	Philippines	41.3	45	Egypt	11.5	
19	Spain	39.4	46	Peru	10.3	
20	Finland	39.2	47	Kenya	10.1	
21	Israel	39.1	48	Ethiopia	10.0	
22	South Korea	37.3	49	Morocco	8.4	
23	Argentina	36.5	50	Cameroon	8.2	
24	Norway	36.2	51	Sudan	5.9	
25	Portugal	33.4	52	Bangladesh	5.5	
26	Cyprus	33.3	53	Gabon	5.4	
27	Malaysia	30.7	54	Algeria	2.0	

SOURCE: F. Hassan, "Intraindustry Trade: Theory and Evidence" (Ph.D. diss., University of Pittsburgh, 1987), Table 4-3, Calculated by author.

year 1983. The measure of intraindustry trade (IIT) employed in this table is given by Formula 5.1:

$$\text{IIT} = 100 - 50 \times \sum_{j=1}^{n} \left| \frac{\text{exports of } j}{\text{total exports}} - \frac{\text{imports of } j}{\text{total imports}} \right| \qquad (5.1)$$

where j is an identifier for a particular industry, and there are n different industries. Theoretically, values of IIT can be as high as 100. This would occur if all the trade of a country were intraindustry and if trade in each product category were exactly balanced (e.g., if exports of cars were equal to imports of cars, exports of computers were equal to imports of computers, etc.). If none of the trade of a country is intraindustry trade but overall trade is balanced, then the value of IIT is zero.

As the data in the table clearly show, there is a wide disparity in the amount of intraindustry trade in the world. In general, countries displaying the highest degree of intraindustry trade are industrialized countries, especially those in Western Europe.

Developing countries in Africa and Central and Southern Asia exhibit a much smaller proportion of intraindustry trade.*

The existence of intraindustry trade would seem to contradict the models of comparative advantage we have studied so far. After all, if a country has comparative advantage in a product, why would it ever import it? Several answers to this question are consistent with models such as the HO model. For instance, consider the role of transportation costs. On the east coast of North America, timber is exported from the United States to Canada. On the west coast, trade in timber flows in the opposite direction. Such trade can be explained by the fact that it is cheaper to transport timber from British Columbia south to the United States than it is to transport it east to Ontario. Thus, Ontario tends to import timber from the United States, even though (western) Canada is relatively well endowed with timberland.

A second explanation for intraindustry trade that is consistent with standard models of comparative advantage has to do with the construction of the data used by economists to measure intraindustry trade. Obviously, there are hundreds of thousands of different types of products that can be traded. (To convince yourself of this, think of all the different kinds of clothing that exist.) How do governments keep track of trade in all these different items?

In some cases, governments aggregate data according to the end-use characteristics of products. Consider desks. All desks serve relatively the same purpose, but they can be manufactured using quite different materials. For instance, they can be made from wood or metal. Countries that have large quantities of metal ores and metal-smelting facilities should have a comparative advantage in the production of metal desks. Countries with large endowments of timber would have a comparative advantage in wooden desks. Thus, even in an HO world it is possible for a country to both export *and* import desks, so long as exports and imports were manufactured using different inputs and so long as consumers view these goods as less than perfect substitutes for each other.

Added to the problem that goods with similar uses can be made in different ways is a second problem: Often there are so many goods that data storage and presentation restrictions require further consolidation of data to include trade in even more dissimilar goods. For example, cotton sweaters are added with wool sweaters to form a category called *sweaters*. Then, sweaters are added with other types of clothing, such as shirts, suits, and dresses, to form a category called *apparel*. The same sort of aggregation occurs in other industry data groupings. Thus, it is easy to imagine that some intraindustry trade is purely a statistical phenomenon, one that would go away if economists had access to highly detailed data on trade (e.g., data on trade in cotton vs. wool sweaters). Unfortunately, even the most highly disaggregated data that

*More recent, but less comprehensive, studies of intraindustry trade include Don P. Clark, "Recent Evidence on Determinants of Intra-industry Trade," *Weltwirtschaftliches Archiv* (1993); David Greenaway, R. Hine, and Chris Milner, "Vertical and Horizontal Intraindustry Trade: A Cross Industry Analysis for the United Kingdom," *The Economic Journal* (1995); and Roy J. Ruffin, "The Nature and Significance of Intra-industry Trade," *Economic & Financial Review* (Federal Reserve Bank of Dallas, 1999).

are available to economists include combinations of items whose potential two-way trade could be explained by factor requirements in production.

INCREASING RETURNS AND IMPERFECT COMPETITION

Despite the examples just presented, there is good reason to think that a considerable proportion of intraindustry trade is not explainable by problems of data aggregation and categorization. Other explanations of intraindustry trade must be explored. One idea that has been receiving increasing amounts of attention by economists has to do with the role of **increasing returns to scale** in the production process. In this section we define increasing returns to scale and describe the implications for the presence of increasing returns to scale on domestic industrial structure. Then, we turn to a discussion of the relationship between increasing returns to scale and international trade.

> **Increasing returns to scale**
> A technological situation in which proportionate increases in the use of productive inputs lead to greater than proportionate increases in output.

Increasing returns to scale are said to exist when a proportionate increase in the use of factors of production results in a greater than proportionate increase in output. For instance, if, by doubling the size of an automobile factory and the number of autoworkers, automobile output more than doubles, then automobile production is said to experience increasing returns to scale. The notion of increasing returns can be applied either for a firm or for an industry as a whole. In either case, the long-run average cost curve of the firm (or industry) falls as its output increases.

Increasing returns to scale may be external or internal to individual firms in an industry. In the first case, as more and more resources are devoted to the production of a good, the cost curves of all firms in the industry shift down. This situation seems to describe well what happened to American agriculture in the nineteenth century. As the Midwest and Great Plains were settled and more and more farms were established, it became profitable to build railroad lines to ship grain to markets and for manufacturers of farm implements to begin production. The growth in the transportation infrastructure and the increased availability of factors of production helped to the lower the costs of production for all farmers.

If one or more industries in an economy exhibit increasing returns to scale technology, this will affect the shape of a country's PPF. To see this, suppose that both soybeans (S) and textiles (T) enjoy external economies and that these two industries use capital and labor in the same proportions. In Figure 5.1 we derive the PPF for this country. Point E (F) represents the maximum amount of S (T) the country can produce if it were to specialize completely in the production of that good. These points determine the end points of the PPF. Now, suppose that beginning from point E, resources are allocated away from S in such a way that each industry ends up with exactly half of all factors of production. We know that output of S will fall by more than one-half its original level. That means that the new level of production of S will be at a point such as point H on the diagram. Because T now has half the available resources, its output will rise. However, because it too enjoys increasing returns to scale, T will produce an output level less than half of what it would produce if it had all available factors. That is, it would produce at a point such as point

FIGURE 5.1   *PPF of a country with increasing returns to scale industries.*

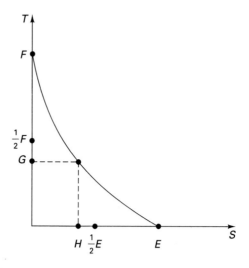

G. Thus, we have established that increasing returns to scale typically result in PPFs that are convex to the origin.*

Figure 5.2 illustrates a country with S and T industries that both exhibit increasing returns to scale. The autarky equilibrium for this country is at point M, where the PPF is tangent to the highest attainable community indifference curve (CIC_0). The autarky relative price is given by the slope of the PPF at the tangency point. Note that autarky is not a very desirable equilibrium for this country. At existing prices, it would be better off by specializing in the production of one good (e.g., good T), maximizing the gains from increasing returns to scale, and trading its surplus production in world markets for the other good. This is illustrated in the diagram by an international trade equilibrium of point N. Figure 5.2 is drawn under the assumption that the international terms of trade are identical with the autarky relative price. This is not required and, indeed, is not likely to happen in the real world. However, the diagram clearly makes the point that, unlike the previous models we have studied, here the benefits from trade occur not because of the opportunity to trade in world markets at prices that are more advantageous than autarky prices but because international trade allows a country to specialize in industries where average costs fall (and therefore productivity rises) as additional resources are utilized. Thus, we see an entirely new reason for international trade. Trade allows countries the oppor-

---

*This need not always be true. However, the conditions wherein concave PPFs occur even with increasing returns to scale are beyond the scope of this book.

FIGURE 5.2   *Increasing returns to scale and gains from trade.*

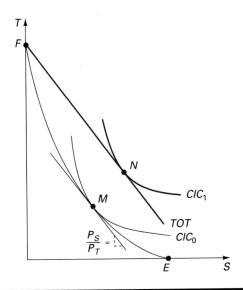

tunity to expand production in order to achieve gains from increasing returns to scale technology.

Note that by assumption the country we have been describing could have specialized in the production of S instead and also experienced gains from trade. As drawn, if it had done so, at constant prices it would have found itself on a CIC between CIC_0 and CIC_1 (not shown in the diagram). Thus, the direction of specialization will determine, in part, the overall gains from trade. What determines in which direction specialization will occur? There is no simple answer to that question. One possibility is historical accident. For instance, an order for merchandise from an overseas customer may occur and cause production in one industry to expand. Once an industry begins to grow, costs begin to fall, and this tends to induce further expansion.*

Increasing returns may also be internal to individual firms in an industry. Under this situation, it usually assumed that the capital investment required for production

---

*The fact that the location of economic activity may be due to historical accident is one of the themes of a strand of research related to trade and geography. This literature emphasizes the importance of increasing returns and decreasing costs due to geographic concentrations of production. U.S. examples of geographic concentration of production include California's Silicon Valley for semiconductors and related products, Detroit for automobiles, and Dalton, Georgia, for carpets. In his book *Geography and Trade* (Cambridge, Mass.: MIT Press, 1991), Paul Krugman makes the case that industrial specialization is rampant, especially in the United States where barriers to trade across states are low. He argues that in places such as the European Union, where internal barriers are falling, specialization and trade will rise.

is "lumpy" in the sense that it cannot be easily altered in size to accommodate different levels of production. For instance, it is often the case that the cost of purchasing and installing larger machines is proportionately less than the cost of smaller machines. Consequently, small firms with low levels of production would have to make capital investments that exceed the level they could profitably afford to make given their projected revenues. On the other hand, firms that produce relatively large amounts of output are able to justify larger capital investments that, in turn, lead to cost savings on a per unit basis. Moreover, because costs fall with scale of production, firms that expand first can undersell competing firms that have not expanded, potentially driving them from the market.

Because the practices of one firm can have effects on the health of another, it is no longer legitimate to assume that perfect competition prevails in this industry. Instead, some form of imperfect competition, such as monopolistic competition, oligopoly, or monopoly, must prevail. The precise market structure that will emerge depends in part on the size of the market, the extent to which firms can expand before the economies of scale run out, and whether the product being produced can be differentiated (by brand name) through slight variations in design and performance.

What does the presence of increasing returns at the level of the firm imply for the pattern or the effects of international trade? Much research aimed at answering that question is currently under way. Several results seem especially important. First, increasing returns to scale and imperfect competition can easily explain intraindustry trade. Consider the following example:

Suppose there are two countries, originally in autarky. In each country there are two goods, food and automobiles. Food is produced under constant cost conditions by perfectly competitive firms. The production of automobiles is subject to increasing returns to scale, and, initially, in each country there are many automobile firms, each producing a slightly different product (red cars, blue cars, green cars, etc.). In each country consumers have diverse tastes. Some prefer red cars, others blue, and so on.

Now, we allow the two countries to engage in trade. What will happen? Several things. First, depending on HO-type arguments, one country will tend to export food in exchange for automobiles. This type of trade is *inter*industry trade. And, if food is labor intensive and automobiles are capital intensive, we would expect that the relatively labor-abundant country would export food.

Nonetheless, we would also expect the labor-abundant country to export some automobiles in exchange for other automobiles. In other words, we would also expect *intra*industry trade. Because barriers to trade have been removed, the markets for cars of different colors are now much larger. Firms in both countries will move to expand their production. If the foreign firm that produces red cars is able to expand first, it can drive its domestic competitor, the local red car producer, out of business. This is because of the assumption of increasing returns to scale. Whichever firms expand first experience a reduction in their costs of production and can thereby lower their prices. Thus, producers of one type of car—say, red cars—will expand in one country at the expense of identical firms in the other. And, perhaps, blue car production will tend to expand in the other country. The pattern and location of such specialization are, in general, impossible to predict. In the end, we would expect to see one country exporting several varieties of automobiles in exchange for food and other varieties of cars.

In the example just described, some interindustry trade took place due to differences in factor endowments. We know from our analysis of the HO model that the more similar any two countries are in terms of factor endowments, the less incentive they have to trade. Thus, the following conclusion applies in the case where at least some goods are produced according to increasing returns: The more similar two countries are in terms of their factor endowments, the greater the likelihood that trade between them will be intraindustry trade. This result helps to explain the high degree of intraindustry trade found to exist between the Western industrialized countries reported in Table 5.3.

A second important result from recent theory on increasing returns and imperfect competition has to do with the welfare effects of free international trade. Up to this time, we have argued that international trade improves the standards of living of both countries. When some goods are produced according to increasing returns to scale, this need no longer be the case. In particular, if free trade leads to an overall contraction in the production of goods subject to increasing returns to scale, then trade can be harmful. This situation seems quite unlikely. Rather, it is more probable that the opposite occurs and that both countries gain from international trade.*

CONCLUSIONS

In this chapter we have discussed the results of several attempts to test theories of the determination of comparative advantage. Tests of the classical proposition that the direction of trade flows can be explained by differences in labor productivity tend to support this idea, but not uniformly so. Tests of the HO proposition perform less well and often produce seemingly paradoxical results. What can we conclude from this discussion?

First, the world is a very complicated place. This is something that we knew all along, of course. The primary reason for model building is to simplify the world to allow us to recognize those forces that are most important in understanding particular phenomena. For instance, the HO model assumes away differences in technology and tastes, tariffs, and economies of scale, and it attempts to explain trade patterns based upon international differences in factor endowments. Tests of this theory, to date, have yielded evidence that, for the most part, tends to contradict predictions of the theory. But these tests do not tell us enough about the world to be able to reject the HO model. That is, the results of the tests may be due to problems in testing procedure, problems with data availability and measurement, and the

---

*The literature on increasing returns to scale and international trade has expanded rapidly over the past decade. A collection of some of the leading papers on the topic is Gene M. Grossman, ed., *Imperfect Competition and International Trade* (Cambridge, Mass.: MIT Press, 1992). An advanced textbook treatment of the topic is Elhanan Helpman and Paul R. Krugman, *Market Structure and Foreign Trade* (Cambridge, Mass.: MIT Press, 1985).

like. Or they may be due to the existence in the real world of systematic violations of the assumptions of the HO model, violations that are so strong that they turn the pattern of trade away from that predicted by the HO model. To date, no one has been able to establish which of these two alternatives is correct.

A second message of this chapter is that it is very hard for economists to develop direct tests of models of comparative advantage. Consider again the tests of the HO model we have discussed. One needs information on national endowments of factors of production. In some cases, these are relatively easy and straightforward measures to obtain (amounts of farmland, timberland, etc.). In other cases, the measures are less comparable. For instance, an unskilled worker in the United States is probably more skilled than an unskilled worker in many developing countries, since he or she probably has had more basic education. In some cases, measures of factors are not comparable at all. This is the case with physical capital, where machines differ from industry to industry but are aggregated together and measured on a monetary-value basis.

The problems in testing HO theory do not end with the difficulties in measuring factor endowments. Knowledge of factor intensities in production is also required. The procedure of Leontief and later of Bowen, Leamer, and Sveikauskas was to assume that U.S. technology (as found in the U.S. input-output table) is representative of the technology used commonly throughout the world. Yet, simple observation should tell us that this cannot possibly be true. In countries where labor is relatively cheap, activities that are capital intensive in the United States (e.g., agriculture) are labor intensive.

Finally, as if these problems were not enough, the way that governments collect and compile data on trade flows can also lead to unwarranted rejections of the theory. That is, if governments aggregate commodity trade statistics according to the end use of products rather than the factor intensities of production, clear-cut tests of the theory may be impossible. Recall, for instance, our example of the problem of measuring trade in desks when these desks could be made of wood or metal.

A third important lesson from the discussion in this chapter is that international economics is an evolutionary science. While some economists have reacted to the results of empirical tests of traditional models by seeking to reconcile the evidence with these models, others have set out to develop and explore new theories of trade. Even though none of these theories is at a stage that would allow it to replace the HO model as the leading paradigm of comparative advantage, much has been learned from these efforts.

SUMMARY

1. Economists test economic theories by comparing the events predicted by their theories with real-world outcomes.

2. Attempts to test both the classical and the HO models of international trade have been at best inconclusive.

3. A test of the classical model conducted by MacDougall produced results that are largely consistent with the classical model. On the other hand, various predictions of the classical model, including complete specialization and no intraindustry trade, are not borne out by the data.

4. Leontief conducted the most famous empirical experiment in economic history when he tested the HO model. He showed the seemingly paradoxical result that U.S. exports were labor intensive, while U.S. imports were capital intensive.

5. More recent tests of the HO model have also produced results inconsistent with the model.

6. The paradoxical results of Leontief have led some economists to abandon the HO model and develop alternative theories of international trade. These models share the common feature that they all attempt to be less general than the HO model. Instead, they try to explain only a subset of international trade, usually trade in manufactured products.

7. One phenomenon that some of the new theories attempt to explain is intraindustry trade. Intraindustry trade, the simultaneous import and export of a product, appears to be quite common, especially in the trade patterns of European industrialized economies.

EXERCISES

1. Why were Leontief's findings considered paradoxical? Explain.

2. Suppose that the following information represents the complete trade data for each country. Use these data to calculate values of IIT for each country.

	Exports	Imports
Country A		
Good X	$10,000	$ 5,000
Good Y	$ 8,000	$ 1,000
Good Z	0	$12,000
Country B		
Good R	$ 5,000	0
Good S	$ 400	$ 6,000
Good T	$ 1,600	$ 1,000
Country C		
Good M	$ 2,000	$ 1,800
Good N	$ 1,000	$ 1,500
Good O	$ 1,500	$ 1,200

3. Discuss various reasons why we might expect countries to engage in intraindustry trade.

4. Explain carefully how Leontief went about testing the HO model. Why is this an incomplete test of the model?

5. Discuss the merits of the alternative reconciliations of Leontief's finding. Why do you think so much effort was expended in trying to reconcile Leontief's findings with the HO model?

6. How else might the HO model be tested? (*Hint:* Factor price equalization.) What would you expect to find if you were to test this proposition with real-world data? Would this necessarily refute the model?

7. Explain how each of the alternative models of comparative advantage explains the Leontief paradox.

8. Would the Linder hypothesis provide a convincing explanation for the pattern of international trade in wheat? In coal? Explain why or why not.

REFERENCES

Deardorff, Alan. "Testing Trade Theories and Predicting Trade Flows." In *Handbook of International Economics,* vol. 1, edited by R. Jones and P. Kenen. Amsterdam: North-Holland Publishers, 1984.

Helpman, Elhanan, and Paul Krugman. *Increasing Returns, Imperfect Competition, and International Trade.* Cambridge, Mass.: MIT Press, 1985.

Leamer, Edward. *Sources of Comparative Advantage: Theory and Evidence.* Cambridge, Mass.: MIT Press, 1984.

INTERNET APPLICATIONS

Please visit our Web site at www.awl.com/husted_melvin for more exercises and readings.

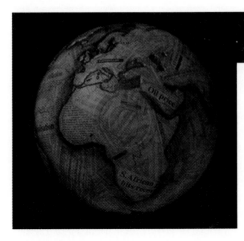

CHAPTER 6

Tariffs

TOPICS TO BE COVERED

Commercial Policy
Tariffs
Welfare Analysis
Deadweight Losses
Optimal Tariff
Effective Rate of Protection

KEY WORDS

Commercial policy
Tariff
Quota
Subsidy
Nontariff barriers
Static gains from trade
Dynamic gains from trade
Political gains from trade
Revenue effect
Protective effect
Most favored nation (MFN) status
Ad valorem tariff

Specific tariff
Compound tariff
Generalized system of preferences
  (GSP)
Consumer surplus
Producer surplus
Deadweight cost of the tariff
Optimal tariff
Trade war
Average tariff
Effective rate of protection (ERP)
Tariff escalation

S o far in this textbook, we have focused our discussion on the causes and consequences of international trade. We have seen that international trade leads to the redistribution of production in an economy. It also affects the returns paid to factors of production. For both of these reasons, some individuals in every society favor government policies aimed at affecting the volume and composition of international trade. In this chapter and the next three, we turn our attention to the role of government in the area of international trade.

Actions taken by a government to influence the volume and composition of trade flows (into or out of a country) are known as **commercial policy**. A government has a variety of options in conducting commercial policy. These options include **tariffs**, which are taxes on imports and/or exports; **quotas**, which are government-imposed limitations on the value or volume of imports or exports; **subsidies**, which are payments by a government to an industry to encourage exports or discourage imports; and **nontariff barriers**, which include a variety of government policies or regulations, such as health and safety standards, or government procurement policies that affect trade flows.

The next four chapters of this text provide an in-depth discussion of various forms of commercial policy. This chapter is largely devoted to a theoretical analysis of tariffs. In Chapter 7 we turn our attention to other forms of trade policy. Then, in Chapter 8, we discuss the commercial policy practices of the United States and other countries as well as various national and international initiatives to set rules on the conduct of commercial policy. Finally, in Chapter 9, we describe the formation of various regional trading blocs, such as the European Union and the North American Free Trade Agreement, and analyze some of the effects these agreements have on member as well as nonmember countries.

Before we begin our analysis of commercial policy, however, it is useful to return one last time to our general equilibrium model of trade to review the benefits from free-trade policies. By focusing on these benefits, we establish a basis for comparison with the benefits accruing to a country that uses commercial policies to distort trade flows.

Commercial policy
Actions taken by a government to influence the quantity and composition of that country's international trade.

Tariff
A tax imposed by a government on either exports or imports.

Quota
A government-mandated limitation on either the quantity or value of trade in a product.

Subsidy
A government payment to an industry based upon the amount it engages in international trade.

Nontariff barriers
A wide range of government policies other than tariffs designed to affect the volume or composition of a country's international trade.

Static gains from trade
Increases in economic well-being, holding resources and technology constant, that accrue to a country engaging in international trade.

THE GAINS FROM FREE TRADE

When a country opens its markets to free international trade, it benefits in several ways. First, it enjoys **static gains from trade.** These gains are illustrated in Figure 6.1. There we depict a country in free-trade equilibrium. Point A in the diagram is the autarky equilibrium point. If we let ρ_F be the free-trade international price, then we know that trade will lead to a change in both consumption and production activities within the country. In particular, consumption moves to point C, while production moves to point X. Our argument is that this is beneficial because the bundle of goods denoted by point C could never have been purchased and enjoyed in the absence of trade.

This gain to the economy can be divided into two parts: consumption gains and production gains. Beginning again in autarky at point A, suppose we open the econ-

FIGURE 6.1   *The gains from free trade.*

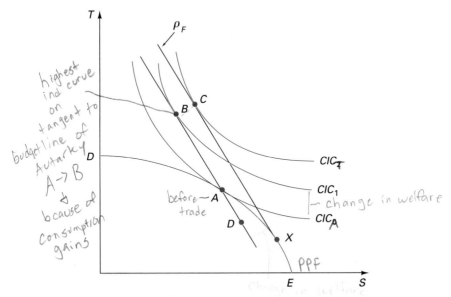

The handwritten annotations read:

highest ind curve on tangent to budget line of Autarky

A → B

because of Consumption gains

before — trade

change in welfare

B → C = higher income

omy up to free trade. Suppose the economy is allowed to trade at the free trade price ρ_F, but production is not allowed to move. Will the country be better off? The answer is yes. In the figure, we have shown this situation by drawing a price line with slope ρ_F through point A. Even though production remains fixed, the opportunity to trade at world prices leads the consumption point to move off the PPF to point B.* Using the *CIC*s as indicators of community welfare, the movement to a higher *CIC* illustrates static consumption gains—the one-time gains from the shift from autarky to trading at world prices.

Once resources are allowed to move away from point A, the economy accrues further economic gains. These gains are reflected in the movement of the consumption point from B to C and, in terms of community welfare, from CIC_1 to CIC_2. These gains come about because productive resources are channeled into the economy's comparative-advantage industries; and because of this redistribution of resources, overall output (GNP) rises. Hence, this second increase in welfare is known as *the static production gains from trade.*

---

*How do we know that consumption will move up the price line from point A to point B rather than down the price line to some point, such as D, once the price changes? The answer is simple: If point D were preferable to point A, then, because the point lies inside the PPF, the economy could choose to be at that point in the absence of trade. The fact that it does not in autarky argues that it will not move there given the opportunity instead to trade.

Dynamic gains from trade

Increases in economic well-being that accrue to an economy because trade expands the resources of a country or induces increases in the productivity of existing resources.

Free trade also leads to **dynamic gains**. These refer to the relationship between trade and economic growth. An economy grows over time either because it experiences increases in its stock of productive factors or because a technological innovation helps a country's existing stock of factors become more efficient. In terms of our model, economic growth refers to an outward shift in a nation's PPF. International trade is related to economic growth in several ways.*

First, trade need not be restricted to trade in final-consumption goods. In fact, as we saw from the data in Table 1.3, the vast bulk of international trade consists of trade in raw materials and intermediate products. There is also considerable trade in capital goods. In effect, when a country imports capital goods in exchange for consumer goods, its productive capacity increases; and once capital is put in place, the country is able to produce more of all goods. To the extent that capital-goods imports lead to a higher overall capital stock than would have occurred in autarky, trade raises the overall rate of growth of the economy.[†]

Second, international trade may enhance the international diffusion of technological advance. Ideas developed in one country for increasing the efficiency of productive activity can be (and often are) licensed to firms in other countries. Through this process, technology is transferred from country to country. In the absence of international trade, such transfers would not take place, and economic growth would be slower.

Third, international trade is procompetitive. That is, once a country opens to trade, local monopolies lose their power over local markets. This creates dynamic gains for two reasons. Greater competition encourages more efficient production, as the discrepancy between price and marginal cost is closed. In addition, as competition destroys industry rents, fewer resources are devoted to wasteful rent-seeking behavior.

Fourth, if economies of scale in production exist, then dynamic gains from international trade accrue because trade expands the size of the market. As the market expands, industries are able to move further down their average-cost curves, bringing down prices in the process. Moreover, expanding the size of the market may encourage industries to step up investments in research and development, since they can spread the costs of these investments over larger levels of output. These investments could, it turn, raise the overall level of technology of the country.

Finally, international trade can enlarge the pool of savings that is available to fund investment purchases. This can occur in several ways. We have seen that trade raises the real income of a country above the level that would exist in autarky. There is considerable evidence to support the hypothesis that higher levels of national income lead to higher levels of savings. Hence, trade increases the amount of

---

*For a survey of the literature on dynamic gains, see U.S. International Trade Commission, *The Dynamic Effects of Trade Liberalization: A Survey* (Washington, D.C.: Government Printing Office, February 1993).

[†]Richard Baldwin provides a technique for measuring the size of this effect. He finds that the dynamic gains from the Europe 1992 initiative were almost as large as the static gains. See Richard Baldwin, "Measurable Dynamic Gains from Trade," *Journal of Political Economy* (1992).

national savings relative to that which would be found in autarky. And the higher the level of savings, the greater the availability of funds for investment spending.

Alternatively, international trade allows a country to borrow savings from other countries. Consider a situation where a country imports more goods than it exports. Under these circumstances, the country is taking in funds from the rest of the world because its export receipts fall short of its expenditures on imports. These funds can be used to finance capital-goods imports.

In sum, a country that engages in international trade enjoys benefits both in terms of immediate improvements in standard of living and in terms of economic growth. The standard of living that is achieved surpasses that which would be available to a competitive economy that operates in autarky. In addition to economic gains from trade, a nation that trades may enjoy **political gains**. These come about because of the likelihood that as countries become more economically interdependent, they are less likely to revert to hostile actions among themselves.

Political gains from trade
Increases in economic well-being that accrue to a country because expanded trade and economic interdependency may increase the likelihood of reduced international hostility.

Despite these obvious benefits, countries apply a variety of measures aimed at altering the amount of trade from the free-trade level. Perhaps the most common method used for distorting trade is the tariff. This is a government-imposed tax on trade flows. Why do countries ignore the obvious benefits of free-trade policies? How do tariffs affect the level of trade and economic welfare of a country? The remainder of this chapter considers answers to these questions.

TARIFFS: AN INTRODUCTION

A tariff is a tax that is imposed by a government on imports or exports. Such taxes are extremely common throughout the world. They also have a long history. Virtually every country of the world imposes tariffs on at least some products. The United States has tariffs on a wide variety of imported items. It does not, however, impose tariffs on exports. This practice was forbidden in the original articles of the Constitution.* Many countries do put a tax on their exports, such as Brazil on its coffee exports.

As we are about to demonstrate, tariffs have several effects on the economy where they are imposed. For instance, tariffs have a **revenue effect**. That is, they are a mechanism for raising government revenue. Tariffs also have a **protective effect**. Consider an import tariff. Since the tariff is applied only on imported products, foreign producers incur a cost not borne by domestic competitors. And to the extent that foreign producers pass on these higher costs to local consumers in the form of higher prices, domestic producers of similar products may find it easier to compete against their foreign rivals. Because tariffs typically provide this protective effect, advocates of tariffs, and for that matter other forms of trade barriers, are often described as *protectionists*.

Revenue effect
The amount of revenue accruing to a government from a tariff.

Protective effect
The amount by which domestic producers are able to expand their output because a tariff is in place.

Generally, both the revenue and the protective effects of a tariff will operate at the same time. However, there are special cases when only one of these effects is

---

*See Chapter 8 for a more complete discussion of the history of U.S. tariff policy.

present. For instance, a tariff that is imposed on an import when no domestic producer exists would be a pure revenue tariff. A prohibitive tariff is one that is so high that no goods are imported and thus is an example of a purely protective tariff—in such a circumstance no government revenue is collected.

Governments in developed economies rarely if ever rely on tariffs as a major source of government revenue.* Consequently, it is difficult to point to an example of a pure revenue tariff collected by the United States or other major industrialized economies. On the other hand, the governments in developing economies depend heavily on trade taxes as a source of revenue. There, examples of pure revenue tariffs abound. Tariffs in developed economies primarily exist because of their protective effect.

To get a better feel for what tariffs are like, consider Table 6.1. There we reproduce one page from the 2000 U.S. tariff schedule. There are many things to note about the information in this table. First, the table is highly specific. The items from this page refer to prepared or preserved fruits, including cherries, peaches, and strawberries. As a whole, the tariff schedule lists tariffs for virtually every imaginable manufactured good, including fireworks, bicycle speedometers, blank cassette tapes, computer chips, compact disks, t-shirts, and so on. It totals several hundred pages in length.[†]

Next, note that for every product there are three possible tariffs. The first column, known as *Column 1 General Rates of Duty,* is the duty category most commonly utilized by customs officials. Tariffs from this category are applied to goods from countries to whom the United States has granted **most favored nation status (MFN)**. If the United States (or any other country) grants another country MFN status, it agrees to charge tariffs against that country's goods that are no higher than those imposed against the goods of any other country.[‡]

Now, consider the numbers in this column of tariffs. These rates illustrate the ways in which tariffs are calculated. For instance, tariffs may be **ad valorem**, which means that the tax is collected as a percentage of the value of the product. Most of the U.S. tariff code is expressed in ad valorem terms. For example, the MFN U.S. tariff rate on imported peach preserves is 17 percent, but the MFN rate on prepared palm hearts is only 0.9 percent. This illustrates the point we made earlier. Imported peach products compete with many domestic varieties. The tariff on these products is high. Few American food processors produce canned palm hearts, and the tariff on these products is almost zero.

Tariffs may be **specific**. That is, the tariff may be a fixed amount of money per unit of goods traded—regardless of the value of an individual unit. Finally, tariffs may be **compound**. Such tariffs have both specific and ad valorem components. In

---

Most favored nation (MFN) status
A country confers MFN status upon another country by agreeing not to charge tariffs on that country's goods that are any higher than those it imposes on the goods of any other country.

Ad valorem tariff
A trade tax equal to a given percentage of selling price.

Specific tariff
A trade tax equal to a fixed amount of money per unit sold.

Compound tariff
A trade tax that has both a specific and an ad valorem component.

---

*For instance, U.S. tariff revenue accounts for less than 2 percent of federal government revenue. Similar ratios apply for other industrial countries. In developing countries, the proportions tend to be much higher. See Table 7.4.
[†]The U.S. tariff schedule is available online at http://www.usitc.gov/taffairs.htm.
[‡]The U.S. government now uses the term *permanent normal trade relations* (PNTA) to denote most favored nation status.

TABLE 6.1   *Harmonized Tariff Schedule of the United States (2000)*

Heading/ Subheading	Stat. Suffix	Article Description	Unit of Quantity	Rates of Duty 1 General	Rates of Duty 1 Special	2
2008 (con.)		Fruit, nuts and other edible parts of plants, otherwise prepared or preserved, whether or not containing added sugar or other sweetening matter or spirit, not elsewhere specified or included (con.):				
2008.40.00		Pears		15.3%	Free (A, CA, E, IL, J, MX)	35%
	20	In other containers each holding less than 1.4 kg	kg			
	40	Other	kg			
2008.50		Apricots:				
2008.50.20	00	Pulp	kg	10%	Free (A, CA, E, IL, J, MX)	35%
2008.50.40	00	Other	kg	29.8%	Free (A, CA, E, IL, J, MX)	35%
2008.60.00		Cherries		6.9¢/kg+ 4.5%	Free (A, CA, E, IL, J, MX)	21¢/kg+ 40%
	20	Maraschino	kg			
		Other:				
	40	Sweet varieties	kg			
	60	Tart varieties	kg			
2008.70.00		Peaches		17%	Free (A, CA, E, IL, J) 4.5% (MX)	35%
	20	In containers each holding less than 1.4 kg	kg			
	40	Other	kg			
2008.80.00	00	Strawberries	kg	11.9%	Free (A, CA, E, IL, J, MX)	35%
		Other, including mixtures other than those of subheading 2008.19:				
2008.91.00	00	Palm hearts	kg	0.9%	Free (A, CA, E, IL, J, MX)	35%
2008.92		Mixtures:				
2008.92.10		In airtight containers and not containing apricots, citrus fruits, peaches or pears		5.6%	Free (A, CA, E, IL, J) 2.1% (MX)	35%
	20	Prepared cereal products	kg			
	40	Other	kg			
2008.92.90		Other		14.9%	Free (A, CA, E, IL, J, MX)	35%

the table, processed cherry products are protected by a compound tariff of 6.9¢ per kilogram (specific) plus 4.5 percent of the product price (ad valorem).

Countries that have not been granted MFN status are charged tariffs based on *Column 2 Rates of Duty*. As the numbers in the table indicate, these rates are substantially higher (sometimes 200 or 300 percent higher) than MFN rates.* For instance, the non-MFN tariff on processed strawberry products is 35 percent, almost three times the MFN rate.

Generalized system of preferences (GSP)
A system where industrialized countries charge preferential lower tariff rates on goods from certain developing countries.

The third set of rates, known as *Column 1 Special Rates of Duty,* are tariffs, even lower than MFN rates, that are applied to certain products from many developing countries or to products from countries with whom the United States has negotiated special trade agreements. An example of the first is the **Generalized System of Preferences (GSP)**, which was instituted by the United States in the early 1970s. Other industrialized countries, including Canada, the European Union (EU), and Japan, have their own GSP programs, many instituted about the same time or before the date of the U.S. plan.† The idea behind the GSP is that by charging lower tariffs on goods from developing countries, importers in the preference-granting countries such as the United States will have an incentive to expand their purchases from the preference-receiving countries. In turn, expanded exports should improve the standards of living for these countries (and raise the demand for imports from industrialized countries such as the United States!). In the table, the letter A in parentheses indicates the GSP rate. Another of the U.S. trade assistance programs is the Caribbean Basin Initiative (CBI), which was begun in the 1980s. This program applies low tariffs on certain goods coming from most nations of the Caribbean Basin. In the table, CBI rates are identified with the letter E in parentheses. For instance, processed peach products from CBI-eligible countries are allowed into the United States duty free.

In addition to special tariffs applied to goods from developing countries, the United States grants tariff concessions to countries with whom it has negotiated preferential trade agreements. In early 2000, the United States had two such agreements in place: the United States–Israel Free Trade Agreement and the North American Free Trade Agreement (NAFTA). These agreements provide for free trade among the signing countries, but with some tariffs going to zero only after a considerable phasing-in period. Examples of rates applied to these countries are identified in Table 6.1 with the letters IL for Israel, CA for Canada, and MX for Mexico.

Before moving on, a word of caution is in order. The tariff rates listed in Table 6.1 are relatively high by U.S. standards. For many manufactured goods, for instance most semiconductors and computers, U.S. MFN tariffs are zero. As we discuss further below, the average U.S. tariff is well under 5 percent.

---

*In fact, the Column 2 rates correspond to the tariff rates as enacted in the Smoot-Hawley tariff of 1930. In 2000, countries without U.S.-granted MFN status were Afghanistan, Cuba, Laos, North Korea, and Vietnam. For more on the Smoot-Hawley tariff see Item 6.2 below and the discussion in Chapter 8.
†Because these tariff concessions are aimed at promoting economic development, the various countries involved have agreed that the concessions do not violate MFN treatment.

TARIFFS: AN ECONOMIC ANALYSIS

To analyze the economic impact of commercial policies including tariffs, it is necessary to develop some new tools of analysis. In particular, we are going to leave our general equilibrium framework to concentrate on the market for a specific product. To avoid confusion with our earlier notation, let's consider the market for grapes (G) in country A. In Figure 6.2 we illustrate the demand curve for grapes (labeled D_G). This curve is the sum of individual demand curves for all the residents of country A. It tells us the maximum amount that people in A would be willing to pay for a given quantity of grapes (good G). For instance, if a monopolist controlled the supply of grapes in A and could sell his or her product 1 unit at a time to the highest bidder, he or she could receive P_1 for the first unit sold, P_2 for the second, and so on. It is seldom the case, however, that products are sold in such a fashion. Rather, one price exists in the market so that all individuals pay the same, even if some were willing to pay more.

Consider Figure 6.2 again. Suppose that P is the market price. The quantity purchased in the market would be Q units. Total expenditure (price times quantity) would be represented by the rectangle $0PAQ$. If, on the other hand, there had been a monopolist selling each unit for what the market would bear, the amount spent on grapes would have been the entire area under the demand curve up to Q units. The difference between what individuals would be willing to pay and the amount that they actually pay is known as **consumer surplus**. In the diagram it is the shaded triangle whose base begins at the market price.

Consumer surplus has an important and useful interpretation. It represents the amount of money people would have been willing spend but did not have to spend

Consumer surplus
The difference between the amount consumers are willing to pay to purchase a given quantity of goods and the amount they have to pay to purchase those goods.

FIGURE 6.2   *Consumer surplus.*

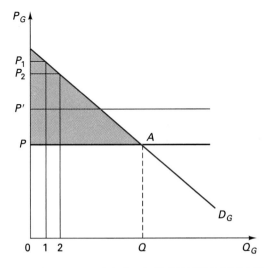

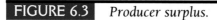

FIGURE 6.3   *Producer surplus.*

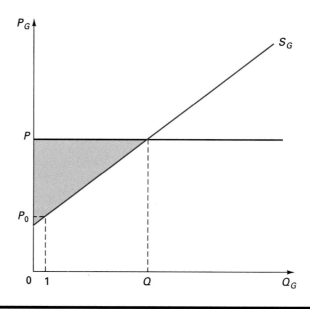

to purchase a particular product. Thus, it provides us with a convenient measure of the gains to consumers from being able to transact in markets. Note that consumer surplus varies inversely with price. That is, if the market price of grapes were to rise to P', consumer surplus would fall. Lower market prices increase the amount of consumer surplus.

Let us turn our attention now to the other side of the market—producers. Consider Figure 6.3. There, we illustrate the market supply curve for domestic producers (labeled S_G). This curve tells us the minimum amount of money producers would accept to place a given quantity of grapes on the market. For instance, to sell 1 unit the market price must be at least P_0. Again, suppose that the market price is P. If so, then for all units supplied to the market up to Q, the industry receives a price in excess of the minimum required to produce and market those units. The difference between what the industry receives and that minimum amount is known as **producer surplus**. Alternatively, it could be thought of as profits. In the diagram, producer surplus is illustrated by the shaded triangle.

Producer surplus
The difference between the price paid in the market for a good and the minimum price required by an industry to produce and market that good.

THE GAINS FROM FREE TRADE: ONE MORE TIME

Consumer surplus and producer surplus are tools that can be used to analyze economic policy. To illustrate that fact, let us return to a discussion of the static benefits of free trade. Let's continue to consider the market for grapes. Figure 6.4 illus-

FIGURE 6.4   *The gains from free trade (imports side).*

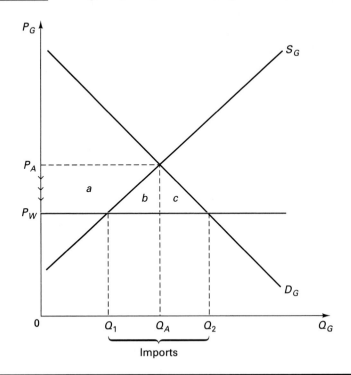

trates this market for an individual country, say country A. In autarky equilibrium, the price of grapes would be P_A, and the quantity produced would be Q_A.

Now, suppose we introduce international trade into this model. Suppose further that country A is economically small. This means that once international trade begins, consumers in A (as a group) can buy all of the grapes they want in world markets without affecting the world price. In other words, we are treating A (for the time being) as a price taker in the world market, just as an individual is in the grocery store. That is, no matter how much A's consumers choose to purchase, their decision has no bearing on the world price. Finally, we assume that the world price of grapes, P_W, is lower than P_A.

Once country A is exposed to trade, the price of grapes in A will fall to P_W. This will cause consumption to expand to Q_2 and domestic production to fall to Q_1. The difference between domestic consumption and domestic production will comprise imports.

What are the economic impacts of these changes in the grape market in country A? Clearly, consumers are better off. They are able to purchase this product at a lower price than in autarky, and they respond by purchasing more. Domestic producers are worse off. The lower price leads some suppliers to reduce the quantity supplied and others to drop out of the market.

TABLE 6.2	Summary of the Welfare Effects in the Import Market of a Move to Free Trade			
Change in consumer surplus		$a	+$b	+$c
Change in producer surplus		−$a		
NET WELFARE CHANGE			$b	+$c

Given that some in the economy are better off than before and some are worse off, how do we evaluate this move to free trade? The answer is through the use of producer and consumer surplus. Changes in producer surplus tell us *in dollar terms* how the fortunes of suppliers have changed. Changes in consumer surplus tell us *in dollar terms* how much consumers have benefited or lost. To analyze this or any other policy that affects the economy, the two surpluses are compared, on an equal dollar basis. That is, it is assumed that a dollar of consumer surplus has equal welfare weight to a dollar of producer surplus.

Let us attempt such an exercise for the situation presented in Figure 6.4. Beginning from the autarky equilibrium, the move to free trade expands consumer surplus by the sum of the areas denoted by the letters *a*, *b*, and *c*. Producer surplus falls

FIGURE 6.5   *The gains from free trade (exports side).*

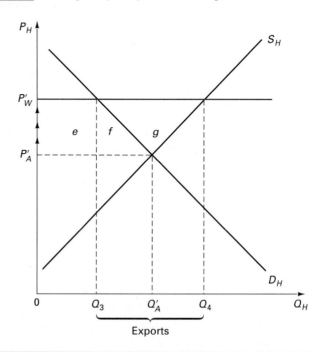

TABLE 6.3	*Summary of the Welfare Effects in the Export Market of a Move to Free Trade*		
Change in consumer surplus	$-\$e$	$-\$f$	
Change in producer surplus	$\$e$	$+\$f$	$+\$g$
NET WELFARE CHANGE			$\$g$

in the economy by the area represented by letter *a*. The net effect of free trade in this instance is for welfare to rise by $\$(b + c)$. These results are summarized in Table 6.2.

The preceding example shows the effect of free trade on the market for an importable. Let us now describe how this analysis would apply in the market for an exportable. Consider Figure 6.5. Suppose this represents the market for honey (*H*). In autarky the price of *H* is determined solely by internal supply and demand, and consequently would equal P'_A. Suppose that the world price of *H* is equal to P'_W. Then, after international trade is introduced, domestic suppliers would move to expand output in response to the now higher price. At the same time, the domestic quantity demanded would fall. The new quantity supplied would be Q_4, while the new quantity demanded would be Q_3 units. The difference represents exports of *H* to the rest of the world.

Let's analyze the welfare implications of this scenario. Because the price has increased, consumer surplus falls. The total reduction of consumer surplus would be $\$(e + f)$. The higher price, however, raises producer surplus. The increase is equal to $\$(e + f + g)$. The net impact, then, in this market is for national welfare to rise by $\$g$. These results are summarized in Table 6.3.

The fact that international trade produces national welfare gains in both the import and the export market is important. It suggests, in no uncertain terms, that *free trade is better for country A than autarky*. The sum of the gains in the two markets, areas $\$(b + c)$ in Figure 6.4 plus $\$g$ in Figure 6.5, are analytically equivalent to the movement to a higher *CIC* brought about by free international trade, illustrated in Figure 6.1. Now, note that we have shown that it is better for *A* to import *G* and export *H* than it is for *A* to remain in autarky. Clearly, since country *B* is on the opposite side of these transactions, *B* must also be better off from trading than remaining in autarky.

THE WELFARE COST OF TARIFFS

Now, let's use the tools we have just developed to analyze the impact of a tariff. We'll consider the imposition of a specific tariff of *t* dollars on imports. Consider Figure 6.6. We illustrate again the domestic market for grapes. Suppose the government of *A* imposes a tariff on imports of grapes of *t* dollars. Because *A* is assumed to be a small country, nothing it can do will affect the world price of grapes. Consequently, the price *A*'s consumers must pay for grapes rises by the full amount of the tariff, from P_W to $P_W + t$. These two prices are illustrated in the diagram.

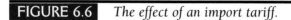

FIGURE 6.6   *The effect of an import tariff.*

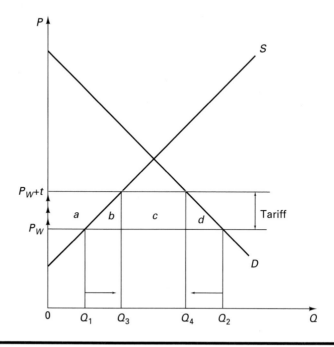

Let's consider the effect of the tariff on production and consumption. Under free trade, domestic production was Q_1 units, while consumption was Q_2 units. Imports represented the difference between these two amounts. After the tariff, production rises from Q_1 to Q_3 units (note arrow). Why? Consider again the effect of the tariff on price. Once the tariff is imposed, it is passed through to the economy in the form of higher prices for the foreign product. Since domestic producers are selling an identical product, they find it in their interests to raise their prices as well; and with higher prices, marginal domestic producers who had previously found it unprofitable now enter the market.

Total consumption of grapes falls. This is due, of course, to the higher price consumers must pay for the product. With higher prices in this market, some consumers choose to switch their consumption to other products. Hence, quantity demanded falls from Q_2 to Q_4 (note arrow).

As the previous discussion has just explained and as the arrows depict in the diagram, the tariff causes a reduction in imports for two reasons. First, domestic output expands. Second, domestic consumption falls. The size of the first effect depends upon the slope (or elasticity) of the domestic supply curve. The amount of the latter depends upon the slope (or elasticity) of domestic demand. Hence, because different goods have different demand and supply characteristics, a given percentage tariff will have different effects on imports of different types of goods.

Let us turn now to the welfare cost of the tariff. Consider again Figure 6.6. Because of the imposition of the tariff, consumers must pay a higher price for the grapes they consume. This implies a loss of consumer surplus. How much is lost? Consumers lose the area under the demand curve that lies between the two price lines. In other words, they lose $a + $b + $c + $d. Domestic producers gain with the tariff. Their profits rise by $a.

Who else gains or loses? Clearly, because the domestic government has found a new source of revenue, it gains. How much does it collect? The answer is $c. Why? Consider again the diagram. The government collects $t per unit of imports. The base of area c is equal to the level of imports when the tariff is in place. The side of area c is equal to the tariff. Consequently, area c is equal to tariff proceeds. If we assume that the government of country A redistributes the tariffs it collects to the economy, then the tariff revenues represent an internal transfer of income and are not lost to the economy. Thus, in our analysis of welfare we shall treat increases (or decreases) in government revenue as having equal welfare weight for the economy as increases (or decreases) in consumer or producer surplus. The net result of the tariff is that consumers lose $a + $b + $c + $d; domestic producers gain $a; and domestic government gains $c. Netting out these changes, we see that the economy *as a whole* has lost $(b + d). This result is summarized in Table 6.4. What does it mean for an economy to lose $(b + d)? How should this loss be interpreted?

The amount $(b + d) is known as the **deadweight cost of the tariff**. This, in effect, is the cost to society of imposing the tariff. And, perhaps surprisingly, it is an amount that goes to no one. It is economic waste. To see what we mean by this statement, consider Figure 6.7. There, we reproduce the information given in Figure 6.6 and add some additional notation. Area b (or, equivalently, $b) is known as the production deadweight cost of the tariff. This amount represents the value of resources required to increase domestic output from Q_1 to Q_3, in excess of what those units could be purchased for in the world market. How do we know this? Examine the graph carefully. We have already established that, because of the tariff, profits to domestic industry will rise by $a. In Figure 6.7 this amount is decomposed into two parts. Area a_1 represents the increased profits on units the industry would have sold even under free trade. That is, with free trade, domestic sales would be Q_1 units, each selling for P_W. With the tariff, each of those units now sells for $P_W + t$.

As we have already noted, the protective effect of the tariff allows the domestic industry to expand its production above free trade levels. This represents a second source of expanded profits to the domestic industry. Sales revenue rises by the amount equal to the increase in production ($Q_1 Q_3$ units) times the price for each

Deadweight cost of the tariff
Value of wasted resources devoted to expanded domestic consumption and expenditures devoted to less desired substitutes brought about by a tariff.

TABLE 6.4	*Welfare Cost of a Tariff Imposed by a Small Country*			
Change in consumer surplus	−$a	−$b	−$c	−$d
Change in producer surplus	$a			
Change in government revenue			$c	
NET WELFARE CHANGE		−$b		−$d

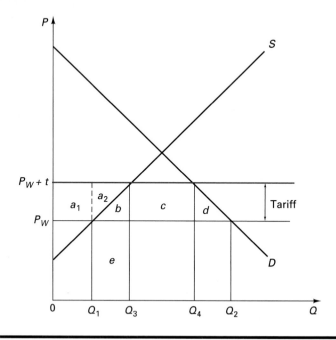

FIGURE 6.7   *Deadweight cost of the tariff.*

unit ($P_W + t$ dollars), or, as labeled in the figure, $\$a_2 + \$b + \$e$. As we have already illustrated, $\$a_2$ is the producer surplus on the expanded output. The cost of the resources required to produce that output is given by areas $b + e$. Without the tariff, those units could have been purchased in the world market for $\$e$. Hence, $\$b$ represents the cost of resources devoted to expanding production in the higher-cost domestic industry rather than having those units provided by a lower-cost foreign producer.

Area d is the consumer deadweight cost of the tariff. This amount represents the value of lost consumer satisfaction due to a shift in consumption to less desired substitutes brought on by the higher price. That is, before the tax, consumers purchased Q_2 units. After the tax, consumption falls to Q_4 units. Consumers lose $\$a + \$b + \$c$ because the amount they now buy costs them more. They lose an additional $\$d$ because their consumption of this product has declined and they shift their purchases to other products. How do we know that consumers are worse off because of this latter effect? The answer is that if Q_4 had been the preferred amount prior to the tariff, consumers could have afforded to buy that many units. In fact, they chose to buy more. Thus, the change in consumption behavior brought on by the tax is the second component of the deadweight cost of the tariff.

In presenting our analysis of the economic costs of tariffs, we have focused on a perfectly competitive market where imports can be purchased in unlimited amounts at constant prices. In such markets, it is easy to carry out the welfare calculations conforming to those illustrated in the diagram. Consider area *b*. From geometry, we know that the area of a triangle is given by the formula 1/2 × base × height. The height of the triangle is equal to the size of the tariff, and the base of the triangle is equal to the expansion in domestic production brought about because of the tariff. Similarly, the area of triangle *d* is given by 1/2 × the tariff (height) × the change in domestic consumption brought about by the tariff (base). Now, note that since the reduction in imports is given by the sum of the change in domestic production (Q_1 to Q_3) and the change in consumption (Q_2 to Q_4), the total deadweight cost of the tariff is simply 1/2 × tariff × reduction in imports.*

Calculation of the welfare effects of tariffs or their removal has become a commonplace activity of trade economists. The formula just described is one of several procedures used by economists both within and outside the government to calculate the economic costs of tariffs.[†] Item 6.1 presents estimates of the welfare impact of recent tariff protection on certain U.S. industries.[‡]

---

*Note that this formula is valid only in the case where demand and supply curves are linear.
[†]For some additional welfare estimates, see Robert Baldwin, Jack Mutti, and David Richardson, "Welfare Effects on the United States of a Significant Multilateral Tariff Reduction," *Journal of International Economics* (1980); Stephen Magee, "The Welfare Effects of Restrictions on U.S. Trade," Brookings Papers on Economic Activity (1972); and David Tarr and Morris Morkre, *Aggregate Costs to the United States of Tariffs and Quotas on Imports: General Tariff Cuts and Removal of Quotas on Automobiles, Steel, Sugar, and Textiles* (Washington, D.C.: U.S. Federal Trade Commission, 1984).
[‡]See the appendix to this chapter for a detailed discussion of a somewhat more complicated model, known as *the imperfect substitutes model*, that has become an increasingly popular model for policy analysis purposes.

ITEM 6.1   The Welfare Costs of Tariffs: Estimates from Certain U.S. Industries

Although current U.S. tariffs are quite low on average, tariffs remain high for some products. In 1994, Gary Hufbauer and Kimberly Ann Elliott from the Institute for International Economics (IIE) undertook an analysis of the welfare costs of tariff protection in those industries where U.S. tariffs are especially high.* Some of their findings are presented in the table below. The information in the table includes consumer cost, the loss in consumer surplus due to the tariff (i.e., in terms of our analysis, $a + $b + $c + $d); producer gain, increased profits due to the tariff (i.e., $a); and deadweight costs of the tariff (i.e., $b + $d). Also included in the table is a

measure of the consumer cost per job "saved" because of the presence of the tariff.

There are two types of *rubber footwear*: protective (e.g., boots) and casual (e.g., tennis shoes). Both segments of this industry have been protected by very high tariffs since 1930, although in recent years tariffs on some of these products have fallen substantially. At the time of the study, ad

---

*For a similar study that reaches many of the same conclusions but for additional industries, see U.S. International Trade Commission, *The Economic Effects of Significant U.S. Import Restraints* (Washington D.C.: U.S. ITC, May 1999).

(Continued)

ITEM 6.1	The Welfare Costs of Tariffs: Estimates from Certain U.S. Industries
	(Continued)

valorem rates on protective footwear ranged from 6.6 percent to 12.5 percent depending upon the category of product. Tariffs on casual rubber footwear ranged from 20 to 67 percent. The average for all types of rubber footwear was 20 percent. The IIE estimates that these duties impose an annual cost to U.S. consumers of $208 million. Because of these tariffs, there are about 1,701 more employed in this industry than would be the case with free trade. The consumer cost of preserving each job is calculated to be $122,300.

U.S. *luggage* manufacturers have had a long history of tariff protection. The Smoot-Hawley tariffs on these products ranged from 35 to 90 percent, depending upon whether the luggage was made of leather or other substances, such as textiles or plastic. Tariffs on these goods currently average about 16.5 percent. These tariffs cost consumers about $211 million per year,

preserving about 225 jobs. The cost to consumers per job saved is almost $1 million.

Finally, consider the case of *frozen orange juice concentrate*. The current tariff on this product stands at 30 percent, down substantially from Smoot-Hawley levels. The cost this tax imposes on consumers exceeds $280 million per year, saving perhaps 600 jobs. The consumer cost per job saved exceeds $450,000.

As these examples indicate, the consumer cost of protection, even on relatively small items in the total consumption basket of the U.S. economy, can be large. Even more dramatic than the overall costs is the extraordinarily high cost imposed upon consumers in order to maintain employment levels in import-competing industries. This illustrates the relative inefficiency of a tariff as a job-creating policy measure.

Industry	Tariff (%)	Consumer Cost (million$)	Producer Gain (million$)	Consumer Cost per Job (thousand$)	Deadweight Cost (million$)
Rubber footwear	20.0	208.0	55.0	122.3	12.0
Women's shoes	10.0	376.0	70.0	101.6	11.0
Ceramic tiles	19.0	139.0	45.0	400.6	2.0
Luggage	16.5	211.0	16.0	933.6	26.0
Frozen orange juice concentrate	30.0	281.0	101.0	461.4	35.0
Glass and glassware	11.0	266.0	162.0	180.1	9.0
Chinaware	11.0	102.0	18.0	244.0	2.0
Women's purses	13.5	148.0	16.0	191.5	13.0
Costume jewelry	9.0	103.0	46.0	96.5	5.0

SOURCE: Gary Clyde Hufbauer and Kimberly Ann Elliott, *Measuring the Costs of Protection in the United States* (Washington, D.C.: Institute for International Economics, 1994). Table constructed by the authors.

SOME COMPLICATIONS

The analysis presented so far has relied on some rather strict assumptions both about the size of the country imposing the tariff and about the number and the nature of the products involved. As a result, some very strong conclusions have been reached about the effect of tariffs on a country. In this section we explore some issues that emerge when we relax these strict assumptions.

The Optimal Tariff

Suppose that the country that imposes a tariff is a large country in the sense that it is a significant importer (or exporter) of the product in question. In that case, as we are about to see, the imposition of a tariff could lead to a welfare improvement for the country, relative to free trade. In essence, because the country has market power, by imposing a tariff it is able to obtain the goods it continues to purchase at a lower world price. By forcing down the world price, the tariff-imposing country, in effect, shifts some of the burden of the tariff onto the exporting country.

Let's assume that country A is an economically large country. That is, A is an important world importer of a certain product—say, lumber (good L). Let country B export good L to A. Consider Figure 6.8. In the left-hand panel we illustrate A's market for L. In the right-hand panel we present country B's market for L. In the absence of trade, the price of L would be P_A in A and P_B in B. Simple inspection of the diagram demonstrates that if trade were allowed to occur, then B would have comparative advantage in L and would export L to A. Clearly, at any price below P_A, country A would import L; at any price above P_B, country B would export L.

FIGURE 6.8 *International free-trade equilibrium.*

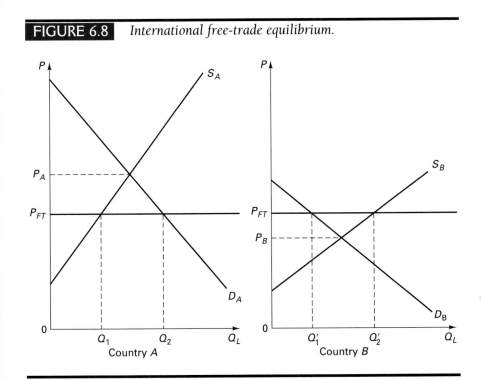

The equilibrium world price is defined as the price at which the quantity that consumers in A want to import is equal to the quantity that producers in B want to export. In the diagram, this price is denoted by P_{FT}. At that price, country A's desired imports equal $Q_1 Q_2$ units, which exactly matches B's desired exports (denoted in the right-hand panel of the diagram as $Q_1' Q_2'$ units). Note carefully that P_{FT} is the only possible candidate for an equilibrium free-trade price. At any price above P_{FT}, the demand for imports will fall in A, while the supply of exports from B will rise. In other words, at free-trade prices above P_{FT}, there will be an excess supply of L in world markets; excess supply will tend to force the price down. By identical reasoning, it is easy to see that at any free-trade price below P_{FT}, there will be international excess demand for L, and the market price for the good will tend to rise.

The fact that the markets in A and B interact in the way just described in order to determine the world price is the source of A's international market power. In particular, a change in A's demand for imported units of L will have a direct effect on the world price. Increases in demand will drive the world price up; decreases in demand will drive it down. To see how this works, consider the following scenario:

Suppose that A imposes a tariff on imports of L that causes imports to fall to $Q_3 Q_4$ units. This is illustrated in the left-hand panel of Figure 6.9 by the increase in price from P_{FT} to P''. Note, now, the effect A's tariff has on country B. Since A is an important customer of B's product, when A uses a tariff to reduce its demand, this

FIGURE 6.9   *Illustration of a tariff for a large country.*

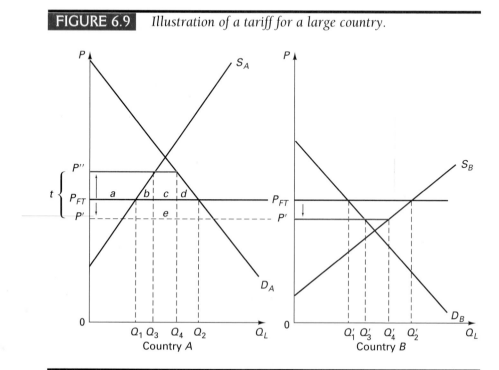

causes the price in B to fall. As drawn, the price will fall until world trade is balanced. This occurs at price P', where B's exports equal $Q_3'Q_4'$, which exactly matches the Q_3Q_4 units of lumber demanded by A after it imposes the tariff.

With the higher price, consumers in A lose $\$a + \$b + \$c + \$d$ in consumer surplus. Producer surplus rises by the amount $\$a$. What about government revenue? How much has it risen by? The answer is that government revenue rises by $\$(c + e)$. To see that, note first that by definition the size of the tariff equals the difference between the price consumers in A pay for the product (P'') and the price producers in B receive (P'). That is, the per unit tariff of $\$t$ equals $P'' - P'$. Thus, we see that in this case the price has gone up in A, but by less than the full amount of the tariff. For example, if the tariff had been $10 per unit, the actual price rise imposed on A's consumers would be less than $10. What has happened is that A is such an important customer of B's product that producers in B attempt to maintain sales by absorbing some of the tariff in the form of price reductions. In the new equilibrium, the price received by producers in B falls from P_{FT} to P'.

This means that the lumber that country A now imports comes into the country at a lower price. Then, once the tariff is imposed, the new price in A is P'' ($= P' + t$). This leads to a convenient interpretation of the amount $\$(c + e)$. $\$c$ represents the tariff proceeds paid (in effect) by A's consumers to the government of A. We know this because the height of rectangle c is equal to the increase in price to A's consumers, and the base equals the level of imports. $\$e$ represents the amount of the tariff paid (in effect) by B's producers. That is, the height of rectangle e represents the amount that B's producers have cut their price, and the base is equal to the level of A's imports (B's exports).

What has been the impact on A's overall welfare due to the tariff? To answer that question, we simply net out the various surpluses. This is illustrated in Table 6.5. The change in welfare in A brought about by the imposition of a tariff equals $\$e - \$(b + d)$. This amount could be positive or negative, depending upon the relative sizes of the two terms. As previously noted, $\$e$ represents the amount of the tariff revenue paid by foreigners because the world price of their exports has fallen. The larger area e is, everything else held constant, the greater is the likelihood that A's welfare has increased because of the imposition of the tariff. The amount $\$(b + d)$ represents the usual deadweight costs of the tariff. The smaller this is, the greater the likelihood of a welfare increase in A.

As Figure 6.9 clearly suggests, the amounts $\$b$, $\$d$, and $\$e$ depend both on the slopes of the various demand and supply curves and on the size of the tariff imposed by country A. Thus, for a given set of demand and supply curves, it should be possible

TABLE 6.5	*Welfare Cost of a Tariff Imposed by a Large Country*			
Change in consumer surplus	$-\$a$	$-\$b$	$-\$c$	$-\$d$
Change in producer surplus	$\$a$			
Change in government revenue			$\$c$	$+\$e$
NET WELFARE CHANGE		$-\$b$	$-\$d$	$+\$e$

Optimal tariff
The size of a tariff that raises the welfare of a tariff-imposing country by the greatest amount relative to free-trade welfare levels.

for the government of A to impose a tariff that raises A's welfare to the largest extent possible. That is, the tariff would be set to a level that maximizes the area $e - $(b + d)$. Such a tariff is known as A's **optimal tariff**.

Under what conditions is a tariff likely to raise a country's welfare? First, the country must be an important participant in the world market. Countries that consume a large amount of traded goods have market power—and can affect world price through import tariffs. Countries that produce a large amount of a particular traded good can influence world price, much as a monopolist can, through an export tariff. Thus, market power is the most important condition for the imposition of an optimal tariff.

A country's market power is determined both by the amounts it consumes (or produces) relative to the overall size of the market and by the slopes of the demand and supply curves in the domestic markets of both the home and the foreign countries. In particular, the more elastic (inelastic) demand and supply conditions are in the home (foreign) markets, the greater the ability of the home country to impose an optimal tariff.*

A second factor that, up to now, we have not taken into account is the reaction the imposition of an optimal tariff will induce from the rest of the world. Clearly, as A's welfare rises with the imposition of a tariff, it comes at the expense of B. This is a decidedly unfriendly policy for A to undertake, and it could produce a set of retaliatory tariff measures on the part of the government of B. When the imposition of tariffs (or other forms of protection) by one country leads to increased protection in the rest of the world, we are said to be in a **trade (or tariff) war**.[†] Trade wars necessarily lead to a reduction in world trade, although it is unlikely that trade would ever disappear entirely. Also, while it is theoretically possible that A's welfare could remain higher than under free trade even after retaliation is imposed by B, there is a much higher probability that welfare in both countries would fall after retaliation has been imposed. Item 6.2 considers some of the ramifications of the last great trade war, the tariff escalation following the imposition of the Smoot-Hawley Tariff of 1930.

Trade (or tariff) war
A general reduction in world trade brought about by increases in trade barriers throughout the world.

Given the likelihood of retaliation, it is often the case that countries do not attempt to impose what would otherwise be optimal tariffs. There is no evidence, for instance, of any efforts by the United States—which certainly has the market power to do so—to exploit its market power in the implementation of commercial policy.[‡] Examples of attempts to impose optimal export tariffs are more common. The Organization of Petroleum Exporting Countries (OPEC) oil price increases of the 1970s, while not represented as such at the time, were qualitatively identical with attempts to raise internal (to OPEC) welfare by forcing the rest of the world to pay the tariff it had imposed.

---

*You are asked to prove this statement in one of the exercises at the end of the chapter.
[†]Trade wars are relatively uncommon. The last followed the imposition by the United States of the Smoot-Hawley Tariff in 1930. See the discussion in Item 6.2 for more detail.
[‡]Recently, however, the United States has shown an increased inclination to impose or to threaten to impose tariffs to encourage foreign governments to end what the United States considers to be "unfair" trade practices. The authority to impose these tariffs is found in Section 301 of the Trade Act of 1974, as amended. For more detail on this point, see Chapter 8.

ITEM 6.2 | The Smoot-Hawley Tariff and Its Aftermath

Article I of the Constitution of the United States gives Congress the sole authority to "regulate commerce with foreign nations" and to "lay and collect . . . duties." From time to time over the first 150 years of the Republic, Congress has used this authority to revise the U.S. tariff code. The last such occasion began in early 1929 at the request of then President Hoover. During his successful election campaign of 1928, he had promised farmers a tariff on agricultural products to try to boost sagging farm prices.* Congress set about to help President Hoover keep his promise.

At first, the tariff revisions were restricted to agricultural products. Soon, however, representatives from manufacturing states began demanding additional tariffs for industries in their districts. The process of pork-barrel politics started in earnest, with representatives promising to vote to protect industries in other districts in return for votes to protect the industries of their districts.

The process of expanding and increasing U.S. tariff barriers took considerable time and effort. In preparing this change in tariff code, the House Ways and Means Committee took over 11,000 pages of testimony. It was not until April 1930 that the bill authorizing the tariff changes, the Tariff Act of 1930, passed both houses of Congress and went to the president for his signature. This bill is also known as the Smoot-Hawley Tariff, named after the principal congressional sponsors of the legislation.

Prior to signing the bill, President Hoover received formal protests from 38 foreign governments, warning of likely retaliation to the U.S. actions. Some countries, anticipating the enactment of the bill, raised their tariffs shortly before its final passage. Over 1,000 American economists wrote the president urging him to veto the bill. On June 17, 1930, the Smoot-Hawley Tariff bill was signed and enacted into law. The result was the highest general tariff structure in the history of the United States. Average tariff levels rose to almost 60 percent of dutiable imports. Tariffs were raised on over 12,000 products.

The reaction was immediate. Charles Kindleberger, in his history of the Great Depression, writes of the

. . . reactions of Spain, concerned about tariffs on grapes, oranges, corn, and onions, which passed the Wais tariff of July 22, 1930; of Switzerland, which objected to increased tariffs on watches, embroideries, and shoes, and undertook a boycott of U.S. exports; of Canada, reacting to tariffs on many food products, logs and timber, which . . . raised tariffs three times between 1930 and 1932; and of Italy, which objected to tariffs on hats and bonnets of straw, wool felt hats and olive oil, and took reprisal against United States . . . automobiles on 30 June 1930. New tariffs were also enacted by Cuba, Mexico, France, Australia, and New Zealand.[†]

Eventually, over 40 nations raised their tariff levels, and these higher barriers, coupled with falling income levels, brought world trade virtually to a halt. By 1933, world trade was only about one-third the level it had been in 1929. U.S. exports collapsed. This is illustrated quite effectively in a diagram designed by Professor Kindleberger and presented as the following Figure 6.10.

---

*Curiously, it is doubtful how much effect these tariffs would have on raising prices, since the products they initially applied to were seldom imported into the United States.

[†]Kindleberger, Charles, *The World in Depression, 1929–1939* (Berkeley and Los Angeles: University of California Press, 1973), 132 (including Figure 6.10).

(Continued)

ITEM 6.2   The Smoot-Hawley Tariff and Its Aftermath *(Continued)*

International trade bottomed out in 1933, along with the depression. Gradually, exports began to rise.* This was helped in part by negotiations to lower trade barriers on a bilateral basis with major trading partners. These talks were undertaken by President Roosevelt and authorized by Congress in the Reciprocal Trade Agree-

ments Act of 1934. This legislation set in motion the modern era of U.S. trade policy, wherein, and from time to time, Congress cedes to the president its authority to alter trade barriers.

_____

*However, they would not return to their 1929 level until 1942.

FIGURE 6.10   *The contracting spiral of world trade, January 1929 to March 1933 (total imports of 75 countries in millions of U.S. dollars).*

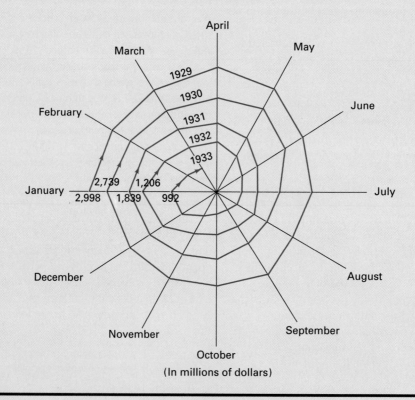

(In millions of dollars)

How High Are Tariffs?

So far we have assumed that tariffs have been imposed on only one good. In reality, however, there are many goods in the world, and countries tend to maintain extensive tariff structures on these products. Table 6.6 presents some post–Tokyo Round average tariff levels for selected countries. The first thing to note about these tariffs is that they differ by product. Some products enjoy large protection, some little or none. Providing a measure of the overall level of tariffs for a country becomes much more problematic when, as is the case for the United States, there are so many individual products with different tariffs that the tariff code is contained in a book roughly the size of the Manhattan telephone directory. Still, this would not be a particularly difficult problem if each country had only one tariff rate (e.g., 10 percent) that it applied to all goods entering a country. This is seldom the case in the real world.*

To come up with a measure of overall tariff protection for a country, the usual practice is to measure the height of its **average tariff**. This calculation involves dividing a country's tariff revenue for a given period (usually one year) by some measure of trade for that country. Typically, one of two measures of trade is employed—total imports or total dutiable imports. Total dutiable imports represents only those products upon which duties are collected. Since many goods are assessed no duties, especially by industrialized countries, average tariff calculations based on dutiable imports are almost always higher than those based on total imports.

Average tariff
A measure of the height of a country's tariff barriers.

A second feature to note in Table 6.6 is that, on average, tariffs tend to be relatively low. The average tariff for most countries shown in the table is around 5 percent. Of these countries, only Australia, Austria, and New Zealand have average tariff levels in excess of 10 percent. These relatively low rates reflect the general reduction in the tariff levels of major industrialized countries that has occurred since the end of World War II. Not shown in the table, however, are data from developing countries. It should be noted that tariff levels for most developing countries are much higher, with average tariff rates often in excess of 20 percent. It is a curious and unresolved phenomenon that small developing countries that have the most to lose from imposing tariffs use them extensively.

Effective Rate of Protection

The production of most goods involves the use of raw-material or semiprocessed-material inputs. Autos require steel, glass, and rubber; computers require semiconductors and electrical wiring; and so on. We have seen that a tariff on a product protects the producers of that good and serves as an incentive to produce more locally.

---

*However, since the 1980s, the World Bank has promoted greater uniformity of tariff rates in developing countries. Recently, Bolivia adopted a uniform tariff rate of 17 percent on virtually all imports. Chile has had a single tariff rate since the late 1970s. Argentina and Mexico have adopted a three-level tariff structure. For a model of the costs and benefits of uniform tariff rates, see Arvind Panagariya and Dani Rodrik, "Political-Economy Arguments for a Uniform Tariff," *International Economic Review,* 1993.

TABLE 6.6 *Post–Tokyo Round Tariff Rates for Selected Industrial Countries and Products*
(PERCENTAGE, WEIGHTED BY OWN-COUNTRY IMPORTS)

	Australia	Austria	Belgium	Canada	Denmark	Finland	France	Germany	Ireland	Italy	Japan	Netherlands	New Zealand	Norway	Sweden	Switzerland	United Kingdom	United States	Mean
Agriculture	7.5	8.6	4.7	2.2	5.0	11.0	4.6	4.7	5.2	6.1	21.8	4.7	3.8	1.5	1.8	5.2	4.5	1.8	6.9
Food, beverages, tobacco	21.9	20.7	10.1	6.1	13.4	23.8	9.1	11.2	10.8	7.7	28.5	10.6	16.2	8.7	3.7	13.3	10.3	4.7	11.0
Textiles	21.2	15.9	7.2	16.7	8.7	22.5	7.3	7.4	7.8	5.6	3.3	8.5	12.3	13.3	10.3	6.6	6.7	9.2	8.5
Wearing apparel	61.8	36.2	13.4	24.2	13.2	36.5	13.2	13.4	13.2	13.2	13.9	13.5	58.5	21.7	14.2	12.4	13.3	22.7	17.5
Leather products	20.3	7.7	2.5	6.3	1.8	9.3	1.6	3.2	1.8	0.7	3.1	3.0	15.3	5.8	4.0	2.1	1.2	4.2	3.0
Footwear	33.8	23.4	11.4	21.9	11.5	17.4	11.3	11.7	11.9	10.4	15.7	11.2	40.7	21.7	13.7	9.0	12.5	8.8	12.0
Wood products	12.5	3.7	2.4	3.2	3.4	0.4	2.4	2.9	2.5	0.8	0.3	2.8	11.4	1.6	0.7	3.2	3.1	1.7	1.9
Furniture	31.2	22.1	5.6	14.3	5.5	5.5	5.6	5.6	5.7	5.6	5.1	5.6	38.3	5.1	4.0	9.2	5.6	4.1	6.9
Paper	7.7	12.3	6.9	6.7	7.9	4.5	5.5	5.2	8.0	2.6	2.9	6.2	20.5	1.9	2.4	4.3	4.9	0.2	4.3
Printing and publishing	1.8	1.5	1.5	1.0	2.8	1.1	2.2	2.1	1.5	1.8	0.1	2.2	1.1	4.3	0.2	0.7	2.1	0.7	1.5
Chemicals	5.4	4.7	8.0	7.5	8.5	1.8	7.6	8.0	7.6	8.1	4.8	8.1	8.1	6.2	4.8	0.9	7.9	2.4	6.4
Petroleum	0.2	4.4	1.5	0.3	3.3	0.1	0.5	1.8	3.8	0.6	2.2	1.0	0.6	0.1	0.0	0.0	1.1	1.4	1.4
Rubber products	11.2	9.9	4.2	6.7	4.4	13.5	3.5	3.8	3.7	2.7	1.1	4.1	9.5	6.6	6.1	1.7	2.7	2.5	4.1
Nonmetallic mineral products	11.5	5.9	3.7	6.4	5.0	2.9	4.7	3.6	4.5	2.8	0.5	3.3	12.7	2.4	2.8	2.5	2.4	5.3	4.0
Glass	18.9	12.9	8.0	7.2	7.5	22.3	7.4	7.9	7.3	7.6	5.1	7.5	13.5	8.0	7.1	3.1	7.9	6.2	8.0
Iron and steel	10.8	5.8	4.6	5.4	5.5	4.2	4.9	4.7	5.9	3.5	2.8	5.6	5.2	1.7	3.7	1.7	4.7	3.6	4.3
Nonferrous metals	4.2	3.3	1.6	3.0	6.6	0.8	2.6	1.9	6.5	1.8	1.1	3.6	4.1	0.9	0.7	2.4	1.7	0.7	1.7
Metal products	23.7	10.4	5.4	8.5	5.5	7.7	5.4	5.5	5.4	5.5	5.2	5.4	26.5	4.4	4.0	2.8	5.6	4.8	6.2
Nonelectric machinery	13.9	6.4	4.3	4.5	4.4	6.1	4.4	4.5	4.3	4.5	4.4	4.3	22.1	5.2	3.5	1.2	4.2	3.3	4.7
Electric machinery	21.6	14.7	7.4	5.8	7.1	6.0	7.7	8.3	7.2	8.0	4.3	7.8	19.6	6.9	4.5	1.6	8.1	4.4	7.1
Transportation equipment	21.2	22.1	7.9	1.6	7.2	3.8	7.9	7.7	10.2	8.8	1.5	9.0	26.8	2.2	5.1	6.1	7.2	2.5	5.9
Miscellaneous manufactures	12.8	8.7	3.0	5.4	6.1	12.6	5.8	5.6	6.5	5.8	4.6	5.2	18.2	7.4	4.6	1.1	3.0	4.2	4.8
MEAN (WEIGHTED BY IMPORTS)	14.8	11.3	5.4	4.6	6.4	6.2	4.9	5.7	6.6	4.4	6.2	5.7	13.8	4.5	3.9	3.5	4.9	3.3	5.2

SOURCE: Alan Deardorff and Robert Stern, *Computational Analysis of Global Trading Arrangements* (Ann Arbor: University of Michigan Press, 1990), Table A8. Reprinted by permission.

Suppose a country imposed a tariff on steel but not on autos. What sort of incentive would this have on the production of autos? A considerable amount of work has been devoted by economists to answering questions such as this one. In general, the challenge of this work has been to calculate the amount of protection afforded to individual products by the tariff *structure* of a country. In other words, what is the **effective rate of protection (ERP)** enjoyed by individual products, because there may or may not be tariffs on these goods or on the goods used in their production?*

To understand effective rates of protection and how they differ from nominal rates of protection, consider the following example:

> **Effective rate of protection (ERP)**
> The amount of protection provided to the domestic content of a product by the tariff structure of a country.

EXAMPLE

Assume that it takes 5 yards of textiles to produce a man's suit. Let the amount paid to domestic primary factors used in the production of suits (e.g., wages, rent, and profits) equal $50 per suit. This amount of money is known as domestic value added. Suppose textiles are available from both domestic and foreign suppliers at a constant world price of $20 per yard. Then, under free trade and perfect competition, we would expect that the price of a suit would be $150 (5 yards at $20 per yard + $50).

Suppose, now, that the government imposes a tariff of 20 percent on imported suits. Such a tariff raises the price of all suits by $30 (0.20 × $150).[†] Because textiles remain available from international sources at the world price of $20 per yard, the increase in revenue per suit in the apparel industry will go to domestic primary factors in the form of higher wages, rents, or profits. That is, after the tariff on suits has been imposed, domestic producers receive $180 for each suit sold, but still pay only $100 for the textiles used to make the suit. The remaining $80 goes to domestic factors. In this case, the tariff allows an increase in domestic value added from $50 to $80. Presumably, it is this increase in value added (including, of course, higher profits) that causes the industry to respond with higher output levels whenever there is an increase in tariff protection.

---

*The amount of literature on effective rates of protection is enormous. A small sample of important papers includes Max Corden, "The Structure of a Tariff System and the Effective Protection Rate," *Journal of Political Economy* (1966); Wilfred Ethier, "The Theory of Effective Protection in General Equilibrium: Effective-Rate Analogues of Nominal Rates," *Canadian Journal of Economics* (1977); and Harry Johnson, "The Theory of Tariff Structure, with Special Reference to World Trade and Development," in *Trade and Development,* ed. Harry Johnson and Peter Kenen (Geneva: Librarie Droz, 1965). Examples of empirical work in this area include Giorgio Basevi, "The U.S. Tariff Structure: Estimates of Effective Rates of Protection of U.S. Industries and Industrial Labor," *The Review of Economics and Statistics* (1966); Alan Deardorff and Robert Stern, "The Effects of the Tokyo Round on the Structure of Protection," in *The Structure and Evolution of Recent U.S. Trade Policy,* ed. Robert Baldwin and Anne Krueger (Chicago: University of Chicago Press, 1984); and the many papers found in Herbert Grubel and Harry Johnson, eds., *Effective Tariff Protection* (Geneva: Graduate Institute for International Studies, 1971).
[†]That is, we are assuming that domestic and imported clothes are perfect substitutes and that the tariff-imposing country is small in world markets for imported clothing and cloth.

Let us define the following terms:

Nominal rate of protection (NRP) = t/P

Effective rate of protection (ERP) = $(v' - v)/v$

where t equals the tariff (in dollars) on the final product (i.e., the product sold to consumers), P equals the (free-trade) price of the final product (in dollars), v equals domestic value added under free trade, and v' equals domestic value added when tariffs are in place. In the example we have been considering,

NRP = \$30/\$150 = 20%

ERP = (\$80 − \$50)/\$50 = 60%

The meaning of the NRP is straightforward. It represents the amount that domestic producers can raise the price of their output and still compete with foreign production. What is the meaning of the ERP? This fraction tells us the amount that domestic value added can rise relative to free-trade levels, while the domestic industry remains able to sell its product in the market. In our example, the tariff allows payments to land, labor, and capital to rise by a total of 60 percent over free-trade levels on a per unit basis.

Suppose now that the government imposes a second tariff—this time on textiles. Let that tariff equal only 10 percent. This tariff results in an increase in the price of textiles of 10 percent, from \$20 to \$22 per yard. The raw-material input cost of making a suit increases from \$100 to \$110 (5 yards at \$22 per yard). Can the suit producer pass these costs on to the public? The answer is no. With a 20 percent tariff on imported suits, foreign suits will still sell for \$180. To remain competitive, domestic suit producers must absorb the higher costs brought about by the tariff (on their input) in the form of lower profits or lower payments to other domestic factors (labor or land). This is made clear by comparing the ERPs for apparel before and after the imposition of the tariff on textiles.

ERP (0% tariff on textiles) = \$30/\$50 = 60%

ERP (10% tariff on textiles) = (\$70 − \$50)/\$50 = 40%

Because of the tariff on textiles, the effective rate of protection afforded to suits has fallen. This is an important lesson. It shows us that protection in one industry is affected not only by tariffs in that industry but by tariffs in related industries as well. In Table 6.7 we continue with this example by illustrating how higher and higher tariffs on imported intermediate products (e.g., textiles) lower the ERP on a final product (e.g., suits). A surprising feature of this table is that even though NRP may be positive for the final product, ERP can be negative! The implication of this is that due to the tariff structure, the cost of imported inputs has become so high that value added must be reduced to below the levels found in free trade for a country to compete with imports of the final product.

TABLE 6.7		*Illustration of Effective Rates of Protection*				
World Price, Suits ($)	Tariff on Suits (%)	World Price, Textiles ($)	Tariff on Textiles (%)	Value Added ($)	NRP, Suits (%)	ERP, Suits (%)
150	0	100	0	50	0	0
150	20	100	0	80	20	60
150	20	100	10	70	20	40
150	20	100	20	60	20	20
150	20	100	30	50	20	0
150	20	100	40	40	20	−20
150	20	100	50	30	20	−40

An upshot of this result is that if an intermediate-goods industry, such as textiles, succeeds in obtaining increases in its NRP, final goods sectors using this product be will likely to demand increases in the tariffs protecting their industries. Thus, tariffs can tend to increase and spread throughout an economy much like a malignant tumor grows in the human body.

The effective rate of protection is an important and useful concept. First, it helps to explain the structure of protection in many countries. For instance, as Table 6.8 illustrates, it is commonplace for industrialized countries to have relatively low or even no protection on raw materials. Tariffs on semimanufactured products tend to be somewhat higher, while tariffs on final products typically are the highest. This structure is known as **tariff escalation by stages of processing**, and it tends to guarantee positive levels of ERP throughout all protected sectors of the economy.

Second, measures of ERP tell us something about the allocation of domestic resources. Factors of production tend to be drawn to those endeavors where rewards are the greatest. Thus, if possible, it would seem likely that resources will leave industries with low levels of ERP for industries with high ERPs. As we have seen from the preceding example, for products that require imported intermediate goods in their production, NRP measures do not tell us much about the amount of protection afforded to domestic value added.

Tariff escalation Tariff rates that rise with stages of processing.

TABLE 6.8	*Tariffs by Stages of Processing, United States, European Union, Japan, and Canada (percentage)*			
	Post–Tokyo Round Tariff Rates			
Industry	United States	EU	Japan	Canada
All industrial products	4.4	4.7	2.8	7.9
Raw materials	0.2	0.2	0.5	0.5
Semimanufactures	3.0	4.2	4.6	8.3
Finished manufactures	5.7	6.9	6.0	8.3

SOURCE: GATT.

Third, effective rates of protection are valuable measures for politicians and especially for trade negotiators, because they tell how changes in the tariff structure would affect incomes received by domestic factors of production. Thus, ERP measures are often calculated. In Table 6.9 we provide measures of NRP and ERP for selected industries for the United States, the European Union, and Japan.

TABLE 6.9 *Nominal and Effective Rates of Protection, United States, European Union, and Japan (percentage)*[1]

	United States Nominal Tariffs	Effective Rate of Protection	EU Nominal Tariffs	Effective Rate of Protection	Japan Nominal Tariffs	Effective Rate of Protection
Traded Goods						
Agriculture, forest products, and fish	1.80 (17)	1.91 (18)	4.86 (12)	4.10 (17)	21.80 (2)	21.40 (4)
Food, beverages, and tobacco	4.70 (7)	10.16 (4)	10.06 (3)	17.83 (3)	28.50 (1)	50.31 (1)
Textiles	9.20 (2)	18.02 (2)	7.17 (8)	8.79 (10)	3.30 (12)	−2.41 (24)
Wearing apparel	22.70 (1)	43.30 (1)	13.37 (1)	19.26 (2)	13.90 (4)	42.20 (3)
Leather products	4.20 (9)	4.95 (12)	2.01 (21)	−2.19 (28)	3.10 (13)	−14.75 (28)
Footwear	8.80 (3)	15.37 (3)	11.63 (2)	20.08 (1)	15.70 (3)	50.02 (2)
Wood products	1.70 (18)	1.72 (19)	2.51 (18)	1.68 (20)	0.30 (21)	−30.59 (29)
Furniture and fixtures	4.10 (11)	5.52 (11)	5.60 (9)	11.30 (8)	5.10 (6)	10.26 (5)
Paper and paper products	0.20 (22)	−0.86 (28)	5.37 (11)	8.29 (12)	2.90 (14)	1.75 (14)
Printing and publishing	0.70 (21)	0.90 (20)	2.06 (20)	−1.03 (26)	0.10 (22)	−1.51 (23)
Chemicals	2.40 (16)	3.66 (15)	7.95 (5)	11.71 (6)	4.80 (8)	6.39 (11)
Petroleum and related products	1.40 (19)	4.69 (13)	1.16 (22)	3.39 (18)	2.20 (16)	4.14 (13)
Rubber products	2.50 (14)	1.95 (16)	3.54 (17)	2.29 (19)	1.10 (18)	−4.99 (27)
Nonmetal mineral products	5.30 (5)	9.23 (6)	3.66 (16)	6.52 (15)	0.50 (20)	−0.54 (19)
Glass and glass products	6.20 (4)	9.77 (5)	7.70 (7)	12.16 (5)	5.10 (7)	8.10 (7)
Iron and steel	3.60 (12)	6.18 (9)	4.67 (14)	11.59 (7)	2.80 (15)	4.34 (12)
Nonferrous metals	0.70 (20)	0.50 (21)	2.13 (19)	8.29 (11)	1.10 (19)	1.73 (15)
Metal products	4.80 (6)	7.86 (7)	5.46 (10)	7.07 (13)	5.20 (5)	9.23 (6)
Nonelectric machinery	3.30 (13)	4.06 (14)	4.37 (15)	4.71 (16)	4.40 (10)	6.74 (9)
Electric machinery	4.40 (8)	6.34 (8)	7.89 (6)	10.79 (9)	4.30 (11)	6.73 (10)
Transportation equipment	2.50 (15)	1.94 (17)	7.95 (4)	12.31 (4)	1.50 (17)	0.03 (16)
Miscellaneous manufactures	4.20 (10)	5.79 (10)	4.67 (13)	6.55 (14)	4.60 (9)	7.30 (8)
Nontraded goods						
Mining and quarrying		−0.47 (26)		−0.51 (22)		−0.99 (22)
Electricity, gas, and water		−0.16 (23)		−0.61 (23)		−0.79 (21)
Construction		−2.88 (29)		−2.96 (29)		−3.64 (25)
Wholesale and retail trade		−0.55 (27)		−1.37 (27)		−0.39 (18)
Transportation, storage, and communication		−0.35 (25)		−0.74 (25)		−0.54 (20)
Finance, insurance, and real estate		−0.09 (22)		−0.46 (21)		−0.16 (17)
Commercial, social, and personal services		−0.28 (24)		−0.61 (24)		−3.69 (26)

[1]Numbers in parentheses are column ranks.

SOURCE: Alan Deardorff and Robert Stern, "The Effects of the Tokyo Round on the Structure of Protection," in *The Structure and Evolution of U.S. Trade Policy,* ed. Robert Baldwin and Anne Krueger (Chicago: University of Chicago Press, 1984), Tables 10.1–10.3. Reprinted by permission.

SUMMARY

1. Tariffs are taxes imposed by countries on either imports or exports. This form of commercial policy is probably the most commonly used tool by governments around the world to regulate their trade flows.

2. The effect of import tariffs is to raise the price of these goods and hence discourage their consumption. At the same time, domestic producers of substitute goods find it easier to raise prices and profits. Thus, tariffs are said to protect domestic producers.

3. In general, tariffs lower the standard of living of a country relative to free trade, because they hurt consumers more than they help producers.

4. Tariffs can increase a country's standard of living if that country has market power in world markets. This result does not apply for most countries and for most products. Even when the requisite conditions hold, improvements in welfare depend crucially on foreign countries not retaliating with increases in their own tariffs.

5. When raw materials and intermediate goods are traded internationally, the amount of protection a manufactured good receives from a tariff depends not only on its own tariff but also on the tariffs on imported inputs.

EXERCISES

1. Prove the following proposition: Free trade is better than no trade.

2. Prove the following: Some trade (trade with tariffs) is better than no trade.

3. Suppose that a country imposes a pure revenue tariff. Diagram the welfare effects of this tariff. How do these effects differ from the usual deadweight costs analyzed in the chapter?

4. The less elastic (i.e., the steeper) is the domestic supply curve, the lower is the production deadweight cost of any tariff. True or false? Demonstrate and explain.

5. The more elastic (i.e., the flatter) is the domestic demand curve, the lower is the consumption deadweight cost of any tariff. True or false? Demonstrate and explain.

6. Use the data in the table in Item 6.1 to calculate U.S. tariff revenues on rubber footwear, women's shoes, and luggage.

7. Given the following information, calculate the cost to consumers, the benefit to producers, the change in government revenue, and the deadweight costs of a proposed 20 percent tariff on personal computers:

Price of computers (free trade)	$2,000
Domestic production (free trade)	100,000
Domestic production (after tariff)	120,000
Domestic consumption (free trade)	150,000
Domestic consumption (after tariff)	140,000

8. The optimal tariff for a small country is zero. Prove this statement geometrically and then explain your results.

9. Prove that the more elastic demand and supply conditions are in a country that is large in world markets, the greater the ability of that country to impose an optimal tariff.

10. Prove that the more inelastic demand and supply conditions are in a foreign country, the greater the ability for a country that is large in world markets to impose an optimal tariff. Use this result to explain why the OPEC price increases of the 1970s had such devastating effects on the economies of the West.

11. Given the following information, find the NRP and the ERP in the personal computer (PC) industry:

World price of PCs	$2,000
Cost of imported memory chips	$500
Domestic value added (free trade)	$1,500
Tariff on PCs	$200
Tariff on memory chips	$0

Suppose the government were to impose a tariff of 30 percent on memory chips. What would happen to the NRP and the ERP in the PC industry? Derive and explain.

12. Suppose a country imposed a specific export tariff of $t on each unit of its exports of a certain product. Describe this situation graphically, and calculate the welfare cost of this policy.

13. In Argentina, there are *export* tariffs both on raw materials, such as soybeans, and on processed soybean products (e.g., oils). Use the theory of effective protection to explain which tariff is likely to be higher.

14. Prove that if a product is made with only domestic factors of production (i.e., there are no imported intermediate components), the NRP equals ERP.

15. Recently, the World Bank has been advising member countries to adopt uniform tariff rates on all imports. Suppose a country such as Chile adopts a uniform tariff of 20 percent ad valorem on all imports. Compare Chile's NRP and ERP under this policy. Why do you suppose the World Bank has been advocating uniform tariff rates?

16. Use the data in Table 6.6 to compare U.S. protectionist policies with those of Japan. In what sectors are protection levels relatively equal? Where do they differ? Try to explain these patterns.

17. Suppose that the domestic demand and supply for shoes in a small open economy are given by

$$P = 100 - 2Q \text{ (demand)}$$
$$P = 5 + Q \text{ (supply)}$$

where P denotes price and Q denotes quantity.
   a. What are the autarky price of shoes and the quantity produced?
   b. What are the levels of domestic production, consumption, and imports if the world price is $10?
   c. How do your answers in part b change if this country were to impose a tariff of $3?

REFERENCES

Deardorff, Alan, and Robert Stern. "The Effects of the Tokyo Round on the Structure of Protection." In Robert Baldwin and Anne Krueger, eds., *The Structure and Evolution of Recent U.S. Trade Policy*. Chicago: The University of Chicago Press, 1984.

Hufbauer, Gary Clyde, and Kimberly Ann Elliott. *Measuring the Costs of Protection in the United States*. Washington, D.C.: Institute for International Economics, 1994.

Kindleberger, Charles. *The World in Depression, 1929–1939*. Berkeley and Los Angeles: University of California Press, 1973.

INTERNET APPLICATIONS

Please visit our Web site at www.awl.com/husted_melvin for more exercises and readings.

APPENDIX 6.1

THE IMPERFECT SUBSTITUTES MODEL

The model presented in the main part of this chapter to calculate welfare costs of a tariff assumes that foreign goods are perfect substitutes in demand for domestically produced items. That is, the typical consumer would essentially be incapable of distinguishing between domestic and foreign products and would treat the two types of goods as being functionally identical. This is obviously a very strong assumption. Furthermore, it is an assumption that applies to a proportionately smaller amount of traded goods, as manufactured-goods trade expands relative to homogeneous-agricultural and other raw-material products.

Consequently, analysts have recently been making greater and greater use of a model known as the imperfect substitutes model, which treats domestic and foreign goods as similar but not identical products. In this appendix, we describe this model and show how it can be used to analyze the welfare implications of tariff protection.

We begin with separate demand and supply diagrams for the foreign and domestic products. Figure A6.1a illustrates equilibrium in the market for the imported good, while Figure A6.1b shows equilibrium for the domestic substitute. Prior to the imposition of an import tariff, the price of imports is P_M, while the price of the domestic good is P_D. Note that since consumers are assumed to view these two

FIGURE A6.1   *Markets for imperfect substitutes.*

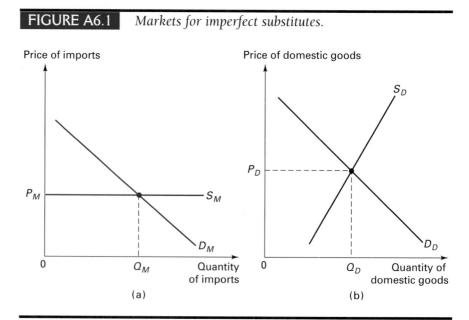

FIGURE A6.2	*Welfare effects of a tariff, imperfect substitutes model.*

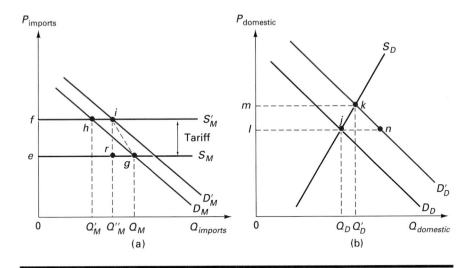

goods as similar but not identical, the prices need not be equal. Returning to the figure, we see that in free trade, Q_M units are imported, while Q_D units of the domestic substitute are produced at home.

Suppose now that the home country imposes a tariff of $\$t$ on imports. This is illustrated in Figure A6.2a. The immediate impact is to shift the world supply curve up by the amount of the tariff. This is shown in panel a as the shift from S_M to S'_M. This induces an initial change in the equilibrium in the import market from point g to point h. However, the story does not end here.

The higher price of imports leads some consumers to switch their demand to the domestic market, causing an outward shift in the demand curve in the market; see panel b. This would tend to raise prices in the domestic goods market (as shown by the movement of equilibrium from j to k), leading to a shift of demand back to the foreign market. The final equilibrium after all these interrelated shifts in demand have occurred is found at points i and k, respectively. In particular, the price of foreign goods had risen (by the amount of the tariff) from e to f. Quantity imported has fallen from Q_M to Q'_M. In the domestic market, price is also higher, rising from l to m. Domestic production also rises, from Q_D to Q'_D.

What are the welfare implications of the imposition of the tariff? Because prices are higher for both goods, consumer surplus falls in both markets. For imports, consumer surplus falls by a dollar amount represented by area *fegi*. In the domestic market, consumer surplus falls by area *lmkj* (dollars). Producer surplus rises due to higher prices in the domestic market. This amount is given by area *lmkj* (dollars). Tariff revenue also rises. This amount is equal to the tariff times the new import level, area *efir*, in panel a. Netting out these latter two gains from consumer loss leaves a deadweight cost of the tariff equivalent to the triangle formed in panel a by the letters *rgi*.

Empirical measurement of the costs of protection in this model is somewhat more difficult than in the case of the perfect substitutes model. What is required is not only detail on the slopes of the relevant demand curves and supply curves but also knowledge of how far the demand curves will shift in the two markets. The slopes of the demand and supply curves can be inferred directly from elasticities of demand and supply. Much statistical analysis of data from various product markets has been undertaken in the past several decades, so that economists have a growing body of knowledge about these numbers. However, this knowledge is incomplete, and many times analysts must rely on educated guesses (especially about supply elasticities) to carry out their calculations.

Knowledge about the magnitude of demand shifts comes from data on cross-price elasticities. Here, the situation is even more problematic. For a variety of reasons, including the lack of data or an inadequate number of observations, good estimates often do not exist.

Due to this uncertainty regarding the magnitudes of the underlying parameters of the model, analysts will often present ranges of welfare cost estimates to government officials. It is not uncommon for the high estimate to be larger than the lower estimate by a factor of 2! Such uncertainty points out the difficulty of welfare cost measurement, especially in highly disaggregated sectors of the economy.

CHAPTER 7

Nontariff Barriers and Arguments for Protection

TOPICS TO BE COVERED

Nontariff Barriers to Trade
Quotas
Similarities Between Tariffs and Quotas
Export Subsidies
Government Procurement Policies
Health and Safety Standards
Protection of Intellectual Property Rights
Arguments for Protection
Tariffs and Government Revenue
Protection and National Defense
Infant Industry Argument for Protection
Protecting the Environment
Strategic Trade Policy

KEY WORDS

Quota
Embargo
Tariff rate quotas (TRQs)
Quota rents
Voluntary export restraint (VER)

Export subsidy
Countervailing duty
"Buy American" acts
Infant industry argument

T he previous chapter was devoted entirely to a discussion of the use of tariffs as barriers to international trade. While tariffs remain the most universal of trade barriers, they are not the only form of commercial policy available to governments. In fact, nontariff barriers (NTBs) in a wide variety of forms are used as instruments of commercial policy by most governments. The amount of trade that is disrupted because of NTBs is large; because of this NTBs have become a major focus of concern in international talks to reduce trade barriers.

In this chapter we explore the nature of various nontariff barriers to international trade.* We focus our discussion especially on *quotas*, which are government-imposed limitations on the quantity or value of trade in a certain product. We also examine other nontariff measures, such as subsidies, health and safety standards, and government procurement policies, all of which are aimed at affecting the level of international trade. Part of our discussion in this portion of the chapter will be on the similarities and differences between these policies and tariffs.

After we have analyzed NTBs, our attention shifts to an analysis of the motivation for imposing barriers to trade. In particular, we focus on the question of what, if any, are the legitimate arguments for protection. That is, governments use a variety of justifications to defend their imposition of trade barriers. These include the preservation of jobs, industry restructuring, national defense, and government revenue. One of the interesting results of this section is that most of the commonly heard arguments for protection have little or no legitimacy. That is, protection fails to lead to the outcome it is supposed to achieve. On the other hand, legitimate arguments for protection exist, but in cases where these arguments apply, protection is seldom the best way to achieve the stated goal.

QUOTAS

⚡ Quota
A government-mandated limitation on either the quantity or the value of trade in a product.

Quotas are government-imposed limits on the quantity or value of goods traded between countries. For example, a government may choose to limit imports of a product (e.g., sugar) to no more than 1.25 million tons in a particular year,[†] or it may decree that no more than $25 million of another product (e.g., cotton blouses) will be allowed into the country.[‡] Because quotas restrict the amount of foreign com-

---

*The classic analysis of nontariff barriers is in Robert Baldwin, *Nontariff Distortions of International Trade* (Washington, D.C.: Brookings Institute, 1970). See also Julio Nogues, Andrzej Olechowski, and L. Alan Winters, "The Extent of Nontariff Barriers to Imports of Industrial Countries," *World Bank Staff Working Papers #789* (1986); James Cassing, "Protectionism and Non-Tariff Barriers," *Portfolio: International Economic Perspectives* (1984); Shailendra Anjaria, Naheed Kirmani, and Arne Petersen, *Trade Policy Issues and Developments* (Washington, D.C.: International Monetary Fund, 1985); and Sam Laird and Alexander Yeats, *Quantitative Methods for Trade-Barrier Analysis* (New York: New York University Press, 1990). For a superb, nontechnical introduction to the topic, see Cletus Coughlin and Geoffrey Wood, "An Introduction to Non-Tariff Barriers to Trade," *Review* (Federal Reserve Bank of St. Louis, 1989).
[†]In fact, this was the level of the U.S. quota on sugar imports for the period from October 1993 through September 1994.
[‡]In practice, quantitative quotas, often based on market shares, are more common than value quotas; hence, they will be the focus of the discussion that follows.

petition in the marketplace, they tend to have effects similar to those of tariffs. That is, after they are imposed, domestic prices rise and, of course, imports fall.

Quotas that entirely eliminate trade in a certain product are known as **embargoes**. Embargoes are sometimes established as a form of economic sanction against the policies or practices of another country. For instance, the United States has had an embargo on the export of U.S. goods to Cuba since 1960 and an embargo on the import of most products from Cuba since 1962. The United States also currently bans most imports from Iran, Iraq, Libya, and North Korea. Sometimes countries will impose embargoes for national defense reasons. For instance, the NATO allies have an agreement that restricts exports of certain "high-tech" goods to countries considered to be unfriendly. Despite these examples, embargoes are relatively scarce.* Rather, quotas are most often set at levels greater than zero so that some, though limited, trade occurs.

Embargo A complete ban on trade in a product or products.

For a variety of reasons that we will soon explore, quotas are viewed as being more restrictive than tariffs. Perhaps as a result of this attitude, quotas on most manufactured products have long been prohibited by the international trade law administered by the World Trade Organization (WTO). And, as part of the 1994 Uruguay Round agreements, signatory countries have begun to replace existing quotas on agricultural products, textiles, and apparel with tariffs or **tariff rate quotas (TRQs)**.[†] TRQs are quota policies that allow a certain quantity of a good into a country at low (often zero) tariff rates, but then apply (often substantially) higher tariffs to quantities that exceed the quota. Despite the movement to replace them with these alternative forms of protection, quotas still exist. Phaseout of worldwide textile and apparel quotas is not scheduled to be completed until 2005. International trade law allows countries to impose quotas to provide temporary protection to aid locally distressed industries or when they have balance-of-payments problems.

Tariff rate quotas (TRQs) Policies that allow a certain quantity of a good into a country at low (often zero) tariff rates, but then apply higher tariffs to quantities that exceed the quota.

As of 2000, the United States had import quotas on many types of textiles and apparel, and TRQs on milk, cream, cheese, butter, margarine, peanuts, sugar, various products containing sugar (including chocolate), cotton, and cotton waste. In addition, it has a law known as the Jones Act of 1920 that requires all shipping between U.S. ports to be carried on American-built, American-owned ships. Examples such as these abound worldwide. For instance, Canada has TRQs on dairy products, eggs, and poultry; Indonesia has banned the export of logs and rattan; Thailand prohibits imports of cigarettes; and Finland has a ban on the import of softwood products.

In addition to formal restrictions, countries have found ways of imposing quotas indirectly by obtaining agreements from exporting countries to "voluntarily" limit exports. These latter agreements are also gradually being phased out under the auspices of the WTO.

---

*For an extensive history and analysis of the use of trade policy as a tool to influence foreign policies, see Gary Hufbauer, Jeffrey Schott, and Kimberly Elliott, *Economic Sanctions Reconsidered: History and Current Policy* (Washington, D.C.: Institute for International Economics, 1985). For details on U.S. sanctions, see U.S. International Trade Commission, *Overview & Analysis of Current U.S. Unilateral Economic Sanctions* (Washington, D.C.: USITC, August 1998).
[†]See Chapter 8 for a complete discussion of WTO and the Uruguay Round.

From the point of view of government officials, quotas are a very flexible tool of commercial policy. They may be imposed against all countries or used against only a few. The internal and external impact of the quota depends in part on how the policy is administered. Sometimes countries announce an unallocated global quota. In these circumstances, customs officials are instructed to maintain a count of the imported product (in terms of quantity or value) as it arrives at the docks from different foreign suppliers. Once the quota has been reached, no more of the product is allowed into the country. Thus, those foreign suppliers who get their product to the domestic market first are able to sell their product. Latecomers are turned away.

Unallocated global quotas are relatively uncommon, especially among industrialized countries—for a variety of reasons. First, because the system rewards those who import early in the quota period, ports of entry into the country tend to be clogged during some parts of the year and empty during other parts. This leads to considerable inefficiency in the use of cargo-handling facilities. In addition, under this type of quota scheme, it is often the case that imports of the product that reach the docks exceed the levels permitted by the quota. Second, because the quota does not discriminate between various potential sources of supply, some foreign producers may lose markets that had traditionally been theirs. This could lead to considerable friction between countries. Finally, because unallocated global quotas can lead to extraordinary profits for those lucky enough to be able to import the product into the country, government officials may want to ensure that certain groups (perhaps including themselves) become the beneficiaries of these policies. Thus, it has become common for quotas to be allocated on the basis of licenses.

Quota licenses provide the bearer with the right to import into the country a specific amount of the product during a specific period of time. Depending upon the quota scheme in force, licenses may be sold or given away. The recipients may be domestic or foreign. As we shall see, the welfare impact of this quota system depends in part on who gets the licenses and how much was paid to obtain them.

In order to understand better the economic effects of a quota, consider Figure 7.1. There we show the market for good *M*—say motorcycles. The curve labeled S_M is the supply curve of domestic producers. The curve labeled D_M is the domestic demand curve. The world price is assumed to be $1,000. Under free trade, residents of this country would consume 50,000 motorcycles; 10,000 of these would be produced locally, and 40,000 would be imported.

Suppose that the government imposes a quota that limits imports to 20,000 units. Because of the reduction in imports, motorcycle prices will start to rise, and this will encourage local producers to expand their output levels. These market forces will bring about a new equilibrium. Where will the equilibrium be located? Consider the diagram. Prices must continue to rise until desired imports fall to the quota level of 20,000 units. In terms of the picture, the price must rise until the difference between domestic demand and supply equals 20,000. As drawn, this occurs at a price of $1,500. At this price, 44,000 units will be purchased; 20,000 of these will be imported, and the remaining 24,000 will be produced locally. Thus, just as with a tariff, quotas serve to limit trade and raise prices. In fact, as drawn in

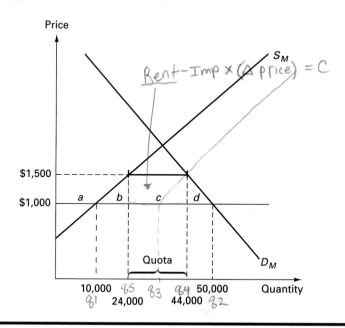

FIGURE 7.1 *Welfare effects of a quota.*

Price

Rent-Imp x (Δ price) = C

$1,500

$1,000   a   b   c   d

Quota

S_M

D_M

10,000   *q5*   *q3*   *q4*   50,000   Quantity
q1   24,000   *q3*   44,000 *q2*

---

the diagram, a quota of 20,000 units appears to be qualitatively identical with a tariff of $500. How apt is this comparison? It is to this question that we now turn.

THE WELFARE EFFECTS OF QUOTAS

One issue we were concerned with in our study of tariffs was the welfare consequences of these policies. What are the welfare effects of a quota? Consider again Figure 7.1. The imposition of the quota raises the domestic price and therefore lowers consumer surplus. Consumers lose the amount $(a + b + c + d)$. Of this lost consumer surplus, a represents higher profits (producer surplus) that accrue to domestic firms. These come about (as with the case of tariffs) because import barriers have lowered the amount of foreign competition faced by domestic firms. Thus, domestic firms are able to raise their prices above the free-trade price without fear of losing their customers to foreign suppliers. The triangles $(b + d)$ represent the deadweight costs of the quota and correspond exactly to the deadweight costs of an equivalent tariff (i.e., a tariff of $500). Consider area c. What does this area represent?

Area c is the value of **quota rents**. Quota rents are profits that accrue to whoever has the right to bring imports into the country and sell these goods in the protected

Quota rents
Profits that come about because a quota has artificially raised the price of imported products.

market. To see this more clearly, consider the rectangle that defines area *c*. The base of that rectangle represents the amount of imports allowed into the country (i.e., 20,000 units). The height of the rectangle is the difference between the world price ($1,000) and the domestic price ($1,500). The difference between these two prices, of course, reflects the per unit (additional) profit that can be earned by whoever has the right to sell the imported product.

This brings us back to the issue of who gets the licenses and how much is spent in obtaining them. We can distinguish between several cases. Suppose the licenses are auctioned by the government. If there is competitive bidding for all licenses, we would expect that the government should be able to collect almost all of area *c*. In this case, area *c* can be thought of as government revenue. Treating $c as an increase in government revenue (assuming that the government returns this revenue to the economy) leads to a straightforward calculation of the economic costs of the quota. In particular, the quota causes a redistribution of income from consumers to domestic producers ($a) and the government ($c). The remaining loss of consumer surplus represents the net deadweight cost to the economy, $(b + d)$. This information is summarized in Table 7.1.

Thus, if we continue to assume that $1 of government revenue has equal welfare weight to $1 of producer or consumer surplus, then, when the government auctions quota licenses, the welfare cost to the economy is identical with the cost imposed by an import tariff that raises the price by the same amount. While tariffs and quotas appear to be identical in this instance, it is necessary to study other scenarios. Surprisingly, it is seldom the case that governments auction import licenses. In particular, only Australia and New Zealand have quota auction programs in place today.*

How big is area *c*? The answer varies according to the country that imposes the quota, the products protected, and the degree of protection. In the mid-1980s, two separate studies provided estimates of how much revenue the United States might raise were it to auction quota rights to the quotas in place at the time. These studies concluded that the U.S. government was forgoing between $3.7 billion and $6.8 bil-

TABLE 7.1	*Welfare Effects of a Quota When a Government Auctions Licenses*			
Change in consumer surplus	−$a	−$b	−$c	−$d
Change in producer surplus	$a			
Change in government revenue			$c	
NET WELFARE COST		−$b		−$d

*For more on the Australian and New Zealand experience with quota auctions, see Fred Bergsten, Kimberly Elliott, Jeffrey Schott, and Wendy Takacs, *Auction Quotas and United States Trade Policy* (Washington, D.C.: Institute for International Economics, 1987).

lion annually in potential revenues by not holding auctions. The bulk of these amounts involved quota licenses on steel and on textiles and apparel.*

When governments give away quota rights, the welfare effects of quota protection depend crucially on who receives the licenses. For instance, when licenses are given to *domestic* producers or importers, the effects are qualitatively identical with those of auctions. The only difference between this situation and auctioning is that in this instance area c becomes part of domestic producer surplus. That is, profits to domestic firms rise by $\$(a + c)$, while government revenue remains unchanged.

A case where quota rents were given to local producers occurred in the United States in the 1960s. The government imposed a quota on imported oil. The purpose of the quota was to drive oil prices up (!) inside the country to increase the competitiveness of U.S. oil fields. Quota rights were given to the U.S. oil industry. The quotas were so restrictive that the domestic industry was able to buy oil in the world market at a price of $1.85 per barrel (delivered from the Persian Gulf to the United States) and sell it inside the United States for $3.10, a 67 percent markup. In 1966, the quota rents accruing to oil importers amounted to $620 million (about $3.1 billion in 1999 dollars).

Now, let us consider the case in which the government gives the quota licenses to foreigners. A classic example of this type of policy is a **voluntary export restraint (VER)** agreement negotiated with a foreign supplier. Under such an agreement, a foreign government restricts the exports of its industries to the importing country. In return, these foreign industries are able to raise their prices, thus earning the quota rents on top of their normal profits. What are the welfare costs of a VER? Again, consumers lose $\$(a + b + c + d)$. Of this amount, $\$a$ is transferred to domestic producers; $\$(b + d)$ again is deadweight loss for the economy; and $\$c$ is a transfer of income from domestic residents to foreign exporters. Hence, it too is a cost to the economy. In sum, with a VER, the economy loses $\$(b + c + d)$. This information is summarized in Table 7.2.

Voluntary export restraint (VER) An agreement reached between importing and exporting countries whereby the exporters agree to limit the amount they export.

TABLE 7.2	*Welfare Effects of a Voluntary Export Restraint*			
Change in consumer surplus	−$a	−$b	−$c	−$d
Change in producer surplus	−$a			
Change in government revenue			0	
NET WELFARE COST[1]		−$b	−$c	−$d

[1] −($b + $d) are the deadweight costs of the VER. − $c represents the transfer of income to foreigners.

---

*See Bergsten et al., *Auction Quotas*; and Congressional Budget Office, "Revenue Estimates for Auctioning Existing Import Quotas" (memorandum, February 1987). Neither of these studies has been updated, so it is unclear what lost auction revenue would be today. In addition, the United States has changed several of its trade restrictions. In particular, quotas on U.S. steel imports are no longer in place.

Thus, we see that if the government negotiates a VER with a foreign government, the welfare costs rise above the costs of a tariff. They also rise above the costs of an auctioned quota system or a system in which quota rights are given to domestic residents. This is why it is important to know how a quota is administered.

THE EQUIVALENCE OR NONEQUIVALENCE OF TARIFFS AND QUOTAS

So far, we have shown that tariffs and quotas are similar in their effects on prices, output, and imports. We have also shown that there is at least one major difference between these two policies—the interpretation of area c and who receives these funds. In fact, the distribution of area c is but one of several differences between quotas and tariffs. In this section we discuss these differences. One reason for knowing that these differences exist, of course, is to understand better why governments might choose one type of policy over another.*

One principal difference between tariffs and quotas concerns the effects of these alternative policies on the behavior of the protected industry. Suppose, for instance, that the domestic industry is a monopoly. With a tariff, the domestic monopolist can charge no more than the world price plus the tariff. Because the monopolist faces potential competition from suppliers in other countries, he or she is unable to exploit his or her domestic monopoly power.

This is not the case with quota protection. Under a quota, the monopolist knows that his or her competition is limited to a specific amount of imports. Thus, he or she merely subtracts the amount of quota-restrained imports from overall market demand and is then free to exercise his or her market power over the remaining part of the domestic market. We now can state a general result: If the domestic firm has market power in its own market, then it will charge higher prices and produce less under quota protection than under tariff protection.

Tariff and quota protection will also be different if market forces change over time. Suppose that domestic demand increases. With tariff protection, the internal price remains the world price plus the tariff. The increased demand will be met by a rise in imports. With quota protection, no new imports are allowed in. The only way the market can reach equilibrium is for the price to adjust. And with higher domestic prices come greater deadweight costs.

---

*There is a considerable body of literature on the equivalence or nonequivalence of different forms of commercial policy. See, for instance, Hirofumi Shibata, "Note on the Equivalence of Tariffs and Quotas," *American Economic Review* (1968); Jagdish Bhagwati, "More on the Equivalence of Tariffs and Quotas," *American Economic Review* (1968); Carlos Rodriguez, "The Non-Equivalence of Tariffs and Quotas under Retaliation," *Journal of International Economics* (1974); Wendy Takacs, "The Nonequivalence of Tariffs, Import Quotas, and Voluntary Export Restraints," *Journal of International Economics* (1978); and Jose Lizondo, "A Note on the Nonequivalence of Import Barriers and Voluntary Export Restraints," *Journal of International Economics* (1984). A summary of research on quotas is found in James E. Anderson, *The Relative Inefficiency of Quotas* (Cambridge, Mass.: MIT Press, 1988).

A third difference between the two forms of protection has to do with administrative difficulties. We have already shown that the welfare impact of a quota depends in part on which of many interested parties obtains the quota rights and whether or not the rights are sold by the government. How is this decision made? There is no clear-cut answer as to why so few governments auction off quota rights. Some economists argue that it is because politicians don't want consumers to know what individuals would be willing to pay for the quota rights. Such information would provide a clear signal of the consumer cost of the quota. Others have argued that in the cases where the goal of protection is temporary shelter from foreign competition, governments would later be reluctant to drop quotas because of the loss in revenues. Less cynical commentators note that in many cases the value of quota rents may be relatively low, especially when compared with the bureaucratic costs of holding an auction.*

Thus, in most cases the issue boils down to a question of how to give away the quota rights. A solution that is often chosen is to give away rights based on traditional market shares.† The problem with this approach is that it freezes the market based on historical relationships. Such divisions do not allow consumers to alter their consumption choices with changes in tastes or on efficiency grounds. There is no legal mechanism to ensure that if, for instance, a country becomes relatively more efficient in producing a good, it can obtain a higher market share. With a tariff, on the other hand, importers are free to search the world market for the best goods. Market shares will change to reflect relative changes in efficiency.

The final problem is that relative to tariffs, quota protection encourages much more graft and corruption. Because of the arbitrary nature of the disposition of quota rights, there is an incentive to bribe authorities to make particular decisions. Moreover, even when authorities are known to resist bribes, potential beneficiaries will devote considerable sums of money on legal methods of persuasion, such as campaign contributions and expensive dinners or weekend vacations with lobbyists. The chase for these valuable quota rents leads, then, to an expenditure of resources. This expenditure brings about no new production of goods generally valued for consumption purposes, and it is an expenditure, therefore, that is considered by many to be economic waste.‡

---

*There may also be considerable bureaucratic resistance to the auctioning of quota licenses. One objection sometimes cited by officials in Washington is that no foreign country would want to be the first to be told that the quota rents it would have been given in previous years are now being auctioned to the highest bidders. Obviously, so long as arguments such as this are invoked and hold sway, quota licenses will never be sold.

†This is the case where either domestic importers or foreign producers are given the rights.

‡There is now a substantial body of literature concerned with the economic effects of rent seeking by potential beneficiaries of government policies. Some important contributions to this literature include Jagdish Bhagwati and T.N. Srinivasan, "Revenue Seeking: A Generalization of the Theory of Tariffs," *Journal of Political Economy* (1980); William Brock and Stephen Magee, "The Economics of Special Interest Politics: The Case of the Tariff," *American Economic Review* (1978); Anne Krueger, "The Political Economy of the Rent Seeking Society," *American Economic Review* (1974); and Gordon Tullock, "The Welfare Cost of Tariffs, Monopolies, and Theft," *Western Economic Journal* (1967).

OTHER NONTARIFF BARRIERS

As we noted in the introduction to this chapter, there are many types of nontariff barriers to trade. In this section, we discuss several examples.

Export Subsidies*

Export subsidy
A payment by a government to an industry that leads to an expansion of exports by that industry.

An **export subsidy** is a direct (or indirect) payment from a country's government to one or more of its export industries. This payment is usually related to the level of exports, and thereby enables exporters to charge a price that is lower than would otherwise be charged. With lower prices, exporters are then able to gain a larger share of the world market. As was the case with quotas, export subsidies on manufactured goods are outlawed by the WTO. Foreign export subsidies are also against U.S. law.[†] The WTO does permit export subsidies on primary (i.e., nonmanufactured) products, and the United States is one of many countries that subsidizes the export of at least some of its agricultural products.

The economic effects of export subsidies are symmetrical with those of import tariffs. Just as tariffs cause production to expand in the import-competing sector, export subsidies lead to a greater level of output of exportables than would otherwise occur. Resources are drawn from import-competing sectors. Economic waste is created because the cost of increasing output to expand export sales exceeds the revenue earned from these sales in the international market.[‡] Furthermore, because export subsidies encourage the diversion of sales away from a country's internal market to the world market, internal prices of exportables rise. Consumers lose in another way as well. Specifically, they become liable for the additional taxes that are required to finance the export subsidy.

Export subsidies take on many forms in the real world. These include tax rebates, subsidized loans to foreign purchasers, insurance guarantees, government funding for research and development, guarantees against losses, and direct grants or subsidized loans. As just noted, both international law and the laws of countries such as the United States proscribe export subsidies. Under both sets of laws, the legal means for dealing with export subsidies is to impose a tariff on the subsidized exports, known as a **countervailing duty**, in order to offset the subsidy and raise the price of the product to the presubsidy price.

Countervailing duty
A tariff imposed by an importing country designed to offset artificially low prices charged by exporters.

The fact that tariff protection is the chosen means to offset foreign subsidies provides domestic industry with an incentive to allege the existence of foreign subsidization. Such allegations are also often aimed at practices that may have only very

---

*For a detailed study on subsidies, see Gary Hufbauer and Shelton Erb, *Subsidies in International Trade* (Washington, D.C.: Institute for International Economics, 1984). For analyses of specific subsidy policies of the United States and other developed countries, see Jack Mutti and Harry Grubert, "The Domestic International Sales Corporation and Its Effects," and Heywood Fleisig and Catharine Hill, "The Benefits and Costs of Official Export Credit Programs," in *The Structure and Evolution of Recent U.S. Trade Policy,* ed. Robert Baldwin and Anne Krueger (Chicago: University of Chicago Press, 1984).
[†]In the next chapter, we discuss in more detail U.S. laws related to foreign export subsidies.
[‡]If this were not the case, exporters would produce more even without the subsidy.

indirect links to exports. Hence, governments are forced to decide whether various foreign government policies constitute export subsidies. Not surprisingly, there is often considerable ambiguity in relation to the issue. For instance, do defense contracts from the U.S. government to domestic aircraft manufacturers, such as Boeing, constitute export subsidies? Some European countries charge that these expenditures are unfair subsidies because, for instance, knowledge gained from research on aircraft design for the military can be used to design new commercial aircraft.

Government Procurement Policies

When governments (federal, state, and local) purchase goods and services, they are often constrained by legislative mandate to purchase from domestic producers. In the United States, for instance, there are "**Buy American**" provisions at all levels of government.

"Buy American" acts Laws that direct purchasing agents of U.S. federal, state, and local governments to purchase American products unless comparable foreign goods are substantially cheaper.

The federal "Buy American" act was first passed in 1933. It requires that U.S. government agencies (except the Department of Defense) purchase domestically produced goods and services unless the domestic price is *more than* 12 percent greater than the foreign price.* By law, the Department of Defense uses a 50 percent rule except on certain military purchases from NATO countries. The obvious implication of the "Buy American" act is that domestic firms can raise prices charged to the government as if there were a tariff of as much as 50 percent on competing imported items. The effect of this type of policy is to raise the cost to government of providing public services, transferring income in the process from taxpayers to domestic producers.

Other countries have policies with similar effects. For instance, for many years the United Kingdom has had a "Buy Britain" policy. Until recently, the government of Japan refused to consider the purchase of U.S. supercomputers, choosing to lease products made by Japanese producers. Also, through the way that contracts for construction projects, such as new airports, are awarded in Japan, it has been able to limit the amount of foreign participation in these projects. In the past, the French government guaranteed that a certain percentage of its purchases of electronics products come from French sources.

In 1979 rules governing international trade were amended to incorporate restrictions on local preferences by government purchasing agents. Basically, it was agreed that countries that signed a special code would grant each other equal access to government contracts. In 1994, as part of the Uruguay Round agreement, the government procurement code was expanded to include government purchases of both goods and services, to cover central government, subcentral governments, and government-owned enterprises, and to follow improvements in procurement procedures. Signatories to this agreement, known as the WTO Agreement on Government Procurement, include the United States, Canada, the EU, Japan, and the Republic of Korea. Each of these countries negotiated the exclusion of certain procurement from

---

*In some cases, the maximum differential is only 6 percent.

obligations imposed by the code. U.S. agencies excluded from the agreement include the Department of Transportation, the Department of Energy, the Tennessee Valley Authority, the Corps of Engineers of the Department of Defense, the Bureau of Reclamation, and the Data and Telecommunications Services of the General Services Administration.

Other federal entities not covered by the code include the U.S. Postal Service, Comsat, Amtrak, and Conrail. In addition, the code does not supersede special programs reserving certain purchases to products of small or minority-owned businesses or to blind-made goods, or to the requirements contained in Department of Defense appropriations acts that certain products (i.e., textiles, clothing, shoes, food, stainless steel flatware, certain specialty metals, buses, hand tools, ships, and major ship components) be purchased only from domestic sources.

Health and Safety Standards

Governments often regulate the production and distribution of products deemed to be hazardous to the health and safety of their citizens. Sometimes, however, such standards are established merely to provide a mechanism for protecting domestic producers from foreign competition. Many such examples exist. For instance, in the mid-1980s, the government of Japan announced that foreign-made skis would not be allowed into Japan because they were unsafe. The reason cited for this regulation was a claim (no doubt encouraged by local manufacturers) that Japanese snow differed from snow in Europe or in the United States. After protest from foreign governments, the ban was rescinded.

The EU also uses such practices to limit trade. In 1989 it imposed an embargo on beef imports containing growth hormones. This ban has had a considerable effect on U.S. beef exports, since most cattle raised in the United States are treated with these (USDA-approved) hormones. The U.S. government has taken the position that the ban represents an illegal trade measure, since there is no conclusive proof that the growth hormone has had any harmful effects on humans. In 1996, the United States initiated formal WTO dispute settlement proceedings with the EU. In 1997, an independent WTO panel ruled in favor of the U.S. position that the EU ban violated obligations made by the EU, since the ban was not based on scientific risk assessment. In 1998, an appellate panel in the WTO reaffirmed the earlier decision. In 1999, the WTO authorized the United States to impose retaliatory, prohibitive tariffs on $117 million of European agricultural exports. As of early 2000, those tariffs were still in place.

In another squabble over health standards, in 1996 the EU introduced new import controls on animals and animal products that threatened to disrupt U.S. exports to the EU. At the heart of this ban was a desire to standardize veterinary inspection practices across the countries of the EU. In turn, these standardized procedures differed from U.S. practice. The two sides to the dispute entered into negotiations in early 1997 and shortly after reached an agreement on a framework for recognizing each other's veterinary inspection systems as equivalent.

In his book on nontariff barriers (see the first footnote in this chapter), Robert Baldwin describes differences in regulations in several European countries in the late 1960s covering the safety of tractors.* The maximum allowable tractor speed for tractors sold in France was 17 miles per hour (mph). In Germany it was 13 mph, and in the Netherlands it was 10 mph. Thus, tractors produced in one country for export to another had to be modified before they could be exported, thereby raising costs and harming competitiveness.

As just noted, the imposition of health and safety standards by national governments is a legitimate form of government behavior. Such standards aim to guarantee that lives are not jeopardized unduly by exposure to the potentially adverse effects associated with certain products. However, as the preceding examples indicate, these codes provide a strong incentive to local producers for insisting that foreign products be made to conform to local standards or that they be restricted from the local markets even in situations where the health or safety of the local populace is not threatened. In either event, the result is for prices to rise and for local producers to claim a larger share of the market.

Failure to Protect Intellectual Property Rights

Intellectual property is defined as the innovative or creative ideas of inventors, artists, or authors. Patent, copyright, and trademark laws exist to provide incentives to create intellectual properties by ensuring that the owners of the intellectual properties maintain exclusive control over these ideas, at least for a certain period of time. For instance, patents allow inventors the opportunity to recover their investment and the costs of creating and marketing inventions. Copyrights give authors control over the reproduction, dissemination, and public performance of their works. Trademarks assure consumers about product characteristics, such as quality.

Different countries provide different levels of intellectual property protection, and this can have significant effects on international trade. For instance, in the mid-1990s the U.S. computer software industry estimated that 49 out of 50 software programs used in China were pirated and calculated its lost export sales to China to stand at $500 million annually. U.S. government measures aimed at Chinese copyright piracy in 1996 almost led to a trade war between the two countries. For more on this dispute, see Item 7.1. In addition, U.S. pharmaceutical companies argue that lax copyright enforcement of their drug patents by Argentina has allowed Argentine firms to make cheap generic substitutes for both home and export markets. The U.S. government maintains that U.S. firms have lost $500 million annually in pharmaceutical exports because of Argentine policy.

Similarly, a growing problem in international trade is trade in counterfeit goods. Such goods are sold in international markets with fraudulent (or counterfeit) trademarks. Firms with valid trademarks lose more than sales due to counterfeit goods.

---

*These standards will be made uniform as a result of the EC 1992 initiative. For more on EC 1992, see Chapter 9.

ITEM 7.1   U.S.–Chinese Disputes Over Intellectual Property Rights

In June 1994 under the provisions of a U.S. trade statute called "Special 301," the United States government designated China as a priority country for failing to provide adequate and effective intellectual property protection and market access to persons that rely on intellectual property protection.* This announcement set in motion a study of the claims by representatives of U.S. software and entertainment companies who were complaining that they were losing significant export sales in Asia due to the failure of the Chinese government to protect their intellectual property rights. In particular it was alleged that Chinese factories were producing pirated copies of music and film compact disks (CDs), laser disks, and CD-ROMs, selling these products throughout China, and exporting some to other markets via Hong Kong. In February 1995, the U.S. government concluded that there was merit to the industry claims and announced that it was prepared to impose punitive tariffs on Chinese goods should the Chinese government fail to correct the problem. Negotiations between the two sides produced an agreement several weeks later, with the Chinese government promising to take action to stop the production of pirated CDs and the U.S. government rescinding its threat of tariffs.

However, despite the agreement, the Chinese government was slow to make changes to its policies, and U.S. firms continued to see their products pirated. In the spring of 1996, the Clinton administration accused the Chinese of shirking the agreement. The U.S. government determined that in the previous year, U.S. firms had lost $2.3 billion in sales due to pirated goods made in China. The administration announced a series of 100 percent tariffs to be imposed on $2 billion of imports of Chinese textiles and other goods. China announced that it would retaliate against U.S. tariffs with prohibitive tariffs of its own on U.S. goods. After five days of talks, the two sides reached a new agreement. As part of this pact, China immediately shut down 15 factories found to be producing counterfeit compact disks, laser disks, and CD-ROMs. It also promised to assign its Ministry of Public Security to help fight piracy, concentrating on production in southern provinces of China, where much of the production was taking place. Finally, it announced that it would increase cooperation between Chinese customs officials and U.S. counterparts to prevent the export of pirated goods. As a result of this agreement, both sides announced their intention to rescind their threats of higher tariffs.

As of early 2000, intellectual property protection in China appears to have greatly improved. According to Chinese government statistics, China has seized some 35 million illegal audiovisual products, and it has shut down or fined 74 assembly operations for pirated video CDs and seized over 20 million smuggled video CDs. Training on intellectual property protection has been a key part of building the necessary infrastructure for continuing enforcement efforts. More than 3,000 judges have received training on the intellectual property rights law, and the subject is now taught at major universities. Nonetheless, end-user piracy of computer software, including within Chinese government ministries, costs U.S. companies millions of dollars per year.

Fraudulent copies are often substandard and perform poorly. Legitimate manufacturers may be blamed for this performance and thereby lose their reputation and further sales of these and other products.

Because of the problems that inadequate intellectual property rights protection can cause, countries such as the United States pushed for and achieved expanded protection as part of the Uruguay Round of trade talks. The agreement on this issue, known as the Trade Related Intellectual Property Rights (TRIPs) agreement, covers patents, trademarks, copyrights, and industrial designs. It provides for minimal standards of protection in all member countries of the WTO, the organization that enforces the agreement. In some areas, such as copyrights, the agreement applies the principles of long-standing international agreements. In other areas, such as patent protection, the agreement provides for higher standards than were previously required.

HOW IMPORTANT ARE NONTARIFF BARRIERS?

The examples just described serve to illustrate the variety of nontariff barriers that exist today. Many other forms exist. These include conditional import authorization, whereby quota licenses are granted conditional on the importer undertaking commitments in other areas, such as reexport; taxes, known as variable levies, that adjust so that the import price equalizes to a decreed internal price; price floors on foreign products; domestic content laws that require minimum percentages of the value of certain products to be of domestic origin; deliberate undervaluation of currencies to discourage imports and encourage exports; and laws that grant special treatment (perhaps on cultural grounds) to local producers.*

All of these provisions are found in varying degrees around the world today. The effect is to distort trade flows, sometimes severely. Economists at the World Bank have been studying the extent and impact of NTBs for some time.[†] Most of their efforts have been concentrated on the import barriers imposed by major industrialized countries (including the United States, the nations of the EU, Switzerland, and Japan). Some of the main results from this research are summarized in Table 7.3.

In the first part of the table, numbers are presented to illustrate the extent and growth of industrialized countries' NTBs on imports by product category. The numbers in the table represent ratios of trade in products protected by NTBs to total imports of those products for the years 1966 and 1986. So, for instance, according to the first number in the table, 61 percent of the all-foods imports of the EU in the 1966 study were affected by NTBs. The table shows several important aspects of

---

*See Laird and Yeats, *Quantitative Methods,* Appendix 4, for a glossary that provides more details on the various types of NTBs.

[†]Several recent studies by these economists include J. Nogues, A. Olechowski, and L. Winters, "The Extent of Nontariff Barriers to Industrial Countries' Imports," *World Bank Economic Review,* September 1986; Laird and Yeats, *Quantitative Methods*; and Sam Laird and Alexander Yeats, "Trends in Nontariff Barriers of Developed Countries, 1966–1986," *Weltwirtschaftliches Archiv* (1990).

TABLE 7.3   *The Extent of Nontariff Barriers in Industrialized Countries*

IMPORTS BY MAJOR PRODUCT GROUP, 1966, 1986 (PERCENTAGE OF OWN IMPORTS AFFECTED BY NTBs)

Importing Country	All Foods		Agricultural Raw Materials		Fuels		Ores and Metals		Manufactures		All Goods	
	1966	1986	1966	1986	1966	1986	1966	1986	1966	1986	1966	1986
EU	61	100	4	28	11	37	0	40	10	56	21	33
Belgium	68	99	1	21	96	90	0	28	21	69	31	74
Denmark	35	100	2	7	9	9	0	37	1	46	5	37
France	56	99	4	37	22	100	0	58	6	61	16	82
Germany	71	92	9	20	7	0	0	47	12	59	24	41
Italy	72	99	0	53	0	0	1	36	9	66	27	30
Netherlands	55	98	0	21	0	93	0	71	8	58	31	79
United Kingdom	2	96	0	0	0	0	0	16	9	44	16	38
Finland	n.a.	70	0	55	67	95	4	3	8	28	15	51
Japan	73	99	0	59	33	28	2	31	48	50	31	43
Norway	43	95	3	16	0	0	0	15	38	22	31	23
Switzerland	53	90	4	55	0	99	0	9	15	39	19	50
United States	32	74	14	45	92	0	0	16	39	71	36	45
All countries	56	92	4	41	27	27	1	29	19	58	25	48

SOURCE: Constructed from data in Table 4 of Sam Laird and Alexander Yeats, "Trends in Nontariff Barriers of Developed Countries, 1966–1986," *Weltwirtschaftliches Archiv* (1990).

TYPE OF NTB MEASURE USED BY INDUSTRIALIZED COUNTRIES, 1986 (PERCENTAGE OF IMPORTS AFFECTED BY NTBs BY NTB TYPE)

Exporting Countries	Tariff Types	Dumping Duties	Decreed Prices	Licensing Regulations	Quotas	VERs	MFA Types
Developed countries	3.6	1.4	1.1	3.7	4.8	7.4	0.1
Developing countries	5.4	1.2	1.6	5.3	5.1	1.5	9.6

SOURCE: Constructed from data in Tables 4.6 and 4.7 of Sam Laird and Alexander Yeats, *Quantitative Methods for Trade-Barrier Analysis* (New York: New York University Press, 1990).

NTB protection. First, the importance of NTB protection has grown dramatically. In 1966, 25 percent of the imports of the industrialized countries were affected by NTB protection. By 1986, the proportion of trade affected by NTBs had grown to 48 percent. The amount (in dollars) of trade corresponding to this percentage was $355 billion. As the table shows, the greatest incidence of NTB protection is found in trade in manufactures, agricultural raw materials, and especially food.

There is a wide variance in the use of NTBs across countries. France places the greatest reliance on NTBs; more than 80 percent of its trade is affected by these measures. NTBs are also prevalent in Belgium and the Netherlands. The United States ranks slightly below the overall levels of all the countries in the table, with 45 percent of its trade affected by NTBs. It has also experienced somewhat slower growth in the use of these measures than many of the other industrialized countries.

For several reasons, many of the numbers in both parts of the table understate the degree of protection. This is due in part to the fact that many forms of NTBs, including government procurement policies, health and safety standards, and domestic subsidies policies, are not included in the analysis. Furthermore, protection is understated because the percentages reflect the amount of restricted goods that are *still* imported even though the protection is in place. The more restrictive are the barriers, the smaller is this amount.

The second part of the table indicates the types of nontariff measures utilized by the industrialized countries. These measures are identified by several categories: *tariff types* include barriers such as tariff-quotas (whereby imports above a certain quantity face higher tariffs than imports within the quota amount), seasonal tariffs, and variable levies; *dumping duties* include both antidumping and antisubsidy countervailing duties; *decreed prices* represent minimum price restrictions imposed on imported goods; *licensing regulations* are arrangements whereby importers must acquire special licenses before goods are allowed into a country; *quotas*; *VERs*; and *MFA types,* which include various quantity restrictions on textile trade, including the multifiber arrangement.

As this part of the table shows, the industrialized countries rely most heavily on quotas and VERs to limit trade among themselves. More than 12 percent of industrialized-country imports from developed countries are affected by one of these two measures. About another 7 percent of imports from these countries is affected by tariff-type NTB protection and restrictive licensing regulations. In contrast, the single most important NTB used by developed countries on their imports from developing countries are restrictions on textile trade. This amounts to almost 10 percent of developed-country imports from the developing world. Quotas, tariff-type measures, and licensing regulations each affect about an additional 5 percent of imports.

ARGUMENTS FOR PROTECTION

We have now concluded our discussion on various forms of protection available to countries. A clear implication of this discussion has been that under many circumstances, protection is harmful to national welfare. If this is so, why do governments impose protection? Putting the question in another way, are there circumstances where protection is a valid means to a particular policy goal? As we demonstrate in the following sections, the answer to the last question is yes. In particular, protection is an appropriate policy to use to achieve certain economic and noneconomic outcomes. However, as we also demonstrate, protection is never the economically most efficient policy to achieve the objectives of the government.

In the next section, we discuss justifications for protection that have been put forward from time to time but that have no logical validity whatsoever.* This discussion

---

*In his book *The Theory of International Trade* (New York: Augustus M. Kelly Publishers, 1968), Haberler differentiates between valid and invalid arguments for protection, referring to the latter as arguments that do not merit serious discussion. For more detail, see Chapter 17 in Haberler's book.

is important because even though these arguments have little logical merit, they appear to have considerable popular support both in government and with the general public. After we have outlined these justifications, we turn to arguments that have greater validity. With these latter arguments we describe not only the role that protection plays in achieving the government objective but also alternative policies that could be used at lower cost to society.

Invalid Arguments*

Patriotism   Sometimes it is said that it is patriotic to erect barriers to foreign competition. Good examples of this point are the bumper stickers that read "Be American Buy American" and the advertising on television that encourages a buyer to look for the "Made in the U.S.A." label found on clothing. Such efforts are legitimate forms of persuasion in the marketplace. However, the appeal to patriotism is somewhat misplaced. This is especially true if one of the reasons why domestic consumers switch to the consumption of locally produced goods is that protection has raised the price of foreign goods. After all, as we have seen, in many circumstances when a country imposes protection, its national well-being falls. True patriots, it would seem, should oppose policies that lower national welfare.

Employment   One of the most often cited arguments for protection is that it creates, or at least preserves, jobs. The naive basis for this claim is that because output expands in the protected sector, employment must rise throughout the country. In general, this argument is false. This is because it ignores effects in other markets (i.e., it ignores general equilibrium effects).

It is certainly true that protection does lead to an expansion in the protected industry. However, where will the resources come from that are required for this expansion? Clearly, the output of other industries must fall. Or, even if there are unemployed resources available for work in the protected sector, the resulting decrease in imports should be expected to lead to a decline in employment in export industries. As Keynes once noted, "Imports are receipts and exports are payments. How as a nation can we expect to better ourselves by diminishing our receipts? Is there anything a tariff can do, which an earthquake could not do better?"[†] In other words, it is more likely that protection serves only to redistribute jobs rather than to create them.

Fallacy of Composition   Sometimes protection is justified on the grounds that because it is good for a protected industry, it must be good for all industries. The length to which such arguments can be taken was illustrated in a brilliant satire composed by Frederic Bastiat in 1854, entitled "The Petition of the Candlemakers":

---

*The examples that follow are not the full set of invalid arguments for protection. Rather, they represent some of the more popular of the current but invalid justifications for protection.
[†]This quotation is taken from Haberler, 246.

We are subjected to the intolerable competition of a foreign rival whose superior facilities for producing light enable him to flood the French market at so low a price as to take away all our customers the moment he appears, suddenly reducing an important branch of French industry to stagnation. This rival is the sun.

We request a law to shut up all windows, dormers, skylights, openings, holes, chinks, and fissures through which the sunlight penetrates. Our industry provides such valuable manufactures that our country cannot, without ingratitude, leave us now to struggle unprotected through so unequal a contest.

Do not repulse our petition as a satire without hearing our reasons. Your protection of artificial lighting will benefit every industry in France. If you give us the monopoly of furnishing light, we will buy large quantities of tallow, coal, oil, resin, wax, alcohol, silver, iron, bronze, and crystal. Greater tallow consumption will stimulate cattle and sheep raising. Meat, wool, leather, and above all manure, that basis of agricultural riches, will become more abundant. . . . In short, granting our petition will greatly develop every branch of agriculture. Navigation will equally profit. Thousands of vessels will soon be employed in whaling. . . . When we and our many suppliers have become rich, our great consumption will contribute to the prosperity of workers in every industry. . . . There is perhaps not one Frenchman, from the rich stockholder to the poorest matchmaker, who is not interested in the success of our petition.*

Fair Play for Domestic Industry   The allegation is often raised that foreign producers do not play fair. Foreign workers sometimes earn lower wages. Foreign firms might not be subject to the same laws regarding pollution control, worker safety, or the like. Whatever the difference, the cry from domestic industry is for "a level playing field" on which to compete. This argument has an appealing sound to it; but like the justifications just presented, it is totally invalid. Commerce (national or international) is not a game; it is business. And, as such, it can be ruthless. The goal of every firm is to outperform its rivals. A surefire way to achieve this end is to produce a better product at a lower price. International trade enhances this competitive process, and thereby benefits the consumer. Appeals for protection on the grounds that "fairness" requires that competition be limited are themselves totally unfair. They would deny domestic consumers the right to choose the widest possible selection of goods in the marketplace.

Preservation of the Home Market   Sometimes it is said that buying from ourselves is better than buying from foreigners because we keep the goods and we keep the money. On the other hand, when we import from abroad, we get the goods but the money flows out of the country.[†] If only this were true! Imagine a world where we could buy all our goods from various countries around the world, with each of

---

*This quotation is taken from Leland Yeager and David Tuerck, *Foreign Trade and U.S. Policy* (New York: Praeger Publishers, 1976), 142–43.
[†]This argument has been falsely attributed to Abraham Lincoln.

these countries wanting only pieces of paper money in return. We would never have to work—except for a few moments every now and then at the printing presses. In fact, this is not the way the world works. Ultimately, goods must pay for goods. The money that flows out comes back to the country to pay for domestic exports, and we must work in order to produce these goods.

Valid Arguments*

Government Revenue   All governments need tax revenues to function. Tariffs produce government revenue. Also, for at least two reasons, tariffs may be especially attractive taxes for some governments to impose. First, there is the possibility that foreigners rather than domestic residents will actually be paying the taxes. In such circumstances domestic welfare rises. As we saw in Chapter 6, however, this would be true only for large countries that have world market power. A second reason why tariffs are a popular source of government revenue for some countries is that they are easy taxes to collect. This is because there are only so many natural ports of entry or exit in a country. All a government has to do to collect tariffs is position customs agents at these ports of entry.

Table 7.4 provides details on the fraction of government revenue accounted for by trade taxes or tariffs. As you can see, in most industrialized countries tariffs generate only a very small percentage of government revenue. The typical tax that is used instead is an income tax or a value-added tax. In developing countries, the story is much different. Tariffs can account for a substantial fraction, sometimes exceeding 50 percent, of the government revenue. This pattern probably reflects the difficulties perceived by the governments of developing countries of instituting and collecting an income or value-added tax.[†]

While in some respects tariffs are an easy tax to collect, using commercial policy for this purpose is wasteful and inefficient. A better policy would be a general income tax. Because they distort the relative prices of goods, tariffs create dead-weight costs. More production is concentrated in the relatively inefficient sectors of the economy. Income taxes tend to have less of this resource reallocation effect. Furthermore, if a goal of the government is to tax rich people at higher rates than poor, a progressive income tax can be easily devised. Finally, if the government is to be efficient in its tariff collection, it would have to know something about the demand and supply curves for every traded good. After all, the amount of tariff revenue (area c) depends upon these slopes.[‡] The information that would be required to maximize

---

[*]Again, as in the preceding section, the arguments that follow are only a limited set of valid arguments for protection. One argument that is excluded from this discussion is the optimal tariff argument. See Chapter 6 for more details.
[†]See Raymond Riezman and Joel Slemrod, "Tariffs and Collection Costs," *Weltwirtschaftliches Archiv* (1987), for a statistical analysis of this issue.
[‡]Convince yourself of this fact by drawing several demand-and-supply diagrams with curves of different slopes.

TABLE 7.4   *Tariffs and Trade Taxes as a Percentage of Government Revenue*

Country	Year	Percentage	Country	Year	Percentage	Country	Year	Percentage
Industrial Countries			Rwanda	1992	31.06p	Slovak Republic	1998	5.20p
United States	1998	1.09	Seychelles	1998	40.47	Turkey	1996	2.32
Canada	1995	1.85	Sierra Leone	1997	46.48	**Middle East**		
Australia	1998	2.56	South Africa	1998	.24p	Bahrain	1998	12.27
Japan	1993	1.24p	Tunisia	1996	25.57	Egypt	1997	11.62
New Zealand	1998	2.45	Zambia	1999	16.50	Iran, I.R. of	1998	9.56
Austria	1997	.34	Zimbabwe	1997	20.06	Israel	1998	.42
Belgium	1997	—	**Asia**			Jordan	1997	22.72
Denmark	1995	.05p	Bhutan	1998	1.59	Kuwait	1998	2.41
Finland	1997	—	China, P.R.:			Lebanon	1998	44.16
France	1997	—	Mainland	1997	7.39	Oman	1998	4.32
Germany	1998	. . .	Fiji	1996	21.37	Syrian Arab		
Greece	1997	.07	India	1998	22.27	Republic	1997	10.59
Iceland	1997	1.18	Indonesia	1998	4.34p	United Arab		
Ireland	1996	—	Korea	1997	6.30	Emirates	1998	—
Italy	1998	.17	Malaysia	1997	12.63	Yemen,		
Luxembourg	1997	—	Maldives	1998	31.65	Republic of	1999	10.27
Netherlands	1997	—	Mongolia	1998	.82	**Western Hemisphere**		
Norway	1997	.52	Myanmar	1997	9.89	Argentina	1997	7.57
Portugal	1997	—	Nepal	1998	27.00	Bahamas, The	1998	57.19
San Marino	1995	1.40	Pakistan	1999	12.21p	Belize	1996	29.32
Spain	1996	—	Papua New Guinea	1994	23.72	Bolivia	1998	6.71
Sweden	1998	.07	Philippines	1997	20.25	Brazil	1994	1.69
Switzerland	1997	1.04	Singapore	1997	.83	Chile	1998	7.92
United Kingdom	1998	—	Sri Lanka	1998	16.09p	Colombia	1998	9.76
			Thailand	1998	8.99	Costa Rica	1996	8.42
Developing Countries			Vietnam	1999	25.15	Dominican		
Africa						Republic	1997	35.79
Algeria	1996	15.49	**Europe**			Ecuador	1994	11.27p
Botswana	1996	12.36	Albania	1998	15.49	El Salvador	1997	11.64
Burkina Faso	1992	. . .	Azerbaijan	1999	8.53	Grenada	1995	16.77
Burundi	1997	15.63	Belarus	1998	7.36	Guatemala	1998	14.21
Cameroon	1995	27.58	Bulgaria	1998	6.00	Mexico	1997	3.87
Congo, Dem.			Croatia	1998	6.74	Netherlands		
Rep. of	1997	27.66	Cyprus	1997	5.57	Antilles	1995	39.16
Congo, Republic of	1997	8.79	Czech Republic	1998	2.29	Nicaragua	1994	20.94
Côte d'Ivoire	1998	50.71	Estonia	1998	—	Panama	1997	. . .
Ethiopia	1995	29.73	Georgia	1998	12.97	Paraguay	1993	12.46
Gambia, The	1993	42.04p	Hungary	1998	3.57	Peru	1998	9.19
Ghana	1993	26.76	Kazakhstan	1998	3.71	St. Kitts and Nevis	1994	36.91p
Guinea	1999	74.65f	Kyrgyz Republic	1998	6.24	St. Vincent &		
Kenya	1996	14.80	Latvia	1998	1.59	Grens.	1998	39.70p
Lesotho	1998	47.67p	Lithuania	1998	2.14	Trinidad and		
Madagascar	1996	53.32	Malta	1997	4.10	Tobago	1995	6.01
Mauritius	1998	30.29	Poland	1998	3.09	Uruguay	1998	3.69
Morocco	1995	14.44	Romania	1997	5.57	Venezuela	1998	11.38
Namibia	1993	30.49f	Russia	1995	8.74			

NOTE: The letter p indicates that data are in whole or in part provisional, preliminary, or projected.

SOURCE: International Montary Fund, *Government Finance Statistics Yearbook* (1999).

tariff proceeds is enormous and simply not available for any country in the world—including the United States.

Income Redistribution   Trade policy can be used to redistribute income from one sector of society to another. That is, it can be used to make some groups in society worse off and other groups better off. The most common example of income redistribution we have noted is from consumers to producers. That is, consumer surplus falls, while the profits of domestic firms rise. The desire on the part of policy makers to boost profits in certain domestic industries probably explains most protection patterns in industrialized countries and much of what we observe in developing countries.

Sometimes, as we have seen, income is transferred between other sectors. Recall the predictions of the Heckscher–Ohlin (HO) model. The HO model argues that trade benefits the abundant factor of production and harms the scarce factor. Thus, it is the scarce factor that may petition the government for protection in order to avoid a loss in income. The HO model would predict, then, that labor and capital tend to take opposite views with regard to commercial policies. Stephen Magee has studied the positions taken by various industry and labor groups in testimony before Congress.* He shows that in many cases, labor and capital take the same sides on the question of trade policy. For instance, both the domestic steel producers and the United Steelworkers union support trade barriers on steel. This commonality of interest suggests that, at least in the short run, the income of both groups would fall if trade barriers were not imposed. Such a situation could arise if capital and/or labor were immobile among various sectors.

In some countries, one of the stated aims of commercial policy is to tax the rich in order to aid the poor. This is done by imposing high tariffs on goods considered to be luxury items and imposing export taxes on goods considered necessities. The idea is that by imposing high import tariffs on luxuries, the rich will pay high taxes to the government. Similarly, export tariffs on necessities keep goods at home and tend therefore to lower their prices. The problem with the use of trade policy in this case is that by imposing barriers on luxuries, their prices are increased and domestic residents are encouraged to move into the production of these items. Furthermore, because necessities are now even cheaper, local producers have less of an incentive to produce them. The long-run impact of protection in this case is for the production of high-priced luxuries to rise and for low-priced necessities to fall. Clearly, this would seem to go against the assumed goals of the government.

All forms of taxation involve transfers of incomes. People who pay taxes see their incomes fall, while recipients of government benefits see their incomes rise. Commercial policy seems to be a particularly appealing mechanism to carry out income redistribution. This is because the direct effects of any particular trade policy on those who are harmed may not be evident. For instance, when a government imposes a quota, prices rise. However, people may not be aware of the existence of

---

*See Stephen Magee, "Three Simple Tests of the Stolper–Samuelson Theorem," in *Issues in International Economics*, ed., Peter Oppenheimer (London: Oriel Press, 1978).

the quota or of its effects in the market. Similarly, tariffs also lead to higher prices, and again these are taxes that fall directly on consumers. But, as opposed to a sales tax, a tariff is rarely collected at the point of retail sale, so that it is not an obvious part of the price of the product being purchased. Thus, through trade policy a government is able to generate benefits for certain special interest groups with taxes that are largely invisible, but no less burdensome, to the general public.

As with government revenue, an income tax is a much better tax system to use to redistribute income among groups. Deadweight costs are reduced. Moreover, the government does not have to deal with difficult issues such as defining in legal terms the concept of a luxury good.

Noneconomic Goals   Sometimes governments impose protection for noneconomic reasons. That is, the aim of the government is to achieve an outcome that is not directly related to economic welfare. A good example is national defense. The argument is often made that the output of local industries vital to the national defense should be protected from international competition. This would guarantee the availability of critical products in the time of war or national emergency—one of the oldest justifications for protection. For instance, Adam Smith, an otherwise free-trade advocate, suggests in *The Wealth of Nations* that this argument is legitimate.*

Indeed, the national defense argument does provide a valid basis for protection of certain domestic markets. Economists cannot dispute the fact that for national defense reasons local production of some items may be necessary. Protection, however, is not the best policy to achieve the goal of a strong national defense.

The first problem with the national defense justification is that it is easily overused. In their book on trade policy, Leland Yeager and David Tuerck describe some of the industries that have testified before Congress as to the importance of their products to the defense effort:

> Gloves, pens, pottery, peanuts, umbrella frames, paper, candles, and thumbtacks are just a few among many industries that have stressed their own strategic importance. The ordinary wood-cased pencil, its manufacturers insist, is essential in conducting all peacetime and wartime activities. . . . Lacemakers once sought increased protection on the grounds that they could convert their machinery to make mosquito netting in case of war in the tropics. A linen thread manufacturer once stressed that the fish netting his industry makes is important to the nation's wartime food supply and that the netting is also used for camouflage. Tuna fishermen have called their boats auxiliary vessels for the Navy. Producers of . . . embroidery have told how they bolster morale by making shoulder patches for soldiers' uniforms.†

---

*For a more recent examination of the national defense argument, see T.N. Srinivasan, "The National Defense Argument for Government Intervention in Foreign Trade," in *U.S. Trade Policies in a Changing World Economy*, ed. Robert Stern (Boston: MIT Press, 1986). See also the comments to this article in this same volume by Michael Intrilligator and Elhanan Helpman and Srinivasan's postscript. An earlier discussion of this issue can be found in Earl Thompson, "An Economic Basis for the 'National Defense Argument' for Aiding Certain Industries," *Journal of Political Economy* (1979).
†Leland Yeager and David Tuerck, *Foreign Trade and U.S. Policy*, 145.

Clearly, as this excerpt suggests, nearly every industry can, if it wants, provide to policy makers a story as to the strategic nature of its product, and in some cases it may be difficult for the policy makers to reject these claims.

A second problem with the national defense argument for protection is that, in some cases, national defense needs might be better served by expanding imports rather than contracting them. That is, the domestic availability of certain products in times of national emergency is what is necessary to ensure defense-related needs. The cheapest way to guarantee that these needs are met might be for the government to purchase large quantities of certain goods in world markets during peacetime and then store these goods so that they would be available during national emergencies. The alternative to this type of program would be trade barriers that serve to guarantee that the product in question is produced on domestic soil. The costs of this program are the usual deadweight losses during both good times and bad. Thus, the national defense argument makes sense only if production on domestic soil is what is required for national defense purposes.

The United States is one of many countries that has special laws to limit the importation of defense-related products.* This authority, provided in Sections 232 and 233 of the Trade Expansion Act of 1962, has been used only on rare occasions, most notably in the case of oil imports and more recently, as the authority to negotiate VERs on machine tools. One of the reasons that this provision is not used more often is probably that the United States has comparative advantage in many defense-related products. In fact, the United States is much more likely to prevent the export of defense products than it is to prevent their import.

A better policy than protection to guarantee that a certain level of domestic production of defense-related products is achieved is through a direct subsidy to the industry coupled with free trade. To understand this point better, consider Figure 7.2. There, we show the market for a product whose continued domestic production is considered vital to the national defense. As the graph clearly shows, if the country were to follow a policy of free trade, domestic output would equal Q_0 units. Suppose policy makers have decided that, for defense reasons, domestic output should increase to Q_1 units. Clearly, one way to achieve that goal would be to impose a tariff of $t.

Consider instead a per unit production subsidy of $t paid by the government to domestic manufacturers coupled with free trade. The effect of the subsidy would be to shift the domestic supply down by the amount of the subsidy—reflecting the lower costs the industry now faces. This is illustrated by the supply curve labeled S'. Because of the subsidy, domestic producers would expand their output to the point where their subsidy-augmented supply curve crosses the world price line. That is, they would choose to produce Q_1 units. What is the economic cost of the subsidy program? First, there is the subsidy itself. From the diagram, we can easily see that producers receive $a + $b. That is, they receive $t (the length of the side of area a) times every unit produced domestically (Q_1 units). Where does the government get

FIGURE 7.2	*Welfare effects of a domestic production subsidy.*

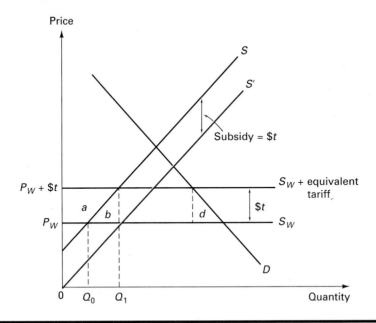

the money needed to finance the subsidy? The answer must be that it is paid by tax-payers, who are assumed to be in the consumer sector.

What do producers gain under the subsidy? The answer is that domestic profits rise by $a. The remainder of the money they receive goes to pay for the additional cost of resources required to expand production from Q_0 to Q_1 units. Thus, just as with tariffs, we can think of $b as a deadweight cost of government policy, in this case the cost of the subsidy program. Putting it all together, consumers lose $a + $b in the form of higher taxes, while producers gain $a in profits. The cost to society is area b, the production deadweight cost of the subsidy. This compares favorably with a tariff of $t that would produce deadweight costs $(b + d). That is, the difference between a tariff and a subsidy is that with the former there is both a production deadweight cost and a consumption deadweight cost. With the subsidy and free trade, goods sell at world prices, so that there is no consumption deadweight cost.

Finally, it is important to note that subsidies are superior to protection in another way: they are more visible. If governments are making payments on a regular basis to domestic industry, it becomes a part of the public record. Unlike with trade barriers, it becomes easy to understand the costs to society of supporting any given industry. Thus, one would expect that industries with only an indirect link to national defense would have a harder time winning subsidy payments than they might gaining import protection.

Infant industry argument
The argument holding that new industries may need temporary protection until they have mastered the production and marketing techniques necessary to be competitive in the world market.

Infant Industry Protection   One of the oldest justifications for protection is the **infant industry argument**.* This basis for protection is built on the notion that certain industries require temporary protection from foreign competition in order to grow and prosper. This may be because the initial costs of production tend to be high. However, given time and access to a protected market, firms will expand production and learn the techniques necessary to lower their costs and to be internationally competitive. In fact, after some period of time, the protection can be removed, and if the government has made the right choices regarding whom to protect, the industry will thrive.

There are a number of problems with the logic of the infant industry argument. First, it presupposes that protected firms will work to lower costs, even though they are destined to face increased foreign competition if they are successful. It would seem more likely that protecting the infant industry provides the infant with an incentive never to grow up.

Second, even if the industry responds by improving its productivity, the argument seems to imply that governments are better able to pick winners than the private market is. After all, it is not uncommon for industries to lose money when they first get started. One of the functions of the financial sector of the private economy is to provide funds to firms to enable them to produce until they become profitable. Moreover, when the initial funding comes from private sources, domestic residents are not subject to the higher prices that are the inevitable result of government-imposed protection.

The validity of the infant industry argument is better confined to those situations where the government is in a superior position to support the development of certain industries. Such a situation comes about on occasion in developing countries when the infant industry is one whose growth will lead to an expansion of the infrastructure of the economy. That is, sometimes firms must build roads, expand airports, extend public utility services, teach workers certain generally applicable work habits, and the like before production can take place. When these improvements are made, society benefits, but the industry may never be compensated for the expense it has incurred in the process. Protection is one means to ensure that the industry is compensated for providing these services to the economy.

Despite the points just discussed, infant industry protection is not the most efficient way to encourage certain industries to develop and grow within an economy. Clearly, as was the case with national defense protection, if the goal is to expand production, then a production subsidy with free trade is more efficient than protection. Moreover, if what the government wants is expanded infrastructure (e.g., improved roads, harbors, airports, or better-trained workers), then under almost all circumstances it would be more efficient for the government to provide these goods directly rather than to impose protection so that they might be provided by the private sector.

---

*For a critique of this argument, see Robert Baldwin, "The Case Against Infant-Industry Tariff Protection," *Journal of Political Economy* (1969). For a possible example from U.S. history, see Douglas Irwin, "Did Late Nineteenth Century U.S. Tariffs Promote Infant Industries? Evidence from the Tin Plate Industry," *NBER Working Paper* #6835 (December 1998).

Domestic Distortions   A well-known theorem in economics states that perfect competition is Pareto optimal. That is, if perfect competition is reached, then no one in the economy can be made better off without hurting someone else. It is virtually always the case that perfect competition is not achieved in the real world. According to the theory of the second best, if there are distortions present in an economy that keep it from achieving perfect competition, then it may be best for governments to choose policies that add more distortions. For instance, government policies are put into place to aid certain groups, and, as a consequence, protection may be required to guarantee that the goals of the program are not undermined or that the program does not become too costly.

Consider, for instance, U.S. farm policy. The government has decided to help domestic farmers through a system of price supports. The effect of this policy is shown in Figure 7.3. In autarky and in the absence of a government program, the product would sell for P_0. The effect of the price support program is to guarantee farmers a price of P_1. This causes production to rise to Q_1, consumption to fall to Q_0, and, consequently, the government to purchase the difference between these two levels, Q_0Q_1 units. Now, let's introduce international trade. Suppose the world price is P_W. Clearly, the government cannot follow a policy of free trade. It has guaranteed to pay P_1 for the product. If trade is allowed, importers would buy farm products at the low world price only to sell these goods at a higher support price. The

FIGURE 7.3   *Price supports and tariffs.*

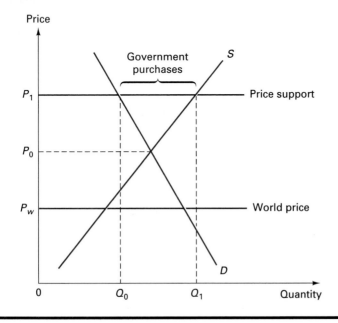

costs of the farm program would become enormous. Thus, due to the existence of a distortionary policy, that is, the price support program, a second distortionary policy, namely, protection, is necessary.

Many protectionist policies are in place in the United States and elsewhere for second-best reasons. But as the name implies, tariffs are not first-best policies. Rather, better policies would attack the distortions (e.g., eliminate the government programs) that have generated the need for protection.

Protecting the Environment

The production of some types of goods can generate negative *externalities*. These are unwanted byproducts of one activity that raise the cost of other activities. For instance, steel production tends to pollute the air, making it harder for other local businesses, such as restaurants or hospitals, to maintain clean establishments. Externalities are an example of market failure. That is, the social cost of producing steel (which would include the additional costs borne by other local businesses) exceeds the actual cost incurred by steelmakers.

Steelmakers do not take these extra costs into account when they decide production levels. Hence, market forces will tend to lead to outcomes where more steel is produced than is socially optimal. Market failures imply a role for government. Using our steel example, the government could impose a pollution tax on the steel plant to discourage its production.

International trade poses new problems for policy makers who attempt to set policies to deal with market failures such as externalities. If production occurs in one country and pollution is thereby transported across its borders, there may be a role for trade policy (e.g., a tariff or quota) by the country receiving the pollution to discourage the polluting industry. However, trade policy will never be the best way to attack the problem. It works well only if the country imposing the policy is a major customer of the country generating the pollution. If not, the policy will have little effect on the foreign country. In either case, absent local pollution taxes, increased trade barriers would also encourage expanded production and pollution at home.*

Alternatively, the fear of environmental decline has been used as an argument for the retention of certain barriers to trade. The debate over the creation of a North American Free Trade Agreement (NAFTA) offers an illustration. Some environmentalists in the United States opposed NAFTA on the grounds that it would raise the level of global pollution. Their argument was essentially as follows: Over the past few years, American firms have been subject to increasing pressure to reduce pollution emissions, through both more intensive regulation and higher taxes. The passage of NAFTA would allow U.S. firms to relocate in Mexico, where environmental standards are lower and currently less well enforced. The end result would be an expansion of pollution in Mexico and a loss of leverage of the U.S. government in

---

*For additional discussion on trade and environmental issues, see Kym Anderson and Richard Blackhurst, eds., *The Greening of World Trade Issues* (Ann Arbor: University of Michigan Press, 1992), and Alison Butler, "Environmental Protection and Free Trade: Are They Mutually Exclusive?" *Review* (Federal Reserve Bank of St. Louis, 1992). Chapter 8 contains a trade policy case study of a role that GATT plays in environmental protection.

trying to curtail environmental degradation. Thus, the environmentalists argued that trade and investment restrictions should remain in place.*

While this reasoning may have some economic validity, it misses a number of important points. First, it assumes that international differences in pollution containment costs are a primary determinant of industrial location. Data on U.S. manufacturing suggests that pollution abatement costs average only 1.38 percent of total value added. Even in those sectors where pollution costs are high, they seldom exceed 5 percent of value added. Thus, everything else held constant, U.S. firms would appear to gain little in competitiveness by relocating even to countries where (unlike in Mexico) there are no pollution standards. Moreover, even if U.S. firms did relocate, it is likely that they would install new capital equipment in their plants. Such equipment is almost uniformly cleaner than older technologies.

Second, from the analysis in Chapters 3 and 4, we know that lower barriers to trade will cause liberalization along the lines of comparative advantage. All available studies suggest that Mexico has comparative advantage in agriculture and labor-intensive manufactures and comparative disadvantage in environmentally dirtier capital-intensive manufactures. Thus, NAFTA will be likely to produce Mexican specialization in relatively "clean" industries, while the United States and perhaps Canada will experience a relatively small increase in the production of dirtier, more capital-intensive industries. Finally, NAFTA will stimulate economic growth and raise the standard of living in Mexico. Recent studies have shown that environmental quality improves as standards of living rise. That is, improving the environment is a luxury good; the richer people are, the more they are willing to spend on it.[†]

In response to this criticism by environmentalists and to help win support for the agreement, the Clinton administration negotiated a side agreement with Mexico that commits all parties to enforce strictly all existing environmental legislation and to guarantee that future environmental laws will not weaken existing standards. The agreement also calls for the establishment of a border environment institution to coordinate and finance action on water and solid waste pollution in regions along the U.S.–Mexico border.

Strategic Trade Policies   In Chapter 5 we noted that recent research in the theory of international trade has explored the role of increasing returns to scale in explaining international trade flows. When increasing returns are present, domestic markets will no longer be characterized by perfect competition. Rather, firms in any given industry will tend to be fewer in number, with the actions of one affecting the actions of another. And, once international trade is allowed in such industries, actions taken by firms in one country will influence the actions of firms in other

---

*For more on NAFTA, see Chapter 9.
[†]These arguments correspond to a series of points made in Gene M. Grossman and Alan B. Kreuger, "Environmental Impacts of a North American Free Trade Agreement," in *The Mexico-U.S. Free Trade Agreement,* ed. Peter M. Garber (Cambridge, Mass.: The MIT Press, 1993). This important article provides an empirical analysis of the likely environmental effects of NAFTA. It concludes that NAFTA may lead to a reduction of pollution in Mexico.

countries.[†] Under these conditions, policies such as import tariffs or export subsidies may be a way of raising domestic welfare. If governments implement trade policy for these reasons, they are said to be engaged in strategic trade policy.

The idea of strategic trade policy may be best illustrated by considering two examples. In the first, suppose that Brazil imports computers from IBM. Suppose further that IBM is the only producer of computers in the world. That is, Brazil is importing from a monopoly. This situation is depicted in Figure 7.4. In the figure, D_B denotes Brazil's demand curve for computers. MR_B denotes the marginal revenue curve corresponding to this demand curve. Let the horizontal line, C, indicate IBM's marginal cost curve. Under free trade, IBM would maximize its profits by equating marginal cost with marginal revenue, exporting Q^* units to Brazil at a price of P^* per computer. The profits IBM would earn would be given by the shaded area in the diagram.

FIGURE 7.4   *Trade policy and foreign monopoly.*

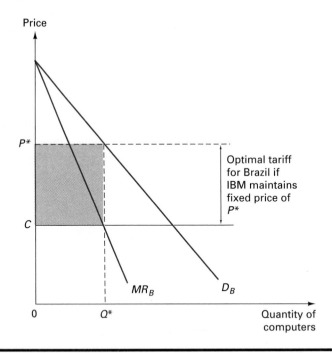

Suppose now that, within Brazil, manufacturers exist that could produce computers profitably if their price were to rise above P^*. That is, so long as IBM does not raise its price above P^*, it has the market all to itself. Under such (extreme) circumstances, Brazil should impose a tariff on computers. What would be the result of this tariff? So long as IBM wants to keep its market to itself, it would not raise its price. Since its price has not changed, neither would its sales to Brazil. Thus, consumers would not be hurt. The only result of the tariff would be that some of IBM's monopoly profits would now remain in Brazil in the form of government revenue. How high should Brazil's tariff be under these conditions? Clearly, Brazil could increase its tariff until it captured all of IBM's monopoly profits, provided that IBM maintains a policy of keeping its price at P^* in order to restrict competition. Note that this is a very special situation. A tariff established by Brazil would impose no deadweight costs on either country because neither prices nor trade levels change. It would merely recapture extraordinary profits that had previously been paid by its citizens to the foreign producer (IBM).

A second example of strategic trade policy is provided by Paul Krugman in his analysis of the legitimacy of arguments for free trade.[†] Suppose that there are two countries capable of building a new passenger jet aircraft, Europe and the United States, and one firm in each country that could produce the good, Airbus and Boeing, respectively. Assume that each firm is faced with the choice of whether or not to enter the market and that so long as only one firm does, it will earn profits from doing so. Finally, assume that all airplane sales of either firm will be to a third country so that producer surplus and national welfare will be identical.

Table 7.5 provides details on the strategic game played by each of the firms. Consider the first matrix. Boeing's (Airbus's) choices to produce or not are denoted by the letters P and N (p and n) along the side (top) of the matrix. Inside each cell of the matrix are the profits that accrue to each firm given its decision and that of the other. Boeing's profits are listed first in each cell.

If each firm makes its decision at the same time, then there is no unique solution to the game. However, if Boeing has a head start, then it will decide to produce the aircraft, and Airbus's best strategy is to stay out of the market. Given this situation, in the absence of any government intervention, Boeing will enter the market, make profits of 100, and deter entry from Airbus.

Is there anything that Europe can do about this situation? The answer is yes. Suppose that Europe guarantees an export subsidy to Airbus of, say, 10, regardless of whether Boeing produces or not. This outcome is illustrated in the second matrix in Table 7.5. In this case, Airbus is assured of profits whether or not Boeing enters the market. Therefore, Airbus will produce the airplane and Boeing's best strategy is not to enter. Thus, the solution of the game moves from the upper right-hand to the lower left-hand cell of the matrix. A subsidy of 10 raises Airbus's profits by 110.

[†]This example is discussed in more detail in Paul Krugman, "Is Free Trade Passé?" *Journal of Economic Perspectives* (Fall 1987). In this important and highly readable article, Krugman concludes that even though economists have found important arguments for imposing protective policies, free trade remains essentially the right policy for governments to pursue.

TABLE 7.5	*The Effects of a Hypothetical Strategic Trade Policy*

Payoff Matrix (no subsidy)

		Airbus			
		p		*n*	
Boeing	P	−5	−5	100	0
	N	0	100	0	0

Payoff Matrix (European subsidy of 10)

		Airbus			
		p		*n*	
Boeing	P	−5	5	100	0
	N	0	110	0	0

Of this, 100 represents a transfer of profits and economic welfare from the United States to Europe.

Economists have explored other situations where strategic trade policies may be applied. Under some market conditions, the appropriate government policy is an import quota. Under others, the correct policy is a subsidy to encourage domestic research and development efforts.*

Given the examples just discussed, it would seem that strategic trade policy is an important and legitimate justification for the use of tariffs and quotas. This may not actually be the case. First, the types of situations where strategic policy should be applied are very specialized and depend crucially on assumptions about how firms behave. If, for instance, two firms compete internationally with each other by changing production levels, the optimal strategic policy may be an export subsidy. This was the case with our airplane example. If these same two firms compete by changing prices, however, the optimal policy becomes an export *tariff*!

Second, even if we know how firms compete with each other, other assumptions that must hold will often be violated in the real world. For instance, our example of the competition between Boeing and Airbus suggests that Europe has an incentive to subsidize airline production. The model as presented, however, ignores the real-world fact that some parts of American airplanes are made by European firms. Moreover, a substantial amount of the component parts of Airbus airplanes are made by American firms. Thus, any European policies aimed against Boeing could end up

---

*For an excellent textbook-level survey of strategic trade policy, see Neil Vousden, *The Economics of Trade Protection* (Cambridge, England: Cambridge University Press, 1990). For a more advanced discussion of these issues, see Elhanan Helpman and Paul Krugman, *Trade Policy and Market Structure* (Cambridge, Mass.: MIT Press, 1989). Real-world experience with strategic trade policy appears to be limited. Douglas Irwin argues in a fascinating paper that the rivalry between the Dutch and the British in the sixteenth century over East India trade represents a classic case of strategic trade policy in action. See Douglas Irwin, "Mercantilism as Strategic Trade Policy: The Anglo-Dutch Rivalry for the East India Trade," *Journal of Political Economy* (1991).

hurting European parts producers and helping American parts producers. Moreover, by eliminating the competition from Boeing, European airline companies might have to pay more for less desirable airplanes. The net result then is ambiguous. It is no longer clear that the export subsidy is the right policy.

Another problem with the use of strategic trade policy is that the gains from these policies depend upon the response of the foreign government. Just as was the case with the optimal tariff argument for protection, if the foreign government retaliates, then any initial gains may be lost. At the very least, they will be reduced.

Finally, even though it is possible to show that in some cases tariffs, quotas, or subsidies are welfare-improving policies when countries apply them strategically, economists have yet to establish that these policies are the best policies that can be implemented. This is an important area for economists to study.

SUMMARY

1. While tariffs are the most universal form of protection found in the world today, nontariff barriers, such as quotas, subsidies, and government policies related to procurement or to health and safety standards, affect a large and growing share of international trade.

2. Quotas are limits on the volume or value of international trade. Because quotas restrict the quantity of goods traded, they generate higher prices, raising domestic profits and deadweight costs to society.

3. The economic effects of quotas depend in part on how they are administered. If quota licenses are auctioned by the government in competitive auctions, then the effects of the quotas are similar to those of tariffs. If the quota licenses are given to foreigners in the form of voluntary export restraints, then quotas produce large deadweight costs.

4. Even if quotas are auctioned, because they restrict quantities rather than prices they tend to be more restrictive than tariffs over time. Moreover, the arbitrary way in which quota levels are determined and quota shares are allocated will have no connection with underlying comparative advantage.

5. Other nontariff barriers present a growing problem to policy makers interested in freeing up international trade. This is because these barriers tend to be product and country specific. It is difficult, if not impossible, to design international rules of conduct that would effectively block many of these practices.

6. Most of the commonly heard and therefore important arguments for protection are totally invalid. That is, in these cases protection fails to achieve its stated justification.

7. There are valid arguments for protection, such as government revenue and national defense, but protection used for these reasons is never the most efficient policy.

EXERCISES

1. In what ways are tariffs and quotas similar in their effects? In what ways do they differ?

2. Suppose that prospective importing firms hire lobbyists to help them secure from government authorities the right to import quota-restricted items into a country. How much would importers as a group be willing to pay lobbyists for their services? Explain. Suppose lobbyists are paid this amount. What happens to domestic welfare in this case?

3. Suppose that a country requires special inspections on all imported food but exempts domestic production from similar inspection. What effect would this have on imports, domestic production, prices, and quantity consumed? Explain fully.

4. Show graphically that a monopolist will charge a higher price and produce at a lower level of output with a quota protection than with a tariff protection that yields the same level of imports.

5. The United States has used quotas to protect its domestic sugar industry. What has been the likely impact of these quotas on the world price of sugar (relative to the price that would exist under free trade)? Explain.

6. Is the optimum tariff argument a valid argument for protection? (Hint: See Chapter 6.) Is it the best policy for this purpose? Explain.

7. Consider the example of airplane building and strategic trade policy described in the text. Suppose that the United States matched Europe's export subsidy with a subsidy of 10 to Boeing. How would this policy affect the solution to the game? What would be the welfare effects of this policy on America and Europe?

8. The United States has recently begun building a new type of television called high-definition television (HDTV). Should the United States impose temporary protection on this product to guarantee U.S. commercial success in this product? Why or why not?

9. Suppose that the domestic demand and supply for hats in a small open economy are given by:

$$Q = 100 - P \quad \text{(demand)}$$

$$Q = 50 + 2P \quad \text{(supply)}$$

where Q denotes quantity and P denotes price.
   a. If the world price is 10, what is the free trade level of imports?
   b. Suppose that the country imposes a quota of 11 units. How much will the domestic price rise?

   c. What will be the welfare effects on this country of a quota of 11 units?

   d. Suppose instead that this country negotiates a VER of 11 units with its chief foreign supplier. What are the welfare effects of this policy?

10. According to the analysis in this chapter, VERs are a more costly form of protection than tariffs or other types of quotas. Why do countries like the United States continue to protect certain industries using this form of protection?

11. Suppose that Guatland protects its motorcycle industry with a quota that raises domestic prices by $100 per unit. If Guatland's government were to then impose a tariff of $90 per motorcycle, what would happen to Guat motorcycle imports? What would be the welfare effects of this tariff on the Guat economy?

12. Under what circumstances can commercial policy be an effective tool to solve world environmental problems? Under what circumstances will commercial policy be not very effective? In general, which set of circumstances is more likely to exist in the real world?

REFERENCES

Baldwin, Robert. *Nontariff Distortions of International Trade*. Washington, D.C.: Brookings Institute, 1970.

Haberler, Gottfried von. *The Theory of International Trade*. New York: Augustus M. Kelly Publishers, 1968.

Krugman, Paul. "Is Free Trade Passé?" *Journal of Economic Perspectives* (Fall 1987): 131–44.

Laird, Sam, and Alexander Yeats. *Quantitative Methods for Trade-Barrier Analysis*. New York: New York University Press, 1990.

———. "Trends in Nontariff Barriers of Developed Countries, 1966–1986." *Weltwirtschaftliches Archiv*, Heft 2 (1990): 299–324.

U.S. House of Representatives, Committee on Ways and Means. *Overview and Compilation of U.S. Trade Statutes*. Washington, D.C.: Government Printing Office, August, 1995.

Yeager, Leland B., and David Tuerck. *Foreign Trade and U.S. Policy*. New York: Praeger Publishers, 1976.

INTERNET APPLICATIONS

Please visit our Web site at www.awl.com/husted_melvin for more exercises and readings.

CHAPTER 8

Commercial Policy:

History and Practice

KEY WORDS

Logrolling
Unconditional most favored nation
    status
Dumping
Predatory dumping
International price discrimination
Dumping margin
Injury test

Countervailing duty
Upstream subsidy
Section 301
Escape clause
Trade adjustment assistance (TAA)
Safeguards protection

We have now studied the various tools of commercial policy as well as some of the arguments made by advocates of trade policy for the imposition of these tools. In this chapter we expand upon this discussion by focusing on recent trade policy initiatives of the United States, the European Union, and Japan. We also discuss in some detail the role of international organizations and agreements, such as the World Trade Organization (WTO), in setting the rules of commercial policy.

There has been a marked trend since the end of World War II for the general levels of trade barriers to fall in the Western industrialized economies. This movement, which has been spurred to a considerable extent by the United States, arose out of a worldwide desire at the end of the war not to repeat the pattern of trade wars and depression witnessed in the years that preceded the war. As a result, international trade has expanded rapidly, and lengthy recessions have been avoided.

With the expansion of trade, however, commercial disputes have also arisen. These disputes have typically centered on trade in specific commodities and, in some cases, have led to the imposition of new barriers to replace those that had been removed. In turn, trade disputes have prompted lawmakers in different countries to modify their trade laws or the administration of these laws to handle changing circumstances. Thus, of particular importance in this chapter will be a discussion of the nature and evolution of U.S. trade laws, including examples of the application of these laws to specific trade problems.

HISTORY OF U.S. COMMERCIAL POLICY

The Constitution of the United States grants to Congress the authority "to regulate commerce with foreign nations." This authority includes the right to impose import tariffs, but it denies Congress the right to institute export tariffs.* Over the nation's history, Congress has exercised its constitutional obligation in this area by passing a series of tariff bills. Some of these bills provided special levels of protection to certain industries. Others were aimed at adjusting either up or down the general level of protection conferred to the nation as a whole.

Tariff bills came at infrequent and irregular intervals during the first 150 years of U.S. history. The last, and probably most famous, of these bills was the Tariff Act of 1930, the Smoot-Hawley Tariff. (See our discussion of this tariff in Chapter 6.) After the passage of this bill and the subsequent collapse of international trade, Congress began to shift its emphasis away from setting general levels of protection toward ensuring that specific industries would be able to obtain relief from certain types of foreign competition. Thus, since 1930, most bills related to commercial policy (known since 1930 as trade bills) have delegated tariff-setting authority to the president, authorizing the chief executive to negotiate lower foreign tariff levels in

---

*The prohibition of export tariffs was written into the Constitution at the insistence of Southern delegates to the Constitutional Convention who feared that without it, the federal government would rely on taxes on exports of cotton as a chief source of government revenue.

exchange for lower U.S. tariff levels. In addition, these bills have increasingly sought to address issues such as the response of the U.S. government to "unfair foreign trade practices" both in the U.S. market and overseas.

Figure 8.1 illustrates the cyclical movements in U.S. tariffs since the founding of the country. In the earliest days of the country, tariffs were relatively low and were aimed at collecting revenue for the federal government.* The first tariff act, passed in 1789, imposed a 5 percent import duty on most goods. Higher tariffs were imposed on luxury goods, with the highest rate equal to 15 percent applied to carriages. During this period, from 1791 to 1807, trade grew rapidly, rising in nominal terms by over 400 percent.

War between England and France helped fuel this growth in trade, as the United States sold agricultural products and other raw materials to both countries. In 1808, this trend was reversed. Both England and France sought to limit the trade of the other by instituting naval blockades of each other's harbors. Ships of neutral countries

FIGURE 8.1   *U.S. tariffs, 1792–1999.*

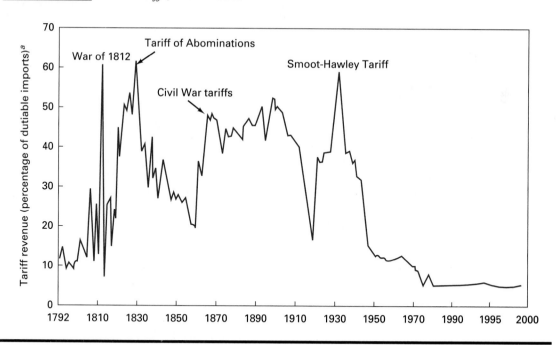

aData before 1821, tariff revenue as a percentage of total imports.

SOURCE: U.S. Bureau of the Census, *Historical Statistics of the United States: Colonial Times to 1970* and U.S. International Trade Commission Web site http://www.usitc.gov/.

*The United States did not institute an income tax until 1913, when the Sixteenth Amendment to the Constitution was ratified.

(such as the United States) were boarded, goods were destroyed, and sailors were taken hostage. The U.S. government reacted by imposing a ban on commerce with England. Eventually this dispute led to the War of 1812. To help fund the war, the U.S. government doubled tariffs. But because of the war, U.S. trade plummeted to its lowest level since 1790, and, despite the higher tariff rates, tariff revenues fell. After the close of the war in 1814, tariffs were raised in 1816 to an average of about 20 percent, again with the goal of securing revenue to pay off the war debts of the government.

The War of 1812 had profound effects on U.S. tariff policy. Because the war caused a cutoff of trade with Europe, U.S. manufacturers of industrial products began to expand their production. These manufacturers were located largely in the northern and central parts of the country. At the end of the war, members of Congress from these regions began to press for continued and higher tariffs on industrial products to protect the "infant industries" of their districts. Compounding this effect was the fact that after the war there was a worldwide depression. This depression led to a fall in agricultural prices and weakened traditional export sectors of the country (the South and the Midwest). With the fall in agricultural prices came additional pressure on Congress from agricultural states of the Midwest to protect the home market with tariffs. Only members of Congress from the South, who feared the loss of foreign markets for cotton exports, opposed higher tariffs. Congress responded in 1824 and again in 1828 with new tariff laws. The latter, known as the *Tariff of Abominations,* raised the average tariff to almost 60 percent.

How the Tariff of Abominations came to be passed is one of the more interesting stories in the history of international trade politics. At the time the bill was written, John Quincy Adams was president and Andrew Jackson was his leading political opponent. Most of the support for Adams came from New England, where tariffs on manufactured goods were popular but tariffs on raw materials were not.* Followers of Jackson controlled the Congress. Some of these members were from the South and wanted lower tariffs. Others were from the North, where tariffs were popular. Jackson's supporters in Congress devised a plan for a new tariff bill that they thought would achieve two goals. First, it would embarrass and weaken Adams and his supporters. Second, it would give both the Northern and the Southern supporters of Jackson something they could vote for (or against) to maximize their own political support. Frank Taussig in his brilliant *Tariff History of the United States* describes the plan as follows:

> A high tariff bill was to be laid before the House. It was to contain not only a high general range of duties, but duties especially high on those raw materials on which New England wanted duties to be low [e.g., imported wool to be used in woolen factories]. It was to satisfy the protective demands of the Western and Middle States, and at the same time to be obnoxious to the New England members. The Jackson men of all shades, the protectionists from the North and the free-traders from the South, were to unite in preventing any amendments; that bill, and no other, was to be voted on. When the final vote came, the Southern men were to turn around and vote against their own measure. The New England men, and the Adams men in general, would be unable to swallow it,

---

*Recall the concept of effective protection discussed in Chapter 6.

and would also vote against it. Combined, they would prevent its passage, even though the Jackson men from the North voted for it. The result expected was that no tariff bill would be passed during the session, which was the object of the Southern wing of the opposition.*

Despite the seeming brilliance of the plan, when Congress finally voted there were enough New England votes in favor of the bill to ensure its passage. And so, the tariff that was not supposed to pass was enacted into law.

Almost immediately, pressures arose to reduce some of the most egregious aspects of the law. Several individual tariffs, such as those on goods that did not compete with U.S. production (e.g., tea, coffee, and cocoa), were lowered. In 1833, Congress passed the Compromise Tariff Act. This law set into motion a series of annual reductions in tariff rates designed to bring about a uniform 20 percent tariff on all goods by 1842. The 20 percent uniform tariff came into effect on July 1, 1842. It remained in force for only two months before Congress, reacting to demands for greater protection from imports, voted increased tariffs on a variety of products.

Between 1842 and the beginning of the Civil War in 1861, Congress passed two more tariff bills. Both of these bills instituted tariff reductions aimed largely at lowering the large surplus in the federal budget. In 1861, 1862, and again in 1864, Congress increased tariffs, ostensibly for the purpose of raising government revenue to help finance the war effort of the North. As they had after the War of 1812, however, tariffs remained high after the end of the Civil War. Tariffs would not fall until 1913, when, supported by Southern Democrats, the Wilson administration sponsored legislation that cut tariffs significantly. Tariffs fell to levels not seen for 60 years.

Unlike previous experiences with wars, tariffs remained low during World War I.[†] Shortly after the war, however, the U.S. economy fell into recession, the Republicans returned to the White House, and tariffs were raised once again. The law that raised these tariffs was the Fordney-McCumber Tariff of 1922. This act restored tariffs to their prewar levels and, by closing off American markets to foreign producers, helped to ensure that the war-torn countries of Europe would have a more difficult time rebuilding their economies.

The last general tariff bill Congress was to write came in 1930. This was, of course, the famous Smoot-Hawley Tariff. In Chapter 6 we described some of the features of the Smoot-Hawley Tariff and the response to the tariff by America's major trading partners. It is worth noting again how the bill came to be written. It began as a measure aimed at imposing tariffs on a limited set of agricultural products. To win passage of the law, its backers sought support for it from fellow members of Congress. The price of this support was to include in the law higher tariffs on goods produced in the congressional districts of these new supporters. This process of voting in favor of one proposal to earn return support for another is known as

---

*This passage is taken from Frank Taussig, *The Tariff History of the United States* (New York: G. P. Putnam's Sons, 1888), 88–89. This book is a fascinating and highly readable account of the economics and politics of protectionism in the United States in the nineteenth century. Taussig lived a long and productive life, and in subsequent editions of his book he analyzed tariffs as recent as the Smoot-Hawley Tariff.

[†]By 1913, the United States had enacted an income tax. Thus, there was less need to rely on tariffs to finance the war effort than there had been in previous wars.

Logrolling
The trading of votes by legislators to secure approval on issues of interest (e.g., tariffs) to each one.

logrolling. The Smoot-Hawley Tariff is a classic example of the logrolling process. More and more members of Congress signaled their willingness to support the bill, demanding in return higher tariffs for products produced in their district. The result was the highest set of tariffs since the Tariff of Abominations.* These were soon followed by the imposition of retaliatory tariffs overseas and a consequent fall in the volume of international trade.

The tariffs of 1828 and 1930 help to illustrate the problems inherent in a country where commercial policy is formulated by the legislative branch of government. When Franklin Roosevelt became president in 1933, his Secretary of State, Cordell Hull, persuaded Congress to cede to the president the authority to negotiate with trading partners to achieve mutual reductions in tariff levels. The mechanism that allowed the president to engage in these negotiations was the Reciprocal Trade Agreements Act of 1934. This act gave the president the authority to negotiate the reduction of any U.S. tariff by up to 50 percent without recourse to Congress. Congress granted tariff-negotiating authority to the president for only three years. The authority was renewed in three subsequent trade bills enacted between 1937 and 1943. By 1945, the United States had negotiated 32 agreements with 27 different countries, reducing tariff rates on average by 44 percent.

Unconditional most favored nation status
The principle of nondiscrimination in international trade.

The basic principle underlying the bilateral tariff negotiations entered into by the United States was that of **unconditional most favored nation status**. Under this rule, any special tariff cuts agreed to by the United States in bilateral negotiations (e.g., with Canada) would apply to the products of all other trading partners whom the U.S. government had designated with most favored nation (MFN) status.[†]

After the end of World War II, several new international organizations and agreements were instituted. One of these was the General Agreement on Tariffs and Trade (GATT). The GATT served two main purposes in the international community. First, it set the rules of conduct of international commerce and served as an arena for hearings to resolve international commercial disputes. There were four key principles to the GATT rules: (a) Trade barriers should be lowered in general and quotas should be eliminated in particular; (b) Trade barriers should be applied on a nondiscriminatory (most favored nation) basis; (c) Once made, tariff concessions could not be rescinded without compensation to affected trade partners, nor could new barriers be erected to replace tariffs that had been lowered; and (d) Trade disputes should be settled by consultation. The GATT trade rules form the basis for current rules of international trade. They are described further in Item 8.1.

The second main purpose of the GATT was to provide a forum for a series of multilateral talks aimed at lowering levels of protection around the world. Between 1947 and 1993, eight rounds of these talks were completed, each of them leading to reductions in tariff levels around the world. In the last, a new international organization, the World Trade Organization (WTO), was created to replace the GATT. Table 8.1 presents details on the results of the various rounds.

---

*For an analysis of the role logrolling played in the formation of the Smoot-Hawley tariff, see Douglas Irwin and Randall Kroszner, "Logrolling and Economic Interests in the Passage of the Smoot-Hawley Tarriff," *NBER Working Paper #5510* (March 1996).
[†]See Chapter 6 for additional discussion on the concept of MFN status.

TABLE 8.1	*U.S. Tariff Reduction Under the GATT (percentage)*			
GATT Conference	Proportion of Dutiable Imports Subjected to Reductions	Average Cut in Reduced Tariffs	Average Cut in All Duties	Remaining Duties as a Proportion of 1930 Tariffs[1]
Pre-GATT, 1934–1947	63.9	44.0	33.2	66.8
First round, Geneva, 1947	53.6	35.0	21.1	52.7
Second round, Annecy, 1949	5.6	35.1	1.9	51.7
Third round, Torquay, 1950–1951	11.7	26.0	3.0	50.1
Fourth round, Geneva, 1955–1956	16.0	15.6	3.5	48.9
Dillon Round, Geneva, 1961–1962	20.0	12.0	2.4	47.7
Kennedy Round, Geneva, 1964–1967	79.2	45.5	36.0	30.5
Tokyo Round, 1974–1979	n.a.	n.a.	29.6	21.2
Uruguay Round, 1986–1993	n.a.	n.a.	33.0	n.a.

NOTE: n.a. = not available.

[1]These percentages do not take into account the effects either of structural changes in trade or of inflation on the average tariff level.

SOURCE: Real Phillipe Lavergne, *The Political Economy of U.S. Tariffs* (Toronto: Academic Press Canada, 1983), Table A2.1, p. 32. Reprinted by permission. Updated by authors.

The last two of these multilateral negotiations to be fully implemented by the member countries were the Kennedy Round talks, held between 1964 and 1967, and the Tokyo Round talks, held between 1974 and 1979. Both sets of talks led to substantial reductions in tariff levels of industrialized countries. The second round also produced some initial agreements on the reduction of certain nontariff barriers to trade. In both cases, the negotiations were preceded by the passage of legislation in the United States enabling the president to send delegates to the talks with specific authority to bargain for lower trade barriers.* The legislation allowing the United States to participate in what would become known as the Kennedy Round was the Trade Expansion Act of 1962. The Trade Reform Act of 1974 authorized U.S. participation in the Tokyo Round talks.† Authority for U.S. representatives to participate in the Uruguay Round talks was first granted in 1979, renewed in the Omnibus Trade Act of 1988, and extended into 1993 by Congress in 1991.

---

*Technically, as the person responsible for conducting foreign policy, the president can always negotiate to lower tariffs or other forms of protection. Whatever is agreed to in these negotiations must be approved by Congress. Thus, it is seldom the case that the president would initiate (or that foreign countries would participate in) negotiations without prior authority from Congress.

†As Table 8.1 shows, GATT conferences did not have names until the Dillon Round, held in 1961. Douglas Dillon was the U.S. Secretary of the Treasury at the time of these talks and the leader of the U.S. delegation. The next round of talks was named for President Kennedy because he was president when the Trade Expansion Act was passed and in tribute to his memory. When President Nixon succeeded in obtaining passage of the Trade Reform Act of 1974, he hoped to have a round named after him, but the Watergate affair intervened. Instead, the round was dubbed the Tokyo Round, not because the negotiations took place in Tokyo—they were held in Geneva—but because Tokyo was where trade ministers met in 1974 and agreed to launch a new round of talks. The practice has been repeated with the naming of the latest round as the Uruguay Round, since Punta del Este (in Uruguay) was where trade ministers met in 1986 and agreed to begin formal talks, which again were held in Geneva.

ITEM 8.1   The GATT Agreement

The Preamble of the General Agreement proposes to raise living standards by reducing trade barriers and, in particular, by eliminating discriminatory trade practices. Part I states the basic principle of nondiscrimination and legally binds members to comply with their tariff concessions. Part II calls for the elimination of nontariff barriers, subject to several qualifications. Part III contains procedural rules, most importantly condoning the formation of free-trade areas. Part IV, added in 1965, addresses the special needs of developing countries.

Part I

MFN. Article I provides that a tariff on an imported product should be applied equally to all members. This affirmation of nondiscrimination is called most favored nation (MFN) treatment.

Binding tariff schedules. Article II legally binds members to their tariff concessions. It states that tariffs should not be increased above the rates in each country's tariff schedule.

Part II

National treatment. Article III prohibits members from circumventing tariff concessions by employing nontariff policies to offset the effect of a tariff reduction. National treatment requires that internal taxes apply equally to domestic and imported products and that regulations treat imported goods "no less favorably" than similar domestic goods.

Customs regulations. Articles V and VII through X curb customs procedures that impede imports. Such activities include rules of transit (Article V), customs valuation (Article VII), customs fees and formalities (Article VIII), and marks of origin (Article IX). Article X states that all laws and regulations regarding trade should be formulated and applied in a transparent manner, which requires public disclosure and the uniform and impartial administration of trade laws.

Antidumping and countervailing duties. Article VI defines dumping, states that both dumping and injury to domestic producers must be proved in order to merit an antidumping duty remedy, and specifies that antidumping duties should not exceed the dumping margin. It provides similar rules for the countervailing duty remedy to offset foreign government subsidies.

Quantitative restrictions. Article XI calls for the general elimination of quantitative restrictions (QRs) to trade, subject to several qualifications. Most importantly, QRs can be used to safeguard the balance of payments (Article XII) and to provide temporary escape clause relief for domestic industries (Article XIX). Developing countries can also use QRs to further developmental goals (Article XVIII and Part IV). Article XIII states that QRs, when employed, must be applied on a nondiscriminatory basis, with some exceptions listed in Article XIV. Article XV regulates the use of currency controls to evade QR restrictions, and coordinates GATT and IMF interests during balance-of-payments emergencies.

Subsidies. Article XVI discourages the use of subsidies in general, and calls for the elimination of export subsidies for nonprimary products in particular. Export subsidies for primary products should not cause a country to achieve more than an equitable share of world export trade in that product.

State-owned enterprises. Article XVII asserts that state-owned enterprises should choose among potential buyers and sellers according to normal business considerations, especially in terms of prices, quality, and procurement.

Government assistance in developing countries. Article XVIII affords developing countries exemptions to most of the requirements of the General Agreement, subject to rigorous criteria. Because of its strict standards, these exemptions have rarely been employed. Instead, developing countries have justified their use of policies such as nontariff barriers and export subsidies as safeguards for balance-of-payments problems.

Escape clause and other exceptions. Articles XIX through XXI provide additional exceptions to the general rules. Article XIX, the escape clause, allows countries to protect, through withdrawal of concessions or other measures, domestic producers from injury resulting from increases in imports. Articles XX and XXI identify other essentially noneconomic justifications for trade restrictions, such as for national security protection.

Consultation and dispute settlement. Articles XXII and XXIII lay out the dispute settlement process of GATT. Consultation between countries is emphasized, but panels of experts can also be asked to review cases on a nonbinding basis.

Part III

Procedural issues. Procedural and other administrative matters are taken up in Articles XXIV through XXXV. Most notably: Article XXIV addresses how free trade areas are to be established; Article XXVIII sets rules for modifying tariff schedules, including a call for periodic tariff negotiations; and Article XXXIII establishes criteria for accession of new members.

Part IV

Trade and development—treatment of developing countries. Article XXXVI acknowledges the special problems confronted by developing countries, and states that developed countries should not expect reciprocity from developing countries. Article XXXVII contains a statement of the intent of developed countries to encourage developing-country exports by unilaterally lowering trade barriers, and Article XXXVIII includes encouragement to stabilize and improve market conditions for primary products.

SOURCE: U.S. Congress, Congressional Budget Office, *The GATT Negotiations and U.S. Trade Policy* (Washington D.C.: Government Printing Office, June 1987), 18–19.

What led Congress initially to cede some of its trade policy authority to the president? Clearly, as we have noted in our discussion of the Smoot-Hawley Tariff, the trade policy formation process had broken down. Any discussion in the halls of Congress to institute even minor changes in tariff law would lead to an army of lobbyists seeking additional changes in tariffs. Tariffs were escalating, and with them came retaliatory tariffs imposed against U.S. goods by U.S. trading partners.

To its credit, Congress realized that the solution to its problems was to transfer some of its authority to the executive branch of the government. The action of Congress was entirely in its own self-interest. That is, by delegating tariff-setting authority to the president, members of Congress were giving "priority to protecting themselves: from the direct, one-sided pressure from producer interests that had led them to make bad trade law."* In the process, the interests of American exporters would

*I. M. Destler, *American Trade Politics: System Under Stress* (Washington, D.C.: Institute for International Economics, 1986), 12.

receive greater attention because the focus of U.S. trade policy would be on opening foreign markets rather than closing domestic markets.

However, Congress did not remain content in its decision to delegate its authority to the president. With each successive trade bill after the 1934 Reciprocal Trade Agreements Act, additional restrictions were placed on the authority of the president. Features were added to bills that allowed, for instance, domestic firms to seek a repeal of tariff cuts, thereby abrogating concessions made to foreign trading partners. In some instances, concessions made to foreign governments hinged on both trade-related concessions *and* non-trade-related political actions, such as cooperation in drug control or enforcement of human rights protection. In general, as trade expanded because of the success of the multilateral trade liberalization talks, Congress instituted new forms of (usually product-specific) protection by mandating procedures for and restrictions on the behavior of the executive branch. As Robert Baldwin notes,

> A rough idea of the increase over the years in the degree of specificity in the authority granted the president can be obtained by noting that the Trade Agreements Act of 1934 was 2 pages long, the 1958 extension 8 pages long, the Trade Expansion Act of 1962, 32 pages, the Trade Act of 1974, 99 pages, the Trade Agreements Act of 1979, 173 pages, and the Trade and Tariff Act of 1984, 102 pages.*

THE URUGUAY ROUND AND THE CREATION OF THE WTO

The Uruguay Round was launched at a meeting of trade ministers in Punta del Este, Uruguay, in October 1986. The formal negotiating process, involving representatives from over 100 countries, began in late 1986 and was expected to last for four or five years. Instead the talks soon became deadlocked over a number of thorny issues; they dragged on until a last minute agreement was struck in December 1993, hours before a U.S. imposed deadline was due to expire. What made the Uruguay Round so contentious was that unlike earlier rounds, which had focused on reducing tariffs, these negotiations were concentrated on reducing nontariff barriers, expanding protection of intellectual property rights, liberalizing trade in services and agriculture, and improving the functioning of the GATT system. Most of these objectives had been ignored in previous rounds for fear that disagreements over these issues would undermine the negotiations, and that was almost the case with the Uruguay Round.

Over the last three years of the talks the biggest stumbling block to an agreement involved liberalization of trade in agricultural products. As written, GATT rules had always applied to trade in agriculture. However, member countries—including the

---

*Robert Baldwin, *The Political Economy of U.S. Import Policy* (Cambridge, Mass.: MIT Press, 1985), 38.

United States, Japan, Korea, and the EU—were able to obtain waivers on these rules. As a consequence, many countries continued to use high tariffs or quotas to protect agriculture, even as protection levels on most manufactured goods came down.

By all accounts the most egregious protectionist policies have been applied by the EU. In order to protect local farmers, the EU operates a system of target prices for various farm products combined with import barriers and export subsidies. This system is known as the Common Agricultural Policy (CAP). The combination of EU import barriers and export subsidies of its surplus agricultural products severely affects world prices. During the negotiations, the CAP came under heavy criticism from the United States and especially a group of agricultural exporting countries known as the Cairns Group. The United States sought a significant reduction in subsidized exports and greater access for U.S. products in EU markets. However, the EU, led by France on this issue, refused to make any major concessions. Finally, in December 1993, the EU and the United States reached a compromise agreement on agriculture, allowing the Uruguay Round to be completed. During these talks other countries also announced liberalization of their agriculture policies. Both Korea and Japan announced the end to long-standing policies of embargoes on imports of rice.

The Uruguay Round also achieved some limited success in liberalizing international trade in services. Production and trade in services, including banking, construction, insurance, data processing, and audiovisual entertainment, have grown rapidly in the past few decades. The WTO estimates that cross-border trade in services totaled $1.3 trillion in 1998, more than three times 1980 levels, and about one-fourth the size of world merchandise trade. The GATT had never set down formal rules of behavior for trade in this area; many countries continue to restrict various types of services trade. This is especially true in developing countries. In March 1992, agreement appeared to be close on rules governing trade in several service sectors, including telecommunications and financial services. However, in the final draft of the Uruguay Round agreement only modest progress was made in extending GATT rules to these or any other service sectors. The agreement calls for countries to write regulations and licensing procedures that treat service companies from other nations the same as domestic companies. But member countries have made only modest commitments to change their rules to reflect these principles. Moreover, some issues, such as a dispute between the United States and the EU over European restrictions and taxes on American television and movies, were left completely unresolved.

Even though many compromises were made that have slowed trade liberalization, the Uruguay Round agreement is having a major impact on the evolving international trade environment. On January 1, 1995, the agreement took effect with a series of tariff cuts made by signatory countries; ultimately tariff levels will come down another 33 percent. Many countries have begun to convert quotas into less restrictive tariffs. Industrial countries are phasing out their quotas on textiles and apparel, and will end them completely by 2005. Trade in some agricultural products, especially fruits, vegetables, and rice, has expanded. The U.S. government estimates that lower trade barriers will generate $5 trillion in additional world output by 2005, with one-fifth of that being produced in the United States.

Perhaps the most substantive achievement of the Uruguay Round was the creation of a new international institution, the WTO.* The WTO replaced the GATT as the international organization responsible for enforcing existing international trade agreements and serving as a host for new talks to liberalize trade. As of late 1999, 135 countries had become members of the WTO; these countries account for more than 90 percent of world trade. Another 30 countries are in the process of applying for membership. The basic rules of the WTO are the principles laid out in the GATT agreement as well as those established in the Uruguay Round. Countries must accept all of the results of the Uruguay Round, without exception, to become WTO members. The WTO is responsible for setting new rules for goods and services trade, international investment, and protection of intellectual property rights. It also operates a strengthened disputes settlement procedure.

The old GATT was often criticized because it lacked an enforcement mechanism. When disputes between countries arose, the members were urged to consult. Should consultations fail, a panel of third-country representatives could be formed to hear the case and issue a ruling. However, the panel rulings were nonbinding on parties. If a country won a GATT case, it could appeal to GATT for permission to retaliate against the offending country. However, the offending country could veto retaliation.

The WTO dispute settlement procedures make more automatic the adoption of the findings of panels charged with settling trade disputes and of an appellate body designed to hear appeals of panel decisions. It provides for cross-retaliation (i.e., withdrawal of benefits in one sector for violations of rules in another). One goal of a stronger dispute settlements mechanism is to limit unilateral determinations that trade rules have been violated by affirming that members shall not themselves make determinations that a violation has occurred.

As of late 1999, the WTO dispute settlements system had been remarkably active and successful. Between January 1995 and January 2000, more than 190 cases had been notified to the dispute settlements process, involving about 150 distinct matters. This total represents more than half the number of cases brought to the GATT during its 50-year history. Of the 190 cases, 32 had been settled or become inactive, 32 had been reviewed by the appellate panel, and 22 had reached an initial panel decision. Roughly half of these cases were under review. The fact that so many cases have been brought to the WTO speaks volumes about the increased effectiveness of this system versus that in place under the GATT. The decisions that have been reached by the panels have sometimes been controversial and therefore labeled as sinister. WTO panel decisions have been portrayed by critics as decisions of a supergovernmental body that forces democratic nations to overturn their own laws in favor of the wishes of multinational corporations. In fact, this is not so. WTO panels do nothing more than try to ensure that national governments do not pass laws that violate the international commercial agreements to which these governments have already agreed. The WTO cannot force member countries to open their economies to trade and investment beyond the levels that have already been chosen. Nonetheless, an effective dispute settlements mechanism means that agreements will

---

*For more on the WTO, visit their Web site at http://www.wto.org/.

be adhered to more closely; this has made the WTO much stronger than the GATT it replaced.

A strong WTO has been viewed by some as possibly detrimental to the world environment. This is because some environmental policies of member countries have been challenged as violating WTO rules.* Indeed, the relationship between environmental and trade policy is of increasing interest to WTO officials. WTO rules currently place no constraints on the ability of countries to implement regulations on production or consumption activities in the domestic economy that could have adverse environmental impacts.

When the environmental problem is due to production or consumption activities in another country, WTO rules do constrain domestic regulatory actions, since they prohibit making market access dependent on changes in the domestic policies or practices of the exporting country. To do otherwise would invite many new trade restrictions as countries either attempt to impose their own domestic environmental standards on other countries or use such an attempt as a pretext for reducing competition from foreign imports.

However, the fact that WTO rules block unilateral use of trade measures as environmental policies does not mean that countries are powerless. They can negotiate multilateral agreements to take common actions. For instance, in 1987 a large number of countries signed the Montreal Protocol, which calls for a ban on trade in products that deplete the ozone layer. In cases where negotiations fail, countries can seek waivers from WTO rules in order to implement their policies. In either case, these options offer the prospect of resolving environmental problems without resorting to the excesses that could result from unilateral actions.

---

*For more on this topic, see Trade Policy Case Study 1: U.S. Tuna Quotas to Save Dolphins.

TRADE POLICY CASE STUDY 1

U.S. Tuna Quotas to Save Dolphins

Dolphins frequently school near stocks of yellowfin tuna in the eastern Pacific; a common way for tuna fishers to search for yellowfin stocks is to hunt for schools of dolphins, which often swim above the tuna. In the process of encircling the tuna, some dolphins are trapped in tuna nets, where they suffocate. There is no commercial market for dolphin meat, so the dead dolphins are discarded.

While the incidental catch of dolphins is an isolated problem—it occurs only in the eastern Pacific—it has long been a concern to animal rights groups, who have complained loudly to Congress. The Marine Mammal Protection Act (MMPA) was passed in 1972 in order to limit tuna harvests that would endanger dolphins. The act called on the government to close the eastern Pacific

(Continued)

fishing area should tuna harvesting result in a catch of dolphins in excess of an annual quota of 20,500. The quota was first reached in October 1986, and the area was closed to the U.S. tuna fleet for the rest of the year. The MMPA also authorized import restrictions on fish from countries that use fishing practices that endanger marine mammals. Imports were permitted from those countries that followed U.S. standards, but amendments to the MMPA in 1984, 1988, and 1990 made it increasingly hard for foreign countries to meet U.S. standards with respect to yellowfin tuna. In April 1990, the U.S. District Court of Northern California imposed an embargo on imports of Mexican tuna under the provisions of the MMPA; the embargo was upheld on appeal in February 1991. Mexico immediately challenged the embargo under the GATT.

Mexico argued that the measures prohibiting imports of yellowfin tuna were quotas, which are prohibited by GATT Article XI. The United States responded that the measures were not quotas but rather internal regulations that applied to all tuna, whether imported or caught by U.S. tuna fishers. The GATT panel found in favor of Mexico in September 1991. It did so on the grounds that the U.S. policy did not treat Mexican and U.S. tuna fishers equally. While the U.S. standard allowed Mexican fishers to kill dolphins in the process of catching tuna, the number of dolphins they were permitted to kill was based on the quantity killed by U.S. fishers—a quantity that would be known only after the fact. Thus, Mexican officials would have no way of knowing, at any point in time, whether they were in conformity with U.S. standards. This unpredictability was not necessary to protect dolphins, the panel found, and could not be justified as an exception to GATT rules. In October 1991, the two countries requested that the panel report be tabled, pending negotiations over a bilateral agreement about the problem.

Shortly thereafter, 10 countries that fish for yellowfin tuna in the eastern Pacific Ocean, including the United States and Mexico, set up a voluntary international dolphin protection program known as the La Jolla Agreement. The agreement was the first to set international limits on dolphin mortality and set a goal of decreasing dolphin deaths to under 5,000 by the year 2000. The program involved 100 percent observer coverage, captain and crew training in dolphin release techniques, and data collection on dolphin biology and by-catch.* The program was so successful that dolphin mortality went from 100,000 deaths per year in 1989 to fewer than 2,700 in 1996.

In 1995, 11 nations, including the United States and Mexico, signed the Panama Declaration. This agreement called on the United States to lift the embargoes on tuna from the eastern Pacific Ocean for those countries participating in the agreement and to change the definition of *dolphin-safe* to include tuna caught in encircling nets that resulted in zero mortality of dolphins in the process. At the time, the dolphin-safe definition meant only that no encircling nets were used to catch the tuna in the eastern Pacific Ocean. Fishermen who caught tuna with other methods—or in other areas of the world—but killed dolphin in the process were still allowed to use the dolphin-safe label.

In 1997 Congress made the Panama Declaration definition legally binding by passing the International Dolphin Conservation Program Act. It officially rescinded the import embargo on tuna caught by encircling nets and required an observer from an international oversight group to accompany every tuna boat using encircling nets. The Commerce Department was then directed to redefine the dolphin-safe label by spring 1999 based on studies to be done on the status of dolphin populations and the effect of stress due to encirclement. Also, under the law the National Marine Fisheries Service was required to pursue further studies and make another review in 2002 on whether the use of large encircling nets to catch tuna causes "significant adverse impact" on dolphin that swim with tuna.

---

*By-catch is the capture of unmarketable or restricted commercial fishing species.

THE CONDUCT OF U.S. COMMERCIAL POLICY

American trade law has a certain schizophrenic quality. On the one hand, in major trade legislation passed since 1934, Congress has authorized systematic reduction in American trade barriers in exchange for negotiated reductions in foreign barriers. On the other, Congress has provided American businesses with alternative mechanisms for seeking and obtaining relief from foreign competition. These procedures define the rules of legal commercial activity and allow for assistance, in the form of higher levels of protection, from either unfair *or* fair foreign competition. In this section we discuss in detail some of these measures.

Dumping

Dumping is defined as selling a product in a foreign country at a price that is lower than the price charged by the same firm in its home market or at a price below costs of production. Sales of this sort are defined in U.S. law to be sales at less than fair value (LTFV).

Dumping
Selling a product in a foreign market at a price that is below fair market value.

Before we discuss the legal procedures involved in dealing with dumping, let's explore a bit further the economics of dumping. Consider Figure 8.2. Suppose this represents the market for automobiles in the United States. Let P_W represent the price of automobiles in world markets as well as the price in the domestic market of the exporting country, say Korea. Under free trade conditions in the United States, the price of autos would also be P_W, and MN units would be imported. Holding everything else constant, if the Koreans were to lower the price they charged for their autos to, say, P_1, then they would be dumping in the U.S. market.

Suppose that the Koreans did dump their cars at price P_1. How would the United States be affected? Clearly, consumers would benefit, and domestic automakers would lose. However, the gain to consumers would exceed the loss to domestic pro-

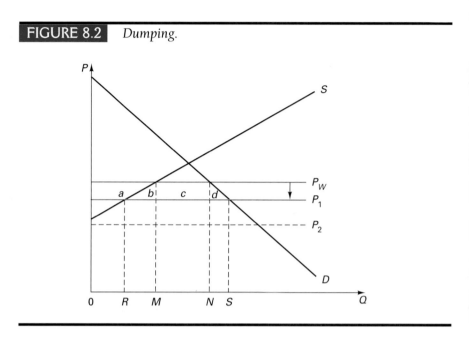

FIGURE 8.2   *Dumping.*

ducers, so that U.S. welfare would rise. An obvious question emerges from this analysis. If foreign dumping is good for America, why does Congress legislate against it? The answer is that in this instance at least, Congress is more interested in preserving the profits of domestic producers than it is in raising U.S. welfare. In addition, there is a fear that foreign dumping may be **predatory.**

Predatory dumping
Dumping in order to drive foreign competitors out of their market so that the market can be monopolized.

Consider what would happen if the Koreans were to charge P_2 instead of P_1. Clearly, U.S. firms would be driven from the market. This is because P_2 is below the minimum price necessary for any domestic production to occur (i.e., it is below the intercept of the domestic supply curve). Without competition from domestic firms, it is sometimes argued that foreign firms would stop charging such low prices and begin to behave as monopolists. Under these circumstances, dumping would be harmful. While this makes a good story, there is no documented evidence that predatory dumping has ever occurred or that it could ever occur. If foreign firms were to begin pricing in a monopolistic fashion, this would certainly entice new firms to enter or old firms to return to the market. Thus, if foreign firms want to maintain the entire U.S. market to themselves, they must keep their prices low enough to discourage entry by U.S. firms.

International price discrimination
Selling a product in two different countries at two different prices.

Under what circumstances is dumping likely to occur? One scenario involves a foreign industry that has some degree of market power both in its domestic market and in its foreign market. Because of this market power, the firm can set its own prices and does so in a fashion that maximizes its profits from selling in the two markets. Now, if the firm faces different demand curves in the two markets, and if it is not possible to resell the goods between markets, then the firm will charge different prices in the two markets. In other words, it will practice **international price dis-**

FIGURE 8.3 *International price discrimination.*

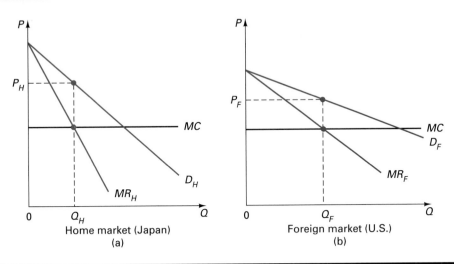

Home market (Japan)
(a)

Foreign market (U.S.)
(b)

crimination. And if demand for its products is more inelastic in the firm's home market, it is quite likely that the price the firm will charge at home will be higher than the price it will charge overseas.*

Consider Figure 8.3. There, we show the two markets faced by a Japanese semiconductor firm. In the left panel of the figure, we show the demand curve in the domestic (Japanese) market for the firm's product. In the right panel, we show the foreign (U.S.) market for this product. The domestic demand curve is shown to be steeper (less elastic), reflecting perhaps greater familiarity with this product in the home market. The U.S. demand curve is shown to be flatter, reflecting the possible existence of locally produced substitutes. Suppose now that the marginal cost of production is identical (and constant) regardless of where the product is to be sold. This is illustrated by the horizontal marginal cost (MC) line with the same height in both panels of the figure. To maximize its profits, the firm will produce at the output levels in each of the two markets where marginal revenue (MR) equals marginal cost (MC). Then, given the output levels it has chosen for the two markets, it will set a price in each market to be able to sell its output. As we have drawn it, the price it charges at home is higher than the price it charges in the United States.[†] In other words, dumping can result from profit-maximizing behavior.

---

*The incentives to price-discriminate exist within a country as well. Think, for instance, of a small brewing company in Pittsburgh that wants to sell some of its beer in Denver. It is reasonable to think that it might charge a lower price (than its Pittsburgh price) to consumers in Denver to convince them to try its product. The only thing the brewer must guard against is the possibility that someone in Denver might buy the beer at the low Denver price and try to resell it in Pittsburgh.

[†]Note that this is not a necessary result; nor is it always possible that a firm will be able to price-discriminate in this manner.

International price discrimination is one possible explanation for dumping. Dumping could also occur if a foreign firm were to receive a production or export subsidy from its government. Such a subsidy would help defray the costs of production, thereby allowing a firm to charge a price below its marginal cost. When a firm dumps in world markets under these circumstances, the taxpayers in the firm's home country, in effect, are picking up part of the tab for consumption that occurs in countries where the good is sold. As many economists have joked, under these circumstances, residents of the country where the dumping occurs should send the foreign taxpayers a thank-you note.

Antidumping Law

Dumping margin
The difference between the market price of a product and its fair market value.

Current antidumping law provides that under certain conditions, a special tariff (in addition to any normal duty) be imposed on foreign goods sold in the United States and priced at less than fair value.* The special tariff should be equal to the difference (known as the **dumping margin**) between the actual (lower) selling price and the (higher) fair market value of the product. To have the special tariff imposed, it is necessary to show that the dumping has materially injured a domestic industry or threatens to injure a domestic industry. The requirement that injury must be present or threatened is known as the **injury test.**

Injury test
An investigation to determine whether an unfair foreign trade practice has caused or threatens to cause harm to a domestic industry.

Antidumping cases begin with a complaint filed simultaneously with the Department of Commerce (DOC) and the International Trade Commission (ITC), both located in Washington, D.C. The complaint could come from anyone, including the secretary of commerce. In general, however, complaints are made by groups, such as firms, trade unions, or industry associations, closely tied to the production of the good competing with the allegedly dumped merchandise. Included in the complaint are evidence that dumping may be occurring and data designed to illustrate injury or threat of injury.

The ITC is an independent, quasi-judicial agency, headed by five presidentially appointed commissioners and staffed by economists and lawyers. The ITC investigates various trade-related issues and provides advice, based on its investigations, to the executive branch of the U.S. government. Its job with respect to antidumping cases is to investigate the question of injury. The ITC collects data on various aspects of the domestic industry and on the prices and quantities of imports. What it looks for is evidence of a link between imports and certain industry characteristics that would suggest that imports of the dumped merchandise have been to blame for the state of the industry. These industry characteristics include losses in the following: sales, market share, profits, productivity, return on investment, and capacity utilization. The ITC also considers effects on employment, inventories, wages, and the ability to raise new capital. Once the data have been collected and analyzed, the five commissioners vote on the question of injury.

---

*The antidumping statute is found in Section 731 of the Tariff Act of 1930, as amended. The first antidumping law was passed in 1916. The basis for the current statute is a law passed in 1921. To our knowledge, there is no U.S. law that prevents U.S. firms from dumping in foreign markets.

While the ITC investigates injury, the DOC investigates whether dumping has actually occurred. The DOC has 160 days to make a preliminary assessment of the question, including a first guess as to the size of the dumping margin. If the DOC finds that there is evidence that dumping might exist, all imports of the product in question are immediately subject to an increased tariff equal to the estimated dumping margin. The DOC then begins a further investigation of whether dumping has occurred and, at the completion of the investigation, makes a final ruling. If, after further study, the DOC finds that dumping has not occurred, then the special duties that had previously been imposed are rebated. Otherwise, the process continues until the ITC makes its final ruling as to the extent of injury.

If the ITC rules in its final report that injury has not occurred, then again the case is terminated and the special duties are rebated. If both the DOC and the ITC rule in favor of the petition, a permanent tariff is put in place, equal to the dumping margin calculated by the DOC in its final investigation.

For the DOC to calculate dumping margins, it must determine the fair market value of a product. U.S. law provides three alternatives. The preferred statistic for the calculation is the price of identical goods sold in the exporter's home market, so long as this price exceeds cost. If no such data exist, then prices in third-country markets are used (again, so long as these prices exceed production costs). If these data are unavailable or if the DOC determines that obtaining information on these prices would take too much time, then the DOC constructs a value based on the costs of production plus at least 10 percent for general expenses *and* at least 8 percent for profits.*

In the past several trade bills, Congress has sought to increase the rate at which antidumping cases are filed and judgments awarded. In 1980, the responsibility for investigating the size of the dumping margin was transferred from the Treasury Department (which had handled these cases since 1921) to the DOC.† It was felt that as the chief advocate for American business in the U.S. government, the DOC was likely to be more aggressive in fighting foreign dumping than the Treasury Department. In addition, in several recent bills, Congress has directed that greater use be made of constructed values rather than foreign prices in calculating fair market value. The use of constructed values clearly makes it more likely that the DOC will find that dumping exists. By requiring rigid expense and profit markups in constructed-value calculations, the law effectively brands as "unfair," and therefore prohibits, standard business practices such as lowering prices and accepting decreased profits when market conditions are poor.

Antidumping laws are one form of the many types of nontariff barriers, which are described in more detail in Chapter 7. Consider how the process works in favor of local firms. If they can convince the DOC and the ITC that there is reason to think

---

*James Bovard, in his book on U.S. trade policy, reports that 13 of the 15 largest companies in the Fortune 500 did not earn 8 percent profits in 1989, thereby failing the standard the DOC mandatorily imposes on foreign firms. See James Bovard, *The Fair Trade Fraud* (New York: St. Martin's Press, 1991).
†The transfer of authority from Treasury to DOC was authorized by the Carter administration under great pressure from Congress. For more on this subject, see I. M. Destler, *American Trade Politics.*

dumping might have occurred, protection is immediately awarded. If there is considerable competition between domestic and foreign firms, then it is quite likely that there will be price and profit cutting on both sides. The presence of antidumping laws puts foreign firms on notice that this competition must be restrained or else they face, at a minimum, the expense of hiring lawyers to defend themselves in antidumping hearings. The law does provide an option for foreign firms. At any time during the process, foreigners can escape the imposition of duties by entering into an agreement with the DOC to either raise their prices or stop selling their goods in the U.S. markets. Thus, antidumping laws tend to place a floor on foreign prices and to limit foreign competition. Finally, note that antidumping laws offer no discretion to government officials. If the DOC finds dumping and the ITC finds injury, tariffs will be imposed. This is so even if the tariffs may harm more U.S. firms than they help. An illustration of this point is given in Trade Policy Case Study 2.

TRADE POLICY CASE STUDY 2

Computer Display Screens

In July 1990, the Advanced Display Manufacturers of America (ADMA), an association of seven small U.S. electronics companies, filed petitions with the DOC and the ITC alleging that imports of Japanese high-definition flat panel computer screens were being sold in the United States at prices below fair market value. Essentially, two types of products were mentioned in the petition. Active matrix (AM) displays are used mainly as laptop and portable computer screens. Electroluminescent (EL) display panels may also be found on portable computers but are more commonly used in avionics, military equipment, and medical instruments. The petitions claimed that unfair prices posed a threat of material injury to U.S. firms. After completing its investigation, the DOC determined that the computer screens were being sold at less than fair value. The DOC set dumping margins of 63 percent on imports of Japanese AM display screens and 7 percent on imports of Japanese EL screens.

At that point, the ITC began its final investigation of injury. The American firms involved in the case were all extremely small. Both of the American AM screen producers aimed their products at military customers and other specialized users. Neither had succeeded in selling displays to U.S. computer manufacturers. In contrast, the Japanese firms named in the petition were some of Japan's largest electronics firms, including Hitachi, Matsushita, Sharp, and Toshiba. They all sent representatives to protest the imposition of antidumping duties. Also in opposition to the petition were a number of American firms, including Apple Computer, IBM, Texas Instruments, and

---

*Anne E. Brunsdale, *Certain High-Information Content Flat Panel Displays and Display Glass Therefore from Japan,* Final Determination, USITC, August 1991, p. 35.

Tandy Corporation. These companies all argued that their U.S. manufacturing operations would be adversely affected if they were forced to pay higher tariffs on any imported computer screens they might use in producing their computers or electronic instruments. Several of these companies reported that they had tried to buy their screens from firms belonging to ADMA, but ultimately chose Japanese suppliers because the American firms could not deliver the product they needed. Indeed, Apple testified that the American company it approached, OIS Optical Imaging Systems, had "zero high volume manufacturing capability, little customer support experience, zero manufacturing flexibility, zero mass production experience and delivery schedule."*

Despite this testimony, as well as threats from several American computer companies to move their manufacturing operations offshore if the tariffs were imposed, the ITC ruled that unfairly low prices were injuring U.S. screen manufacturers. In particular, the ITC appeared to be concerned that the prices were so low that American firms were discouraged from entering this area of manufacturing.

One year later, in November 1992, OIS Optical Imaging Systems petitioned the DOC to remove the antidumping duties on AM displays. Even with the duties in place, business for OIS had not improved. In the previous 12 months, it had lost $5.7 million on sales of only $5.8 million. During this period, new owners of the company replaced the original OIS management. The new managers began to make business overtures to Apple Computer and other American manufacturers. These new ties to laptop producers appear to have influenced the decision to request removal of the tariffs, although no direct evidence was presented from the firm regarding its rationale for the move. In June 1993, the duties were lifted.

American firms make considerable use of antidumping laws. Between 1992 and 1995, 123 antidumping petitions were filed—almost 70 percent more than in the previous four-year period. Between 1996 and 1998 another 86 petitions were filed, 50 in 1998 alone. Of the 50 cases filed in 1998, the DOC ruled—at least in its preliminary findings—that pricing at less than fair value had occurred in every case but one, and, in every case where dumping was detected, the ITC made a preliminary finding of injury to domestic firms. In final rulings over the 1980–1998 period, only 36 percent of antidumping cases were disposed of without duties being imposed or foreign prices increased.

As of December 31, 1998, 315 antidumping duties were in place against foreign products. Products involved in these cases included a wide variety of steel products from many countries: shop towels from Bangladesh; pencils, paper clips, and garlic from China; semiconductors from Korea; and kiwi fruit from New Zealand. Of the duties, 86 percent (271) were imposed after 1985. Products from Asia were the most often targeted, with 51 duties in place against Japan, 41 against China, 22 against Taiwan, and 18 against Korea. On average, antidumping duties are 10 to 20 times higher than MFN tariffs. Tariffs this high are a remarkable effective mechanism to reduce foreign competition. In a recent study, Thomas Prusa argues that U.S. antidumping duties cause the value of imports to fall by 30–50 percent.*

Countervailing Duty Law

As we previously noted, one possible cause of dumping is the provision of production or export subsidies by foreign governments to their firms or industries. Congress views such subsidies as an unfair trade practice regardless of whether or not dumping actually occurs. U.S. trade law provides for **countervailing duties** to offset the effects of any subsidy allocated for the production or export of a good that is subsequently imported into the United States.

Countervailing duty
A tariff designed to raise the price of an imported product to its fair market value.

Countervailing duty (CVD) cases are handled much like antidumping cases. There are two main differences. First, foreign firms that receive a subsidy need not be practicing international price discrimination for domestic firms to receive protection. Second, in some cases, no injury test is required. In these cases, if a subsidy is shown to exist, the duty is imposed—even if domestic industry has not been harmed or even threatened with harm.

Petitions are filed with the DOC and, in situations where an injury test is required, with the ITC. The DOC investigates whether a subsidy exists and, if so, its size. According to the law, subsidies are direct and/or indirect grants for the production or export of goods. They can take many forms, including direct cash payments, tax credits, or loans with artificially low interest rates. Current law also applies to **upstream subsidies**. An upstream subsidy is said to exist if a foreign manufacturer is able to purchase an input at an artificially low price because the government of that country has subsidized the use of this input.

Upstream subsidy
A subsidy that lowers the cost of an input for a manufacture.

In addition to U.S. law against subsidies, the WTO administers a subsidies agreement reached as part of the Uruguay Round negotiations. The agreement establishes three categories of subsidies: those that are *prohibited*; those that are *actionable*; and those that are *non-actionable*. In general terms, prohibited subsidies are those that are made available contingent upon export performance or upon the use of domestic over imported goods. Prohibited subsidies are subject to dispute settlement procedures that include an expedited timetable for action by the WTO dispute settlement body. If it is found that the subsidy is indeed prohibited, it must be immediately withdrawn. If this is not done within the specified time period, the complaining member is authorized to take countermeasures. With respect to actionable subsidies, the starting point is that no member of the WTO should cause, through the use of subsidies, adverse effects to the interests of other members. Members affected by actionable subsidies may refer the matter to the dispute settlement body. In the event that it is determined that adverse effects exist, the subsidizing member

*See Thomas J. Prusa, "On the Spread and Impact of Antidumping," *NBER Working Paper #7404* (October 1999).

must withdraw the subsidy or remove the adverse effects. Non-actionable subsidies could either be non-specific subsidies, or specific subsidies involving assistance to industrial research and pre-competitive development activity, assistance to disadvantaged regions, or certain types of assistance for adapting existing facilities to new environmental requirements imposed by law and/or regulations. Where another member believes that an otherwise non-actionable subsidy is resulting in serious adverse effects to a domestic industry, it may seek a determination and recommendation on the matter.

The agreement also contains provisions on the use of countervailing measures. Thus it sets out disciplines on the initiation of countervailing cases, investigations by national authorities and rules of evidence to ensure that all interested parties can present information and arguments.

Disciplines on the calculation of the amount of a subsidy are outlined, as is the basis for the determination of injury to the domestic industry. The agreement requires that relevant economic factors be taken into account in assessing the state of the industry and that a causal link be established between the subsidized imports and the alleged injury. All countervailing duties have to be terminated within five years of their imposition unless the authorities determine on the basis of a review that the expiry of the duty would be likely to lead to continuation or recurrence of subsidization and injury.

Subsidies may play an important role in developing countries and in the transformation of centrally planned economies to market economies. Least-developed countries and developing countries with less than $1,000 per capita GNP are thus exempted from disciplines on prohibited export subsidies, and have a time-limited exemption from other prohibited subsidies. For other developing countries, export subsidy prohibition takes effect in 2003, while exemption from the other prohibited subsidies will be curtailed more quickly than for the poorer countries. Countervailing investigations of products originating from developing-country members will terminate if the overall level of subsidies does not exceed 2 percent (and from certain developing countries 3 percent) of the value of the product, or if the volume of the subsidized imports represents less than 4 percent of the total imports for the like product in the importing member.

Unfair Foreign Practices: Section 301

Up to this point, our discussion has centered on U.S. trade law provisions to deal with unfair foreign trade practices in U.S. markets. U.S. trade law has also provided a means to combat perceived unfair practices in foreign markets. **Section 301** of the Trade Act of 1974 provides authority to the president to enforce U.S. rights under international agreements and to respond to certain unfair trade practices in foreign markets. That is, the emphasis in these cases is on the actions of foreign governments taken in their own markets against U.S. firms. If foreign governments engage in policies or practices that burden, restrict, or discriminate against U.S. commerce, the United States may impose import restrictions against the products of that country in the event that an agreement cannot be reached to end the offensive practices.

Section 301
A provision in U.S. trade law that requires the U.S. government to negotiate the elimination of foreign unfair trade practices and to retaliate against offending countries if negotiations fail.

Section 301 cases are administered by the office of the U.S. Trade Representative (USTR). USTR is an agency within the executive branch that is charged with advising the president on trade policy matters and coordinating the U.S. government in its trade negotiations. It is headed by a cabinet-level official whose title is also the U.S. Trade Representative (the USTR).*

Petitions to begin a Section 301 case are presented to USTR. They can be filed by anyone, including cases self-initiated by the U.S. government. The USTR has a short period of time (usually about six weeks) to decide whether to accept a case. If it is accepted, negotiations begin between the U.S. government and the government against whom the complaint has been filed. When the dispute involves practices of another WTO member country over products or practices covered under any of the WTO agreements, consultations and negotiations take place in the WTO as part of the WTO dispute settlement process. In other situations, the WTO is not brought into the picture. In these latter cases, if no agreement is reached in the negotiations, the statute requires action by the USTR within one year of the onset of the case. The action may be to continue the talks, to drop the case for lack of merit, or to impose retaliation by closing U.S. markets to exporters in the foreign country to persuade the country to end its practices.

Between 1975 and August 1999, 119 Section 301 cases were undertaken by the U.S. government. Roughly half of these have been resolved successfully in that the offending foreign practice was eliminated or modified in some way, although less than half of these have resulted in any significant expansion in U.S. exports of the product in question. Thirteen have resulted in retaliation by the United States against foreign products, in the form of higher tariffs or stricter quotas. Many cases dragged on for years, either because the old GATT process was slow and cumbersome or because the (private) parties to the dispute had become happy with the status quo. Several cases were dropped after investigations failed to show that U.S. commerce was adversely affected by the foreign practices. Trade Policy Case Study 3 provides an example of a Section 301 case that resulted in retaliation.

Congress is eager to see Section 301 used more often, and recent trade legislation has included measures that would make retaliation more automatic and would place stricter time limits on the negotiation process. By making retaliation more automatic, the feeling in Congress is that the United States will have more leverage in its negotiations to remove foreign trade barriers. If used wisely, Section 301 can lead to welfare increases in the United States and possibly overseas. That is, if the *threat* of retaliation is sufficient to lower foreign barriers, the United States clearly gains. If the alternative that the foreign country faces is retaliation, it almost certainly gains by lowering its trade barriers. If retaliation is actually imposed, the United States loses: The foreign barriers remain in place and U.S. consumers face higher tariffs on certain imports.

---

*To avoid confusion (we hope), we refer to the office as USTR and to the individual as *the* USTR. Charlene Barshefsky currently serves as the USTR.

TRADE POLICY CASE STUDY 3

U.S.–EU Bananas Dispute

Bananas grow in countries with tropical climates all over the world. The most productive areas for banana production are the countries of Central America and certain countries in South America. Over the past several decades banana production has been growing rapidly, up 24 percent in the 1990s alone. Despite this vast increase in production, bananas are very expensive in the countries of the EU; they retail for twice the price paid in stores in the United States. The reason for this is a complicated system of tariffs and quotas that the EU imposed in 1993 to control imports of bananas. The stated purpose of this policy is to support banana production in countries that are former European colonies located in the Caribbean, Asia, and Africa; these countries were given a substantial share of the quota licenses. Without this policy, the EU argues, banana production in these countries would be wiped out. This is because these former colonies are far less well suited to produce the fruit than are Central and South American countries.

In 1996 USTR self-initiated a Section 301 investigation against EU banana import policies. It did so because the world's three largest banana companies, Dole Food Company, Inc.; Chiquita Brands, Inc.; and Fresh Del Monte Produce Inc.—all based in the United States—had lost significant market share in the EU because of the quota policy. As a result of the Section 301 investigation, the dispute was taken to the WTO. In 1997 the WTO ruled in favor of the U.S. position, and later that year a WTO appellate panel also ruled in favor of the United States. To try to head off a major trade dispute, the two sides took the case to arbitration. But in early 1999 the WTO arbitration panel also ruled in favor of the United States. When the EU announced that it would not change its banana policy, the United States received permission from the WTO to impose 100 percent tariffs on certain imports from the EU. These tariffs went into place in March 1999.

A critical analysis of the EU policy points to the enormous inefficiency of the EU policy at trying to achieve its stated goal. It is estimated that in any given year consumers in the EU pay $2 billion in quota rents because of the policy while the favored developing countries received $150 million in additional profits. In other words, EU consumers paid $13.25 for every $1 transferred to banana producers in their former colonies. The rest of the money went to a few trading companies that owned the import licenses and were able to charge the artificially high prices for bananas in the EU. As of early 2000, both the EU policy and the U.S. tariffs remain in place.*

---

*For more on this case, see Martin Wolf, "Going Bananas," *Financial Times,* Wednesday March 24, 1999, and Gordon Fairclough and Darren McDermott, "Why Bananas, a Rotten Business, Set Off a Trade War Far and Wide," *Wall Street Journal,* August 9, 1999.

It is ironic that in perhaps the most egregious of situations, Section 301 threats are almost always destined to fail. This is because Section 301 is clearly an intrusion by the United States into the policies of foreign governments. Foreign political leaders may not want to appear to be vulnerable to U.S. threats and may resist mutually beneficial agreements in order to preserve national pride. Thus, foreign governments are most likely to give in to U.S. demands over issues that have little economic or political significance but to resist in situations involving larger trade volumes or more politically sensitive product areas. Another problem faced by U.S. negotiators is the (potentially) embarrassing existence of similar trade barriers in the United States. For instance, currently the United States imposes severe limits on imports of textiles, steel, and sugar. To the extent that U.S. practices inspire foreign trade barriers, the U.S. negotiation position may be weakened. A potentially more successful way to lower foreign barriers to trade might be to offer reductions in U.S. barriers on goods that are currently limited.

The Escape Clause: Section 201

Escape clause
A measure in U.S. trade law that allows for temporary protection against fairly traded foreign imports.

So far, we have considered provisions in U.S. trade law designed to offset unfair foreign trade practices. U.S. law also provides a mechanism for domestic firms to seek protection from fairly traded foreign goods. This mechanism is known as the **escape clause**. The escape clause, in various forms, has been part of U.S. trade law since the early 1940s. It provides that the president may withdraw or modify trade concessions made to foreign countries and impose restrictions on imports of any article that causes or threatens serious injury to a domestic industry producing a similar or directly competitive good.

Present escape clause language stresses that the increased protection of domestic industry be of a temporary nature. Trade restrictions can be increased for an initial period of no more than five years and should be phased down over this interval. The use of temporary protection is for two reasons. First, it helps slow the contraction of domestic industry, thereby providing more time for resources to be smoothly transferred to other sectors of the economy. Second, by increasing domestic profits it may provide incentives to domestic firms to reinvest in their industry so as to be better able to compete with foreign producers.*

To obtain escape clause protection, a representative of an industry (i.e., firms, labor, or the industry trade association) files a petition with the ITC. The petition must state the purpose of seeking trade relief, such as facilitating the transfer of resources from the industry or adjusting the industry to better face foreign competition. Upon receipt of the petition, the ITC begins an injury investigation. According to the law as it is now written, the ITC must investigate whether imports have caused, or threaten to cause, injury to the domestic industry. For purposes of its

---

*For an excellent analysis of escape clause protection and whether this protection has been successful, see U.S. Congress, Congressional Budget Office, *Has Trade Protection Revitalized Domestic Industries?* (Washington D.C.: Government Printing Office, 1986).

investigation, the ITC may define the domestic industry as only that portion producing the like article.

The ITC has six months to complete its investigation. If it finds that injury has occurred or might occur, it recommends to the president the amount and nature of import relief necessary to remedy or prevent the injury. The president must then decide whether or not to provide the relief. In general, relief is provided unless the president determines it is not in the national economic interest.

The escape clause has been used relatively rarely over the past few years. The ITC has considered 70 petitions since 1975. Of these, it found injury in 38 cases, and the president imposed restrictions in only 14. The most recent case where protection was imposed involved imports of lamb meat. American producers complained that they could not compete with low-priced Australian and New Zealand lamb meat products. In July 1999 President Clinton established a temporary tariff rate quota (TRQ) on lamb meat. Under this plan, the first-year quota was set at 31.9 million kilograms (the level of U.S. imports in 1998). The quota will rise by 0.8 million kilograms for each of the next two years. Quota licenses were distributed to Australia and New Zealand according to 1998 market shares. Tariffs within the quota levels were raised to 9 percent in the first year, 6 percent in the second, and 3 percent in the third. Tariffs on imports beyond the quota levels were set at 40 percent in the first year, 32 percent in the second, and 24 percent in the third. Prior to the TRQ, the U.S. tariff on lamb meat had been 0.2 percent.

As an alternative to higher protection, the ITC may rule that workers or firms in the industry receive **trade adjustment assistance (TAA)**. The assistance is designed to help workers who, because of competition from imports, have entered into long-term unemployment. TAA provides funds to allow workers to participate in worker training programs, to supplement their incomes while they search for new jobs, or to relocate. TAA paid to firms consists of technical assistance to establish industry-wide programs for new product development, process development, or export development.

Trade adjustment assistance was used extensively in the late 1970s as an alternative to the imposition of protection. Many autoworkers and steelworkers received TAA benefits as supplements to unemployment compensation. The enormous budget cost of the program led Congress to change the emphasis of the program from income supplements to worker retraining. Because of these changes, the use of TAA has declined dramatically in recent years.

Trade adjustment assistance (TAA) Payments made by the government to help factors retrain or retool after they have been displaced by foreign competition.

Other Measures

Current U.S. trade law contains other measures designed to offer protection against either fair or unfair competition. There is a provision (Section 337) that restricts unfair methods of competition, such as patent or copyright infringement. Section 337 has been used extensively by U.S. firms, mainly to charge foreigners with patent infringement. If the domestic firm wins its case, the foreign product is barred from entry into the United States. In one case, certain Cabbage Patch dolls were restricted from importation because, unlike their domestic counterparts, these dolls did not have adoption papers—a copyrighted feature of dolls to be marketed in the United States.

There is also a measure (Section 406) that provides relief from market disruption by imports from Communist countries. Section 406 cases are much like escape clause cases, except that the test for injury is much weaker. These cases are rare, especially since the dissolution of the USSR and communist Eastern Europe.

There are restrictions on trade in goods considered vital to the national defense. For instance, the government recently extended voluntary export restraint agreements (VERs) with foreign producers of machine tools. Several agencies of the U.S. government must discriminate in favor of American goods according to the federal "Buy American" act.

Comparisons with Policies in Other Countries

Most of the policies just described have counterparts in the policies of many foreign countries, especially in industrialized economies. Foreign countries make substantial use of antidumping statutes. There are also many examples of efforts to protect industries imperiled by fairly traded foreign products. This latter protection, similar to the escape clause in U.S. legislation, is known as **safeguards protection**. The sum total of all of these actions involving antidumping statutes, countervailing duties, safeguards protection, and the like makes up a substantial share of the nontariff barriers in the world today.

Safeguards protection
A general name for measures such as the escape clause.

From 1987 through 1997, 2,196 antidumping cases were initiated worldwide, with more than half resulting in higher duties. With the exception of 1995, more than 200 new cases were filed in various countries each year from 1991 through 1997. In the 1980s, the primary users of antidumping laws were the United States, the EU, Australia, Canada, and New Zealand. During the 1990s a number of developing countries began to make increasing use of this form of protection. Indeed, the United States government has sent teams of experts to various countries, including Egypt and Indonesia, to train officials in the establishment and administration of this type of trade law. Table 8.2 provides data on the countries involved in antidumping cases during 1997. As the table shows, Australia had the most cases that year, followed closely by the EU. Ranking third was South Africa, which had not had an antidumping law before 1994. Countries of the EU were the targets of the most antidumping cases. China ranked second, with Korea and Taiwan tied for third among countries targeted by these cases.

Although a number of countries have laws that authorize the use of countervailing duties to offset foreign export subsidies, the imposition of these duties is relatively common only in the United States. At the end of 1998, the United States had in place more than 59 orders imposing countervailing antisubsidy duties on various goods. The use of countervailing duty laws seems to have declined in recent years. For instance, in 1995 the United States initiated only two new cases, and only twelve new cases were initiated worldwide. Other countries initiating new cases in 1995 included Australia (3), Canada (4), and New Zealand (1). Countries most often accused of providing subsidies to their exporters were the EU and the United States.

TABLE 8.2	Antidumping Cases Initiated Worldwide, 1997	
	Number of Antidumping Cases	
Country	By	Against
Australia	42	1
European Union[1]	41	57
Argentina	15	n.a.[2]
Brazil	11	5
Canada	14	3
China	0	31
Japan	0	12
Korea	n.a.	16
Mexico	6	n.a.
New Zealand	5	0
South Africa	23	n.a.
Taiwan	n.a.	16
United States	16	15
Others	60	77
TOTALS	233	233

[1]Antidumping actions are taken by the EU, not by individual member states. Actions against the E.U. are against member countries.

[2]not available

SOURCE: Constructed by the authors from data in Thomas J. Prusa, "On the Spread and Impact of Antidumping," Tables 1 and 2.

WTO members may take safeguard actions to protect a specific domestic industry from an increase of imports of any product that is causing, or is likely to cause, serious injury to the industry. Such safeguard measures were always available under GATT. However, they were infrequently used; some governments, such as the United States and the EU, preferred to secure protection for domestic industries through VERs and other market-sharing devices in product areas as diverse as automobiles, steel, videotape recorders, and televisions.

The WTO agreement broke new ground in establishing a prohibition against VERs and in setting a sunset clause on all safeguard actions. The agreement stipulates that members shall not seek, take, or maintain any VERs, orderly marketing arrangements, or any other similar measures on the export or the import side.

In principle, safeguard measures have to be applied irrespective of the source of the imports. However, the agreement lays down the manner in which decisions on the allocation of a quota should be made including in the exceptional circumstances where imports from certain WTO members have increased disproportionately quickly. The duration of a safeguard measure should not exceed four years, though this can be extended up to eight years, subject to a determination by competent national authorities that the measure is needed and that there is evidence the industry is adjusting. Measures imposed for more than a year must be progressively liberalized.

SUMMARY

1. Commercial policy is the set of barriers and/or subsidies a country puts in place to affect its international trade.

2. The U.S. Constitution confers authority to the Congress for the development of commercial policy. Over much of the first 200 years of the United States, Congress exercised this authority by passing comprehensive tariff-setting bills. The last bill of this sort was the Smoot-Hawley Tariff of 1930.

3. Since 1930, in a series of trade bills, Congress has delegated authority to the president for limited periods of time to reach agreements with foreign trading partners to lower trade barriers on a mutual basis.

4. At first, the president negotiated with foreign countries on an individual basis. Since the end of World War II, however, trade liberalization negotiations have been held from time to time on a multilateral basis under the auspices of the GATT. The most well-known and successful of these talks were the Kennedy Round in the 1960s, the Tokyo Round in the 1970s, and the Uruguay Round in the 1980s and early 1990s.

5. Also included in these trade bills have been a variety of provisions that make it possible for industries on an individual basis to receive continued or expanded protection. These provisions include measures (e.g., antidumping provisions, countervailing duty laws, and Section 301) ostensibly aimed at unfair trade practices of foreign countries as well as provisions (e.g., the escape clause) designed to provide protection from fairly traded imports.

6. Over time, the Congress has expanded the ability of American businesses to make use of these special provisions, and the number of such cases has grown enormously.

EXERCISES

1. Examine Figure 8.1 carefully. In what periods were U.S. tariffs high? When were they low? How do you explain these patterns?

2. What is the WTO? What services does it perform? Explain carefully.

3. What is dumping? What are the welfare costs of dumping? Why would firms ever dump? Explain carefully.

4. Compare and contrast how the U.S. government handles antidumping and countervailing duty cases.

5. What is Section 301 of U.S. trade law? Describe how it works. Do you think it is likely to be very effective? Comment.

6. In 1988, Senator Ernest Hollings of South Carolina was quoted as saying that "going the 201 route is for suckers." By this, he appeared to mean that Ameri-

can firms seeking protection from foreign competition would do better by using other trade remedies. Given your knowledge of how Section 201 and alternative forms of U.S. trade laws are administered, do you agree with the senator's statement? Why or why not?

7. A former ITC commissioner, Alfred Eckes, has written, "In battling dumping, trade administrators not only help sustain political support for an open global trading system, but they also bring benefits to consumers as well as producers. I remember well how imposition of U.S. antidumping duties against Korean television makers prompted them to lower high home market prices in order to avoid the payment of U.S. dumping duties." Comment on Mr. Eckes's statement. Do you agree or disagree with its general thrust? Support your answer with examples from how U.S. policy is applied and recent world experience with such policies.

8. Milton Friedman has often written that instead of imposing countervailing duties on subsidized foreign goods, the United States should write a note of thanks to foreign taxpayers. Do you agree? Why or why not? Illustrate with a simple diagram.

9. What are the benefits and costs of U.S. antidumping laws?

10. How likely is dumping to be predatory? Discuss.

REFERENCES

Council of Economic Advisers. *Economic Report of the President.* Washington, D.C.: Government Printing Office, 1987, 1988, and 1992.

Destler, I. M. *American Trade Politics: System Under Stress.* Washington, D.C.: Institute for International Economics, 1986.

Jackson, John. *The World Trading System.* Cambridge, Mass.: MIT Press, 1989.

Taussig, Frank. *The Tariff History of the United States.* New York: G. P. Putnam's Sons, 1888.

U.S. House of Representatives, Committee on Ways and Means. *Overview and Compilation of U.S. Trade Statutes.* Washington, D.C.: Government Printing Office, August 1995.

U.S. International Trade Commission. *Operation of the Trade Agreements Program.* Washington, D.C.: Government Printing Office, 1998.

INTERNET APPLICATIONS

Please visit our Web site at **www.awl.com/husted_melvin** for more exercises and readings.

CHAPTER 9

Preferential Trade

Arrangements

Since the end of World War II, trade barriers have fallen and international trade has grown rapidly. Part of the reduction in trade barriers has come about because of the multilateral trade talks sponsored by GATT. In addition to this movement toward trade liberalization, various countries have agreed to reduce even further barriers to trade among themselves. Such agreements are known as preferential (or discriminatory) trade arrangements, or, because they are likely to be established between neighboring countries, regional trade liberalization. Today, virtually all of the 130 WTO member countries participate in at least one of the 109 preferential agreements that have been officially recognized by the WTO.*

Free-trade area (FTA)
An agreement among several countries to eliminate internal barriers to trade but to maintain existing barriers against nonmember countries.

The two main types of preferential trade arrangements are **free-trade areas (FTAs)** and **customs unions (CUs)**.[†] The basic difference between FTAs and CUs is how the member countries treat nonmember countries. In particular, a CU is an association of countries that agrees to eliminate barriers to trade among its members and to form a common barrier against nonmember countries. Countries that form an FTA also agree to eliminate trade barriers among themselves, but they maintain their own individual trade barriers against nonmember countries.

Customs unions (CU)
An agreement among several countries to eliminate internal barriers to trade and to erect common barriers against nonmember countries.

The best-known example of a CU is the **European Union (EU)**.[‡] The EU was founded in 1957 as a customs union agreement among six countries: France, West Germany, Italy, and the Benelux nations (Belgium, Netherlands, and Luxembourg). Since then, the EU has added nine new members: the United Kingdom, Ireland, and Denmark in 1973; Greece in 1981; Spain and Portugal in 1986; and Austria, Finland, and Sweden in 1995. The population of the EU now stands at over 375 million people, and the EU countries *as a group* rank as the largest exporters and importers in the world.

European Union (EU)
A CU among most of the nations of Western Europe.

In theory, the EU is a sort of united states of Europe: individual countries tied together by a common commercial policy and internal free trade, much like the free trade that exists among California, Kansas, and New York. In practice, that is not the case. While the agreement eliminated most tariffs among the member countries, it left in place a maze of nontariff barriers. In early 1986, the member countries agreed to begin a process aimed at the removal of these nontariff barriers by the end of 1992. Implementation of these reforms has been slowed by the complexity of the process and by EU expansion; over 1,400 measures are involved, often requiring leg-

---

*For a description and analysis of existing preferential trade agreements, circa mid-1992, see Norman S. Fieleke, "One Trading World or Many: The Issue of Regional Trading Blocs," *New England Economic Review* (Federal Reserve Bank of Boston, 1992). For more detail on the relationship between preferential trade agreements and the WTO, see "Customs Unions and Free Trade Areas Since 1948," *WTO Focus Newsletter* (World Trade Organization, May–June 1995).
†Some authors refer to a third type of preferential trade agreement known as a common market (CM). A CM is a CU that has freedom of movement for all factors of production within the area defined by the member states. In the remainder of this chapter, we do not distinguish between CMs and CUs.
‡Over the course of its existence, the EU has had a variety of names. It was first called the European Common Market. Later, it became the European Economic Community (EEC). More recently, it has been designated as the European Community (EC). In November 1993, the EC became the EU, in recognition of the goal of expanded cooperation between its individual sovereign governments.

islation in each of the 15 countries. As of November 1999, member states had enacted 87 percent of these measures.

In 1993, the United States, Canada, and Mexico agreed to form one of the world's largest FTAs. This arrangement, known as the **North American Free Trade Agreement (NAFTA)**, went into effect on January 1, 1994. In some ways, NAFTA merely represents an expansion of a previously existing FTA between the United States and Canada to include Mexico. Over time, virtually all tariffs on trade among the three countries will fall to zero; trade in services will be liberalized, as will rules on international mobility of investment flows. An international commission that was established by the United States and Canada to review antidumping and counter-vailing duty decisions made by the national institutions on either side of the border became a trilateral commission that also handles disputes arising among the countries over implementation of the agreement.

The NAFTA also goes beyond the earlier agreement in several important dimensions. Most notably, it includes two side accords that seek to enforce environmental and labor laws and provide funding for labor retraining and environmental cleanup. It also calls on each country, but particularly Mexico, to adopt measures to enforce intellectual property rights.

Why are preferential trade agreements so important in the current world trading system? What are the economic effects of these agreements? How do these arrangements accord with the WTO? The goal of this chapter is to provide answers to all these questions. We begin by developing a simple model of preferential trade arrangements that spells out some of their costs and benefits. We then go on to provide greater detail on several existing agreements.

> **North American Free Trade Agreement (NAFTA)**
> An FTA among Canada, Mexico, and the United States.

PREFERENTIAL TRADE ARRANGEMENTS: ECONOMIC ANALYSIS

The economic implications of regional trade liberalization such as FTAs or CUs are essentially identical. In order to understand these implications, suppose that there exist three countries in the world: A, B, and C. We begin by assuming that A is the world high-cost producer of a product, say beer, and that initially A protects its producers with an ad valorem tariff of 100 percent against all foreign producers. Suppose that, in autarky, beer would cost $5.00 per bottle in A and that B would be willing to export beer to A for $2.00 per bottle, while C, the low-cost world producer, is willing to export beer at a price of $1.50 per bottle.

Figure 9.1 illustrates the market for beer in A. The lines S_B and S_C denote the export supply curves to A's market from countries B and C, respectively. Under free trade, A would import IJ bottles of beer from C, at a price of $1.50 each. Since A can buy beer from C at $1.50, there is no demand for beer from B, which is priced at $2.00.

Now, recall that we have assumed that A has a 100 percent tariff in place. The effect of this tariff is to double the price of imported beer. Thus, the price of beer imported from C rises to $3.00 per bottle. This is lower than the $4.00 price ($2.00

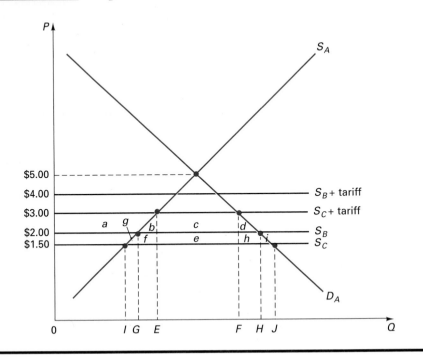

FIGURE 9.1   *Regional trade liberalization.*

plus $2.00 tariff) of beer that could be imported from B. So A continues to import beer only from C, EF bottles at $3.00 each.

Suppose that A were to negotiate an FTA with country B. Under such an arrangement, goods coming to A from country B would not be charged a tariff. The tariff would remain on any goods coming from country C. Suppose the tariff on beer from B were dropped—what would happen? Clearly, consumers in A could buy beer from B at a price of $2.00. If they were to buy from C instead, the price would be $3.00. Thus, there would be a natural tendency for A to switch its beer purchases from C to B. In the process, imports would expand from EF bottles to GH bottles. All of these would come, however, from country B rather than country C.

As this example shows, the formation of an FTA (or a CU) can have two effects on international trade. First, there is the shift in the source of trade from C, the lowest-cost world producer, to B, the lowest-cost FTA member country. This shift in the source of trade is known as **trade diversion**. In general, trade diversion is viewed as welfare reducing for the world. The intuition for thinking this is that A no longer imports from the country that has a natural comparative advantage (i.e., country C). Instead, it has agreed to discriminate in favor of its fellow FTA partner, country B. In the process, resources are directed away from beer production in the low-cost

Trade diversion

A shift in the pattern of trade from low-cost world producers to higher-cost CU or FTA members.

world producer, country C, and directed toward beer production in the higher-cost partner, country B.

The second effect of the formation of the FTA is that trade expands for country A. Imports rise from EF to GH. This comes about because consumers are able to pay a lower price for imports (although, in this example, not the lowest). The expansion of trade that results from FTA (or CU) formation is known as **trade creation**. From a world welfare point of view, trade creation is good. This is because the highest-cost producer (country A, in this example) is availing itself to a greater extent of the benefits available from international trade.

Trade creation
An expansion in world trade that results from the formation of a preferential trade arrangement.

Whether or not the creation of an FTA is beneficial to the member countries depends (in the static sense) on the relative strengths of the forces of trade creation and trade diversion. Consider again Figure 9.1. Let's calculate the welfare impact on country A of the creation of an FTA between A and B. If A forms an FTA with country B, consumers in A benefit. The price they pay falls from $3.00 to $2.00. Consumer surplus rises by $(a + b + c + d)$. Producer surplus falls by a, while tariff revenue falls by $(c + e)$. Netting out these changes in surpluses yields a welfare impact on A of $(b + d) − \$e$. (See Table 9.1.)

Because of the trade diversion, A no longer trades with country C. The impact of this is for tariff revenues to fall. Part of this loss of tariff revenues, c, accrues to domestic residents in the form of lower prices. The remainder, e, represents a loss to A. This loss occurs because the FTA between A and B means that consumers in A must pay a higher price to producers in B than they would pay for the same goods purchased from C. The side of area e represents the amount that the price has risen (here 50 cents) and the base of area e is the quantity of trade diverted away from C by the FTA. Thus, e is the increased amount that B's producers receive relative to what C's producers had received prior to the FTA. This is the cost to A of the trade diversion.

Because trade expands, however, there is an offsetting gain. Consumers in A pay a lower price to purchase the good, and hence, trade expands. The benefits of international trade are the familiar (we hope!) triangles equal in value to $b + \$d$. To interpret these areas in the context of this example note that the height of these triangles represents the amount that the retail price of imports has fallen because the FTA was formed (here $1). The lengths of the bases of the two triangles sum to equal the amount that trade has increased because of the FTA (i.e., the amount of trade creation). Thus, the sum of these two triangles represents the gains to A from trade

---

TABLE 9.1 *The Welfare Effects on Country **A** of an FTA between Countries **A** and **B***

Change in consumer surplus	$a	+$b	+$c	+$d
Change in producer surplus	−$a			
Change in government revenue			−$c	−$e
CHANGE IN WELFARE (FOR A)		$b	+$d	−$e

creation. Overall, *A* is better off if the benefits of trade creation exceed the costs of trade diversion, but there is nothing in the diagram to guarantee that this will occur.

What about the other countries? Clearly, *B* gains on the export side from this arrangement. It obtains export markets in *A* that it had previously been unable to penetrate. On the other hand, if *A* is a higher-cost producer of goods than *C*, then when *B* lowers its tariffs on goods from *A*, it too faces ambiguous welfare prospects. Meanwhile, country *C* loses because its producers have lost markets. Clearly, since the effect on *A* and *B* is ambiguous and *C* loses, the worldwide welfare effect of the formation of FTAs or other preferential trading relationships is anything but certain.* The world could gain, or it could lose. What will make the difference?

In general, preferential trading arrangements that maximize trade creation (or minimize trade diversion) will have the greatest positive world welfare effect. Let's return to Figure 9.1 and consider an FTA between country *A* and country *C*. In this case, *A* would eliminate its tariffs with respect to country *C*. The price of beer would fall to $1.50, and imports (from *C*) would expand to *IJ*. The increase in imports represents pure trade creation. That is, in this example, trade diversion would be zero, since, both before and after the agreement, *A* trades with *C*. For *A*, the welfare gains of the formation of an FTA (with country *C*) relative to tariffs are $(b + f + g + d + h + i)$. Country *C* gains as well, because its exports rise. *B* neither gains nor loses in this case, because its trade has not been affected.

An obvious question is, Why would *A* ever form an FTA with *B* if it could improve its welfare more by forming one with *C*? There are many answers to that question, none of them completely satisfactory. One view is that to explain the formation of preferential trading relationships, one needs to go beyond calculations of static gains and losses (i.e., trade creation and trade diversion) to a calculation of dynamic gains. In particular, suppose that there are economies of scale in production in various goods. Then, when *A* and *B* form an FTA, the size of the market expands for the manufacturers in these two countries, allowing producers in both countries to expand production and lower prices. Presumably, then, what keeps the FTA from expanding to include *C* so that there is universal free trade is that these economies of scale are fully exploited within the narrower FTA.

A second view is that preferential trading arrangements are formed for political (noneconomic) reasons. The formation of the EU, for instance, can be viewed as an attempt by European political leaders to integrate their economies so completely that the temptations to go to war, which could not be resisted twice in the twentieth century, would diminish substantially. In addition, the Generalized System of Preference (GSP) schemes that have been instituted among various industrialized and developing countries clearly have a strong political motivation. These plans provide limited (usually by product on a quantity and value basis) special trade preferences

---

*Technically, this is not quite correct, because, for ease of exposition, we have assumed that *A* is a small country so that the supply curves it faces from all possible exporters are horizontal. In such cases, by imposing tariffs, *A* hurts only itself, and, by removing them, it helps only itself. *C* would definitely be hurt if *A* (or the combination of *A* and *B*) had any world market power at all. Then, as it quits trading with *C*, the price *C* receives for its product falls.

(usually zero tariffs) to goods produced in developing countries. Many of these plans were begun in the early 1970s by industrialized countries under pressure from developing countries who wanted help in their development process.*

NORTH AMERICAN FREE TRADE AGREEMENT

On January 1, 1994, the North American Free Trade Agreement (NAFTA) among Canada, Mexico, and the United States officially came into force. This agreement contains a negotiated schedule for tariff reductions on NAFTA origin goods that is to be fully implemented by the year 2004 for most manufactured goods and 2008 for agricultural products. As of late 1999, six annual stages of scheduled tariff reductions had already been implemented, and many other goods were put on an accelerated schedule for tariff reductions. By 2008, NAFTA will lead to virtual free trade in almost all goods and services among the three countries. To understand better the forces that led to this agreement, it is necessary to describe first some of the events that took place in Mexico in the years just before the negotiation of the accord.

For most of the past 50 years, the government of Mexico has followed policies that sought to achieve economic growth and industrialization through import substitution.[†] It encouraged domestic production of manufactured goods by providing direct subsidies to local enterprises and by restricting imports with high tariffs and a variety of nontariff barriers. And, to prevent foreign firms from benefiting from these policies by relocating to Mexico, the Mexican government restricted direct investment in and foreign ownership of Mexican assets. It also assumed control of over 1,000 Mexican companies and administered the activities of most of the rest of the Mexican economy through a complicated maze of regulations. At first, these policies seemed to succeed as Mexico achieved impressive rates of economic growth throughout the first 30 years after World War II.

However, by the mid-1970s, problems began to beset the Mexican economy. The government had maintained a high level of social services and continued to subsidize inefficient local enterprises. It financed these expenditures by printing money, which ultimately led to inflation. High inflation and an overvalued local currency, in turn, brought on balance-of-payments problems as local residents sought to protect the value of their financial assets by converting them to foreign currency and depositing them overseas.[‡] As budget deficits continued to grow, the Mexican government borrowed huge amounts of money in world capital markets.

---

*The literature on preferential trading arrangements is enormous. A good introduction to the extent of these arrangements, circa 1985, is found in Richard Pomfret, "Discrimination in International Trade: Extent, Motivation, and Implications," *Economia Internazionale* (1985), and a relatively nontechnical discussion of the economic theory behind these arrangements in Richard Pomfret, "Preferential Trading Arrangements," *Weltwirtschaftliches Archiv* (1986). A more recent and much more critical analysis of preferential trading agreements is found in Jagdish Bhagwati and Arvind Panagariya (eds.), *The Economics of Preferential Trade Agreements* (Washington, D.C.: The AEI Press, 1996).
[†]For more on import substitution development policies, see Chapter 10.
[‡]This phenomenon is known as capital flight. For more on capital flight, see Chapter 16.

At first, Mexico appeared to be an excellent credit risk. The Mexican government controlled the production of oil, and revenue from oil exports were thought by most experts to be sufficient to guarantee repayment of the loans. But in the early 1980s, oil prices began to fall and so did oil export revenue. In addition, Mexico was hit by three other events: The worldwide recession in the early 1980s reduced the demand for Mexican nonpetroleum exports; tight money policies in the United States and elsewhere led to large increases in the rate of interest on Mexican debts; and a fall in the value of the Mexican peso led to a rise in the U.S. dollar value of Mexican debt. By 1982, Mexico had amassed $86 billion in debt to foreign countries. Service on this debt (i.e., interest and principal repayments) required one-third of Mexico's annual export revenue. In August of that year, the Mexican government announced that it could not make scheduled debt payments.

The Mexican government, under the leadership of President Miguel de la Madrid, began a series of reforms aimed at revitalizing the Mexican economy. The president recognized that one of the chief problems faced by the country was the incredible waste and inefficiency created by the past policies of import substitution. Therefore, to stimulate competition, tariffs were cut and regulations on local business were eased. The government set out to divest its ownership of private enterprises, privatizing more than 750 firms in six years. Despite these efforts, economic growth stagnated and inflation continued to soar.

In his last year as president, de la Madrid initiated a program to carry out a wider set of economic reforms. A major objective was to reduce the rate of inflation. The pact called for a freeze on wages and prices and for reductions in government spending and the government deficit. The plan also placed restrictions on the rate of growth of the money supply. The Mexican economy began to turn around. At about this time, the United States and Mexico signed an agreement that recognized Mexico's need to expand exports to repay foreign debt and called for the creation of a mechanism for trade consultation, dispute resolution, and mutual reduction of trade and investment barriers.

President de la Madrid was followed in office by Carlos Salinas in December 1988. President Salinas set about to accelerate the pace of liberalization, viewing this process as a key to help stabilize the economy and promote growth and efficiency. Mexico reduced its highest tariff rate to 20 percent, down from 100 percent in the mid-1980s. The average tariff rate fell from 25 percent to about 12 percent over this period. Quotas were eliminated and other nontariff barriers were reduced. Mexican economic growth picked up, and inflation declined rapidly. President Salinas came to Washington, D.C., in June 1990 to meet with President Bush. The two leaders reviewed the progress made by Mexico in liberalizing its economy and determined that a comprehensive FTA would be the best vehicle to broaden bilateral economic relations and to commit Mexico to continued economic liberalization. Both leaders asked their legislatures for permission to begin formal negotiations. Shortly after, Canada, which had already established an FTA with the United States, expressed an interest in joining the talks.

On August 12, 1992, the three countries announced that they had reached agreement on the details of the NAFTA. The initial draft of the pact called for the creation of a free-trade area over a 15-year period starting on January 1, 1994; substantial liberalization of trade in services; strengthened intellectual property rights protection; and expanded opportunities for international investment among the three countries. The NAFTA was signed by the leaders of the three countries on December 17, 1992. But President Bush left office before the document could be sent to Congress for its approval.

During the 1992 presidential campaign, then candidate Clinton announced general support for the NAFTA but called for the negotiations to be reopened to consider environmental and labor issues of the agreement. Talks began on these side agreements in January 1993 and were concluded on August 13, 1993. These measures along with the main agreement were then sent to the legislatures of the respective countries for passage. Each country ratified the agreement in late 1993. For more on the specifics of NAFTA, see Item 9.1.

ITEM 9.1	Details of the NAFTA

The NAFTA took effect on January 1, 1994. Since it is an FTA, each country continues to maintain its own tariff and other trade barriers against nonmember countries. Moreover, the NAFTA does not include any agreement to form common foreign policies, stabilize exchange rates, or coordinate welfare or immigration policies. The NAFTA offers preferential treatment to most goods and services that are produced in and then traded between any of the member countries.

The fact that the agreement calls for the United States to give special consideration to goods made in Canada or Mexico requires an agreement among the members over what constitutes the national identity of a product. That is, how much of a good must be made in, say, Canada for it to be called Canadian? Laws that provide answers to this question are a necessary part of any preferential trade arrangement; they are known as *rules of origin*. These rules differ from one agreement to the next and are often the subject of intense negotiations.

For instance, according to the NAFTA, some goods, like televisions, textiles, apparel, and automobiles, not only must be assembled in the member countries but also must be built partly or entirely from North American–made component parts to receive preferential treatment. For

instance, textiles and apparel will be free of duty so long as they are made in North America with yarn or fiber that also comes from NAFTA countries. The nationality of the factory's owners does not matter—a Japanese-owned automobile factory in the United States will qualify for trade preferences so long as at least 62.5 percent of the parts used in its factory come from NAFTA countries.

Basic Agreements

Tariffs

The agreement phases out tariffs on goods traded between any of the three countries. Many tariffs were eliminated at the onset of the agreement. Others will be reduced, depending on the product, over 5, 10, or 15 years. Among the goods for which trade is now tariff free are computers, medical equipment, agricultural equipment, internal combustion engines, and telephone switching equipment, all of which previously faced tariffs of 10 percent or more in the Mexican market. NAFTA will also eliminate quotas and import licenses that are not essential for such purposes as protecting health or safety.

(Continued)

Safeguards protection

If any one of the three countries finds that a surge of imports is harming local industry, it may temporarily raise the tariff on that product back to its original level. The country raising the tariff must compensate the exporting country by lowering other tariffs more quickly.

Investment

No financial investment from an individual or corporation based in another NAFTA member country can be seized without full compensation. Investors are guaranteed the right to convert their profits into another currency and repatriate them. Mexico is allowed to retain its ban on foreign ownership of oil and natural gas reserves, but American firms will also be allowed to conduct oil exploration and share in the profits from any oil discoveries. American firms will be allowed to acquire majority stakes in Mexican trucking companies in the year 2000 and to own them entirely in 2003.

Health and safety standards

Current inspections of imported food and other products will continue as before. Existing American standards for pesticide residues and other hazards will remain intact but could be challenged by other member countries as unfair trade barriers if they discriminate against imports. To win an appeal, the challenger must demonstrate that there is no scientific basis for the standard.

Services

Mexico has agreed to dismantle its virtual ban on American banks operating inside Mexico. American banks will be allowed to capture up to 15 percent of the Mexican market by January 1, 2000, and up to 25 percent by 2004. All remaining limits disappear by 2007. American securities firms will be allowed to control up to 30 percent of the market for brokerage services in Mexico by 2004. As with banking, all remaining limits disappear by 2007.

Intellectual property protection

Virtually all types of inventions, including pharmaceutical and agricultural chemicals, are protected under NAFTA provisions that require patents to be granted for both products and processes developed by firms in member countries. The agreement also protects copyrights for computer programs and databases, and rental rights for computer programs and sound recordings. Service marks and trade secrets are also covered, along with integrated circuit masks both directly and as components of other products.

The Side Agreements

North American Agreement on Environmental Cooperation

The aim of this agreement is to guarantee the right of each country to safeguard its environment. NAFTA maintains all existing U.S. health, safety, and environmental standards and allows local governments to enact even tougher standards. The side agreement creates a new North American Commission on Environmental Cooperation, with a council made up of the three countries' top environmental officials. There is a "layered" enforcement mechanism to ensure that countries obey their own environmental laws. The mechanism starts with "sunshine" provisions that guarantee that the public be notified of and participate in monitoring the enforcement of local laws. Trade sanctions are then provided for, if other avenues are insufficient to resolve disputes. The commission will spend up to $8 billion to clean up air and water pollution and toxic waste dumps along the U.S.–Mexican border, and a North American Development Bank will be created to provide additional funding for environmental cleanup as well as development projects on either side of the border.

North American Agreement on Labor Cooperation

This agreement seeks to manage the terms of potential change in labor markets brought about by the accord. It involves such issues as restrictions on child labor, health and safety standards, and minimum wages. The supplemental labor agreement is centered on three fundamental principles: (a) enhanced collaboration, cooperation, and exchange of information among the three countries; (b) increased efforts to make each country's labor laws and their implementation explicit and highly visible; and (c) increased use of effective mechanisms to encourage the enforcement of national labor laws. The agreement establishes procedural mechanisms for enforcement. If a solution cannot be reached, the agreement provides for binding arbitration and assessment of penalties. For its part, Mexico has pledged to link increases in its minimum wage to increases in productivity.

NAFTA and the U.S. Economy: Six Years Later

In the United States, NAFTA was and remains very controversial. Although past and present national leaders and most newspapers supported passage, some leading politicians and pundits from both political parties opposed the agreement. Labor unions and certain environmental groups were also against the deal.* Passage was in doubt, especially in the House of Representatives, until only a few days before the final vote. In the end, the Clinton administration succeeded in winning enough votes from House Democrats to ratify the agreement.[†]

Why was NAFTA so contentious? The principal answer has to do with the differences in standards of living that exist among the three countries and with concerns, especially in the United States, that trade liberalization with Mexico would mean a loss of U.S. manufacturing jobs. Lower wages in Mexico, it was argued, would give Mexican firms comparative advantage over their U.S. counterparts and thereby encourage U.S. manufacturers to relocate their factories in Mexico in order to remain competitive. A leading opponent of NAFTA, H. Ross Perot, used this reasoning to argue that almost 6 million American manufacturing jobs (out of a total 18 million) were at risk and warned of NAFTA producing a "giant sucking sound" as U.S. jobs were lost to firms located south of the U.S.–Mexico border.[‡]

Table 9.2 provides some comparative data on aspects of the economies of the NAFTA countries. As the table clearly shows, the standards of living of Mexico are much lower than those found in the other two countries. At current exchange rates, Mexico's economy is less than two-thirds the size of Canada's, despite having more

---

*For more on the objections to NAFTA raised by environmentalists, see Chapter 7.
[†]The final House vote was 234 in favor and 200 opposed; 102 Democrats and 132 Republicans supported the pact.
[‡]For more on Perot's objections to NAFTA, see H. Ross Perot and Pat Choate, *Save Your Job, Save Our Country: Why NAFTA Must Be Stopped—Now!* (New York: Hyperion, 1993).

TABLE 9.2   *Economic Characteristics of NAFTA Countries*

(1998 DATA)

Country	Population (in millions)	GDP (billions of U.S.$)	Exports to United States (billions of U.S.$)	Imports from United States (billions of U.S.$)	Wages[a] (U.S.$ per hour)
Canada	31	612	175 (83%)[b]	164 (76%)	$15.69
Mexico	96	381	95 (88%)	74 (74%)	$1.83
United States	270	9364	—	—	$18.56

SOURCE: Constructed by the authors from Table 1.1, Bureau of Labor Statistics, Foreign Labor Statistics Table 2 (found at http://stats.bls.gov/news .release/ichcc.t02.htm) and the CIA's *World Factbook* (http://www.cia.gov/cia/publications/factbook/index.html).

NOTES: [a]Average hourly compensation of manufacturing workers including mandated benefits.

[b]Numbers in parentheses denote percentage of total trade flows of that country.

than three times its population. Manufacturing wages in Mexico currently stand at only about 10 percent of comparable U.S. and Canadian wages. But, as we learned in Chapter 3, even in the case where labor is the only factor of production, comparative advantage is not determined by wage levels alone. In fact, consider again the data in Table 9.2. Even though Mexican wages are substantially lower than Canadian wages, the United States imports almost twice as much merchandise from Canada as it does from Mexico.

Recall from our study of the classical model that, even with free trade, wage rates will differ across countries so long as there are international differences in labor productivity. The evidence is that Mexican labor is significantly less productive than U.S. or Canadian counterparts. A simple demonstration of this point is given by a cross-country comparison of per capita GDP. According to the table, 1998 per capita GDP for Mexico was $3,969, about one-fifth the level of per capita GDP in Canada and one-ninth of that found in the United States.* The World Bank has calculated that Mexican labor productivity is about one-fourth of the U.S. level. And, in 1993 alone, several large American manufacturers, including Cummins Engine Co., General Motors, and Quality Coils, announced that they were moving manufacturing operations from Mexico back to the United States because Mexico's low wages did not offset lower worker productivity.

What accounts for Mexico's low productivity levels? First, Mexican workers are largely untrained and have limited amounts of capital with which to work. Another factor is the relatively small scale of manufacturing operations of a typical Mexican firm. That is, for years Mexican firms produced only for the local market, and the volume of sales was quite low. The market was not large enough for most firms to expand to a size sufficient to exploit economies of scale. In contrast, the typical

---

*To calculate per capita GDP from the numbers in Table 9.2, take the values in column 2, multiply by 1000, and then divide by the comparable number in column 1. Note that the resulting number is measured in $_{US}$ and hence does not give an accurate picture of standards of living. According to the information in Table 1.1, if purchasing power parity exchange rates are used to calculate per capita GDP, the numbers for Mexico and Canada would be about 206 percent and 22 percent higher, respectively.

American firm is much larger and thus can achieve internal economies through mass production. Other factors that contribute to the relatively low productivity levels in Mexico include a crumbling infrastructure and a general shortage of qualified managers. Highways are in poor shape or nonexistent, although new toll roads are being built. Capital goods are in short supply, and the legal system is unreliable.

These factors argue against the wholesale relocation of U.S. capital to Mexico and the consequent loss of U.S. jobs as the NAFTA is implemented, although some U.S. capital will be attracted to those sectors where Mexican labor is relatively more productive. Rather, it seems more likely that some American firms that established operations in Mexico in order to avoid high Mexican tariffs may find it more cost effective to relocate in the United States, especially as Mexican tariffs fall.

After its first six years, what effect has NAFTA had on the U.S. economy? So far, the answer seems to be not much. U.S. trade with both countries has grown enormously, but so has U.S. trade with other countries. U.S. exports to Mexico have doubled from $40 billion in 1993 to $81 billion in 1999. U.S. imports from Mexico have more than doubled, from $39 billion to $109 billion over the same period. Critics have pointed to the current U.S. trade deficit with Mexico as an indication of the failure of the agreement. However, the growth in that deficit is more likely due to the effects of the devaluation of the Mexican peso in December 1994 and the subsequent sharp downturn of the Mexican economy than it is to lower U.S. trade barriers.* A study by economists at the North American Integration and Development (NAID) Center at UCLA estimates that on average 37,000 U.S. jobs per year are at risk due to Mexican imports, and 57,000 jobs per year are at risk due to Canadian imports. Since the U.S. economy creates over 200,000 jobs per month, the small job impact from NAFTA trade is apparent.[†]

Why have the effects of NAFTA so far been so small? First, U.S. trade barriers on most goods are already low, even against goods from countries that do not have FTAs with the United States. Thus, lowering barriers against Mexican goods offers Mexico only a small competitive edge over other countries that export to the United States, and the amount of trade diversion caused by the agreement appears to be minimal. Second, the Mexican economy is small relative to that of the United States. According to a study by Edward Leamer, the largest share that Mexican producers enjoy of any U.S. commodity imports is 10 percent.[‡] In many cases, U.S. imports from Mexico account for no more than 2 or 3 percent of total U.S. imports. Thus, even with a reduction in U.S. tariffs, it seems unlikely that Mexico will be able to expand its share of the U.S. market to have any significant effects on price. Leamer goes on to show that if Mexico were able to displace foreign competition in the U.S. market and devote its entire manufacturing capacity to producing goods for U.S. export, it would not be able to satisfy U.S. demand for foreign-produced goods. This

---

*For more on the devaluation of the peso, see Chapter 19.

[†]See Ojeda et al., "The U.S. Employment Impacts of North American Integration after NAFTA: A Partial Equilibrium Approach," NAID Working Paper, January 2000. This paper is available on the Web at http://naid.sppsr.ucla.edu/pubs&news/nafta2000.html.

[‡]For more details, see Edward Leamer, "Wage Effects of a U.S.–Mexican Free Trade Agreement," in *The Mexico–U.S. Free Trade Agreement*, ed. Peter Garber (Cambridge, Mass.: MIT Press, 1993).

turns out to be true even in sectors such as apparel, shoes, and leather goods, thought to be comparative-advantage industries for Mexico.

Things could change, however, as time progresses. NAFTA will cause Mexican industry to expand in industries that are intensive in unskilled labor or minerals (i.e., along the lines of Mexican comparative advantage). Such industries include textiles, shoes, nonmetallic mineral manufactures, leather, and pottery. If foreign capital is attracted to these sectors and productivity rises, then Mexico may ultimately capture a significant share of the U.S. market. This would lead to lower U.S. prices for these goods and imply a reduction in payments to the U.S. factors that are intensive in the production of these goods. That is, wages paid to low-skilled U.S. workers will fall; Leamer predicts that annual low-skilled wages may decline by $1,000 over the next decade.

Other U.S. industries stand to benefit from NAFTA. These include producers of capital-intensive and/or skilled-labor-intensive goods such as computers, aircraft, high-tech electronics, and professional services such as banking, finance, law, and medicine. Leamer estimates that the long-term movement of resources into these sectors could raise annual high-skilled wages by as much as $6,000 and annual payments to capital owners by 1.3 percent.

EUROPEAN UNION

With 15 member countries and a combined population of 375 million, the European Union (EU) is the world's largest CU, and many other countries would like to join. In 1997 the EU received applications from 10 countries. Negotiations got under way in 1998 with the first wave of six countries: Cyprus, the Czech Republic, Estonia, Hungary, Poland, and Slovenia. These will be followed by a second wave of five countries: Bulgaria, Latvia, Lithuania, Romania, and Slovakia. In September 1998 Malta reactivated an application it had previously filed with the EU. Also that month the EU launched efforts to prepare Turkey for accession. Currently many of these countries have associate member status with the EU and receive certain trade preferences. Two others, Norway and Switzerland, were approved for membership in the 1990s but did not join following negative votes in national elections on the membership issue.

Single European Act
An act passed by the EU to remove various NTBs between the member countries.

The EU is more than a simple CU agreement. The ultimate goal of the member countries is to achieve a level of integration so complete that the EU becomes a "united states of Europe." Early on, the EU put in place a government to make and enforce its statutes and to operate its common agricultural and commercial policies. In the mid-1980s, the EU enacted the **Single European Act**. The goal of this policy is to develop a uniform system of product standards for the member states and to remove a wide range of physical, technical, and fiscal barriers that impinge on the free flow of goods and services between the countries of the EU. The EU has set in motion a series of additional reforms that liberalize intraunion migration of labor and capital. A capstone achievement in the process of unifying the internal EU market was the January 1, 1999, launch of the euro, a common currency that is used by 11 of the 15 EU countries.

The EU Government

The EU government is headquartered in Brussels and comprises four main institutions: the European Commission, the Council of the European Union (formerly known as the Council of Ministers), the Court of Justice, and the European Parliament. The council and the commission are the chief administrative agencies of the EU. The other two agencies are the judicial and legislative branches of the EU government.

The **European Commission** serves as the chief guardian of the EU treaty. Its primary task is to ensure that EU law is applied by member states and EU institutions. It also initiates policy, drafts measures needed for its implementation, and steers legislative proposals through the European Parliament. It represents the EU in international trade negotiations, such as WTO rounds, and it sets common policies in fields such as agriculture or in the move to reduce internal trade barriers.

The commission is made up of 20 members, 2 each from Germany, France, Italy, the United Kingdom, and Spain and 1 each from the other EU countries. Commissioners are appointed by their respective governments to renewable four-year terms; in performing their duties, the commissioners are independent of their home governments. The commission is headed by a president and six vice-presidents who hold office for a two-year renewable term. Decisions of the commission are made by majority vote.

The **Council of the EU** is the other body of the EU government in charge of executing EU policy. Each country has one representative on the council. Member states are normally represented by their country's foreign minister. In addition, there is a wide range of specialized council meetings, attended by the ministers of agriculture, transport, economics, finance, and so forth. The office of the President of the Council is held for a term of six months by each member state in turn, in alphabetical order. In 1993, the presidential term cycle was inverted to ensure that each country holds the office in the first half of the year, when decisions about sensitive issues, such as farm price support levels, are decided. Particularly important or controversial policy issues are dealt with in the "European Council," which meets twice a year. The European Council comprises the heads of state or government of the member countries, accompanied by their foreign ministers and the president of the European Commission. The presidency of the European Council rotates every six months conforming to that of the Council of the EU.

Any act of general legal importance must be issued by the council, usually on the basis of a commission proposal. Commercial policy issues are decided by a qualified majority (roughly 70 percent of total votes). Directives that aim at the harmonization of national laws can be passed only by unanimous council vote. The same is true of new policies that are not explicitly provided for by the EU treaty. During trade policy negotiations with third countries, the council forms a special committee to assist the commission in the talks.

The **European Court of Justice** decides on the legality of council or commission acts (i.e., regulations, directives, or decisions) in the light of EU treaties. It also reviews cases of possible infringement of the EU treaties brought by the commission against member states. With respect to status or procedure, the court is comparable

European Commission
One of two executive offices of the EU government; its chief responsibility is to draft and enforce EU laws.

Council of the EU
One of two executive offices of the EU government; it has the power to make decisions about European Commission proposals and to issue directives and regulations to the member states.

European Court of Justice
Chief judiciary body of the EU that decides on the legality of council or commission actions.

with the highest courts of appeal of the member countries. Cases may be brought to the court by member states, by one of the EU institutions, or by individuals that are affected by a decision or regulation.

European Parliament
Legislative branch of the EU government and the chief representative of the populace in the process of setting EU policy.

The **European Parliament** is the legislative body of the EU and acts as the chief representative of the people in the process of setting EU policy. The parliament is composed of 626 members, each elected for five-year terms. The number of representatives an individual member country has in the parliament is determined by population and the size of the member country's economy. Germany has the most representatives with 99; France, Italy, and the United Kingdom each have 87 members. Spain is next with 64. No other country has more than 35. The parliament's administrative seat is in Luxembourg, but plenary sessions are now held in Strasbourg, France.

Relative to national parliaments, the European Parliament has limited powers. It can scrutinize but not initiate legislation. Draft proposals from the commission go to the parliament for its opinion and suggestions. It can amend certain expenditures of the EU budget, and it sets its own agenda to debate issues it views as important. Most recently, the parliament acquired the power to reject or amend council decisions regarding the Single European Act. It also holds veto power over applications for EU membership from potential new entrants.

The Europe 1992 Initiative

Since its founding, the goal of the EU has been to allow free trade of goods, services, capital, and labor among the member countries. However, the reality has been much different. Each member state has had its own regulations and standards covering virtually every facet of commercial activity. These standards, which range from such seemingly trivial issues as the wheat content of pasta, the minimum sugar levels in raspberry jam, and the maximum noise levels of lawn mowers to more important issues such as emissions standards for automobiles, have served to limit trade among the member states. In addition, the countries of the EU have maintained other types of nontariff barriers among themselves, including quotas, different border and value-added taxes, and individual subsidy and procurement programs.

In 1986 the EU set out to remove these nontariff barriers. It passed the Single European Act that calls on the member states to enact into law or implement 280 directives that would eliminate border checkpoints for intra-EU trade, dismantle internal quotas, harmonize technical standards and tax codes, and deregulate various economic activities, especially with respect to transportation and financial services.* The goal of the EU was to have these changes in place by the end of 1992 or at least begin the phase-in process for these changes by that date. However, the

---

*For more on the Europe 1992 initiative, see Janice Boucher, "Europe 1992: A Closer Look," *Economic Review* (Federal Reserve Bank of Atlanta, 1991). For an extensive discussion of the effects on the United States, see ITC, *The Effects of Greater Economic Integration within the European Community on the United States* (U.S. International Trade Commission, 1989), and several follow-up reports to this document.

implementation of these changes has been slower than planned. As of early 2000, only about 88 percent of the reforms have been enacted by the member countries.

The benefits from these deregulations could be substantial for the member countries. Gains in the form of cost reductions will accrue due to the removal of border controls and excess paperwork, the standardization brought on by a common set of technical regulations, and the efficiency enhancements adopted by firms that must operate in a more competitive environment. Another source of gains will arise when government procurement is opened to EU-wide bidding. Perhaps the greatest gains will occur as firms begin producing for a larger market, thereby becoming able to exploit economies of scale in production. One study estimates the potential gains to be as much as $255 billion, roughly 5.3 percent of EU GDP and equal to $810 per resident.

Parallel to the market integration process, the member countries have taken other steps to link their countries still further. In December 1991, at a conference in Maastricht, the Netherlands, the EU countries agreed to form an economic and monetary union (EMU) with a single currency by the end of the 1990s. An element of this plan would be the creation of the European Central Bank, a new institution that would conduct monetary policy for all the member countries. Despite some early threats to implementing this agreement due to speculative pressures on individual currencies, the EMU was successfully launched in January 1999. As of early 2000, only 11 of the 15 countries participate in the EMU; Denmark, Greece, Sweden, and the United Kingdom do not yet belong. Exchange rates between currencies of the EMU countries are now immutably locked, just as the exchange rate between nickels and dimes is. The new currency, the euro, will replace individual currencies in all transactions by 2002.

A second treaty signed in Maastricht aims to strengthen political ties among the members. It defines a new social charter and calls for a closer political union with common foreign and defense policies. This agreement allows residents of any one country freedom to live anywhere in the EU's member countries. It also establishes a common set of standards for worker rights and strengthens international networks to fight crime.

REGIONALISM VERSUS MULTILATERALISM

The EU and NAFTA are two examples of the many preferential trade arrangements that are currently in place in the world. Item 9.2 describes many other such agreements. It is important to remember that regional trade liberalization is very much different from the process of multilateral liberalization that is the cornerstone of the WTO. In regional trade agreements, countries lower their trade barriers only for a small group of partner countries and discriminate against the rest of the world. Within the WTO, trade liberalization by any one member country is extended to all other members on an unconditional MFN basis; here, there is essentially no discrimination. Do these two types of trade liberalization go hand in hand, or does the

ITEM 9.2	Other Preferential Trade Arrangements

Many countries of the world currently participate in one or more preferential trade arrangements. In this section, we provide some detail on several of the trade arrangements in effect as of early 1997. We organize this information by geographic region. Many of these agreements have been in existence for several decades, but few have been commercially viable. This is especially true for preferential arrangements between developing countries. Talks often break down over disagreements about how the perceived gains and losses are to be distributed and over compensation to be provided by countries that gain to poorer, losing countries.

AFRICA

1. The *West African Economic Community (CEAO)* is a CU agreement launched in 1959. Its current members are Benin, Burkina Faso, Côte d'Ivoire, Mali, Mauritania, Niger, and Senegal. This agreement called for a common tariff, equal distribution of tariff revenue, and harmonization of tax policies. None of these goals has been achieved.

2. The *Economic and Customs Union of Central Africa (UDEAC)* was founded in 1964 as a CU among Cameroon, Central African Republic, Chad, Congo, Equatorial Guinea, and Gabon. In 1990 a common external tariff was introduced by four of the six members (Cameroon, Congo, Central African Republic, and Gabon).

3. The *Economic Community of West African States (ECOWAS)* is a CU agreement among Benin, Burkina Faso, Cape Verde, Côte d'Ivoire, The Gambia, Ghana, Guinea, Guinea-Bissau, Liberia, Mali, Mauritania, Niger, Nigeria, Senegal, Sierra Leone, and Togo. This agreement also allows for the free movement of labor and capital among the member countries. It was launched in 1981. Progress within ECOWAS at lowering barriers and expanding trade has been slowed by the participation of its members in other preferential trade arrangements such as CEAO and UDEAC that impose obligations incompatible with those assumed under ECOWAS. The resulting inconsistency of members' commercial policies has led to a virtual paralysis in the reduction of barriers.

4. The *Economic Community of Central African States (CEEAC)* also is a CU that allows free movement of labor and capital among member countries. Founded in 1981, its members include Burundi, Cameroon, Central African Republic, Chad, Congo, Equatorial Guinea, Gabon, Rwanda, Sao Tome and Principe, and Zaire.

5. The *Arab Maghreb Union (AMU)* has five members: Algeria, Libya, Mauritania, Morocco, and Tunisia. Launched in 1989, the AMU is a CU arrangement with free mobility of labor and capital.

ASIA

1. The *Association of Southeast Asian Nations (ASEAN)* is an FTA among Brunei, Indonesia, Malaysia, Philippines, Singapore, and Thailand. It was founded in 1967. Despite its lengthy existence, progress has been slow in reducing trade barriers among member countries. This is because negotiations have been carried out on a product-by-product rather than an across-the-board basis. In 1991 the ASEAN countries agreed to establish an FTA by 2008, a timetable subsequently shortened to 2003. The product coverage of the proposed FTA excludes unprocessed agricultural products, natural resources, and services.

2. The *Australia–New Zealand Closer Economic Relations Trade Agreement (ANZCERT)* is an FTA founded between the two countries in 1983. The agreement covers all merchandise trade; tariffs and quotas were eliminated between the two countries by 1990. Coverage of the agreement was extended to include services in 1988. In 1992 the two countries exempted each other's products from antidumping actions.

EUROPE

1. The *European Free Trade Association (EFTA)* is an FTA among Iceland, Liechtenstein, Norway, and Switzerland. It was formed in 1960. Many of its original members, including Austria, Denmark, Portugal, and the United Kingdom, have left EFTA to join the EU. Three of EFTA's four members, Iceland, Liechtenstein, and Norway, are participants in the European Economic Area (EEA) accord, a free trade agreement linking EFTA and EU countries in the world's largest and most comprehensive multilateral trading area. The EEA goes beyond a standard FTA in that it extends beyond free trade in goods and most services to include the creation of a single labor market. The EFTA countries that belong to the EEA have adopted various EU laws but maintain separate agricultural regimes and some special provisions on fisheries, energy, and transport. The EFTA countries have concluded free trade agreements with 10 Central and East European countries: Bulgaria, the Czech Republic, Hungary, Poland, Romania, Slovenia, the Slovak Republic, and the three Baltic states, Estonia, Latvia, and Lithuania. In addition, EFTA has signed free trade agreements with Turkey and Israel.

2. The *Central European Free Trade Area (CEFTA)* is an FTA agreement among the Czech Republic, Hungary, Poland, and the Slovak Republic. It was founded in 1992. The CEFTA covers trade in manufactured goods and raw materials. The agreement was expected to be fully implemented by the end of 1997. In addition to this agreement, in 1993 the Czech and Slovak Republics formed a CU between their two economies that prohibits the introduction of any new tariffs or NTBs on trade in agricultural or manufactured goods. The agreement also covers services and protects intellectual property rights.

LATIN AMERICA

1. The *Central American Common Market (CACM)* is a CU whose members include Costa Rica, El Salvador, Guatemala, Honduras, Nicaragua, and Panama. It was formed in 1960 but collapsed when war broke out between Honduras and El Salvador in 1969. The five members agreed to reestablish the agreement in 1991, and the CU was reactivated in 1993.

2. The *Andean Pact* is a CU among Bolivia, Colombia, Ecuador, and Venezuela. It is the descendant of an earlier pact among these same countries and Peru, known as the Andean Common Market, that was formed in 1969 but was never viable. The new agreement was reached in 1991, with Peru as an initial member. It "temporarily" pulled out of the agreement in 1992. In 1994 the members, including Peru, agreed on a four-tier common external tariff structure of 5, 10, 15, and 20 percent.

3. The *Southern Cone Common Market (MERCOSUR)* is a CU agreement among Argentina, Brazil, Paraguay, and Uruguay. It was formed in 1991. In 1995 a common external tariff was implemented.

pursuit of one adversely affect on the other? This question remains unanswered and is the focus of much current attention in trade policy circles.

At the end of World War II, the United States was the leading world advocate for multilateral trade liberalization. It fought against a GATT amendment that would permit discriminatory trade agreements between member countries; in the end, it supported a compromise amendment—Article XXIV—that allows FTAs and CUs, but only with 100 percent reduction of all internal trade barriers among members.* Later on, the United States backed the formation of the EU, which it viewed as a long-term solution to the problem of political and economic instability that had plagued Western Europe.

In the mid-1980s, the United States began to change its position on multilateralism and started to espouse the benefits of regional accords. It negotiated FTAs with Israel and Canada prior to the NAFTA accord and has since invited negotiations with other countries, especially those in the Western Hemisphere. The reason for this change in position is unclear. Jagdish Bhagwati attributes it to the "diminished giant syndrome." He argues that the rise of East Asia (especially Japan) has caused an erosion of America's predominant status in the world economy. This diminution of power as well as persistent trade imbalances has fueled protectionist sentiments in the United States and a demand for an end to multilateralist principles.[†] Bhagwati views increased emphasis on the creation of regional agreements as a dangerous trend that will undermine the WTO. Moreover, regionalism is harmful because it encourages trade diversion. In contrast, the official U.S. position is that the formation of regional agreements complements the process of multilateral liberalization promoted by the WTO. Since overall barriers to trade are now quite low, regional agreements are not likely to divert much trade. Thus, the goals of regional liberalization are not inconsistent with the WTO, and achievements in this area may stimulate progress in multilateral negotiations. Indeed, after more than seven fractious years of negotiations, the Uruguay Round was completed less than one month after NAFTA passed in the House of Representatives.

Which view is correct? Paul Krugman argues that there are elements of truth to both sides. The formation of NAFTA and the Europe 1992 initiative are two parts of a process that he predicts will ultimately produce three major world trading blocs: Europe, North America, and East Asia. This process has diverted attention from multilateral trade liberalization. However, Krugman maintains, the prospect of trade diversion from FTAs is low, because the trading blocs are really "natural" trading areas. These areas will tend to have high amounts of intraregion trade because of proximity and similarities of cultures and standards of living. Therefore, regional arrangements merely serve to stimulate trade that would have occurred even in the

---

*As we have seen, existing agreements such as NAFTA and the EU have not achieved 100 percent liberalization; despite that, they have come close enough to receive WTO approval. Article XXIV also requires that trade barriers against nonmembers are not higher or more restrictive than those previously in effect and that interim arrangements leading to the FTA or CU are employed for only a reasonable length of time.

[†]For a cogent presentation of this argument, see Jagdish Bhagwati, "U.S. Trade Policy at Crossroads," *World Economy* (1989).

absence of an agreement. Thus, existing FTAs may be even better in practice than they are in theory.*

SUMMARY

1. Preferential trading arrangements are agreements among a limited number of countries to provide special trade benefits to each other.

2. The two main types of preferential trade arrangements are free-trade areas and customs unions. The European Union (EU) is an example of a customs union. The United States, Canada, and Mexico recently formed the North American Free Trade Agreement (NAFTA), an example of a free-trade area.

3. Preferential trading arrangements may or may not be beneficial to world welfare. They are more likely to be beneficial if, after their conclusion, world trade grows (i.e., trade is created) but there is little trade diversion (i.e., world trade patterns do not change much).

4. NAFTA went into effect on January 1, 1994. The agreement calls for the elimination of most barriers to trade among the three countries by the year 2009. It also liberalizes trade in services, and international flows of investment capital. The NAFTA includes two side accords that seek to enforce environmental and labor laws and to provide funding for labor retraining and environmental cleanup.

5. NAFTA is the world's first FTA between industrialized and developing countries. As such, its passage was very controversial in the United States. However, most of the economic impact of NAFTA will be felt in Mexico, as lower Mexican trade barriers lead to a substantial redistribution of resources.

6. With 15 member countries, the EU is the world's largest and richest CU. The EU is more than a simple CU agreement. The ultimate goal of the member countries is to achieve a level of integration so complete that it becomes a "united states of Europe."

EXERCISES

1. What is the difference between free-trade areas and customs unions? Provide examples of each.

2. Comment on the observation that the sign of a successful customs union is that world trade expands after it is formed.

---

*Krugman's analysis is presented in Paul Krugman, "The Move toward Free Trade Zones," in *Policy Implications of Trade and Currency Zones* (Kansas City: Federal Reserve Bank of Kansas City, 1991). For a dissenting view, see C. Fred Bergsten, "Comment on the Move toward Free Trade Zones," in the same volume.

3. Discuss the pros and cons of multilateral trade liberalization under the principle of unconditional MFN status versus the formation of regional trade arrangements.

4. Why was the formation of NAFTA so controversial in the United States but much less so in Canada?

5. Why was the formation of NAFTA so controversial in the United States, while the formation of the Canada–U.S. FTA was little noticed by most Americans?

6. What conditions are likely to lead to a trade-diverting customs union? To a trade-creating customs union?

7. Why is trade diversion considered harmful and trade creation considered beneficial?

8. Consider the following data detailing the situation for Guatland before and after it forms an FTA with Mexland:

Pre-FTA

Imports from Eurland	100 million units
Imports from Mexland	0 units

Post-FTA

Imports from Eurland	0
Imports from Mexland	270 million units

How much trade was diverted by this agreement? How much trade was created? Suppose that Eurland charges $5 for this product and Mexland charges $6. Suppose that Guatland's original tariff was $2 per unit. Calculate the welfare gain or loss to Guatland from forming this FTA.

REFERENCES

Bhagwati, Jagdish, and Arvind Panagariya, eds. *The Economics of Preferential Trade Agreements.* Washington, D.C.: The AEI Press, 1996.

World Trade Organization. *Regionalism and the World Trading System.* Geneva: WTO, April 1995.

INTERNET APPLICATIONS

Please visit our Web site at www.awl.com/husted_melvin for more exercises and readings.

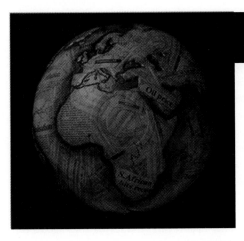

CHAPTER 10

International Trade
and Economic Growth

TOPICS TO BE COVERED

Trade and Development
Neutral Economic Growth
Protrade Biased Growth
Antitrade Biased Growth
Immigration
Capital Flows
Multinational Corporations

KEY WORDS

Economic development
Primary-export-led development
  strategies
Linkage effects
Import-substitution development
  strategies
Outward-looking development
  strategies
Neutral economic growth
Protrade biased growth
Antitrade biased growth

Neutral technical change
Labor-saving technical change
Capital-saving technical change
Immizerizing growth
Guest workers
Brain drain
Multinational corporation (MNC)
Marginal product of labor
Diminishing returns to labor
Value marginal product of labor

**Economic
development**
The achievement of a
quality of life for the
average citizen of a
country that is
comparable to that
enjoyed by the average
citizen of a country
with a modern
economy.

An economy is said to grow when the amount of output produced in the economy (i.e., the economy's gross domestic product, or GDP) rises. Economic growth is of fundamental importance to all economies. Recall that in Chapter 2 we argued that per capita GDP provides a useful measure of a country's standard of living. Since virtually all countries experience growth in population over time, growth in GDP is required simply to maintain current standards of living. In fact, if standards of living are to rise over time, then GDP must grow faster than the population.

Economic growth is also critical for **economic development.** Economic development refers to the achievement of a quality of life for the average citizen of a country that is comparable to that enjoyed by the average citizen of a country with a modern economy, such as the United States. Economic development is characterized by such things as high levels of consumption, broad-based educational achievement, adequate housing, and access to high-quality health care. Achieving these goals can come about only after long periods of sustained high levels of economic growth.

International trade can affect the level of economic growth of an economy. With unemployed resources, an increase in export sales will lead to an overall expansion in production and an accompanying fall in the unemployment rate. International trade also allows for the purchase of capital goods from foreign countries and exposes an economy to technological advances achieved around the globe. Conversely, economic growth can affect the types of goods a country is able to trade. A technological advance in a country's import-competing sector could, for instance, lead to an overall reduction in the volume of trade of a country. Thus, international trade and economic growth are closely linked.

In this chapter we will explore various relationships between trade and growth. First, we will briefly consider aspects of the relationship between trade and economic development. Then, we will examine how economic growth affects international trade patterns. Finally, we will explore an additional link between trade and growth, international flows of factors of production. That is, each year labor and capital move from one country to another. We will discuss some of the economic consequences of these international flows of factors of production. In particular, we will consider the effects of the international migration of labor. We will also discuss international flows of physical capital, exemplified by the multinational corporation.

TRADE AND DEVELOPMENT*

Roughly 75 percent of the world's population lives in the low- or middle-income developing countries of the world.[†] The typical developing country is characterized

---

*This section is meant to provide only a brief introduction to the topic of trade and development. For a more complete textbook discussion, see Michael Todaro, *Economic Development,* 7th ed. (Reading, Mass.: Addison-Wesley, 1999). For additional detail, see Chapter 5 of World Bank, *World Development Report 1991* (Oxford: Oxford University Press, 1991).
[†]For a list of many of these countries as well as data on some of their basic characteristics, see Table 1.1 in Chapter 1.

by low per capita GDP, high levels of illiteracy, high birthrates, and inadequate housing and sanitation. Most of these countries devote a much larger share of their economy to agricultural production than do industrialized countries. These countries are plagued by shortages of physical capital. Their export sectors tend to be concentrated in only a few items, usually primary products, such as agricultural goods, petroleum, and minerals, or basic manufactures, such as textiles and shoes.

In order to improve their economic circumstances, many developing countries have undertaken large-scale development plans. These plans almost always involve massive government intervention into the economy. For instance, to encourage the growth of industry, governments will impose high taxes on farmers, using the proceeds to subsidize industry. These taxes also serve to encourage workers to leave agriculture for urban areas where industrial jobs are being created. Another common feature of these plans is the extensive use of trade policy. The types of strategies undertaken by these countries generally fall into one of several categories and are examined in the next few sections.

Primary-Export-Led Development Policies

Many developing countries are blessed with abundant natural resources or substantial amounts of land that are ideal for the production and export of natural-resource or land-intensive products. A **primary-export-led development strategy** involves government programs designed to exploit natural comparative advantage by increasing production of a few export goods most closely related to the country's resource base and exporting them in return for manufactured goods produced elsewhere. The hope is that, just as we described in the early chapters of this book, standards of living will rise due to specialization along the lines of comparative advantage (i.e., the static gains from trade).

In addition to the usual static gains from trade, there may be several benefits to the primary-export-led growth. First, in the absence of trade, it is quite possible that certain factors would be underutilized or perhaps not used at all. For instance, without international trade, a country with large amounts of fertile land might not put all of its land into cultivation. This would mean that in autarky the country would be at a production point inside its production possibility frontier (PPF). Opening the economy up to trade would encourage more intensive use of existing factors of production.*

Second, this type of development strategy can serve to entice the inflow of foreign capital. Foreign firms could locate in the country in order to help it to expand its export sectors. In time, as development occurs, other foreign investment might situate in related sectors, thereby helping to facilitate the development of other industries. In either event, the inflow of foreign capital would cause the PPF of the developing country to shift out.

Finally, this type of growth may have **linkage effects.** Linkage effects refer to the benefits to other industries or sectors of an economy that occur as one industry

> **Primary-export-led development strategies**
> Government programs designed to exploit natural comparative advantage by increasing production of a few export goods most closely related to a country's resource base.

> **Linkage effects**
> Benefits to other industries or sectors of an economy that occur as one industry expands.

---

*This point suggests that trade serves as a vent for surplus. Hla Myint stresses this feature of primary-export-led growth in "The 'Classical Theory' of International Trade and the Underdeveloped Countries," *Economic Journal* (1959).

expands. For instance, the growth of a large-scale mining sector could encourage the development of a local mining-equipment industry. This type of effect is known as a backward linkage. A second type of linkage occurs when the development of an export sector leads to the provision or development of economic infrastructure, such as roads, railroads, harbors, telecommunications, electricity, and the like. The development of this infrastructure then serves to lower the costs of other industries operating in the country, further promoting development.

Primary-export-led growth strategies count on the benefits from static and dynamic gains from trade to be the primary forces to promote economic growth and development. It has been argued that Australia, Canada, and the United States achieved economic development in just this fashion. More recently, countries that have pursued a primary-export-led growth strategy with at least some success include Colombia (coffee), Mexico and Nigeria (petroleum), and Malaysia (rubber).

Despite these examples, some economists and many government leaders have been critical of primary-export-led growth strategies. Their opposition to such policies includes the following points: First, it is argued that the world markets for primary products do not grow fast enough to support development. That is, the largest markets for primary products are the industrialized countries of the world. As these countries grow, so too does their demand for primary products, but not at the same rate. Over time, one would expect that primary products would represent a declining share of industrialized countries' imports.

A second and related problem to primary-export-led development strategies is the claim that exporters of primary products face a secular deterioration in their terms of trade.* That is, it is argued that over time the price of primary-product exports relative to manufactured-goods imports will tend to fall. This fall could occur for either of two reasons. First, if demand for primary goods is sluggish in the industrialized countries, then there will be downward pressure on the growth of primary-product prices. Second, if governments in the developing countries pursue export-expansion policies, then supplies of these products will rise on world markets, again tending to deflate prices. In either event, the upshot is that a trend deterioration in the terms of trade suggests that developing countries may enjoy a decreasing share of the gains from trade as trade continues through time. Whether or not this is the case depends not only on price but on the quantity of exports. That is, suppose Brazil increases its exports of coffee. This will tend to lower world coffee prices. If world demand is sufficiently elastic, then Brazil's export earnings will rise. If export earnings rise relative to the price of imports, then Brazil can purchase more imports than before, and its welfare will have risen.

The issue of whether or not the terms of trade of primary-product exporters have been deteriorating through time has not yet been fully resolved. A relatively recent

---

*This argument has been attributed to Hans Singer, "The Distribution of Trade between Investing and Borrowing Countries," *American Economic Review* (1950); and to Raul Prebish, primary author of United Nations, *The Economic Development of Latin America and Its Principal Problems* (1950).

study of the data over the 70-year period from 1900 to 1970 finds no evidence that a decline has occurred.* However, analysis of data from 1950 onward does seem to support the hypothesis of a decline in the terms of trade. A more recent study, using very modern statistical methodology and data from 1900 to 1983, again finds no evidence of any deterioration over the long run.[†]

Figure 10.1 provides some detail on the behavior of the terms of trade of oil exporting and non-oil-exporting developing countries from 1964 to 1994. As the figure shows, the terms of trade for these two groups of countries have behaved very differently over this period. Oil exporters have seen three sharp increases in their terms of trade, in 1974, 1979, and again in 1990. The first two coincide with the two large increases in petroleum prices engineered by the Organization of Petroleum Exporting Countries (OPEC). The third reflects the sharp rise in oil prices at the time that Iraq invaded Kuwait. In the 1980s, between the last two increases, oil prices fell sharply and so too did the terms of trade of the oil exporters. This pattern has been repeated since the end of the Gulf War in 1991. The terms of trade of the non–oil exporters have shown much less fluctuation. There are two significant downturns,

FIGURE 10.1   *Terms of trade of developing countries.*

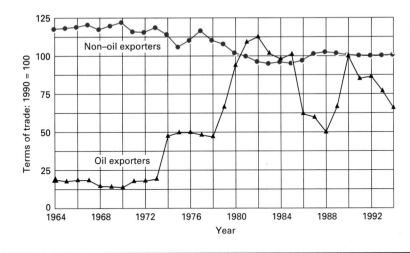

NOTE: 1985 = 100.

SOURCE: International Monetary Fund, *International Financial Statistics Yearbook* (1990).

*See John Spraos, "The Statistical Debate on the Net Barter Terms of Trade between Primary Commodities and Manufactures," *Economic Journal* (1980).
[†]See John Cuddington and Carlos Urzua, "Trends and Cycles in the Net Barter Terms of Trade: A New Approach," *Economic Journal* (1989).

coinciding with the OPEC oil price increases. Otherwise, the terms of trade appear to be quite stable, with a slight downward trend over time.*

The recent experience described in Figure 10.1 offers some additional insights on the terms of trade debate. First, if a group of developing countries has significant market power over a product that is inelastically demanded in world markets, it can improve its terms of trade by restricting supply. This is the counterpart on the export side to the effect of an optimal import tariff.[†] As the figure also shows, the ability to raise one's terms of trade may not be permanent. That is, over time, consumers of the more expensive product will cut back consumption even as the higher price encourages increased production from other sources. As consumption falls and new production rises, the price of the expensive product will fall. Second, the major short-run deteriorations in the terms of trade of non–oil exporters in the past several decades were more likely caused by the policies of other developing countries (i.e., the nations involved in OPEC) than by market conditions in developed countries.

Import-Substitution Development Policies

Import-substitution development strategies
Policies that seek to promote rapid industrialization by erecting high barriers to foreign goods to encourage local production.

For a variety of reasons, many developing countries have ignored primary-export-led growth strategies in favor of **import-substitution development strategies.** These policies seek to promote rapid industrialization and therefore development by erecting high barriers to foreign goods to encourage local production. Ideally, this approach to development applies the infant industry argument for protection to one or more targeted industries in the developing country. That is, the government determines those sectors best suited for local industrialization, raises barriers to trade on the products produced in these sectors in order to encourage local investment, and then lowers the barriers over time as the industrialization process takes hold. If the government has targeted the "correct" sectors, the industries in these sectors will continue to thrive even as protection comes down.

In practice, however, the barriers rarely do come down. Corporate managers who convinced politicians that protection should be imposed in the first place recognize the strong link between profits and protection. Any change in the market that would cause profits to fall leads these managers back to the government for additional protection. In the end, countries that follow import-substitution strategies tend to be characterized by high barriers to trade that grow over time.

Import-substitution policies have other problems. First, they tend to limit the development of industries that supply inputs to the protected industries. That is, it is often the case that the industries targeted for initial protection are producers of consumer goods. Managers in these industries would be very much opposed to any government policies that increased the costs of their inputs. Thus, they would tend

---

*A statistical analysis of these data suggests an average annual decline of 0.77 percent in the terms of trade of non-oil-exporting developing countries over the period 1964–1994.
[†]See Chapter 6 for a discussion of optimal import tariffs.

to oppose protection for these other industries or demand still more protection for their products.*

Second, because countries that pursue import-substitution strategies tend not to apply high tariffs to capital goods, imported capital goods are used extensively in local production. Coupled with other local policies (e.g., minimum wages that tend to raise labor costs), local managers utilize relatively capital-intensive production techniques. This means that employment in the newly industrializing sector does not grow as fast as might otherwise be the case.

Finally, because the whole development strategy depends upon the choices made by government officials, considerable resources are devoted to convincing officials of the merits of various cases. Alternatively, officials are bribed. In either event, the resources used in these activities could have been devoted to productive enterprises and hence represent additional economic waste over and above the usual deadweight costs of protection.

Outward-Looking Development Policies

In contrast to import-substitution policies, some developing countries have adopted **outward-looking development strategies.** These policies involve government targeting of sectors in which the country has potential comparative advantage. Thus, if a country is well endowed with low-skilled labor, the government would encourage the development of labor-intensive industries in the hope of promoting exports of these products. This type of strategy includes government policies such as keeping relatively open markets so that internal prices reflect world prices, maintaining an undervalued exchange rate so that export prices remain competitive in world markets, and imposing only minimal government interference on factor markets so that wages and rents reflect true scarcity. In addition, successful exporters often enjoy additional benefits, including special preference for the use of port facilities, communications networks, and lower loan and tax rates.

Outward-looking development strategies Government support for manufacturing sectors in which a country has potential comparative advantage.

Only a few countries have followed outward-oriented development strategies for extensive periods of time, but those that have done so have been very successful. They include Japan in its post–World War II reconstruction and the newly industrialized countries (NICs) of Asia: Hong Kong, South Korea, Singapore, and Taiwan. In part because of their success and because of the high economic cost of import-substitution policies, many other countries have recently begun to adopt more outward-oriented policies. Table 10.1 describes some of the recent trade-liberalizing measures adopted by developing countries. Item 10.1 compares the experiences of some countries that have followed each approach to development.†

---

*You should recall the concept of the effective rate of protection developed in Chapter 6 and the fact that tariffs tend to escalate by stages of processing.
†For an extended analysis of the benefits of outward-oriented development policies, see Jeffrey Sachs and Andrew Warner, "Economic Reform and the Process of Global Integration," *Brookings Papers on Economic Activity,* 1995.

TABLE 10.1	Trade Reforms in Selected Developing Countries
Country	**Reforms**
Argentina	Average tariff level was reduced from 18 percent to 11 percent in 1991. The highest tariff rate was cut by 15 percentage points in 1992. Import licensing restrictions were substantially eased in 1991.
Bangladesh	Average tariff rate recently reduced to 25 percent.
Brazil	Average tariff level was reduced from 32 percent in 1990 to 21 percent in 1992. Stringent computer protection ended in October 1992; most NTBs were removed in March 1990.
Chile	Substantial reform began in 1973, with elimination of quotas and a uniform tariff of 10 percent on all goods except automobiles. Following an economic crisis in the early 1980s, the uniform tariff rate was raised to 15 percent.
China	An agreement was concluded in 1992 to begin significant liberalization of imports, including a phaseout of almost 90 percent of all NTBs by 1998.
Colombia	Average import duty was reduced from more than 33 percent to less than 13 percent in 1992.
Ecuador	In June 1992, a new tariff range for most products of 5 to 20 percent replaced the previous range of 5 to 35 percent.
Egypt	An import ban was reduced from 37 percent of tradable goods in 1990 and 23 percent in 1991 to 10 percent in 1992. In 1993, a new tariff range of 5 to 80 percent replaced the previous range of 5 to 100 percent.
Ghana	As part of a reform effort that started in the mid-1980s, NTBs were reduced, and a uniform tariff was introduced on most goods.
India	Restrictive import licensing requirements covering 70 percent of all imports were eliminated in 1992. In 1993, the average peak tariff rate was reduced from 110 percent to 85 percent.
Indonesia	Trade reforms begun in 1986. By 1989, only about 20 percent of imports were subject to special licensing provisions.
Jamaica	Reforms begun in 1984. Quotas have been eliminated and tariffs lowered to between 20 and 30 percent for most items.
Mexico	Substantial reduction in quotas begun in 1985. Tariffs reduced to an average 11 percent, with a maximum rate of 20 percent.
Pakistan	In 1992, tariffs on consumer durables were cut from between 80 and 90 percent to 50 percent, and some machinery tariffs were cut in half. Lists of banned imports were reduced by 50 percent.
Peru	Reforms begun in 1990. Quotas have been eliminated and tariffs simplified to include three rates (15 percent, 25 percent, and 50 percent). In 1991, the top rate was cut to 20 percent.
Philippines	Trade reform package was adopted in 1991 to reduce average tariff rate from 28 percent to 20 percent over four years. Some quotas were also lifted.
Senegal	Removed most quotas during 1986–1988. Also made selective cuts in tariffs.
Tunisia	NTBs reduced on many items by mid-1990. Maximum tariff reduced from 220 percent to 43 percent.
Turkey	Substantial tariff reductions were enacted in 1992.

SOURCE: Based on Table 1 in Dani Rodrick, "The Rush to Free Trade in the Developing World: Why So Late? Why Now? Will It Last?" *NBER Working Paper, #3947* (January 1992), and Table 1 in Susan Hickok, "Recent Trade Liberalization in Developing Countries: The Effects on Global Trade and Output," *Quarterly Review,* Federal Reserve Bank of New York (Autumn 1993).

| ITEM 10.1 | Outward-Looking Versus Import-Substitution Growth Policies |

When Ghana became independent in 1957, it was a major exporter of cocoa. One-fifth of Ghana's GDP came from the sales of this product in world markets. Upon independence, Ghana began a program of import-substitution (IS) policies aimed at expanding its industrial base. Tariffs were raised, and resources were drawn from cocoa production into other sectors. The result was a sharp reduction in cocoa exports. Because of the economic distortions required to implement the industrial policy, Ghana's GDP per capita fell (in constant dollar terms) from $500 in 1957 to $310 in 1983. By contrast, the neighboring country of the Côte d'Ivoire, with resources similar to those in Ghana, followed a policy of encouraging the production and export of a variety of primary products, including coffee, cocoa, and wood. Between 1960 and 1980, export growth averaged almost 7 percent per year, and per capita GDP grew to almost twice that of Ghana's.

Very few countries have been able to implement successful IS policies. One that has enjoyed some success is Kenya. There, between 1960 and 1983, real per capita GDP grew more than 5 percent per year, while the ratio of imports to GDP fell. There is no clear reason why Kenya's IS policies have been relatively successful, while Ghana's appear to have failed. One difference between the two policies is that, in Kenya, much less emphasis was placed on replacing agricultural production with manufacturing. And, despite the impressive growth statistics just described, by 1983 Kenya's GDP per capita had grown to only about the level to which Ghana's had fallen.

The most successful export-promotion policies have been followed by Japan and the newly industrialized countries (NICs) of the Pacific Basin. The NICs (i.e., Hong Kong, Singapore, South Korea, and Taiwan) have followed similar policies and have enjoyed similar spurts of growth. Consider South Korea, for example. Between 1960 and 1983, exports grew on average 24 percent per year, and GDP per capita rose by 6 percent per year. In Singapore, over roughly the same period, GDP per capita rose almost 8 percent per year.

TRADE AND GROWTH*

Irrespective of government policies, there is always a tendency for economic growth to occur. Increases in population imply a growing labor force. Investment in new plant and equipment by firms implies a larger and larger capital stock. Over time, technological advances occur that allow for greater efficiency in production. Despite the fact that these general tendencies for growth occur around the world, actual patterns of factor growth and technical innovation differ quite substantially across various countries. (Recall, e.g., the data in Table 1.1.) Moreover, the manner in which a country grows will have implications for its pattern of trade as time progresses. It is to these issues that we now turn.

---

*The next two sections can be omitted without loss of continuity.

Because growth can occur in a variety of ways, we shall break up our analysis into several specific cases.* For each of these cases, we assume that the economy in question produces two goods, S (soybeans) and T (textiles), by means of two factors of production, L (labor) and K (capital). We make the long-run assumption that these two factors are always fully employed, so that the economy's production point will always be somewhere on the nation's production possibility frontier (PPF). Growth will be depicted as a shift outward in the PPF. We assume that the production of soybeans (textiles) is relatively capital (labor) intensive, and that the economy is relatively abundant—at least initially—in labor. Hence, by HO-type arguments, the country initially has a comparative advantage in textiles and exports these goods to the rest of the world in exchange for soybeans. Finally, we assume that the country in question is small, so that it takes world prices as given, and that it follows free-trade policies.

Economic growth can be described graphically as an outward shift in a nation's PPF. How will the shift occur? As we saw from our discussion in Chapter 4 of the Rybczynski theorem, if only one factor of production grows, then the PPF will expand largely in the direction of the commodity whose production is relatively intensive in the growing factor.† Suppose both factors grow. Then, as the PPF tends to expand more uniformly in all directions, the closer are the rates of growth of the two factors. If the two factors grow at exactly the same rates, then the overall capital/labor ratio in the economy will remain unchanged over time. In this situation, the PPF will preserve its original shape as it becomes larger.

International trade is the difference between a nation's production and its consumption. As we have seen, growth necessarily affects production. It also affects consumption. This is because the price line that is tangent to the PPF will also be shifting out with growth, reflecting the fact that a nation with a growing endowment of productive resources is able to undertake a growing amount of consumption. Thus, since growth affects both production and consumption, it tends to affect international trade.

Consider Figure 10.2. There, we depict an economy before growth occurs.‡ The nation's production point is at A_0, and its consumption point is at C_0. The international price of S is given by the slope of the price line PP. At that price, the country exports A_0B_0 units of T in exchange for B_0C_0 units of S. Consider the line (denoted

---

*For a taxonomic treatment of all the ways an economy can grow and the effects of this growth on international trade, see Harry Johnson, "Economic Development and International Trade," in *Readings in International Economics,* ed. Richard Caves and Harry Johnson (Homewood, Ill.: Richard D. Irwin, 1968).

†Recall that the Rybczynski theorem states that at constant prices, if a country experiences an increase in the supply of one factor, it will produce more of the product whose production is intensive in that factor and less of the other product. See also Figure 4.7 for an illustration of economic growth when only one factor has increased in supply.

‡In the extended discussion that follows, we model growth as increases in the supplies of factors of production. It is equally interesting to discuss technological changes that make existing factors more productive. So long as any technological change is not industry specific, the two causes of growth are analytically identical. Later, we discuss briefly the case of industry-specific technological change.

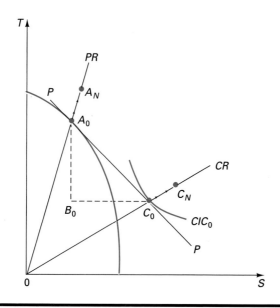

FIGURE 10.2   *Patterns of production and consumption with neutral growth.*

by *PR*) emanating from the origin (point 0) and passing through point A_0. The slope of the *PR* line represents the initial ratio of production of the two goods in the economy. Similarly, the slope of the *CR* line provides the ratio in which the two goods are consumed prior to economic growth in the country. The type of growth a country experiences can be categorized according to where, in relation to the *PR* and *CR* lines, the new production and consumption points are located after growth has occurred.

Neutral economic growth is a situation where, after growth has taken place, the new production and consumption points lie further to the right along the original *PR* and *CR* lines, respectively. In other words, after growth the economy continues to produce and consume the two goods in the same ratios as it had before growth. Such a situation would be illustrated in Figure 10.2 if the production point were to move outward, say to A_N, with a corresponding movement of the consumption point to C_N. As it turns out, in this case exports and imports will both rise by amounts proportional to the increase in production.*

Neutral economic growth
A proportionate increase in all factors and consumption so that trade expands proportionately to the growth of the economy.

---

*To convince yourself of the validity of this last statement, trace out the new trade triangle for the economy based on production occurring at A_N and consumption at C_N. Then, compare the size of this triangle with that of the old trade triangle.

What are the underlying economic circumstances necessary for economic growth to be neutral? First, it must be the case that the new PPF must look exactly like the old PPF, but bigger. Only in this case will the new production point lie on the same *PR* as the old production point. This statement requires some discussion. Recall that we have assumed that world prices stay constant. If output prices remain constant, so will input prices. Constant input prices, in turn, imply that after growth each industry will want to use capital and labor in the same mixes that were used prior to growth. Consequently, for output to grow by equiproportionate amounts in the two industries, factors must grow in supply so that they can continue to be divided between the two industries in precisely the same fashion they were before growth occurred. Thus, if the ratio of new capital to new labor equals the preexisting overall capital/labor ratio in the economy, then output of the two goods will expand proportionately.

The second condition for neutral growth is that the consumption of the two goods rises along the *CR* line. This will happen only if the consumption of both rises by the same proportion. What brings about the changes in consumption? Clearly, the answer is that because of economic growth, the economy is at a higher income (GDP) level.* In your Principles of Economics course, you probably learned about a measure of the relationship between changes in demand and changes in income. This measure is known as the *income elasticity of demand.* We denote the formulas for the income elasticity of demand for *S* and *T*, respectively, as

$$\eta_S = \frac{\text{percentage change in consumption of } S}{\text{percentage change in income (GDP)}}$$

and

$$\eta_T = \frac{\text{percentage change in consumption of } T}{\text{percentage change in income (GDP)}}$$

For consumption of each good to rise in the same proportion, as is required to remain on the *CR* line, the two income elasticities must be equal. That is, $\eta_S = \eta_T$. Moreover, since there is nothing else to purchase, the percentage changes in the consumption of both products must equal the percentage change in income. That is, it must also be the case that both elasticities equal 1.[†] This is the second requirement of neutral economic growth.

A numerical example of neutral economic growth is provided in Table 10.2. We assume that the economy begins with a production level of 1,000 units of *T* and that it consumes 600 of these. The difference of 400 is exported to the rest of the world.

---

*Recall that we are maintaining an assumption of fixed prices.
[†]Recall from your Principles of Economics course that income elasticities of demand may be positive or negative. If they are negative, goods are said to be inferior. If they are positive, goods are normal. Goods with very high (positive and greater than 1) elasticities are sometimes described as luxuries. This is because an increase in income leads to a large increase in consumption of these products. Goods with income elasticities less than 1 are sometimes described as necessities.

TABLE 10.2	*Example of Neutral Economic Growth*		
	Before Growth	After Growth	Percentage Change
Production of T	1,000	1,600	60
Consumption of T	600	960	60
Exports of T	400	640	60
Production of S	800	1,280	60
Consumption of S	1,600	2,560	60
Imports of S	800	1,280	60
Slope of PR line	$5/4^1$	$5/4^2$	0
Slope of CR line	$3/8^3$	$3/8^4$	0
Terms of trade	2	2	0
GDP[5]	2,800	4,480	60

[1]Calculated as production of T/production of S = 1,000/800.

[2]Calculated as production of T/production of S = 1,600/1,280.

[3]Calculated as consumption of T/consumption of S = 600/1,600.

[4]Calculated as consumption of T/consumption of S = 960/2,560.

[5]Measured in units of S.

We assume that the world price of T in terms of S is 2, so that when this country exports 400 units of T, it receives 800 units of S in return. Adding these imports to its (assumed) production of 800 units of S allows the country to consume 1,600 units of S. The GDP for this country is calculated by adding together the level of T production (measured in units of S) and the level of S production. Hence, initial GDP equals 2,800 ($2 \times 1{,}000 + 800$).

Suppose that growth in the supplies of capital and labor leads to a 60 percent change in the outputs of S and T. Consumption of each good must also rise by 60 percent. If both production and consumption of a good rise by 60 percent, so too will the amount of trade in this good. This growth is illustrated by the figures in the second column of the table. Our example provides a compelling illustration of why this type of growth is called neutral. Every aspect of the economic activity in this economy has expanded by the same proportion.

With the case of neutral economic growth established as a reference point, we are now in a position to consider other forms of economic growth. To cut down on the number of cases that could be illustrated, we shall assume that after growth, consumption continues to occur along the original CR line. In other words, we assume that $\eta_S = \eta_T = 1$ throughout.*

Suppose the supply of labor were to increase by a greater percentage than the supply of capital.† What will happen to the output of the two goods? Since T is a

---

*We leave as an exercise the effects on international trade if this were not the case.

†The limiting case of this type would be the Rybczynski case where only labor increased in the economy.

FIGURE 10.3   *Location of production following protrade biased growth.*

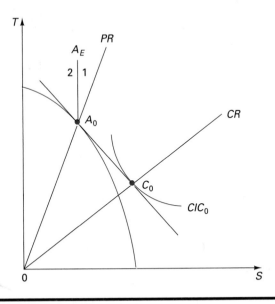

labor-intensive industry, and, by assumption, economic growth has made the country relatively more labor abundant, the PPF will tend to grow proportionately more along the T axis than along the S axis. Holding prices constant, the new production point will lie above the old PPF, with the new PR line rotating to the left of the original PR line. This is indicated by the regions denoted 1 and 2 in Figure 10.3. If the new production point is located in region 1, then the outputs of both T and S rise, but that of T rises in a greater proportion. If the new production point occurs in region 2, then, after growth, the output of T rises, but that of S falls. Finally, if the new production point occurs on the boundary line between these two regions (denoted by $A_0 A_E$), the output of T rises, but the output of S remains constant. Where will the production point end up? The answer is that it depends on the relative growth of labor and capital.

Recall that the T industry is assumed to be more labor intensive than the S industry. Now, we consider the case where the economy receives an infusion of new labor and capital, but at a rate that will lower the overall capital/labor ratio of the economy. The ratio of new capital to new labor will determine what happens to the outputs of S and T. If the ratio of new capital to new labor equals the original capital-to-labor ratio in industry T, then the new production point will lie on the vertical line segment above A_0. That is, the output of T will rise after growth, while the output of S will remain constant. The intuition behind this result is relatively straightforward. The economy has received new factors of production in precisely the combination that is used to produce *T*. Hence, these factors can be allocated efficiently to the *T* industry without affecting production in the *S* industry.*

Consider now the case where the proportion of new factors is different from the ratio in which they are used in the *T* industry. That is, suppose that the ratio of new capital to new labor exceeds (is less than) the original capital/labor ratio in the *T* industry. Then, the new production point will lie in region 1 (2).[†] Again, the logic of this is relatively straightforward. If the ratio of new capital to new labor is less than the ratio used in the *T* industry, then for *T* to be able to employ these new factors, it will need some additional capital. This capital can come only from the *S* industry. Hence, the output of *S* must fall, and, graphically, the production point moves into area 2. Conversely, if the ratio of new capital to labor exceeds that used in the *T* industry, the *T* industry could expand, but it would not want to hire factors in the proportion available to it. There would be a tendency to employ less than the fully available amounts of new capital. However, these factors would become employed if the *S* industry were to expand. Hence, in this case, the production point of the economy would tend to move into area 1.

No matter whether the new production point is in area 1, in area 2, or on the line between, after growth has occurred there will be a tendency for the economy to produce relatively more *T* and relatively less *S* than before growth occurred. If, as we have assumed, the economy still wants to consume *S* and *T* in the same ratios as before, then there will be a tendency for a large expansion in both exports and imports. Consider the case where the economy moves into area 2. Production of *T* has risen, production of *S* has declined, but GDP has expanded. Hence, the demand for both products has risen. Clearly, because the output of *S* has declined while the demand for it has risen, imports must rise (a lot!). Since, by assumption, the international price of imports has remained unchanged, the only way the economy can expand its imports of *S* is through an expansion in exports of *T*. We have now established the following result: *When an economy grows because of a relative expansion in the supply of the factor used intensively in the production of exportables, there will be a tendency for the output of exportables to rise relative to the output of importables and for international trade to rise in percentage terms by an amount greater than the percentage expansion of GDP.* This type of growth is called **protrade biased growth.**

Note carefully the implication of protrade biased growth on an economy. If the amount that a country trades is growing over time at a rate that exceeds that country's growth in GDP, then the relative importance of trade to that economy (as measured by, e.g., the ratio of exports to GDP) is also growing. Graphically, the *PR* line rotates away from the *CR* line so that the production point moves further and further away from the consumption point. As we saw in Chapter 1, since World War

Protrade biased growth
Growth that results in an expansion of trade that exceeds the rate of growth of GDP.

---

*Recall that, by assumption, prices are fixed. This means that new supplies of factors have no effect on factor prices. Thus, each industry will want to employ new factors in the same ratio as before growth.
[†]In the Rybczynski case, this clearly holds because only labor increases. Therefore, the ratio of new capital to new labor is zero. This must be less than the original capital/labor ratio in the *T* industry; and hence, by the theorem, the output of *T* will rise, while the output of *S* will fall.

TABLE 10.3	*Example of Protrade Biased Growth*		
	Before Growth	After Growth	Percentage Change
Production of *T*	800	1,100	37.5
Consumption of *T*	500	600	20.0
Exports of *T*	300	500	66.7
Production of *S*	200	100	−50.0
Consumption of *S*	500	600	20.0
Imports of *S*	300	500	66.7
Slope of *PR* line	4	11	175.0
Slope of *CR* line	1	1	0.0
Terms of trade	1	1	0.0
GDP	1,000	1,200	20.0

II, trade has tended to grow faster than GDP for most countries. This indicates a general tendency for protrade biased growth in the world.

A numerical example of protrade biased growth is provided in Table 10.3. In this example, we assume that capital and labor grow in such a fashion that the output of *T* rises and of *S* falls. That is, we illustrate a movement into area 2 of Figure 10.3. We also assume that *S* and *T* have the same nominal price, so that the relative price of *S* is 1. This allows a simple calculation of how much growth has actually occurred in the economy. In particular, in the example, *T* has risen by 300, but *S* has fallen by 100. Because the two goods have the same price, we can add these physical changes to find the overall change in GDP (measured in units of *S*). Since GDP has grown by 20 percent, given our assumption that $\eta_S = \eta_T = 1$, consumption of both *S* and *T* will rise by 20 percent. Combining the effects of changes in production and consumption of the two goods yields the effect of growth on exports and imports.

It is also possible that a country could grow so that its relative endowment of initially scarce factors increases. For instance, in our example, the capital-scarce country could experience a relative expansion in its overall ratio of capital to labor. As might be expected from our preceding discussion, if this were to occur, there would be a tendency for an expansion of *S* production relative to *T* production. In fact, *production of* T *could even fall* if the ratio of new capital to new labor were greater than that used originally in the *S* industry. If we assume that consumption rises in proportion to the overall growth in the economy, then, because the production of *S*, the importable, is rising faster than the overall growth of the economy, the amount this country will trade will fall. When an economy grows because of a relative expansion in the supply of the factor used intensively in the production of importables, there will be a tendency for the output of importables to rise relative to the output of exportables and for the international trade of this country to fall. This type of growth is called **antitrade biased growth.**

An implication of antitrade biased growth is that, over time, the economy produces a bundle of goods that more and more closely matches the bundle that it

Antitrade biased growth
Growth that results in a reduction of trade relative to the size of the economy.

TABLE 10.4	*Example of Antitrade Biased Growth*		
	Before Growth	After Growth	Percentage Change
Production of *T*	2,000.0	2,100.0	5.0
Consumption of *T*	1,500.0	1,687.5	12.5
Exports of *T*	500.0	412.5	−17.5
Production of *S*	1,000.0	1,200.0	20.0
Consumption of *S*	1,250.0	1,406.25	12.5
Imports of *S*	250.0	206.25	−17.5
Slope of *PR* line	2.0	1.75	−12.5
Slope of *CR* line	1.2	1.2	0.0
Terms of trade	0.5	0.5	0.0
GDP	2,000.0	2,250.0	12.5

wants to consume. That is, the *PR* line rotates toward the *CR* line. In these circumstances, the importance of international trade to this economy tends to decline. In other words, there is a general tendency toward autarky.

Table 10.4 provides an example of a country that experiences antitrade biased growth. Here, we assume that increases in the supplies of capital and labor lead to a greater percentage growth in *S* than in *T* (i.e., 20 percent vs. 5 percent). Overall, the economy grows by 12.5 percent. Because of our continuing assumption about unitary income elasticities of demand for each good, consumption of *S* and of *T* rises by 12.5 percent. Note the effects of this type of growth on international trade. Consider industry *T* first. There, production has grown by less than consumption. Hence, the amount of *T* available for export must fall. In the *S* industry, production has grown by more than consumption. This implies that the demand for imports has fallen. Thus, this country wants to trade less after growth than before.

Note something else about antitrade biased growth. In this situation, over time the economy tends to produce relatively less of its traditional export good and relatively more of its traditional import good. Would it ever be possible that growth could lead to a switch in trade patterns? The answer is yes. If, for instance, supplies of capital were to continue to rise much faster than labor in the country we have been considering, then eventually, this country could be expected to stop exporting (importing) *T* (*S*) and begin to import (export) it.

TRADE AND GROWTH: SOME ADDITIONAL COMMENTS

The analysis we have conducted so far has made a number of quite restrictive assumptions about the sources of economic growth, the size of the country, and the trade policies that it follows. In this section, we briefly indicate how the results we have established so far change when some of the assumptions we have made are relaxed.

Technological Change

Technological (technical) change is said to occur when the same amount of output can be produced by fewer factor inputs, or, equivalently, when the same amount of inputs can produce greater amounts of output. Technical change can occur in a variety of ways. **Neutral technical change** is defined as innovation that reduces by an equiproportionate amount the quantity of factors required to produce a given level of output. **Labor-saving (capital-saving) technical change** is said to occur if the invention leads to a reduction in the use of labor (capital) at the original factor prices.

Technical change can be specific to an industry, or it can be economywide. Thus, the combination of the location of the innovation and the way in which the innovation saves on the use of resources will have implications for the postgrowth shape of the country's PPF. If neutral technical change occurs to the same degree in all industries of an economy, then that country's PPF shifts out in a manner that preserves its original shape. More likely, however, is that innovations will be industry and factor specific.

A complete treatment of all of the possibilities for industry-specific technical change is beyond the scope of this text. However, the following general results have been established in the special case where world prices remained fixed.*

If neutral technical progress occurs in one industry, the output of that industry will rise at the expense of the other. This will be even more the case if the innovation leads to a reduction in the per unit use of the relatively intensive factor of an industry. For instance, we would expect the output of T to rise substantially if a labor-saving innovation were introduced in the T industry. Why is this so? The effect of the innovation is to reduce the amount of labor industry T needs to produce its original level of output. At initial levels of output, this is just as if the economy were given an increase in its endowment of labor. Recall from the Rybczynski theorem that when an economy experiences an increase in the quantity of one factor, the output of the industry that uses that factor relatively intensively must rise, and the output of the other industry will fall.

If technical progress allows an industry to save on the use of the factor it uses relatively less intensively, then almost anything can happen. The output of the industry where the innovation occurred could rise, or it could fall. This is because there are two opposing effects at work. The effect of the innovation is to lower costs to the industry where the innovation occurred. This would tend to lead to an expansion in output of that industry. Working against this is the Rybczynski effect—the output of the other industry must rise to absorb the factor that is "saved" by the innovation.

Growth, Prices, and Welfare

Suppose that the country in question is large in world markets rather than small. In that case, the way in which the country grows will have strong implications for

Neutral technical change
An innovation that results in an equiproportionate reduction in the use of all factors in the production of one unit of output.

Labor-saving (capital-saving) technical change
An innovation that results in a more than proportionate reduction in the use of labor (capital) relative to other factors in the production of one unit of output.

---

*See Ronald Findlay and Harry Grubert, "Factor Intensity, Technological Progress, and the Terms of Trade," *Oxford Economic Papers* (1959), for a complete treatment of the effects of technical change on production and international trade.

world prices. For instance, suppose A is a large country that is relatively abundant in capital. As we have seen, if it undergoes neutral economic growth, then, over time, it will want to export more S and import more T. Because A is a large country, the increase in supply of S on world markets and the increase in demand for T will tend to lower the world price of S relative to T. In other words, in the case of neutral economic growth for a large country, the terms of trade for that country (the price of its exports relative to its imports) will tend to decline as it grows.

Biased economic growth will also have effects on a large country's terms of trade. Protrade biased growth will cause the terms of trade to deteriorate even more than neutral growth. This is because growth has caused a more than proportionate increase in the supply of exports to the world market and in the demand for imports from the world market. On the other hand, antitrade biased growth will lead to an improvement in the growing country's terms of trade.

Changes in a country's terms of trade have implications for the welfare level of the country. Economic growth at constant prices shifts a country's price line out, thereby expanding its consumption possibilities set and raising its standard of living. For a large country, this effect is diminished to some extent if growth leads to a deterioration in its terms of trade.

The fact that, for a large country, growth has both positive and potentially negative welfare effects means that it might be possible for growth to actually make a country worse off. In a classic paper, Jagdish Bhagwati has shown the conditions for **immizerizing growth,** growth that makes a country worse off.* In Figure 10.4 we

Immizerizing growth
Economic growth that results in a reduction in national economic welfare.

FIGURE 10.4   *Immizerizing growth.*

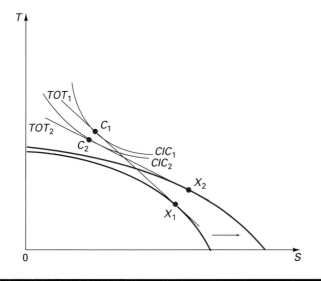

---

*See Jagdish Bhagwati, "Immizerizing Growth: A Geometrical Note," *Review of Economic Studies* (1958).

illustrate a situation of immizerizing growth. Initially, the economy is in free-trade equilibrium, producing at point X_1 and consuming at point C_1. Its welfare level in this equilibrium is denoted by the community indifference curve CIC_1, and the world price in this equilibrium, by the price line labeled TOT_1. Suppose there is strong protrade biased growth in the country. This will cause the PPF to shift out along the S axis and will produce a large expansion in the desired level of exports of the country. Suppose further that the demand for this good in the rest of the world is relatively inelastic. In this case, the world price of that product must fall substantially. This is shown by the fall in price from TOT_1 to TOT_2. Under these circumstances, consumption moves to C_2, and the country's welfare level falls to CIC_2. The deterioration in the growing country's terms of trade has been so great as to lower overall welfare below its pregrowth level.

Is immizerizing growth a common phenomenon? Probably not. This is for two reasons. First, precise conditions on both the nature of growth and world demand must hold for immizerizing growth to occur. Second, as we learned from our discussion of the optimal tariff in Chapter 6, if a country has the ability to affect world prices with its tariff policy, it can improve its welfare. This is clearly the situation here. If, in particular, the world price of the growing country's exports is falling, the government of that country can act to prevent this by imposing an export tariff. Thus, government policy can be used to mitigate any potential negative consequences of growth. A phenomenon somewhat similar to immizerizing growth is perhaps more common. This is known as the *Dutch disease*. Item 10.2 describes in more detail some of the history and implications of the Dutch disease.

ITEM 10.2 The Dutch Disease

In the 1960s, large deposits of natural gas were discovered in the Netherlands. Natural gas soon became a leading Dutch industry in terms both of production and exports. Because of the plentiful supplies of natural gas, other Dutch industries adopted energy-intensive production techniques. In the 1970s, the world experienced two oil-price shocks. The effects of these shocks on the Netherlands were especially profound.

The higher price of oil led to higher prices of substitute forms of energy, including natural gas. As prices rose in the natural gas sector of the economy, so did wages. This encouraged workers to leave other jobs for the expanding natural gas sector. Manufacturers in other sectors were forced to offer higher wages to hold on to their employees. Higher wages coupled with higher energy costs forced some manufacturers out of business. As if this were not enough, the fact that the Netherlands was relatively energy independent led foreign-exchange traders to bid up the value of the Dutch currency. This made it even more difficult for Dutch manufacturers to compete in world markets, and so higher energy prices led to the demise of a significant portion of the Dutch manufacturing sector. And because of downward rigidities in wages in the Netherlands, unemployment rose.

Other countries besides the Netherlands have had similar experiences with booming resource sectors. The fact that good fortunes for one part of a country's economy can lead to very bad times for the economy as a whole has become known as the *Dutch disease*. This notion has usually been associated with the implications of a boom in the market for a particular commodity and the effects of this boom on an economy that has large endowments of the commodity in question.

Economists have become interested in the various ramifications of the Dutch disease phenomenon. In particular, they are interested in whether other sectors in the economy must necessarily be made worse off when the resource boom occurs (in other words, whether these other sectors must necessarily catch the "disease"). They have shown that whenever a resource boom occurs, other sectors stand to be affected. This is what one would expect given constraints on the availability of resources. However, it need not be the case, as it was in the Netherlands, that a resource boom leads to de-industrialization. Export sectors such as agriculture may absorb the burden of the boom by providing the resources to the expanding sector. In addition, sectors specializing in the provision of goods that do not enter into international trade (e.g., the government, many services) could stand to gain from a resource boom, because these industries can raise their prices without fear of international competition.*

---

*For more discussion of the Dutch disease, see Max Corden and Peter Neary, "Booming Sector and De-Industrialization in a Small Open Economy," *Economic Journal* (1982); James Cassing and Peter Warr, "The Distributional Impact of a Resource Boom," *Journal of International Economics* (1985); and the papers in Peter Neary and Sweder van Wijnbergen, eds., *Natural Resources and the Macroeconomy* (Cambridge: MIT Press, 1986).

INTERNATIONAL FLOWS OF FACTORS

Labor

Up to this point, we have modeled economic growth as originating from within the growing country. Countries can also grow because they receive factor inputs from other countries. Consider the case of the United States. It is estimated that about 64 million people migrated to the United States from foreign countries between 1820 and 1997. Table 10.5 highlights the pattern of U.S. immigration over the past 175 years. Measured in terms of total flows, the peak level of immigration occurred between 1901 and 1910, the decade just prior to World War I. Then, in each subsequent decade until the 1940s, immigration fell.* Measured in terms of the ratio of immigrants to total population, again the highest proportion of immigrants in the population was found during the first decade of the twentieth century, but immigration was also very high relative to total population during the 1840s, the 1850s, and the 1880s.

This influx of new population helped to expand the labor force of the United States just at the time when other factors, such as land (through purchase, conquest, and expropriation) and capital (through domestic- and foreign-sourced investment),

---

*Some of this reduction can be explained by the enactment, in 1921, of the first in a series of laws to limit immigration into the United States.

TABLE 10.5	*U.S. Immigration, 1820–1997*[1]				
	Total			**Total**	
Year(s)	Number	Rate[2]	Year(s)	Number	Rate[2]
1820–1990	57,090	3.5	1931–1940	528	0.4
1820–1830[3]	152	1.2	1941–1950	1,035	0.7
1831–1840[4]	599	3.9	1951–1960	2,515	1.5
1841–1850[5]	1,713	8.4	1961–1970	3,322	1.7
1851–1860[5]	2,598	9.3	1971–1980[7]	4,493	2.1
1861–1870[6]	2,315	6.4	1981–1990	7,338	3.0
1871–1880	2,812	6.2	1991–1997	6,943	3.8
1881–1890	5,247	9.2	1993[8]	904	3.5
1891–1900	3,688	5.3	1994[8]	804	3.1
1901–1910	8,795	10.4	1995[8]	720	2.7
1911–1920	5,736	5.7	1996[8]	916	3.5
1921–1930	4,107	3.5	1997[8]	798	3.0

[1]In thousands, except rate. Through 1976, for years ending June 30, except as noted; beginning 1977, ending September 30. For definition of immigrants: 1820–1867, alien passengers arriving; 1868–1891 and 1895–1897, immigrants arriving; 1892–1894 and 1898 to the present, immigrants admitted. Rates based on Bureau of the Census estimates as of July 1 for resident population through 1929, and for total population thereafter (excluding Alaska and Hawaii prior to 1959). See also *Historical Statistics, Colonial Times to 1970,* series C89.

[2]Annual rate per 1,000 U.S. population, 10-year rate computed by dividing sum of annual immigration totals by sum of annual U.S. population totals for same 10 years.

[3]October 1, 1819, to September 30, 1830.

[4]October 1, 1830, to December 31, 1840.

[5]Calendar years.

[6]January 1, 1861, to June 30, 1870.

[7]Includes transition quarter, July 1 to September 30, 1976.

[8]Includes persons who were granted permanent residence under the legalization program of the Immigration Reform and Control Act of 1986.

SOURCE: Jagdish Bhagwati, "Global Interdependence and International Migration," in *Capital, Technology, and Labor in the New Global Economy,* ed. James Cassing and Steven Husted (Washington, D.C.: American Enterprise Institute, 1988), Table 1, reprinted by permission; and *Statistical Abstract of the United States, 1999* (Washington, D.C.: U.S. Government Printing Office, 1999), Table 5.

were also growing. Thus, immigration played a large part in the emergence of the United States as a leading world economy by the end of the nineteenth century.

The United States is not the only country to have experienced large inflows of migrants. For instance, between 1960 and 1980, Canada, Australia, and New Zealand took in 5.7 million immigrants, roughly one-third of the permanent world immigration during this period. Moreover, because these countries have much smaller populations, the proportion of immigrants to total population is much higher there than it is in the United States.

In addition to moves that migrants view as essentially permanent, a considerable amount of temporary immigration occurs today. These temporary moves are often the result of specific policies instituted by governments in host countries. Under these programs, workers from foreign (source) countries are invited to relocate in host countries for short time spans to work in various industries. Beginning in the

1960s and extending through at least 1975, rich Western European countries invited **guest workers** (or *gastarbeiter*) from neighboring poorer countries, such as Italy, Spain, Portugal, Turkey, Greece, and Yugoslavia. All in all, about 6.3 million workers were invited to move to Western Europe, and they composed a substantial proportion of the workforces there. At one point, 18 percent of Switzerland's labor force was made up of guest workers. The amount of workers participating in this program tended to reduce by substantial proportions the workforces in the source countries. Portugal, for example, exported more than 10 percent of its labor force. In addition to the guest worker programs in Western Europe, the OPEC countries of the Middle East have imported large numbers of workers from countries such as Egypt, Jordan, Pakistan, India, and even Korea. And also, for many years migrant workers from Mexico have crossed the border to work in the United States during agriculture harvests.

Guest workers
Foreign workers who are invited to temporarily relocate in a country to work in a certain sector of an economy.

Migration occurs for many reasons and follows a variety of paths. The majority of international relocations happen because the migrant is seeking at least one of three things: better economic circumstances, refuge from political tyranny or devastation, or reunion with other family members. Much of the migrant flow, such as in the guest worker programs, is from poor countries to rich countries. These flows are largely motivated by the opportunity workers have to earn higher wages and to enjoy the benefits of greater job security. Poor country to poor country and rich country to rich country flows are also relatively common. Rich country to poor country flows are not.

Migrants possess different skills. Much of the rich country to rich country migration that occurs involves skilled labor.* A substantial amount of migration from poor countries to rich countries also involves skilled labor. The process whereby skilled workers leave their homeland and relocate abroad is known as **brain drain.** The notion of a brain drain became an important focus of study in the 1960s. Then, the concern was that Europe's most skilled workers, including its best scientists, doctors, and engineers, were abandoning Europe for the United States, Canada, and elsewhere. Today, that flow has diminished and in some instances may have reversed its direction. More recently, concern has grown that rich industrialized countries may be draining skilled labor from poor developing countries, where, at the margin, the contribution of skilled labor to economic development may be quite high.†

Brain drain
The permanent relocation of skilled workers from one country to another.

Because of relatively higher wage levels and general standards of living, poor country to rich country movements of low-skilled workers are a common phenomenon. This pattern of migration describes well the flows of workers from Southern and Eastern Europe to the United States in the early part of the twentieth century and the migration of workers from Mexico and Southeast Asia to the United States today. The outflow of unskilled workers has sometimes been described as a *brawn drain.*

---

*This is due in part to the fact that many host countries have immigration laws that limit the inflow of people. A feature of these laws is that it is often easier for people with special skills to immigrate.
†The issue of whether or not the brain drain is a problem goes beyond the scope of this text. For an excellent overview of the issues on the brain drain, see Jagdish Bhagwati, "Global Interdependence: International Migration," in *Capital, Technology, and Labor in the New Global Economy,* ed. James Cassing and Steven Husted (Washington, D.C.: AEI, 1988), and the references cited therein.

Capital

Labor is not the only factor that flows across international boundaries. Capital, both in financial and in physical forms, does as well. In fact, international flows of capital have become an everyday fact of life in the international economy and, because of their enormous size, are probably much more important than labor flows in influencing rates of economic growth and the location of economic activity.

Again, we consider the case of the United States. Throughout the nineteenth century, it was a capital-importing country.* Other countries, most notably the United Kingdom, lent a substantial proportion of the financial capital that enabled the construction of railroads, factories, and communication systems, thereby helping to propel the U.S. economy to the status of an industrial giant. Imports of European-made capital goods (in exchange for U.S. agricultural products) also helped promote the development of the U.S. industrial base.

For much of the twentieth century, the United States was a capital exporter. That is, it lent financial capital to countries throughout the world, becoming by 1980 the world's largest net creditor. Since the 1980s, this trend has reversed. American firms, citizens, and especially the U.S. government have been borrowing in record amounts from foreigners. In the process, the United States has moved from being the world's largest net creditor to being the world's largest net debtor.[†]

Even though, of late, the United States has been importing more capital than it has been exporting, the United States still supplies substantial amounts of capital to the rest of the world. Firms in the United States have taken the lead in a particular form of international transfer of capital known as *direct foreign investment.* This happens when a domestic (e.g., U.S.) firm acquires ownership or control over the operations of a foreign subsidiary firm. According to U.S. definitions, a (parent) firm is said to directly invest abroad if it has a direct or indirect ownership interest of 10 percent or more in a foreign business enterprise (foreign affiliate corporation). American firms have engaged in direct foreign investment by setting up (or buying previously existing) production and marketing facilities in foreign countries, or by becoming minority owners of competing foreign corporations. Firms that own and operate capital in one or more foreign countries are known as **multinational corporations (MNCs).**

Multinational corporation (MNC) A corporation that operates production or marketing facilities in more than one country.

Virtually all of America's most well-known corporations, such as Ford, General Motors, IBM, McDonald's, and Coca-Cola, are MNCs. Many lesser-known American companies are MNCs as well. In 1997, worldwide sales of U.S. MNCs totaled almost $6.1 *trillion,* and worldwide employment of U.S. MNCs stood at 26.4 million people. The American (parent corporation) shares of these totals were $4.9 trillion in sales and 19.9 million employees, respectively. Table 10.6 provides detail on an

---

*In the real world, capital tends to flow both into and out of a country. That is, some agents (citizens, firms, or governments) borrow in international markets, while others lend. A capital importing (exporting) country is one where its citizens borrow (lend) more in international financial markets than they lend (borrow).

[†]See Chapter 12 for a more complete account of these events as well as an analysis of what this means for the United States.

TABLE 10.6 Employment of Nonbank U.S. MNCs, Selected Years (worldwide, parent, and affiliate)

| | Number of Employees (thousands) | | | | | | | | | Affiliates as a Percentage of Total Employment |
| | Worldwide | | | Parent | | | Affiliate | | | |
	1982	1989	1997	1982	1989	1997	1982	1989	1997	1997
All industries	23,727.0	23,879.4	26,392.8	18,704.6	18,765.4	19,867.4	5,022.4	5,114.0	6,525.4	25
Petroleum	1,600.1	786.0	660.2	1,225.3	579.8	483.2	374.8	206.2	177.0	27
Manufacturing	14,247.3	13,791.1	12,842.8	10,532.8	10,127.0	8,622.7	3,714.5	3,664.1	4,220.1	33
Food and kindred products	1,436.1	1,473.1	1,094.6	1,011.2	1,135.8	732.8	424.9	337.3	361.8	33
Chemicals and allied products	2,032.7	1,881.1	1,667.2	1,364.6	1,255.0	966.8	668.1	626.1	700.4	42
Primary and fabricated metals	1,223.0	843.2	852.1	976.2	684.6	611.4	246.8	158.6	240.7	28
Nonelectrical machinery	1,972.0	1,905.0	1,838.5	1,457.9	1,249.9	1,103.8	514.1	655.1	734.7	40
Electric and electronic equipment	2,107.2	1,479.4	1,760.2	1,619.5	1,093.3	1,175.1	487.7	386.1	585.1	33
Transportation equipment	2,332.0	2,851.9	2,442.9	1,687.3	2,104.4	1,657.6	644.7	747.5	785.3	32
Other manufacturing	3,144.3	3,357.4	3,187.3	2,416.0	2,604.0	2,375.2	728.3	753.4	812.1	25
Wholesale trade	522.5	582.6	1,166.4	396.7	434.2	756.9	125.8	148.4	409.5	35
Finance (except banking) Insurance and real estate	1,316.2	1,408.0	1,290.2	1,004.0	1,107.6	1,052.1	312.2	300.4	238.1	18
Services	1,121.1	2,014.6	3,710.2	993.8	1,700.0	3,024.3	127.3	314.6	685.9	18
Other industries	4,919.7	5,297.1	6,723.0	4,551.9	4,816.7	5,928.3	367.8	480.4	794.7	12

SOURCE: Raymond J. Mataloni, Jr., "U.S. Multinational Companies: Operations in 1997," Survey of Current Business (U.S. Department of Commerce, July 1999).

TABLE 10.7	*Employment of U.S. MNC Foreign Affiliates, by Area, 1997*			
	Number of Employees (thousands)		Number of Employees (thousands)	
All countries	6,525.4	**Developing countries**	1,956.5
Developed countries	4,568.9	Latin America	1,229.1
Canada	858.3	*Of which:*	
Europe	2,988.6	Mexico	530.7
Of which:		Africa	58.6
France	438.6	Middle East	42.9
Germany	579.0	Asia and Pacific	613.8
United Kingdom	897.0	*Of which:*	
Japan	409.0	India	38.4
Australia, New Zealand,		South Korea	31.8
and South Africa	312.9	**International**	12.1

SOURCE: Raymond J. Mataloni, Jr., "U.S. Multinational Companies: Operations in 1997," *Survey of Current Business* (U.S. Department of Commerce, July 1999).

industry-by-industry breakdown of MNC activity, as measured by employment, both in the United States and in foreign locations. Clearly, the manufacturing sector accounts for the largest share of MNC employment both in the Unites States and overseas. Within this category, a considerable fraction of overseas employment is in the transportation equipment sector, largely employees of the "big three" U.S. automakers in foreign assembly plants.

Table 10.7 provides some information on the location of foreign affiliates of U.S. MNCs, again measured by levels of employment. According to this table, almost 70 percent of foreign U.S. MNC employment is in developed countries, with the greatest share of this in Western Europe. The greatest amount of U.S. MNC employment in developing countries is found in Latin America.

Foreign MNCs exist, and most operate in the United States. U.S. companies that are affiliates of foreign MNCs sold $1.7 trillion in goods and services in 1997 and employed more than 5.2 million people. European-based corporations accounted for the greatest share of U.S. affiliate employment (62 percent). United Kingdom- and Japanese-based firms were the largest employers of workers in the United States, with 19 percent and 16 percent, respectively. Canadian firms accounted for almost 12 percent.*

Why some firms choose to become MNCs is an interesting and unresolved question in economics. Clearly, firms that operate in foreign countries are at a disadvan-

*For more information on the activities of foreign MNCs in the United States, see William J. Zeile, "Foreign Direct Investment in the United States," *Survey of Current Business* (U.S. Department of Commerce, August 1999).

tage relative to their locally based foreign competitors. That is, they face additional costs, including the costs of coordinating activities over long distances, that their competitors do not incur. Economic theory suggests, then, that there must be special advantages to being multinational, or else these firms would cease such operations. What sort of special advantages might there be? First, MNCs might have access to special technology. Control over this technology would enable the MNC to compete successfully with local firms. A second possibility is that there may be increasing returns to scale that accrue to a firm that operates plants in many locations.*

As we noted in our discussion of NAFTA, some have argued that trade liberalization between rich and poor countries will induce firms in high-wage countries to relocate their manufacturing operations to low-wage countries. In the process, employment would fall in high-wage countries and production would be replaced by imports from low-wage countries. The numbers in Tables 10.6 and 10.7 suggest that, to date, U.S. MNCs have not made widespread use of this practice. First, across all types of industries the vast bulk of U.S. MNC employment remains inside the United States. Second, more than two-thirds of overseas U.S. MNC employment is in the high-wage foreign countries of Europe, Canada, and Japan. In addition, studies of MNC-related trade flows suggest that intrafirm trade shares of U.S. exports and imports of goods have changed little over the past two decades.† All of this seems to suggest that the location of overseas production by U.S. MNCs appears to be determined more by access to markets than by access to low-wage labor or natural resources.

Economic Analysis

In this section, we end our discussion of international flows of factors by developing and analyzing a simple model that allows one to understand some of the economic implications of these flows. The model we develop is sufficiently general to allow us to apply it to international flows either of labor or of capital. For concreteness, however, we shall discuss labor migration. We leave as an exercise the application of this model to the study of international capital mobility.

We begin by assuming that there is one country, America, that produces one good, Y (or GDP), by means of fixed amounts of capital and labor. The first thing we want to establish is the level of labor demand in America under this situation. We define the **marginal product of labor** (MP_L) in America as the additional amount (in physical units) of output that can be produced with the addition of one more worker to the production process. What are the properties of the MP_L? Recall that we have assumed that there is a fixed stock of capital in America. If the capital stock is fixed, it seems plausible that, as more and more workers are added to the production pro-

Marginal product of labor
The additional amount of output (in physical terms) that is produced because one more worker is added to the production process.

---

*For a more complete discussion on the economics of MNCs, see John Dunning, "The Determinants of International Production," *Oxford Economic Papers* (1973); and Chapter 20 in James Markusen and James Melvin, *The Theory of International Trade* (New York: Harper and Row, 1988).
†See William J. Zeile, "U.S. Intrafirm Trade in Goods," *Survey of Current Business* (U.S. Department of Commerce, February 1997).

Diminishing returns to labor
The fact that as workers are added to the production process, holding all other factors fixed, the marginal product of labor declines.

cess, the MP_L will exhibit **diminishing returns to labor.** That is, the increase in output due to an increase in labor will become smaller and smaller. This is because a fixed amount of machines is being shared by a larger and larger work force.

Suppose that Y sells for P dollars per unit in the output market and that the market is competitive. Then, we define the **value marginal product of labor** (VMP_L) as the amount of money producers receive from selling the amount that was produced because the last worker was hired. In other words,

Value marginal product of labor
The monetary value of the marginal product of labor.

$$VMP_L = P \times MP_L \qquad (10.1)$$

where VMP_L represents the marginal revenue to producers from hiring the last worker.

Let's now consider the profit-maximizing decision by producers in determining their labor input. Suppose the going wage rate for workers is W; W can be thought of as the marginal cost of the last worker. The profit-maximizing rule, then, is simple. Producers should hire workers until the marginal cost of the last worker equals the marginal revenue that accrues because that worker was hired. That is, firms should equate marginal revenue with marginal cost.

Given information on the value of P and values of MP_L for different levels of employment, it is possible to develop a graph of the VMP_L. Such a graph appears in Figure 10.5. This curve slopes downward, reflecting the diminishing marginal product of labor. The VMP_L curve can be thought of as the demand-for-labor curve. We denote the fixed supply of workers in the economy by distance $0A$ in the diagram. The interaction of demand and supply in the labor market determines the wage rate,

FIGURE 10.5   *Distribution of income between labor and capital.*

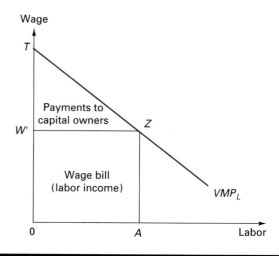

W'. Note, then, that the rectangular area defined by the letters $0W'ZA$ is the total value of labor earnings in the economy. This is determined by the fact that there are $0A$ workers, each earning $0W'$. The remaining area under the VMP_L curve, the triangle $W'TZ$, represents payments to the other factor of production, capital. How do we know this? Recall that at any point the height of the VMP_L curve represents the marginal revenue earned by producers because that worker was hired. The worker was paid \$$0W'$. The remainder is the amount left over that is available to pay owners of the capital stock also used in the production process. The combined areas represent total labor income and total income paid to capital owners, in other words, the value of GDP.

We are now in a position to consider migration. Let's assume that America allows an inflow of foreign workers and that these workers are as skilled as their American counterparts. The obvious effect of this policy is to increase the supply of labor. We denote this increase by the distance AB in Figure 10.6. There are several economic implications to the immigration of foreign workers.

First, as the diagram shows, there is a wage effect. Because of the expansion in the supply of labor (and the assumption that everything else, including the capital stock, has been held constant), wages are driven down to W'''. There is also an output effect. The expansion in the labor force means that more goods can be produced. The value of expanded production is shown in the diagram as the area of the trapezoid $AZZ''B$. Of this amount, the triangle $ZZ'Z''$ represents payments to capital, while the rectangle $ABZ''Z'$ represents the wages paid to foreign workers.

Finally, there is an income-redistribution effect. Domestic labor experiences a drop in the wage rate from $0W'$ to $0W'''$, and total domestic labor earnings fall from

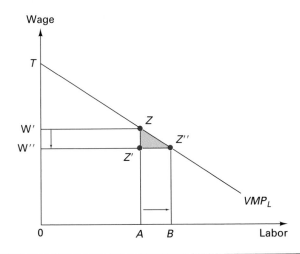

FIGURE 10.6   *The economic effects of labor immigration.*

$0W'ZA$ to $0W''Z'A$. The difference between the areas of these two rectangles represents the value of lost earnings to domestic labor. This amount is not lost to the economy, however. Rather, it reverts back to capital owners (assumed to be domestic residents). Capital owners benefit from the immigration of foreign labor because the resulting expansion in output leads to a more intensive use of capital and therefore to a rise in rental rates.

Thus, it is clear that even though foreign labor immigration leads to greater domestic output, not all in society benefit from this inflow. Domestic labor loses. Domestic capital owners gain. Exactly the opposite occurs in the source country. This can be seen from the diagram by considering an outflow of workers equivalent to the distance AB. In this case, labor has become somewhat more scarce. Its wage rises and total output falls. Capitalists in the labor-exporting country are made worse off because of this emigration of labor from their country.

We can draw several conclusions from this analysis. First, if we were to generalize the results of this model to many goods and factors of production, the following result obtains: *International factor flows tend to lower the incomes of those factors in the host country that most directly substitute for this factor and tend to raise the incomes of other factors.* This could mean that some types of labor in the host country could benefit from foreign migration. For instance, an influx of foreign unskilled labor into the United States may result in higher incomes for (domestic) skilled workers. Second, because factor flows have effects on the distributions of income in host and source countries, these countries often impose policies to limit factor flows. Such policies include restrictions on immigration and limits on capital outflows. The former are more common in rich countries, while the latter are more common in poor countries.

SUMMARY

1. International trade and economic growth are related to each other in many ways. Expanded exports tend to raise the level of GDP. The way in which a country grows affects the way it trades.

2. *Economic development* refers to the attainment of a high standard of living for the average citizen of an economy. Economic growth is essential for economic development.

3. Because of the relationship between trade and growth, some developing countries pursue outward-looking or primary-export-led development strategies that encourage the production of exports. Some of these countries have been the most successful in achieving economic development over the past several decades.

4. Other developing countries have pursued import-substitution policies to encourage development. These policies involve high tariffs or quotas on many items in order to protect local industry. In practice, these policies have not been very successful.

5. When a country is at full employment, growth occurs because of an expansion in factors of production or because of technological innovations.

6. The way in which a country grows affects its pattern of international trade. A country can experience *neutral growth,* in which exports and imports grow at the same rate as GDP; *protrade biased growth,* in which trade grows faster than GDP; or *antitrade biased growth,* in which international trade may even fall.

7. A country can also grow because it acquires factors from other countries. For instance, the growth of the United States in the last century was due in large part to the considerable immigration of foreign workers to the United States as well as to an inflow of foreign capital.

8. Factor inflows from foreign countries tend, as a whole, to raise welfare in the host country and to lower welfare in the source country.

EXERCISES

1. Compare and contrast the types of trade policy actions taken by governments that pursue import-substitution policies versus those that pursue outward-looking strategies.

2. Many Latin American countries have followed import-substitution policies. Many of these same countries have also experienced long periods of high inflation. Explain some of the possible linkages between import-substitution policies and high inflation.

3. According to Table 10.1, many developing countries have begun to replace quotas with tariffs as they adopt more outward-looking strategies. Discuss some possible motives for these changes.

4. Describe how import-substitution policies can encourage the escalation of tariffs by stages of processing.

5. Explain carefully how international trade can affect the rate of growth of an economy.

6. Suppose that in country A the income elasticity of demand for good S is less than one and that the income elasticity of demand for good T is greater than one. Suppose also that A exports good S and imports good T, that S is relatively capital intensive in its production, and that A is relatively capital abundant. What would happen to A's trade pattern if, alternatively,
   a. A were to experience equiproportionate growth in K and L?
   b. A were to experience a relative increase in K versus L?
   c. A were to experience a relative increase in L versus K?

7. Compare the costs of an MNC operating in a foreign country with the costs of domestic firms operating in that country. Explain how an MNC can compete under these circumstances.

8. Suppose that *A* is a small open economy that takes world prices as given. What would be the effect on wages and rents in *A* if it were to experience an inflow of foreign capital? Use a diagram to explain your answer. Which groups would favor this capital inflow? Which would oppose? Explain.

9. What is immizerizing growth? Do you think it is likely to occur in the real world? Explain.

REFERENCES

Bhagwati, Jagdish. "Global Interdependence and International Migration." In *Capital, Technology, and Labor in the New Global Economy,* edited by James Cassing and Steven Husted. Washington, D.C.: American Enterprise Institute, 1988.

Todaro, Michael P. *Economic Development,* 7th ed. Reading, Mass.: Addison-Wesley Publishing Co., 2000.

 ## INTERNET APPLICATIONS

Please visit our Web site at www.awl.com/husted_melvin for more exercises and readings.

CHAPTER 11

An Introduction to International Finance

TOPICS TO BE COVERED

The Balance of Payments
Exchange Rates
Prices and Exchange Rates
Interest Rates and Exchange Rates
Additional Major Topics

KEY WORDS

Trade surplus
Trade deficit
Exchange rate

The first ten chapters of the text deal with international trade in goods and services. Now we turn to trade in financial assets. Such trade may be related to the financing of goods and services trade, but it may also be related to investors altering their portfolios, multinational firms transferring assets from one subsidiary to another, governments buying and selling different currencies to change exchange rates, or any of a myriad of daily events taking place.

This chapter will provide an overview of the subject matter to be covered in the remainder of the text. This body of knowledge is sometimes called "international monetary economics" as well as "international finance." In either case, we are addressing the financial or monetary issues related to international transactions. Let's take a brief look at some of the issues involved.

THE BALANCE OF PAYMENTS

Our study of international finance begins with the balance of payments. Here we learn how nations record transactions with the rest of the world. Terms like "trade surplus" and "deficit" have become newsworthy as public interest grows in knowing whether we sell more to the rest of the world than we buy. As we shall learn, a country with a **trade surplus** exports more goods than it imports, while a country with a **trade deficit** imports more than it exports.Figure 11.1 illustrates how the trade balance differs across countries over time. The United States has consistently run balance of trade deficits, with the last surplus year coming in 1975. Germany and Japan have consistently run balance of trade surpluses, as has Canada. Mexico, on the other hand, has experienced periods of trade surpluses in the 1980s followed by trade deficits in the early 1990s. The coming chapters devote much time to the causes and consequences of balance of payments fluctuations.

Trade surplus
Merchandise exports exceed imports

Trade deficit
Merchandise imports exceed exports

EXCHANGE RATES

Mexicans use pesos, Japanese use yen, Austrians use euros, and this use of different monies by different countries results in the need to exchange one money for another to facilitate trade between countries. Monies are traded in the foreign exchange market and the price of one money in terms of another is called the **exchange rate.**

Table 11.1 shows that foreign exchange trading volume tends to be concentrated in just a few places. The United Kingdom, specifically London, is the world leader due to both the historical leadership of British institutions in international finance and a favorable location straddling both European and North American business hours. The data in Table 11.1 come from a survey taken by the Bank for International Settlements every three years. In April 1998, U.K. banks reported a daily average foreign exchange trading volume of $637.3 billion. Other major foreign exchange trading centers are located in New York and Tokyo. After these three locations, the volume of activity drops off significantly, although a few additional Asian and European countries handle sizeable levels of activity.

Exchange rate
The price of one money in terms of another

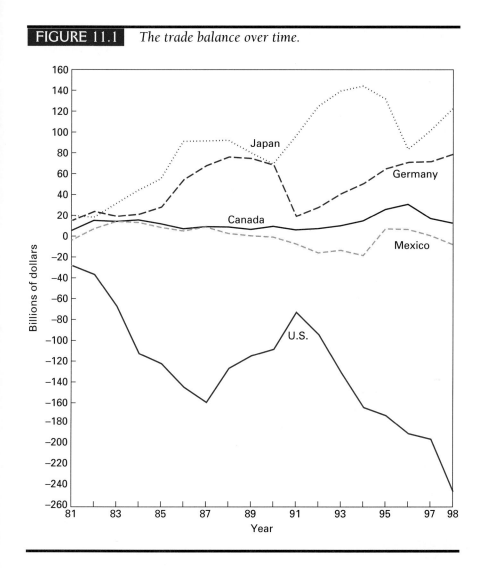

FIGURE 11.1 *The trade balance over time.*

Table 11.1 shows that the average daily volume of currencies traded internationally in all locations equals $1,981.6 billion. This volume of almost 2 trillion dollars per day makes the foreign exchange market the world's largest financial market. The table also shows how rapid the growth of this market has been. In April 1989, total volume in all locations averaged $717.9 billion per day. By 1995, volume had doubled.

While the United Kingdom has the largest volume of foreign exchange trading, this does not mean that the British pound is the most commonly traded currency. Table 11.2 lists the percentages of trading volume involving a currency on one side of a transaction. To understand this table, consider that if you trade U.S. dollars for German marks, then both the mark and the dollar are involved in that transaction.

TABLE 11.1	Foreign Exchange Market Trading Volume							
	April 1989		April 1992		April 1995		April 1998	
Country	Amount	Percentage share	Amount	Percentage share	Amount	Percentage share	Amount	Percentage share
United Kingdom	184.0	26	290.5	27	463.8	30	637.3	32
United States	115.2	16	166.9	16	244.4	16	350.9	18
Japan	110.8	15	120.2	11	161.3	10	148.6	8
Singapore	55.0	8	73.6	7	105.4	7	139.0	7
Germany	—	—	55.0	5	76.2	5	94.3	5
Hong Kong	48.8	7	60.3	6	90.2	6	78.6	4
Switzerland	56.0	8	65.5	6	86.5	6	81.7	4
France	23.2	3	33.3	3	58.0	4	71.9	4
Australia	28.9	4	29.0	3	39.5	3	46.6	2
Canada	15.0	2	21.9	2	29.8	2	36.8	2
Netherlands	12.9	2	19.6	2	25.5	2	41.0	2
Denmark	12.8	2	26.6	2	30.5	2	27.3	1
Belgium	10.4	1	15.7	1	28.1	2	26.5	1
Italy	10.3	1	15.5	1	23.2	1	28.2	1
Sweden	13.0	2	21.3	2	19.9	1	15.4	1
Luxembourg	—	—	13.2	1	19.1	1	22.2	1
Spain	4.4	1	12.3	1	18.3	1	19.3	1
Austria	—	—	4.4	0	13.3	1	10.5	1
Ireland	5.2	1	5.9	1	4.9	0	10.1	1
Norway	4.3	1	5.2	0	7.6	0	8.8	0
New Zealand	—	—	4.2	0	7.1	0	6.9	0
Finland	3.4	0	6.8	1	5.3	0	4.2	0
South Africa	—	—	3.4	0	5.0	0	8.8	0
Greece	0.4	0	1.1	0	3.3	0	7.2	0
Bahrain	3.0	0	3.5	0	3.1	0	2.4	0
Portugal	0.9	0	1.3	0	2.4	0	4.4	0
Total volume	717.9	100	1,076.2	100	1,571.8	100	1,981.6	100

SOURCE: Bank for International Settlements, *Central Bank Survey of Foreign Exchange and Derivatives Market Activity*, Basle: May 1999.

TABLE 11.2	Use of Currencies on One Side of the Transaction as a Percentage of Total Foreign Exchange Market Volume

Currency	Percentage share
U.S. dollar	87
German mark	30
Japanese yen	21
British pound	11
Swiss franc	7
French franc	5
Canadian dollar	4
Australian dollar	3
ECU and other	
EMS currencies	17
Other currencies	15

This is why the percentages in Table 11.2 sum to 200 percent. Each transaction involves two currencies, so both would be counted in Table 11.2 for each transaction. The table clearly shows the popularity of the U.S. dollar, as the dollar is traded on one side of transactions in 87 percent of the total amount traded. After the dollar, the next highest trading volume involves the German mark and the Japanese yen. Trading marks for dollars is the most popular trade in the foreign exchange market.

Table 11.2 lists "ECU" among the currencies. This stands for European Currency Unit, which is an artificial currency that reflects the average value of some Western European currencies. Similarly, "EMS" in Table 11.2 stands for European Monetary System. This is an organization of Western European countries that will be discussed in detail in Chapter 19. Now, the EMS member countries have one money (called the euro), which has replaced their individual national monies resulting in a system much like the individual states of the United States sharing the use of the dollar. In 1998 at the time of the survey, ECUs and national monies like marks were still traded. It is reasonable to expect that the trading in euros should reflect the value of trading formerly done in the currencies of EMS member countries.

Several chapters address the topics of why exchange rates change and the effects of such change. We shall learn that there are several competing views of the important determinants of exchange rates. Regardless of what one believes to be a key factor in changing exchange rates, it is clear that exchange rate changes are largely unexpected, so there is an important element of risk in multinational transactions that domestic transactions lack.

PRICES AND EXCHANGE RATES

If a hamburger sells for 1 dollar in Los Angeles and 100 yen in Tokyo, what exchange rate between the U.S. dollar and the Japanese yen would yield the same hamburger price when dollars are converted into yen or yen are converted into dollars? If the exchange rate is 100 yen per dollar, then 1 dollar is worth 100 yen and the hamburger costs the same in Tokyo and Los Angeles. In this case, we say that "purchasing power parity" holds for the yen and dollar because the purchasing power of the two currencies is the same. Chapter 14 will analyze the relationship between prices and exchange rates. We shall see that there are good reasons why purchasing power parity should not hold at any point in time, so that the Tokyo hamburger need not sell for the same value as the Los Angeles hamburger.

Table 11.3 reports how well purchasing power parity held for McDonald's Big Mac hamburger prices from 1987 to 1995.* The column labeled Big Mac Inflation Differential gives the percentage change in the price of a Big Mac in the country listed in the left column minus the percentage change in the price of a Big Mac in the United States. The column labeled Exchange Rate Change gives the percentage change in the value of a U.S. dollar in terms of the country's currency. For instance,

---

*This information comes from Michael R. Pakko and Patricia S. Pollard, "For Here or To Go? Purchasing Power Parity and the Big Mac," *Federal Reserve Bank of St. Louis Review* (1996).

TABLE 11.3	*Big Mac Purchasing Power Parity*	
Country	Big Mac Inflation Differential*	Exchange Rate Change**
Australia	26%	−1%
Belgium	−18%	−39%
Britain	9%	−8%
Canada	33%	11%
Denmark	−15%	−28%
France	−25%	−33%
Germany	−25%	−38%
Italy	−6%	24%
Japan	8%	−39%
Netherlands	−15%	−39%

*Percentage change in price of Big Mac in listed country − percentage change in U.S. price of Big Mac.

**Percentage change in the listed country's currency price of a U.S. dollar.

SOURCE: Michael R. Pakko and Patricia S. Pollard, "For Here or To Go? Purchasing Power Parity and the Big Mac," *Federal Reserve Bank of St. Louis Review* (Jan/Feb 1996).

if the price of a Big Mac was $1 in the United States and ¥100 in Japan and the yen/dollar exchange rate was 100, then Big Mac purchasing power parity holds, because $1 is equal in value to ¥100. If the price of a Big Mac increased to ¥110 in Japan but remained constant at $1 in the United States, then there is a 10 percent Big Mac inflation in Japan but no Big Mac inflation in the United States. So the Big Mac inflation differential between the two countries equals 10 percent. If the exchange rate increased 10 percent also, from ¥100 per dollar to ¥110 per dollar, then purchasing power parity would still hold. Purchasing power parity holds when the inflation differential equals the percentage change in the exchange rate. Looking at Table 11.3, we see that Big Mac purchasing power parity holds in no case. For instance, the price of a Big Mac increased 8 percentage points more in Japan than the United States, yet the yen price of a U.S. dollar fell by 39 percent over the same period. We shall see that there are good reasons why such a divergence of prices and exchange rates from purchasing power parity is not limited to Big Macs.

INTEREST RATES AND EXCHANGE RATES

Interest rates can differ greatly across countries at a point in time and also differ for a single country over time. Figure 11.2 plots interest rates in the 1990s for four countries. Notice how even countries with extensive economic ties like Canada and the United States can have independent movements in interest rates. While there is increasingly an important global factor that affects interest rates in all countries, a nation's interest rates may still largely reflect a nation's economic conditions. In Chapter 15 we will analyze the determinants of interest rates and learn how interest rates are linked globally. This analysis will allow us to sort out why interest rates change and how changes in one country's rates can affect other countries. The following example illustrates an important linkage between national interest rates that will be studied in detail later.

If a depositor can earn an interest rate of 25 percent on a bank deposit in Mexico and only 5 percent on a bank deposit in the United States, why would anyone deposit money in U.S. banks? The answer has to do with expected exchange rate changes. Since the Mexican deposit is denominated in Mexican pesos and the U.S. deposit is in U.S. dollars, changes in the peso/dollar exchange rate will change the actual return to depositors. For instance, suppose you are a U.S. resident and deposit $100

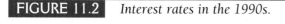

FIGURE 11.2 *Interest rates in the 1990s.*

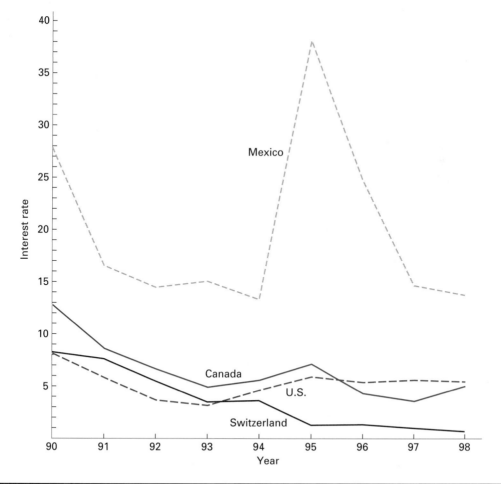

SOURCE: Data are bank deposit rates from the International Monetary Fund, *International Financial Statistics*, February, 1997.

in a Mexican bank when the exchange rate is 10 pesos per dollar. Your $100 is worth 1,000 pesos at the time of the deposit. After one year, at a 25 percent rate of interest, your 1,000 pesos has grown in value to 1,250 pesos. However, since you are a resident of the United States, you will exchange the 1,250 pesos for dollars. Now we see how a change in the exchange rate can offset the interest differential existing between Mexican and U.S. bank deposits. If the exchange rate has changed from 10 pesos per dollar to 12.5 pesos per dollar, the 1,250 pesos will now be worth 1,250/12.5 = 100 dollars. Since you deposited $100 initially, your actual rate of interest in dollar terms turns out to zero, even though the Mexican bank deposit paid 25 percent interest in pesos.

Interest differentials between countries reflect expected exchange rate changes. In the previous example, Mexican bank deposits offer higher interest rates than dollar deposits. This indicates that people expect the peso to fall in value relative to the dollar. In Figure 11.2, we see that in 1995, the Mexican interest rate was about 40 percent while the U.S. rate was about 6 percent. This interest differential of 34 percent could be wiped out if the peso depreciated against the dollar by 34 percent over the same period. In that case, the return to a U.S. investor from a Mexican deposit would be equivalent to the return on a U.S. deposit. At the beginning of the year, one would not know what the actual change in the exchange rate would be, but it turns out that over this year the peso actually fell in value by more than 40 percent against the dollar. So a U.S. investor depositing dollars in a Mexican bank would have had the higher Mexican interest rate wiped out by the falling value of the peso; the Mexican deposit would have actually given a U.S. investor a lower return on his or her deposit than if the money had been deposited in a U.S. bank. Sometimes exchange rates change more than we expect, and sometimes they change less. One thing that seems clear is that exchange rates often move in surprising ways.

Interest differentials may reflect more than just expected exchange rate changes. They could also reflect a premium for risk. Just as high-risk borrowers pay a higher interest rate for a car loan than do low-risk borrowers, countries where investors have greater uncertainty regarding the future value of their investment will be countries that must offer higher interest rates to compensate investors for bearing risk.

ADDITIONAL MAJOR TOPICS

In addition to the areas mentioned so far, the following chapters will address all the key issues related to the monetary or financial side of international economics. A brief list of some of the topics to be covered include:

> *Foreign exchange risk* Since exchange rates change in surprising ways, future monetary amounts to be paid or received that are denominated in foreign currency involve risk. For instance, suppose Tokyo Textbook Importers has agreed to buy $10,000 worth of textbooks from Addison Wesley Co. in Boston. At the time the contract is signed, 1 dollar is worth 100 yen so $10,000 would cost Tokyo Textbook Importers 1 million yen. But if payment is not due for 90 days and over the 90-day period the dollar rises in value from 100 yen to 105 yen, then the textbooks

would cost 1,050,000 yen. The cost of the textbooks rose by 50,000 yen because of the exchange rate change.

There are several ways that business firms and individuals can protect themselves from the risk of an unexpected exchange rate change. Tokyo Textbook Importers could lock in a certain yen price of the books at the time the sales contract is signed so that there is no risk of the price of the textbook purchase changing due to exchange rate change. We will learn about forward, future, and options markets for currency that may be used to eliminate risk.

International investment The returns and risks of investing in foreign countries' financial assets are an important aspect of international finance. We shall see that there is a gain from international diversification in that the risk of an investment portfolio may be reduced without reducing the expected return from holding the portfolio. In addition to purchasing foreign assets such as stocks and bonds, international investment also includes the establishment of foreign subsidiaries of domestic firms and the outright purchase of foreign firms. There are many possible reasons why a firm would establish a foreign operating subsidiary. Japanese auto manufacturers located factories in the United States to avoid the exchange-rate induced fluctuations in the dollar price of cars imported from Japan. During periods when the yen appreciated in value against the dollar, the dollar price of imported cars rose. When the cars are built in the United States, the exchange rate is no longer a major source of price volatility. Other motivations for establishing foreign subsidiaries are that multinational firms may seek to better serve foreign markets, the multinational firm may want to prevent domestic firms from entering into a business that the multinational dominates, or they may simply be seeking to avoid tariffs or quotas on international trade.

International monetary systems The evolution of the international monetary system has progressed from a gold standard 100 years ago, to a fixed exchange rate system over fifty years ago, to the modern era of exchange rate flexibility. We trace the history of major developments in this evolution and then analyze the key issues in choosing floating or fixed exchange rates. This issue is of importance today because not all countries have floating exchange rates. Many countries choose to limit the flexibility of their exchange rate for good economic reasons, which will be covered in later chapters. An important example of an exchange rate arrangement with limited flexibility is the European Monetary System's drive to a single currency. We shall examine the important factors in determining whether or not a region can have a successful arrangement of fixed exchange rates among a group of countries.

International banking Since the early 1950s, banking across national borders has grown rapidly. Whether we call it "offshore banking," the "Eurocurrency market," or simply international banking, we are talking about a business where huge amounts of money are deposited and loaned. We shall see that there is nothing especially "Euro" about the Eurocurrency market other than its historical origins. Our discussion includes a look at the period of the international financial crises of the 1990s along with an analysis of the assessment of risk in lending to foreign countries. International bankers must conduct an assessment of creditworthiness when lending across international borders just as they do when lending domestically. The added dimension of international lending involves political and social factors as well as economic.

International macroeconomics Often called "open-economy macroeconomics," the determination of the equilibrium level of national income, interest rates, and exchange rates in a global setting takes one beyond the restrictive models used in principles of economics courses, where it is commonly assumed that only one country exists. Now we can see how policy choices such as fixed or floating exchange rates can impact an economy and can analyze the roles of fiscal and monetary policy in a world of interdependent economies. This interdependency creates incentives for coordination of economic policy across countries to avoid having policy decisions of some countries adversely affect others.

The goal of this half of the text is to provide a solid foundation in the financial side of international economics. The most up-to-date issues are covered in an applied structure that always stresses the real-world implications of theory. This is not an "ivory-tower" subject suitable for the classroom only. Public policy and private business deal daily with the topics covered in the following chapters, and some of the major policy controversies of our times lie on the financial side of international economics.

SUMMARY

1. The balance of payments is a record of a nation's transactions with the rest of the world.

2. Currencies are traded in the foreign exchange market, and the price of one money in terms of another is called the exchange rate.

3. Purchasing power parity holds between two currencies when the inflation differential based on goods prices matches the percentage change in the exchange rate.

4. Interest differentials between two countries may be offset by exchange rate changes so that it is not necessarily true that the higher interest rate will offer the best return.

EXERCISES

1. When does a country have a trade surplus? When does it have a trade deficit?

2. Which country has the largest volume of foreign exchange traded?

3. What are the most commonly traded currencies?

4. Create an example of automobile prices in London and New York where purchasing power parity holds. Assume initially that the exchange rate is 2 U.S. dollars per British pound and that a particular kind of automobile sells for

$20,000 in New York and £10,000 in London. Create new prices and a new exchange rate that will yield purchasing power parity for the dollar and pound.

5. A U.S. resident can earn 6 percent interest on a one-year bank deposit of $100,000 at home. Alternatively, she can convert the $100,000 into euros and earn 4 percent on a one-year bank deposit in Germany. If the exchange rate is initially 1.5 euros per dollar and then changes to 1.45 euros per dollar in one year, which deposit would have given the U.S. resident a higher return?

INTERNET APPLICATIONS

Please visit our Web site at www.awl.com/husted_melvin for more exercises and readings.

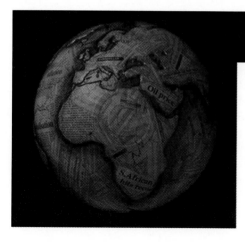

CHAPTER 12

The Balance

of Payments

TOPICS TO BE COVERED

Current Account
Financing the Current Account
Additional Summary Measures
Transactions Classification
Balance-of-Payments Equilibrium and
    Adjustment

KEY WORDS

Balance-of-payments deficit
Balance-of-payments surplus
Balance of trade
Basic balance
Liquidity balance

Official settlements balance
Balance-of-payments equilibrium
Flexible exchange rates
Fixed exchange rates

We have all heard of the balance of payments. Unfortunately, common usage does not allow us to discuss the balance of payments because there are several ways to measure the balance, and the press often blurs the distinction among these various measures. In general, the balance of payments records a country's trade in goods, services, and financial assets with the rest of the world. Such trade is divided into useful categories that provide summaries of a nation's trade. A distinction is made between private (individuals and business firms) and official (government) transactions. Balance-of-payments data are reported quarterly for most developed countries. Table 12.1 presents the balance of payments as reported by the U.S. Department of Commerce. This rather imposing document is of great use to economists, but it provides more detail than we need be concerned with here. To identify the popular summary measures of the balance of payments, we are interested only in broad definitions. Table 12.2 presents a simplified balance of payments.

The balance of payments is an accounting statement based on double-entry bookkeeping. Every transaction is entered on both sides of the balance sheet, as a credit and a debit. Credit entries are those entries that will bring foreign exchange into the country, whereas debit entries record items that would mean a loss of foreign exchange. In Table 12.1 debit balances are recorded as a negative value. For instance, suppose we record the sale of a machine from a U.S. manufacturer to a French importer, and the manufacturer allows the buyer 90 days' credit to pay. The machinery export is recorded as a credit in the merchandise account, whereas the credit extended to the buyer is a debit to short-term capital. The capital we speak of is financial capital. Thus, credit extended belongs in the same broad account with stocks, bonds, and other financial instruments of a short-term nature. If, for any particular account, the value of the credit entries exceeds the debits, we say a **surplus** exists. On the other hand, where the debits exceed the credits, a **deficit** exists. Note that a surplus or a deficit can apply only to a particular area of the balance of payments, since the sum of the credits and debits on all accounts will always be equal—the balance of payments will always balance. This will become apparent in the following discussion.

Balance-of-payments deficit (surplus)
Balance-of-payments debit items exceed (are less than) the credit items in value.

Let us consider some of the popular summary measures of the balance of payments.

CURRENT ACCOUNT

The current account is defined as including the value of trade in merchandise, services, income, and unilateral transfers. Merchandise is the obvious trade in tangible commodities. Services refers to trade in the services of factors of production: land, labor, and capital. Included in this category are travel and tourism, royalties, transportation costs, and insurance premiums. The payment for the services of physical capital, or the return on investments, is listed separately, apart from other services. Interest and dividends paid internationally are large and growing rapidly as the world financial markets become more integrated.

The unilateral transfers component of the balance of payments includes transfers such as U.S. foreign aid, gifts, and retirement pensions, along with interest payments

TABLE 12.1 *U.S. International Transactions (millions $)*

Line	(Credits +; debits −)	1960	1970	1980	1990	1998
1	Exports of goods, services, and income	30,556	68,387	343,241	652,936	1,192,231
2	Merchandise, adjusted, excluding military	19,650	42,469	224,269	389,550	670,246
3	Services	6,290	14,171	47,584	133,295	263,661
4	Transfers under U.S. military agency sales contracts	2,030	4,214	9,029	9,899	17,155
5	Travel	919	2,331	10,588	40,579	71,250
6	Passenger fares	175	544	2,591	12,251	19,996
7	Other transportation	1,607	3,125	11,618	22,407	25,518
8	Royalties and license fees	837	2,331	7,085	15,291	36,808
9	Other private services	570	1,294	6,276	32,173	92,116
10	U.S. Government miscellaneous services	153	332	398	695	818
11	Income receipts	—	—	—	—	258,324
11a	Compensation of employees	—	—	—	—	1,857
11b	Income receipts on U.S. assets abroad	4,616	11,748	71,388	130,091	256,467
12	Direct investment receipts	3,621	8,169	37,146	54,444	102,846
13	Other private receipts	646	2,671	31,680	65,702	150,001
14	U.S. Government receipts	349	907	2,562	9,945	3,620
15	Imports of goods, services, and income	−23,670	−59,901	−333,774	−722,730	−1,368,718
16	Merchandise, adjusted, excluding military	−14,758	−39,866	−249,750	−497,665	−917,178
17	Services	−7,674	−14,520	−41,491	−106,919	−181,011
18	Direct defense expenditures	−3,087	−4,855	−10,851	−17,119	−12,841
19	Travel	−1,750	−3,980	−10,397	−38,671	−56,105
20	Passenger fares	−513	−1,215	−3,607	−8,963	−19,797
21	Other transportation	−1,402	−2,843	−11,790	−23,463	−30,457
22	Royalties and license fees	−74	−224	−724	−2,644	−11,292
23	Other private services	−593	−827	−2,909	−13,819	−47,670
24	U.S. Government miscellaneous services	−254	−576	−1,214	−2,240	−2,849
25	Income payments	—	—	—	—	−270,529
25a	Compensation of employees	—	—	—	—	−7,106
25b	Income payments on foreign assets in the United States	−1,238	−5,515	−42,532	−118,146	−263,423
26	Direct investment payments	−394	−875	−8,635	−1,782	−43,441
27	Other private payments	−511	−3,617	−21,214	−78,494	−128,863
28	U.S. Government payments	−332	−1,024	−12,684	−37,870	−91,119
29	Unilateral transfers, net	−4,062	−6,156	−8,349	−22,329	−44,075
30	U.S. Government grants	−3,367	−4,449	−5,486	−17,486	−13,057
31	U.S. Government pensions and other transfers	−273	−611	−1,818	−2,947	−4,350
32	Private remittances and other transfers	−423	−1,096	−1,044	−1,896	−26,668
33	U.S. assets abroad, net (increases/capital outflow(−))	−4,099	−9,337	−86,118	−57,706	−292,818
34	U.S. official reserve assets, net	2,145	2,481	−8,155	−2,158	−6,784
35	Gold	1,703	787	—	—	−
36	Special drawing rights	—	−851	−16	−192	−149
37	Reserve position in the International Monetary Fund	442	389	−1,667	731	−5,118
38	Foreign currencies	—	2,156	−6,472	−2,697	−1,517
39	U.S. Government assets, other than official reserve assets, net	−1,100	−1,589	−5,162	2,976	−429
40	U.S. credits and other long-term assets	−1,214	−3,293	−9,860	−7,319	−4,676
41	Repayments on U.S. credits and other long-term assets, net	642	1,721	4,456	10,327	4,102
42	U.S. foreign currency holdings and U.S. short-term assets, net	−528	−16	242	−32	145
43	U.S. private assets, net	−5,144	−10,229	−72,802	−58,524	−285,605
44	Direct investment	−2,940	−7,590	−19,222	−33,437	−132,829
45	Foreign securities	−663	−1,076	−3,568	−28,476	−102,817

(Continued)

TABLE 12.1	U.S. International Transactions (millions $) (Continued)					
Line	(Credits +; debits −)	1960	1970	1980	1990	1998
46	U.S. claims on unaffiliated foreigners reported by U.S. nonbanking concerns	−394	−596	−3,174	−1,944	−25,041
47	U.S. claims reported by U.S. banks, not included elsewhere	−1,148	−967	−46,838	5,333	−24,918
48	Foreign assets in the United States, net (increase/capital inflow (+))	2,294	6,359	58,112	86,303	502,637
49	Foreign official assets in the United States, net	1,473	6,908	15,497	32,425	−21,684
50	U.S. Government securities	655	9,439	11,895	29,310	−3,625
51	U.S. Treasury securities	655	9,411	9,708	28,643	−9,957
52	Other	—	28	2,187	667	6,332
53	Other U.S. Government liabilities	215	−456	615	1,703	−3,113
54	U.S. liabilities reported by U.S. banks, not included elsewhere	603	−2,075	−159	2,998	−11,469
55	Other foreign official assets	—	—	3,145	−1,586	−3,477
56	Other foreign assets in the United States, net	821	−550	42,615	53,879	524,321
57	Direct investment	315	1,464	16,918	37,213	193,375
58	U.S. Treasury securities	−364	81	2,645	1,131	46,155
59	U.S. securities other than U.S. Treasury securities	282	2,189	5,457	1,781	218,026
60	U.S. liabilities to unaffiliated foreigners reported by U.S. nonbanking concerns	−90	2,014	6,852	3,779	9,412
61	U.S. liabilities reported by U.S. banks, not included elsewhere	678	−6,298	10,743	9,975	40,731
62	Allocations of special drawing rights	—	867	1,152	—	—
63	Statistical discrepancy (sum of above items with sign reversed)	−1,019	−219	25,736	63,526	10,126
63a	*Of which* seasonal adjustment discrepancy				—	
	Memoranda:					
64	Balance on merchandise trade (lines 2 and 16)	4,892	2,603	−25,481	−108,115	−246,932
65	Balance on services (lines 3 and 17)	−1,385	−349	6,093	26,376	82,650
66	Balance on goods and services (lines 64 and 65)					−164,282
67	Balance on income (lines 11 and 25)	3,379	6,233	28,856	11,945	−12,205
68	Balance on goods, services, and income (lines 1 and 15 or lines 66 and 67)	6,886	8,486	9,467	−69,794	−176,487
69	Unilateral transfers, net (line 29)	−4,062	−6,156	−8,349	−22,329	−44,075
70	Balance on current account (lines 1, 15, and 29 or lines 68 and 69)	2,824	2,331	1,119	−92,123	−220,562

TABLE 12.2	Simplified U.S. Balance of Payments for 1998 (millions $)		
	Credits	Debits	Net
Merchandise	670,246	917,178	− 246,932
Services	263,661	181,011	82,650
Income	258,324	− 270,529	− 12,205
Unilateral transfers			− 44,075
Current Account			**− 220,562**
U.S.–owned assets abroad			− 292,818
Foreign-owned assets in the United States			502,637
Capital Account			**209,819**
Statistical Discrepancy			**10,126**

to foreigners on their holdings of U.S. government debt. The United States generally records a large deficit on these items.

Figure 12.1 illustrates how the various account balances have changed over time. The merchandise and current account deficits of the 1980s were unprecedented. The $167 billion current account deficit of 1987 is the sum of a $160 billion merchandise trade deficit, a $7 billion services surplus, a $7 billion income surplus, and a $23 billion transfers deficit. From 1946 to 1970, the United States ran a merchandise trade surplus. Following a $2 billion deficit in 1971, the merchandise account has been in deficit every year since except 1973 and 1975. Even with this persistent merchandise trade deficit, U.S. earnings from foreign investments (or income) have had sizable surpluses so that the current account realized a surplus in 1973–1976 and 1980–1981.

We can draw a line in the balance of payments to sum the debit and credit items above the line. If we "draw the line" at the current account balance, all the entries below the line amount to financing the merchandise, services, income, and unilateral transfers (gifts), so that the current account indicates whether a country is a net borrower from or lender to the rest of the world. A current account surplus implies that a country is running a net deficit below the line, so that the country is a net lender to the rest of the world.

The current account excludes capital account transactions—purchases and sales of financial assets. Because the items "below the line" of the current account must be equal in value (but opposite in sign) to the current account balance, we can see how the current account balance indicates financial activity (below the line) as well as the value of trade in merchandise, services, income, and unilateral transfers that are recorded above the line. In a period (year or quarter) during which a current account deficit is recorded, the country must borrow from abroad an amount sufficient to finance the deficit.

Since the balance of payments always balances, the massive current account deficits of the mid-1980s are matched by massive capital account surpluses. This means that foreign investment in U.S. securities has been at very high levels. Some analysts have expressed concern over the growing foreign indebtedness of the United States. The next section reviews this issue.

Financing the Current Account: The Capital Account

Large current account deficits imply large capital account surpluses. The capital account transactions are recorded below the current account items in the balance of payments. Referring to Table 12.1, lines 33 through 61 record capital account transactions. We see that capital account transactions include both official and private transactions.

Before reviewing the recent history of U.S. international capital flows, we should consider the definitions of the individual capital account items:

Direct Investment:	Private financial transactions that result in the ownership of 10 percent or more of a business firm.

FIGURE 12.1   *U.S. international transactions, 1946–1998*

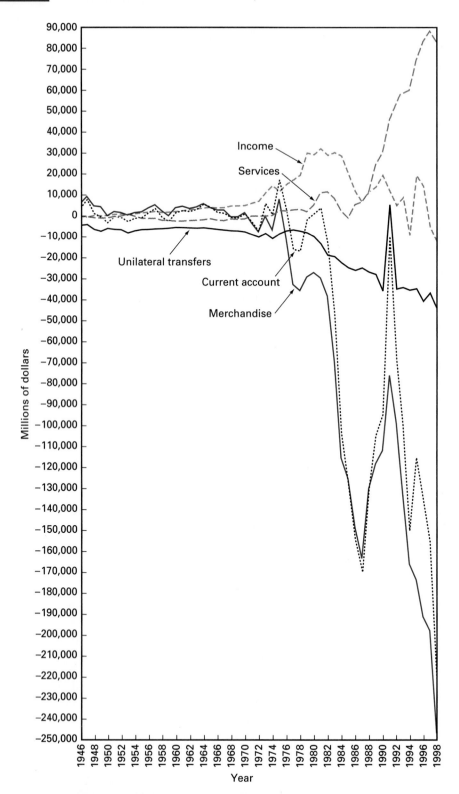

Security Purchases:	Private-sector net purchases of equity (stock) and debt securities.
Bank Claims and Liabilities:	Claims: loans, collections outstanding, acceptances, deposits abroad, claims on affiliated foreign banks, foreign government obligations, and foreign commercial and finance papers; liabilities: deposits, certificates of deposit, liabilities to affiliated foreign banks, and others.
U.S. Government Assets Abroad:	Changes in U.S. official reserve assets (gold, SDRs, foreign currency holdings, and reserve position in the IMF; all assets that can be used to settle debts between countries).
Foreign Official Assets in the United States:	Net purchases of U.S. government securities, obligations of U.S. government corporations and agencies, securities of U.S. state and local governments, and changes in liabilities to foreign official agencies reported by U.S. banks.

Some capital account transactions are a direct result of trade in merchandise and services. For instance, many goods are sold using trade credit. The exporter allows the importer a period of time—typically 30, 60, or 90 days—before payment is due. This sort of financing will generally be reflected in bank claims and liabilities, since such transactions are handled by the exporter's bank. Other capital account items are a result of portfolio management by international investors. Security purchases would fall into this category. Official transactions involve governments and are motivated by a host of economic and political considerations.

In terms of financing current account deficits, the deficits of the 1970s were financed in a different manner from that of the recent deficits. In the 1970s, foreign official capital inflows largely financed the current account deficit. This was a period of large foreign-exchange market intervention by foreign central banks aimed at supporting the dollar. U.S. government securities serve as an interest-bearing reserve asset for foreign governments accumulating dollar assets, so there were sizable official purchases during the late 1970s.

In the 1980s and 1990s, current account deficits were financed by private capital flows. Security purchases in the United States by foreigners increased dramatically. Also, U.S. bank claims on foreigners fell dramatically until the mid-1980s before rising again. This reflects an inward turn by U.S. banks. U.S. bank lending abroad fell between 1982 and 1985 as banks responded to the high returns and low risk available through domestic lending. Rapid economic growth in the United States coupled with large government borrowing requirements resulted in a rising demand for credit at home to which U.S. banks responded. As the U.S. fiscal deficit and interest rates fell, U.S. bank lending to foreigners increased.

One implication of capital account transactions pertains to the net creditor or debtor position of a nation. A net debtor owes more to the rest of the world than it is owed, while a net creditor is owed more than it owes. As Item 12.1 discusses, the United States became a net international debtor in 1985 for the first time since World War I. The high current account deficits of the 1980s were matched by high capital account surpluses. This rapid buildup of foreign direct investment and purchases of U.S. securities led to a very rapid drop from being a net creditor of $147 billion in 1982 to holding a net debtor status by 1985. Once again, we see that the current account is a useful measure, as it summarizes the trend with regard to the net debtor position of a country. For this reason, international bankers focus on the current account trend as one of the crucial variables to consider when evaluating loans to foreign countries.

National Saving, Investment, and the Current Account

In principles of economics classes, students learn the national income accounting identity:

$$Y = C + I + G + X \qquad (12.1)$$

where Y is national income or gross domestic product (GDP), C is consumption spending, I is investment spending, G is government spending, and X is net exports or the current account. We can rearrange Equation 12.1 as:

$$Y - C - G = S = I + X \qquad (12.2)$$

where $Y - C - G$ is domestic income less consumption and government spending at home, which we may call national saving S. Equation 12.2 indicates that national saving is equal to the sum of investment spending plus the current account. This relationship implies that the current account must be equal to the national saving (S) minus investment spending (I):

$$X = S - I \qquad (12.3)$$

If domestic saving exceeds investment, there will be a current account surplus (positive X). If saving is less than investment, there will be a current account deficit (negative X).

Now we can understand how domestic spending and saving behavior is reflected in the balance of payments. A country where spending is greater than income has investment greater than saving, and a current account deficit. The excess of spending over income must be financed by foreign investment, so there will be a capital account surplus to match the current account deficit.

This analysis indicates that balance of payments values will be affected by changes in international spending and saving behavior. This behavior may be on the part of households and business firms or it may be on the part of government. To

ITEM 12.1	The World's Largest Debtor

On September 16, 1985, the U.S. Commerce Department announced that the United States was a debtor nation for the first time since World War I. The magnitude of the current account deficit for 1985 and 1986 made the United States the largest international debtor in the world, with debts exceeding those of developing country debtors such as Brazil and Mexico.

It is interesting to note that the United States reached its all-time high as a net creditor in 1982, with net international investment of $147 billion. The rapid fall from 1982 to 1985 followed more than sixty years as a net creditor. In the 1950s and 1960s, U.S. foreign direct investment led the push for the net creditor improvement. In the 1970s, U.S. bank lending abroad increased the net creditor position.

Prior to the emergence of the United States as the major financial power in the world, Britain was the world's great creditor nation. In the nineteenth century and early twentieth century, England financed much of world trade and permitted access to British markets for debtor nations to earn the foreign exchange needed to service the debt. The rise of protectionist sentiment in the 1920s and 1930s led to barriers to trade that made it difficult for international debtors to repay their debts. The drop in world trade during the 1930s marked the end of Britain's dominance as an international lender. After World War II, the United States emerged as the dominant financial leader. How did the United States turn from a net creditor to a net debtor in the course of three years?

The U.S. story is recorded in the massive current account deficits and corresponding capital account surpluses of the early 1980s. To consume more at home than is produced (this is what you do when you run a current account deficit), the United States must borrow from abroad. In the

U.S. case, the borrowing was at such a high level that the record net creditor position of 1982 was eliminated in just three years.

Behind the accounting record of the balance of payments lies the economic causes of the change. The world debt crisis had caused a reduction in U.S. foreign lending as banks sought to lower their exposure to default risk. Record U.S. federal budget deficits made lending at home more attractive to U.S. banks as the deficits contributed to relatively high returns on U.S. loans. These same high returns, along with the perception of the United States as a "safe haven" for investment, made U.S. securities more attractive to foreign lenders.

There is nothing wrong with being a net debtor as long as the borrowed funds contribute to a more productive economy. Considering the magnitude of federal government borrowing in the 1980s, without the large inflow of foreign funds, U.S. interest rates would have been higher and investment would probably have been lower. If the borrowing has allowed a higher growth rate, then future generations, who share the burden of repaying the debt, will also enjoy a higher standard of living.

In the early 1980s an appreciating dollar and high interest rates signaled the incentive for foreign investment in the United States. The large current account deficits and capital account surpluses have continued since then. If foreign portfolios reach a point where dollar-denominated assets are no longer desired, then the dollar will tend to depreciate, and interest rates will tend to fall. A falling capital account surplus will be matched by a falling current account deficit. Ultimately, conditions could change so that the United States once again becomes a net lender, and the title of "world's largest debtor" would fall to another.

better understand the link between saving behavior and the current account, we can think of two kinds of saving: private and government. Private saving is equal to domestic income less taxes (*T*) and consumption, and government saving is equal to taxes less government spending, so that:

$$S = (Y - T - C) + (T - G) \qquad (12.4)$$

or national saving equals private saving plus government saving. For many years, the United States has had positive private saving and negative government saving (or government dissaving). Note that government saving is the negative of the government budget deficit. A government that spends more than its tax revenue will create government dissaving and contribute to a larger current account deficit. The current account deficit and capital account surplus could be reduced by reducing the government budget deficit so that government dissaving falls.

We now see how balance of payments values are determined by the same things that affect national income, spending, and national saving. So rather than just think in terms of international trade and determinants such as tariffs, quotas, and international trade policies, we must think in broader macroeconomic terms to understand fluctuations in the current account. Reducing the current account deficit requires increasing domestic saving relative to investment and (saying the same thing in different terms) increasing domestic output relative to domestic spending.

ADDITIONAL SUMMARY MEASURES

So far, we have focused on the current account of the balance of payments. In terms of practical importance to economists, government policy makers, and business firms, this emphasis on the current account is warranted. However, there are other summary measures of balance-of-payments phenomena. Within the current account categories, the balance on merchandise trade is often cited in the popular press (because it is reported on a monthly basis by the United States). The **balance of trade** (line 2 plus line 16 in Table 12.1) records a surplus when merchandise exports exceed imports. Domestic business firms and labor unions often use the balance of trade to justify a need to protect the domestic market from foreign competition. When a country is running a large balance-of-trade deficit, local industries that are being hurt by import competition will argue that the trade balance reflects the harm done to the economy. Because of the political sensitivity of the balance of trade, it is a popularly cited measure.

Beyond the items recorded in the current account, there are still broader summary measures of the balance of payments that are purported to reflect important economic relationships.

If we add the balance on long-term capital to the current account, we get the **basic balance**. This measure is supposed to emphasize long-run trends in the balance of payments, since everything below the line represents short-term items that are thought to be related to financing trade.

Balance of trade
The value of merchandise exports minus imports.

Basic balance
The current account plus long-term capital.

The logic just presented is faulty on at least two accounts: (a) Short-term capital includes more than just credit extended for delaying payment on goods and services; it also includes short-term investment portfolio items and (b) long-term capital includes volatile portfolio items that represent long-run trends no better than the investment elements of short-term capital. The limited usefulness of the basic balance explains why the official balance-of-payments table (Table 12.1) omits it.

Adding short-term capital held by the United States plus errors and omissions ("Statistical discrepancy," line 63 in Table 12.1) to the basic balance yields the **liquidity balance.** This is supposed to measure the potential pressure on U.S. reserves (holdings of gold and foreign currencies that can be used to settle international debts) insofar as it indicates the total dollars accruing to foreigners by putting all liquid liabilities (dollars or anything else that is readily convertible into dollars) below the line. The problem here is that many of the supposed nonliquid liabilities, such as securities held, are also readily converted into dollars. As a result, the liquidity balance is not shown in the official balance of payments (Table 12.1).

Liquidity balance
The basic balance plus short-term capital plus errors and omissions.

In any case, just because foreigners accumulate claims against the United States in the form of dollar holdings does not mean that they will want to sell the dollars for gold or other currencies and thus deplete U.S. reserves. There might possibly be an international demand for the dollars so that the outstanding balances are willingly held.

The **official settlements balance** (reported on lines 34 and 49 less line 53 in Table 12.1) yields a value of the balance of payments as if only short-term capital held by foreign monetary agencies and official reserve asset transactions fall below the line.

Official settlements balance
The value of the change in short-term capital held by foreign monetary agencies and official reserve asset transactions.

The official settlements balance serves as a measure of potential foreign exchange pressure on the dollar, in that official institutions will not hold increasing stocks of dollars but would rather sell them, thereby driving down the foreign-exchange value of the dollar. Yet this approach is subject to the same criticism applied to the liquidity balance: There may be a demand for the dollar so that official stocks of dollars build without any foreign-exchange pressure. Furthermore, in the modern day it is not always clear whether official holdings are what they seem to be, because (as we shall see in a later chapter) the Eurodollar market allows central banks to turn official claims against the United States into private claims.

Still, monetary economists have found the official settlements balance to be useful, because changes in international reserves impinge on the money stock due to the fact that reserves are one element on which the nation's money supply depends. (We shall learn subsequently that "high-powered money" has a domestic credit component and an international reserves component.)

For most countries, foreign monetary-agency holdings of their liabilities are trivial, so that the official settlements balance essentially measures international reserve changes. In the case of the United States, the official settlements balance primarily records changes in short-term U.S. liabilities held by foreign monetary agencies. This demand for dollar-denominated short-term debt by foreign central banks is what allows the United States to finance current account deficits largely with dollars. Other countries must finance such deficits by selling foreign currency. As a result, they face a greater constraint on their ability to run deficits as they eventually deplete their stocks of foreign currency.

TRANSACTIONS CLASSIFICATION

So far, we have defined the important summary measures of the balance of payments and developed an understanding of the various categories included in a nation's international transactions. The actual classification of transactions is often confusing to those first considering such issues. To aid in understanding the problems, we will analyze five transactions and their placement in a simplified balance of payments.

First, we must remember that the balance of payments is a balance sheet, so at the bottom line, total credits equal total debits. This means that we use double-entry bookkeeping—every item involves two entries, a credit and a debit, to the balance sheet. The credits record items leading to inflows of payments. Such items are associated with a greater demand for domestic currency or a greater supply of foreign currency to the foreign-exchange market. The debits record items that lead to payments outflows. These are associated with a greater supply of domestic currency or a greater demand for foreign currency in the foreign-exchange market. Now consider the following five hypothetical transactions and their corresponding entry in Table 12.3 for the U.S. balance of payments.

1. A 10-year loan of $1 million is made to Romania. The loan is funded by creating a $1 million deposit for Romania in a U.S. bank.

   (*Note:* The loan represents a long-term capital outflow [long-term since it is over one year] and is recorded as a debit to long-term capital. The new deposit is recorded as a credit to short-term capital, since an increase in foreign-owned bank deposits in U.S. banks is treated as a short-term capital inflow.)

TABLE 12.3	*Balance of Payments*		
	Credit (+)	Debit (−)	Net Balance
Merchandise	$1,000,000 (2) 100,000 (5)		
Services		$10,000 (4)	
Income	10,000 (3)		
Unilateral transfers		100,000 (5)	
Current account			$ + 1,000,000
Short-term capital	10,000 (4) 1,000,000 (1)	10,000 (3) 1,000,000 (2)	
Long-term capital		1,000,000 (1)	
TOTALS	$2,120,000	$2,120,000	

NOTE: The numbers in parentheses refer to the five hypothetical transactions discussed in the chapter.

2. A U.S. firm sells $1 million worth of wheat to Romania. The wheat is paid for with the bank account created in transaction 1.

   (*Note:* The wheat export represents a merchandise export of $1 million, and thus we credit merchandise $1 million. Payment using the deposit creates a $1 million debit to short-term capital since a decrease in foreign-owned deposits in U.S. banks is treated as a short-term capital outflow.)

3. A U.S. resident receives $10,000 in interest from German bonds she owned. The $10,000 is deposited in a German bank.

   (*Note:* Earnings on international investments represent a credit on the income account. The increase in U.S.–owned foreign bank deposits is considered a short-term capital outflow and is recorded by debiting short-term capital $10,000.)

4. A U.S. tourist travels to Europe and spends the $10,000 German deposit.

   (*Note:* Tourist spending is recorded in the service account. U.S. tourist spending abroad is recorded as a $10,000 debit to the service account. The decrease in U.S.–owned foreign deposits is considered a short-term capital inflow and is recorded by a $10,000 credit to short-term capital.)

5. The United States gives $100,000 worth of grain to Nicaragua.

   (*Note:* The grain export is recorded as a $100,000 credit to the merchandise account. Since the grain was a gift, the balancing entry is unilateral transfers; in this case, there is a debit of $100,000 to unilateral transfers.)

Note that the current account balance is found as the sum of the merchandise, services, income, and unilateral transfers accounts. Summing the credits and debits, we find that the credits sum to $1,110,000, whereas the debits sum to $110,000, so that there is a positive, or credit, balance of $1 million.

The short-term capital entries are typically the most confusing, particularly those relating to changes in bank deposits. For instance, the third transaction just discussed recorded the deposit of $10,000 in a German bank as a debit to the short-term capital account of the United States. The fourth transaction recorded the U.S. tourist spending the $10,000 German bank deposit as a credit to the short-term capital account of the United States. This may seem confusing, because early in the chapter it was suggested that credit items are items that bring foreign exchange into a country whereas debit items involve foreign exchange leaving the country, yet neither of these transactions affected bank deposits in the United States, just foreign deposits. The key is to think of the deposit of $10,000 in a German bank in transaction 3 as if the money had come from a U.S. bank account. Increases in U.S.–owned deposits in foreign banks are debits, whether or not the money was ever in the United States. What matters is not whether the money is physically ever in the United States, but the country of residence of the owner. Similarly, decreases in U.S.–owned foreign deposits are recorded as a credit to short-term capital, whether or not the money is actually brought from abroad to the United States.

The item "Statistical discrepancy" (line 63) recorded in the actual balance of payments of Table 12.1 is not the result of not knowing where to classify some transactions. The international transactions that are recorded are simply difficult to measure accurately. Taking the numbers from customs records and surveys of business firms will not capture all of the trade that actually occurs. Some of this may be due to illegal or underground activity, but in the modern dynamic economy, we would expect sizable measurement errors even with no illegal activity. It is simply impossible to observe every transaction, so we must rely on a statistically valid sampling of international transactions.

BALANCE-OF-PAYMENTS EQUILIBRIUM AND ADJUSTMENT

So far, we have focused on the accounting procedures and definitions that apply to the balance of payments. Now we want to consider the economic implications of the balance of payments. For instance, since merchandise exports earn foreign exchange whereas imports involve outflows of foreign exchange, we often hear arguments for policy aimed at maximizing the trade, or current account, surplus. Is this in fact desirable? First, it must be realized that because one country's export is another's import, it is impossible for everyone to have a surplus—on a worldwide basis, the total value of exports should equal the total value of imports, or there is globally balanced trade. However, the global current account balance has summed to a deficit in recent years. The problem seems to involve inaccurate measurement of international financial transactions. Merchandise trade is measured fairly accurately, and the global sum of trade balances is roughly zero. But service transactions are more difficult to observe, and investment income flows seem to be the major source of global current account discrepancies. Yet even with these bookkeeping problems facing government statisticians, the essential economic point is still true: Not all nations can have a trade surplus.

Since some country must always have a trade deficit when another has a trade surplus, is it necessarily true that surpluses are good and deficits bad, so that one country benefits at another's expense? In one sense, it seems that imports should be preferred to exports. In terms of current consumption, merchandise exports represent goods no longer available for domestic consumption, but goods that will be consumed by the importers. As we learn from studying international trade theory, the benefits of free international trade are more efficient production and increased consumption. If trade between nations is voluntary, then it is difficult to argue that deficit countries are harmed while surplus countries benefit by trade.

In general, it is not obvious whether a country is better or worse off running payments surpluses rather than deficits. Consider the following simple example of a world with two countries, A and B: Country A is a wealthy creditor country that has extended loans to poor country B. For country B to repay these loans, B must run trade surpluses with A to earn the foreign exchange required for repayment. Would you rather live in rich country A and experience trade deficits or in poor country B and experience trade surpluses? Although this is indeed a simplistic example, there are real-world analogues of rich creditor countries with trade deficits and poor debtor nations with trade surpluses. The point here is that you cannot analyze the balance of payments apart from other economic considerations. Deficits are not inherently bad, nor are surpluses necessarily good.

    Balance-of-payments equilibrium is a concept that has several alternative definitions. A useful definition is that it is a condition where exports equal imports or credits equal debits on some particular subaccount, such as the current account or official settlements account. If we had a current account equilibrium, the nation would find its net creditor or debtor position unchanging, as there would be no need for any net financing—the current account export items are just balanced by the current account import items. Equilibrium on the official settlements basis would mean no change in short-term capital held by foreign monetary agencies and reserve assets. For most countries, this would simply mean that their stocks of international reserves are unchanging.

    What happens if there is a disequilibrium in the balance of payments, say, the official settlements basis? Now, there will be reserve asset losses from deficit countries and reserve accumulation by surplus countries. International reserve assets are composed of gold, IMF special drawing rights (a credit issued by the IMF and allocated to countries on the basis of their level of financial support for the IMF), and foreign exchange. To simplify matters (although this is essentially the case for most countries), let us consider foreign exchange alone. Chapter 13 will discuss the foreign-exchange market, where currencies are traded internationally, in detail. For now, we must simply know that an exchange rate is the price of one money in terms of another. For instance, 1 British pound might be worth 1.50 U.S. dollars. The concept of balance-of-payments equilibrium may be linked to a familiar diagram from principles of economics courses—the supply and demand diagram. Figure 12.2 depicts the hypothetical supply and demand diagram for the dollar/pound foreign-exchange market. To further simplify matters, let's assume that Britain and the United States are the only two countries in the world.

    Initially, there is an official settlements balance-of-payments equilibrium and foreign-exchange market equilibrium at point A in Figure 12.2. At this point the dollar price of the pound is 1.60, and quantity $£_0$ (we don't care about a specific number here) is bought and sold. Note that the demand is a familiar downward-sloping demand curve. In this case, the demand for pounds comes from the U.S. demand for British goods or financial assets. The higher the dollar price of the pound, the more expensive British goods and the smaller the quantity of pounds demanded will be. The supply curve is the supply of pounds to this market from British buyers of U.S. goods or financial assets. The upward-sloping supply curve reflects the fact that as the pound appreciates in value (so that the exchange rate, $/£, rises), U.S. products are cheaper to British buyers, and more pounds will be supplied to this market.

    Suppose the initial equilibrium at point A is disturbed by a change in British preferences for U.S. goods. For instance, suppose British buyers now believe that U.S. automobiles are of higher quality and now demand more auto imports from the U.S. The supply of pounds to this market will shift to the right to S', so at every level

Balance-of-payments equilibrium
Credits equal debits for a particular account.

FIGURE 12.2 *Balance-of-payments disequilibrium as reflected in the foreign-exchange market.*

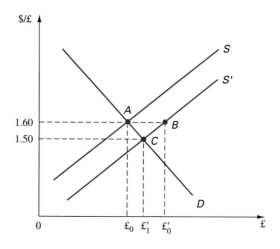

---

of the exchange rate, more pounds are offered for dollars. In terms of the U.S. balance of trade, there is now a surplus resulting from the higher British demand for U.S. cars. Great Britain, on the other hand, now has a balance-of-payments deficit.

Figure 12.2 suggests an obvious way for restoring equilibrium to the foreign-exchange market and the balance of payments: Let the pound depreciate to $1.50 per pound. At $/£ = 1.50, equilibrium is restored at point C. A new equilibrium quantity of pounds ($£_1'$) is traded at the new exchange rate. With the appreciation of the dollar, U.S. buyers are willing to buy more from the United Kingdom to balance the increased purchases of U.S. autos by British buyers. In this case of **flexible exchange rates,** where the exchange rate is determined by the free-market supply and demand, balance-of-payments equilibrium is restored by the operation of the free market.

Flexible exchange rates
Free-market supply and demand determines the value of currencies.

Fixed exchange rates
Central banks peg exchange rates at desired levels.

As we will learn in Chapter 19, exchange rates are not always free to adjust to changing market conditions. With **fixed exchange rates,** central banks set exchange rates at a particular level. If the exchange rate is fixed at 1.60, then, after the shift in the supply curve, the pound will be overvalued, there will be an excess supply of pounds ($£_0' - £_0$) on the foreign-exchange market, and the United Kingdom will run a balance-of-trade deficit, while the United States runs a surplus. The central banks must now finance the trade imbalance by international reserve flows. Specifically, the Federal Reserve (or the Bank of England) must sell dollars for pounds to support the deficit. In this case, the British deficit could continue only as long as the U.K. stock of dollars lasts. Once the United Kingdom has depleted its stock of foreign exchange, the pound would have to be devalued to $1.50 per pound, at which time the trade imbalance would end and there would again be equilibrium in the foreign-exchange market.

Besides these methods of adjusting to balance-of-payments disequilibrium, countries sometimes use direct controls on international trade to shift the supply and demand curves by government-mandated quotas or prices that induce balance-of-payments equilibrium. Such policies are particularly popular in developing countries where chronic shortages of international reserves will not permit financing the free-market-determined trade disequilibrium at the government-supported exchange rate.

The mechanism of adjustment to balance-of-payments disequilibrium is one of the most important practical problems in international economics. The discussion here is but an introduction, as much of the analysis of Chapters 17 and 18 is related to this issue.

SUMMARY

1. If the value of the credit items on a particular balance-of-payments account exceeds (is less than) the debit items, a surplus (deficit) exists.

2. The current account is the sum of the merchandise, services, income, and unilateral transfers accounts.

3. Current account deficits are offset by capital account surpluses.

4. The United States became a net international debtor in 1985.

5. Merchandise exports minus imports equals the balance of trade.

6. The official settlements balance is equal to changes in short-term capital held by foreign monetary agencies and official reserve asset transactions.

7. Increases (decreases) in U.S.–owned deposits in foreign banks are debits (credits) to U.S. short-term capital. Increases (decreases) in foreign-owned deposits in U.S. banks are credits (debits) to short-term capital.

8. Deficits are not necessarily bad, nor are surpluses necessarily good.

9. With floating exchange rates, balance-of-payments equilibrium is restored by exchange rate changes.

10. With fixed exchange rates, central banks must finance deficits, allow a devaluation, or else use trade restrictions to restore equilibrium.

EXERCISES

1. If we sum the trade balance of every nation, we find a nonzero world trade balance. Is this balance positive or negative, and why doesn't the balance equal zero?

2. Classify the following transactions in the Mexican balance of payments:

    a. A Mexican auto parts manufacturer sells Ps500,000 of parts to a U.S. firm, allowing 30 days' trade credit until payment is due.

    b. The United States gives Ps10,000,000 of corn to Mexico to help feed earthquake victims in Mexico City.

    c. A U.S. tourist travels to Mazatlán, Mexico, and spends Ps10,000 on hotels and tequila while on vacation. He pays with a check drawn on a Phoenix, Arizona, bank.

    d. Señor de la Madrid in Mexico City receives Ps80,000 in interest from a deposit in a Houston, Texas, bank. He deposits the Ps80,000 in Bank of America in San Francisco.

3. What is the value of the current account in the preceding problem?

4. Analyze the following quotation: "A nation is enriched as its balance-of-trade surplus grows, so policy should always be aimed at maximizing the trade surplus."

5. What is a balance-of-payments disequilibrium? How are such disequilibriums eliminated? In other words, what forces bring about a restoration of balance-of-payments equilibrium?

6. How did the United States become the world's largest debtor nation in the 1980s?

7. How reasonable is it for every country to follow policies aimed at increasing net exports?

8. Use the information in the following table on Switzerland's 1998 international transactions to answer the questions below (amounts are millions of U.S. dollars):

Balance-of-Payments Account	Amount
Merchandise imports	$92,871
Merchandise exports	$93,859
Services imports	$15,406
Services exports	$26,683
Investment income receipts	$43,720
Investment income payments	$27,702
Unilateral transfers	−$3,736

    a. What is the balance of trade?

    b. What is the current account?

    c. Did Switzerland become a larger international net creditor during 1998?

9. People sometimes talk about "twin deficits" where the twins are the current account and the government budget deficit. Carefully explain how these two deficits are related economically so that changes in one are reflected in changes in the other.

REFERENCES

The Balance of Payments of the United States: Concepts, Data Sources, and Estimating Procedures. Washington, D.C.: U.S. Department of Commerce, May 1990.

Gill, Mahinder S., and Jack Bame. "IMF Balance of Payments Manual Adapts to a Changing World." *Finance and Development* (March 1994): 31.

Glick, Reuven. "The Largest Debtor Nation." *FRBSF Weekly Letter,* February 14, 1986.

Gonnelli, Adam. *The Basics of Foreign Trade and Exchange.* New York: Federal Reserve Bank of New York, 1993.

International Monetary Fund. *Report on the World Current Account Discrepancy.* Washington, D.C.: IMF, September 1987.

Motala, John. "Statistical Discrepancies in the World Current Account." *Finance and Development* (March 1997): 24–25.

INTERNET APPLICATIONS

Please visit our Web site at www.awl.com/husted_melvin for more exercises and readings.

CHAPTER 13

The Foreign-Exchange Market

TOPICS TO BE COVERED

Spot Rates
Arbitrage
Forward Rates
Swaps
Futures
Options
Central-Bank Intervention
Black Markets and Parallel Markets

KEY WORDS

Exchange rate	Foreign exchange swap
Spread	Hedging
Spot market	Margin
Cross rate	Call option
Depreciate	Put option
Appreciate	Striking price
Forward exchange market	Exercise price
Forward premium	Black market
Forward discount	Parallel market

Foreign-exchange trading refers to trading one country's money for that of another country. The need for such trade arises due to tourism, the buying and selling of goods internationally, or investment across international boundaries. The kind of money that is specifically traded is bank deposits or bank transfers of deposits denominated in foreign currency. The *foreign-exchange market,* as we usually think of it, refers to large commercial banks in financial centers, such as New York or London, trading foreign-currency-denominated deposits with each other. Actual *bank notes,* like dollar bills, are relatively unimportant insofar as they rarely physically cross international borders. In general, only tourism or illegal activities would lead to the international movement of bank notes.

SPOT RATES

Exchange rate
The price of one money in terms of another.

Table 13.1 provides foreign-exchange rate quotations for a particular day. An **exchange rate** is the price of one money in terms of another. In the table, we see that on Tuesday, January 11, 2000, Swiss francs were selling for $0.6416. Note that this exchange rate is quoted at a specific time, 4:00 P.M., since rates will change throughout the day as supply and demand for the currencies change. Note also that these exchange rates are quotes based on large trades ($1 million or more) in what is essentially a wholesale market for money. The smaller the quantity of foreign exchange purchased, the higher the price. For instance, if a U.S. importer is buying watches from Switzerland at the dollar price of $10,000, his or her local bank would sell $10,000 worth of francs for more than $0.6416 per franc. Suppose the bank charges $0.65 per franc. The importer would then buy SF15,385 ($10,000/$0.65) to settle the account with the Swiss exporter. An individual buying even smaller amounts of francs would pay a higher rate still.

In the example just considered, the U.S. importer found that $10,000 was equivalent in value to SF15,385. We calculated this by dividing the total dollar value of the purchase ($10,000) by the dollar price of one franc ($0.65). Note that the foreign-exchange quotations also list quotes in terms of foreign-currency units per dollar. In Table 13.1, we see that on Tuesday, January 11, the Swiss franc sold for $0.6416. By looking farther to the right, we also see that the dollar was worth SF1.5585. It will always be true that when we know the dollar price of the franc ($/SF), we can find the franc price of the dollar by taking the reciprocal (SF/$). Of course, this relationship works in the opposite direction as well. If the franc price of the dollar is SF1.5585, then the dollar price of the franc is found as the reciprocal (1/1.5585 = $0.6416).

In the example of the U.S. watch importer, if the bank is selling francs for $0.65, then what is the implied franc price of the dollar? To find this, we simply calculate the reciprocal: 1/0.65 = SF1.5385. Had we initially been given the exchange rate quote in terms of francs per dollar, we could have found the franc equivalent of $10,000 by multiplying $10,000 by the franc price of one dollar: 10,000 × 1.5385 = SF15,385.

TABLE 13.1	*Foreign-Exchange Rate Quotations*

CURRENCY TRADING

EXCHANGE RATES
Tuesday, January 11, 2000

The New York foreign exchange midrange rates below apply to trading among banks in amounts of $1 million and more, as quoted at 4 p.m. Eastern time by Reuters and other sources. Retail transactions provide fewer units of foreign currency per dollar. Rates for the 11 Euro currency countries are derived from the latest dollar-euro rate using the exchange ratios set 1/1/99.

Country	U.S. $ equiv.	Currency per U.S. $
Argentina (Peso)	1.0001	.9999
Australia (Dollar)	.6581	1.5196
Austria (Schilling)	.07509	13.318
Bahrain (Dinar)	2.6525	.3770
Belgium (Franc)	.0256	39.0415
Brazil (Real)	.5488	1.8220
Britain (Pound)	1.6478	.6069
1-month forward	1.6479	.6068
3-months forward	1.6478	.6069
6-months forward	1.6472	.6071
Canada (Dollar)	.6863	1.4570
1-month forward	.6869	1.4558
3-months forward	.6878	1.4539
6-months forward	.6891	1.4512
Chile (Peso) (d)	.001917	521.75
China (Renminbi)	.1208	8.2795
Colombia (Peso)	.0005244	1907.00
Czech. Rep. (Koruna)		
Commercial rate	.02875	34.784
Denmark (Krone)	.1388	7.2053
Ecuador (Sucre)		
Floating rate	.0004028	24825.00
Finland (Markka)	.1738	5.7544
France (Franc)	.1575	6.3485
1-month forward	.1579	6.3338
3-months forward	.1586	6.3057
6-months forward	.1596	6.2652
Germany (Mark)	.5283	1.8929
1-month forward	.5295	1.8885
3-months forward	.5319	1.8802
6-months forward	.5353	1.8681
Greece (Drachma)	.003123	320.19
Hong Kong (Dollar)	.1286	7.7786
Hungary (Forint)	.004057	246.48
India (Rupee)	.02298	43.525
Indonesia (Rupiah)	.0001379	7250.00
Ireland (Punt)	1.3122	.7621
Israel (Shekel)	.2435	4.1076

Country	U.S. $ equiv.	Currency per U.S. $
Italy (Lira)	.0005336	1873.96
Japan (Yen)	.009429	106.05
1-month forward	.009477	105.52
3-months forward	.009569	104.50
6-months forward	.009717	102.91
Jordan (Dinar)	1.4085	.7100
Kuwait (Dinar)	3.2916	.3038
Lebanon (Pound)	.0006640	1506.00
Malaysia (Ringgit)	.2632	3.8000
Malta (Lira)	2.4765	.4038
Mexico (Peso)		
Floating rate	.1051	9.5170
Netherland (Guilder)	.4689	2.1328
New Zealand (Dollar)	.5174	1.9327
Norway (Krone)	.1256	7.9596
Pakistan (Rupee)	.01927	51.898
Peru (new Sol)	.2850	3.5083
Philippines (Peso)	.02451	40.800
Poland (Zloty)	.2460	4.0655
Portugal (Escudo)	.005154	194.03
Russia (Ruble) (a)	.03499	28.580
Saudi Arabia (Riyal)	.2666	3.7503
Singapore (Dollar)	.5993	1.6687
Slovak Rep. (Koruna)	.02443	40.934
South Africa (Rand)	.1641	6.0925
South Korea (Won)	.0008726	1146.00
Spain (Peseta)	.006210	161.04
Sweden (Krona)	.1191	8.3979
Switzerland (Franc)	.6416	1.5585
1-month forward	.6441	1.5526
3-months forward	.6486	1.5419
6-months forward	.6553	1.5260
Taiwan (Dollar)	.03252	30.755
Thailand (Baht)	.02657	37.635
Turkey (Lira)	.00000185	539600.00
United Arab (Dirham)	.2723	3.6730
Uruguay (New Peso)		
Financial	.08592	11.639
Venezuela (Bolivar)	.001536	651.25
– – –		
SDR	.7280	1.3736
Euro	1.0333	.9678

Special Drawing Rights (SDR) are based on exchange rates for the U.S., German, British, French, and Japanese currencies. Source: International Monetary Fund.

a-Russian Central Bank rate. Trading band lowered on 8/17/98. b-Government rate. d-Floating rate; trading band suspended on 9/2/99.

The 3-month and 6-month forward rates for France, Germany, Japan, and Switzerland appearing in the Foreign Exchange column were incorrectly calculated for the period beginning with August 13 and ending with October 7. Corrected data is available from

SOURCE: *Wall Street Journal*, January 11, 2000.

The importer buys this quantity of francs from the bank and actually pays for the watches with a check drawn on the bank (or a foreign associate of his or her bank).

Note that the exchange rate quotes in Table 13.1 are "midrange" quotes. This is the average of the banks' buying and selling prices. Banks bid to buy foreign exchange at lower rates than they sell, and the difference between selling and buying

TABLE 13.2	*London Closing Spreads, January 11, 2000*
United Kingdom[1]	1.6468–1.6476
Ireland[1]	1.3073–1.3078
Canada	1.4565–1.4575
Netherlands	2.1395–2.1404
Belgium	39.1650–39.1802
Denmark	7.2227–7.2244
Germany	1.8989–1.8996
Portugal	194.643–194.718
Spain	161.540–161.603
Italy	1879.87–1880.60
Norway	7.9760–7.9800
France	6.3685–6.3710
Sweden	8.4089–8.4182
Japan	105.750–105.800
Austria	13.3595–13.3647
Switzerland	1.5626–1.5635
Euro[1]	1.0296–1.0300

[1]Quotes for the United Kingdom, Ireland, and the euro are in terms of U.S. dollars per British pound, Irish punt, and euro, respectively. All other quotes are domestic-currency units per U.S. dollar.
SOURCE: *Financial Times*, January 12, 2000.

Spread
The difference between the buying and selling price of a currency.

rates is called the **spread**. Table 13.2 lists the spreads at the close of business on Tuesday, January 11, in London. We see that at the time the London market closed, the Swiss franc price a bank would pay for dollars was SF1.5626 per dollar. Dollars would be sold for francs by the bank at SF1.5635 per dollar. This spread of less than 1/10 of 1 percent (1.5635 − 1.5626)/1.5626 = .0006 is indicative of the normal spread in the market for major traded currencies. The existing spread in any currency will vary according to the individual currency trader, the currency being traded, and the trading bank's overall view of conditions in the foreign-exchange market. The spread quoted will tend to increase for more thinly traded currencies (i.e., currencies that do not generate a large volume of trading) or when the bank perceives that the risks associated with trading in a currency at a particular time are rising. The discussion of the South African rand in Item 13.1 is a good example of how uncertainty can change the spread on a currency.

The large trading banks, such as Citibank or Deutsche Bank, stand ready to "make a market" in a currency by offering buy (bid) and sell (ask) rates on request. Actually, currency traders do not quote all the numbers indicated in Table 13.2. For instance, the table lists the spread on Canadian dollars as Can$1.565 to Can$1.4575. In practice, this spread is quoted as Can$1.4565–75, or, in words, the Canadian dollar per U.S. dollar rate is one forty-five-sixty-five to seventy-five. The listener then recognizes that the bank is willing to bid Can$1.4565 to buy U.S. dollars and will sell U.S. dollars at Can$1.4575.

ITEM 13.1   Bid-Ask Spreads and Politics: The South African Rand

The spread between the price a bank will pay for a currency and the price at which it will sell will swing up and down as the risk of trading the currency varies. When conditions in a nation are unsettled politically, there is a greater potential for change that could lead to large shifts in the exchange rate. Banks will charge a wider spread in such situations to protect against unexpected exchange rate movements.

The South African rand provides an excellent example of how bid-ask spreads vary with political crises. Figure 13.1 plots the spread on the rand/dollar exchange rate in the London market

(Continued)

FIGURE 13.1   *South African rand bid-ask differences.*

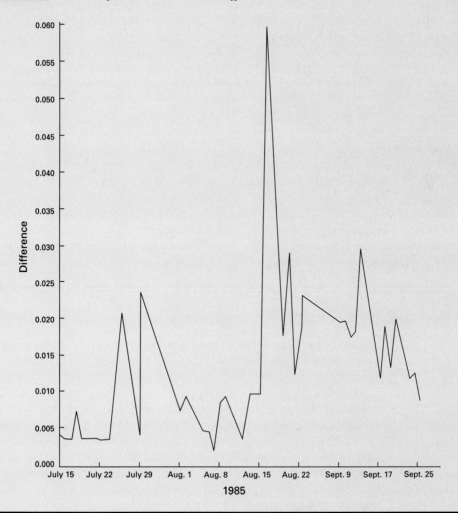

ITEM 13.1   Bid-Ask Spreads and Politics: The South African Rand (Continued)

from July 15, 1985, to September 25, 1985. On July 15, the bid price was 1.9130 and the ask was 1.9170, so the spread was 0.004. After the imposition of a "state of emergency" giving police near absolute powers of arrest and detention, the spread jumped to 0.0208 on July 26. The spread moved around erratically until a dramatic jump to 0.0600 on August 16, 1985. This jump in the spread followed a speech by the South African president. The speech followed the worst week of racial violence in South African history and was expected to include announced modifications in national policy. Instead, the president rejected any idea of concessions to the black majority. The market reacted to this news by pushing the rand to an all-time low against the dollar (the bid price was now 2.3800) and greatly widening the spread.

Financial market participants react to increased risk associated with a financial asset by decreasing demand for the asset. The new uncertainty that resulted from the president's speech reduced the demand to hold the rand and resulted in a rand depreciation.

It is interesting to note that the jumps in the spreads on July 26 and August 16 both occurred on Fridays. Since the financial markets are closed on Saturday and Sunday, banks seek a wider spread on Friday to insure against any further surprises that might occur over the weekend. In both the July 26 and August 16 cases, the spread fell considerably on the following Mondays.

The South African government suspended trading in the nation's stock and foreign-exchange markets from August 28 through September 2 in response to foreign investors clamoring to liquidate their South African investments. The heavy selling of the rand for foreign currencies had pushed the rand/dollar rate to 2.7700 on August 27. The foreign-exchange trading ban stopped the depreciation, and when the market reopened September 2, the rand regained some of its lost value.

The South African rand case is interesting because it is so dramatically tied to identifiable domestic events. Such an analysis of foreign-exchange market spreads could be applied to any country whose currency is openly traded. Our purpose is to recognize the importance that political uncertainty may play in the foreign-exchange market.

Thus far, we have discussed trading Swiss francs and Canadian dollars using the symbols SF and Can$, respectively. Table 13.3 lists the commonly used symbols for several currencies along with their international standard (ISO) code letters. Exchange rate quotations are generally available for all freely traded currencies. In the cases where free markets are not permitted, the state typically conducts all foreign-exchange trading at the official price, regardless of current market conditions.

So far, we have been discussing the buying and selling of foreign exchange to be delivered on the spot (actually, deposits traded in the foreign-exchange market generally take two working days to clear); this is called the **spot market**. In our example of the U.S. watch importer, the importer wants to buy $10,000 worth of Swiss francs for current payment. If the importer purchases the francs in the spot market today, in two days the bank will reduce the importer's checking account balance by

Spot market
Where currencies are traded for current delivery.

TABLE 13.3	*Commonly Used Symbols for Several Currencies*		
Country	Currency	Symbol	ISO Code
Australia	dollar	A$	AUD
Austria	schilling	Sch	ATS
Belgium	franc	BF	BEF
Canada	dollar	Can$	CAD
Denmark	krone	DKr	DKK
Euro countries	euro	€	EUR
Finland	markka	FM	FIM
France	franc	FF	FRF
Germany	deutsche mark	DM	DEM
Greece	drachma	Dr	GRD
India	rupee	Rs	INR
Iran	rial	RI	IRR
Italy	lira	Lit	ITL
Japan	yen	¥	JPY
Kuwait	dinar	KD	KWD
Mexico	peso	Ps	MXP
Netherlands	guilder	Fl	NLG
Norway	krone	NKr	NOK
Saudi Arabia	riyal	SR	SAR
Singapore	dollar	S$	SGD
South Africa	rand	R	ZAR
Spain	peseta	Pts	ESP
Sweden	krona	SKr	SEK
Switzerland	franc	SF	CHF
United Kingdom	pound	£	GBP
United States	dollar	$	USD

$10,000 and wire the SF15,385 to be drawn on a Swiss bank by the exporter (for relatively small transactions, the two-day delay may not be necessary).

We shall soon consider the important issues that arise when the trade contract involves payment at a future date. First, we consider in more detail the nature of the foreign-exchange market in general.

ARBITRAGE

The foreign-exchange market is a market where price information is readily available by telephone or computer terminals. Since currencies are homogeneous goods (a dollar is a dollar regardless of where it is traded), it is very easy to compare prices in different markets. Exchange rates tend to be equal worldwide. If this were not so, there would be profit opportunities for simultaneously buying a currency in one market while selling in another. This activity, known as arbitrage, would raise the exchange rate where it is too low, because this is the market you would buy in, and the increased demand for the currency would result in a higher price. The market where the exchange rate is too high is the one in which you would sell, and this increased selling activity would result in a lower price. Arbitrage occurs until the exchange rates in different locales are so close that it is not worth the costs incurred from any further buying and selling. When this situation occurs, we say that the rates are transaction costs close, because any remaining deviation in rates will not cover the costs of additional arbitrage transactions, so the arbitrage activity ends.

For instance, suppose that in New York the German mark is selling for $0.63, while in London the mark is quoted at $0.64. A profit-seeking arbitrager would buy marks where they are relatively cheap (New York) and simultaneously sell them where they are relatively expensive (London), thereby earning a profit of 1 cent per mark traded. The trader's net profit will be determined by the transaction cost incurred in the activity.[*] If the transaction cost exceeded 1 cent, then no arbitrage activity would take place. Otherwise, the arbitragers work to keep exchange rates the same in all markets. In the present example, the increased demand for marks in New York will raise the dollar price of marks in New York, while the increased supply of marks in London will lower the dollar price of marks in London. In this manner, arbitrage ensures that the dollar-mark exchange rate is almost identical across countries.

Arbitrage could involve more than two currencies. When we consider that the bulk of foreign-exchange trading involves the U.S. dollar, we note the role of comparing dollar exchange rates for different currencies to determine if the implied third exchange rates are in line. Since banks quote foreign-exchange rates with respect to the dollar (the dollar is said to be the "numeraire" of the system), such comparisons are readily made. For instance, if we know the dollar price of pounds ($/£) and the dollar price of Swiss francs ($/SF), we can infer the corresponding pound price of francs (£/SF). Note that, from now on, we shall explicitly write the units of our exchange rates to avoid the confusion that can easily arise. For instance, $/£ = $2.00 is the exchange rate in terms of dollars per pound.

Cross rate
The third exchange rate implied by any two exchange rates involving three currencies.

Suppose in London $/£ = $2.00, while in New York $/SF = $0.40. The corresponding **cross rate** is the £/SF rate. Simple algebra shows that if $/£ = $2.00 and $/SF = 0.40, then £/SF = ($/SF)/($/£) = 0.40/2.00 = 0.2. If we observe a market where one of the three exchange rates—$/£, $/SF, or £/SF—is out of line with the other two, there is an arbitrage opportunity. Suppose in Zurich the exchange rate is £/SF = 0.2, while in New York $/SF = 0.40, but in London $/£ = $1.90. Astute traders in the foreign-exchange market would observe the discrepancy, and quick action would be rewarded. The trader could start with dollars and buy £1 million in

*Several studies have estimated the transaction costs in the foreign-exchange market; Mohsen Bahmani-Oskooee and Satya P. Das, "Transaction Costs and the Interest Parity Theorem," *Journal of Political Economy* 93 (August 1985): 793–99, and Kevin Clinton, "Transaction Costs and Covered Interest Arbitrage: Theory and Evidence," *Journal of Political Economy* 96 (April 1988): 358–70, are good examples. Clinton estimates transaction costs of approximately 0.06 percent of the value of the transaction. More recent studies have considered 0.05 percent as realistic. Such studies include Richard Levich and Lee Thomas, "The Significance of Technical Trading-Rule Profits in the Foreign Exchange Market: A Bootstrap Approach," *Journal of International Money and Finance* 12 (October 1993): 451–74 and Christopher J. Neely, "Technical Analysis in the Foreign Exchange Market: A Layman's Guide," *Federal Reserve Bank of St. Louis Review* 79 (Sept/Oct 1997): 23–38.

London for $1,900,000, since $/£ = $1.90. The pounds could be used to buy francs at £/SF = 0.2, so that £1,000,000 = SF5,000,000. The SF 5 million could then be used in New York to buy dollars at $/SF = $0.40, so that SF5,000,000 = $2,000,000. Thus, the initial $1,900,000 could be turned into $2,000,000 with the *triangular arbitrage* action, earning the trader $100,000. (Costs associated with the transaction should be deducted to arrive at the true arbitrage profit.)

As in the case of the two-currency arbitrage covered earlier, a valuable product of this arbitrage activity is the return of the exchange rates to internationally consistent levels. If the initial discrepancy was that the dollar price of pounds was too low in London, the selling of dollars for pounds in London by the arbitragers will make pounds more expensive, raising the price from $/£ = $1.90 back to $2.00. (Actually, the rate would not return to $2.00, because the activity in the other markets will tend to raise the pound price of francs and lower the dollar price of francs so that a dollar price of pounds between $1.90 and $2.00 will allow a new equilibrium among the three currencies.)

Table 13.4 gives the cross rates for several currencies on January 11, 2000. Effective arbitrage will ensure that by knowing any two exchange rates, we are able to infer a third. For instance, we find that £/$ = 0.60690 by looking across the U.K. row for the $ column, which happens to be the first column. To find the pound price of Swiss francs, we glance across the U.K. row for the SFranc column and note that £/SF = .38941. The implied cross rate for $/SF is determined by division: $/SF = (£/SF)/(£/$) = .38941/.60690 = .64164. We can look at the U.S. row and the SFranc column to see the cross rate of .64164.

Since there is active trading between the dollar and many currencies, we can look to any two exchange rates involving dollars to infer the cross rates. So even if there is limited trading directly between, for instance, Mexican pesos and the yen, by using $/Ps and $/¥, we can find the implied Ps/¥ rate. The depth of foreign-

TABLE 13.4

FOREIGN-EXCHANGE CROSS RATES, JANUARY 11, 2000[1]

	Dollar	Euro	Pound	SFranc	Guilder	Peso	Yen	Lira	D-Mark	FFranc	CdnDlr
Canada	1.4570	1.5055	2.4008	0.9349	.68314	.15309	.01374	.00078	.76972	.22950	....
France	6.3485	6.5599	10.4611	4.0735	2.9766	.66707	.05986	.00339	3.3538	....	4.3572
Germany	1.8929	1.9559	3.1191	1.2146	.88752	.19890	.01785	.00101	....	.29816	1.2992
Italy	1874.0	1936.4	3087.9	1202.4	878.64	196.26	17.669	....	989.99	295.18	1286.2
Japan	106.06	109.59	174.77	68.053	49.728	11.144	....	.07560	56.030	16.706	72.792
Mexico	9.5170	9.8339	15.682	6.1065	4.4622	....	.08973	.00508	5.0277	1.4991	6.5319
Netherlands	2.1328	2.2038	3.5144	1.3685	....	.22410	.02011	.00115	1.1267	.33595	1.4638
Switzerland	1.5585	1.6104	2.5681	....	.73073	.16376	.01469	.00083	.82334	.24549	1.0697
U.K.	.60690	.6271	....	.38941	.28454	.06377	.00572	.00032	.32060	.09559	.41652
Euro	.96780	....	1.5947	.62096	.45376	.10169	.00912	.00052	.51126	.15244	.66422
U.S.	....	1.0333	1.6478	.64164	.46887	.10508	.00943	.00053	.52829	.15752	.68634

[1]Exchange rates are the number of units of the currency listed in the left-hand column per unit of the currency listed in the top row.

SOURCE: Reuters.

exchange trading involving dollars often makes it cheaper to go through dollars to get from some currency X to another currency Y when X and Y are not widely traded, as transaction costs are higher for lightly traded currencies. Thus, if a business firm in Mexico wants to buy Indian rupees to pay for merchandise imports from India, it may well be cheaper to sell Mexican pesos for dollars and then use dollars to buy rupees rather than try to trade pesos for rupees directly.

Although arbitrage will tend to equalize exchange rate quotes worldwide, we must remember that the different financial centers operate in different time zones. Therefore, it only makes sense to compare quotations at a time when the markets overlap. As Figure 13.2 indicates, we could not compare $/¥ quotes in New York with those in Tokyo because there is no overlap between the trading hours. Figure 13.2 illustrates the 24-hour dimension of the foreign-exchange market. We can determine the hours each market is open by the country bars at the top of the figure. Time is measured as Greenwich Mean Time (GMT). For instance, the Tokyo market is open from 0000 to 0800 or 9:00 A.M. to 5:00 P.M. local time. The New York market is open from 1200 (7:00 a.m. New York time) to 2000 (3:00 P.M. New York time). While there is no overlap between Tokyo and New York, the figure indicates the extent to which other trading centers are open simultaneously.

FORWARD RATES

Suppose we now return to our example of the U.S. watch importer. Earlier, the importer purchased Swiss francs in the spot market to settle a contract payable now. Yet much of international trade is contracted in advance of delivery and payment. It would not be unusual for the importer to place an order for Swiss watches for delivery at a future date. For instance, suppose the order calls for delivery of the goods and payment of the invoice in three months. Specifically, let's say that the order is for SF100,000.

What options does the importer have with respect to payment? One option is to wait three months and then buy the francs. A disadvantage of this strategy is that the exchange rate could change over the next three months in a way that makes the deal unprofitable. Looking back at Table 13.1, we see that the current spot rate (on January 11) is $0.6416 = SF1. At the current spot rate, SF100,000 = $64,160. Yet there is no guarantee that this exchange rate (and consequent dollar value of the contract) will prevail in the future. If the dollar should **depreciate** against the franc, then it would take more dollars to buy any given quantity of francs. For instance, suppose the future spot rate (which is currently unknown) is $.70 = SF1. Then, it would take $70,000 to purchase SF100,000, and the watch purchase would not be as profitable for the importer. Of course, if the dollar should **appreciate** against the franc, then the profits would be larger. As a result of this uncertainty regarding the dollar-franc exchange rate in the future, the importer may not want to choose the strategy of waiting three months to buy francs.

Another alternative is to buy the francs now and hold or invest them for three months. This alternative has the advantage that the importer knows exactly how

Depreciate
The value of one currency falls relative to another.

Appreciate
The value of one currency rises relative to another.

FIGURE 13.2 *The world of foreign-exchange dealing.*

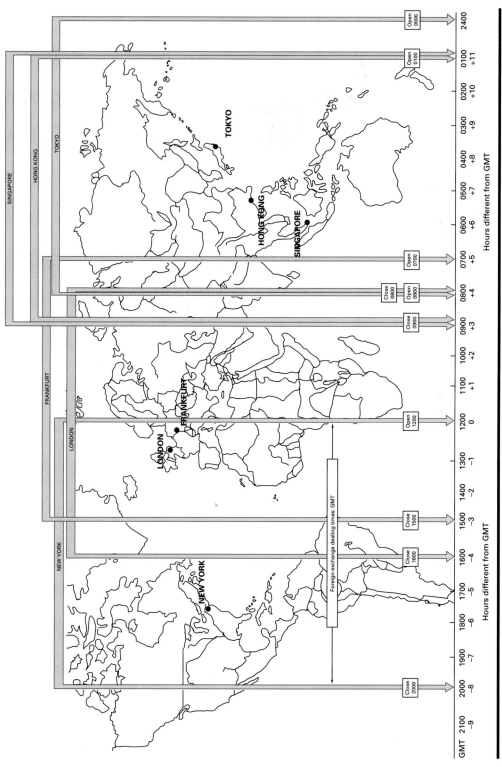

Information on trading hours has been provided by R.D. Dave of Olsen & Associates, Zurich.

Forward exchange market
Where currencies may be bought and sold for delivery in a future period.

many dollars are needed to buy SF100,000. But the importer is faced with a new problem of investing the francs for three months. Another alternative that ensures a certain dollar price of francs is using the **forward exchange market**. As will be shown in a later chapter, there is a close relationship between the former alternative of buying francs now and investing them for three months and the forward market. For now, we focus on the operation of the forward market.

The forward exchange market refers to buying and selling currencies to be delivered at a future date. Table 13.1 includes forward exchange rates for the major traded currencies, including the Swiss franc. Note that the three-month forward rate on the franc is $.6486 = SF1. To buy francs for delivery in three months would cost $.6486 per franc. Note that one-month and six-month forward rates are also quoted.

The advantage of the forward market is that we have established a set exchange rate between the dollar and the franc and do not have to buy the francs until they are needed in three months. This may be preferred to buying francs now and investing them for three months, because it is necessary neither to part with any funds now nor to have knowledge of investment opportunities in francs. (However, the selling bank may require that the importer hold "compensating balances" until the three-month period is up, that is, leave funds in an account at the bank, allowing the bank to use the money until the forward date.)

Forward premium
The forward exchange rate exceeds the spot rate.

Forward discount
The forward exchange rate is less than the spot rate.

If the forward exchange price of a currency exceeds the current spot price, that currency is said to be selling at a **forward premium**. A currency is selling at a **forward discount** when the forward rate is less than the current spot rate. The forward rates in Table 13.1 indicate that all the major traded currencies except the pound are selling at a premium against the dollar. The implications of a currency selling at a discount or premium are explored in coming chapters. In the event that the spot and forward rates are equal, as for three-month pounds in Table 13.1, the currency is said to be *flat*.

SWAPS

Foreign exchange swap
An agreement to trade currencies at one date and reverse the trade at a later date.

Commercial banks rarely use forward exchange contracts for interbank trading; instead, swap agreements are arranged. A **foreign exchange swap** is a trade that combines both a spot and a forward transaction into one deal (some swaps combine two forward transactions, and are called *forward-forward swaps*). For example, suppose Citibank wants pounds now. It could borrow the pounds, arranging to repay them in three months. Then, it could buy pounds in the forward market to ensure a certain price to be paid when the pounds are needed in three months. Alternatively, Citibank could enter into a swap agreement whereby it trades dollars for pounds now and pounds for dollars in three months. Thus, a swap serves as a borrowing and a lending operation combined in one deal. The terms of the arrangement are obviously closely related to conditions in the forward market, since the swap rates will be determined by the discounts or premiums in the forward exchange market.

Suppose Citibank wants pounds for three months and works a swap with Lloyds. Citibank will trade dollars to Lloyds and in return will receive pounds. In three months, the trade is reversed. Citibank will pay out pounds to Lloyds and receive dollars. (Of course, there is nothing special about the three-month period used here—swaps can be for any period.) Suppose the spot rate is $/£ = $2.00, and the three-month forward rate is $/£ = $2.10, so that there is a $0.10 premium on the pound. These premiums or discounts are actually quoted in basis points when serving as swap rates (a basis point is 1/100 percent, or 0.0001). Thus, the $0.10 premium converts into a swap rate of 1,000 points, which is all the swap participants are interested in; they do not care about the actual spot or forward rate, since only the difference between them matters for a swap.

Swap rates are usefully converted into percent per annum terms to make them comparable to other borrowing and lending rates (remember, a swap is the same as borrowing one currency while lending another currency for the duration of the swap period). The swap rate of 1,000 points, or 0.1000, was for a three-month period. To convert this into annual terms, we find the percentage return for the swap period and then multiply this by the reciprocal of the fraction of the year for which the swap exists:

$$\text{Percentage return for the swap period} = \text{premium (discount)/spot rate} = \$0.10/\$2.00 = 0.05$$

$$\text{Fraction of year for which swap exists} = 3 \text{ months}/12 \text{ months} = 1/4$$

$$\text{Reciprocal of fraction} = 1/(1/4) = 4$$

$$\text{Percent per annum premium (discount) or swap rate} = 0.05 \times 4 = 0.20$$

This swap then yields a return of 20 percent per annum, which can be compared with the other opportunities open to the bank.

Swaps are an efficient way to meet a bank's need for foreign currencies because they combine two separate transactions into one. We shall learn later that a bank avoids any foreign-exchange risk by matching the liability created by borrowing foreign currencies with the asset created by lending domestic currency, both to be repaid at the known future exchange rate. This is known as **hedging** the foreign-exchange risk.

Hedging
An activity to offset risk.

Table 13.5 presents data on the volume of activity in the foreign-exchange market. Approximately 38 percent of the $1,529 billion traded were spot transactions. Swaps composed about 48 percent of the business, with forward purchases or sales of a single currency composing around 8 percent of total transactions. We can see that foreign-exchange activity is dominated by the spot and swaps markets.

The United Kingdom (specifically, London) is the largest center for foreign-exchange trading, with an average daily volume of $637 billion compared with the U.S. figure of $351 billion and Japan's $149 billion. In terms of percentage shares, the United Kingdom does about 32 percent of the total daily foreign-exchange market volume, followed by the United States (18 percent), Japan (8 percent), Singapore (7 percent), and Germany (5 percent).

It should be pointed out that banks do not trade strictly among themselves. Nonbank customers include multinational firms and governments, and much of the interbank trade occurs through brokers. If a bank wants to buy a particular currency,

TABLE 13.5	Average Daily Volume of Bank Foreign-Exchange Market Activity	
	Billions of Dollars	Percentage Share
Spot	578	38
Swaps	734	48
Forwards	130	8
Options	87	6
Total	1,529	100

SOURCE: *Central Bank Survey of Foreign Exchange and Derivatives Market Activity* (Basle: Bank for International Settlements, May 1999).

several other banks could be called for quotes, or the bank representative could call a broker who is in contact with many banks and able to reveal the best price at the current time among those banks with whom he or she conducts business. If a bank contacts the broker with an offer to buy a currency and the broker has no offers to sell, then the broker will call around and try to find an interested seller. The broker's role, obviously, is to reduce the information costs of the banks. While trading in the broker's market is in progress, the names of the banks making bids and offers are not known until a deal is reached. This anonymity may be very important to the trading banks, because it allows banks of different sizes and market positions to trade on an equal footing. The broker's reward, the commission, is split between the buyer and the seller and is usually less than 0.01 percent of the selling price. In recent years automated brokerage services (computerized order matching) have become increasingly important, taking business away from human voice brokers. In the United Kingdom approximately 25 percent of the spot foreign-exchange transactions volume is arranged through automated brokers. In the United States and Japan, the number is even higher, at 33 percent and 36 percent respectively.

THE FUTURES MARKET

The foreign-exchange market as discussed so far (spot, forward, and swap transactions) is a global market. Commercial banks, business firms, and governments in various locations buy and sell, using telephones and computer terminals with no geographic market location. However, additional institutions that have not yet been covered exist—one of which is the foreign-exchange futures market. The futures market is a market where foreign currencies may be bought and sold for delivery at a future day. The futures market differs from the forward market in that only a few currencies are traded, trading occurs in standardized contracts, and trading occurs in a specific geographic location, such as the International Monetary Market (IMM) of the Chicago Mercantile Exchange, the largest currency futures market.

International Monetary Market futures are traded on the British pound, Australian dollar, Canadian dollar, Japanese yen, Swiss franc, Mexican peso, euro, and German

TABLE 13.6

FOREIGN CURRENCY FUTURES PRICES, JANUARY 11, 2000

CURRENCY

	Open	High	Low	Settle	Change	Lifetime High	Lifetime Low	Open Interest
JAPAN YEN (CME)-12.5 million yen; $ per yen (.00)								
Mar	.9600	.9642	.9498	.9535	−.0071	1.0018	.8369	74,958
June	.9673	.9710	.9667	.9692	−.0071	1.0175	.8619	3,197
Sept	....	....	....	.9847	−.0071	1.0272	.9838	244
Est vol 23,866; vol Mon 14,597; open int 78,406, −152.								
DEUTSCHEMARK (CME)-125,000 marks; $ per mark								
Mar	.5270	.5304	.5270	.5304	+.0036	.5611	.5144	5,382
Est vol 3; vol Mon 46; open int 5,419, +4.								
CANADIAN DOLLAR (CME)-100,000 dlrs.; $ per Can $								
Mar	.6882	.6886	.6865	.6879	−.0004	.6952	.6425	54,458
June	.6895	.6898	.6885	.6894	−.0004	.6964	.6547	5,486
Sept	.6898	.6910	.6898	.6906	−.0004	.6970	.6630	1,263
Dec	.6905	.6920	.6905	.6917	−.0004	.6980	.6640	514
Est vol 4,335; vol Mon 5,193; open int 61,755, +59.								
BRITISH POUND (CME)-62,500 pds.; $ per pound								
Mar	1.6366	1.6490	1.6364	1.6480	+.0112	1.6810	1.5570	35,401
Est vol 5,154; vol Mon 4,881; open int 35,409, +294.								
SWISS FRANC (CME)-125,000 francs; $ per franc								
Mar	.6421	.6464	.6412	.6459	+.0038	.7086	.6292	45,795
June	.6494	.6537	.6494	.6532	+.0038	.7040	.6360	201
Est vol 7,569; vol Mon 8,896; open int 46,028, +1,578.								
AUSTRALIAN DOLLAR (CME)-100,000 dlrs.; $ per A.$								
Mar	.6571	.6595	.6540	.6588	+.0018	.6704	.6268	29,075
Est vol 1,197; vol Mon 2,060; open int 29,097, +1,693.								
MEXICAN PESO (CME)-500,000 new Mex. peso; $ per MP								
Mar	.10335	.10358	.10300	.10305	−.00650	.10450	.08135	13,507
June	.10015	.10015	.09975	.09975	−.00600	.10075	.08350	2,194
Sept	....	....	....	.09675	−.00600	.10295	.08500	158
Dec	.09465	.09465	.09450	.09405	−.00600	.09465	.09200	101
Est vol 2,186; vol Mon 5,677; open int 15,960, +851.								
EURO FX (CME)-Euro 125,000; $ per Euro								
Mar	1.0304	1.0380	1.0295	1.0373	+.0069	1.1242	1.0089	59,664
June	....	....	....	1.0444	+.0069	1.1077	1.0166	176
Sept	....	....	....	4.0509	+.0069	1.1136	1.0226	97
Est vol 12,651; vol Mon 14,401; open int 59,951, +3,628.								

SOURCE: *Wall Street Journal*, January 12, 2000.

mark. The contracts involve a specific amount of currency to be delivered at specific maturity dates. Table 13.6 displays the foreign-exchange futures quotes for January 11, 2000. In this market, contracts mature on the third Wednesday of March, June, September, and December. In the forward market, contracts are typically 30, 90, or 180 days long and are maturing every day of the year. Forward market contracts are written for any amount agreed upon by the parties involved. In the futures market, the contracts are written for fixed amounts, as indicated in Table 13.6: £62,500, A$100,000, Can$100,000, ¥12,500,000, SF125,000, Ps500,000, €125,000 and DM125,000.

The first column of Table 13.6 gives the maturity month of the contract; the remaining columns yield the following information:

Open:	Price of contract at beginning of business that day.
High:	High price of contract on that trading day.
Low:	Low price of contract on that trading day.
Settle:	Price at which contracts are settled at the close of trading that day.
Change:	Change in the settlement price from the previous day.
Lifetime high:	Highest price at which this contract has ever traded.
Lifetime low:	Lowest price at which this contract has ever traded.
Open interest:	Number of outstanding contracts on the previous trading day.

To review each of these values specifically, consider the March pound contract. On January 11, the contract began trading at $1.6366 per pound (so, for £62,500, the contract value was $102,287.50). Over the course of the day, the price rose to a high of $1.6490, sank to a low of $1.6364, and settled at $1.6480. The settlement price was up $.0112 from the previous day. Over the life of trading in this contract, the highest price ever was $1.6810. The lowest price ever was $1.5570. On the previous day there were 35,401 outstanding contracts.

The daily settlement is an interesting feature of futures markets. Traders are required to realize any losses in cash on the day they occur. To trade in the futures market, a trader must deposit money with a broker. The amount required varies with the broker and the contract, and is called the **margin** requirement. Suppose the March pound contract requires an initial margin of $2,000. If the price fell $0.0175 on one day, then the fall in the settlement price of $0.0175 represents a loss of $1,093.75 on the £62,500 contract ($0.0175 \times 62,500 = 1,093.75$). The daily settlement involves deducting this daily loss from the margin deposited with the broker. If the value of the margin account falls below a certain level (typically 75 percent of the initial margin), the trader must deposit sufficient funds to raise the margin to its initial level. With a $2,000 margin, the loss of $1,093.75 in a single day reduces the margin account to $906.25—a value that would warrant a call for additional funds.

The last line for each currency in Table 13.6 provides information regarding the estimated volume of trading on the current day, the actual volume on the previous

Margin
A deposit with a broker required for trading in the futures market.

day, the current number of contracts (open interest) across all maturity dates for this currency, and the change in the number of contracts since the previous day.

Futures markets provide a hedging facility for firms involved in international trade as well as a speculative opportunity. Speculators will profit when they accurately forecast a future price for a currency that differs significantly (by more than the transaction cost) from the current contract price. For instance, if we believe that in March the pound will sell for $1.45, and the March futures contract is currently priced at $1.5000, we would sell a March contract. Then, at maturity, we will receive $1.5000 per pound, or $93,750. If the actual price of the pound falls below $1.5000, we realize a profit (less transaction costs). Suppose the actual price in March is $1.45. We could then buy £62,500 for $90,625. The difference of $93,750 − 90,625 = $3,125, less transaction costs, will be our profit.

Since futures contracts involve daily cash flow settlements while forward contracts do not, prices in the two markets will differ slightly, even for the same contract maturity date. Futures contracts are for smaller amounts of currency than forward contracts are and therefore serve as a useful hedging vehicle for relatively small firms. Forward contracts are within the realm of wholesale banking activity and are typically used only by large financial institutions and other large business firms that deal in very large amounts of foreign exchange.

FOREIGN-CURRENCY OPTIONS

Besides forward and futures contracts, there is an additional market where future foreign-currency assets and liabilities may be hedged—the options market. A foreign-currency option is a contract that provides the right to buy or sell a given amount of currency at a fixed exchange rate on or before the maturity date (these are known as "American" options; "European" options may be exercised only at maturity). A **call option** gives the right to buy currency, and a **put option** gives the right to sell. The price at which currency can be bought or sold is the **striking price**, or **exercise price**.

Call option
An option to buy currency.

The use of options for hedging purposes is straightforward. Suppose a U.S. importer is buying equipment from a German manufacturer with a DM1,000,000 payment due in three months. The importer can hedge against a mark appreciation by buying a call option that confers the right to purchase marks over the next three months at a specified price. Specifically, assume that the current spot exchange rate is $0.57 per mark. At this exchange rate, DM1,000,000, would cost $570,000. If the mark appreciated to $0.62 over the next three months, then using the spot market in three months would change the value of the imports to $620,000 (0.62 × DM1,000,000), an increase in the price of the imports of $50,000. The call option will provide insurance against such change. To add realism to our example, refer to the options quotes displayed in Table 13.7.

Put option
An option to sell currency.

Striking price
(exercise price)
The price of currency stated in an option contract.

Table 13.7 reports foreign-currency options prices for January 11. Foreign-currency options have been traded only since December 1982, when the Philadelphia

TABLE 13.7

FOREIGN-CURRENCY OPTIONS, PHILADELPHIA EXCHANGE

OPTIONS PHILADELPHIA EXCHANGE

Strike	Month	Calls Vol.	Calls Last	Puts Vol.	Puts Last
Euro					102.53
62,500 Euro-cents per unit.					
104	Mar	10	1.60	...	...
106	Jan	2	0.01	...	...
106	Mar	1	1.00	...	0.01
British Pound					164.72
31,250 Brit. Pounds-European Style.					
160	Mar	32	5.05	...	0.01

Strike	Month	Calls Vol.	Calls Last	Puts Vol.	Puts Last
Euro					102.53
62,500 Euro-European Style.					
102	Mar	1	3.20	...	0.01
Japanese Yen					95.00
6,250,000 J.Yen-100ths of a cent per unit.					
92 1/2	Feb	...	0.01	10	0.42
95	Mar	...	...	10	1.84
99	Mar	225	0.75	...	
6,250,000 J.Yen-European Style.					
74 1/2	Feb	20	0.54	...	0.01

Strike	Month	Calls Vol.	Calls Last	Puts Vol.	Puts Last
Swiss Franc					63.71
62,500 Swiss Francs-European Style.					
64	Jan	...	...	16	0.30
65	Jan	...	0.01	16	1.10
Swiss Francs-cents per unit.					
65	Jan	...	...	5	0.90
65	Mar	3	0.92	3	1.62
65 1/2	Jan	8	0.03	...	...
66	Feb	...	...	5	1.90

Call Vol 675   Open Int ... 15,151
Put Vol 705   Open Int ... 13,367

SOURCE: *Wall Street Journal*, January 12, 2000.

Stock Exchange offered a market. The Philadelphia exchange offers contracts for A$50,000, £31,250, Can$50,000, ¥6,250,000, €62,500 and SF62,500. The first row of the options quotations gives the currency being traded and its current spot exchange rate. The first column lists alternative striking prices available. The next column lists the different maturity months. The next two columns list the number of call contracts traded and prices of different maturity months. The final two columns list the put option volumes and prices for different maturity months.

An option is said to be "in the money" if the striking price is less than the current spot rate for a call or greater than the current spot rate for a put. Note that the prices of options rise in Table 13.7 for those that are in the money.

Let's consider an example of a U.S. importer buying SF1,000,000 of Swiss watches to be paid for in three months. The current spot rate is $0.6371 per franc. At this rate, SF1,000,000 is equal to $637,100. To hedge against unexpected exchange rate change, the importer could buy a March option. Suppose he or she wants a striking price of $0.65, so that the upper bound on the value of the imports is $650,000. In Table 13.7, a March call option with a strike price of $0.65 sells for $0.0092 or 0.92 cents per franc, so one contract for SF62,500 costs $575. To cover SF1 million, the importer must buy 16 contracts (16 × 62,500 = 1 million) at a cost of $9,200. If the franc appreciates above $0.65, the option will be exercised. For instance, if the March spot price is $0.68, then using the spot market would mean a cost of $680,000 for the imports. Exercising the option contracts ensures a price of $650,000, so that the firm saves $30,000 less the $9,200 premium compared with what would occur with an unhedged position. If the franc does not appreciate to the level of the striking price, then the option is allowed to expire. For instance, if the March spot price is $0.63, then using the spot market would mean a cost of $630,000 for the imports. This is $20,000 less than the cost using the option contracts. In this case, the firm is out the $9,200 it paid for the options.

If we knew with certainty what the future exchange rate would be, there would be no market for options, futures, or forward contracts. In an uncertain world, risk-averse traders willingly pay to avoid the potential loss associated with adverse movements in exchange rates. An advantage of options over futures or forwards is greater flexibility. A futures or forward contract is an obligation to buy or sell at a set exchange rate. An option offers the right to buy or sell if desired in the future and is not an obligation.

CENTRAL-BANK INTERVENTION

Thus far, we have not explicitly introduced government into the foreign-exchange market; but, of course, central banks and national treasuries play a large role in the market. Because the exchange rate is the price of one money in terms of another, changes in exchange rates will affect the prices of goods and services traded internationally. This is a major reason for official intervention in the foreign-exchange market. Central banks, such as the Federal Reserve in the United States, buy and sell currencies to drive the value of their money to levels other than what the free market would establish. Let's use the foreign exchange market supply and demand diagram of Figure 13.3 to illustrate how intervention works. In this diagram, the demand for pounds in exchange for dollars comes from the U.S. demand for British goods, services, and financial assets. The supply of pounds in exchange for dollars comes from the British demand for U.S. goods, services, and financial assets. For instance, if initially the dollar-per-pound exchange rate is $/£ = 1.60, and then the U.S. demand for British goods increases, this causes the demand for pounds to increase from D to D' in Figure 13.3. As a result, the pound begins to appreciate against the dollar, and U.S. imports from England would become more expensive. This is clearly seen if we assume that the exchange rate has changed from $/£ = 1.60 at point A to $/£ = 1.70 at point C. A product selling for £100 in England would find its dollar price in the United States changing from $160 to $170. To help stimulate U.K. exports, the Bank of England may desire to halt the appreciation of the pound by selling pounds on the foreign-exchange market. If the supply curve shifted to the right to S', then a new equilibrium at point B would be established so that 1.60 is again the equilibrium exchange rate, but now a higher quantity of pounds $£_0'$ is being traded. As the supply of pounds to the market increases, the price of pounds tends to fall, just the same as an increase in the supply of apples lowers the price of apples.

In the case of a depreciating domestic currency, central banks often sell foreign currencies in exchange for domestic currency to halt the depreciation. For example,

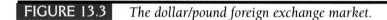

FIGURE 13.3   *The dollar/pound foreign exchange market.*

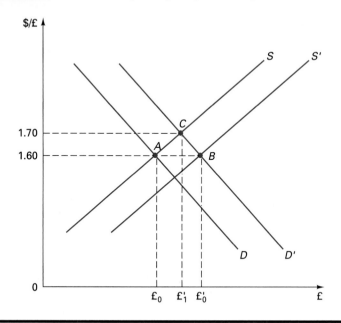

instead of the Bank of England selling pounds to stop the pound appreciation in Figure 13.3, the Federal Reserve could have sold pounds. Because they often do not hold sufficient stocks of the desired foreign currencies, swap arrangements are used as an efficient way to borrow from foreign official institutions. The Federal Reserve has established line-of-swap arrangements with other institutions that may be drawn upon when the need arises. Any sizable central-bank interventions in the foreign-exchange market will involve either the Federal Reserve or a foreign central bank drawing currency balances from the swap facility; these are then replenished at a later date after the value of the currency has stabilized.

Official institutions appear in the foreign-exchange markets for reasons other than intervening in the determination of exchange rates. In the course of the normal operations of government, it is often necessary to use the foreign-exchange market to facilitate the transfer of goods and services internationally. The role of the various central banks is to conduct foreign-exchange operations for central governments.

BLACK MARKETS AND PARALLEL MARKETS

So far, we have discussed the foreign-exchange market as a market where currencies are bought and sold openly by individuals, business firms, and governments. For the major developed countries, this is an accurate description. However, developing countries generally do not permit free markets in foreign exchange and impose many restrictions on foreign-currency transactions. These restrictions take many forms, such as government licensing requirements, limited amounts of foreign currency that may be purchased, a limited time after the receipt of foreign currency before it must be sold to the central bank, or even outright prohibitions of foreign-currency use by private concerns.

As a result of government restrictions or legal prohibitions on foreign-exchange transactions, illegal markets in foreign exchange develop to satisfy trader demand. These illegal markets are known as **black markets**. In many countries, such illegal markets exist openly with little or no government enforcement of legal prohibitions. In other countries, foreign-exchange laws are strictly enforced and lawbreakers receive harsh sentences when caught.

Black market
An illegal market in foreign exchange.

Often, the government sets an official exchange rate that deviates widely from what the free market would establish. If the government will purchase foreign exchange only at the official rate but private citizens are willing to pay the market-determined rate, there will be a steady supply of foreign exchange to the black market. Obviously, government policy creates the black market. The demand arises because of legal restrictions on buying foreign exchange, and the supply exists because of government-mandated official exchange rates that offer less than the free market. Ironically, governments defend the need for foreign-exchange restrictions based on conserving scarce foreign exchange for high-priority uses. But such restrictions work to reduce the amount of foreign exchange that flows to the government as traders turn to the black market instead. Item 13.2 provides an example of the workings of a black market in Iraq.

In many countries facing economic hardship, the illegal markets have allowed normal economic activities to continue through a steady supply of foreign exchange. Some governments have unofficially acknowledged the benefits of a black market by allowing the market to openly exist. For instance, Guatemala had an artificially low official exchange rate of one quetzale per dollar for more than three decades. However, a black market was allowed to flourish openly in front of the country's main post office, where the exchange rate fluctuated daily with market conditions. In many Latin American countries, the post office is a center for black-market trading since relatives living in the United States send millions of dollars in checks and money orders home. In Guatemala, the government allowed such activity openly, as foreign-currency traders called to people leaving the post office, offering to buy dollars. This sort of government-tolerated alternative to the official exchange market is often referred to as a **parallel market**.

Parallel market
A free market allowed to coexist with the official market.

While many other anecdotes could be included, the point is to note the fact that foreign-exchange trading has a dimension beyond the open trading and single exchange rate that exist for the major developed countries. In developing countries, foreign-exchange transactions are generally heavily regulated activities. In many countries, the official exchange rate has no relation to current economic reality, so we should expect black markets or parallel markets to flourish.

ITEM 13.2	Dollars for Dinars

To check economic conditions in Iraq, all one has to do is walk down a narrow side street and watch how the black market exchange rate is changing between the U.S. dollar and Iraqi dinar. In a 1996 *Wall Street Journal* article,[*] activity in the market is described as being highly sensitive to foreign news reports on the Iraqi economy, which domestic residents hear on short-wave radios. The article describes activity on a recent day as follows:

"'I've got a book,' shouts a changer, using code for the clutch of 100 hundred dollar bills he is hoisting. 'Who wants it for 12 million?' Several prospective buyers huddling on the sidewalk call out, and one man grabs the changer by the elbow, hustling him away with an anxious glance over his shoulder. The deal is done behind a parked Toyota. Then the changer, struggling under the weight of three burlap sacks packed with Iraqi currency, makes his way back to his closet-sized storefront, where he masquerades as a cigarette merchant, to tune in to the foreign news on his short-wave radio. What he hears out of Washington or New York, and how he interprets it, will decide what he offers for dollars during his next venture onto the street-side trading floor.

"A U.S. missile strike? That will boost the dollar by 800 Iraqi dinars at least. A visit to the city by the United Nations weapons-inspection team? That's possibly good news, and merits about a 10-dinar decrease.... A statement by Madeline Albright, U.S. ambassador to the U.N. on the suspended pact to allow Iraq to sell oil to buy food? Hardly worth trading on.... 'We care more about action than words,' says Ali, at age 21 a self-taught political analyst and one of the thousands of illicit money-changers in Baghdad whose assessment of the news determines the price of everything from Jordanian light bulbs to home-grown hummus.

"... Depending on how traders interpret what they hear on their ubiquitous short-wave radios,

or what they read in the five newspapers published daily in this city, the value of the Iraqi currency can change by the hour, in times of crisis by the minute.... The money market fluctuates so wildly because it is all based on people's wavering expectations of when Iraq will be able again to export oil—its sole foreign-currency earner—and because virtually everything in Iraq nowadays is imported. When oil flows, Iraq is awash in dollars, which the government sells to the people at inexpensive rates ... so the less likely it appears that oil will flow again soon, the more despondent people become and the more determined they are to buy ever-scarcer dollars on the black market, which means bad news makes the dollar rise against the dinar; good news makes it fall.

"The system drives merchants to distraction, and has created a class of reluctant political junkies. 'We're forced to become experts in international politics,' says Bashar Hashim, a flour and rice dealer. He telephones the money-changers as often as twice an hour to check on the dinar's status, shouting into the receiver the question posed by his colleagues throughout the country countless times a day, 'What's the new price?' Mr. Hashim also spends far more time than he would like with his ear pressed up against the speaker of his ancient Iraqi-made radio, calculating the impact the news will have on his costs and how much he must charge his clients."

Black market exchange rates are set by the free market forces of supply and demand. The Iraqi case, described above, is illustrative of how prices rise and fall as people expect the supply and demand for the currencies traded to increase or decrease over time.

---
[*]Anne Reifenberg, "Dialing for Dinars: Iraqis Turn On Radio To Set Exchange Rate," *Wall Street Journal*, September 20, 1996, p. A1.

SUMMARY

1. The foreign-exchange market is a global market where foreign-currency-denominated deposits are traded. Trading in actual currency notes is generally limited to tourism or illegal activities.

2. The spot market is for current delivery, and the forward market is for delivery of foreign exchange at a future date.

3. Arbitrage ensures that exchange rates are transaction costs close in all markets.

4. If the forward price of a currency exceeds (is below) the spot price, the currency is said to sell at a premium (discount).

5. Besides the forward market, foreign-exchange assets and liabilities may be hedged in the futures market and the options market.

6. Central banks intervene in the foreign-exchange market when they feel that exchange rates should be changed.

7. Black markets or parallel markets in foreign exchange arise due to government regulation of the foreign-exchange market.

EXERCISES

1. As a treasurer of a large U.S. corporation, you must decide how best to manage the firm's cash flows to maximize profits, subject to maintaining an acceptable level of risk. Your firm has an account payable to a French firm of €2,000,000 due in 180 days. Review the options available for managing this foreign-currency liability. Is there any reason to prefer one course of action over another?

2. In the following examples, is the dollar selling at a premium or at a discount?

Spot	Three-Month Forward
(a) $/£ = 1.77	$/£ = 1.78
(b) $/¥ = 0.004	$/¥ = 0.005
(c) $/DM = 0.40	DM/$ = 2.50
(d) €/$ = 6.60	$/€ = 0.15
(e) $/SF = 0.51	SF/$ = 1.94

3. Suppose £1 = $2.4110 in New York, $1 = FF3.997 in Paris, and FF1 = £0.1088 in London.
    a. If you begin by holding £1, then how could you profit from these exchange rates?
    b. Ignoring transaction costs, what is your arbitrage profit per pound initially traded?

4. You could analyze changes in foreign-exchange rates by using supply and demand diagrams. Construct an example for the $/£ exchange rate wherein the dollar appreciates relative to the pound. Carefully label your diagram and have the initial exchange rate equal to 1.60. What might cause the supply and/or demand curve to move in the manner illustrated (what are the underlying

reasons for exchange rate movements)? Then, indicate what sort of central-bank intervention would be necessary to prevent the exchange rate from moving away from the initial equilibrium.

5. What is the difference between an American option and a European option? When is an option "in the money"?

6. Suppose you are the treasurer of a firm importing calculators from Japan. You have a ¥62,500,000 payable due in 90 days. The current spot rate is $0.005 per yen, but you expect the yen to appreciate against the dollar over the next 90 days and buy a call option contract on yen. The premium on the option is 0.0002, and the striking price is 0.0055. What is the dollar cost of the contract? If the spot rate in 90 days is 0.0052, do you exercise the option or let it expire? What was your dollar gain or loss from holding the option contract? If the spot rate in 90 days is 0.0057, do you exercise the option or let it expire? What was your dollar gain or loss from holding the option contract?

7. A bicycle manufactured in the United States costs $100. Using the exchange rates listed in Table 13.1, what would the bicycle cost in each of the following countries?
   a. Argentina
   b. Brazil
   c. Canada
   d. Hong Kong
   e. Italy
   f. Mexico
   g. Philippines

8. The U.S. dollar price of a Swedish krona changes from $.1572 to $.1730.
   a. Has the dollar depreciated or appreciated against the krona?
   b. Has the krona appreciated or depreciated against the dollar?

REFERENCES

Central Bank Survey of Foreign Exchange and Derivatives Market Activity. Basle: Bank for International Settlements, May 1999.

Coy, Peter, De'Ann Weimer, and Amy Barrett, "Perils of the Hedge Highwire," *Business Week,* October 26, 1998, pp. 74–76.

Gonnelli, Adam, *The Basics of Foreign Trade and Exchange.* Federal Reserve Bank of New York, 1993.

Volcker, Paul A., and Toyoo Gyohten, *Changing Fortunes.* New York: Times Books, 1992.

INTERNET APPLICATIONS

Please visit our Web site at www.awl.com/husted_melvin for more exercises and readings.

APPENDIX 13.1

EXCHANGE RATE INDEXES

Suppose we want to consider the value of a currency. One measure is the bilateral exchange rate—say, the yen value of the dollar or the lira value of the mark. However, if we are interested in knowing how a currency is performing globally, we need a broader measure of a currency's value against many other currencies. This is analogous to looking at a consumer price index to measure how prices in an economy are changing. We could look at the price of shoes or the price of a loaf of bread, but such single-good prices will not necessarily reflect the general inflationary situation—some prices may be rising while others are falling.

In the foreign-exchange market, it is common to see a currency rising in value against one foreign money while it depreciates relative to another. As a result, *exchange rate indexes* are constructed to measure the average value of a currency relative to several other currencies. An exchange rate index is a weighted average of a currency's value relative to other currencies, wherein the weights are typically based on the importance of each currency to international trade. If we want to construct an exchange rate index for the United States, we would include the currencies of those countries that are the major trading partners of the United States.

If half of U.S. trade were with Canada and the other half were with Mexico, then the percentage change in the trade-weighted dollar exchange rate index would be found by multiplying the percentage change in both the Canadian dollar/dollar and Mexican peso/dollar exchange rates by 1/2 and summing the result. Table A13.1 lists two popular exchange rate indexes and their weighting schemes. The indexes listed are those of the Federal Reserve Board (FRB) and the Federal Reserve Bank of Atlanta (FRBA).

Since the different indexes are constructed using different currencies, should we expect them to tell a different story? It is entirely possible for a currency to be appreciating against some currencies while depreciating against others. Therefore, not all the exchange rate indexes will move identically, but all will show the same general trends. Figure A13.1 plots the movement of the indexes from 1980 to 1999.

Figure A13.1 indicates that the value of the dollar generally rose in the early 1980s and then fell in the late 1980s—a conclusion we draw regardless of the exchange rate index used. This suggests that for discerning broad trends in the value of a currency, all indexes tell much the same story. Yet for shorter-term movements, where the magnitude of the change is important, there can be differences across exchange rate indexes. Since different indexes assign a different importance to each foreign currency, this is not surprising.

Exchange rate indexes are commonly used tools of analysis in international economics. When changes in the average value of a currency are important, bilateral exchange rates (between only two currencies) are unsatisfactory. Neither economic theory nor practice gives a clear indication of which exchange rate index is best. In fact, for some questions there is little to differentiate one index from another. In many cases, however, the best index to use will depend on the question addressed.

TABLE A13.1 *Percentage Weights Assigned to Major Currencies in Two U.S. Dollar Exchange Rate Indexes*

	Exchange Rate Index	
Country	FRBA	FRB
Canada	24.6	18.0
Euro area	16.6	18.2
Japan	15.6	20.4
Mexico	11.0	4.7
China	5.5	2.3
United Kingdom	5.1	5.2
Taiwan	4.2	5.3
Korea	4.1	4.8
Singapore	3.0	2.2
Malaysia	2.3	1.1
Hong Kong	2.1	3.0
Brazil	1.9	2.4
Saudi Arabia	1.4	0.9
Switzerland	1.3	2.4
Australia	1.3	1.9
Other	—	7.1
TOTAL	100.0	100.0

FIGURE A13.1 *U.S. dollar exchange rate according to two indexes, 1980–1999.*

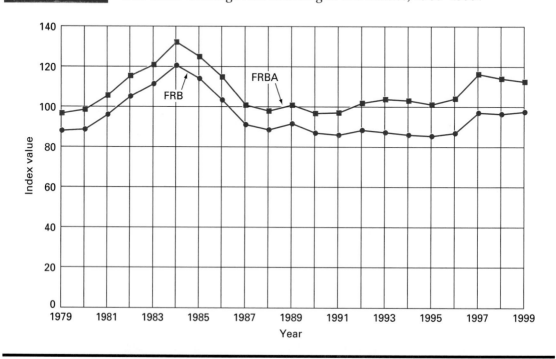

CHAPTER 14

Prices and Exchange Rates: Purchasing Power Parity

KEY WORDS

Nominal value
Law of one price
Relative price change
Random
Endogenous variable
Exogenous variable

Shock
News
Spurious relationship
Overvalued currency
Undervalued currency

Chapter 13 discussed the role of foreign-exchange-market arbitrage in keeping foreign-exchange rates the same in different locations. If the dollar price of a yen is higher at Bank of America in San Francisco than at Morgan Guaranty Bank in New York, we would expect traders to buy yen from Morgan Guaranty and simultaneously sell yen to Bank of America. This activity would raise the dollar/yen exchange rate quoted by Morgan Guaranty and lower the rate at Bank of America until the exchange rate quotations are transaction costs close. Such arbitrage activity is not limited to the foreign-exchange market. We would expect arbitrage to be present in any market where similar goods are traded in different locations. For instance, the price of gold is roughly the same worldwide at any point in time. If gold sold at a higher price in one location than in another, arbitragers would buy gold where it is cheap and sell where it is high until the prices are equal (allowing for transaction costs). Similarly, we would expect the price of tractors or automobiles or sheet steel to be related across geographically disparate markets. However, as we shall see in this chapter, there are good economic reasons why some goods prices are more similar across countries than others.

This tendency for similar goods to sell for similar prices globally provides a link between prices and exchange rates. If we wanted to know why exchange rates change over time, one obvious answer is that as prices change internationally, exchange rates must also change to keep the prices measured in a common currency equal across countries. In other words, exchange rates should adjust to offset differing inflation rates between countries. This relation between goods and services prices and exchange rates is known as purchasing power parity (PPP). Although we are hesitant to refer to purchasing power parity as a theory of the exchange rate, for reasons that will be made apparent subsequently, it is important to study the relationship between price levels and exchange rates to understand the role of goods markets (as separate from financial-asset markets) in international finance.

ABSOLUTE PURCHASING POWER PARITY

The first view of purchasing power parity to be considered is absolute purchasing power parity. Here, we consider the exchange rate to be given by the ratio of price levels between countries. If E is the spot exchange rate (domestic-currency units per foreign unit), P the domestic price index, and P^F the foreign price index, the absolute PPP relation is written as

$$P/P^F = E \tag{14.1}$$

For those readers who are not familiar with price indexes, P and P^F may be thought of as consumer price indexes, or producer price indexes, or price indexes used to convert the gross domestic product (GDP) from nominal to real magnitudes—known as GDP deflators. A price index is supposed to measure average prices in an economy and therefore is subject to the criticism that, in fact, it measures the actual prices faced by no one. To construct such an index, we must first determine which prices to include, that is, which goods and services are to be monitored. Then, these various items need to be assigned weights reflecting their importance in total spending. Thus, the consumer price index would weight housing prices very heavily, but bread prices would have a very small weight. The final index is a weighted average of the prices of the goods and services surveyed. Item 14.1 describes the actual weighting of items in the U.S. consumer price index.

Phrased in terms of price indexes, absolute PPP, as given in Equation 14.1, indicates that the exchange rate between any two currencies is equal to the ratio of their price indexes. Thus, the exchange rate is a **nominal value,** dependent on prices. When using real-world price index data, we should be careful that the various national price indexes we use are comparable in terms of goods and/or services covered as well as base year (the reference year used for comparisons over time). If

Nominal value
A value dependent on current price levels.

ITEM 14.1 | The U.S. Consumer Price Index

It is easy to understand the problems that arise when making comparisons of different nations' prices by considering how the consumer price index (CPI) in the United States is measured. To construct a single value for "the price level," it is necessary to calculate a weighted average of individual product and service prices that the typical household might consume.

One problem that arises is the appropriate measure of housing costs (what kind of house?), clothing costs (what sort of clothes?), or the costs of any other particular category of goods. Assuming such problems are solved, each individual product price must be weighted according to its importance in the typical consumer budget. So, housing takes the largest weight, while other products are assigned smaller weights. The percentage breakdown across items included in the CPI for the United States is given in the following table:

The Relative Importance of Components of the Consumer Price Index

All items	100.0
Food and beverages	16.3
Housing	39.6
Apparel and upkeep	4.9
Transportation	17.6
Medical care	5.6
Entertainment	6.1
Education and communication	5.5
Other goods and services	4.3

The table indicates that housing accounts for over 39 percent of the typical household budget. Transportation takes approximately 18 percent, while food accounts for about 16 percent. Obviously, every household in the United States is different, so the CPI is a crude indicator of the prices facing your household. Imagine the problems if we compare a Japanese or Mexican price index with the U.S. index. Will the typical Japanese or Mexican household buy the same goods as the U.S. household will? Is housing, food, or transportation going to claim the same fraction of the U.S., Japanese, or Mexican consumer budget? The answer to these questions is no! Since people in different countries consume different goods and spend their incomes differently, we must be cautious in drawing conclusions based on comparisons of price indexes across countries.

changes in the world were only nominal, due to price-level change, then we would expect PPP to hold if we had true price indexes. The significance of this last sentence will be illustrated soon.

Equation 14.1 can be rewritten as

$$P = EP^F \tag{14.2}$$

Law of one price
Similar goods sell for the same price worldwide.

so that the domestic price level is equal to the product of the domestic-currency price of foreign currency and the foreign price level. Equation 14.2 is called the **law of one price** and indicates that goods sell for the same price worldwide. For instance, we might observe a shirt selling for $10 in the United States and for £4 in the United Kingdom. If the $/£ exchange rate is $2.50 per pound, then $P = EP^F = (2.50)(4) = 10$. Thus, the price of the shirt in the United Kingdom is the same as the U.S. price once we convert the pound price into dollars, using the exchange rate, and compare prices in a common currency.

Unfortunately for this analysis, the world is more complex than the simple shirt example. The real world is characterized by differentiated products, costly information, and all sorts of impediments to the equalization of goods prices worldwide. Certainly, the more homogeneous goods are, the more we expect the law of one price to hold. Some commodities, which retain essentially the same form worldwide, provide the best example of the law of one price. Gold, for instance, is quoted in dollar prices internationally, and thus we would be correct in stating that the law of one price holds quite close for gold. However, shirts come in different styles, brand names, and prices, and we do not expect the law of one price to hold for shirts domestically, let alone internationally.

Economists have questioned why we would ever expect PPP to hold, since we know that international trade involves freight charges and tariffs. Given these costs associated with shipping goods, we would not expect PPP to hold for any particular good, so why would we anticipate the relationship phrased in terms of price indexes to hold, as in Equation 14.1? Furthermore, not all goods are traded internationally, yet the prices of these goods are captured in the national price indexes. As the nontraded goods prices change, the price indexes change. Yet the exchange rates may not vary, since the changing prices of nontraded goods would not give rise to international trade flows, and so no change in the supply and demand for currencies need result.* Recently, economists have added many refinements to the analysis of PPP, which we need not consider here. The important lesson to be learned is the potential problem associated with using price indexes to explain exchange rate changes.

---

*In Michael Melvin and David Bernstein, "Trade Concentration, Openness, and Deviations from Purchasing Power Parity," *Journal of International Money and Finance* (December 1984), a study of 87 countries revealed that purchasing power parity holds better for more open economies (where internationally traded goods constitute a large fraction of GDP) than for more closed economies (where traded goods are a similar fraction of GDP). In P. G. J. O'Connell, "Market Frictions and Real Exchange Rates," *Journal of International Money and Finance* (February 1998), the role of impediments to trade is discussed.

So far, we have emphasized variations in the exchange rate brought about by changing price indexes or nominal changes. However, it is reasonable to believe that much of the week-to-week change in exchange rates is due to real rather than nominal events. Besides variations in the price level due to general inflation, we can also identify **relative price changes.** Inflation results in an increase in all prices, but relative price changes indicate that not all prices move together. Some prices increase faster than others, and some rise while others fall. An old analogy that students often find useful is to think of inflation as an elevator carrying a load of tennis balls representing the prices of individual goods. As the inflation continues, the balls are carried higher by the elevator, which means that all prices are rising. But as the inflation continues and the elevator rises, the balls, or individual prices, are bouncing up and down. So, while the elevator raises all the balls inside, the balls do not bounce up and down together. The balls bouncing up have their prices rising relative to the balls going down.

Relative price change The price of one good relative to another good changes.

If we think of different elevators as representing different countries, then, if the balls were still and the elevators rose at the same rate, the exchange rate would be constant, as suggested by purchasing power parity. Also, if we looked for sufficiently long intervals, we could ignore the bouncing balls, because the large movements in the elevators would dominate the exchange rate movements. If, however, we observed very short intervals during which the elevators move only slightly, we would find that the bouncing balls, or relative price changes of individual goods, will largely determine the exchange rate.

Exchange rates can change due to real economic events, even with average price levels constant. Since PPP is usually discussed in terms of price indexes, we find that real events, such as the relative price changes brought about by a poor harvest, will cause deviations from absolute PPP as the exchange rate changes, even if the price indexes remain constant.

The previous discussion has illustrated why absolute PPP probably fails to hold at most points in time. Saying that the level of the exchange rate is equal to the ratio of price indexes is quite a strong statement to make. In the next section, a less restrictive relationship between prices and exchange rates is discussed.

RELATIVE PURCHASING POWER PARITY

There is an alternative view of PPP besides the absolute PPP just discussed. Relative PPP is said to hold when

$$\hat{E} = \hat{P} - \hat{P}^F \tag{14.3}$$

where a caret ($\wedge$) over a variable denotes percentage change. So, Equation 14.3 says that the percentage change in the exchange rate ($\hat{E}$) is equal to the percentage change in the domestic price level ($\hat{P}$) minus the percentage change in the foreign price level ($\hat{P}^F$). Therefore, although absolute PPP states that the exchange rate is equal to the ratio of the price indexes, relative PPP deals with percentage changes in these variables.

We usually refer to the percentage change in the price level as the rate of inflation. So, another way of stating the relative PPP relationship is that the percentage change in the exchange rate is equal to the inflation differential between the domestic and foreign countries. If we say that the percentage change in the exchange rate is equal to the inflation differential, then we can ignore the actual levels of E, P, and P^F and consider the changes, which is not so strong an assumption as absolute PPP. It should be noted that if absolute PPP holds, then relative PPP will also hold. But if absolute PPP does not hold, relative PPP still may. This is because the level of E may not equal P/P^F, but the change in E could still equal the inflation differential.

Having observed in the last section how relative prices can determine exchange rates, we can, with reason, believe that these relative price changes will, over time, decrease in importance as compared with inflation rates, so that, in the long run, inflation differentials will dominate exchange rate movements. The idea is that real events causing relative price movements are often **random** and short-run in nature. By *random* we mean they are unexpected and equally likely to raise or lower the exchange rate. Given this characterization, it follows that these random relative price movements will tend to cancel out over time (otherwise, we would not consider them equally likely to raise or lower E).

Random

Moving in an unpredictable manner.

TIME, INFLATION, AND PPP

Several researchers have found that PPP holds better for high-inflation countries.* When we say "holds better," we mean that the equalities stated in Equations 14.1 and 14.3 are more closely met by actual exchange rate and price-level data observed over time in high-inflation countries compared with low-inflation countries. In high-inflation countries, changes in exchange rates are highly correlated with inflation differentials because the sheer magnitude of inflation overwhelms the relative price effects, whereas in low- or moderate-inflation countries, the relative price effects dominate exchange rate movements and lead to discrepancies from PPP. In terms of our earlier example, when the elevator is moving faster (high inflation), the movement of the balls inside (relative prices) is less important; however, when the elevator is moving slowly (low inflation), the bouncing balls will be quite important. Item 14.2 describes the experience with hyperinflation in Bolivia. In such an environment, the rapid inflation overwhelms any relative price movements and becomes the important factor determining the exchange rate.

Besides the rate of inflation, the period of time analyzed will also have an effect on how well PPP holds. We expect PPP to hold better for annual data than for monthly data because the longer time frame will allow for more inflation, so that the random relative price effects are relatively unimportant and we find exchange rate

---

*Studies in this area include Jacob Frenkel, "Purchasing Power Parity: Doctrinal Perspective and Evidence from the 1920s," *Journal of International Economics* (May 1978); and Shang-Jin Wei and David Parsley, "Purchasing Power Disparity during the Floating Rate Period: Exchange Rate Volatility, Trade Barriers, and Other Culprits," National Bureau of Economic Research Working Paper no. 5032 (February 1995).

ITEM 14.2 Hyperinflation in Bolivia

The highest inflation rate in the 1980s belonged to Bolivia. In 1982, consumer prices increased by 133 percent. This doubling of prices in a single year is shocking to most residents of developed countries, but by 1985, 100 percent inflation would have been welcome in Bolivia. During 1985, the inflation rate was 11,750 percent. As the Bolivian rate of inflation started to skyrocket, the value of the peso Boliviano relative to the U.S. dollar started to plummet. At the end of 1982, 1 dollar cost 196 pesos. At the end of 1985, 1 dollar cost 1,692,000 pesos. It is safe to say that when a currency depreciates by more than 13,000 percent in 3 years, relative price change is irrelevant. The depreciation is a result of policies that created the tremendous inflation differential between the peso Boliviano and the dollar.

In 1985 Bolivia, prices increased daily or even hourly. The *Wall Street Journal* reported that in 1 week, the price of one egg increased from 3,000 pesos to 10,000 pesos. In the same article, a pharmacist stated that she bought a new Toyota in 1982 for the same number of pesos that she now charges for three boxes of aspirin. As the price level rose in Bolivia, the purchasing power of the peso fell at home. Because the peso bought less at home, arbitrage ensured that it also bought less in other countries. As the value of the peso fell on the foreign-exchange market, the purchasing power of the peso fell in terms of other nations' prices.

While relative price change can be an important factor in exchange rate movements, you can bet that relative price changes were unimportant in the Bolivian experience of 1985, where customers would have needed to carry 68 pounds of 1,000-peso bills to the store to buy an average television set.

changes closely related to inflation differentials. Using the elevator analogy again, the longer the time frame analyzed, the farther the elevator will move; and the more the elevator moves, the less important will be the individual bouncing balls inside. This suggests that studies of PPP covering many years will be more likely to yield evidence of PPP than studies based on data of a few years only.

The literature on PPP is voluminous and tends to confirm the statements just made. There is evidence that real relative price shifts can have an important role in the short run, but over time the random nature of the relative price changes minimizes the importance of these unrelated events.* Several studies have analyzed long periods of time (100 years or more) and concluded that PPP holds well in the long run.†

---

*See Hali J. Edison, "Purchasing Power Parity in the Long Run: A Test of the Dollar/Pound Exchange Rate (1890–1978)," *Journal of Money, Credit, and Banking* (August 1987).
†See Lawrence Officer, "Effective Exchange Rates and Price Ratios over the Long Run: A Test of the Purchasing Power Parity Theory," *Canadian Journal of Economics* (May 1980); Niso Abuaf and Philippe Jorion, "Purchasing Power Parity in the Long Run," *Journal of Finance* (March 1990); Yoon-bai Kim, "Purchasing Power Parity in the Long Run: A Cointegration Approach," *Journal of Money, Credit, and Banking* (November 1990); Francis X. Diebold, Steven Husted, and Mark Rush, "Real Exchange Rates under the Gold Standard," *Journal of Political Economy* (December 1991); and James R. Lothian and Mark P. Taylor, "Real Exchange Rate Behavior: The Recent Float from the Perspective of the Past Two Centuries," *Journal of Political Economy* (June 1996).

Figure 14.1 demonstrates the difference between examining PPP on a monthly basis versus an annual basis. In panel a of the figure, the annual percentage change in the exchange rate ($\hat{E}$) is plotted along with the inflation differential between Japan and the United States ($\hat{P}_J - \hat{P}_U$). In panel b, the monthly data for each variable are plotted. There are two obvious lessons in this figure: First, the exchange rates are much more variable than the inflation differentials; and second, deviations from PPP are much more apparent for monthly data than for annual data.

In this figure, deviations from PPP are indicated by a divergence between the $\hat{E}$ line and the $\hat{P}_J - \hat{P}_U$ line. If relative PPP held perfectly, then $\hat{E} = \hat{P}_J - \hat{P}_U$ (as in Equation 14.3), and the two lines would merge into one line. When the percentage change in the exchange rate differs from the inflation differential, there is a deviation from PPP. A glance at Figure 14.1 indicates that such deviations are more pronounced for monthly data than for annual data. The next section provides an analysis of the economic basis for such deviations.

DEVIATIONS FROM PPP

So far, the discussion has included several reasons why deviations from PPP occur. When we discussed the role of arbitrage in goods markets, we said that the law of one price would not apply to differentiated products or to products that are not traded internationally. Also, since international trade involves shipping goods across national borders, prices may differ due to shipping costs or tariffs. Relative price changes have been emphasized as a reason why PPP would hold better in the long run than the short run. Such relative price changes are due to real economic events, such as changing tastes, bad weather, or government policy. The law of one price could hold for individual goods, yet PPP could be violated for a price index. This, of course, just points out a problem in using price indexes rather than individual goods prices to measure PPP. Since consumers in different countries consume different goods, price indexes are not directly comparable internationally. We know that evaluating PPP between the United States and Japan using the U.S. and Japanese consumer price indexes is weakened by the fact that the typical Japanese consumer will buy a different basket of goods than the typical U.S. consumer. In this case, the law of one price could hold perfectly for individual goods, yet we would observe deviations from PPP using the consumer price index for Japan and the United States.

Recognizing that there are problems in using national price indexes to measure PPP might lead us to believe that PPP, or the law of one price, should hold well for individual goods. Yet there is evidence that PPP does not hold well for many individual goods traded internationally.* There are several reasons why this may be true.

---

*See Peter Isard, "How Far Can We Push the Law of One Price?" *American Economic Review* (December 1977); Aris A. Protopapadakis and Hans R. Stoll, "The Law of One Price in International Commodity Markets: A Reformulation and Some Formal Tests," *Journal of International Money and Finance* (September 1986); Alberto Giovannini, "Exchange Rates and Traded Goods Prices," *Journal of International Economics* (February 1988); and Charles Engel and John H. Rogers, "How Wide Is the Border?" *American Economic Review* (December 1996).

FIGURE 14.1 *U.S.–Japan purchasing power parity.*

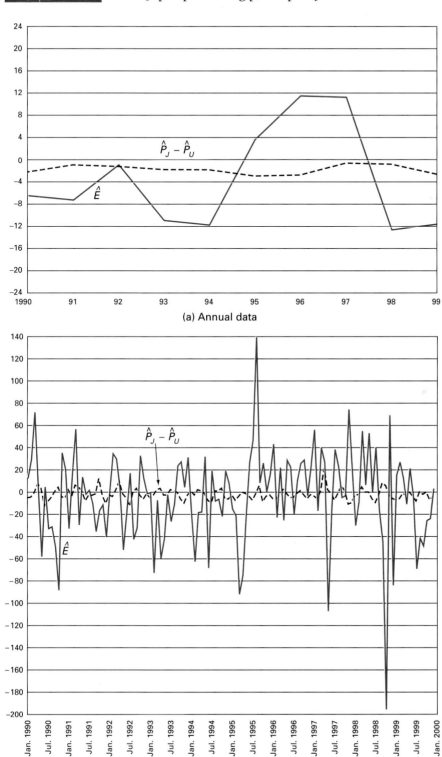

(a) Annual data

(b) Monthly data

Endogenous variable
A variable whose value is determined by some given factors.

Exogenous variable
A variable whose value is given to the economic system by an outside force, such as government or nature.

Shock
An unexpected change.

News
Unexpected information.

First of all, it is important to realize that PPP is not a theory of exchange rate determination. In other words, inflation differentials do not *cause* exchange rate change. PPP is an equilibrium relationship between two **endogenous variables.** When we say that prices and exchange rates are endogenous, we mean that they are simultaneously determined by other factors, such as bad weather or government policy (variables considered to be **exogenous**). Given a change in an exogenous variable, like poor weather and a consequent poor harvest, both prices and exchange rates will change. Deviations in measured PPP will occur if prices and exchange rates change at different speeds. Evidence indicates that, following some exogenous **shock,** changes in exchange rates precede changes in prices.

Such a finding can be explained by theorizing that the price indexes used for PPP calculations move slowly because commodity prices are not so flexible as financial-asset prices (the exchange rate is the price of monies). We know that exchange rates vary throughout the day as the demand and supply for foreign exchange varies. But how often does a department store change the price of furniture, or how often does an auto parts store change the price of tires? Since the prices that enter into published price indexes are slower to adjust than exchange rates are, it is not surprising that exchange rate changes seem to lead price changes. Yet if exchange rates change faster than goods prices, we have another reason why PPP should hold better in the long run than the short run. When economic **news** is received, both exchange rates and prices may change. For instance, suppose the Federal Reserve announces today that it will promote a 100 percent increase in the U.S. money supply over the next 12 months. Such a change would cause greater inflation, as more money in circulation leads to higher prices. The dollar would also fall in value relative to other currencies, as the supply of dollars rises relative to the demand. Following the Fed's announcement, would you expect goods prices in the United States to rise before the dollar depreciates on the foreign-exchange market? While there are some important issues in exchange rate determination that must wait until later chapters, we generally can say here that the dollar would depreciate immediately after the announcement. If traders believe that the dollar will be worth less in the future, they will attempt to sell dollars now, and this selling activity drives down the dollar's value today. There should be similar forces at work in the goods market, as traders expecting higher prices in the future buy more goods today. But for most goods, the immediate short-run result will be a depletion of inventories at constant prices. Only over time will most goods prices rise. Figure 14.2 illustrates how the exchange rate will shift with news. The figure illustrates the quantity of dollars bought and sold on the horizontal axis and the yen price of the dollar on the vertical axis. Initially, the foreign-exchange-market equilibrium occurs where the demand curve D_0 intersects the supply curve S_0, at an exchange rate of 140 yen per dollar with quantity $\$_0$ of dollars being bought and sold. Suppose the Federal Reserve now issues a statement causing people to expect the U.S. money supply to grow more rapidly in the future. This causes foreign-exchange traders to expect the dollar to depreciate in the future. As a result, they attempt to sell more dollars now, shifting the supply curve out to S_1 in Figure 14.2. This shift in supply, with constant demand, causes the dollar to depreciate now down to 120 yen per dollar. At this new exchange rate, quantity $\$_1$ is traded.

Suppose that PPP holds initially, so that $E = 140 = P^{JA}/P^{US}$. The announced change in monetary policy has an immediate effect on the exchange rate because currencies are traded continuously throughout the day. Prices of goods and services will change much more slowly. In the short run, the ratio of the price level in Japan to the price level in the United States may remain unchanged at 140. So, while E falls today to 120 in Figure 14.2, the ratio of the national price levels is still equal to the initial exchange rate of 140, and there is an apparent deviation from PPP.

Therefore, periods with important economic news will be periods when PPP deviations are large—the exchange rate adjusts while prices lag behind.* In addition to the differential speed of adjustment between exchange rates and prices, periods dominated by news are likely to be periods involving much relative price change, so that PPP deviations would tend to appear even when exchange rates and prices do not change at different speeds.†

Another reason why deviations from PPP are likely is that international trade involves lags between order and delivery. Prices are often set by contract today for goods that are to be delivered several months later. If we compare goods prices and

FIGURE 14.2 *Shifts in the foreign-exchange market and deviations from PPP.*

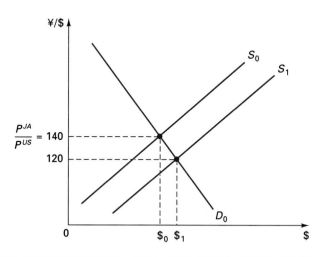

*This story is nicely demonstrated in Jacob A. Frenkel, "The Collapse of Purchasing Power Parities during the 1970s," *European Economic Review* (May 1981).
†This relative price effect is linked to "news" in Nurhan Davutyan and John Pippenger, "Purchasing Power Parity Did Not Collapse during the 1970s," *American Economic Review* (December 1985).

exchange rates today to evaluate PPP, we are using the exchange rate applicable to goods delivered today with prices that were set at some time in the past. Ideally, we should compare contract prices in each country at the time contracts are signed with the exchange rate that is expected to prevail in the future period when goods are actually delivered and payment is made. If the exchange rate actually realized in the future period is the same as that expected when the goods prices were agreed upon, then there would be no problem in using today's exchange rate and today's delivered goods prices. The problem is that, realistically, exchange rates are very difficult to forecast, so that seldom would today's realized exchange rate be equal to the trader's forecast at some past period.

Let's consider a simple example. Suppose on September 1, Ms. U.S. agrees to buy books from Mr. U.K. for £1 per book. At the time the contract is signed, books in the United States sell for $2, and the current exchange rate of $E_{\$/£} = 2$ ensures that the law of one price holds—a £1 book from the United Kingdom is selling for the dollar equivalent of $2 (the pound book price of £1 times the dollar price of the pound of $2). If the contract calls for delivery and payment on December 1 of £1 per book and Ms. U.S. expects the exchange rate and prices to be unchanged until December 1, she *expects* PPP to hold at the time the payment is due. Suppose on December 1 the actual exchange rate is £1 = $1.50. An economist researching the law of one price for books would compare book prices of £1 and $2 with the exchange rate of $E_{\$/£} = \$1.50$ and examine if

$$E_{\$/£} = P^{US}/P^{UK}$$

Spurious relationship
Not a genuine
relationship.

Since $\$1.50 \neq 2/1$, he or she would conclude that there are important deviations from PPP. Yet these deviations are **spurious.** At the time the prices were set, PPP was expected to hold. We generate the appearance of PPP deviations by comparing exchange rates today with prices that were set in the past.*

The possible explanations for deviations from PPP include factors that would suggest permanent deviations (shipping costs and tariffs), factors that would produce temporary deviations (differential speed of adjustment between financial-asset markets and goods markets or real relative price changes), and factors that cause the appearance of deviations where none may actually exist (comparing current exchange rates with prices set in the past or using national price indexes when countries consume different baskets of goods). Since PPP measurements convey information regarding the relative purchasing power of currencies, such measurements have served as a basis for economic policy discussions. The next section will provide an example of policy-related information contained in PPP measurement.

---

*The analysis of such a problem is found in Stephen P. Magee, "Contracting and Spurious Deviations from Purchasing Power Parity," in *The Economics of Exchange Rates,* ed. Jacob A. Frenkel and Harry G. Johnson (Reading, Mass.: Addison-Wesley, 1978).

"OVERVALUED" AND "UNDERVALUED" CURRENCIES

If we observe E, P, and P^F over time, we find that the absolute PPP relationship does not hold very well for any pair of countries. If, over time, P^F rises faster than P, we would expect E, the domestic-currency price of the foreign currency, to fall. If E does not fall by the amount suggested by the lower P/P^F, then we could say that the domestic currency is **undervalued** or (the same thing) the foreign currency is **overvalued**.

In the early 1980s, there was much talk of an "overvalued" dollar. The foreign-exchange value of the dollar appeared to be too high relative to the inflation differentials between the United States and the other developed countries.* The term *overvalued* suggests that the exchange rate is not where it should be; yet, if the free-market supply and demand factors are determining the exchange rate, then the "overvalued" exchange rate is actually the free-market equilibrium rate. In this case, the term *overvalued* might suggest that this equilibrium is but a temporary deviation from PPP, and over time the exchange rate will fall in line with the inflation differential.

Figure 14.3 illustrates what the pattern of percentage changes in exchange rates and price levels meant for the actual level of the mark/dollar exchange rate. Prior to 1981, the dollar appears to be undervalued in that the actual exchange rate is below that implied by PPP as measured by inflation differentials. In other words, the line labeled "PPP exchange rate" measures the values the exchange rate would take so that the percentage change in the exchange rate would equal the inflation differential between Germany and the United States. Figure 14.3 indicates that the actual exchange rate was below the PPP level—thus, the undervalued dollar. After 1981, the dollar appreciated against the mark at a faster rate than the inflation differential, so the dollar becomes "overvalued." By 1985, the dollar begins to depreciate against the mark and move toward the PPP value of the exchange rate.

Since we know that PPP does not hold well for any pair of countries in the short run with moderate inflation, we must always have currencies that appear "overvalued" or "undervalued" in a PPP sense. The issue becomes important when the deviation persists for some time and has significant macroeconomic consequences. The major political issue in the U.S. experience was that the "overvalued" dollar was hurting export-oriented industries. U.S. goods were rising in price to foreign buyers as the dollar appreciated. The problem was made visible by a large balance-of-trade

Undervalued currency
Currency worth less than PPP value.

Overvalued currency
Currency worth more than PPP value.

---

*During this period, several articles appeared addressing this apparent overvaluation. For instance, Jeffrey Frankel, "The Dazzling Dollar," *Brookings Papers on Economic Activity* 1 (1985); Paul Krugman, "Is the Strong Dollar Sustainable?" *Federal Reserve Bank of Kansas City* (1985); and Ronald I. McKinnon, "Dollar Overvaluation against the Yen and Mark in 1983: How to Coordinate Central Bank Policies" (Center for Economic Policy Research, discussion paper 7, May 1983). James R. Lothian, "Some New Stylized Facts of Floating Exchange Rates," *Journal of International Money and Finance* (February 1998), ranks the behavior of the dollar in the early 1980s as "one of the important puzzles of the past 25 years" (p. 29).

FIGURE 14.3   *The actual mark/dollar exchange rate and the PPP-implied exchange rate.*

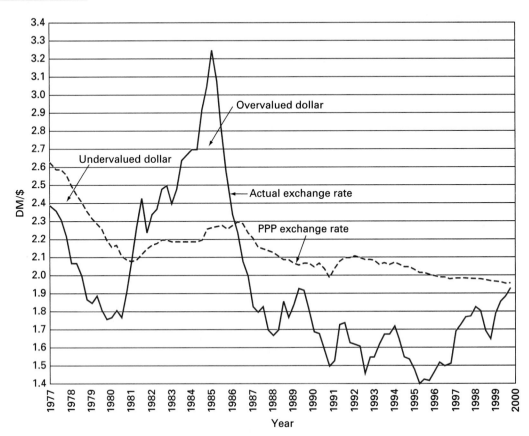

deficit that became a major political issue. In 1985, coordinated central bank intervention in the foreign-exchange market contributed to a dollar depreciation that reduced the PPP-implied dollar overvaluation.

Besides the dollar overvaluation relative to the currencies of the other developed countries, many developing countries have complained, from time to time, that their currencies are overvalued against the developed country currencies, and thus their balance of trade sustains a larger deficit than would otherwise occur. If PPP should apply only to internationally traded goods, then we can show how lower labor productivity in developing countries could contribute to the appearance of overvalued currencies. For nontraded goods, we assume that production methods are similar worldwide. It may make more sense to think of the nontraded goods sector as being largely services. In this case, the more productive countries tend to have higher wages and thus higher prices in the service sector than the less productive, low-wage countries. We now have a situation where the price indexes used to calculate PPP vary with productivity and hence with wages in each country. If we assume that exchange rates are determined by traded goods prices only (the idea being that if a good does not enter into international trade, there is no reason for its price to be equalized internationally and thus no reason for changes in its price to affect the exchange rate), then we can find how price indexes can vary with service prices while exchange rates are unaffected. For instance, the price of a haircut in Paris should not be affected by an increase in Los Angeles haircut prices. So if the price of haircuts should rise in Los Angeles, other things being equal, the average price level in the United States increases. But this U.S. price increase should not have any impact on the dollar per franc exchange rate. If, instead, the price of an automobile rises in the United States relative to French auto prices, we would expect the dollar to depreciate relative to the franc, as demand for French autos, and thus francs, increases, while U.S. auto, and thus dollar, demand decreases.

If the world operates in the way just described, then we would expect that the greater the traded goods productivity differentials between countries, the greater will be the wage differentials reflected in service prices, and thus the greater will be the deviations from absolute PPP over time. Suppose that developing countries, starting from lower absolute levels of productivity, have higher growth rates of productivity. If per capita income differences between countries give a reasonable measure of the productivity differences, then we would anticipate that as developing country per capita incomes increase relative to developed country per capita incomes, the price indexes of the developing countries will grow faster than those of the developed countries. At the same time, the depreciation of the developing country currencies will lag behind the inflation differentials, as measured by the average price levels in each country that include traded and nontraded goods prices. Thus, other things being equal, over time the currencies of the developing countries will tend to appear increasingly overvalued (the foreign-exchange values of developing country money have not depreciated as called for by the average price levels), whereas the developed country currencies will appear increasingly undervalued (the exchange values of foreign money have not appreciated enough).

The original studies linking productivity to PPP were written by Balassa and Samuelson in the 1960s.* Today, people sometimes refer to the hypothesis linking productivity differentials to PPP as the "Balassa–Samuelson effect." Evidence suggesting that the deviations from PPP as previously mentioned do indeed occur systematically with changes in per capita income has appeared in several studies.[†]

---

*Bela Balassa, "The Purchasing Power Parity Doctrine: A Reappraisal," *Journal of Political Economy* (December 1964) and Paul A. Samuelson, "Theoretical Notes on Trade Problems," *Review of Economics and Statistics* (February 1964).
[†]Examples are R. Summers and A. Heston, "The Penn World Table (Mark 5): An Expanded Set of International Comparisons, 1950–88," *Quarterly Journal of Economics* (May 1991); Jose DeGregorio, Alberto Giovanni, and Hoger Wolf, "International Evidence on Tradables and Nontradables Inflation," *European Economic Review* (June 1994); and Kenneth Rogoff, "The Purchasing Power Parity Puzzle," *Journal of Economic Literature* (June 1996).

What is the bottom line of the foregoing consideration? National price indexes are not particularly good indicators of the need for exchange rate adjustments. In this respect, it is not surprising to find that many studies since Balassa's have shown that absolute PPP does not hold. The idea that currencies are undervalued or overvalued can be misleading if exchange rates are free to change with changing market conditions. Only if the central-bank or government intervention interrupts the free adjustment of the exchange rate to market-clearing levels can we really talk about a currency as being overvalued or undervalued (and, in many such instances, black markets develop where the currency is traded at free-market prices). The fact that changes in PPP over time present the appearance of an undervalued currency in terms of the price indexes of two countries is perhaps more an indicator of the limitations of price indexes than of any real market phenomenon.

SUMMARY

1. If the exchange rate is equal to the ratio of the price indexes, absolute PPP holds.

2. If the percentage change in the exchange rate is equal to the inflation differential between two countries, relative PPP holds.

3. PPP holds better for high-inflation countries or long time periods when the movement of price levels overwhelms any relative price changes.

4. Deviations from PPP may arise from the presence of nontraded goods prices in price indexes, differentiated goods, shipping costs, tariffs, relative price changes, different consumption bundles across countries (and thus different goods included in national price indexes), prices fixed by contract, or differential speeds of adjustment of exchange rates and goods prices.

5. Currencies are said to be overvalued (undervalued) if they have appreciated more (less) than the difference between the domestic and foreign inflation rates.

EXERCISES

1. Answer true, false, or uncertain, and then *explain* your answer.
   a. Purchasing power parity holds better in the long run than in the short run.
   b. Purchasing power parity is no theory of exchange rate determination.
   c. If nontradable goods prices rise faster in country A than in country B, and if nontradable goods prices rise faster than prices in general, the currency of country A will appear to depreciate by more than is called for by PPP, as measured by price indexes. (Assume countries A and B are similar in other respects.)

2. For what type of goods does the law of one price hold quite well?

3. Why should purchasing power parity hold quite well during a hyperinflation?

4. List four reasons why deviations from PPP might occur; then, carefully explain how each reason causes such deviations.

5. Since PPP rarely holds at any point in time, is there any substantive meaning to the terms *overvalued* or *undervalued* currency?

6. Write an equation that describes PPP, and then explain the equation.

7. Suppose that on January 1, the yen price of the dollar is 120. Over the year, the Japanese inflation rate is 5 percent, and the U.S. inflation rate is 10 percent. If the exchange rate is $1 = ¥130 at the end of the year, does the yen appear to be overvalued, undervalued, or at the PPP level? Explain your answer.

8. In 1960, a U.S. dollar sold for 620 Italian lire. If PPP held in 1960, what would the PPP value of the exchange rate have been in 1987 if Italian prices rose 12 times and U.S. prices rose 4 times between 1960 and 1987?

9. Suppose at the beginning of the year, a best-selling book sells for EUR60 in Paris, France, and USD60 in New York City, and PPP holds. Over the year, there is an inflation rate of 10 percent in France and no inflation in the United States. What exchange rate would maintain PPP at the end of the year?

REFERENCES

Edison, Hali, Joseph Gagnon, and William Melick, "Understanding the Empirical Literature on Purchasing Power Parity, the Post–Bretton Woods Era," *Journal of International Money and Finance* (February 1997).

Froot, Kenneth A., and Kenneth Rogoff, "Perspectives on PPP and Long-Run Real Exchange Rates," in *Handbook of International Economics,* vol. 3, ed. G. Grossman and K. Rogoff (Amsterdam: Elsevier, 1995).

Koedijk, Kees, "The Pendulum of Exchange Rate Economics," *Journal of International Money and Finance* (February 1998).

Officer, L.H. *Purchasing Power Parity and Exchange Rates: Theory, Evidence, and Relevance* (Greenwich, Conn.: JAI Press, 1982).

INTERNET APPLICATIONS

Please visit our Web site at www.awl.com/husted_melvin for more exercises and readings.

CHAPTER 15

Exchange Rates,

Interest Rates, and

Interest Parity

TOPICS TO BE COVERED

Interest Parity
Interest Rates and Inflation
Exchange Rates, Interest Rates, and Inflation
Expected Exchange Rates and the Term Structure
    of Interest Rates

KEY WORDS

Covered return
Interest rate parity
Effective return
Uncovered interest parity

Nominal interest rate
Real interest rate
Fisher equation
Term structure of interest rates

International trade occurs in both goods and financial assets. Exchange rates change in a manner to accommodate this trade. Chapter 14 described a relationship between exchange rates and prices known as purchasing power parity. If markets for real goods could be costlessly arbitraged, we might expect PPP to hold, so that the price of a good in one country would be equal to the exchange-rate-adjusted price (so that the good is measured in terms of a common currency across countries) in another country. As we learned in Chapter 14, there are many reasons why PPP does not hold.

In this chapter, we study the relationship between interest rates and exchange rates. Instead of the goods market analysis of the last chapter, we now consider how exchange rates accommodate equilibrium in financial markets. In the PPP analysis of the last chapter we had a problem of comparing a financial-asset price—the exchange rate—with a ratio of real product prices. Since financial-asset prices typically adjust to new information more quickly than goods prices, PPP may not hold well in periods characterized by important economic news. However, because interest rates are the return to holding interest-bearing financial assets, we might expect interest rates to adjust quickly to new information, just as exchange rates do. We shall derive the interest parity relationship using an example of international investor behavior.

INTEREST PARITY

The interest parity relationship results from profit-seeking arbitrage activity, specifically *covered interest arbitrage*. Let us go through an example of how covered interest arbitrage works. For expositional purposes,

$i_\$$ = interest rate in the United States
$i_£$ = interest rate in the United Kingdom

F = forward exchange rate (dollars per pound)
E = spot exchange rate (dollars per pound)

where the interest rates and the forward rate are the same term to maturity (e.g., 3 months or 1 year). An investor in the United States can earn $1 + i_\$$ at home by investing $1 for one period (for instance, 1 year). Alternatively, the U.S. investor can invest in the United Kingdom by converting dollars to pounds and then investing the pounds. One dollar is equal to $1/E$ pounds. Thus, by investing in the United Kingdom, the U.S. resident can earn $(1 + i_£)/E$. This is the quantity of pounds resulting from the 1 dollar invested. Remember, $1 buys $1/E$ pounds, and £1 will return $1 + i_£$ after one period. Thus, $1/E$ pounds will return $(1 + i_£)/E$ after one period. Since the investor is a resident of the United States, the investment return will ultimately be converted to dollars. But because future spot exchange rates are not known with certainty, the investor can eliminate the uncertainty regarding the future dollar value of $(1 + i_£)/E$ by *covering* the £ currency investment with a forward contract. By selling

$(1 + i_£)/E$ pounds to be received in the future period in the forward market today, the investor has guaranteed a certain dollar value of the pound investment opportunity. The **covered return** is equal to $(1 + i_£)F/E$ dollars. The U.S. investor can earn either $1 + i_\$$ dollars by investing \$1 at home or $(1 + i_£)F/E$ dollars by investing \$1 in the United Kingdom. Arbitrage between the two investment opportunities results in

Covered return
The domestic-currency value of a foreign investment when the foreign-currency proceeds are sold in the forward market.

$$1 + i_\$ = (1 + i_£)\frac{F}{E}$$

which may be rewritten as

$$\frac{1 + i_\$}{1 + i_£} = \frac{F}{E} \tag{15.1}$$

Equation 15.1 can be put in a more useful form by first subtracting 1 from both sides, giving the **interest rate parity** equation:

$$\frac{i_\$ - i_£}{1 + i_£} = \frac{F - E}{E} \tag{15.2}$$

Interest rate parity
The forward premium or discount is equal to the interest differential.

which is sometimes approximated as

$$i_\$ - i_£ = \frac{F - E}{E} \tag{15.3}$$

The smaller $i_£$, the better the approximation of Equation 15.3 to Equation 15.2. Equation 15.3 indicates that the interest differential between a comparable U.S. and U.K. investment is equal to the forward premium or discount on the pound (we must remember that since interest rates are quoted at annual rates or percent per annum, the forward premiums or discounts must also be quoted at annual rates). Now, let's consider an example.

Ignoring bid-ask spreads, we observe the following interest rates:

EXAMPLE

\$: 7%

£: 5%

The exchange rate is quoted as the dollar price of pounds and is currently $E = 2.00$. Given the preceding information, what do you expect the 12-month forward rate to be?

Using Equation 15.3, we can plug in the known values for the interest rates and spot exchange rate and then solve for the forward rate:

$$0.07 - 0.05 = \frac{F - 2.00}{2.00}$$

$$0.02 = \frac{F - 2.00}{2.00}$$

$$0.04 = F - 2.00$$

$$F = 2.04$$

Thus, we expect a 12-month forward rate of $2.04 to give a 12-month forward premium equal to the 0.02 interest differential.

Suppose the actual 12-month forward rate is not $2.04 but $2.06 instead. What would profit-seeking arbitragers do? They could buy pounds spot, then invest and sell the pounds forward for dollars, since the forward price of pounds is higher than that implied by the interest parity relation. These actions would tend to increase the spot rate and lower the forward rate, thereby bringing the forward premium back in line with the interest differential. The interest rates could also move, because the movement of funds into pound investments would tend to depress the pound interest rate, whereas the shift out of dollar investments would tend to raise the dollar rate.

Effective return
The foreign interest rate plus the forward premium or discount.

The interest parity relationship can also be used to illustrate the concept of the **effective return** on a foreign investment. Equation 15.3 can be rewritten so that the dollar interest rate is equal to the pound rate plus the forward premium:

$$i_\$ = i_\pounds + \frac{F - E}{E} \qquad (15.4)$$

Interest parity ensures that Equation 15.4 will hold. But suppose an investor does not use the forward market, yet he or she is a U.S. resident who is buying a U.K. bond? The interest rate on the bond, $i_\pounds$, is not the relevant return measure, since this is the return in terms of a U.K. investment. The effective return on the bond is given by the interest rate plus the expected change in the exchange rate. In other words, the return on a U.K. investment plus the expected change in the value of U.K. currency is our expected return on a pound investment. If the forward exchange rate is equal to the expected future spot rate, then the forward premium is also equal to the expected change in the exchange rate and **uncovered interest parity** would hold. (The next chapter introduces a reason this might not hold—foreign-exchange risk.)

Uncovered interest parity
The expected change in the exchange rate is equal to the interest differential.

Even though foreign-exchange traders quote forward rates based on interest differentials and current spot rates so that the forward rate will yield a forward premium equal to the interest differential, we may ask, "How well does interest rate parity hold in the real world?" Since deviations from interest rate parity would seem to present profitable arbitrage opportunities, we would expect profit-seeking arbitragers to eliminate any deviations. Still, careful studies of the data indicate that small deviations from interest rate parity do occur. Do these deviations indicate unexploited profit opportunities for an astute investor? It appears that the answer is no. There are several reasons why interest rate parity may not hold exactly, and yet investors can earn no arbitrage profits from the situation. The most obvious reason is the cost of transacting in the markets. Since buying and selling foreign exchange and international securities involves a cost for each transaction, deviations from interest rate parity may exist that are equal to or smaller than these transaction costs. In this case speculators cannot profit from these deviations because the price of buying and selling in the market would wipe out any apparent gain. Studies indicate that for comparable financial assets that differ only in terms of currency of denomination (e.g., dollar- and pound-denominated deposits in a London bank), 100 percent of the deviations from interest rate parity can be accounted for by transaction costs.*

Besides transaction costs, there are other reasons interest rate parity may not hold perfectly. These include differential taxation, government controls, political risk, and time lags between observing a profit opportunity and actually trading to realize the profit. If taxes differ according to an investor's residence, which they surely do, then the same investment opportunity will yield a different return to residents of different countries.[†] Thus, it will be misleading to simply consider pretax effective returns to decide if profitable arbitrage is possible. The appendix to this chapter incorporates taxes in the interest rate parity condition.

If government controls on financial-capital flows exist, an effective barrier between national markets is in place. If an individual cannot freely buy or sell the currency or securities of a country, then the free-market forces that work in response to effective return differentials will not function. Indeed, even the serious threat of controls, or, more generally, any national emergency impinging on international trade in financial assets, could make the political risk of investing in a country prohibitive. Political risk is often mentioned as a reason why interest rate parity does not hold.[‡] We should note at this point that the external or Eurocurrency market often serves as a means of avoiding political risk, since an individual can borrow and lend foreign currencies outside the home country of each currency. For instance, the Eurodollar market provides a market for U.S. dollar loans and deposits in major

---

*Several papers have argued that transaction costs may be smaller than previously thought, so that other factors may account for some deviations from interest rate parity. See Mohsen-Bahmani-Oskooee and Satya P. Das, "Transaction Costs and the Interest-Parity Theorem," *Journal of Political Economy* (August 1985); Kevin Clinton, "Transactions Costs and Covered Interest Arbitrage: Theory and Evidence," *Journal of Political Economy* (April 1988); Mark P. Taylor, "Covered Interest Parity: A High-Frequency, High-Quality Data Study," *Economica* (November 1987); and Helen Popper, "Long-Term Covered Interest Parity: Evidence from Currency Swaps," *Journal of International Money and Finance* (August 1993).

[†]The importance of taxation is demonstrated in several articles, including Maurice Levi, "Taxation and Abnormal International Capital Flows," *Journal of Political Economy* (June 1977); Menachem Katz, "Impact of Taxation on International Capital Flows: Some Empirical Results," in *Taxation, Inflation, and Interest Rates*, ed. Vito Tanzi (International Monetary Fund, 1984); David G. Hartman, "Taxation and the Effects of Inflation on the Real Capital Stock in an Open Economy," *International Economic Review* (June 1979); David H. Howard and Karen H. Johnson, "Interest Rates, Inflation, and Taxes: The Foreign Connection," *Economics Letters* 2 (1982); J. Harold McClure, "PPP, Interest Rate Parities, and the Modified Fisher Effect in the Presence of Tax Agreements: A Comment," *Journal of International Money and Finance* (September 1988); and Tamim Bayoumi and Joseph Gagnon, "Taxation and Inflation: A New Explanation for Current Account Imbalances," *International Finance Discussion Papers* (Federal Reserve Board, January 1992).

[‡]The effect of political risk in causing deviations from interest rate parity is discussed in a well-known article: Robert Z. Aliber, "The Interest Rate Parity Theorem: A Reinterpretation," *Journal of Political Economy* (November 1973): 1451–59. The role of political risk in deviations from interest rate parity between the Mexican peso and the dollar is explored in Michael Melvin and Don Schlagenhauf, "A Country Risk Index: Econometric Formulation and Application to Mexico," *Economic Inquiry* (October 1985). A German mark example is provided by Michael P. Dooley and Peter Isard, "Capital Controls, Political Risk and Deviations from Interest Rate Parity," *Journal of Political Economy* (April 1980). A general application is Daniel Bachman, "The Effect of Political Risk on the Forward Exchange Bias: The Case of Elections," *Journal of International Money and Finance* (April 1992).

financial centers outside the United States. We investigate in detail the Eurocurrency markets in Chapter 20.

INTEREST RATES AND INFLATION

To better understand the relationship between interest rates and exchange rates, we shall consider how inflation can be related to both. To link exchange rates, interest rates, and inflation, we must first understand the role of inflation in interest rate determination. Economists distinguish between real and nominal rates of interest. The **nominal interest rate** is the rate actually observed in the market. The **real interest rate** is a concept that measures the return after adjusting for inflation. If you lend someone money and charge that person 5 percent interest on the loan, the real return on your loan is negative if the inflation rate exceeds 5 percent. For instance, if the rate of inflation is 10 percent, then the debtor is repaying the loan with dollars that are worth less, so much less that the loan is going to wind up providing you, the creditor, with less purchasing power after you are repaid the principal and interest than you had when you initially made the loan. Item 15.1 provides an example of nominal versus real interest rates.

Nominal interest rate
The rate actually observed in the market.

Real interest rate
The nominal interest rate minus inflation.

This all means that the nominal rate of interest will tend to incorporate inflation expectations to provide lenders with a real return for the use of their money. This inflation-expectation effect on the nominal interest rate is often called the Fisher effect (after Irving Fisher, an early pioneer of the determinants of interest rates), and the relationship between inflation and interest rates is given by the **Fisher equation:**

Fisher equation
The nominal interest rate is equal to the real interest rate plus expected inflation.

$$i = r + \pi \tag{15.5}$$

where i is the nominal interest rate, r is the real rate, and π is the expected rate of inflation. Thus, an increase in π, the expected rate of inflation, will tend to increase i, the nominal rate of interest. The fact that interest rates in the 1970s and 1980s were much higher than in the 1950s and 1960s is due to the higher inflation rates. Across countries at a point in time we should expect interest rates to vary with inflation. Table 15.1 shows that nominal interest rates tend to be higher in countries with higher rates of inflation.

TABLE 15.1   *Interest Rates and Inflation Rates for Selected Countries, 1995*[1]

Country	Inflation Rate (%)	Interest Rate (%)
Japan	0.1	0.17
Switzerland	0.0	0.56
Mexico	19.0	13.4
Ecuador	42.3	53.2
Russia	97.0	90.0

[1]Inflation rate is annual rate of change in consumer price index. Interest rate is annual average of bank deposit rates.

ITEM 15.1 | Lenders and Borrowers, Losers and Winners

Suppose Mr. Smith lends Ms. Jones $100 for one year at 10 percent simple interest. At the end of one year, Ms. Jones repays the $100 principal plus $10 interest. What has Mr. Smith gained from the loan? He now has $110 and he lent only $100 a year ago, yet he may or may not be gaining from making the loan. To evaluate the gain from the loan, we must consider the value of money. The value of a dollar is the goods and services that may be purchased with the dollar. As prices rise, one dollar will buy fewer goods and services, so the value of money falls.

Suppose prices are constant over the year of the Smith-Jones loan. With constant prices, the $10 interest plus the $100 principal provides Mr. Smith with command over more goods and services than the original $100. So Mr. Smith has a real gain from making the loan, and Ms. Jones has a real cost. The use of the *real* indicates that the interest plus principal repaid will allow Mr. Smith to consume more real goods and services than he could have with his initial $100, while Ms. Jones will have to give up the consumption of real goods and services in order to have the use of the $100 for one year.

Suppose prices rise 10 percent over the year instead of remaining constant. If prices rise 10 percent, it now takes $110 to buy what $100 would buy in the earlier period. In this case, Ms. Jones is repaying a sum of money that is equal in a purchasing power sense to the initial sum borrowed. She bears no real interest cost. Mr. Smith, however, now has no real gain. The $110 he receives upon repayment will buy the same quantity of goods and services after prices have risen 10 percent as the initial $100 principal. If prices had risen by more than 10 percent, then it would take more than $110 to buy what $100 could buy in the initial period. Suppose prices increased 20 percent. Now $120 is needed to

buy what $100 would initially buy. If Mr. Smith receives only $110 after a year, he is losing purchasing power. In this case, Mr. Smith is earning a negative real return from the loan, and Ms. Jones is paying a negative real interest rate. After the loan is repaid, in terms of real goods and services, it is as though the lender paid the borrower some real goods to borrow the money.

Do we ever observe negative real interest rates in the real world? The accompanying table lists the nominal interest rate on a one-year U.S. Treasury bill purchased in January of each year from 1975 to 1999. The third column gives the inflation rate over the following year. Subtracting the realized inflation rate from the nominal interest rate gives the realized real interest rate in the final column. Note that in 5 of the 22 years, the real return from holding the T-bill was negative. Of course, in January, when the T-bills were purchased, the future inflation rate was not known. Investors have some notion of what they expect inflation to be, but no one knows exactly. Many analysts claim that the negative real interest rates of the late 1970s were a result of unexpectedly high inflation. Subsequently, the early 1980s were characterized by unexpectedly low inflation, so that realized real interest rates were high. Whatever the cause of shifts in real interest rates, the table illustrates that there have been real-world cases of negative real interest rates, where borrowers gain and lenders lose. When the inflation rate turns out to be higher than expected, debtors generally gain at the expense of creditors. With unexpectedly low inflation, creditors gain at the expense of debtors. Over the long run, on average, creditors must earn a positive real return on their loans, or else no loans would be made.

(Continued)

| ITEM 15.1 | Lenders and Borrowers, Losers and Winners *(Continued)* |

REALIZED REAL INTEREST RATES ON U.S. TREASURY BILLS

Month Purchased	Nominal Interest Rate (%)	Subsequent Inflation Rate (%)	Realized Real Interest Rate (%)
1/99	4.34	1.7	2.67
1/98	5.09	1.6	3.46
1/97	5.05	3.0	2.01
1/96	5.09	2.7	2.39
1/95	7.05	2.7	4.35
1/94	3.54	2.8	0.74
1/93	3.35	2.8	0.55
1/92	3.95	3.1	0.85
1/91	6.25	3.1	3.15
1/90	7.38	6.1	1.28
1/89	8.37	4.6	3.77
1/88	6.52	4.4	2.12
1/87	5.44	4.0	1.44
1/86	7.31	1.5	5.81
1/85	8.33	3.9	4.43
1/84	9.07	3.6	5.47
1/83	8.01	4.1	3.91
1/82	12.77	3.6	9.17
1/81	12.62	8.4	4.22
1/80	10.96	11.7	−0.74
1/79	9.54	13.9	−4.36
1/78	6.80	9.3	−2.50
1/77	5.00	6.8	−1.80
1/76	5.44	5.2	0.24
1/75	6.27	6.8	−0.53

SOURCE: *Federal Reserve Bulletin.*

EXCHANGE RATES, INTEREST RATES, AND INFLATION

If we combine the Fisher equation (Equation 15.5) and the interest parity equation (Equation 15.3), we can determine how interest rates, inflation, and exchange rates are all linked. First, consider the Fisher equation for the United States and the United Kingdom:

$$i_\$ = r_\$ + \pi_\$ \quad i_£ = r_£ + \pi_£$$

If the real rate of interest is the same internationally, then $r_\$ = r_\pounds.$* In this case, the nominal interest rates, $i_\$$ and $i_\pounds$, differ solely by expected inflation, so we can write

$$i_\$ - i_\pounds = \pi_\$ - \pi_\pounds \tag{15.6}$$

The interest parity condition of Equation 15.3 indicates that the interest differential is also equal to the forward premium, or

$$i_\$ - i_\pounds = \pi_\$ - \pi_\pounds = \frac{F - E}{E} \tag{15.7}$$

Equation 15.7 summarizes the link between interest, inflation, and exchange rates. In words, we could say that real interest rates are equalized across countries when the Fisher equation, interest rate parity, and relative purchasing power parity all hold.

In the real world, the interrelationships summarized by Equation 15.7 are determined simultaneously, because interest rates, inflation expectations, and exchange rates are jointly affected by government policy changes and other new events and information. For instance, suppose we begin from a situation of equilibrium where interest parity holds. Then, there is a change in U.S. policy that leads to expectations of a higher U.S. inflation rate. The increase in expected inflation will cause dollar interest rates to rise. At the same time, exchange rates will adjust to maintain interest parity. If the expected future spot rate is changed, we would expect F to carry much of the adjustment burden. If the expected future spot rate is unchanged, the current spot rate would tend to carry the bulk of the adjustment burden. Finally, if central-bank intervention is "pegging" exchange rates at fixed levels by buying and selling so as to maintain the fixed rate, both the domestic- and foreign-currency interest rates will have to rise to maintain parity levels. The fundamental point is that the initial U.S. policy change leads to changes in inflationary expectations, interest rates, and exchange rates simultaneously, since they all adjust to new equilibrium levels.

EXPECTED EXCHANGE RATES AND THE TERM STRUCTURE OF INTEREST RATES

There is no such thing as *the* interest rate for a country. Interest rates within a country vary for different investment opportunities and for different maturity dates on similar investment opportunities. The structure of interest rates existing on investment

---

*There is evidence that real interest rates may not be equal across countries; see John J. Merrick and Anthony Saunders, "International Expected Real Interest Rates," *Journal of Monetary Economics* (November 1986): 313–22; or Nelson C. Mark, "Some Evidence on the International Inequality of Real Interest Rates," *Journal of International Money and Finance* (June 1985): 189–208. Reasons for inequality are given in Barry K. Goodwin and Thomas J. Grennes, "Real Interest Equalization and the Integration of International Financial Markets," *Journal of International Money and Finance* (February 1994).

Term structure of interest rates
The pattern of interest rates over different terms to maturity.

opportunities over time is known as the **term structure of interest rates**. For instance, in the bond market we observe 3-month, 6-month, 1-year, 3-year, and still longer-term bonds. If the interest rates rise with the term to maturity, then we observe a rising term structure. If the interest rates are the same regardless of term, then the term structure is flat. We describe the term structure of interest rates by describing the slope of a line connecting the various points in time at which we observe interest rates.

There are several competing theories of the term structure of interest rates, which we briefly discuss:

1. *Expectations.* This theory suggests that the long-term interest rate tends to equal an average of short-term rates expected over the long-term holding period. In other words, an investor could buy a long-term bond or a series of short-term bonds, so that the expected return from the long-term bond will tend to be equal to the return generated from holding the series of short-term bonds.

2. *Liquidity premium.* Here we have the idea of long-term bonds incorporating a risk premium, as risk-averse investors would prefer to lend short-term. The premium on long-term bonds would tend to result in interest rates rising with the holding period of the bond.

3. *Preferred habitat.* This approach contends that the bond markets are segmented by maturities. In other words, there is a separate market for short- and long-term bonds, and the interest rates are determined by supply and demand in each market.

Although we could use these term-structure theories to explain the term structure for interest rates in any one currency, in international finance we can use the term structures on different currencies to infer expected exchange rate changes. For instance, if we compared Eurodollar and Euromark deposit rates for different maturities, such as 1-month and 3-month deposits, the difference between the two term structures should reflect expected exchange rate changes. Of course, if there are capital controls, then the various national markets become isolated, and there will not be any particular relationship between international interest rates.

Figure 15.1 plots the deposit rates for 1- through 12-month Eurocurrency deposits at a particular point in time. First, we know from our previous discussion that when one country has higher interest rates than another country, the high-interest-rate currency is expected to depreciate relative to the low-interest-rate currency. Since effective returns will tend to be equal everywhere, the only way an interest rate can be above another one is if the high-interest-rate currency is expected to depreciate, so that the effective rate $i + (F - E)/E$ (as shown in Equation 15.4, with the forward rate used as a predictor of the future spot rate) is lower than the observed rate i, due to the expected depreciation of the currency ($F < E$).

If the distance between two of the term-structure lines is the same at each point, then the expected change in the exchange rate is constant. To see this more clearly, let us once again consider the interest parity relation given by Equation 15.3:

FIGURE 15.1   *Eurocurrency (market-closing) interest rates for January 11, 2000.*

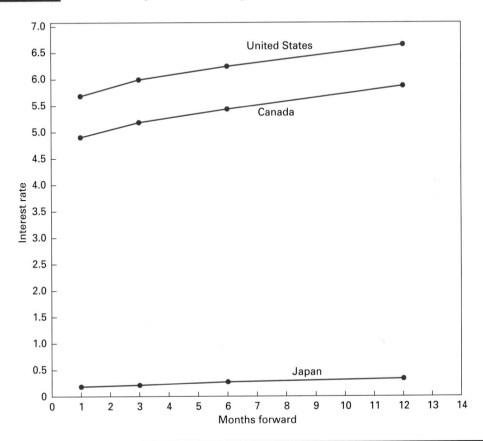

$$i_\$ - i_£ = \frac{F - E}{E}$$

This expression indicates that the difference between the interest rates in two countries will be equal to the forward premium or discount when the interest rates and
the forward rate are for the same term to maturity. If the forward rate is considered
a market forecast of the future spot rate, which it often is, then we can say that the
interest differential is also approximately equal to the expected change in the spot
rate. This means that at each point in the term structure, the difference between the
national interest rates should reflect the expected change in the exchange rate for the
two currencies being compared. By examining the different points in the term structure, we can determine how the exchange rate expectations are changing through
time. One implication of this is that even if we did not have a forward exchange

market in a currency, the interest differential between the interest rate on that currency and the interest rate on other currencies would allow us to infer expected future exchange rates.

Now we can understand why a constant differential between two interest rates implies that future changes in the exchange rate are expected to occur at some constant rate. Thus, if two of the term-structure lines are parallel, the exchange rate changes are expected to be constant (the currencies will appreciate or depreciate against each other at a constant rate). On the other hand, if two term structure lines are diverging, or moving farther apart from one another, then the high-interest-rate currency is expected to depreciate at an increasing rate over time. For term structure lines converging, or moving closer together, the high-interest-rate currency is expected to depreciate at a declining rate relative to the low-interest-rate currency.

In Figure 15.1, we see that the term structure lines for the United States and Canada are roughly parallel to each other and are relatively close together. Therefore, at this time the U.S. dollar was expected to depreciate against the Canadian dollar by a small and relatively constant rate over time. On the other hand, the term structure lines for the United States and Japan are relatively far apart and diverging. At this time, the U.S. dollar was expected to depreciate against the yen at a faster rate than for the Canadian dollar, and the rate of depreciation was expected to increase over time. At the end of the business day in London on January 11, 2000, the day that the interest rates were sampled, the one-year forward premium on the Canadian dollar against the U.S. dollar was 0.7 percent while the one-year forward premium on the yen against the U.S. dollar was 6.1 percent. The term structure lines approximately reflect expected exchange rate changes.

SUMMARY

1. The interest parity relation indicates that the interest differential between investments in two currencies will equal the forward premium or discount between the currencies.

2. Covered interest arbitrage ensures interest parity.

3. Deviations from interest rate parity could be due to transaction costs, differential taxation, government controls, and/or political risk.

4. The real interest rate is equal to the nominal interest rate minus expected inflation.

5. If real interest rates are equal in two countries, then the interest differential on their currencies will equal the inflation differential, which will equal the forward premium or discount.

6. Differences between the term structure of interest rates in two countries will reflect expected exchange rate changes.

EXERCISES

1. The French franc is selling in the spot market for $0.18, while in the 90-day forward market it sells for $0.16.
   a. Is the dollar selling at a premium or a discount?
   b. What is the forward premium (discount) on the franc (at an annual rate)?

2. The 1-year interest rate on Swiss francs is 5 percent, and the dollar interest rate is 8 percent.
   a. If the current $/SF spot rate is $0.60, what would you expect the spot rate to be in 1 year?
   b. Why is there no observable expected future spot rate?
   c. Suppose U.S. policy changes and leads to an expected future spot rate of $0.63. What would you expect the dollar interest rate to be now? (Assume no change in the Swiss interest rate.)

3. Why might interest rate parity hold better than purchasing power parity over time?

4. State whether the following quotation is true or false, and then carefully explain your answer: "Lenders benefit from unexpected inflation, but borrowers are hurt by it."

5. Show how the forward premium can be equal to the expected inflation differential between two currencies. What assumptions are needed for this to be true?

6. Should we believe that interest differentials cause exchange rate changes, or that exchange rate changes cause interest differentials?

7. Assume the 3-month interest differential for Swiss francs minus British pounds is equal to −0.05. The 6-month interest differential is equal to −0.03. Is the British pound selling at a premium or a discount relative to the Swiss franc? How is the expected rate of pound appreciation or depreciation changing over time?

8. List and explain all factors that might cause deviations from interest rate parity.

9. Suppose the term structure of interest rates is rising for the United States and falling for Germany. If this is all you know, what can you say about the expected change in the mark/dollar exchange rate?

10. If two countries had identical term structures of interest rates, how would you expect the forward premium or discount to change over time?

REFERENCES

Aliber, Robert Z. "The Interest Rate Parity Theorem: A Reinterpretation." *Journal of Political Economy* (November 1973): 1451–59.

"Capital Goes Global," *The Economist* (October 25, 1997).

Hansson, Ingemar, and Charles Stuart. "The Fisher Hypothesis and International Credit Markets." *Journal of Political Economy* (December 1986): 1330–37.

McKinnon, Ronald I. *Money in International Exchange.* New York: Oxford University Press, 1979.

Solnik, Bruno. "International Parity Conditions and Exchange Risk." *Journal of Banking and Finance 2* (1978): 281–93.

Throop, Adrian W. "Linkages of National Interest Rates." *FRBSF Weekly Letter* (September 2, 1994).

 INTERNET APPLICATIONS

Please visit our Web site at www.awl.com/husted_melvin for more exercises and readings.

APPENDIX 15.1

TAXATION AND INTEREST RATE PARITY

Chapter 15 ignores the taxation of investment income in the derivation of interest rate parity. This is commonly done, even by advanced researchers in international finance. Yet we know that investors do not ignore taxes. Investor behavior should be based on expected after-tax returns. In this appendix, we derive the interest rate parity relation incorporating taxation.

In Chapter 15, we considered a U.S. investor facing an investment opportunity in the United States and the United Kingdom. Let us now reconsider the framework used earlier, where

$i_\$$ = interest rate in the United States
$i_£$ = interest rate in the United Kingdom
F = forward exchange rate (dollars per pound)
E = spot exchange rate (dollars per pound)
t_y = normal income tax rate
t_k = capital gains tax rate

The percentage return from investing a dollar at home for one period is $i_\$(1 - t_y)$. The term $1 - t_y$ is the fraction of income retained after taxes, so $i_\$(1 - t_y)$ is the percentage return on the dollar investment when interest is taxed as ordinary income. Alternatively, the U.S. investor can invest in the United Kingdom by converting dollars to pounds and then investing the pounds. In Chapter 15, we ignored taxes and wrote the value of the foreign investment at maturity as $(1 + i_£)F/E$. The percentage return on the foreign investment is $[(1 + i_£)F/E] - 1$. This percentage return may be decomposed into two parts: $i_£$, the interest rate on the U.K. asset; and $(1 + i_£)(F - E)/E$, the percentage foreign-exchange gain or loss on principal plus interest. Since interest is taxed as ordinary income, the after-tax interest return is $i_£(1 - t_y)$. The foreign-exchange gain or loss is often (in many countries) taxed at a lower capital gains tax rate (t_k), so that the after-tax return on foreign-exchange gain or loss is

$$(1 - t_k)(1 + i_£)\left(\frac{F - E}{E}\right)$$

Equating the after-tax domestic return with the after-tax foreign return yields

$$i_\$(1 - t_y) = i_£(1 - t_y) + (1 - t_k)(1 + i_£)\left(\frac{F - E}{E}\right)$$

Rearranging this expression, we have

$$\frac{F - E}{E} = \frac{i_\$ - i_£}{1 + i_£} \frac{1 - t_y}{1 - t_k}$$

In this form, we see that if there are no taxes, then $t_y = t_k = 0$, and we have the interest parity equation as shown in Equation 15.2. If foreign-exchange gains are taxed as ordinary income, then $t_y = t_k$, and $(1 - t_y)/(1 - t_k) = 1$, so that again the problem collapses to the interest parity equation of Chapter 15. The tax effect becomes important only when t_y does not equal t_k. It is common for countries to allow foreign-exchange gains to be taxed at a lower rate than interest income. Ignoring taxes could, then, give a misleading conclusion regarding how well interest rate parity holds or the incentives for international investment. With respect to the latter effect, there would be a greater incentive to invest in countries with a large forward premium, since foreign-exchange rates without the effect of differential taxation will miss the greater return to a dollar of foreign-exchange gain relative to a dollar of interest.

We have seen how taxation can be added to the covered interest arbitrage analysis. When interest income and foreign-exchange gains are taxed at the same rate, it is correct to ignore taxes; otherwise, to be strictly correct, we should include the effect of taxation in interest rate parity analysis.

CHAPTER 16

Foreign-Exchange Risk, Forecasting, and International Investment

TOPICS TO BE COVERED

Types of Foreign-Exchange Risk
Foreign-Exchange Risk Premium
Market Efficiency
Foreign-Exchange Forecasting
International Investment and Portfolio
    Diversification
Direct Foreign Investment
Capital Flight
Capital Inflow Issues
International Lending and Crises

KEY WORDS

Exchange risk exposure
Risk premium
Risk aversion
Efficient market
Long position
Short position
Diversified portfolios

Variance
Covariance
Systematic risk
Nonsystematic risk
Home bias
Contagion effect
Capital flight

397

International business involves foreign-exchange risk because the value of transactions in different currencies is sensitive to exchange rate changes. Although it is possible to manage a firm's foreign-currency-denominated assets and liabilities so as to avoid exposure to exchange rate changes, the cost involved is not always worth the effort.

The appropriate strategy for the corporate treasurer and the individual speculator will be at least partly determined by expectations of the future path of the exchange rate. As a result, exchange rate forecasts are an important part of the decision-making process of international investors.

In this chapter, we first consider the issues of foreign-exchange risk and forecasting. It is the presence of risk arising from uncertainty regarding the future that makes forecasting necessary. If future exchange rates were known with certainty, there would be no foreign-exchange risk. After discussing risk and forecasting, we then turn to international investment and the international capital flows that arise as a result of investment decisions.

TYPES OF FOREIGN-EXCHANGE RISK

One problem we encounter when trying to evaluate the effect of exchange rate changes on a business firm is determining the appropriate concept of exposure to foreign-exchange risk.

Exchange risk exposure

Translation, transaction, and economic exposure are three concepts of exposure to foreign-exchange risk.

We can identify three popular concepts of **exchange risk exposure**:

1. *Translation exposure.* This is also known as accounting exposure and can be found as the difference between foreign-currency-denominated assets and foreign-currency-denominated liabilities.

2. *Transaction exposure.* This is exposure resulting from the uncertain domestic-currency value of a foreign-currency-denominated transaction to be completed at some future date.

3. *Economic exposure.* This is the exposure of the value of the firm to changes in exchange rates. If the value of the firm is measured as the present value of future after-tax cash flows, then economic exposure is concerned with the sensitivity of the real domestic-currency value of long-term cash flows to exchange rate changes.

Economic exposure is the most important to the firm. Rather than worry about how accountants will report the value of international operations (translation exposure), it is more important to the firm (and to rational investors) to focus on the purchasing power of long-run cash flows insofar as these determine the real value of the firm.

As an example, let us consider the situation of a hypothetical firm to illustrate the differences among the alternative exposure concepts. Suppose we have the balance sheet of XYZ-Saudi Arabia, a foreign subsidiary of the parent U.S. firm XYZ Inc. The balance sheet in Table 16.1 initially shows the position of XYZ-Saudi Arabia in terms

TABLE 16.1	Balance Sheet of XYZ-Saudi Arabia, May 31		
Cash	SAR1,000,000	Debt	SAR5,000,000
Accounts receivable	3,000,000	Equity	6,000,000
Plant and equipment	5,000,000		
Inventory	2,000,000		
	SAR11,000,000		SAR11,000,000
Dollar Translation on May 31, SAR4 = $1			
Cash	$250,000	Debt	$1,250,000
Accounts receivable	750,000	Equity	1,500,000
Plant and equipment	1,250,000		
Inventory	500,000		
	$2,750,000		$2,750,000
Dollar Translation on June 1, SAR5 = $1			
Cash	$200,000	Debt	$1,000,000
Accounts receivable	600,000	Equity	1,200,000
Plant and equipment	1,000,000		
Inventory	400,000		
	$2,200,000		$2,200,000

of Saudi riyals (ISO code SAR). A balance sheet is simply a recording of a firm's assets (listed on the left side) and liabilities (listed on the right side). A balance sheet must balance. In other words, the value of assets must equal the value of liabilities, so that the sums of the two columns are equal. Equity is the owner's claim on the firm and is a sort of residual in that the value of equity will change to keep liabilities equal to assets.

Although the balance sheet at the top of Table 16.1 is stated in terms of riyals, the parent U.S. company, XYZ Inc., consolidates the financial statements of all foreign subsidiaries into its own statements. Thus, the riyal-denominated balance sheet items must be translated into dollars to be included in the parent company's balance sheet.

Assume that, initially, the exchange rate equals SAR4 = $1. The balance sheet in the middle of Table 16.1 uses this exchange rate to translate the balance sheet items into dollars. The middle set of figures in Table 16.1 gives us the position of the firm on May 31. However, suppose there is a devaluation of the riyal on June 1 from SAR4 = $1 to SAR5 = $1. The balance sheet in terms of dollars will change as illustrated by the new translation at the bottom of the table. Note that now the owner's claim on the firm in terms of dollars has fallen from $1,500,000 to $1,200,000. Given the current method of translating exchange rate changes, when the currency used to denominate the foreign-subsidiaries statements is depreciating relative to the dollar, then the owner's equity will fall. We must realize that this drop in equity does not necessarily represent any real loss to the firm or any real drop in the value of the firm.

Since the balance sheet translation of foreign assets and liabilities does not, by itself, indicate anything about the real economic exposure of the firm, we must look beyond the balance sheet and the translation exposure. Transaction exposure can be viewed as a kind of economic exposure, since the susceptibility of future transactions profitability to exchange rate change can have a big effect on future cash flows, and hence on the value of the firm. Suppose XYZ-Saudi Arabia has contracted to deliver goods to a Korean firm and allows 30 days' credit before payment is received. Furthermore, suppose at the time the contract was made, the exchange rate was 120 South Korean won per riyal (KRW120 = SAR1). Suppose also the contract called for payment in won of exactly KRW120,000 in 30 days. At the current exchange rate, the value of KRW120,000 is SAR1,000. But if the exchange rate changes in the next 30 days, the value of KRW120,000 would also change. Should the won depreciate unexpectedly, then in 30 days XYZ-Saudi Arabia will receive KRW120,000, but this will be worth less than SAR1,000, so that the transaction is not so profitable as originally planned. This is transaction exposure. XYZ-Saudi Arabia has committed itself to this future transaction, thereby exposing it to exchange risk. Had the contract been written to specify payment in riyals, then the transaction exposure to XYZ-Saudi Arabia would have been eliminated, but the Korean importer would now have a transaction exposure. Firms can, of course, hedge against future exchange rate uncertainty in the forward exchange market. The Korean firm could buy riyals in the forward market to be delivered in 30 days and thus eliminate the transaction exposure.

The example of transaction exposure just reviewed illustrates how exchange rate uncertainty can affect the future profitability of a firm. The possibility that exchange rate changes can affect future profitability, and therefore the current value of the firm, is indicative of economic exposure. Managing foreign-exchange risks involves the sorts of operations considered in our earlier chapter on foreign-exchange markets. There, we covered the use of forward markets, swaps, and borrowing and lending in international currencies. Consequently, we shall not repeat that information here. We note, however, that firms should manage cash flows very carefully with an eye toward expected exchange rate changes and should not always try to avoid all risks, because risk taking can be profitable. Firms practice risk minimization subject to cost constraints and eliminate foreign-exchange risk only when the expected benefits from it exceed the costs.

Although forward exchange contracts may be an important part of any corporate hedging strategy, other alternatives exist that are frequently used. For example, suppose a firm has both assets and liabilities denominated in weak currency X, which is expected to depreciate, and strong currency Y, which is expected to appreciate. The firm's treasurer would try to minimize the value of accounts receivable denominated in X, which could mean tougher credit terms for customers paying currency X. The firm may also delay the payment of any accounts payable denominated in X, because it expects to be able to buy X for repayment at a cheaper rate in the future. Insofar as possible, the firm will try to reinforce these practices on payables and receivables by invoicing its sales in currency Y and its purchases in X. Although institutional constraints may exist on the ability of the firm to specify the invoicing currency, it would certainly be desirable to implement such policies.

We see, then, that corporate hedging strategies involve more than simply minimizing holdings of currency X and currency-X-denominated bank deposits. Managing cash flows, receivables, and payables will be the daily activity of the financial officers of a multinational firm. In instances where the firm cannot successfully hedge a foreign-currency position internally, there is always the forward exchange market. If the firm has a currency-Y-denominated debt and it wishes to avoid the foreign-exchange risk associated with the debt, it can always buy Y currency forward and thereby eliminate the risk. Alternatively, the firm could use the futures or options market to hedge the foreign-currency debt.

In summary, foreign-exchange risk may be hedged or eliminated by the following:

1. The forward, futures, or options market.

2. Invoicing in the domestic currency.

3. Speeding (slowing) payments of currencies expected to appreciate (depreciate).

4. Speeding (slowing) collection of currencies expected to depreciate (appreciate).

FOREIGN-EXCHANGE RISK PREMIUM

Let us now consider the effects of foreign-exchange risk on the determination of forward exchange rates. As mentioned previously, the forward exchange rate may serve as a predictor of future spot exchange rates. We may question whether the forward rate should be equal to the expected future spot rate, or whether there is a **risk premium** incorporated in the forward rate that serves as an insurance premium inducing others to take our risk, in which case the forward rate would differ from the expected future spot rate by this premium.* The empirical work in this area has dealt with the issue of whether the forward rate is an unbiased predictor of future spot rates. An unbiased predictor is one that is correct on average, so that over the long run the forward rate is just as likely to overpredict the future spot rate as it is to underpredict it. The property of unbiasedness does not imply that the forward rate is a good predictor. For example, there is the story of an old lawyer who says, "When I was a young man, I lost many cases that I should have won; when I was older, I won many that I should have lost. Therefore, on average, justice was done." Is it comforting to know that, on average, the correct verdict is reached when we are concerned with the verdict in a particular case? Likewise, the forward rate could be unbiased and "on average" correctly predict the spot rate without ever actually predicting the future-realized spot rate. All we need for unbiasedness is that the forward rate is just as likely to guess too high as it is to guess too low.

Risk premium
The difference between the forward rate and the expected future spot rate.

---

* Many studies have attempted to identify the presence of a risk premium in the forward exchange rate. Good reviews of this literature are provided by Robert J. Hodrick, *The Empirical Evidence on the Efficiency of Forward and Futures Foreign Exchange Markets,* Chur: Harwood, 1987, and Charles Engel, "The Forward Discount Anomaly and the Risk Premium: A Survey of Recent Evidence," *Journal of Empirical Finance* (September 1996): 123–192.

Risk aversion
The tendency of investors to prefer less risk.

The effective return differential between two countries' assets should be dependent on the perceived risk on each asset and the **risk aversion** of the investors. Now let us clarify what we mean by *risk* and *risk aversion*. The risk associated with an asset is the contribution of that asset to the overall portfolio risk of an investor. Modern finance literature has commonly associated the riskiness of a portfolio with the variability of the returns from that portfolio. This is reasonable in that investors are concerned with the future value of any investment, and the more variable the return from an investment is, the less certain we can be about its value at any particular future date. Thus, we are concerned with the variability of any individual asset insofar as it contributes to the variability of our portfolio return (our portfolio return is simply the total return from all our investments).

Risk aversion is the real-world phenomenon of preferring less risk to more risk. In terms of investments, two individuals may agree on the degree of risk associated with two assets, but the more risk-averse individual would require a higher interest rate on the more risky asset to induce him or her to hold it than the less risk-averse individual would. Risk aversion implies that people must be paid to take risk; that is, individuals and corporations with bad credit must pay a higher interest rate than those with good credit. The interest differential is required to induce creditors to make loans to the bad credit risks.

We previously stated that the effective return differential between assets of two countries is a function of risk and risk aversion. The effective return differential between a U.S. security and a security in the United Kingdom is

$$i_{U.S.} - \frac{E^*_{t+1} - E_t}{E_t} - i_{U.K.} = f(\text{risk aversion, risk}) \tag{16.1}$$

The left-hand side of the equation is the effective return differential measured as the difference between the U.S. return, $i_{U.S.}$, and the foreign return, $(E^*_{t+1} - E_t) / E_t + i_{U.K.}$. We must remember that the effective return on the foreign asset is equal to the interest rate in terms of foreign currency plus the expected change in the exchange rate, where E^*_{t+1} is the expected dollar spot price of pounds next period. The right-hand side of Equation 16.1 indicates that the return differential is a function of risk aversion and risk. To say in this case that the return differential is a function of risk and risk aversion means that changes in risk and risk aversion are associated with changes in the return differential.

We can view the effective return differential shown in Equation 16.1 as a risk premium. Let us begin with the covered interest parity relation

$$i_{U.S.} - i_{U.K.} = \frac{F - E_t}{E_t} \tag{16.2}$$

To convert the left-hand side to an effective return differential, we must subtract the expected change in the exchange rate. But since this is an equation, whatever is done to the left-hand side must also be done to the right-hand side:

$$i_{U.S.} - \frac{E^*_{t+1} - E_t}{E_t} - i_{U.K.} = \frac{F - E_t}{E_t} - \frac{E^*_{t+1} - E_t}{E_t} \tag{16.3}$$

or

$$i_{U.S.} - \frac{E_{t+1}^* - E_t}{E_t} - i_{U.K.} = \frac{F - E_{t+1}^*}{E_t}$$

Thus, we find that the effective return differential is equal to the percentage difference between the forward and expected future spot exchange rate. The right-hand side of Equation 16.3 may be considered a measure of the risk premium in the forward exchange market. Therefore, if the effective return differential is zero, then there would appear to be no risk premium. If the effective return differential is positive, then there is a positive risk premium on the domestic currency, because the expected future spot price of pounds is less than the prevailing forward rate. In other words, traders offering to sell pounds for dollars in the future will receive a premium, in that pounds are expected to depreciate (relative to dollars) by an amount greater than the current forward rates. Conversely, traders wishing to buy pounds for delivery next period will pay a premium to the future sellers to ensure a set future price.

EXAMPLE

Suppose $E_t = \$2.10$, $E_{t+1}^* = \$2.00$, and $F = \$2.05$. The foreign-exchange risk premium is

$$\frac{F - E_{t+1}^*}{E_t} = \frac{\$2.05 - \$2.00}{\$2.10} = 0.024$$

The expected change in the exchange rate is equal to

$$\frac{E_{t+1}^* - E_t}{E_t} = \frac{\$2.00 - \$2.10}{\$2.10} = -0.048$$

The forward discount on the pound is

$$\frac{F - E_t}{E_t} = \frac{\$2.05 - \$2.10}{\$2.10} = -0.024$$

Thus, the dollar is expected to appreciate against the pound by approximately 4.8 percent, but the forward premium indicates an appreciation of only 2.4 percent if we use the forward rate as a predictor of the future spot rate. The discrepancy is due to the presence of a risk premium that makes the forward rate a biased predictor of the future spot rate. Specifically, the forward rate overpredicts the future dollar price of pounds in order to allow the risk premium.

Given the positive risk premium on the dollar, the expected effective return from holding a U.K. bond will be less than the domestic return to U.S. residents from U.S. bonds. This nonzero effective return differential can be an equilibrium result consistent with rational investor behavior.

EXAMPLE

To continue the previous example, let us suppose that the U.K. interest rate is 0.124, whereas the U.S. rate is 0.100. Then, the interest differential is

$$i_{U.S.} - i_{U.K.} = -0.024$$

The expected return from holding a U.K. bond is

$$i_{U.K.} + \frac{E^*_{t+1} - E_t}{E_t} = 0.124 - 0.048 = 0.076$$

The return from the U.S. bond is 0.10, which exceeds the effective return on the foreign bond, yet this can be an equilibrium solution given the risk premium. Investors are willing to hold U.K. investments yielding a lower expected return than comparable U.S. investments, because there is a positive risk premium on the dollar. Thus, the higher dollar return is necessary to induce investors to hold the riskier dollar-denominated investments.

MARKET EFFICIENCY

Efficient market
A market where prices reflect all available information.

A market is said to be an **efficient market** if prices reflect all available information. In the foreign-exchange market, this means that spot and forward exchange rates will quickly adjust to any new information. For instance, an unexpected change in economic policy by the United States that informed observers feel will be inflationary (e.g., an unexpected increase in money-supply growth) will lead to an immediate depreciation of the dollar. If markets were inefficient, then prices would not adjust quickly to the new information, so that it would be possible for a well-informed investor to make profits consistently from foreign-exchange trading that are excessive relative to the risk undertaken.

With efficient markets, the forward rate would differ from the expected future spot rate by only a risk premium. If this were not the case, then if the forward rate exceeded the expected future spot rate by more than a risk premium, an investor could realize certain profits by selling forward currency now, being able to buy the currency in the future at a lower price than the forward rate at which the currency will be sold. Although profits are most certainly earned from foreign-exchange speculation in the real world, it is also true that there are no sure profits. The real world is characterized by uncertainty regarding the future spot rate, since the future cannot be perfectly foreseen. Yet forward exchange rates adjust to the changing economic picture based on revisions of what the future spot rate is likely to be (as well as on changes in the risk attached to the currencies involved). It is this ongoing process of price adjustments in response to new information in the efficient market that rules out any certain profits from speculation. Of course, the fact that the future will bring unexpected events ensures that profits and losses will result from foreign-exchange speculation. Should an astute investor possess an ability to forecast exchange rates better than the rest of the market, the profits resulting would be enormous. Foreign-exchange forecasting is discussed in the next section.

Many studies have tested the efficiency of the foreign-exchange market.* The fact that they have often reached different conclusions regarding the efficiency of the market emphasizes the difficulty involved in using statistics in the social sciences. Such studies have usually investigated whether the forward rate contains all the relevant information regarding the expected future spot rate. They test whether the forward rate alone predicts the future spot rate well or if additional data will aid in the prediction. If further information adds nothing beyond that already embodied in the forward rate, the market is said to be efficient. On the other hand, if some data are found that would permit a speculator consistently to predict the future spot rate better than the forward rate allows (including a risk premium), then this speculator would earn a consistent profit from foreign-exchange speculation, and one could conclude that the market is not efficient.

It must be recognized that such tests have their weaknesses. Although a statistical analysis must make use of past data, speculators must actually predict the future. The fact that a researcher can find a forecasting rule that would beat the forward rate in predicting past spot rates is not particularly useful for current speculation and does not rule out market efficiency. The key point is that such a rule was not known during the time in which the data were actually being generated. So, if a researcher in 2001 claims to have found a way to predict the spot rates observed in 2000 better than the 2000 forward rates, this does not mean that the foreign-exchange market in 2000 was necessarily inefficient. Speculators in 2000 did not have this forecasting rule developed in 2001, and thus could not have used such information to outguess the 2000 forward rates consistently.

FOREIGN-EXCHANGE FORECASTING

Because future exchange rates are uncertain, participants in international financial markets can never know for sure what the spot rate will be 1 month or 1 year ahead. As a result, forecasts must be made. If we could forecast more accurately than the rest of the market, the potential profits would be enormous. An immediate question is, What makes a good forecast? In other words, how should we judge a forecast of the future spot rate?

---

*Since tests of a risk premium in the forward market are also tests of market efficiency, the studies cited in the previous footnote are also relevant here. In addition, one could read Paul Boothe and David Longworth, "Foreign Exchange Market Efficiency Tests: Implications of Recent Empirical Findings," *Journal of International Money and Finance* (June 1986): 135–52; David Backus, Allan Gregory, and Chris Telmer, "Accounting for Forward Rates in Markets for Foreign Currency," *Journal of Finance* (December 1993); William Crowder, "Foreign Exchange Market Efficiency and Common Stochastic Trends," *Journal of International Money and Finance* (October 1999); Karen Lewis, "Puzzles in International Financial Markets," in *Handbook of International Economics,* vol. III, ed. G. Grossman and K. Rogoff (Amsterdam: North Holland, 1995); and Richard Lyons and Andrew Rose, "Explaining Forward Exchange Bias . . . Intraday," *Journal of Finance* (September 1995).

We can certainly raise objections to rating forecasts on the basis of simple forecast errors. Even though we should prefer a smaller forecast error to a larger one, other things being equal, in practice, other things are not equal. To be successful, a forecast should be on the correct side of the forward rate. For instance, consider the following example of two forecasts predicting the spot rate 1 year from now:

Current spot rate:	¥150 = $1
Current 12-month forward rate:	¥145 = $1
Ms. A forecasts:	¥130 = $1
Mr. B forecasts:	¥148 = $1
Future spot rate realized in 12 months:	¥144 = $1

A Japanese firm will receive a $1-million payment in 12 months and uses the forecasts to help decide whether to cover the dollars with a forward contract or to wait and sell the dollars in the spot market in 12 months. In terms of forecast errors, Ms. A's prediction of ¥130 = $1 yields an error of 9.7 percent, with a realized future spot rate of ¥144. Mr. B's prediction of ¥148 = $1 is much closer to the realized spot rate, with an error of only 2.8 percent. While Mr. B's forecast is closer to the rate eventually realized, this is not the important feature of a good forecast. Mr. B forecasts a future spot rate in excess of the forward rate, so, following his prediction, the Japanese firm would wait and sell the dollars in the spot market in 12 months (or would take a **long position** in dollars). Unfortunately, since the future spot rate of ¥144 = $1 is less than the forward rate at which the dollars could be sold (¥145 = $1), the firm receives ¥144 million rather than ¥145 million for the $1 million.

Following Ms. A's forecast of a future spot rate below the forward rate, the Japanese firm would sell dollars in the forward market (or take a **short position** in dollars). The firm would then sell dollars at the forward rate of ¥145 per dollar rather than wait and receive only ¥144 per dollar in the spot market. The forward contract yields ¥1 million more than the uncovered position. The lesson is that it is more important for a forecast to be on the correct side of the forward rate than to have a small forecast error. Corporate treasurers or individual speculators want a forecast that will give them the direction by which the future spot rate will deviate from the forward rate.

If the foreign-exchange market is efficient so that prices reflect all available information, then we may wonder why anyone would pay for forecasts. There is some evidence that advisory services have been able to "beat the forward rate" at certain times. If such services could consistently offer forecasts that are better than the forward rate, what could we conclude about market efficiency? Evidence that some advisory services can consistently beat the forward rate is not necessarily evidence of a lack of market efficiency. If the difference between the forward rate and the forecast represents transaction costs, then there is no abnormal return from using the forecast. Also, if the difference is due to a risk premium, then any returns earned from the forecasts would be a normal compensation for risk bearing. Finally, we

Long position
Buying currency for future delivery.

Short position
Selling currency for future delivery.

must realize that the services are rarely free. Although the economics departments of large banks sometimes provide free forecasts to corporate customers, professional advisory services charge anywhere from several hundred to many thousands of dollars per year for advice. If the potential profits from speculation are reflected in the price of the service, then once again service customers cannot earn abnormal profits from the forecasts.

Although the returns to a superior forecaster would be considerable, there is no evidence to suggest that abnormally large profits have been produced by following the advice of professional advisory services. But then, if you ever developed a method that consistently outperformed other speculators, would you tell anyone else?*

INTERNATIONAL INVESTMENT AND PORTFOLIO DIVERSIFICATION

In the early 1960s, international investment was thought to be motivated by interest differentials among countries. If the interest rate in one country exceeded that in another, financial capital was expected to flow between the countries until the rates were equal. Modern capital-market theory has provided a new basis for analysis. There were obvious problems with the old theory, since interest differentials can explain one-way flows of capital, from the low- to the high-interest-rate country, yet, realistically, capital flows both ways between most countries.

There is no doubt that the differences in the returns on various countries' assets will provide an incentive for capital flows. However, we would not expect interest rates to be equalized worldwide, since risk differs among assets. Also, we would anticipate a certain random component of international capital flows, because money flows to new investment opportunities as they open up in various countries. Given the short time needed to shift funds around the world, the expected profit (adjusted for risk differences) from investing in different assets should be equal. If this were not the case, money would flow internationally until it was true.

Yet even with constant interest rates internationally, there would still be an incentive for international capital flows. This additional incentive is provided by the desire to hold **diversified portfolios**. It is this diversification motive that leads to the two-way flows of capital between countries. Besides the return on an investment, investors are also concerned with the risk attached to the investment. It is very unlikely that an individual who has $100,000 to invest will invest the entire amount in one asset. By choosing several investment alternatives and holding a diversified portfolio, the investor can reduce the risk associated with his or her investments.

Diversified portfolios
Assets denominated in several currencies.

---

*There is a body of scholarly literature on exchange rate forecasting that offers conflicting evidence on the ability to forecast better than the forward rate. Representative studies include Richard A. Meese and Kenneth Rogoff, "Empirical Exchange Rate Models of the Seventies: Do They Fit out of Sample?" *Journal of International Economics* (February 1983); Mary G. Finn, "Forecasting the Exchange Rate: A Monetary or Random Walk Phenomenon?" *Journal of International Money and Finance* (June 1986); and Nelson Mark, "Exchange Rates and Fundamentals: Evidence on Long-Horizon Predictability," *American Economic Review* (March 1995).

The modern finance literature has emphasized the concept of variability of return as a measure of risk. This is reasonable, in that investors are interested in the future value of their portfolio; and the more variable the value of the portfolio is, the less certain investors can be of the future value.

By diversifying and selecting different assets (including assets of different countries) for a portfolio, an investor can reduce the variability of the portfolio. To see the effects of diversification, let us consider a simple example of an investor facing a world with two investment opportunities: asset A and asset B. The investor will hold a portfolio of A and B, with the share of the portfolio devoted to A denoted by a and the share devoted to B denoted by b. If the investor holds only A, then $a = 1$ and $b = 0$. If only B is held, then $a = 0$ and $b = 1$. Most likely, the investor will choose some amount of diversification by holding both A and B.

The return on the portfolio, R_p, can be written as a weighted average of the returns on the individual assets, R_A and R_B:

$$R_p = aR_A + bR_B \tag{16.4}$$

The expected future return on the portfolio will then be determined by the expected future return on the individual assets:

$$R_p^* = aR_A^* + bR_B^* \tag{16.5}$$

where R_p^*, R_A^*, and R_B^* are the expected values of the portfolio and the individual asset returns, respectively. We said earlier that the idea of portfolio risk was associated with the variability of the return on the portfolio. The measure of the degree to which a variable varies about its mean, or average, value is known as the **variance**. The variance of the portfolio will depend on the portfolio share taken by the assets and the variance of the individual assets, as well as their **covariance**. Specifically,

Variance
A measure of the dispersion of a variable about its mean value.

$$\text{var}(R_p) = a^2\,\text{var}(R_A) + b^2\,\text{var}(R_B) + 2ab\,\text{cov}(R_A, R_B) \tag{16.6}$$

Covariance
A measure of how two variables fluctuate about their means together.

where *var* stands for variance and *cov* stands for covariance. The covariance is a measure of the degree to which the two assets move together. If, when one return is higher than average, the return on the other asset is lower than average, the covariance is negative. Looking at Equation 16.6, we see that a negative covariance could contribute greatly to reducing the overall portfolio variance and therefore the risk.

To see the effects of diversification more clearly, let us use a simple example:

Probability	R_A(%)	R_B(%)
0.25	−2	16
0.25	9	9
0.25	19	−4
0.25	14	11

NOTE: $R_A^* = 10\%$; $R_B^* = 8\%$; var$(R_A) = 0.00605$; var(R_B) $= 0.00545$; cov$(R_A, R_B) = -0.004825$.

This table is a hypothetical assessment of the investment opportunity that is available. If we hold only asset A, our expected return is 10 percent, with a variance of 0.00605. If we hold only asset B, our expected return is 8 percent, with a variance of 0.00545. By holding 50 percent of our portfolio in A and 50 percent in B, our expected return is $R_p = 0.5(10$ percent$) + 0.5(8$ percent$) = 9$ percent, with a variance as follows (using Equation 16.6):

$$\text{var}(R_p) = 0.25(0.00605) + 0.25(0.00545) + 2(0.25)\ (-0.004825) = 0.0004625$$

We need not be concerned with the statistical theory underlying the example. The important result for our use is the large reduction in variability of return achieved by diversification. By investing half of our wealth in A and half in B, we expect to receive a return on our portfolio that is halfway between what we would expect from just holding A or B alone. However, the variance of our return is much less than half the variance of either R_A or R_B. The substantially lower risk achieved by diversification will lead investors to hold many different assets, including assets from different countries.

As the size of an investor's portfolio grows, the investor will want to buy more assets in the proportions that are already held to maintain the desired degree of diversification. This means that as wealth increases, we would anticipate international capital flows between countries as investors maintain these optimal portfolios. Thus, even with constant international interest rates, we should expect to observe two-way flows of capital as international wealth increases.

We should recognize that diversification does not eliminate all risk to an investor. There still exists **systematic risk**, the risk present in all investment opportunities. For instance, in the domestic context we know that different industries have different time patterns of performance. While one industry is enjoying increasing sales and profits, another industry is languishing in the doldrums. At some later period, the reverse may be true. This is similar to the example of opportunities A and B previously presented. The negative covariance between them indicates that when one is enjoying better than average times, the other is suffering, and vice versa. Yet there is still a positive portfolio variance even when we diversify and hold both assets. The variance that can be eliminated through diversification is called the **nonsystematic risk**. This is the risk that is unique to a particular firm or industry. The systematic risk is common to all firms and remains even in diversified portfolios. Systematic risk is due to events that are experienced jointly by all firms, such as the overall business cycle of recurrent periods of prosperity and recession that occurs at the national level.

Systematic risk
The risk common to all investments.

Nonsystematic risk
The risk that can be eliminated with diversification.

We can gain by international diversification by extending our investment alternatives internationally. Systematic risk at the national level can be reduced with international portfolio diversification. Business cycles do not happen uniformly across countries, so when one country is experiencing rapid growth, another may be in a recession. By investing across countries, we eliminate part of the cyclical fluctuation in our portfolio that would arise from the domestic business cycle. Therefore, some of what would be considered systematic risk in terms of strictly domestic investment opportunities becomes nonsystematic risk when we broaden our opportunities to include foreign as well as domestic investment. We sum up the discussion thus far with the following statement: Not only will investors tend to diversify their portfolio holdings across industries, but they can realize additional gains by diversifying across countries.

Given the diversification gains just discussed, it is surprising to learn that recent research indicates that investors seem to greatly favor domestic assets and invest much less in foreign assets than one would expect given the expected gains from diversification. This has come to be known as **home bias**. Why might home bias exist? Let us consider some possible alternatives:

Home bias

Investors prefer domestic securities to foreign securities.

- *Taxes.* It is unlikely that taxes on foreign securities can explain home bias, as taxes paid to foreign governments can usually be credited against domestic taxes.
- *Transaction costs.* Costs associated with buying and selling foreign securities would include monetary costs, such as commissions and bid-ask spreads, and implicit costs, such as regulations, language differences, and lack of information about foreign markets. Familiarity with domestic assets and lower explicit costs of trading at home may lead to home bias. However, it has been found that investors trade their foreign securities more frequently than domestic securities, which is inconsistent with higher costs of trading foreign securities being a significant problem.*
- *Small gains from international diversification.* Maybe the gains from buying international assets are not so great as one might think. Perhaps one can gain the advantages of holding foreign assets by buying shares of domestic mutual funds that are internationally diversified. Or maybe there is less domestic income variability to be reduced through diversification than simple fluctuations in domestic production would indicate.

Research continues on sorting out the source of home bias in the face of seemingly significant gains from diversification. Perhaps some combination of the factors discussed above can best explain investor behavior.

Although the investor risk considered so far has focused on the variability of portfolio return, it should be realized that in international investment there is always a potential for country risk involving the confiscation of foreigners' assets. Chapter 20 explicitly considers the analysis of such a risk and includes a recent ranking of countries in terms of the perceived political risk attached to investments made in those countries.

---

*Recent studies on the issue of home bias include Linda Tesar and Ingrid Werner, "Home Bias and High Turnover," *Journal of International Money and Finance* (August 1995); Joshua Coval and Tobias Moskowitz, "Home Bias at Home: Local Equity Preference in Domestic Portfolios," *Journal of Finance* (December 1999); and Vihang Errunza, Ked Hogan, and Mao-Wei Hung, "Can the Gains from International Diversification be Achieved without Trading Abroad?" *Journal of Finance* (December 1999).

DIRECT FOREIGN INVESTMENT

So far, we have considered international investment in the form of portfolio investment, such as the purchase of a stock or bond issued in a foreign currency. There is, however, another type of international investment activity called direct foreign investment. Direct foreign investment is the spending of domestic firms for establishing foreign operating units. The growth of direct investment spending corresponds to the growth of the multinational firm. Although direct investment is properly emphasized in international trade discussions of the international movement of factors of production, you should be able to distinguish portfolio investment from direct investment.

The motives for portfolio investment are easily seen in terms of the risk and return concepts already examined. In a general sense, such a concern with a firm's return subject to risk considerations may be thought to motivate all firm decisions, including those of direct investment. However, a body of literature has developed to offer more specific motives for desiring domestic ownership of foreign production facilities.* Theories of direct foreign investment typically explain the incentive for such investment in terms of some imperfection in free-market conditions. If markets were perfectly competitive, then the domestic firm should just as well buy foreign securities to transfer capital abroad rather than actually establish a foreign operating unit. One line of theorizing on direct investment is that individual firms may not maximize profits, which would be in the interest of such a firm's stockholders, but, instead, they maximize growth in terms of firm size. This is a concept that relies on an oligopolistic nature of industry that would allow a firm to survive without maximizing profits. In this case, direct investment is preferred, because firms cannot depend on foreign-managed firms to operate in their best interests.

Other reasons for direct foreign investment are based on the superior skills, knowledge, or information of domestic firms as compared with foreign firms. Such advantages would allow the foreign subsidiary of the domestic firm to earn a higher return than is possible by a foreign-managed firm.

Let's consider, in more detail, reasons for direct investment by analyzing the following issues affecting the profitability of the multinational firm:

---

*For reviews of this literature, see Sara L. Gordon and Francis A. Lees, *Foreign Multinational Investment in the United States,* Chapter 3 (New York: Quorum, 1986); Rachel McCulloch, "U.S. Direct Foreign Investment and Trade: Theories, Trends, and Public Policy Issues," in *Multinationals as Mutual Invaders,* ed. Asim Erdilek (London: Croom Helm, 1985); Constantine Michalopoulos, "Private Direct Investment, Finance, and Development," *Asian Development Review* 2 (1985); and Alan M. Rugman, "New Theories of the Multinational Enterprise: An Assessment of Internationalization Theory," *Bulletin of Economic Research* 2 (1986). Other useful articles include John Dunning, *International Production and the Multinational Enterprise* (London: George Allen Unwin, 1981); K.A. Froot and J.C. Stein, "Exchange Rates and Foreign Direct Investment: An Imperfect Capital Markets Approach," *Quarterly Journal of Economics* (November 1991); R.H. Pettway, "Japanese Mergers and Direct Investment in the U.S.," in *Japanese Financial Market Research,* ed. W.T. Ziemba, W. Bailey, and Y. Hamao (Amsterdam: Elsevier, 1991); and Padma Mallampally and Karl P. Sauvant, "Foreign Direct Investment in Developing Countries," *Finance and Development* (March 1999).

Technology transfer A major reason why firms invest in foreign countries is to transfer a superior technology they possess into another market. The technological advantage may confer lower production costs relative to rivals or even allow the introduction of new products. But why should a firm locate a production unit in a foreign country rather than simply produce the product at home and export to foreign markets? One motivation is to avoid tariffs that would apply to exports but can be avoided by a subsidiary producing in the foreign country. Another incentive is to utilize a cost advantage available in a foreign country. For instance, the firm may have leading technology that requires low-skilled labor for at least part of the production process. In this case, we might see a multinational firm in one country, say the United States, producing products in Mexico to take advantage of low wages, and then exporting the products from Mexico into the United States. Direct investment need not be undertaken solely with a goal of selling in foreign markets.

Economies of scale Some industries may have production requirements that allow firms with multiple plants to realize cost advantages over other firms with only a single plant. Such multiplant economies of scale are driven by activities of the firm that involve major expenditures and are not directly related to production but indirectly support the production process of one or more plants. In this case, spreading the costs of the supportive activities over many plants lowers the production costs of the firm relative to firms with only a single plant. What kinds of production support activities might generate such multiplant economies of scale? Marketing expenses, research and development, financial management, or any expense that can be utilized across plants could be the basis for the scale economies. While the domestic market of the firm may not support enough plants to allow the economies of scale to be realized, direct investment that establishes plants in different countries confers the advantages of multiplant economies that reduce costs per plant relative to rivals.

Appropriability Suppose a firm possesses a technological advantage over its rivals but believes that eventually other firms will be able to copy the technology and enter the market. Direct investment may be used to forestall the entry of the potential competitors. By establishing production units in foreign countries, the firm "appropriates" the foreign market before foreign competitors can copy the technology and begin production. Here the firm uses direct investment to defend itself against potential competition from foreign rivals.

The ideas covered here suggest that direct investment results from some advantages to the multinational firm that accrue to ownership of production units in foreign countries. The target countries of such investment must also provide location-specific advantages that complement the investing firm's expertise. So to fully understand the evolution of direct investment expenditures, we must consider the geographic advantages of locating production in certain countries in tandem with the technological or other advantages owned by the multinational firm.

Direct investment has changed over time as a source of finance for developing countries. Prior to the rapid growth of bank lending following the oil price shocks of 1973–1974, direct investment was more relevant than bank lending as a source of funds in developing countries. Through the late 1970s, bank lending grew in magnitude and came to dominate direct investment by the early 1980s. In 1970, direct investment in developing countries accounted for 19 percent of money inflows.

By 1980, this figure fell to 12 percent. More recently, direct investment has risen in importance again.

The growth of bank lending was a result of the growth of the Eurodollar market associated with the "recycling" of dollars earned by oil exporters through international banks to developing country borrowers. Bank lending was preferred by developing countries because it allowed great flexibility in the use of funds in the borrowing country. Direct investment has often been politically unpopular in developing countries because it is associated with an element of foreign control over domestic resources. Nationalist sentiment, combined with a fear of exploitation, has often resulted in laws restricting direct investment. In such a setting, it is understandable that countries readily embraced the low-cost availability of bank loans in the 1970s. In contrast to direct investment decisions made by foreign firms, funds lent by banks could be used by the nation to follow whatever economic or political strategy existed.

In the mid-1980s, bank lending to large-debtor developing countries was sharply curtailed due to problems of nonrepayment. As a result, direct investment has once again become an important source of funds in developing countries. Table 16.2 shows how direct investment changed in importance over the 1990s. In 1990, direct investment and portfolio investment were roughly of equal importance to developing countries. However, in the early 1990s, direct investment was overshadowed by the growth of portfolio investment. The volatility of investment is driven by several factors. In the early 1990s, there was great interest in investing in "emerging market" securities. Large investment fund managers bought sizable amounts of developing country financial assets to meet the demands of their customers. Then in 1994, a financial crisis in Mexico resulted in a surprising devaluation of the Mexican peso and a dramatic drop in Mexican stock prices. The crisis in Mexico caused investors to reevaluate the risks of developing country portfolio investment and resulted in a **contagion effect** where other developing country financial markets were also hit by declining values as if the Mexican crisis were a contagious disease spreading throughout the developing world. This rippling drop in the value of developing country securities following the Mexican crisis is often referred to as the "Tequila Effect."

Contagion effect
A crisis in one country spills over into other countries.

As a result of the Mexican crisis of 1994, portfolio investment and bank lending in developing countries, viewed as riskier, dropped in importance while the more

TABLE 16.2	*Net Capital Flows to Developing Countries (fraction of total)*				
	1990	1992	1994	1996	1998
Direct investment	0.38	0.30	0.54	0.54	2.04
Portfolio investment	0.36	0.43	0.69	0.38	0.57
Other*	0.25	0.27	−0.23	0.08	−1.61

*Other includes loans, bank deposits, and trade credit.

SOURCE: International Monetary Fund, *International Capital Markets,* September 1998.

long-term direct investment became more important. This shift was not only due to changes in investor preferences, but was also welcomed by the host countries. Portfolio investment is shorter term than direct investment and may contribute to financial crisis as investors move money in and out of nations. Direct investment is not as sensitive to short-term changes in economic conditions as it is viewed more as a long-term commitment. In addition, direct investment may offer the host country advantages relative to bank loans. It may be that direct investment contributes more to economic development than bank loans, as more of the funds go to actual investment in productive resources. Bank loans to sovereign governments were (and are) often used for consumption spending rather than investment. In addition, direct investment may involve new technologies and productive expertise not available in the domestic economy. If foreign firms make a bad decision regarding a direct investment expenditure, the loss is sustained by the foreign firm. If the domestic government uses bank loans inefficiently, the country still faces a repayment obligation to the banks.

Table 16.2 indicates that in both 1994 and 1998 the Other category was negative. Since the table reports *net* capital flows, in 1994 and 1998 we see that in the Other category (largely bank loans) more money flowed out of the developing countries than flowed in. In 1994 this was due to the "Tequila crisis." In 1997–1998 an Asian financial crisis occurred when several Asian countries had surprising currency devaluations along with large drops in securities prices that resulted in investors withdrawing money from these countries. Later in this chapter, we will discuss the issue of financial crises in more detail.

CAPITAL FLIGHT

In the discussion of portfolio investment, we emphasized expected risk and return as determinants of foreign investment. When the risk of investment in a country rises sharply and/or the expected return falls, we sometimes observe large outflows of investment funds, so that the country experiences massive capital account deficits. Such outflows of funds are often descriptively referred to as **capital flight**. The change in the risk-return relationship that gives rise to capital flight may be due to political or financial crisis, tightening capital controls, tax increases, or fear of a domestic-currency devaluation.*

Capital flight
Large capital outflows resulting from unfavorable investment conditions in a country.

Table 16.3 provides estimates of the magnitude of capital flight over the 1977–1987 international debt crisis period for selected countries. The third column,

---

*The threat of an increased tax burden is emphasized in Jonathan Eaton, "Public Debt Guarantees and Private Capital Flight" (discussion paper, Development Research Department, World Bank, September 1986). An overvalued exchange rate (implying an expected future devaluation) is identified as a major incentive for capital flight in Chile, Mexico, Uruguay, and Argentina in the early 1980s in John T. Cuddington, "Capital Flight: Estimates, Issues, and Explanations" (discussion paper, Country Policy Department, World Bank, November 1985). A good review article is Mohsin S. Khan and Nadeem Ul Haque, "Capital Flight from Developing Countries," *Finance and Development* (March 1987).

TABLE 16.3	*Estimated Capital Flight, International Debt Crisis Period 1977–1987 (billions of U.S. dollars)*	
Country	Capital Flight	Gross External Debt (1984)
Argentina	20	46
Brazil	20	104
Mexico	45	97
Venezuela	28	34
Nigeria	9	20
Philippines	8	24

SOURCE: Morgan Guaranty Trust Company and World Bank.

Gross External Debt (1984), is provided to indicate the size of the capital flows relative to the debt incurred. One of the issues arising from the developing country debt crisis of the 1980s was an assertion by bankers that some of the borrowed money was not put to use in the debtor nations, but instead was misappropriated by individuals and deposited back in the developed countries. In addition to alleged misappropriated funds, wealthy individuals and business firms often shipped capital out of the debtor nations at the same time that these nations were pleading for additional funds from developed country banks.

Table 16.3 suggests that over the 1977–1987 period, $20 billion of flight capital left Argentina. This $20 billion is almost half the total debt of $46 billion incurred through 1984. Since some of the debt was accumulated prior to 1977, the data suggest crudely that for every $1 borrowed by Argentina, almost 50 cents came out of the country as flight capital. Similar statements might be made for the other countries in the table. An important aspect of the capital outflows is that less resources are available at home to service the debt, and more borrowing is required. In addition, capital flight may be associated with a loss of international reserves and greater pressure for devaluation of the domestic currency.

The discussion of capital flight serves to highlight the importance of economic and political stability for encouraging domestic investment. Business firms and individuals respond to lower risk and higher return. A stable, growing developing country faces little, if any, capital flight and attracts foreign capital to aid in expanding the productive capacity of the economy. Several of the countries listed in Table 16.3 saw a repatriation of flight capital as their economies stabilized in the late 1980s and 1990s.

CAPITAL INFLOW ISSUES

The early 1990s were characterized by a surge of capital inflows to developing countries. Interest in countries with emerging financial markets stimulated both direct and portfolio investment in these countries. The inflows were welcome in that they helped poor countries finance domestic infrastructure to aid in development, and they also provided additional opportunities for international diversification for investors. However, some countries that experienced particularly large capital inflows exhibited problems that could reduce the positive effects of the capital flows.

A large capital inflow in a short period of time can lead to an appreciation of the recipient country's currency. This appreciation may reduce the competitiveness of the nation's export industries and cause a fall in output and rise in unemployment in these industries. A large rise in the capital account surplus will be accompanied by a large rise in the current account deficit. The capital inflow may also be associated with a rapid increase in the country's money supply, which would create inflationary conditions. As a result of potential problems associated with capital inflows, some countries have imposed policies aimed at limiting the effects of these inflows.

Table 16.4 lists the policy responses of countries facing large capital inflows over the 1988–1994 period. Fiscal restraint is a policy of cutting government expenditures, or raising taxes, so that the expansionary effect of the capital flows is partially offset by the contractionary fiscal policy. The table indicates that Chile, Malaysia, and Thailand followed such policies. All countries but Argentina used some sort of exchange rate policy measures. Generally, these involved an appreciation of the currency in countries where the exchange rate has maintained little flexibility. Allowing the currency to appreciate may hurt export industries, but it allows the money supply to be insulated from the capital flow so that inflationary monetary policy does not occur. Some countries also permitted greater exchange rate flexibility as a way to insulate the domestic money supply from the capital flows. Four of the nine countries imposed capital controls to limit the inflow of capital. Such measures include taxes and quality quotas in capital flows, increased reserve requirements on bank borrowing on foreign currency, or limits on foreign exchange transactions. Finally, Table 16.4 shows that surging capital inflows have been associated with a liberalization or freeing of capital outflows and international trade in some countries. In Colombia, Malaysia, Mexico, and Thailand, rising capital inflows were associated with a reduction in restrictions on both capital outflows and international trade.

TABLE 16.4	*Policy Responses to Capital Inflows, 1988–1994*				
Country	Fiscal restraint	Exchange rate policy	Controls on capital inflows	Liberalization of capital outflows	Trade liberalization accelerated
Argentina (1991)	No	No	No	No	No
Chile (1990)	Yes	Yes	Yes	Yes	No
Colombia (1991)	No	Yes	Yes	Yes	Yes
Indonesia (1990)	No	Yes	Yes	No	No
Malaysia (1989)	Yes	Yes	Yes	Yes	Yes
Mexico (1990)	No	Yes	No	Yes	Yes
Philippines (1992)	No	Yes	No	Yes	No
Sri Lanka (1991)	No	Yes	No	No	Yes
Thailand (1988)	Yes	Yes	No	Yes	Yes

SOURCE: *International Capital Markets,* Washington, D.C.: International Monetary Fund, August 1995, 12.

Overall, the experience of the 1990s created an awareness that capital inflows can be both a blessing and a curse. The attempts to manage the risks associated with such inflows met with varied degrees of success and further studies of the experiences of countries that followed different policies will yield suggestions for appropriate government policy measures.

INTERNATIONAL LENDING AND CRISIS

In many ways international lending is similar to domestic lending. Whether they are lending across town or across international borders, lenders care about the risk of default and the expected return from making loans. However, international lending has been plagued by recurrent horror stories of regional financial crises that have imposed large losses on lenders. During a Latin American debt crisis in the 1980s, many countries were unable to service the international debts they had accumulated. In the 1994–1995 Mexican financial crisis, Mexico devalued the peso dramatically and required a large loan from the IMF and the U.S. Treasury to avoid defaulting on international debts. More recently, the Asian financial crisis of 1997–1998 began with the devaluation of the Thai baht in July 1997 and was followed by financial panic that spread to Malaysia, Indonesia, the Philippines, and, to a lesser extent, South Korea.

All of these crises imposed large losses on international investors and led to banks turning inward for a while, devoting fewer resources to international lending, particularly in developing countries. Table 16.5 illustrates the commitment of U.S. banks to lending in each of the crisis areas. As the table indicates, the situation from the perspective of U.S. banks was much more dire in the 1982 Latin American crisis than in the more recent cases.

TABLE 16.5   *U.S. Bank Loans in Financial Crisis Countries (as a percent of U.S. bank capital)*

Latin America in 1982:	
Argentina	12%
Brazil	26%
Chile	9%
Mexico	37%
Mexico in 1994:	11%
Asia in 1997:	
Indonesia	2%
Korea	3%
Thailand	1%

SOURCE: Steve Kamin, "The Asian Financial Crisis in Historical Perspective: A Review of Selected Statistics," Working Paper (Board of Governors of the Federal Reserve System, 1998).

In contrast to the heavy exposure of international banks to Latin American borrowers in 1982, the Asian financial crisis of 1997 involved a much more manageable debt position. Many international investors lost money in the Asian crisis, but the crisis did not threaten the stability of the world banking system to the extent the 1980s crisis did.

The causes of the recent Asian financial crisis are still being debated. Yet, is it safe to say that certain elements are essential in any explanation. These include external shocks, domestic macroeconomic policy, and domestic financial system flaws. Let's consider each of these in turn.

1. *External shocks.* Following years of rapid growth, in the mid-1990s the East Asian economies faced a series of external shocks that may have contributed to the crisis. The Chinese renminbi and the Japanese yen were both devalued, making other Asian economies less competitive relative to China and Japan. Since electronics manufacturing is an important export industry in East Asia, another factor contributing to a drop in exports and national income was the sharp drop in semiconductor prices. As exports and incomes fell, loan repayment became more difficult and property values started to fall. Since real property is used as collateral in many bank loans, the drop in property values made many loans of questionable value, so that the banking systems were facing many defaults.

2. *Domestic macroeconomic policy.* The most obvious element of macroeconomic policy in most crisis countries was the use of fixed exchange rates. Fixed exchange rates encouraged international capital flows into the countries, and many foreign currency debts were not hedged due to the lack of exchange rate volatility. Once pressures for devaluation began, countries defended the pegged exchange rate by central bank intervention—buying domestic currency with dollars. Since each of these countries had a finite supply of dollars, they also raised interest rates to increase the attractiveness of investments denominated in domestic currency. Finally, some countries resorted to capital controls, restricting foreigners' access to domestic currency to curb speculation. For instance, if investors wanted to speculate against the Thai baht, they could borrow baht and exchange them for dollars, betting that the baht would fall in value against the dollar. This increased selling pressure on the baht could be reduced by capital controls that limit foreigners' ability to borrow baht. However, ultimately the pressure to devalue is too great, as even domestic residents are speculating against the domestic currency and the fixed exchange rate is abandoned. This occurs with great cost to the domestic financial market. Since international debts are denominated in foreign currency, and most are unhedged due to a fixed exchange rate, the domestic currency burden of the debt is increased in proportion to the size of the devaluation. To aid in repaying the debt, countries turn to other governments and the IMF for aid.

3. *Domestic financial system flaws.* The Asian crisis countries were characterized by banking systems in which loans were not always made on the basis of prudent

business decisions. Political and social connections were often more important than expected return and collateral when applying for a loan. As a result, many bad loans were extended. During the boom times of the early to mid-1990s, the rapid growth of the economy covered such losses. However, once the growth started to falter, the bad loans started to adversely affect the financial health of the banking system. A related issue is that banks and other lenders expected the government to bail them out if they ran into serious financial difficulties. This situation of implicit government loan guarantees created a *moral hazard* situation. A moral hazard exists when one does not have to bear the full cost of bad decisions. This creates excessive risk taking as the institution or individual taking the risk knows that they will not be held liable if a bad decision results. So if banks believe that the government will cover any significant losses due to loans to political cronies that are not repaid, they will be more likely to extend such loans.

Once a country found itself with severe international debt repayment problems, it had to seek additional financing. Since international banks are not willing to commit new money where prospects for repayment are slim, the IMF becomes an important source of funding.

SUMMARY

1. Foreign-exchange risk may be analyzed as translation exposure, transaction exposure, or economic exposure.

2. Exchange risk hedges are accomplished by using the forward, futures, or options market; invoicing in domestic currency; speeding (slowing) payments of currencies expected to appreciate (depreciate); and speeding (slowing) collection of currencies expected to depreciate (appreciate).

3. The foreign-exchange risk premium is equal to the percentage difference between the forward rate and the expected future spot rate.

4. Prices reflect all available information in an efficient market.

5. A good spot rate forecast should be on the correct side of the forward rate.

6. International investment is motivated by risk and return considerations.

7. Nonsystematic risk may be diversified away so that only systematic risk remains.

8. Direct foreign investment involves the establishment of foreign operating units.

9. Capital outflows in response to economic or political crises are referred to as capital flight.

10. Capital inflows are good in the additional financing they provide, but they also may have some harmful effects on output and employment of certain industries.

11. Sources of financial crises may be found in external shocks, domestic macro-economic policy, and domestic financial system flaws.

EXERCISES

1. Distinguish among translation exposure, transaction exposure, and economic exposure. Define each concept, and then indicate how they may be interrelated.

2. The 1-year interest rate in the United States is 10 percent; in Switzerland, it is 12 percent. The current spot rate (dollars per franc) is $0.40.
   a. What do you expect the 1-year forward rate to be?
   b. Is the franc selling at a premium or a discount?
   c. If the expected spot rate in 1 year is $0.38, what is the risk premium?

3. We discussed risk aversion as being descriptive of investor behavior. Can you think of any real-world behavior that you might consider evidence of the existence of risk preferrers?

4. Does an efficient market rule out all opportunities for speculative profits? If so, why? If not, why not?

5. Data indicate that there is a "home bias" in international investment where investors appear to hold fewer foreign stocks and hold more domestic stocks than is optimal. Why might this occur?

6. What would be necessary to have a portfolio of four stocks provide the same variance of returns as a portfolio of only one (any one) of the stocks?

7. If foreign stock markets are efficient, why should this allow us to buy foreign stocks as safely as we buy domestic stocks?

8. What sort of factors could make foreign stock markets less efficient to investors than the domestic market?

9. What is the difference between foreign direct investment and portfolio investment?

10. What can a government do to provide a permanent solution to the problem of capital flight?

11. Suppose IBM's subsidiary in Germany has contracted to deliver DM1,000,000 worth of computers to a retailer in France with payment due in 90 days. The current spot exchange rate is DM0.38 per franc, and the 90-day forward rate is quoted at DM0.25 per franc. The accountant for the French retailer has

hired two market analysts who make the following forecasts of the spot rate in 90 days:

Ms. Delors predicts DM0.35 per franc.

Mr. Mitterand predicts DM0.20 per franc.

The actual realized spot rate in 90 days is DM0.32 per franc. Who had the better forecast? Explain why.

12. Suppose the U.S. dollar currently sells at DM1.50, and the 90-day forward premium on the dollar is 5 percent. Calculate the 3-month DM/$ forward rate. What is the expected spot rate in 90 days if the risk premium is 0.03? Is the expected return from holding a U.S. bond greater than or less than the expected return from holding a German bond?

13. It has been said that the Asian financial crisis of the late 1990s was less of a threat to international banks than the debt crisis of the 1980s. In what sense is this true? Besides a threat to international banking, what other harm might spread from a financial crisis?

REFERENCES

Ariyoshi, Akira, Karl Habermeier, Bernard Laurens, Inci Otker-Robe, Jorge Ivan Canales-Kirilenko, and Andrei Kirilenko. *Country Experiences with the Use and Liberalization of Capital Controls.* International Monetary Fund, 1999.

Engel, Charles, "The Forward Discount Anomaly and the Risk Premium: A Survey of Recent Evidence." *Journal of Empirical Finance* (September 1996).

Grauer, Robert R., and Nils H. Hakkansson. "Gains from International Diversification: 1968–85 Returns on Portfolios of Stocks and Bonds." *Journal of Finance* (July 1987).

Kasa, Kenneth. "Measuring the Gains from International Portfolio Diversification." *Federal Reserve Bank of San Francisco Weekly Letter* (April 8, 1994).

Khan, Mohsin S., and Nadeem Ul Haque. "Capital Flight from Developing Countries." *Finance and Development* (March 1987).

Solnik, Bruno. *International Investments*, 4th ed. Reading, Mass.: Addison-Wesley, 2000.

INTERNET APPLICATIONS

Please visit our Web site at www.awl.com/husted_melvin for more exercises and readings.

CHAPTER 17

Basic Theories

of the Balance

# of Payments

E arlier chapters are full of discussions involving foreign-exchange rates and the balance of payments. We now know the definitions and uses of these two important international financial terms, but we have yet to consider what determines their values at any particular point in time. Why do some countries run a surplus balance of payments, while others run deficits? How is it that some currencies appreciate in value during one period yet depreciate in another? These are very important questions that are central to international monetary economics. It is worth noting that financial institutions, central banks, and governments invest many resources in trying to predict exchange rates and international payments balances. The kinds of theories introduced in this chapter have shaped the way that economists, investors, and politicians approach such problems.

We shall first discuss theories of the balance of trade and then proceed to discuss the determinants of the balance of payments and exchange rates.

THE ELASTICITIES APPROACH TO THE BALANCE OF TRADE

Economic behavior involves satisfying unlimited wants with limited resources. One implication of this fact of budget constraints is that consumers and business firms will substitute among goods as prices change to stretch their budgets as far as possible. For instance, if Japanese-made shoes and U.S.–made shoes are good substitutes, then as the price of U.S. shoes rises relative to Japanese shoes, buyers will substitute away from the higher-priced U.S. shoes toward the lower-priced (in relative terms) Japanese shoes. The crucial concept for determining consumption patterns is **relative price**, the price of one good relative to another (originally introduced in Chapter 2).

Relative price
The ratio of two product prices.

Relative prices change as relative demands for and supplies of individual goods change. Such changes may be due to changes in tastes or production technology, government taxes or subsidies, or many other possible sources. If the changes involve prices of goods at home changing relative to foreign prices, then international trade patterns may be altered. The elasticities approach to the balance of trade is concerned with how changing relative prices of domestic and foreign goods will change the balance of trade.

A change in the exchange rate will change the domestic-currency price of foreign goods. Suppose, initially, a pair of shoes sells for $50 in the United States and ¥5,000 in Japan. At an exchange rate of ¥100 = $1 (or ¥1 = $0.01), the shoes sell for the same price in each country when expressed in a common currency. If the yen is devalued to ¥120 = $1 and shoe prices remain constant in the domestic currency of the producer, then shoes selling for ¥5,000 in Japan will now cost U.S. buyers $41.67. After the devaluation, ¥1 = $0.0083, so ¥1 = $41.67, and the price of Japanese shoes to U.S. buyers has fallen. Conversely, the price of $50 U.S. shoes to Japanese buyers has risen from ¥5,000 to ¥6,000. The relative price effect of the yen devaluation should increase U.S. demand for Japanese goods and decrease Japanese demand for U.S. goods. How much the quantity demanded changes in response to the relative price change is determined by the elasticity of demand.

In your beginning economics courses, you probably learned that **elasticity** measures the responsiveness of quantity to changes in price. The elasticities approach to the balance of trade provides an analysis of how devaluations will affect the balance of trade depending on the elasticities of supply and demand for foreign exchange and/or foreign goods.

Elasticity
The responsiveness of quantity to changes in price.

When demand or supply is elastic, it means that the quantity demanded or supplied will be relatively responsive to the change in price. An inelastic demand or supply indicates that the quantity is relatively unresponsive to the price changes. We can make things more precise by using coefficients of elasticity. For instance, letting ϵ_d represent the coefficient of elasticity of demand, we can write ϵ_d as

$$\epsilon_d = \% \, \Delta Q \, / \, \% \, \Delta P \qquad (17.1)$$

This implies that the coefficient of elasticity of demand is equal to the percentage change in the quantity demanded, divided by the percentage change in price. If the price increases by 5 percent and the quantity demanded falls by more than 5 percent, then ϵ_d exceeds 1 (in absolute value), and we say that demand is elastic. If, when the price increases by 5 percent, the quantity demanded falls by less than 5 percent, we would say that demand is inelastic, and ϵ_d would be less than 1.

Just as we can compute a coefficient of elasticity of demand, ϵ_d, so we can compute a coefficient of elasticity of supply, ϵ_s, as the percentage change in the quantity supplied divided by the percentage change in price. If ϵ_s exceeds 1, the quantity supplied is relatively responsive to price, and we say that supply is elastic. For ϵ_s, less than 1, the quantity supplied is relatively unresponsive to price, so that the supply is inelastic.

Elasticity will determine what happens to total revenue (price times quantity) following a price change. With an elastic demand, the quantity changes by a greater percentage amount than the price, so the total revenue will move in the opposite direction from the price change. Suppose the demand for black velvet paintings from Mexico is elastic. If the peso price rises 10 percent, the quantity demanded falls by more than 10 percent, so that the revenue received from sales will fall after the price change. If the demand for Colombian coffee is inelastic, then a 10 percent increase in price will result in a fall in the quantity demanded of less than 10 percent. The higher coffee price more than makes up for the lost sales, so that coffee sales revenues rise after the price change. Obviously, elasticity of demand will be of great importance in determining export and import revenues as international prices change.

Now let us consider an example of supply and demand in the foreign-exchange market. Figure 17.1 provides an example of the supply and demand for U.K. pounds. The demand curve labeled D_0 is the demand for pounds, arising from the demand for British exports. The familiar downward slope indicates that the higher the price of pounds is, the fewer pounds will be demanded. The supply curve labeled S is the supply of pounds to the foreign-exchange market. The upward slope indicates the positive relationship between the foreign-exchange price of pounds and the quantity of pounds supplied. The point where the supply and demand curves intersect is the equilibrium point, where the quantity of pounds demanded just equals the quantity supplied. Suppose initially we have an equilibrium at E_0 and

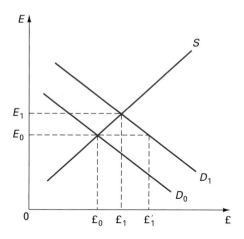

FIGURE 17.1   *Supply and demand in the foreign-exchange market.*

$£_0$. That is, $£_0$ is the quantity of pounds that are bought and sold at the exchange rate E_0. Now, suppose there is an increase in demand for pounds (e.g., due to an increase in demand for U.K. exports). There are several responses possible to this shift in demand:

1. The pound will appreciate, with freely floating exchange rates, so that the exchange rate rises to E_1, and $£_1$ are bought and sold.

2. Central banks can peg the exchange rate at the old E_0 by providing $£_1' - £_0$ from their reserves (and thereby artificially shifting out the supply of pounds).

3. The supply and demand curves can be artificially shifted by imposing controls or quotas on the supply of or demand for pounds.

4. Quotas or tariffs could be imposed on foreign trade to maintain the old supply of and demand for pounds.

The elasticities approach recognizes that the effect of an exchange rate change on the equilibrium quantity of currency being traded will depend on the elasticities of the supply and demand curves involved. It is important to remember that the elasticities approach is a theory of the balance of trade and can be a theory of the balance of payments only in a world without capital flows.

Suppose, in Figure 17.1, E is the dollar price of pounds, and the U.S. central bank decides to meet the increase in demand for pounds by supplying pounds to the market from U.S. reserves. Now, the old exchange rate E_0 is maintained due to the central bank's addition of $£_1' - £_0$ to the market supply. If it becomes apparent that the increase in demand is a permanent change, then the Federal Reserve will devalue the dollar, driving up the dollar price of pounds. This, of course, means that U.K. goods will be more expensive to the United States, whereas U.S. goods will be

FIGURE 17.2 *The J curve.*

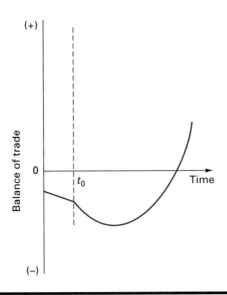

cheaper to the United Kingdom. Will this improve the U.S. trade balance? It all depends on the elasticities of supply and demand. With inelastic demands, it is possible to get *J* **curve effects**, where at first the price of imports to the United States increases, but the quantity of imports demanded changes little so that total payments to the United Kingdom actually increase. Likewise, with an inelastic demand for U.S. exports in the United Kingdom, the price of imports from the United States could fall, yet few more are demanded. In this case, the U.S. balance-of-trade deficit and the excess demand for pounds could actually increase following a devaluation. The *J* curve previously mentioned refers to the pattern of the balance of trade following a devaluation. If the balance of trade is viewed over time, the initial decrease in the trade balance, due to the inelastic demands followed by a growing trade balance, results in the time pattern of the trade balance tracing out a path similar to the letter *J*, as shown in Figure 17.2. Note in the figure that the trade balance is initially negative and falling over time. The devaluation occurs at the point in time t_0. After the devaluation, the balance of trade falls for a while before finally turning upward. The initial fall is due to low elasticities in the short run. Over time, elasticities increase, so that the balance of trade improves. This general pattern of the balance of trade falling before increasing traces out a pattern that resembles the letter *J*.

J **curve effects**
After a devaluation, the balance of trade falls for a while before increasing.

ELASTICITIES AND J CURVES

Devaluation is conventionally believed to be a tool for increasing a country's balance of trade. Yet the *J* curve effect indicates that when the devaluation increases the price of foreign goods to the home country and decreases the price of domestic goods to foreign buyers, there is a short-run period when the balance of trade falls. Is this pattern to be expected, or is the *J* curve simply a theoretical curiosity with no real-world importance? Before reviewing the evidence on this matter, let us investigate the factors that should be important in determining foreign trade elasticities in the short run to see what the possible underlying reasons for a *J* curve are.

We can identify different periods following a devaluation where the ability of traders to respond to the new set of prices is at first limited but over time becomes complete.*

The Currency-Contract Period

Currency-contract period
The period immediately following a devaluation when contracts signed prior to the devaluation are settled.

Immediately after a devaluation, contracts that were negotiated prior to the exchange rate change become due. Let us refer to this as the **currency-contract period**. Figure 17.3 illustrates the timing of events. Contracts are signed at time t_1. After the contracts are established, there is a currency devaluation at time t_2. Then the payments specified in the contracts are due at a later period t_3. The effects of such existing contracts on the balance of trade depend on the currency in which the contract is denominated. For instance, let us suppose that the United States devalues the dollar. Before the devaluation, the exchange rate is $1 per unit of foreign currency (to simplify matters, we will assume only one foreign currency); afterward, the rate jumps to $1.25. If a U.S. exporter has contracted to sell $1 worth of goods to a foreign firm payable in dollars, the exporter will still earn $1. However, if the export contract was written in terms of foreign currency (let FC stand for foreign currency), then the exporter expected to receive FC1, which would be equal to $1. Instead, the devaluation leads to FC1 = $1.25, so the U.S. exporter receives an unexpected gain from the dollar devaluation. On the other hand, consider an import contract in which a U.S. importer contracts to buy from a foreign firm. If the contract calls for payment of $1, the U.S. importer is unaffected by the devaluation. If the contract had been written in terms of foreign currency, so that the U.S. importer owes FC1, then the importer would have to pay $1.25 to buy the FC1 that the exporter receives. In this case, the importer faces a loss due to the devaluation.

FIGURE 17.3	*The currency-contract period.*

Contracts Signed	Currency Devaluation	Payments Due	
t_1	t_2	t_3	Time

---

* A useful approach to analyzing the short-run period following a devaluation is provided by Stephen P. Magee, "Currency Contracts, Pass-Through, and Devaluation," *Brookings Papers on Economic Activity* 1 (1973): 303–25.

TABLE 17.1	*U.S. Trade Balance Effects during the Currency-Contract Period Following a Devaluation*	

U.S. Export Contracts Written in	U.S. Import Contracts Written in	
	Dollars	Foreign Currency
Foreign currency	I. Exports increase Imports constant	II. Exports increase Imports increase
	Balance of trade increases	Initial surplus: balance of trade increases Initial deficit: balance of trade decreases
Dollars	III. Exports constant Imports constant	IV. Exports constant Imports increase
	Balance of trade unchanged	Balance of trade decreases

In the simple world under consideration here, we would expect sellers to prefer to contract in the currency expected to appreciate, whereas buyers would prefer contracts written in terms of the currency expected to depreciate. Table 17.1 summarizes the possible trade balance effects during the currency-contract period.

Table 17.1 divides the effects into four sections. Section I represents the case where U.S. export contracts are written in terms of foreign currency, although import contracts are denominated in dollars. In this case, the dollar value of exports will increase, since the foreign buyer must pay in foreign currency, which is worth more after the devaluation. Since imports are paid for with dollars, the devaluation will have no effect on the dollar value of U.S. imports. As a result, the balance of trade must increase.

Section II indicates the trade balance effects when U.S. exports and imports are paid for with foreign currency. Since the dollar devaluation increases the value of foreign currency, the dollar values of both exports and imports will increase. The net effect on the U.S. trade balance depends on the magnitude of U.S. exports relative to imports. If exports exceed imports, so that there is an initial trade surplus, then the increase in export values will exceed the increase in import values, so that the balance of trade increases. Conversely, if there is an initial trade deficit, so that imports exceed exports, then the increase in import values will exceed the increase in export values, so that the balance of trade decreases.

If both exports and imports are payable in dollars, the balance of trade is unaffected by a devaluation, as indicated in section III. But if exports are payable in dollars, although imports require payment in foreign currency, the dollar value of exports will be unaffected by the devaluation, while import values will increase, so that the trade balance decreases, as in section IV. Note that only in the case of section IV must there be a decline in the trade balance during the currency-contract period following a devaluation. A decline could also occur in section II, although only if there is an initial trade deficit. The key feature of Table 17.1 is that foreign-currency-denominated imports provide a necessary condition for the U.S. trade balance to take the plunge observed in the *J* curve phenomenon during the currency-contract period.

The Pass-Through Period

The currency-contract period refers to that period following a devaluation when contracts negotiated before the devaluation come due. During this time, it is assumed that goods prices do not adjust instantaneously to the change in currency values. Eventually, of course, as new trade contracts are negotiated, goods prices will tend toward the new equilibrium. The **pass-through analysis** considers the ability of prices to adjust in the short run. The kind of adjustment expected is an increase in the price of import goods in the devaluing country and a decrease in the price of the country's exports to the rest of the world. If goods prices do not adjust in this manner, spending patterns will not be altered; as a result, the desirable balance-of-trade effects of devaluation do not appear.

Pass-through analysis
The adjustment of domestic and foreign prices to devaluation.

Devaluation is normally a response to a persistent and growing balance-of-trade deficit. As import prices rise in the devaluing country, fewer imports should be demanded. At the same time, the lower price of domestic exports to foreigners should increase the demand for exports. The combination of a higher demand for domestic exports and a lower domestic demand for imports should bring about an improvement in the trade balance. In the short run, however, if the response to the new prices is slow, so that the quantities traded don't change much, the new prices could contribute to the *J* curve. For instance, if the demand for imports is inelastic, buyers will be relatively unresponsive to the higher price of imports, and thus the total import bill could rise rather than fall after the devaluation. Such behavior is not unreasonable, since it takes time to find good substitutes for the now higher-priced import goods. Eventually, such substitutions will occur, but in the short run buyers may continue to buy imports in large enough quantities so that the now higher price results in greater, rather than smaller, domestic import values after the devaluation. The same explanation could be told on the other side of the market if foreign demand for domestic exports is inelastic. In this case, foreign buyers will not buy much more in the short run, even though the price of domestic exports has fallen.

Table 17.2 summarizes the possible effects following a U.S. devaluation during the brief pass-through period before quantities adjust. Quantities are held fixed because of inelastic demands or supplies. Each section in the table is discussed in turn.

Section IV—The U.S. balance of trade decreases   The worst case is presented in section IV. With an inelastic demand for U.S. imports and an inelastic demand for U.S. exports, there will be a full pass-through of prices. This means that the dollar prices of U.S. imports rise by the full amount of the devaluation while the foreign currency prices of U.S. exports fall by the full amount of the devaluation. The dollar value of U.S. imports increases because U.S. buyers do not change the quantity of goods they import but foreign sellers now want more dollars for their goods since the dollar is worth less. The foreign currency prices of U.S. exports fall because U.S. exporters are now willing to accept a lower foreign currency price since foreign currency is worth more. The drop in the foreign currency price offsets the change in the exchange rate, leaving the dollar price unchanged. Since the quantity of goods

TABLE 17.2	*U.S. Trade Balance Effects during the Pass-Through Period following a Devaluation*	
	U.S. Imports	
U.S. Exports	Inelastic Supply	Inelastic Demand

Inelastic supply	I. Exports increase
	    Imports constant
	
	    Balance of trade increases
		II. Exports increase
		     Imports increase
		
		     Initial surplus: balance of
		     trade increases
		
		     Initial deficit: balance of
		     trade decreases

Inelastic demand	III. Exports constant
	     Imports constant
	
	     Balance of trade constant
		IV. Exports constant
		     Imports increase
		
		     Balance of trade decreases

foreigners want to buy is fixed and the dollar price is also unchanged, U.S. exporters find the dollar value of exports constant. The increase in imports coupled with constant exports results in a fall in the U.S. balance of trade.

EXAMPLE

Suppose there are two countries: the United Kingdom and the United States. Initially, the exchange rate was $2 = £1. At this exchange rate, U.S. exporters sold 100 units of goods at $1 each so the dollar value of exports was $100. U.S. exports of $100 cost U.K. buyers £50. Now there is a 10 percent devaluation of the dollar so that the exchange rate changes to $2.20 = £1. Since the U.K. demand for U.S. exports is inelastic, there will still be 100 units of goods traded. If U.S. exporters still want $100 for the goods they sell, they can now charge a price of £45.45 for the exports since at the new exchange rate of $2.20 = £1, £45.45 = $100. There is a full pass-through of the devaluation since the British pound price of U.S. exports falls by the 10 percent amount of the devaluation.

On the U.S. import side, British sellers now want to charge a higher dollar price for goods sold to the United States since dollars are now worth less. Suppose initially, 50 units of goods are imported from the U.K. into the U.S. If the price is £1 per unit, then U.S. imports from the U.K. were worth £50. At the old exchange rate of $2 = £1, this was worth $100. After the dollar devaluation, U.S. importers still buy 50 units of goods due to the inelastic demand for imports, but at the new exchange rate of $2.20 = £1, U.K. sellers must charge U.S. importers $110 in order to still have the British pound value of U.S. imports equal to £50. There has been a full pass-through of the devaluation to U.S. import prices since the dollar price of U.S. imports rises by the 10 percent amount of the devaluation.

Since U.S. exports are constant at $100 both before and after the devaluation, but U.S. imports rise from $100 to $110, the dollar value of the U.S. trade balance falls. As summarized in section IV of Table 17.2, this case of inelastic demands for both U.S. exports and imports will be associated with a decrease in the U.S. balance of trade.

Section III—The U.S. balance of trade is constant   If we pair the inelastic demand for U.S. exports just discussed with an inelastic supply of U.S. imports, then a devaluation of the dollar will have no impact on the U.S. trade balance. We know that with an inelastic demand for U.S. exports, there will be no change in the dollar value of U.S. exports. An inelastic supply of U.S. imports means that foreign sellers will offer the same quantity of goods for sale regardless of price. The devaluation raises the dollar price of foreign currency and reduces the U.S. demand for imports so that the foreign currency price will fall by the full amount of the devaluation and offset the exchange rate change. In this case, the dollar value of imports is left unchanged and there is no pass-through of the devaluation to prices paid by U.S. importers. With a constant dollar price of imports and an unchanged quantity of goods imported due to the inelastic supply curve, the dollar value of U.S. imports is unchanged by the devaluation. Since the devaluation changes neither the dollar values of exports nor imports, the balance of trade is constant during the pass-through period.

Section II—Balance of trade may increase or decrease   In this case, we couple the inelastic demand for U.S. imports discussed in regard to section IV with an inelastic supply of U.S. exports. The inelastic demand for U.S. imports causes the dollar value of imports to rise following the devaluation. The inelastic supply of U.S. exports means that U.S. sellers will offer the same quantity of goods for sale before and after the devaluation. However, the dollar price of U.S. exports will rise since foreign buyers are willing to pay a higher dollar price due to the exchange rate change making dollars cheaper to them. Since the same quantity is being exported at a higher dollar price, the dollar value of exports will rise after the devaluation. If the dollar value of exports and imports both rise by the same percentage amount as the devaluation, what will happen to the balance of trade? It depends on the initial condition. If initially there is a trade surplus so that exports exceed imports, then an equal percentage increase in both will mean exports increase more in dollar value than imports, and the balance of trade will increase. If initially there is a trade deficit so that imports exceed exports, then an equal percentage increase in both will mean imports increase more in dollar value than exports, and the balance of trade will decrease.

Section I—Balance of trade increases   If quantities are fixed in the short run because of inelasticities of supply for both exports and imports, then the balance of trade will increase during the pass-through period. As discussed in regard to section III, the inelastic supply of U.S. imports will keep imports constant. The discussion of section II indicated that an inelastic supply of U.S. exports will cause exports to rise. In this case, the balance of trade will increase during the pass-through period when quantities are fixed but prices change.

The portrayal of perfectly inelastic supply and demand curves is done for illustrative purposes. We cannot argue that, in the real world, there is absolutely no quantity response to changing prices in the short run. The important contribution of the pass-through analysis is to indicate how changing goods prices in the short run, when the quantity response is likely to be quite small, can affect the balance of trade. If it is more reasonable to expect producers to be less able to alter the quantity supplied than buyers can alter the quantity demanded, then section I of Table

17.2 is the most likely real-world case. In this instance, the supplies of U.S. imports and exports are inelastic, so that the U.S. trade balance should improve during the pass-through period.

Item 17.1 provides a view of the pass-through effect that illustrates why we should expect variation across industries.

THE EVIDENCE FROM DEVALUATIONS

The preceding discussion has shown the possible short-run effects of a devaluation on the trade balance through the currency-contract and pass-through periods. What does the evidence of past devaluations have to offer regarding the *actual* effects? Unfortunately, the evidence available suggests that the effects of devaluation differ across countries and time, so that no strong generalizations are possible. Some studies show that devaluation improves the trade account in the short run, while others disagree. The reasons for such disagreement come from different researchers using different sample periods and different statistical methodology.

As introduced in Item 17.1, several researchers have recently focused on the manner in which producers in different countries adjust the profit margins on exports to partially offset the effect of exchange rate changes. This appears to be an important factor in explaining differences in the pass-through effect across countries. For instance, if the Japanese yen appreciates against the U.S. dollar, the yen appreciation would tend to be passed through to U.S. importers as a higher dollar price of Japanese exports. Japanese exporters could limit this pass-through of higher prices by reducing the profit margins on their products and lowering the yen price to counter the effect of the yen appreciation. This **pricing to market** behavior has been found to be especially prevalent among Japanese and German exporters but is much less common among U.S. exporters. For example, Joseph Gagnon and Michael Knetter analyzed automobile trade and estimated that a 10 percent depreciation of the dollar against the yen would result in Japanese auto firms reducing their prices so that the dollar price to U.S. importers would rise by only 2.2 percent. There was no similar evidence of U.S. auto firms reducing prices for exported autos in response to dollar appreciation. The Japanese resistance to allowing pass-through effects is another reason why the Japanese balance of trade may be less responsive to exchange rate changes than the United States trade balance.

Pricing to market
Adjusting export prices in response to exchange rate changes in order to limit changes in the prices paid by importers.

THE ABSORPTION APPROACH
TO THE BALANCE OF TRADE

The elasticities approach showed that it is possible for a country to improve its balance of trade through devaluation. Once the exchange rate effects pass through to import and export prices, imports should fall while exports increase, stimulating production of goods and services and income at home. If a country is at the full employment level of output prior to the devaluation, then it is producing all it can already, so that no further output is forthcoming. What happens in this case after a

ITEM 17.1   The Pass-Through Effect and Profits

In Chapter 14, we learned that the law of one price relates the domestic-currency price (P) of a good to the foreign-currency price (P^F) times the exchange rate (E), or $P = EP^F$. If the domestic currency depreciates (E increases) and P^F remains constant, P will increase in proportion of the exchange rate change. This view of the law of one price involves a full pass-through of exchange rate changes to domestic prices.

An alternative view recognizes that industries differ in terms of competitiveness, so that profit margins may be higher in some industries than in others. Suppose we analyze a product that is produced in a foreign country at cost (C^F) plus profit margin (M^F), so that $P^F = C^F + M^F$. Now, the law of one price is $P = E(C^F + M^F)$. In this setting, there may be less than full pass-through, as M^F may vary as E varies. For instance, the domestic currency could depreciate, yet P may not change if M^F falls to offset the rise in E.

Evidence regarding U.S. trade suggests that changing profit margins may be an important factor in explaining the magnitude of the pass-through effect. Catherine Mann compared prices and profit margins over the 1977–1980 period of dollar depreciation with those of the 1980–1985 period of dollar appreciation.* The accompanying table summarizes her findings for U.S. imports and exports. First, looking at the data on imports, it is apparent that during the period of dollar depreciation, foreign producers generally lowered profit margins. This is demonstrated for every industry except "Certain steels," where

profit margins increased 14.6 percent. Over the 1980–1985 period of dollar appreciation, foreign producers raised their profit margins on goods sold to the United States. This all means that foreign sellers cut their profit margins M^F when the dollar was depreciating so that the dollar price P would not rise by the full amount of the dollar depreciation. When the dollar was appreciating, foreign profit margins M^F increased so that the dollar price P of foreign goods would not fall by the full amount of the dollar appreciation.

The lower section of the table examines U.S. exports. Considering the 74.9 percent appreciation of the dollar over the 1980–1985 period and the 15.5 percent depreciation over the 1977–1980 period, the relatively small changes in profit margins make it appear that profit margins in U.S. export industries were relatively insensitive to changes in the exchange rate. This may be due to the large size of the domestic market in the United States. Pricing decisions by U.S. firms may be more closely related to market conditions at home than to international factors.

We should expect pricing policies to differ across industries as industry competitiveness varies.† Yet the evidence considered here suggests that foreign-currency prices of U.S. exports are more likely to have a significant pass-through of exchange rate changes than the dollar prices of U.S. imports are. This indicates that when the dollar depreciates, the responsiveness of U.S. imports may be much slower and smaller than the simple law of one price would have us believe.

---

*Catherine L. Mann, "Prices, Profit Margins, and Exchange Rates," *Federal Reserve Bulletin* (June 1986).
†There are many studies that address this issue. A small sample includes Robert M. Dunn, Jr., "Flexible Exchange Rates and Oligopoly Pricing: A Study of Canadian Markets," *Journal of Political Economy* (January–February 1970); Eric O'N. Fisher, "A Model of Exchange Rate Pass-Through" (International Finance Discussion Papers No. 302, Board of Governors of the Federal Reserve System, February 1987); Michael W. Klein, "Macroeconomics Aspects of Exchange Rate Pass-Through," *Journal of International Money and Finance* (December 1990); Michael M. Knetter, "Is Export Price Adjustment Asymmetric? Evaluating the Market Share and Marketing Bottlenecks Hypotheses," *Journal of International Money and Finance* (February 1994); and Pinelopi Goldberg and Michael Knetter, "Goods Prices and Exchange Rates: What Have We Learned?" *Journal of Economic Literature* (September 1997).

Percentage Change in Profit Margins, Selected Industries

Industry	1977 to 1980[1]	1980 to 1985[2]
Exchange value of the dollar[3]	−15.5	74.9
Imports (foreign currency)		
Leather footwear	−4.2	87.3
Certain textiles[4]	−9.1	28.0
Construction machinery	−9.2	11.6
Paper products	−2.3	17.6
Certain apparel[5]	−4.9	4.1
Canned fruits and vegetables	−14.1	6.8
Certain steels[6]	14.6	4.1
Exports (dollars)		
Semiconductors[7]	−5.9	−9.6
Power-driven hand tools[8]	−5.0	−6.9
Pulp mill products	4.6	−17.1
Internal combustion engines[9]	−4.5	4.2
Valves and pipe fittings[10]	−2.7	8.7
Oil-field and gas-field equipment[8]	−2.0	1.0
Printing trades machinery[10]	−3.9	5.3
Farm machinery[9]	−2.9	4.5
Meat packing and preparation[8]	−3.6	17.7

[1] Percentage change between the 1977 four-quarter average and the 1980 four-quarter average
[2] Percentage change between the 1980 four-quarter average and the 1985 four-quarter average
[3] Based on the G-10 multilateral trade-weighted exchange rate
[4] Silk and synthetic fibers
[5] Men's and boys' suits and coats
[6] Rolled and electrometallurgical steels, 1978 four-quarter average
[7] 1979 three-quarter average
[8] 1977 three-quarter average
[9] 1978 three-quarter average
[10] 1978 two-quarter average

devaluation? We now turn to the absorption approach to the balance of trade to answer this question.

The absorption approach is a theory of the balance of trade that emphasizes how domestic spending on domestic goods changes relative to domestic output. In other words, the balance of trade is viewed as the difference between what the economy produces and what it takes, or absorbs, for domestic use. As commonly treated in introductory economics classes, total output Y is written as being equal to total expenditures, or

$$Y = C + I + G + (X - IM) \qquad (17.2)$$

where C is consumption, I is investment, G is government spending, X is exports, and IM is imports. We can define absorption A as being equal to $C + I + G$, and net exports as $X - IM$; thus, we can write

$$Y = A + X - IM$$

or

$$Y - A = X - IM \qquad (17.3)$$

Absorption A is supposed to represent total domestic spending, so that if total domestic production Y exceeds absorption, the amount of the output consumed at home, then the nation will export the rest of its output and run a balance-of-trade surplus. On the other hand, if absorption exceeds domestic production, then $Y - A$ is negative. Thus, by Equation 17.3 we note that $X - IM$ will also be negative, which has the commonsense interpretation that the excess of domestic demand over domestic production will be met through imports.

The analysis of the absorption approach is really broken down into two categories, depending on whether the economy is at full employment or has unemployed resources. If we have full employment, then all resources are being used, so that the only way for net exports to increase is to have absorption fall. On the other hand, with unemployment, Y is not at its maximum possible value, and thus A could remain fixed and Y could increase due to increases in domestic sales to foreigners, X.

The absorption approach is generally concerned with the effects of devaluation on the trade balance. If we begin from the case of unemployed resources, we know that domestic output Y could increase, so that a devaluation would tend to increase net exports (if the elasticity conditions discussed in the last section are satisfied) and bring about an increase in output (given a constant absorption). If we start from full employment, then output Y is at the full employment level, so that it is not possible to produce more goods and services. If we devalue, then net exports will tend to increase, and the end result is strictly inflation. When foreigners try to spend more on our domestic production, and yet there is no increase in output forthcoming, the only result will be a bidding-up of the prices of the goods and services currently being produced.

Of course, we must realize that the absorption approach is providing a theory of the balance of trade, as did the elasticities approach before. The absorption approach can be viewed as a theory of the balance of payments only in a world without capital flows.

THE MONETARY APPROACH TO THE BALANCE OF PAYMENTS

The elasticities approach and the absorption approach are theories of the balance of trade that have been popular for over 40 years. As we have seen, these are theories that emphasize trade in real goods and have little to say about the capital account. For some purposes, these theories can still provide useful intuition. However, the world today is characterized by well-developed financial markets and large-scale international capital flows. To fully understand international economic linkages, we must look beyond merchandise trade and incorporate the important role of financial assets. It was in this spirit that the monetary approach to the balance of payments (MABP) came to popularity in the 1970s.* The MABP emphasizes the monetary aspects of the balance of payments.

We may draw the line in the international accounts (see Chapter 12 for a review of balance-of-payments concepts) so that the current and capital accounts are above the line and only those items that directly affect the money supply are below the line (specifically, official holdings of gold, foreign exchange, special drawing rights [SDRs], and changes in reserves at the International Monetary Fund [IMF]—but do not worry about these terms now). This allows us to concentrate on the monetary aspects of the balance of payments.

The basic premise of the MABP is that any balance-of-payments disequilibrium is based on monetary disequilibrium, that is, differences existing between the amount of money people wish to hold and the amount supplied by the monetary authorities. In very simple terms, if people demand more money than is being supplied by the central bank, then the excess demand for money is satisfied by inflows of money from abroad. On the other hand, if the central bank (the Federal Reserve, in the United States) is supplying more money than is demanded, the excess supply of money is eliminated by outflows of money to other countries. Thus, the MABP analysis emphasizes the determinants of money demand and money supply, since these will also determine the balance of payments.

The monetary approach has a long and distinguished history, so that the recent popularity of the approach can be viewed as a rediscovery rather than a modern innovation. In fact, the recent literature often makes use of a quote from *Of the Balance of Trade,* written by David Hume in 1752, to indicate the early understanding of the problem. Hume wrote:

> Suppose four-fifths of all money in Great Britain to be annihilated in one night, and the nation reduced to the same condition, with regard to specie, as in the reigns of the Harrys and Edwards, what would be the consequence? Must not the price of all labour and commodities sink in proportion, and everything be sold as cheap as they were in these ages? What nation could then dispute with us in any foreign market, or pretend to navigate or to sell manufactures at the same price, which to us would

---

*The literature on the MABP is too voluminous to permit more than a very small sample of articles to be cited. A few of the many papers that provide a good introduction include Jacob A. Frenkel, "A Monetary Approach to the Exchange Rate: Doctrinal Aspects and Empirical Evidence," in *The Economics of Exchange Rates: Selected Readings,* ed. Jacob A. Frenkel and Harry G. Johnson (Reading, Mass.: Addison-Wesley, 1978); Lance Girton and Don Roper, "A Monetary Model of Exchange Market Pressure Applied to the Postwar Canadian Experience," *American Economic Review* (September 1977); Michael R. Darby, "The Monetary Approach to the Balance of Payments: Two Specious Assumptions," *Economic Inquiry* (April 1980); Jeffrey A. Frenkel, "Monetary and Portfolio-Balance Models of Exchange Rate Determination," in *Economic Interdependence and Flexible Exchange Rates,* ed. Jagdeep Bhandari and Bluford Putnam (Boston: MIT Press, 1983); and the papers found in Jacob A. Frenkel and Harry G. Johnson, eds., *The Monetary Approach to the Balance of Payments* (Toronto: University of Toronto Press, 1976).

afford sufficient profit? In how little time, therefore, must this bring back the money which we had lost, and raise us to the level of all the neighboring nations? Where after we have arrived, we immediately lose the advantage of the cheapness of labor and commodities; and the farther flowing in of money is stopped by our fullness and repletion.

Hume's analysis is a strict monetary approach to prices and then to the balance of payments. If England's money stock were suddenly reduced by four-fifths, we know from principles of economics courses that the price level would fall dramatically. The falling price level would give England a price advantage over its foreign competitors, so that its exports would rise and its imports fall. As the foreign money (gold, in Hume's day) poured in, England's money supply would rise and its price level would follow. This process would continue until England's prices reached the levels of its competitors, after which the system would be back in equilibrium.

Thus far, we have discussed the monetary approach only with respect to the balance of payments, which is fine for a world with fixed exchange rates or a gold standard. For a world with flexible exchange rates, we have the monetary approach to the exchange rate (MAER). The dichotomy between fixed and floating exchange rates is an important one. When exchange rates are fixed between countries, we observe money flowing between countries to adjust to disequilibrium. With floating exchange rates, the exchange rates are allowed to fluctuate with the free-market forces of supply and demand for each currency. The free-market-equilibrium exchange rate occurs at a point where the flow of exports just equals the flow of imports, so that no net international money flows are required. International economists refer to this choice of money flows or exchange rate changes as the choice of an international **adjustment mechanism**. With fixed exchange rates, the adjustment to changes in international monetary conditions comes through international money flows, whereas with floating rates, the adjustment comes through exchange rate changes. To organize our thoughts and provide a convenient framework for distinguishing the analysis under the MABP and MAER, we outline a simple economic model relating money demand, money supply, the balance of payments, and exchange rates.

Before turning to the model, we should consider some basic concepts and assumptions. In principles of macroeconomics we learn that the Federal Reserve controls the money supply by altering **base money** (currency plus commercial bank reserves held against deposits). As base money changes, the lending ability of commercial banks changes. Increases in base money tend to result in an expansion of the money supply, whereas decreases in base money tend to contract the money supply. For MABP purposes, it is useful to divide base money into domestic and international components. The domestic component of base money is called **domestic credit**, whereas the remainder is made up of **international reserves** (money items that can be used to settle international debts, primarily foreign exchange). The international money flows that respond to excess demands or excess supplies of goods or financial assets at home affect base money and then the money supply. For instance, if a U.S. exporter receives payment in foreign currency, this payment will be presented to a U.S. commercial bank to be converted into dollars and deposited in the exporter's account. If the commercial bank has no use for the foreign currency, the bank will exchange the foreign currency for dollars with the Federal Reserve (the Fed).

Adjustment mechanism
The process by which international disequilibria are eliminated.

Base money
Currency plus commercial bank reserves, which is also equal to international reserves plus domestic credit.

Domestic credit
The domestic component of base money.

International reserves
The portion of base money used to settle international debts.

The Fed creates new base money to buy the foreign currency by increasing the commercial bank's reserve deposit with the Fed. Thus, the Fed is accumulating international reserves, and this reserve accumulation brings about an expansion of base money. In the case of an excess supply of money at home, either domestic credit falls to reduce base money, or else international reserves will fall in order to lower base money to the desired level.

Now we are ready to construct a simple model of the MABP along the lines of the "minimum monetary model" suggested by Michael Connolly.* The usual assumption is that we are analyzing the situation of a **small, open economy**. It is small because we want to assume that this country cannot affect the international price of goods or the interest rate it faces. Openness implies that this country is an active participant in international economic transactions. We could classify nations according to their degree of openness, or the degree to which they depend on international transactions. The United States would be relatively closed, considering the size of the U.S. GDP relative to the value of international trade, whereas Belgium would be relatively open.

Small, open economy An economy that cannot affect the international price of goods or the foreign interest rate.

We can begin our model by writing the demand for money as

$$L = kPY \qquad (17.4)$$

where L is the demand for money, P is the domestic price level, Y is real income or wealth, and k is a constant fraction indicating how money demand will change given a change in P or Y. Equation 17.4 is often stated as "money demand is a function of prices and income," or "money demand depends on prices and income." The usual story is that the higher the income, the more money people will hold to buy more goods. The higher the price level, the more money is desired to buy any given quantity of goods. So, the demand for money should rise with an increase in either P or Y.

A strong assumption of the monetary approach is that there is a stable demand for money. This means that the relationship among money demand, income, and prices does not change significantly over time. Without a stable demand for money, the monetary approach will not provide a useful framework for analysis.

Letting M stand for money supply, R for international reserves, and D for domestic credit, we can write the money supply relationship as[†]

$$M = R + D \qquad (17.5)$$

Letting P stand for the domestic price level, E for the domestic currency price of foreign currency, and P^F for the foreign price level, we can write the law of one price as

$$P = EP^F \qquad (17.6)$$

---

*In Michael Connolly, "The Monetary Approach to an Open Economy: The Fundamental Theory," in *The Monetary Approach to International Adjustment*, ed. Bluford Putnam and D. Sykes Wilford (New York: Praeger, 1978).
[†]We are assuming that base money and the money supply are equal. Realistically, the money supply is some multiple of base money. We assume that this multiple is 1 in order to simplify the analysis.

Finally, we need the assumption that equilibrium in the money market holds so that money demand equals money supply, or

$$L = M \tag{17.7}$$

The adjustment mechanism that ensures the Equation 17.7 equilibrium will vary with the exchange rate regime. With fixed exchange rates, money supply adjusts to money demand through international flows of money via balance-of-payments imbalances. With flexible exchange rates, money demand will be adjusted to a money supply set by the central bank via exchange rate changes. In the case of a managed float, where theoretically we have floating exchange rates but the central banks intervene to keep exchange rates at desired levels, we have both international money flows and exchange rate changes. All three cases will be analyzed subsequently.

Now, we develop the model in a manner that will allow us to analyze the balance of payments and exchange rates in a monetary framework. We begin by substituting Equation 17.6 into Equation 17.4:

$$L = kEP^F Y \tag{17.8}$$

Substituting Equations 17.8 and 17.5 into 17.7 we obtain

$$kEP^F Y = R + D \tag{17.9}$$

Finally, we want to discuss Equation 17.9, money demand and money supply, in terms of percentage changes. Since k is a constant, the change is zero, and thus k drops out of the analysis and we are left with*

$$\hat{E} + \hat{P}^F + \hat{Y} = \hat{R} + \hat{D} \tag{17.10}$$

where the hat (ˆ) over a variable indicates percentage change.

Since the goal of this analysis is to be able to explain changes in the exchange rate or balance of payments, we should have $\hat{R}$ and $\hat{E}$ on the left-hand side of the equation. Rearranging Equation 17.10 in this manner gives

$$\hat{R} - \hat{E} = \hat{P}^F + \hat{Y} - \hat{D} \tag{17.11}$$

This indicates that the percentage change in reserves (the balance of payments) minus the percentage change in exchange rates is equal to the foreign inflation rate plus the percentage growth of real income minus the percentage change in domes-

---

*If $a = bc$, the percentage change in a is equal to the sum of the percentage change in b plus the percentage change in c: $\hat{a} = \hat{b} + \hat{c}$. In Equation 17.10, $\hat{R} + \hat{D}$ is actually the change in $R + D$ as a fraction of the money supply, or the change in reserves plus the change in domestic credit divided by the money supply, so $\hat{R} = \Delta R/M$ and $\hat{D} = \Delta D/M$.

tic credit. With fixed exchange rates, $\hat{E} = 0$, and we have the monetary approach to the balance of payments:

$$\hat{R} = \hat{P}^F + \hat{Y} - \hat{D} \qquad (17.12)$$

Therefore, with fixed exchange rates, a percentage increase in domestic credit, with constant prices and income (and thus constant money demand), will lead to a percentage decrease in international reserves. This means that if the central bank expands domestic credit, creating an excess supply of money, there will be a bigger balance-of-payments deficit or a smaller surplus as people spend to lower the excess cash balances. Conversely, a decrease in domestic credit would lead to an excess demand for money as money demand is unchanged for a given $\hat{P}^F$ and $\hat{Y}$, yet $\hat{D}$ is falling so that $\hat{R}$ will increase to bring money supply equal to money demand.

In the case of flexible exchange rates with no central-bank intervention, we assume reserve flows $\hat{R}$ equal zero, whereas exchange rate changes are nonzero. The general Equation 17.11 is now written for the monetary approach to the exchange rate as

$$-\hat{E} = \hat{P}^F + \hat{Y} - \hat{D} \qquad (17.13)$$

With the MAER, an increase in domestic credit, given a constant $\hat{P}^F$ and $\hat{Y}$ (so that money demand is constant), will result in a depreciation of the domestic currency. Examining Equation 17.13, we see that $\hat{D}$ and $\hat{E}$ both have a negative sign. Thus, if $\hat{D}$ increases, $\hat{E}$ will also increase, and since $\hat{E}$ is domestic-currency units per foreign-currency unit, an increase in $\hat{E}$ means that domestic currency is either appreciating at a slower rate or depreciating at a faster rate. Under the MAER, domestic monetary policy will not cause flows of money internationally but will lead to exchange rate changes.

The fact that $\hat{P}^F$ and $\hat{Y}$ have signs opposite that of $\hat{E}$ in Equation 17.13 indicates that changes in inflation and income growth will cause changes in exchange rates in the opposite direction. For instance, if $\hat{P}^F$ and/or $\hat{Y}$ increase, we know that money demand increases. With constant domestic credit, we have an excess demand for money. As individuals try to increase their money balances, we observe a decrease in $\hat{E}$ or faster appreciation of the domestic currency.

So far, we have discussed the case of fixed or flexible exchange rates, but what is the framework for analysis of a managed float? Remember, a managed float means that although exchange rates are theoretically flexible and determined by the market forces of supply and demand, central banks intervene at times to peg the rates at some desired level. Thus, the managed float has the attributes of both a fixed and a floating exchange rate regime, because changing supply and demand will affect exchange rates, but the actions of the central bank will also allow international reserves to change. To allow for reserve changes, as well as for exchange rate changes, we can simply return to the initial Equation 17.11. Thus, we can see that given money demand or money supply changes, the central bank can choose to let $\hat{E}$ adjust to the free-market level; or, by holding E at some disequilibrium level, it will allow $\hat{R}$ to adjust.

Given the framework just developed, we can now consider some of the implications and extensions of the monetary approach. First, the assumption of purchasing power parity implies that the central bank must make a policy choice between an exchange rate or a domestic price level. Since $P = EP^F$, under fixed exchange rates E is constant, so that maintaining the pegged value of E implies that the domestic price level will correspond to that of the rest of the world. This is the case in which people discuss imported inflation. If the foreign price level is increasing rapidly, then our price must follow if we are to maintain the fixed E. On the other hand, with flexible rates, E is free to vary to whatever level is necessary to clear the foreign-exchange market, so that we can choose our domestic rate of inflation independent of the rest of the world. If we select a lower rate of inflation than foreigners do, then PPP suggests that our currency will tend to appreciate. This issue of choosing either the domestic inflation rate or a preferred exchange rate has important economic as well as political implications and is not made without much thought and consultation by central bankers.

We can summarize the policy implications of the monetary approach as follows:

1. Balance-of-payments disequilibria are essentially monetary phenomena. Thus, countries would not run long-term (or structural, as they are called) deficits if they did not rely so heavily on inflationary money-supply growth to finance government spending.

2. Balance-of-payments disequilibria must be transitory. If the exchange rate remains fixed, eventually the country must run out of reserves by trying to support a continuing deficit.

3. Balance-of-payments disequilibria can be handled with domestic monetary policy rather than with adjustments in the exchange rate. Devaluation of the currency exchange rate is a substitute for reducing the growth of domestic credit in that devaluation lowers the value of a country's money to the rest of the world (conversely, an appreciation of the currency is a substitute for increasing domestic-credit growth). Following any devaluation, if the underlying monetary cause of the devaluation is not corrected, future devaluations will be required to offset the continued excess supply of the country's money.

4. Domestic balance of payments will be improved by an increase in domestic income via an increase in money demand, if not offset by an increase in domestic credit.

SUMMARY

1. Consumption decisions respond to changes in relative prices.

2. The elasticity of supply or demand measures the responsiveness of quantity to changes in price.

3. A devaluation of the domestic currency should raise the price of foreign goods relative to domestic goods prices.

4. The J curve describes the pattern of the balance of trade following a devaluation where the trade balance first falls before rising.

5. Immediately after a devaluation, the invoicing currency used for contracts written prior to the devaluation becomes an important determinant of the value of the trade account.

6. The pass-through of devaluation to domestic and foreign prices depends on elasticities of supply and demand for international trade.

7. The evidence regarding the effects of devaluation on the balance of trade indicates no standard pattern.

8. The balance of trade can improve only if income increases relative to absorption.

9. The monetary approach analyzes the balance of payments and exchange rates in terms of money supply and money demand.

10. With fixed exchange rates, money supply adjusts to money demand through international reserve flows.

11. With floating exchange rates, money demand adjusts to money supply through exchange rate changes.

12. With a managed float, monetary disequilibrium is eliminated through exchange rate changes and balance-of-payments flows.

EXERCISES

1. What does a *J* curve refer to, and how does it arise?

2. Assume the following to be true:

   Export contracts are denominated in domestic currency.
   Import contracts are denominated in foreign currency.
   The domestic supply of exports is inelastic.
   The foreign supply of exports (domestic imports) is inelastic.

   What will happen to the domestic trade balance following a devaluation of the domestic currency? Explain carefully the effects during the currency-contract period and the pass-through period, and be sure to explain why these effects occur.

3. Using the monetary approach model developed in the text, explain how the following events will affect the foreign-exchange value of the domestic currency (assume flexible exchange rates):
   a. The foreign inflation rate decreases.
   b. A natural disaster destroys a significant fraction of domestic industry and therefore destroys productive capacity.
   c. The domestic central bank decreases the growth rate of the domestic credit component of base money to try to reduce the domestic inflation rate.
   d. A foreign oil cartel succeeds in doubling the market price of oil, and the domestic economy is heavily dependent on imported oil.

4. Both the elasticities and absorption approaches have drawbacks as theories of the balance of payments. What is the most notable drawback shared by each?

5. The monetary approach suggests that long-term, or "chronic," balance-of-payments deficits are caused by . . . ?

6. How do the implications of the absorption approach differ depending on whether or not there is full employment?

7. According to the absorption approach, what happens to a country's trade balance following an increase in domestic spending? How does this differ from an increase in income under the monetary approach?

8. Assume the following to be true:

   Export and import contracts are denominated in domestic currency.
   The domestic demand for imports is inelastic.
   The foreign demand for domestic exports is inelastic.

   What will happen to the domestic trade balance following a devaluation of the domestic currency? Explain carefully the effects during the currency-contract period and the pass-through period, and be sure to explain why these effects occur.

REFERENCES

Betts, Caroline, and Michael Devereux, "The Exchange Rate in a Model of Pricing to Market," *European Economic Review* (1996).

Fullerton, Thomas, W. Charles Sawyer, and Richard L. Sprinkle, "Latin American Trade Elasticities," *Journal of Economics and Finance* (2000).

Gagnon, Joseph E., and Michael M. Knetter, "Markup Adjustment and Exchange Rate Fluctuations: Evidence from Panel Data on Automobile Exports," *Journal of International Money and Finance* (April 1995).

Goldstein, Morris, and Mohsin S. Khan. "Income and Price Effects in Foreign Trade." In *Handbook of International Economics,* Vol. 2, Edited by Ronald W. Jones and Peter B. Kenen. Amsterdam: North-Holland, 1985.

Marquez, Jaime, and Caryl McNeilly. "Income and Price Elasticities for Exports of Developing Countries." *Review of Economics and Statistics* (May 1988).

Rose, Andrew, "Are All Devaluations Alike?" *Weekly Letter,* Federal Reserve Bank of San Francisco, February 9, 1996.

INTERNET APPLICATIONS

Please visit our Web site at www.awl.com/husted_melvin for more exercises and readings.

APPENDIX 17.1

STABLE FOREIGN-EXCHANGE MARKETS AND THE MARSHALL-LERNER CONDITION

The elasticities approach to the balance of trade emphasizes that the effect of an exchange rate change on the equilibrium quantity of currency being traded will depend on the elasticities of the supply and demand curves involved. Normally, we expect a devaluation of the domestic currency to increase the demand for domestic products and reduce the demand for foreign products. Consequently, the supply of foreign currency to be exchanged for domestic currency should increase as the domestic demand for foreign currency falls.

Chapter 17 considered the possibility of J curves, where low trade elasticities could lead to a fall in the domestic trade balance following a devaluation. Let us consider an example of how low elasticities could actually result in a fall in the supply of foreign currency to the domestic market following a devaluation.

Suppose we face a perfectly elastic supply curve for our imports (e.g., we import good X). The demand for our imports is the domestic excess demand for X, that is, the amount of X demanded in excess of the amount supplied at home. Let us assume that we are in the United States, and we import X from the United Kingdom. If we devalue the dollar, the dollar price of pounds increases, making our imports from the United Kingdom more expensive. Figure A17.1 illustrates the possible result of this devaluation.

In Figure A17.1, the perfectly elastic supply curve means that we can buy all the good X we want from the United Kingdom at the U.K. pound price of $P_X^\pounds$ (which is the pound price of good X). Note that the price in Figure A17.1 is the price of X existing in the United Kingdom. The demand curves are the U.S. demand for imports of X and are drawn holding the exchange rate fixed and varying the U.K. price. A dollar devaluation will shift the demand curve to the left, such as the shift from D_0 (drawn at the old exchange rate E_0) to D_1 (drawn at the new exchange rate E_1). We then have the familiar result of a devaluation lowering imports.

Figure A17.2 illustrates the market for exports of good Y. The perfectly elastic supply of exports indicates that we are willing to sell to the United Kingdom all it wants to buy at a given price, such as $P_{Y_0}^\pounds (E_0)$ for the original supply curve S_0. Note that once again the curves are drawn holding exchange rates fixed and varying the pound price. If we devalue, say from E_0 to E_1 (a higher dollar price of pounds), then the foreign-price equivalent of the constant domestic price will drop. If $P = EP^F$, then, holding P constant, an increase in E implies a reduction in P^F to make this equality hold. In Figure A17.2, we see the supply curve shifting to S_1 in recognition of the fact that now a lower foreign price is consistent with the constant domestic price. Of course, this shift in supply and the corresponding drop in the pound price

FIGURE A17.1   *The effect of devaluation on domestic imports with a perfectly elastic supply.*

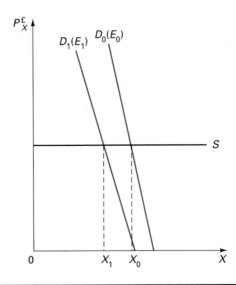

FIGURE A17.2   *The effect of devaluation on domestic exports with a perfectly elastic supply.*

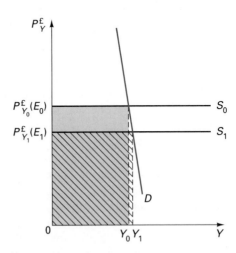

to U.K. buyers of U.S. Y exports indicates that the quantity of Y demanded by U.K. residents will increase, as seen in the shift from equilibrium quantity Y_0 to Y_1.

The interesting feature of Figure A17.2 is the implication of the change in exchange rates for export revenue to the United States. If the U.K. demand for U.S. exports is inelastic, then the increase in sales from Y_0 to Y_1 will not "make up" for the reduction in price in terms of pound export earnings. Originally, U.K. importers were paying $P_{Y_0}^{\pounds} \times Y_0$ (the shaded area) in total export expenditures. After the devaluation, they pay $P_{Y_1}^{\pounds} \times Y_1$ (the area with slanted lines) for exports. If we visually inspect the results, we observe that the loss of revenue when the price falls (the shaded area above $P_{Y_1}^{\pounds}$) is larger than the gain in revenue from the increased sales (the lined region to the right of Y_0). Thus, there has been a drop in total U.K. pound revenue from exports as a result of the devaluation, which implies that the U.K. demand for U.S. exports is inelastic. This also indicates that the foreign-exchange supply curve to the United States will be negatively sloped, as illustrated in Figure A17.3.

In Figure A17.3, the negatively sloped supply curve shows that a devaluation of the dollar, say from E_0 to E_1, will result in a smaller quantity of pounds supplied to the United States from $\pounds_0$ to $\pounds_s$. We know that the devaluation will also decrease the quantity of pounds demanded from $\pounds_0$ to $\pounds_d$, since U.S. residents will want to buy less from the United Kingdom (as in Figure A17.1). However, if the demand curve has a steeper slope than the supply curve (due to the fact that U.S. demand for U.K. exports is inelastic relative to the U.K. demand for U.S. exports) so that the demand curve intersects the supply curve from above the supply curve, then a devaluation

---

FIGURE A17.3   *Foreign-exchange supply and demand when trade elasticities are low.*

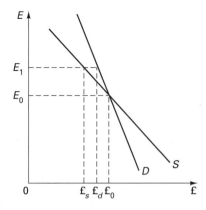

will increase the excess demand for pounds $£_d - £_s$, as illustrated in Figure A17.3. This would be a surprising finding because we tend to believe that a devaluation will result in a lower excess demand for foreign currencies, thereby stabilizing the foreign-exchange market.

The shapes of the supply and demand curves for foreign currency as shown in Figure A17.3 are derived from the goods markets supply and demand curves as indicated in Figures A17.1 and A17.2. The more inelastic the U.S. demand for U.K. exports is, the less responsive will be the U.S. demand for pounds, given a change in the dollar price of pounds, and the more likely that the slope of the demand curve in Figure A17.3 will be steeper. The more inelastic the U.K. demand for U.S. exports is, the more likely it is that the foreign-exchange supply curve in Figure A17.3 will be negatively sloped.

The *Marshall–Lerner condition* is a condition under which a devaluation will improve a country's balance of trade, and the foreign-exchange market will be stable. This condition may be illustrated using our example where the U.S. imports good X from the United Kingdom and exports good Y to the United Kingdom. The supply curves for X and Y are perfectly elastic, so the importing country can buy as much as desired at the going price. In Figure A17.1, the leftward shift in the U.S. demand for imports of X will depend on the elasticity of demand for X in the United States. If the dollar price of good X to U.S. buyers is increased 10 percent by a dollar devaluation, then an inelastic demand for X would mean that the quantity of X demanded would fall by less than 10 percent, while an elastic demand would mean that the quantity of X would fall by more than 10 percent. The more elastic the U.S. demand for imported good X, the greater the reduction in U.S. imports of X and the greater the improvement in the U.S. balance of trade following a dollar devaluation.

In Figure A17.2, the more elastic the U.K. demand for the U.S. export good Y, the greater the increase in Y demanded when the dollar is devalued and the pound price to U.K. buyers falls. With an inelastic demand, as drawn in Figure A17.2, the increase in Y demanded is not great enough to make up for the reduction in the pound price, so that the total quantity of pounds supplied will fall, as in Figure A17.3. For instance, if the shift in supply from S_0 to S_1 in Figure A17.2 lowers the pound price by 10 percent yet the quantity demanded changes by only 5 percent, then the total supply of pounds will fall by 5 percent. With such an inelastic demand, whenever the dollar depreciates, the quantity of pounds supplied falls, and the U.S. balance of trade falls after the dollar devaluation. If the U.K. demand for Y is elastic, then a 10 percent fall in the pound price of Y would increase the quantity demanded by more than 10 percent, so that the total supply of pounds to the market would increase after a dollar devaluation, and the U.S. trade balance would improve. This "normal looking," upward-sloping supply curve is depicted in Figure A17.4.

Suppose the exchange rate is initially E_0, where $£_0$ is the quantity of pounds supplied and demanded. If the dollar is devalued so that the new exchange rate is E_1, there will be an excess supply of pounds, as $£_S$ is the new quantity supplied by U.K. residents, and $£_d$ is the quantity demanded by U.S. residents. This is in contrast to

| FIGURE A17.4 | *Foreign-exchange supply and demand when the Marshall–Lerner condition is met.* |

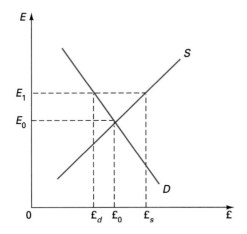

the unstable foreign-exchange-market equilibrium of Figure A17.3, where dollar devaluation created an excess demand for pounds and caused the U.S. trade deficit to increase.

Obviously, the greater the elasticities of U.S. demand for U.K. imports and U.K. demand for U.S. exports, the greater the improvement in the U.S. trade balance after a dollar devaluation. The Marshall–Lerner condition indicates that the devaluation will improve the U.S. trade balance and provide a stable foreign-exchange market if the elasticity of demand for U.S. imports plus the elasticity of demand for U.S. exports exceeds 1. If the sum of the two elasticities is less than 1, the foreign-exchange market will be unstable and the devaluation will cause the trade balance to fall. If the sum of the elasticities is equal to 1, there is no change in the balance of trade after a devaluation. With the perfectly elastic supply curves of our example, it does not matter whether the individual demand curves are inelastic or elastic. All we need to know is the sum of the two. If they sum to greater than 1, then we know that after a dollar devaluation, the U.S. balance of trade will improve because the quantity of pounds supplied to the United States will increase relative to the quantity of pounds demanded.

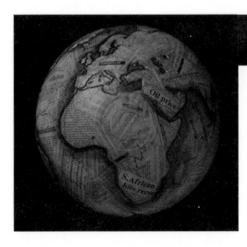

CHAPTER 18

Exchange Rate

Theories

KEY WORDS

Perfect capital mobility   Sterilized intervention
Portfolio-balance approach   Currency union

Prior to the monetary-approach emphasis of the 1970s, it was common to emphasize international trade flows as primary determinants of exchange rates. This was due, in part, to the fact that governments maintained tight restrictions on international flows of financial capital. The role of exchange rate changes in eliminating international trade imbalances suggests that we should expect countries with current trade surpluses to have an appreciating currency, whereas countries with trade deficits should have depreciating currencies. Such exchange rate changes would lead to changes in international relative prices that would work to eliminate the trade imbalance.

In recent years, it has become clear that the world does not work in the simple way just considered. For instance, with financial liberalization we have seen that the volume of international trade in financial assets now dwarfs trade in goods and services. Moreover, we have seen some instances where countries with trade surpluses have depreciating currencies, whereas countries with trade deficits have appreciating currencies. Economists have responded to such real-world events by devising several alternative views of exchange rate determination. These theories place a much greater emphasis on the role of the exchange rate as one of many prices in the worldwide market for financial assets. This chapter considers some of the recent advances in exchange rate theory.

THE ASSET APPROACH

Modern exchange rate models emphasize financial-asset markets. Rather than the traditional view of exchange rates adjusting to equilibrate international trade in goods, the exchange rate is viewed as adjusting to equilibrate international trade in financial assets. Because goods prices adjust slowly relative to financial asset prices and financial assets are traded continuously each business day, the shift in emphasis from goods markets to asset markets has important implications. Exchange rates will change every day or even every minute as supplies of and demands for financial assets of different nations change.

An implication of the asset approach is that exchange rates should be much more variable than goods prices. This seems to be an empirical fact. Table 18.1 lists the standard deviations of percentage changes in prices and exchange rates for two countries. In the 1990s period covered in the table, we observe that spot rates for

TABLE 18.1	*Standard Deviations of Prices and Exchange Rates*[1]		
Country	Price	Exchange Rate	
Canada	.003	.013	
Switzerland	.003	.038	

[1]The table reports the standard deviations of the percentage changes in the consumer price index and the spot exchange rate of each country's currency against the U.S. dollar for the period March 1990 to March 1999.

the countries were much more volatile than prices. Comparing the prices with the exchange rates, we find that the volatility of exchange rates averaged anywhere from 4 to 12 times the volatility of prices. Such figures are consistent with the fact that exchange rates respond to changing conditions in financial-asset markets and are not simply reacting to changes in international goods trade.

Exchange rate models emphasizing financial-asset markets typically assume **perfect capital mobility.** In other words, capital flows freely between nations as there are no significant transactions costs or capital controls to serve as barriers to investment. In such a world, covered interest arbitrage will ensure covered interest rate parity:

$$\frac{i - i_f}{1 + i_f} = \frac{F - E}{E}$$

where i is the domestic interest rate and i_f is the foreign interest rate. Since this relationship will hold continuously, spot and forward exchange rates as well as interest rates adjust instantaneously to changing financial-market conditions.

Within the family of asset-approach models, there are two basic groups: the monetary approach and the **portfolio-balance approach.*** The monetary approach to the exchange rate was introduced in Chapter 17. As we stated there, in the monetary approach the exchange rate for any two currencies is determined by relative money demand and money supply between the two countries. Relative supplies of domestic and foreign bonds are unimportant. The portfolio-balance approach allows relative bond supplies and demands as well as relative money-market conditions to determine the exchange rate. Table 18.2 summarizes the differences between the two approaches.

The essential difference is that monetary-approach (MA) models assume domestic and foreign bonds to be perfect substitutes, whereas portfolio-balance (PB) models assume imperfect substitutability. If domestic and foreign bonds are perfect substitutes, then demanders are indifferent toward the currency of denomination of the bond as long as the expected return is the same. In this case, bond holders do not require a premium to hold foreign bonds—they would just as soon hold foreign bonds as domestic ones—so there is no risk premium, and uncovered interest rate parity holds in MA models.

Perfect capital mobility
A situation in which there are no barriers to international capital flows.

Portfolio-balance approach
A theory of exchange rate determination arguing that the exchange rate is a function of relative supplies of domestic and foreign bonds.

---

*Early "classics" in the monetary-approach group include Jacob Frenkel, "A Monetary Approach to the Exchange Rate: Doctrinal Aspects and Empirical Evidence," *Scandinavian Journal of Economics* (May 1976); Michael Mussa, "The Exchange Rate, the Balance of Payments, and Monetary and Fiscal Policy under a Regime of Controlled Floating," *Scandinavian Journal of Economics* (May 1976); and John Bilson, "The Monetary Approach to the Exchange Rate: Some Evidence," *IMF Staff Papers* (March 1978). Some early portfolio-balance classics are William Branson, Hanna Halttunen, and Paul Masson, "Exchange Rates in the Short Run: The Dollar-Deutschemark Rate," *European Economic Review* 3 (1977); Pentti Kouri and Jorge de Macedo, "Exchange Rates and the International Adjustment Process," *Brookings Papers on Economic Activity* 1 (1978); Stanley Black, "International Money Markets and Flexible Exchange Rates," *Princeton Studies in International Finance* (March 1973); and Polly Allen and Peter Kenen, *Asset Markets, Exchange Rates, and Economic Integration* (New York: Cambridge University Press, 1980).

	TABLE 18.2	*The Asset Approach to the Exchange Rate*	
Characteristic		Monetary Approach	Portfolio-Balance Approach
Perfect capital mobility (implies covered interest rate parity)		Yes	Yes
Domestic and foreign bonds perfect substitutes (implies uncovered interest rate parity and no foreign-exchange risk premium)		Yes	No

With imperfect substitutability, demanders have preferences for distributing their portfolio over the assets of different countries. That is, asset holders have a desired portfolio share for any particular country's assets due to the portfolio diversification incentives discussed in Chapter 16. If the supply of one country's assets increases, they will hold a greater proportion of that country's assets only if they are compensated. This requires a premium to be paid on these assets. In general, then, PB models have risk premiums in the forward exchange rate that are a function of relative asset supplies. As the supply of country *A*'s financial assets rises relative to *B*'s, there will be a higher premium paid on *A*'s assets. An implication of this premium is that uncovered interest rate parity will not hold because risk premiums will exist in the forward market. This premium is missing in the MA model because there it is assumed that investors don't care whether they hold country *A* or country *B* bonds or in what mix they are held.

We might guess that the PB approach is more relevant if we doubt the MA assumption of perfect substitutability of assets internationally. In such cases, we would view the exchange rate as being determined by relative supplies of domestic and foreign bonds as well as domestic and foreign money. We may then modify the monetary approach to the exchange rate equation found in Chapter 17 to incorporate this additional effect. The basic floating exchange rate MA equation presented in Chapter 17 is

$$-\hat{E} = \hat{P}^F + \hat{Y} - \hat{D} \tag{18.1}$$

where $\hat{E}$ is the percentage change in the exchange rate, $\hat{P}^F$ is the foreign inflation rate, $\hat{Y}$ is the percentage change in domestic income, and $\hat{D}$ is the percentage change in domestic credit. Equation 18.1 has the change in the exchange rate as a function of money supply $\hat{D}$ and money demand $\hat{P}^F + \hat{Y}$ variables. If domestic and foreign bonds are perfect substitutes, then Equation 18.1 is a useful MA description of exchange rate determination. The PB approach assumes that assets are imperfect substitutes internationally because investors perceive foreign-exchange risk to be attached to foreign-currency-denominated bonds. As the supply of domestic bonds rises relative to foreign bonds, there will be an increased risk premium on the domestic bonds that will cause the domestic currency to depreciate in the spot market. If the spot exchange rate depreciates today, and if the expected future spot rate is unchanged, the expected rate of appreciation (depreciation) over the future increases (decreases).

For instance, if the dollar-pound spot rate is initially $E_{\$/£} = 2.00$ and the expected spot rate in one year is $E_{\$/£} = 1.90$, then the expected rate of dollar appreciation is 5 percent $[(1.90 - 2.00)/2.00]$. Now, suppose an increase in the outstanding stock of dollar-denominated bonds results in a depreciation of the spot rate today to $E_{\$/£} = 2.05$. The expected rate of dollar appreciation is now approximately 7.3 percent $[(1.90 - 2.05)/2.05]$.

If the spot exchange rate is a function of relative asset supplies, then the MA equation, Equation 18.1, should be modified to include the percentage change in the supply of foreign bonds $\hat{B}^F$ relative to the percentage change in the supply of domestic bonds $\hat{B}$:

$$- \hat{E} = \hat{P}^F + \hat{Y} - \hat{D} + \hat{B}^F - \hat{B} \qquad (18.2)$$

An increase in foreign-bond supplies $\hat{B}^F$ causes the domestic currency to appreciate at a faster rate ($\hat{E}$ falls) or depreciate at a slower rate. An increase in domestic-bond supplies $\hat{B}$ causes the domestic currency to depreciate at a faster rate ($\hat{E}$ increases) or appreciate at a slower rate. This broader PB view might be expected to explain exchange rate changes better than the MA equation, Equation 18.1. However, the empirical evidence is not at all clear on this matter.* One potential problem for analyzing the MA and PB models of exchange rate determination is central-bank activities aimed at insulating the domestic money supply from international events. The next section discusses the importance of this issue.

STERILIZATION

In recent years, an important topic of debate has emerged from the literature on the monetary approach regarding the ability of central banks to sterilize reserve flows. Sterilization refers to central banks offsetting international reserve flows to follow an independent monetary policy. Under the monetary approach to the balance of payments (with fixed exchange rates), if a country had an excess supply of money, this country would tend to lose international reserves or run a deficit until money supply equals money demand. If, for some reason, the central bank desires this higher money supply and reacts to the deficit by further increasing the money supply, then the deficit will increase and persist as long as the central bank tries to maintain a money supply in excess of money demand. For an excess demand for money, the process is reversed. The excess demand results in reserve inflows to equate money supply to money demand. If the central bank tries to decrease the money supply so that the excess demand still exists, its efforts will be thwarted by further

---

*Several researchers have shown that it is difficult to demonstrate that one model of exchange rate determination clearly dominates all others. An example is Ronald MacDonald and Mark P. Taylor, "Exchange Rate Economics: A Survey," *International Monetary Fund Staff Papers* (March 1992).

reserve inflows persisting as long as the central bank tries to maintain the policy of a money supply less than money demand. The discussion so far relates to the standard monetary-approach theory with no sterilization.

If sterilization is possible, then the monetary authorities may, in fact, be able to determine the money supply in the short run without having reserve flows offset the monetary authorities' goals. This would be possible if the forces that lead to international arbitrage are slow to operate. For instance, if there are barriers to international capital mobility, then we might expect international asset return differentials to persist after a change in economic conditions. In this case, if the central bank wants to increase the growth of the money supply in the short run, it can do so regardless of money demand and reserve flows. In the long run, when complete adjustment of asset prices is possible, the money supply must grow at a rate consistent with money demand; in the short run, the central bank can exercise some discretion.

The use of the word *sterilization* is due to the fact that the central bank must be able to neutralize, or sterilize, any reserve flows induced by monetary policy if the policy is to achieve the central bank's money-supply goals. For instance, if the central bank is following some money-supply growth path and then money demand increases, leading to reserve inflows, the central bank must be able to sterilize these reserve inflows to keep the money supply from rising to what it considers undesirable levels. This is done by decreasing domestic credit by an amount equal to the growth of international reserves, thus keeping base money and the money supply constant.

In Chapter 17 the fixed exchange rate monetary approach to the balance-of-payments equation was

$$\hat{R} = \hat{P}^F + \hat{Y} - \hat{D} \tag{18.3}$$

where $\hat{R}$ is the percentage change in international reserves. Given money demand, an increase in domestic credit would be reflected in a fall in $\hat{R}$, or lower growth of reserves. If sterilization occurs, then the causality implied in Equation 18.3 is no longer true.

Instead of the monetary-approach equation previously written, where changes in domestic credit $\hat{D}$ (on the right-hand side of the equation) lead to changes in reserves $\hat{R}$ (on the left-hand side), with sterilization we also have changes in reserves inducing changes in domestic credit to offset the reserve flows. With sterilization, the causality implied in Equation 18.3 with domestic credit causing reserve changes must be reconsidered. Sterilization means that there is also a causality flowing from reserve changes to domestic credit, as in

$$\hat{D} = \alpha - \beta \hat{R} \tag{18.4}$$

where β is the sterilization coefficient, ranging in value from 0 (when there is no sterilization) to 1 (complete sterilization). Equation 18.4 states that the percentage change in domestic credit will be equal to some constant amount α determined by the central bank's domestic-policy goals minus some number β times the percentage change in reserves; β reflects the central bank's ability to use domestic credit to offset reserve flows. Of course, it is possible that the central bank cannot fully offset international reserve flows, yet some sterilization is possible, in which case β will lie between 0 and 1. Evidence has, in fact, suggested both extremes as well as intermediate values for β. It is reasonable to interpret the evidence regarding sterilization as indicating that central banks are able to sterilize a significant fraction of reserve flows in the short run.* This means that the monetary authorities are likely to choose the growth rate of the money supply in the short run, although long-run money growth must be consistent with money-demand requirements.

So far, we have discussed sterilization in the context of fixed exchange rates. Now, let's consider how a sterilization operation might occur in a floating exchange rate system. Suppose the Japanese yen is appreciating against the dollar, and the Bank of Japan decides to intervene in the foreign-exchange market to increase the value of the dollar and stop the yen appreciation. The Bank of Japan increases domestic credit in order to purchase U.S.-dollar-denominated bonds. The increased demand for dollar bonds will mean an increase in the demand for dollars in the foreign-exchange market. This results in the higher foreign-exchange value of the dollar. Now, suppose the Bank of Japan has a target level of the Japanese money supply that requires the increase in domestic credit to be offset. The central bank will sell yen-denominated bonds in Japan to reduce the domestic money supply. The domestic Japanese money supply was originally increased by the increase in domestic credit used to buy dollar bonds. The money supply ultimately returns to its initial level as the Bank of Japan uses a domestic open-market operation (the formal term for central-bank purchases and sales of domestic bonds) to reduce domestic credit. In this case of managed floating exchange rates, the Bank of Japan uses **sterilized intervention** to achieve its goal of slowing the appreciation of the yen with no effect on the Japanese money supply. Sterilized intervention is ultimately an exchange of domestic bonds for foreign bonds. We may well ask how sterilized intervention could cause a change in the exchange rate if money supplies are unchanged. It is difficult to explain in terms of a monetary-approach model but not in terms of a portfolio-balance approach. Equation 18.2 showed that the exchange rate will be determined in part by the relative growth of domestic and foreign asset supplies. When the Bank of Japan buys dollar assets, the supply of dollar assets relative to yen assets available to private-market participants is reduced. This should cause the yen to depreciate, an effect that is reinforced by the open-market sale of yen securities by the Bank of Japan.

Even in a monetary-approach setting, it is possible for sterilized intervention, with unchanged money supplies, to have an effect on the spot exchange rate if money demand changes. The intervention activity could alter the private-market view of what to expect in the future. If the intervention changes expectations in a

Sterilized intervention
A foreign exchange market intervention that leaves the domestic money supply unchanged.

---

*Evidence is presented in Michael Connolly and Dean Taylor, "Exchange Rate Changes and Neutralization: A Test of the Monetary Approach Applied to Developed and Developing Countries," *Economica* (August 1979); Kathryn M. Dominguez and Jeffrey A. Frankel, *Does Foreign Exchange Intervention Work?* (Washington, D.C.: Institute for International Economics, 1993); and Geert Almekinders, *Foreign Exchange Intervention: Theory and Evidence* (International Monetary Fund, Washington, D.C.; Edward Elgar, 1995).

manner that changes money demand (e.g., money demand in Japan falls because the intervention leads people to expect higher Japanese inflation), then the spot rate could change.*

Equation 18.2 can be used to analyze the intervention process just described. Assume Japan is the domestic country and the United States is the foreign country so that $\hat{E}$ represents the yen per dollar exchange rate. The Bank of Japan increases domestic credit to purchase dollar-denominated bonds. As $\hat{D}$ increases and $\hat{B}^F$ decreases, $\hat{E}$ increases. The yen was initially appreciating against the dollar, or $\hat{E}$ was negative. Due to the central-bank intervention, $\hat{E}$ will rise, or the yen will appreciate at a slower rate than before (perhaps even depreciate, if $\hat{E}$ becomes positive).

If the intervention is sterilized, domestic bonds are exchanged for money. In Equation 18.2, $\hat{D}$ falls and $\hat{B}$ increases. Therefore, even if $\hat{D}$ returns to its initial level, $\hat{B}$ will be higher, so that $\hat{E}$ remains higher than initially.

The portfolio-balance model permits sterilized intervention to alter the exchange rate, even though money supplies are ultimately unchanged. In the monetary approach, the relative bond supplies are deleted from Equation 18.2. The only way that a sterilized intervention could change the exchange rate would be if money demand changed so that income or prices (or perhaps the interest rate, if we added that as a determinant of money demand) changed as well.

EXCHANGE RATES AND THE TRADE BALANCE

The introduction to this chapter discussed the recent shift in emphasis away from exchange rate models that rely on international trade in goods to exchange rate models based on financial assets. However, there is still a useful role for trade flows in asset-approach models, since trade flows have implications for financial-asset flows.

If balance-of-trade deficits are financed by depleting domestic stocks of foreign currency, and trade surpluses are associated with increases in domestic holdings of foreign money, we can see the role for the trade account. If the exchange rate adjusts so that the stocks of domestic and foreign money are willingly held, then the country with a trade surplus will be accumulating foreign currency. As holdings of foreign money increase relative to domestic money, the relative value of foreign money will fall, or the foreign currency will depreciate.

Although realized trade flows and the consequent changes in currency holdings will determine the current spot exchange rate, the expected future change in the spot rate will be affected by expectations regarding the future balance of trade and its implied currency holdings. An important aspect of this analysis is that changes in

---

*Useful papers on the effects of sterilized intervention include Kenneth Rogoff, "On the Effects of Sterilized Intervention," *Journal of Monetary Economics* (September 1984); Bonnie E. Loopesko, "Relationships among Exchange Rates, Intervention, and Interest Rates: An Empirical Investigation," *Journal of International Money and Finance* (December 1984); and Kathryn Dominguez, "Market Responses to Coordinated Central Bank Intervention," *Carnegie-Rochester Series on Public Policy 32* (Spring 1988). A good review of this literature is found in Hali Edison, "The Effectiveness of Central-Bank Intervention: A Survey of the Literature after 1982," *Princeton Special Papers in International Economics* (July 1993).

the future expected value of a currency can have an immediate impact on current spot rates. For instance, if there is suddenly a change in the world economy that leads to expectations of a larger trade deficit in the future—say, an international oil cartel has developed so that the domestic economy will have to pay much more for oil imports—then forward-looking individuals will anticipate a decrease in domestic holdings of foreign money over time. This anticipation will, in turn, cause expectations of a higher rate of appreciation in the value of foreign currency in the future, or an equivalently faster expected depreciation of the domestic currency, because foreign currency will be relatively more scarce. This higher expected rate of depreciation of the domestic currency leads to an immediate attempt by individuals and firms to shift from domestic to foreign money. Because at this moment the total available stocks of foreign and domestic money have not changed, the attempt to exchange domestic for foreign money will cause an immediate appreciation of the foreign currency to maintain equilibrium so that the existing supplies of domestic and foreign money are willingly held. The point is that events that are anticipated to occur in the future have effects on prices today.

We note that current spot exchange rates are affected by changes in expectations concerning future trade flows, as well as by current international trade flows. As is often the case in economic phenomena, the short-run effect of some new event determining the balance of trade can differ from the long-run result. Suppose the long-run equilibrium under floating exchange rates is balanced trade, where exports equal imports. If we are initially in equilibrium and then experience a disturbance like the oil cartel formation, in the short run we expect large balance-of-trade deficits; but in the long run, as all prices and quantities adjust to the situation, we return to the long-run equilibrium of balanced trade. The new long-run equilibrium exchange rate will be higher than the old rate, because foreigners will have larger stocks of domestic currency, while domestic residents will hold less foreign currency due to the period of the trade deficit. The exchange rate need not move to the new equilibrium immediately. In the short run, during which trade deficits are experienced, the exchange rate will tend to be below the new equilibrium rate. Thus, as the outflow of money from the domestic economy proceeds with the deficits, there is steady depreciation of the domestic currency to maintain the short-run equilibrium, where quantities of monies demanded and supplied are equal. Figure 18.1 illustrates the effects just discussed. Some unexpected event occurs at time t_0 that causes a balance-of-trade deficit. The initial exchange rate is E_0. With the deficit and the consequent outflow of money from home to abroad, the domestic currency will depreciate. Eventually, as prices and quantities adjust to the changes in the structure of trade, a new long-run equilibrium is reached at E_1, where trade balance is restored. This move to the new long-run exchange rate E_1 does not have to come instantaneously, because the deficit will persist for some time. However, the forward rate could jump to E_1 at time t_0, as the market now expects E_1 to be the long-run equilibrium exchange rate. The dashed line in Figure 18.1 represents the path taken by the spot exchange rate in the short run. At t_0, there is an instantaneous jump in the exchange rate even before any trade deficits are realized, because individuals try to exchange domestic money for foreign in anticipation of the domestic-currency depreciation. Over time, as the trade deficits occur, there is a steady depreciation of

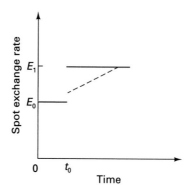

FIGURE 18.1   *The path of the exchange rate after a new event causing balance-of-trade deficits.*

the domestic currency, with the exchange rate approaching its new long-run steady-state value E_1 as the trade deficit approaches zero.

The inclusion of the balance of trade as a determinant of exchange rates allows us to reconcile the modern theory of exchange rate determination with accounts in the popular press, which often emphasize the trade account in explanations of exchange rate behavior. As previously shown, it is possible to make sense of balance-of-trade flows in a model where the exchange rate is determined by desired and actual financial-asset flows, so that the role of trade flows in exchange rate determination may be consistent with the modern asset approach to the exchange rate.*

OVERSHOOTING EXCHANGE RATES

Figure 18.1 indicates that, with news regarding a higher trade deficit for the domestic country, the spot exchange rate will jump immediately above E_0 with the news and will then rise steadily until the new long-run equilibrium E_1 is reached. It is possible that the exchange rate may not always move in such an orderly fashion to the new long-run equilibrium after a disturbance.

We know that purchasing power parity does not hold well under flexible exchange rates. Exchange rates exhibit much more volatile behavior than prices do. We might expect that, in the short run, following some disturbance to equilibrium,

---

*See Peter Hooper and John E. Morton, "Fluctuations in the Dollar: A Model of Nominal and Real Exchange Rate Determination," *Journal of International Money and Finance* (April 1982); and Carlos Alfredo Rodriguez, "The Role of Trade in Exchange Rate Determination: A Rational Expectations Approach," *Journal of Political Economy* (December 1980).

prices will adjust slowly to the new equilibrium level, whereas exchange rates and interest rates will adjust quickly. This different speed of adjustment to equilibrium allows for some interesting behavior regarding exchange rates and prices.

At times, it appears that spot exchange rates move too much given some economic disturbance. Also, we have observed instances when country A has a higher inflation rate than country B, yet A's currency appreciates relative to B's. Such anomalies can be explained in the context of an "overshooting" exchange rate model.* We assume that financial markets adjust instantaneously to an exogenous shock, whereas goods markets adjust slowly over time. With this setting, we analyze what happens when country A increases its money supply.

For equilibrium in the money market, money demand must equal money supply. Thus, if the money supply increases, something must happen to increase money demand. We assume that people hold money for transactions purposes, and they also hold bonds that pay an interest rate i. These assumptions allow us to write a money-demand equation of the form

$$L = aY + bi \tag{18.5}$$

where L is the real stock of money demanded (the nominal stock of money divided by the price level), Y is income, and i is the interest rate. Money demand is positively related to income, so a exceeds zero. As Y increases, people tend to demand more of everything, including money. Since the interest rate is the opportunity cost of holding money, there is an inverse relation between money demand and i, or b is negative. It is commonly believed that, in the short run, following an increase in the money supply, both income and the price level are relatively constant. As a result, interest rates must drop to equate money demand to money supply. Now, let's bring into our analysis a second country.

The approximate interest rate parity relation for countries A and B may be written as

$$i_A = i_B + (F - E)/E \tag{18.6}$$

Thus, if i_A falls, given the foreign interest rate i_B, $(F - E)/E$ or the forward premium on currency B must fall. When the money supply in A increases, we expect that eventually prices in A will rise, because we have more A currency chasing the limited quantity of goods available for purchase. This higher future price in A will imply a higher future exchange rate to achieve purchasing power parity. We may think of a long-run value of the exchange rate E_{LR} that will be consistent with purchasing power parity:

$$E_{LR} = P_A/P_B \tag{18.7}$$

*Examples of overshooting models are provided by Rudiger Dornbusch, "Expectations and Exchange Rate Dynamics," *Journal of Political Economy* (December 1976); Robert A. Driskill, "Exchange Rate Dynamics: An Empirical Investigation," *Journal of Political Economy* (April 1981); David H. Papell, "Activist Monetary Policy, Imperfect Capital Mobility, and the Overshooting Hypothesis," *Journal of International Economics* (May 1985); and Jay H. Levin, "Trade Flow Lags, Monetary and Fiscal Policy, and Exchange Rate Overshooting," *Journal of International Money and Finance* (December 1986).

Since P_A is expected to rise over time, given P_B, E will also rise. This higher expected future spot rate will be reflected in a higher forward rate now. But if F rises while at the same time $F - E$ must fall to maintain interest rate parity, the current E will have to increase more than F. Then, once prices start rising, real money balances fall, so that the domestic interest rate rises. Over time as the interest rate increases, E will fall to maintain interest rate parity. Therefore, the initial rise in E will be in excess of the long-run E_{LR}, or E will overshoot its long-run value. Note that the overshooting exchange rate model revolves around two crucial assumptions: that purchasing power parity does not hold in the short run, and that the spot rate is much more volatile than the forward rate.

If the discussion seems overwhelming at this point, the reader will be relieved to know that a concise summary can be given graphically. Figure 18.2 summarizes the discussion thus far. The initial equilibrium is given by E_0, F_0, P_0, and i_0. When the money supply increases at time t_0, the domestic interest rate falls, and the spot and forward exchange rates increase, while the price level remains fixed. The eventual long-run equilibrium price P_{LR} and exchange rate E_{LR} will rise in proportion to the increase in the money supply. Although the forward rate will move immediately to its new equilibrium F_1, the spot rate will increase above the eventual equilibrium E_{LR}

FIGURE 18.2   *The time path of the forward and spot exchange rate, interest rate, and price level after an increase in the domestic money supply at time t_0.*

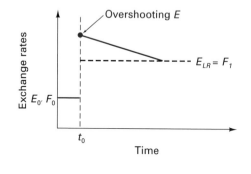

Key:

——— Depict the actual path of the variables.

- - - - Represent the long-run equilibrium values to which the variables converge.

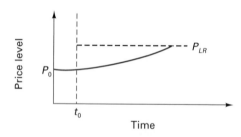

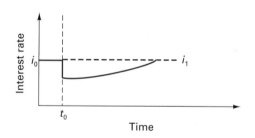

due to the need to maintain interest parity (remember, i has fallen in the short run). Over time, as prices start rising, the interest rate increases, and the exchange rate converges to the new equilibrium E_{LR}.

As a result of the overshooting E, we observe a period where country A has rising prices relative to the fixed prices of country B, yet A's currency appreciates along the solid line converging to E_{LR}. We might explain this period as one in which fixed prices increase, lowering real-money balances and raising interest rates. Country A experiences capital inflows in response to the higher interest rates, so that A's currency appreciates steadily at the same rate as the interest rate increase to maintain interest rate parity.

CURRENCY SUBSTITUTION

As is discussed in Chapter 19, economists have long argued that one of the advantages of flexible exchange rates is that countries become independent in terms of their ability to formulate domestic monetary policy. This is obviously not true when exchange rates are fixed. If country A must maintain a fixed exchange rate with country B, then A must follow a monetary policy similar to that of B. Should A follow an inflationary policy where prices are rising 20 percent per year, whereas B follows a policy aimed at price stability, then a fixed rate of exchange between the money of A and B will prove very difficult to maintain. Yet with flexible exchange rates, A and B can each choose any monetary policy they like, and the exchange rate will simply change over time to adjust for the inflation differentials.

This independence of domestic policy under flexible exchange rates may be reduced if there is an international demand for monies. Suppose country B residents desire to hold currency A for future transactions or simply to hold as part of their investment portfolio. As demand for money shifts between A and B currency, the exchange rate will shift as well. In a region with substitutable currencies, shifts in money demand between currencies will add an additional element of exchange rate variability.*

---

*There is a large and growing literature on currency substitution and its relevance (or, in some cases, irrelevance). Michael Bordo and Ehsan U. Choudhri, "Currency Substitution and the Demand for Money: Some Evidence for Canada," *Journal of Money, Credit, and Banking* (February 1982); John T. Cuddington, "Currency Substitution, Capital Mobility, and Money Demand," *Journal of International Money and Finance* (August 1983); Betty C. Daniel and Harold O. Fried, "Currency Substitution, Postal Strikes, and Canadian Money Demand," *Canadian Journal of Economics* (November 1983); Russell S. Boyer and Geoffrey H. Kingston, "Currency Substitution under Finance Constraints," *Journal of International Money and Finance* (September 1987); Alan G. Isaac, "Exchange Rate Volatility and Currency Substitution," *Journal of International Money and Finance* (June 1989); and Jeffrey H. Bergstrand and Thomas P. Bundt, "Currency Substitution and Monetary Autonomy: the Foreign Demand for U.S. Demand Deposits," *Journal of International Money and Finance* (September 1990). A good review of the literature is found in Alberto Giovannini and Bart Turtelboom, "Currency Substitution," in *The Handbook of International Macroeconomics,* ed. Fredrick Van Der Ploeg (Cambridge, Mass.: Blackwell Economics Handbooks, July 1994).

With fixed exchange rates, central banks make currencies perfect substitutes on the supply side. They alter the supplies of currency to maintain the exchange rate peg. The issue of currency substitution deals with the substitutability among currencies on the demand side of the market. If currencies were perfect substitutes to money demanders, then all currencies would have to have the same inflation rates, or demand for the high-inflation currency would fall to zero (since the inflation rate determines the loss of purchasing power of a money). Perfectly substitutable monies indicates that demanders are indifferent between the use of one currency or another. For instance, people in the United States are basically indifferent as to whether they have a dime or two nickels. The relative values are fixed, and as long as everyone believes that they will remain fixed, people don't worry about whether they should keep dimes or nickels in their pocket. The same would be true of two countries' monies that were fixed in value relative to each other. As long as everyone believes that the exchange value of currency A relative to currency B will never change, then money demanders will be indifferent between holding A or B. If this is no longer true, currency substitution becomes an additional source of exchange rate change. If the cost of holding currency A rises relative to the cost of holding B, say due to a higher inflation rate for currency A, then demand will shift away from A to B if A and B are substitutes. This would cause the A currency to depreciate even more than initially called for by the inflation differential between A and B.

For instance, suppose Indonesia has a 10 percent annual inflation rate, while Australia has a 5 percent rate. With no currency substitution, we would expect the Indonesian rupiah to appreciate against the Australian dollar on purchasing power parity grounds. Now suppose that Indonesian citizens hold stocks of Australian currency, and these dollars are good substitutes for rupiah. The higher inflation rate on the rupiah means that stocks of rupiah held will lose value more rapidly than dollars, so there is an increased demand for Australian dollar currency. This attempt to exchange rupiah currency for dollars results in a further depreciation of the rupiah. Such shifts in demand between currencies can result in volatile exchange rates and can be very unsettling to central banks desiring exchange rate stability. Therefore, one implication of a high degree of currency substitution is a need for international coordination of monetary policy. In Chapter 18 we discuss in more detail the incentives and benefits of **currency unions**, where central banks coordinate monetary policy and fix exchange rates, but we may realize now how a high degree of substitutability between monies might lead to a currency union. If money demanders substitute between currencies to force each currency to follow a similar inflation rate, then the supposed independence of monetary policy under flexible exchange rates is largely illusory. Although central banks may attempt to follow independent monetary policies, money demanders will adjust their portfolio holdings away from high-inflation currencies to low-inflation currencies. This currency substitution leads to more volatile exchange rates, because not only does the exchange rate adjust to compensate for the original inflation differential, but it also adjusts as currency portfolios are altered.

Currency union
An agreement between countries to fix exchange rates and coordinate monetary policies.

We should expect currency substitution to be most important in a regional setting where there is a relatively high degree of mobility of resources between countries. For instance, countries using the euro in Western Europe represent a European currency union and may be evidence of a high degree of currency substitution that once existed among the individual European currencies replaced by the euro.* Alternatively, there is evidence of a high degree of currency substitution existing between the U.S. dollar and Latin American currencies.[†] In many Latin American countries, dollars serve as an important substitute currency, both as a store of value (the dollar being more stable than the typical Latin American currency) and as a medium of exchange used for transactions. This latter effect is particularly pronounced in border areas.

THE ROLE OF NEWS

Considering the theories of exchange rate determination discussed so far, we might believe that with all this knowledge, experts should be quite adept at forecasting future exchange rates. In fact, forecasting future spot exchange rates is difficult. Although researchers have shown the theories we have covered to be relevant in terms of explaining systematic patterns of exchange rate behavior, the usefulness of these theories for predicting future exchange rates is limited by the propensity for the unexpected to occur. The real world is characterized by unpredictable shocks or surprises. When some unexpected event takes place, we refer to this as news. Since interest rates, prices, and incomes are often affected by news, it follows that exchange rates too will be affected by news. By definition, the exchange rate changes linked to news will be unexpected. We find great difficulty in predicting future spot rates because we know that the exchange rate will be, in part, determined by events that cannot be foreseen.

That the predicted change in the spot rate, as measured by the forward premium, varies less over time than the actual change does indicates how much of the change in spot rates is unexpected. Periods dominated by unexpected announcements or realizations of economic policy changes will have great fluctuations in spot and forward exchange rates as expectations are revised subject to the news.

The news also has implications for purchasing power parity. Because exchange rates are financial-asset prices that respond quickly to new information, news will have an immediate impact on exchange rates.[†] Prices of goods and services, how-

---

*See Michael Melvin, "Currency Substitution and Western European Monetary Unification," *Economica* (February 1985).

[†]See Guillermo Ortiz, "Currency Substitution in Mexico: The Dollarization Problem," *Journal of Money, Credit, and Banking* (May 1983); Jaime Marquez, "Money Demand in Open Economies: A Currency Substitution Model for Venezuela," *Journal of International Money and Finance* (June 1987); Michael Melvin, "The Dollarization of Latin America as a Market Enforced Monetary Reform: Evidence and Implications," *Economic Development and Cultural Change* (April 1988); John H. Rogers, "Convertibility Risk and Dollarization in Mexico: A Vectorautoregressive Analysis," *Journal of International Money and Finance* (April 1992); and Paul D. McNelis and Carlos Asilis, "A Dynamic Simulation Analysis of Currency Substitution in an Optimizing Framework with Transactions Costs," *Revista de Análisis Económico,* (June 1992).

[†]Yin-Wong Cheung and Menzie Chinn in "Currency Traders and Exchange Rate Dynamics: A Survey of the U.S. Market," *Journal of International Money and Finance* (forthcoming) survey foreign exchange traders and find that the majority of traders believe that exchange rates fully adjust to most economic news within one minute.

ever, will not be affected by the news in such a rapid manner. One reason is that goods and services are often contracted for in advance, so that prices are inflexible for the duration of the contract. A more basic and general reason is that financial assets, like foreign exchange, have long lives relative to the goods and services that are incorporated in national price indexes. This is important because longer-lived assets or durable-goods prices are more sensitive to changes in expectations than nondurable or relatively short-lived assets are. For this reason, during periods dominated by news, we observe exchange rates varying a great deal relative to prices, so that large deviations from purchasing power parity are realized. The differences between prices and exchange rates are illustrated in Table 18.1. As was discussed earlier, in the context of asset models of exchange rate determination, exchange rates change much more than goods prices do. Periods when many unexpected economic events occur (oil price shocks and international debt problems are two examples) will be periods of large unexpected exchange rate changes and will also be periods when large deviations from PPP occur. For instance, if the Federal Reserve announced a new policy that was expected to increase U.S. inflation, the dollar would immediately depreciate on the foreign exchange market, but prices of goods and services would increase slowly over time.

It is important to realize that the variability of the exchange rate is a result of new developments.* In recent years, research indicates that news regarding unemployment rates has the biggest effect on exchange rates of any regularly scheduled macroeconomic announcement. Volatile exchange rates simply reflect turbulent times. Even with a good knowledge of the determinants of exchange rates, as discussed in this chapter, without perfect foresight exchange rates will always prove to be difficult to forecast in a dynamic world full of surprises.

FOREIGN EXCHANGE MARKET MICROSTRUCTURE

The determinants of the exchange rate discussed so far identify the fundamentals that should cause changes in exchange rates. As news related to money supplies, trade balances, or fiscal policies is received by the market, exchange rates will change to reflect this news. We might think of the discussion as being macro, as such news affects the entire economy and other prices change along with exchange rates. However, there is also a micro level, at which exchange rates are determined by interac-

---

*This is demonstrated in Takatoshi Ito and V. Vance Roley, "News from the U.S. and Japan: Which Moves the Yen/Dollar Exchange Rate?" *Journal of Monetary Economics* (March 1987); Gikas A. Hardouvelis, "Economic News, Exchange Rates, and Interest Rates," *Journal of International Money and Finance* (March 1988); Keivan Deravi, Philip Gregorowicz, and Charles E. Hegji, "Balance of Trade Announcements and Movements in Exchange Rates," *Southern Economic Journal* (October 1988); Kedreth C. Hogan, Jr., and Michael Melvin, "Sources of Meteor Showers and Heat Waves in the Foreign Exchange Market," *Journal of International Economics* (November 1994); and Torben Andersen and Tim Bollerslev, "Deutsche Mark-Longer-Run Dependencies," *Journal of Finance* (February 1998).

tions among traders. Beyond the macro news or public information shared by all, there also exists private information from which some traders know more than others about the current state of the market. Understanding the "market microstructure" allows us to explain the evolution of the foreign exchange market in an intradaily sense, in which foreign exchange traders adjust their bid and ask quotes throughout the business day in the absence of any macro news.

A foreign exchange trader may be motivated to alter his or her exchange rate quotes in response to changes in their position with respect to orders to buy and sell a currency. For instance, suppose Jose Smith is a foreign exchange trader at Citibank who specializes in the euro/dollar market. The bank management controls risks associated with foreign currency trading by limiting the extent to which traders can take a position that would expose the bank to potential loss from unexpected changes in exchange rates. If Smith has agreed to buy more euros than he has agreed to sell, he has a long position in the euro and will profit from euro appreciation and lose from euro depreciation. If Smith has agreed to sell more euros than he has agreed to buy, he has a short position in the euro and will profit from euro depreciation and lose from euro appreciation. His position at any point in time may be called his inventory. One reason traders adjust their quotes is in response to inventory changes. At the end of the day most traders balance their position and are said to go home "flat." This means that their orders to buy a currency are just equal to their orders to sell.

Suppose Jose Smith has been buying and selling euros for dollars throughout the day. By early afternoon his position is as follows:

dollar purchases:	$100,000,000
dollar sales:	$80,000,000

In order to balance his position Smith will adjust his quotes to encourage fewer purchases and more sales. For instance, if the euro is currently trading at $1.0250–60, then Jose could raise the bid quote relative to the ask quote to encourage others to sell him euros in exchange for his dollars. For instance, if he changes the quote to 1.0255–60, then someone could sell him euros (or buy his dollars) for $1.0255 per euro. Since he has raised the dollar price of a euro, he will receive more offers from people wanting to sell him euros in exchange for his dollars. When Jose buys euros from other traders, he is selling them dollars, and this helps to balance his inventory and reduce his long position in the dollar.

This *inventory control* effect on exchange rates can explain why traders may alter their quotes in the absence of any news about exchange rate fundamentals. Richard Lyons studied the deutsche mark/dollar market and estimated that, on average, foreign exchange traders alter their quotes by 0.00008 for each $10 million of undesired inventory. So a trader with an undesired long mark position of $20 million would, on average, raise his quote by 0.00016.

In addition to the inventory control effect, there is also an *asymmetric information* effect, which causes exchange rates to change due to traders' fears that they are quoting prices to someone who knows more about current market conditions than they do. Even without news regarding the fundamentals discussed earlier in the chapter, information is being transmitted from one trader to another through the act of trading. If Jose posts a quote of 1.0250–60 and is called by Ingrid Schultz at Chase asking to buy $5 million of euros at Jose's ask price of 1.0260, Jose then must wonder whether Ingrid knows something he doesn't. Should Ingrid's order to trade at Jose's price be considered a signal that Jose's price is too low? What superior information could Ingrid have? Every bank receives orders from nonbank customers to buy and sell currency. Perhaps Ingrid knows that her bank has just received a large order from DaimlerChrysler to sell dollars, and she is selling dollars (and buying euros) in advance of the price increase that will be caused by this nonbank order being filled by purchasing dollars from other traders.

Jose does not know why Ingrid is buying euros at his ask price, but he protects himself from further euro sales to someone who may be better informed than he is by raising his ask price. The bid price may be left unchanged because the order was to buy his euros; in such a case the spread increases, with the higher ask price due to the possibility of trading with a better-informed counterparty. Richard Lyons estimated that the presence of asymmetric information among traders resulted in the average change in the quoted price being 0.00014 per $10 million traded. At this average level, Jose would raise his ask price by 0.00007 in response to Ingrid's order to buy $55 million of euros.

The inventory control and asymmetric information effects can help explain why exchange rates change throughout the day, even in the absence of news regarding the fundamental determinants of exchange rates. The act of trading generates price changes among risk-averse traders who seek to manage their inventory positions to limit their exposure to surprising exchange rate changes and limit the potential loss from trading with better-informed individuals.

SUMMARY

1. Modern exchange rate models emphasize financial-asset markets.

2. Asset-approach models may be divided into monetary-approach models, assuming perfect substitutability of assets internationally, and portfolio-balance models, assuming imperfect substitutability.

3. Portfolio-balance models of exchange rate determination add relative asset supplies as a determinant.

4. Central-bank sterilization occurs when domestic credit is changed to offset international reserve flows.

5. Since balance-of-trade flows are balanced by financial-asset flows, changes in the trade balance have a role in asset-approach views of exchange rate determination.

6. If financial-asset markets clear fast relative to goods markets, then the exchange rate may overshoot the new long-run equilibrium after some shock to the system.

7. International currency substitution will add an additional source of exchange rate variability.

8. A high degree of currency substitution breeds currency union.

9. Exchange rates are difficult to forecast because the market is continually reacting to unexpected events or news.

10. Even in the absence of any major news, exchange rates adjust through the day as foreign exchange dealers manage their inventories and respond to trades with others who may be better informed.

EXERCISES

1. Suppose country X discovers a new technology that will result at some time in the future in a doubling of X's exports. As a result, country X moves from a position of balance-of-trade deficits to expected long-term surpluses. How will the foreign-exchange value of X's currency be affected? Do you expect any difference between the long run and the short run?

2. A major complaint regarding flexible exchange rates is that the exchange rates are too volatile when they float. Explain how each of the topics considered in this chapter—the trade balance, currency substitution, differential speed of adjustment of asset markets versus goods markets, and news—contributes to exchange rate volatility.

3. Suppose the domestic central bank unexpectedly lowers the money supply. In a world of exchange rate overshooting, how would the spot rate, forward rate, interest rate, and price level change in response? Draw graphs representing the expected time paths. Why does your exchange rate path have the shape that it does?

4. Carefully monitor the local newspaper (better still, the *Wall Street Journal*) for news that should have an impact on the foreign-exchange market. Keep a list of each news event, the effect on the value of the domestic currency you would expect (and why), and the actual effect.

5. Suppose the Federal Reserve in the United States wants to increase the value of the British pound against the dollar. How might it intervene in the foreign-exchange market to accomplish this? If the Fed wants to leave the U.S. money supply unchanged by the foreign-exchange market intervention, how will it conduct a sterilized intervention?

6. Why might governments in small developing countries worry about their citizens substituting among currencies?

7. Explain why overshooting occurs in overshooting exchange rate models. What does it imply about the short-run validity of interest rate parity and purchasing power parity?

8. What is the difference between the monetary approach and the portfolio-balance approach to exchange rate determination? What are the similarities between the two approaches?

9. According to the portfolio-balance approach to exchange rate determination, what will happen to the values of the domestic currency if the supply of foreign bonds rises relative to the supply of domestic bonds? Why?

10. Suppose Taka is a yen-dollar trader who is currently quoting ¥110.20–110.30 for the dollar. So for today he has bought $60,000,000 and sold $30,000,000 of yen. How would he change his quote in order to square his position (equalize amounts bought and sold)?

REFERENCES

Aivazian, Varouj A., Jeffrey L. Callen, Itzhak Krinsky, and Clarence C.Y. Kwan. "International Exchange Risk and Asset Substitutability." *Journal of International Money and Finance* (December 1986).

Calvo, Guillermo, and Carlos H. Végh. "Currency Substitution in Developing Countries: An Introduction." *Revista de Análisis Económico* (June 1992).

Humpage, Owen F. "Exchange Market Intervention: The Channels of Influence." *Economic Review* (Federal Reserve Bank of Cleveland, 3rd quarter, 1986).

Isard, Peter. *Exchange Rate Economics.* Cambridge: Cambridge University Press, 1995.

Lyons, Richard K. *The Microstructure Approach to Exchange Rates.* Cambridge: MIT Press, forthcoming.

Taylor, Mark. "The Economics of Exchange Rates." *Journal of Economic Literature* (March 1995).

INTERNET APPLICATIONS

Please visit our Web site at www.awl.com/husted_melvin for more exercises and readings.

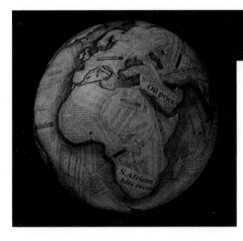

CHAPTER 19

Alternative

International

Monetary Standards

KEY WORDS

Gold standard   Destabilizing speculation
Commodity money standard   Seigniorage

Like most areas of public policy, international monetary relations are subject to frequent proposals for change. The international monetary system is the arrangement existing among countries regarding exchange rates and money flows. Fixed exchange rates, floating exchange rates, commodity-backed currency—all have their advocates. Before considering the merits of alternative international monetary systems, we should understand the background of the international monetary system. Although an international monetary system has been in existence since monies have been traded, it is common for most modern discussions of international monetary history to start in the late nineteenth century. It was during this period that the **gold standard** began.

Gold standard
Currencies have fixed values in terms of gold.

THE GOLD STANDARD: 1880–1914

Although an exact date for the beginning of the gold standard cannot be pinpointed, we know that it started during the 1880–1890 period.* Under a gold standard, currencies are valued in terms of a gold equivalent known as the mint parity price (an ounce of gold was worth $20.67 in terms of the U.S. dollar over the gold standard period). Then, because each currency is defined in terms of its gold value, all currencies are linked together in a system of fixed exchange rates. For instance, if 1 unit of currency A is worth 0.10 ounce of gold, whereas 1 unit of currency B is worth 0.20 ounce of gold, then 1 unit of currency B is worth twice as much as A, and thus the exchange rate of 1 currency B = 2 currency A is established.

Maintaining a gold standard requires a commitment from participating countries to be willing to buy and sell gold to anyone at the fixed price. To maintain a price of $20.67 per ounce, the United States had to buy and sell gold at that price. If the government does not stand willing to buy and sell at the mint parity price, then the price will fluctuate with changes in the supply of and demand for money relative to gold. With fluctuating gold prices, currencies would not be linked together at fixed exchange rates.

Gold was used as a monetary standard because it is a homogeneous commodity worldwide (could you have a fish standard?) that is easily storable, portable, and divisible into standardized units, such as ounces. Since gold is costly to produce, it possesses another important attribute—governments cannot easily increase its supply. A gold standard is a **commodity money standard.** Money has a value that is fixed in terms of the commodity gold.

Commodity money standard
The value of money is fixed relative to a commodity.

One aspect of a money standard based on a commodity with a relatively fixed supply is long-run price stability. Since governments must maintain a fixed value of

---

*Some countries had backed their currency with gold or silver long before 1880. The practice became widespread around 1880. Interesting discussions of the gold standard are found in Robert Triffin, "The Myth and Realities of the So-Called Gold Standard," in *International Finance*, ed. R.N. Cooper (Baltimore: Penguin, 1969); Barry Eichengreen, *The Gold Standard in Theory and History* (London: Methuen, 1985); and Michael David Bordo, "The Classical Gold Standard: Lessons from the Past," in *The International Monetary System: Choices for the Future*, ed. Michael B. Connolly (New York: Praeger, 1982).

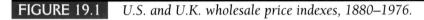

FIGURE 19.1   *U.S. and U.K. wholesale price indexes, 1880–1976.*

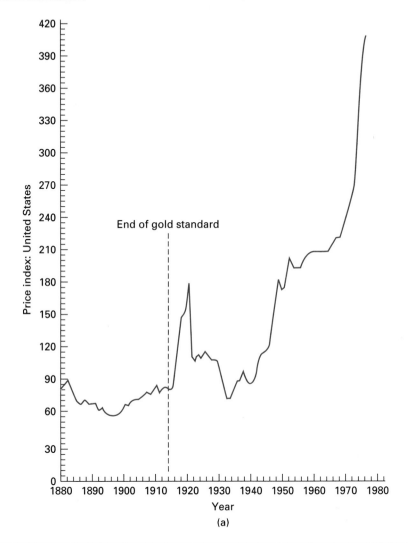

Year
(a)

SOURCE: Roy W. Jastram, *The Golden Constant* (New York: Wiley & Sons, 1977).

their money relative to gold, the supply of money is restricted by the supply of gold. Prices may still rise and fall with swings in gold output and economic growth, but the tendency is to return to a long-run stable level. Figure 19.1 illustrates graphically the relative stability of U.S. and U.K. prices over the gold standard period as compared with later years. Since currencies were convertible into gold, national money supplies were constrained by the growth of the stock of gold. As long as the gold

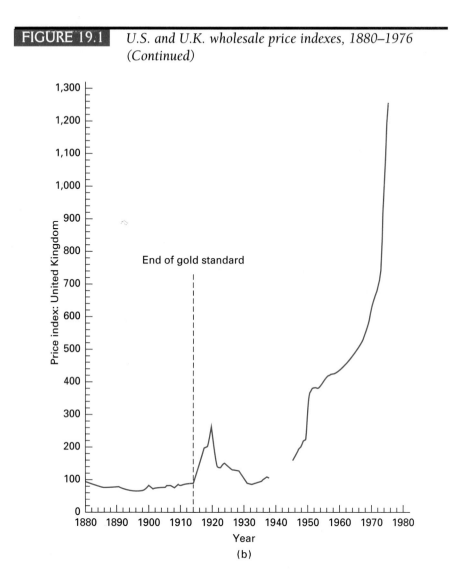

FIGURE 19.1   *U.S. and U.K. wholesale price indexes, 1880–1976 (Continued)*

(b)

stock grew at a steady rate, prices would also follow a steady path. New discoveries of gold would generate discontinuous jumps in the price level, but the period of the gold standard was marked by a fairly stable stock of gold.

People today often look back on the gold standard as a "golden era" of economic progress. It is common to hear arguments supporting a return to the gold standard. Such arguments usually cite the stable prices, economic growth, and development of world trade during this period as evidence of the benefits provided by such an orderly international monetary system. Others have suggested that the economic development and stability of the world economy in these years are not necessarily due to the existence of the gold standard, but rather a result of the lack of any significant real shocks, such as war.

Although people may disagree on the merits of returning to a gold standard, it seems fair to say that the development of world trade was encouraged by the systematic linking of national currencies and the price stability of the system.

Because during a gold standard gold is like a world money, we can easily understand how a balance-of-payments disequilibrium may be remedied. A country running a balance-of-payments deficit would find itself with net outflows of gold, thus reducing its money supply and, in turn, its prices. A surplus country would find gold flowing in and expanding its money supply, so that prices would rise. The fall in prices in the deficit country would lead to greater net exports (exports minus imports), and the rise in prices in the surplus country would reduce its net exports, so that balance-of-payments equilibrium would be restored.

In practice, actual flows of gold were not the only, or even necessarily the most important, means of settling international debts during this period. Since London was the financial center of the world and England the world's leading trader and source of financial capital, the pound also served as a world money. International trade was commonly priced in pounds, and trade that never passed through England was often paid for with pounds.

THE INTERWAR PERIOD: 1918–1939

World War I ended the gold standard. International financial relations are greatly strained by war, because merchants and bankers must be concerned about the probability of countries suspending international capital flows. At the beginning of the war, both the patriotic response of each nation's citizens and legal restrictions stopped private gold flows. Because wartime financing required the hostile nations to manage international reserves very carefully, private gold exports were considered unpatriotic. Central governments encouraged (and sometimes mandated) that private holders of gold and foreign exchange sell these holdings to the government. Governments financed wartime expenditures by printing money—the result was that the prewar parities would no longer hold.

Because much of Europe had experienced rapid inflation during the war and the period immediately afterward, it was not possible to restore the gold standard at the old exchange values. However, the United States had experienced little inflation and thus returned to a gold standard by June 1919 at the old parity. The war ended Britain's financial preeminence; the United States had risen to the status of the world's dominant banker country. In the immediate postwar years, the pound fluctuated freely against the dollar in line with purchasing power parity considerations.*

---

*A good review of the interwar years is given in Ragnar Nurkse, *International Currency Experience* (Geneva: League of Nations, 1944).

In 1925, England returned to a gold standard at the old prewar pound per gold exchange rate even though prices had risen since the prewar period. As John Maynard Keynes had correctly warned, the overvalued pound hurt U.K. exports and led to a deflation of British wages and prices. Due to the low price of gold, the British money supply contracted as citizens exchanged money for government gold. By 1931, the pound was declared inconvertible; the government would no longer exchange gold for pound currency, due to a run on British gold reserves (a large demand to convert pounds into gold), thus ending the brief U.K. return to a gold standard. However, once the pound was no longer convertible into gold, free-market attention centered on the U.S. dollar. The United States now faced a large demand to exchange gold for dollars. This "run" on U.S. gold at the end of 1931 led to a 15 percent drop in U.S. gold holdings. Although this did not lead to an immediate change in U.S. policy, by 1933 the United States raised the official price of gold to $35 an ounce to halt the gold outflow.

The depression years were characterized by international monetary warfare. In trying to stimulate domestic economies by increasing exports, country after country devalued, so that the early to middle 1930s may be characterized as a period of competitive devaluations. Governments also resorted to foreign-exchange controls in the attempt to manipulate net exports in a manner that would increase GDP. Of course, with the onslaught of World War II, the hostile countries utilized foreign-exchange controls to aid the war-financing effort.

THE GOLD EXCHANGE STANDARD: 1944–1970

Memories of the economic warfare of the interwar years led to an international conference at Bretton Woods, New Hampshire, in 1944. At the close of World War II, there was a desire to reform the international monetary system to one based on mutual cooperation and freely convertible currencies. The result of this conference was an agreement to tie the values of all currencies together. The Bretton Woods agreement required that each country fix the value of its currency in terms of gold (this established the "par" value of each currency and was to ensure parity across currencies). The U.S. dollar was the key currency in the system, and $1 was defined as being equal in value to 1/35 ounce of gold. Since every currency had a defined gold value, all currencies were linked in a system of fixed exchange rates.

Nations belonging to the system were committed to maintaining the parity value of the currency within ±1 percent of parity. The various central banks were to achieve this goal by buying and selling their currencies (usually against the dollar) on the foreign-exchange market. When a country was experiencing difficulty maintaining its parity value due to balance-of-payments disequilibrium, it could turn to a new institution created at the Bretton Woods Conference: *the International Monetary Fund (IMF)*. The IMF was created to monitor the operation of the system and provide short-term loans to countries experiencing temporary balance-of-payments difficulties. Item 19.1 describes the operation of the IMF. The Fund's loans were (and still are) subject to IMF conditions requiring changes in domestic economic

ITEM 19.1   The International Monetary Fund

The IMF was created at the Bretton Woods Conference held July 1–22, 1944, in Bretton Woods, New Hampshire, and began operation on December 27, 1945, with headquarters in Washington, D.C. Country membership in the IMF has grown from 39 countries to 182 countries.

Originally, the Fund was mainly concerned with overseeing members' exchange rate practices to ensure the efficient operation of the system of fixed exchange rates adopted at the Bretton Woods Conference. In the 1950s the Fund began reviewing the balance-of-payments situation of members and macroeconomic policy decisions that might have an impact on the balance of payments. Countries having balance-of-payments problems can borrow from the IMF to finance their deficits. Such borrowing is supposed to be short-term in duration (repayment within three to five years) to ease the burden of temporary problems. More fundamental long-term problems are supposed to require exchange rate devaluations and macroeconomic adjustment policies in consultation with the Fund.

The IMF gains leverage over countries through its "conditionality" requirements. Countries asking for loans from the IMF must agree to conditions set by the IMF to receive their funds. The conditions address recommended exchange rates and domestic policies aimed at improving the countries' international payments imbalance. Fund conditions have sometimes become contro-versial political issues in borrowing countries, as nationalistic pride and domestic-policy goals may be hurt by the policies required by the IMF. For instance, a frequent condition imposed is reducing government subsidies of domestic consumer goods and allowing more free markets. It may be very difficult, politically, for a government to raise the price of bread or milk in a poor country, but such loan conditions are a recognition that the nation's problems arise from excessive government spending.

In 1969, the IMF acquired the power to issue special drawing rights (SDRs). This is a unit of account that functions as a money and may be used to settle debts between member countries. In the late 1960s, there had been a growing concern over the increased use of the U.S. dollar to finance world trade. Many felt that a new kind of international money was required to supplement the use of dollars. The SDR was the response offered by the IMF. However, the SDR has not become a major asset used in world payments as originally envisioned.

In summary, the activities of the IMF generally involve the following areas:

1. Overseeing exchange rate policies.

2. Monitoring international payments imbalances.

3. Providing temporary loans for balance-of-payments financing.

policy aimed at restoring balance-of-payments equilibrium. In the case of a fundamental disequilibrium, where the balance-of-payments problems were not of a temporary nature, a country was allowed to devalue its currency, resulting in a permanent change in the parity rate of exchange. Table 19.1 summarizes the history of exchange rate adjustments over the Bretton Woods period for the major industrialized countries.

TABLE 19.1	*Exchange Rates of the Major Industrialized Countries over the Period of the Bretton Woods Agreement*
Country	**Exchange Rates[1]**
Canada	Floated until May 2, 1962, then pegged at Can$1.081 = $1. Floated again on June 1, 1970.
France	No official IMF parity value after 1948 (although the actual rate hovered around FF350 = $1) until December 29, 1958, when the rate fixed at FF493.7 = $1 (old francs). One year later, rate was FF4.937 = $1 when the new franc (1 new franc was equal to 100 old francs) was created. Devaluation to FF5.554 = $1 on August 10, 1969.
Germany	Revalued on March 6, 1961, from DM4.20 = $1 to DM4.0 = $1. Revalued to DM3.66 = $1 on October 26, 1969.
Italy	Pegged at Lit625 = $1 from March 30, 1960, until August 1971.
Japan	Pegged at ¥360 = $1 until 1971.
Netherlands	Pegged at F13.80 = $1 until March 7, 1961, when revalued at F13.62 = $1.
United Kingdom	Devalued from $2.80 = £1 to $2.40 = £1 on November 11, 1967.

[1]Relative to the U.S. dollar.

We note, then, that the Bretton Woods system, although essentially a fixed or pegged exchange rate system, allowed for changes in exchange rates when economic circumstances warranted such changes. In actuality, the system is best described as an adjustable peg. The system may also be described as a gold exchange standard because the key currency, the dollar, was convertible into gold for official holders of dollars (e.g., central banks and treasuries).

The Bretton Woods system worked well through the 1950s and into the early part of the 1960s. In 1960 there was the first of several dollar crises. The United States had been running large balance-of-payments deficits in the late 1950s. This meant that dollars had been piling up in foreign central banks. Concern over large foreign holdings of dollars led some central bankers to exchange their dollar holdings for U.S. gold reserves, and U.S. gold holdings began to fall. The fall in U.S. gold reserves led to fears that the dollar would be devalued in terms of gold. This fear led to a higher demand for gold in private gold markets also. Central-bank cooperation managed to stabilize gold prices at the official rate, but still, the pressures fermented. Although the problem of chronic U.S. deficits and Japanese and European surpluses could have been remedied by revaluing the undervalued yen, mark, and franc, the surplus countries argued that it was the responsibility of the United States to restore balance-of-payments equilibrium.

The failure to realign currency values in the face of fundamental economic change spelled the beginning of the end for the gold exchange standard of the Bretton Woods agreement. By the late 1960s, the foreign dollar liabilities of the United States were much larger than the U.S. gold stock. The pressures of this "dollar glut" finally culminated in August 1971, when President Nixon declared the dollar to be inconvertible. This action, known as "closing the gold window," provided a close to the Bretton Woods era of fixed exchange rates and convertible currencies.

THE TRANSITION YEARS: 1971–1973

In December 1971, an international monetary conference was held at the Smithsonian Institute in Washington, D.C., to realign the foreign-exchange values of the major currencies. The Smithsonian agreement provided for a change in the dollar per gold exchange value from $35 to $38 per ounce of gold. At the same time that the dollar was being devalued by about 8 percent, the surplus countries saw their currencies revalued upward. After the change in official currency values, the system was to operate with fixed exchange rates, whereby the central banks would buy and sell their currencies to maintain the exchange rate within ±2.25 percent of the stated parity.

Although the realignment of currency values provided by the Smithsonian agreement allowed a temporary respite from foreign-exchange crisis, the calm was short-lived. Speculative flows of capital began to put downward pressure on the pound and lira. In June 1972, the British government allowed the pound to float according to supply and demand conditions. Countries experiencing large inflows of speculative capital, such as Germany and Switzerland, applied legal controls to slow further movements of money into their countries.

Although the gold value of the dollar had been officially changed, the dollar was still inconvertible into gold, and thus the major significance of the dollar devaluation was with respect to the foreign-exchange value of the dollar, not with respect to official gold movements. In 1972 and early 1973, currency speculators began selling dollars in massive amounts. This pressure led to a further devaluation of the dollar in February 1973, when the U.S. government raised the official price of an ounce of gold from $38.00 to $42.22. Despite the devaluation, speculative capital flows persisted. Country after country announced that it would abandon fixed exchange rates. By March 1973, the major currencies were all floating.

FLOATING EXCHANGE RATES: SINCE 1973

Although we refer to the exchange rate system in existence since 1973 as a floating rate system, exchange rates have not been determined solely by the free-market forces of supply and demand. The system as operated is best described as a managed float, wherein central banks intervene at times to obtain a politically desirable exchange rate apart from that which would be determined by free-market supply and demand. Such managed floating does not apply to all countries and currencies; we observe several different exchange rate policies followed by countries today. Table 19.2 lists the exchange rate practices of the IMF member countries. Some countries, such as the United States, allow their currencies to float freely, whereas others, such as Aruba, choose to maintain a fixed value (or peg) relative to a single currency, such as the dollar or pound, and still others, such as Botswana, choose to peg to a composite or basket of currencies. There are several reasons for choosing a basket peg. For instance, if trade is not heavily concentrated with one country but is instead diversified across several countries, then it may make more sense to alter the currency value relative to a weighted average of foreign currencies rather than any single currency.

TABLE 19.2   *Exchange Rate Arrangements*

(AS OF JANUARY 1, 2000)

Crawling pegs (6)	Exchange rates within crawling bands (9)	Managed floating with no preannounced path for exchange rate (25)	Independently floating (48)
Angola	Chile	Algeria	Afghanistan, Islamic State of
Bolivia	Colombia	Azerbaijan	Albania
Costa Rica	Honduras	Belarus	Armenia
Nicaragua	Hungary	Cambodia	Australia
Tunisia	Israel	Czech Rep.	Brazil
Turkey	Poland	Dominican Rep.	Canada
	Sri Lanka	Ethiopia	Congo, Dem. Rep. of the
	Uruguay	Jamaica	Ecuador
	Venezuela	Kenya	Eritrea
		Kyrgyz Republic	Gambia, The
		Lao P.D.R.	Georgia
		Malawi	Ghana
		Mauritania	Guatemala
		Nigeria	Guinea
		Norway	Guyana
		Pakistan	Haiti
		Paraguay	India
		Romania	Indonesia
		Russia	Japan
		Singapore	Kazakhstan
		Slovak Rep.	Korea
		Slovenia	Liberia
		Suriname	Madagascar
		Tajikistan	Mauritius
		Uzbekistan	Mexico
			Moldova
			Mongolia
			Mozambique
			New Zealand
			Papua New Guinea
			Peru
			Philippines
			Rwanda
			Sào Tomé and Principe
			Sierra Leone
			Somalia
			South Africa
			Sudan
			Sweden
			Switzerland
			Tanzania
			Thailand
			Uganda
			United Kingdom
			United States
			Yemen
			Zambia
			Zimbabwe

Sources: IMF staff reports.

Exchange arrangements with no separate legal tender (37)	Currency board arrangements (8)	Other conventional fixed peg arrangements (including de facto peg arrangements under managed floating) (44)	Exchange rates within horizontal bands (8)
Another currency as legal tender	Argentina	*Against a single currency (30)*	*Within a cooperative arrangement ERM II (2)*
Kiribati	Bosnia and	Aruba	Denmark
Marshall Islands	Herzegovina	Bahamas	Greece
Micronesia	Brunei Darusalam	Bahrain	*Other band*
Palau	Bulgaria	Barbados	*arrangements (6)*
Panama	Djibouti	Belize	Croatia
San Marino	Estonia	Bhutan	Cyprus
CFA franc zone	Hong Kong SAR	Cape Verde	Iceland
WAEMU	Lithuania	China	Libya
Benin		Comoros	Ukraine
Burkina Faso		Egypt	Vietnam
Côte d'Ivoire		El Salvador	
Guinea-Bissau		Iran, Islamic Rep. of	
Mali		Iraq	
Niger		Jordan	
Senegal		Lebanon	
Togo		Lesotho	
CAEMC		Macedonia, FYR	
Cameroon		Malaysia	
Central African Rep.		Maldives	
Chad		Namibia	
Congo, Rep. of		Nepal	
Equatorial Guinea		Netherlands Antilles	
Gabon		Oman	
Euro Area		Qatar	
Austria		Saudi Arabia	
Belgium		Syrian Arab Republic	
Finland		Swaziland	
France		Trinidad and Tobago	
Germany		Turkmenistan	
Ireland		United Arab Emirates	
Italy		*Against a composite (13)*	
Luxembourg		Bangladesh	
Netherlands		Botswana	
Portugal		Burundi	
Spain		Fiji	
		Kuwait	
		Latvia	
		Malta	
		Morocco	
		Myanmar	
		Samoa	
		Seychelles	
		Solomon Islands	
		Tonga	
		Vanuatu	

The various headings in Table 19.2 indicate quite a variety of exchange rate arrangements. We provide a brief description of each:

Crawling pegs   The exchange rate is adjusted periodically in small amounts at a fixed, preannounced rate or in response to certain indicators (such as inflation differentials against major trading partners).

Crawling bands   The exchange rate is maintained within certain fluctuation margins around a central rate that is periodically adjusted at a fixed, preannounced rate or in response to certain indicators.

Managed floating   The monetary authority (usually the central bank) influences the exchange rate through active foreign exchange market intervention with no preannounced path for the exchange rate.

Independently floating   The exchange rate is market determined, and any intervention is aimed at moderating fluctuations rather than determining the level of the exchange rate.

No separate legal tender   Either another country's currency circulates as the legal tender, or the country belongs to a monetary union where the legal tender is shared by the members (like the euro).

Currency board   A fixed exchange rate is established by a legislative commitment to exchange domestic currency for a specified foreign currency at a fixed exchange rate. New issues of domestic currency are typically backed in some fixed ratio (like one-to-one) by additional holdings of the key foreign currency.

Fixed peg   The exchange rate is fixed against a major currency or some basket of currencies. Active intervention may be required to maintain the target pegged rate.

Horizontal bands   The exchange rate fluctuates around a fixed central target rate. Such target zones allow for a moderate amount of exchange rate fluctuation while tying the currency to the target central rate.

THE CHOICE OF AN EXCHANGE-RATE SYSTEM

A system of perfectly fixed or pegged exchange rates would work much like a gold standard. All countries would fix their exchange rate in terms of a single currency, say the dollar, and thereby would fix their exchange rate in terms of all other currencies. Under such an arrangement, countries would be required to buy or sell their currency in foreign-exchange markets to keep its price fixed.

Flexible or floating exchange rates occur when the exchange rate is determined by the market forces of supply and demand. As the demand (supply) for a currency increases relative to supply (demand), that currency will appreciate (depreciate). Central banks do not intervene to affect the exchange value of their money.

Economists do not agree on the advantages and disadvantages of a floating versus a pegged exchange rate system. For instance, some would argue that a major advantage of flexible rates is that each country can follow domestic macroeconomic policies independent of the policies of other countries. To maintain fixed exchange rates, countries have to share a common inflation experience, or else PPP becomes increasingly violated. Common inflation rates across countries, in turn, require similar monetary policies. The failure of this condition to hold was often a source of problems under the post–World War II system of fixed exchange rates. For instance, in the late 1960s the U.S. government was following very expansionary policies relative to Germany as it sought to fight two wars: one on poverty, the other in Vietnam. Thus, the existing pegged rate could not be maintained. Yet with flexible rates, each country can choose a desired rate of inflation, and the exchange rate will adjust accordingly. If the United States chooses 8 percent inflation whereas Germany chooses 3 percent, there will be a steady depreciation of the dollar relative to the mark (absent any relative price movements). Given the different political environment and cultural heritage existing in each country, it is reasonable to expect different countries to follow different monetary policies. Floating exchange rates allow for an orderly adjustment to these differing inflation rates.

Still, there are those economists who argue that the ability of each country to choose an inflation rate is an undesirable aspect of floating exchange rates. These proponents of fixed rates indicate that fixed rates are useful in providing an international discipline on the inflationary policies of countries. Fixed rates provide an anchor for countries with inflationary tendencies. By maintaining a fixed rate of exchange to the dollar (or some other currency), each country's inflation rate would be "anchored" to the inflation rate in the United States and thus would follow the policy established for the dollar.

Critics of flexible exchange rates have also argued that flexible exchange rates would be subject to **destabilizing speculation.** By *destabilizing speculation*, we mean that speculators in the foreign-exchange market will cause exchange rate fluctuations to be wider than they would be in the absence of such speculation. The counterargument is that logic suggests that if speculators expect a currency to depreciate, they will take positions in the foreign-exchange market that will cause the depreciation as a sort of self-fulfilling prophecy. But speculators should lose money when they guess wrong, so that only successful speculators will remain in the market, and the latter should serve a useful role by "evening out" swings in the exchange rate. For instance, if a speculator expects a currency to depreciate or decrease in value next month, he or she could sell the currency now, which results in a current depreciation. This will lead to a smaller future depreciation than would otherwise occur. Thus, the speculator spreads the exchange rate change more evenly through time and tends to even out big jumps in the exchange rate. If the speculator had bet on future dollar depreciation by selling the dollar now and holding francs, the speculator will lose if the dollar appreciates instead of depreciates. The francs will be converted back into fewer dollars than originally exchanged, so the speculator loses and will eventually be eliminated from the market if such mistakes are repeated. Despite

Destabilizing speculation
Speculators increase the variability of exchange rates.

the talk of destabilizing speculation, there is no evidence that this has ever been a serious problem.

Research has shown that there are systematic differences between countries choosing fixed exchange rates and those choosing floating rates.* One important characteristic is country size (measured in terms of economic activity or GDP). Large countries tend to be more independent and less willing to subjugate their own domestic-policy goals to maintain a fixed rate of exchange with foreign currencies. Because foreign trade tends to constitute a smaller fraction of GDP in larger countries, it is perhaps understandable that these countries are less attuned to foreign-exchange rate concerns than smaller countries are.

The openness of an economy is another important factor. By *openness*, we mean the degree to which the country depends on international trade. The greater the fraction of tradable (i.e., internationally tradable) goods in GDP, the more open the economy will be. A country with little or no international trade is referred to as a closed economy. As previously mentioned, openness is related to size. The more open an economy is, the greater will be the importance of tradable-goods prices in the behavior of the overall national price level, and therefore the greater will be the impact of exchange rate changes on the national price level. To minimize such foreign-related shocks to the domestic price level, the more open economy tends to follow a pegged exchange rate.

Remembering the purchasing power parity (PPP) relation, we can understand why countries that choose to allow higher rates of inflation than their trading partners do will have difficulty maintaining fixed exchange rates with those countries. Since prices are rising faster in the high-inflation countries, their currency must depreciate to keep their goods prices comparable to those of other countries. These high-inflation countries will choose floating rates or a crawling-peg type of system wherein the exchange rate is adjusted at short intervals to compensate for the inflation differentials.

Countries that trade largely with a single foreign country tend to peg their exchange rate to the foreign country's currency. For instance, the United States accounts for the majority of Barbadian trade. By pegging its currency, the Barbadian dollar, to the U.S. dollar, Barbados imparts a degree of stability to the prices of its exports and imports that would otherwise be missing. Countries with diversified trading patterns will not find exchange rate pegging so desirable, because only trade with the country to which their currency is pegged would gain price stability, while trade with all other important trading partners would have prices fluctuating.

The evidence from previous studies indicates quite convincingly the systematic differences between peggers and floaters. These characteristics are summarized in Table 19.3. It must be realized that there are exceptions to these generalities because neither all peggers nor all floaters have the same characteristics. We can safely say that, in general, the larger a country is, the more likely it is to float its exchange rate,

---

*See Hali Edison and Michael Melvin, "The Determinants and Implications of the Choice of an Exchange Rate System," in *Monetary Policy for a Volatile Global Economy*, ed. W. Haraf and T. Willett (Washington, D.C.: American Enterprise Institute, 1990).

TABLE 19.3	*Characteristics Associated with Countries Choosing to Peg or Float*	
Peggers	**Floaters**
Small size	Large size
Open economy	Closed economy
Harmonious inflation rate	Divergent inflation rate
Concentrated trade	Diversified trade

and the more closed an economy is, the more likely the country will float, and so on. The point is that economic phenomena, and not just political maneuvering, ultimately influence foreign-exchange rate practices.

Recently, researchers have focused on how the choice of an exchange rate system will affect the stability of an economy.* If the domestic-policy authorities seek to minimize unexpected fluctuations in the domestic price level, then they will choose an exchange rate system that best minimizes such fluctuations. For instance, the greater foreign tradable-goods price fluctuations are, the more likely it is that authorities will choose to float, since a floating exchange rate helps to insulate the domestic economy from foreign price disturbances.

The greater the domestic money-supply fluctuations are, the more likely it is that there will be a peg, since international money flows serve as a shock absorber that reduces the domestic price impact of domestic money-supply fluctuations. With a fixed exchange rate, an excess supply of domestic money will cause a capital outflow because some of this excess supply is eliminated via a balance-of-payments deficit. With floating rates, the excess supply of money is contained at home and reflected in a higher domestic price level and depreciating domestic currency. Once again, the empirical evidence supports the notion that real-world exchange rate practices are determined by such economic phenomena.

OPTIMUM CURRENCY AREAS

In the 1960s, a literature emerged on the choice of an exchange rate system called the *optimum currency area*. Since references are still made to that body of knowledge, we should briefly review the major points. First, a currency area is an area where exchange rates are fixed within the area and floating exchange rates exist against currencies outside the area. The "optimum" currency area is the best grouping of countries to achieve some objective, such as ease of adjustment to real or nominal shocks.

---

*See Harvey E. Lapan and Walter Enders, "Random Disturbances and the Choice of Exchange Regimes in an Intergenerational Model," *Journal of International Economics* (May 1980); Michael Melvin, "The Choice of an Exchange Rate System and Macroeconomic Stability," *Journal of Money, Credit, and Banking* (November 1985); and Andreas Savvides, "Real Exchange Rate Variability and the Choice of Exchange Rate Regime by Developing Countries," *Journal of International Money and Finance* (December 1990).

How should currency areas be chosen so that exchange rate practices best allow the pursuit of economic goals, such as full employment and price stability?

A popular theory suggests that the optimum currency area is the region characterized by relatively costless mobility of the factors of production (labor and capital).* As an illustration of this theory, suppose we have two countries, A and B, producing computers and cotton, respectively. Now, there is a change in tastes resulting in a shift of demand from computers to cotton. Country A will tend to run a trade deficit and have an excess supply of labor and capital because the demand for computers has fallen, whereas country B will tend to run a surplus and have an excess demand for labor and capital due to the increase in demand for its cotton. What are the possibilities for international adjustment to these changes?

1. Factors of production could move from country A to country B and thereby establish new equilibrium wages and prices in each region.

2. Prices in A must fall relative to B, and the relative price change will eliminate the balance-of-trade disequilibrium if labor and capital cannot move between the countries. (We are ignoring the capital account now, in order to assume zero capital flows.)

3. The exchange rate could change and bring about the required change in relative prices if A and B have different currencies.

Now we can understand why the optimum currency area is characterized by mobile factors of production. If factors can freely and cheaply migrate from an area lacking jobs to an area where labor is in demand, then the factor mobility will restore equilibrium because the unemployment in the one area is removed by migration. Thus, fixed exchange rates within the area will be appropriate because relative price movements are not the only means for restoring equilibrium.

When factors are immobile, so that equilibrium is restored solely through relative price change, there is an advantage to flexible exchange rates. If the monetary authorities in each country tend to resist any price changes, then the easiest way to adjust is with flexible exchange rates because the adjustment can go largely through the exchange rate rather than through prices. Looking at the real world, we might suggest that North America and Western Europe appear to be likely currency areas given the geographic position of Canada, Mexico, and the United States as well as the geographic position of the Western European nations. Since exchange rates between the U.S. and Canadian dollars and the Mexican peso seem closely linked (certainly, the peso and the U.S. dollar had a long history of fixed exchange rates), we might expect these three countries to maintain pegged exchange rates with each other and to float versus the rest of the world. Western Europeans have, in fact, explicitly adopted such a regional optimum-currency-area arrangement. The European Monetary System (EMS) is characterized by fixed rates within the system and floating rates between the EMS and the rest of the world.

---

*This theory is developed in Robert A. Mundell, "A Theory of Optimum Currency Areas," *American Economic Review* (September 1961).

THE EUROPEAN MONETARY SYSTEM AND THE EURO

The optimum currency area literature suggests that in a regional setting like Western Europe a system of fixed exchange rates might be appropriate. While the establishment of the common euro currency may be viewed as a kind of permanently final exchange rate, prior to the euro there already had been a system in place to link currencies and limit exchange rate flexibility since the late 1970s. In March 1979, the European Monetary System (EMS) was established to maintain exchange rate stability in Western Europe. The EMS exchange rate mechanism (ERM) required that each nation maintain the value of its currency within 2.25 percent of a fixed value against the currencies of the other member countries (the Italian lira was allowed to fluctuate within a 6 percent band). The exchange rates were to be kept within these narrow bands by central-bank intervention. For instance, if the French franc threatened to fall below the lower bands of its value against the German mark, then the German and French central banks would buy francs to keep the currency within the ERM limits.

While such intervention worked to stabilize exchange rates, sometimes the realities of the market forced a realignment of the ERM values when it became clear that there were fundamental changes in the values of the currencies. For instance, Germany and the Netherlands typically had lower inflation than the other member countries, so realignments were generally aimed at depreciation of the other currencies against the German mark and the Dutch guilder.

The removal of capital controls restricting international financial transactions (including foreign-exchange transactions) played an important role in the breakdown of the system in 1992. Capital controls that helped keep national financial markets insulated from outside pressures made central bank currency management easier. The removal of such controls, as required by the Single European Act of 1986, allowed for much greater capital mobility among the European nations. In addition, the pursuit of domestic-macroeconomic-policy goals at the expense of exchange rate management put additional pressures on the ERM. In September 1992, as some currencies, particularly the British pound and the Italian lira, neared the bottom of their ERM exchange rate limits, speculators began betting heavily on another realignment that would devalue these currencies. This heavy selling of the pound and lira resulted in the British government pulling the pound out of the ERM on September 16, 1992. A few hours after the British move, the Italian government pulled the lira out of the ERM. The currency crisis resulted in a widening of the ERM bands for exchange rate fluctuations to 15 percent in August 1993.

A major step toward a single European money occurred in December 1991, when the Maastricht Treaty, calling for a single European central bank and single money, was signed. The treaty spelled out the evolution that the EMS followed to approach monetary union. The specific steps taken were as follows:

1. The immediate removal of restrictions on European flows of capital and greater coordination of monetary and fiscal policy.

2. The establishment of a European Monetary Institute (EMI) in January 1994 to coordinate monetary policies of the individual central banks and make technical preparations for a single monetary policy.

3. The irrevocable fixing of exchange rates among all member countries, with a single (euro) currency and a single European Central Bank.

This last step did not occur until January 1999. The countries that moved to this last step of monetary union required their macroeconomic policy to converge to that of the other EMS countries. Convergence was defined as occurring when (a) the country's inflation rate did not exceed the average of the lowest three member country rates by more than 1.5 percentage points; (b) its interest rate on long-term government bonds did not exceed those of the three lowest-inflation members by more than 2 percentage points; and (c) the country's government budget deficit did not exceed 3 percent of GDP, and outstanding government debt did not exceed 60 percent of GDP.

The new European currency, the euro, made its debut on January 1, 1999. The symbol is a €, and the ISO code is EUR. Euro notes and coins will begin to circulate on January 1, 2002. In the transition years, people are using the euro as a unit of account, denominating financial asset values and transactions in euro amounts. Bank accounts are available in euros and credit transactions may be denominated in euros. However, actual cash transactions cannot be made with euros until euro cash starts circulating in 2002.

From January 1 until July 1, 2002, the euro currency will circulate jointly with national monies and both may be used for cash transactions. During this period, the euro cash will slowly take over cash business, and the national monies will be slowly withdrawn from circulation. After July 1, 2002, the national monies (like the German mark, French franc, and Italian lira) will no longer be a legal tender and only euros may be used.

TARGET ZONES

Exchange rate arrangements like the old EMS, where there is limited flexibility around some central fixed value, are sometimes called *target zones*. In this setting, the exchange rate is allowed to change with changes in the fundamental determinants of exchange rates like money supplies, incomes, and prices, but the amount of change allowed is limited by the width of the bands permitted by the target zone arrangement.

Figure 19.2 illustrates the essentials of a target zone system. For purposes of example, let's assume that the United States and the United Kingdom have agreed on a target zone for the dollar/pound exchange rate where the exchange rate will be kept between 2.04 and 1.96 dollars per pound. The vertical axis of Figure 19.2 measures the exchange rate in dollars per pound. The upper bound of the target zone is shown in the figure as $E_{max} = 2.04$. The lower bound is shown as $E_{min} = 1.96$. The horizontal axis measures the value of the "fundamentals" like the net effect of money supply, income, prices, and any other fundamental determinants of exchange rates.

If instead of a target zone there were a fixed exchange rate at $2 per pound, what would that look like in the figure? A fixed exchange rate would be represented by one point in the figure at the origin where $E = 2$. This means that, as other funda-

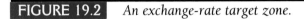

FIGURE 19.2   *An exchange-rate target zone.*

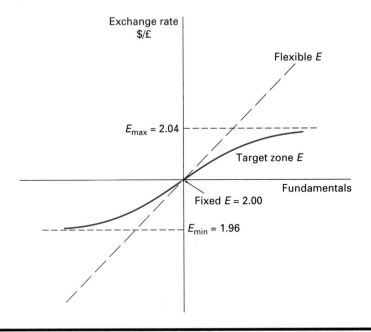

mentals change, the central banks change the money supply to offset the effects of the other fundamentals so that the exchange rate is left unchanged.

If instead of a target zone there were a flexible exchange rate system, what would that look like in the figure? A flexible exchange rate would be represented by the 45 degree line. This indicates that the exchange rate changes match changes in the fundamentals as the central banks do not attempt to offset the effects of the fundamentals. Also, note that a flexible exchange rate may rise or fall without bounds if pushed by the fundamentals.

With a target zone system, the central banks are committed to intervening so that the exchange rate rises no higher than $E = 2.04$ and falls no lower than $E = 1.96$. If people believe that this zone will be enforced by the government authorities, then the exchange rate will lie along the S-shaped line in Figure 19.2.* Note that this line is flatter than the 45 degree line of the flexible exchange rate. This S-shape is due to

---

*There are technical details of target zone analysis that lie beyond the scope of this text but are discussed in the following sample of the large target zone literature: Paul Krugman, "Target Zones and Exchange Rate Dynamics," *Quarterly Journal of Economics* (August 1991); Lars E.O. Svensson, "An Interpretation of Recent Research on Exchange Rate Target Zones," *Journal of Economic Perspectives* (Fall 1992); Hans Lindberg and Paul Söderlind, "Testing the Basic Target Zone Model on Swedish Data, 1982–1990," *European Economic Review* (August 1994); and Peter Garber and Lars E.O. Svensson, "The Operation and Collapse of Fixed Exchange Rate Regimes," in *Handbook of International Economics,* ed. Gene M. Grossman and Kenneth Rogoff (Amsterdam: North Holland, 1995).

the fact that the closer the exchange rate gets to the upper or lower limit, the greater the probability of intervention. For instance, suppose the exchange rate is rising and approaches the upper limit of 2.04. The probability of a central bank intervention is increased so that people will expect a greater probability of the exchange rate dropping with the intervention rather than continuing to rise. As a result, the exchange rate line flattens to give the top of the *S*-shape. Continued increases in the fundamentals result in smaller and smaller dollar depreciation as the threat increases of central bank intervention aimed at dollar appreciation. In this sense, a target zone backed by credible government policies helps to stabilize the exchange rate relative to a floating exchange rate.

CURRENCY BOARDS

The discussion of target zones mentioned the *credibility* of the government authorities as a factor in determining the effectiveness of the arrangement. However, it often appears that financial market participants believe that some governments are lacking the credibility required to create confidence in the system. In particular, developing countries with a long history of unstable exchange rates often find it difficult to convince the public that government policy will maintain stable exchange rates in the future. This lack of credibility on the part of a government can be overcome if some sort of constraint is placed on the discretionary policy-making ability of the authorities with control over monetary and exchange rate policy. One such form of constraint is a *currency board*. A currency board is a government institution that exchanges domestic currency for foreign currency at a fixed rate of exchange.

The typical demise of a fixed exchange rate system comes when the central bank runs out of foreign currency to exchange for domestic currency and ends up devaluing the domestic currency. Item 19.2 discusses how international reserve losses can result in *speculative attacks* on the central bank that force a devaluation. Currency boards achieve a credible fixed exchange rate by holding a stock of the foreign currency equal to 100 percent of the outstanding currency supply of the nation. As a result of such foreign currency holdings, people believe that the board will always have an adequate supply of foreign currency to exchange for domestic currency at the fixed rate of exchange.

For instance, Argentina has a currency board where the exchange rate is fixed to the U.S. dollar at 1 peso per dollar. Since the supply of pesos can only be increased if the dollar holdings of the currency board increase, and there is guaranteed convertibility of pesos into dollars at the fixed exchange rate, a currency board system is quite similar to a gold standard. If Argentina runs an official settlements balance-of-payments surplus so that its international reserve holdings increase, it can issue more pesos. If Argentina runs a deficit and loses international reserves, the outstanding supply of dollars must shrink. Critics of currency boards point to the requirement of large foreign currency holdings as a cost of operating a currency board. However, since currency boards hold largely interest-bearing short-term securities denominated in foreign currencies rather than non-interest-bearing actual currency, the interest earnings tend to make currency boards profitable.

ITEM 19.2	Speculative Attacks and the Mexican and Asian Financial Crises

The maintenance of fixed exchange rates or target zones of limited flexibility is dependent on government willingness to buy or sell domestic currency for foreign currency at the targeted rate of exchange. The ability to maintain the exchange rate requires the central bank to possess an adequate stock of international reserves in order to meet the demand by the public to sell domestic currency for foreign currency at the fixed exchange rate. If the public believes that the central bank's stock of international reserves has fallen to a point where the ability to meet the demand to exchange domestic currency for foreign currency at a fixed exchange rate is threatened, then a devaluation of the domestic currency is expected. This expectation often leads to a *speculative attack* on the central bank's remaining stock of international reserves. The attack takes the form of massive sales of domestic currency for foreign currency so that the loss of international reserves is hastened and the devaluation is forced by the reserve loss.

In December 1994, the Mexican government faced just such a speculative attack on its U.S. dollar reserves. The result was a peso devaluation followed by a float of the peso/dollar exchange rate. Prior to the period of the attack, the peso/dollar exchange rate was being maintained in a target zone. Following the assassination of the leading presidential candidate, Colosio, the exchange rate stayed near the upper limit of the band. In order to maintain the exchange rate within the target zone, the central bank (Banco de Mexico) had to exchange dollars for pesos at a rate that created substantial international reserve (dollar) losses in October and November of 1994. Even though the Mexican government did not publicly announce the reserve losses until after the peso devaluation of December 20, 1994, some investors obviously knew there was a problem as there was massive selling of pesos for dollars—the speculative attack—prior to the devaluation. After the 15 percent peso devaluation on December 20, investors continued to attack the government's international reserves with more peso sales, believing that the government lacked the necessary stock of dollars to support the new exchange rate. As a result of the reserve losses, the Mexican peso was allowed to float against the dollar on December 22. The move to a floating exchange rate, combined with a new injection of dollars borrowed from the U.S. Treasury and the IMF, ended the speculative attack.

More recently, the Asian financial crisis of 1997–1998 involved speculative attacks on the Thai baht, Malaysian ringgit, and Indonesian rupiah. In each case, speculators correctly bet that the governments would be unwilling to lose substantial dollar reserves in order to maintain fixed exchange rates. The devaluations of the currencies were followed by much public debate over the merits of fixed versus flexible exchange rates.

Countries with currency boards may also have central banks that regulate and provide services to the domestic banking system. However, these central banks have no discretionary authority over the exchange rate. If they did, then the public would likely doubt the credibility of the government in maintaining the fixed exchange rate. As shown in Table 19.2, eight countries maintain currency boards. Clearly, for countries that desire fixed exchange rates but face a problem in creating public confidence in the long-run viability of the fixed rate, a currency board may be a reasonable way to establish a credible exchange rate system.

INTERNATIONAL RESERVE CURRENCIES

In the world economy, there are (almost) as many monies as there are countries. Due to several types of costs, many of these monies are not used in international commerce. Rather, only a few monies (or even one) serve the role of money in the international economy in a fashion similar to the role money plays in a domestic economy. These monies are known as reserve currencies. In domestic monetary theory, economists often identify three roles of money. Money is said to serve as (a) a unit of account, (b) a medium of exchange, and (c) a store of value. Likewise, in an international context we can explain the choice of a reserve currency according to criteria relevant for each role.*

Table 19.4 summarizes the roles of a reserve currency. First, the role of the international unit of account is due to information costs. We find that the prices of primary goods, such as coffee, tin, or rubber, are quoted in terms of dollars worldwide. Since these goods are homogeneous, at least relative to manufactured goods, information regarding their value is conveyed more quickly when prices are quoted in terms of one currency. The private use as an invoicing currency in international trade contracts arises from the reserve currency's informational advantage over other currencies. Besides being a unit of account for private contracts, the reserve currency also serves as a base currency to which other currencies peg exchange rates.

The role of a reserve currency as an international medium of exchange is due to transaction costs. In the case of the U.S. dollar, the dollar is so widely traded that it is often cheaper to go from currency *A* to dollars to currency *B* than directly from cur-

TABLE 19.4	*Roles of a Reserve Currency*		
Function	Due to	Private Role	Official Role
1. International unit of account	Information costs	Invoicing currency	Pegging currency
2. International medium of exchange	Transaction costs	Vehicle currency	Intervention currency
3. International store of value	Stable value	Banking currency	Reserve currency

*Useful discussions are provided in Paul Krugman, "The International Role of the Dollar: Theory and Prospect," in *Exchange Rate Theory and Practice*, ed. John F.O. Bilson and Richard C. Marston (Chicago: University of Chicago Press, 1984); and Stephen P. Magee and Ramesh K.S. Rao, "Vehicle and Nonvehicle Currencies in International Trade," *American Economic Review* (May 1980).

rency *A* to currency *B*. Thus, it is efficient to use the dollar as an international medium of exchange, and the dollar serves as a "vehicle" for buying and selling nondollar currencies. The private (mainly interbank) role as a vehicle currency means that the dollar (or the dominant reserve currency) will also be used for central-bank foreign-exchange-market intervention aimed at achieving target levels for exchange rates.

The role of a reserve currency as an international store of value is due to its stability of value. In other words, certainty of future value enhances a currency's role as a store of purchasing power. The private-market use of the dollar for denominating international loans and deposits indicates the role of the dominant reserve currency in banking. In addition, countries will choose to hold their official reserves largely in the dominant reserve currency.

As the preceding discussion indicates, market forces, and not government decree, determine a currency's international role. It is important to realize, however, that just as the market chooses to elevate a currency, such as the U.S. dollar, to reserve-currency status, it can also take away some of that status, which happened to the U.K. pound earlier in this century and which has happened to the dollar to a lesser extent since the 1960s.

International reserves are the means of settling international debts. Under the gold standard, gold was the major component of international reserves. After World War II, we had a gold exchange standard wherein international reserves included both gold and a reserve currency, the U.S. dollar. The reserve-currency country was to hold gold as backing for the outstanding balances of the currency held by foreigners. These foreign holders of the currency were then free to convert the currency into gold if they wished. However, as we observed with the dollar, once the convertibility of the currency becomes suspect, or once large amounts of the currency are presented for gold, the system tends to fall apart.

This appears to describe the dollar after World War II. At the end of the war and throughout the 1950s, the world demanded dollars for use as an international reserve. During this time, U.S. balance-of-payments deficits provided the world with a much needed source of growth of international reserves. As the rest of the world developed and matured, U.S. liabilities to foreigners continued to grow, eventually reaching a level that greatly exceeded the gold reserves backing these liabilities. Yet as long as the increase in demand for these dollar reserves equaled the supply, the lack of gold backing was irrelevant. Through the late 1960s, U.S. political and economic events began to cause problems for the dollar's international standing. Continuing U.S. deficits were not matched by a growing demand for dollars, so that pressure to convert dollars into gold and a consequent falling gold reserve resulted in the dollar being declared officially no longer exchangeable for gold in August 1971.

The dollar is not the only currency that serves as a reserve currency, although it is the dominant reserve currency. Table 19.5 illustrates the diversification of the currency composition of foreign-exchange reserves since the mid-1980s. There was a period of a falling share devoted to U.S. dollars followed by a rising share.

At first glance, it may appear very desirable to be the issuer of the reserve currency and have other countries accept your balance-of-payments deficits as a necessary means of financing world trade. The difference between the cost to the reserve

TABLE 19.5	*Share of National Currencies in Total Identified Official Holdings of Foreign Exchange, End of Year (percentage)*[1]						
	1987	1989	1991	1993	1995	1997	1998
All countries							
U.S. dollar	56.0	51.9	50.9	56.2	56.4	57.1	60.3
Pound sterling	2.2	2.6	3.4	3.1	3.4	3.3	3.9
Deutsche mark	13.4	18.0	15.7	14.1	13.7	12.3	12.1
French franc	0.8	1.4	2.8	2.2	1.8	1.3	1.3
Swiss franc	1.8	1.4	1.2	1.2	0.9	0.6	0.7
Netherlands guilder	1.2	1.1	1.1	0.6	0.4	0.4	0.4
Japanese yen	7.0	7.3	8.7	8.0	7.1	4.8	5.1
ECU	14.2	10.5	10.0	8.3	6.5	5.1	0.8
Unspecified currencies[2]	3.4	5.7	6.2	6.2	9.7	15.1	15.5
Industrial countries							
U.S. dollar	54.8	48.4	43.8	50.5	52.8	57.9	64.3
Pound sterling	1.0	1.2	1.8	2.2	2.1	1.9	3.1
Deutsche mark	14.1	20.6	18.3	16.4	15.7	15.8	14.7
French franc	0.3	1.1	3.0	2.5	2.1	0.9	1.4
Swiss franc	1.5	1.1	0.8	0.3	0.1	0.1	0.2
Netherlands guilder	1.1	1.1	1.1	0.4	0.2	0.2	0.3
Japanese yen	6.3	7.5	9.7	7.9	6.9	5.7	7.0
ECU	19.9	15.0	15.8	14.7	12.3	10.9	1.8
Unspecified currencies[2]	1.0	4.0	5.7	5.2	7.8	6.4	7.3
Developing countries							
U.S. dollar	59.1	60.5	63.3	63.8	60.5	56.5	57.1
Pound sterling	5.4	5.8	6.2	4.4	4.9	4.5	4.6
Deutsche mark	11.5	11.7	11.0	11.1	11.4	9.3	10.1
French franc	2.0	2.1	2.3	1.8	1.5	1.6	1.2
Swiss franc	2.7	2.2	2.1	2.4	1.8	1.0	1.0
Netherlands guilder	1.3	1.0	1.0	1.0	0.8	0.5	0.4
Japanese yen	8.6	6.9	7.0	8.1	7.3	4.0	3.7
ECU	—	—	—	—	—	—	—
Unspecified currencies[3]	9.5	9.9	7.1	7.6	11.8	22.7	21.9

NOTE: Components may not sum to total because of rounding.

[1]Note that European currency units (ECUs) are treated as a separate currency. In 1999 with the euro introduction, we should expect the share of reserves going to the euro to grow relative to ECUs. At the time this text went to press, 1999 data were not available. Only Fund member countries that report their offical holdings of foreign exchange are included in this table.

[2]The residual is equal to the difference between total foreign exchange reserves of Fund member countries and the sum of the reserves held in the currencies listed in the table.

[3]The calculations here rely to a greater extent on Fund staff estimates than do those provided for the group of industrial countries. Growth in recent years reflects the fact that some new IMF member countries do not yet report their reserve holdings by currency.

SOURCE: International Monetary Fund, *Annual Report*, 1999, p.133.

Seigniorage
The difference between the exchange value of a money and its cost of production.

country of creating new balances and the real resources the reserve country is able to acquire with the new balances is called **seigniorage**. Seigniorage, then, is a financial reward accruing to the reserve currency as a result of its being used as a world money.

Although the dollar has lost some of its reserve-currency market share since the 1970s, the dollar is still, by far, the dominant reserve currency. Inasmuch as the U.S.

international position has been somewhat eroded in the past few decades, the question arises, Why have we not seen the German mark, Japanese yen, or Swiss franc emerge as the dominant reserve currency? Although the mark, yen, and Swiss franc have been popular currencies, the respective governments in each country have resisted a greater international role for their money. Besides the apparent low seigniorage return to the dominant international money, there is another reason for these countries to resist. The dominant money producer (country) finds that international shifts in the demand for its money may have repercussions on domestic monetary policy. For a country the size of the United States, domestic economic activity overwhelms international activity, so that international capital flows of any given magnitude have a much smaller potential to disrupt U.S. markets than Japanese, German, or Swiss markets, where foreign operations are much more important. In this sense, it is clear why these countries have withstood the movement of the yen, mark, and Swiss franc to reserve-currency status. Over time, we may find that the euro emerges as a dominant reserve currency as the combined economies of the euro-member countries provide a very large base of economic activity.

COMPOSITE RESERVE CURRENCIES

A composite currency is an artificial currency made up as an average of several real currencies. Examples include the SDR, a composite created by the IMF, made up of five currencies, and the ECU, created by the European Monetary System prior to the euro, made up of European currencies. Despite the overwhelming use of individual major currencies in both official and commercial transactions between countries, sometimes it may be preferred to denominate bank accounts or trade contracts or to peg to a combination or composite of currencies. With regard to exchange rate pegging practices, Table 19.2 indicated that 13 countries pegged to the SDR or some other composite of currencies.

There are many reasons why a country might choose to peg to an average of several currencies rather than a single currency. If a nation's trade is diversified across several countries rather than concentrated with a single country, it may make sense to peg to an average of the trading partners' currencies rather than to a single currency. In denominating bank deposits or bonds, there is a diversification gain to using a composite currency instead of a single currency. This comes about because the value of the composite currency generally is more stable than that of a single currency. Let's now consider the best known composite, the SDR, in more detail.

SDRs began as issues of new international reserves to the member countries of the IMF (see Item 19.1). The value of the SDR is a weighted average of the value of five major currencies—the U.S. dollar, German mark, French franc, Japanese yen, and U.K. pound. These reserves had no physical form. They were merely accounting entries at the Fund. Therefore, originally SDRs were just traded between central banks. When a country needed a particular currency, it could swap some of the SDRs allocated to it by the IMF for the desired currency. There is a very limited private use of SDRs, as private banks have issued SDR-denominated deposits and loans. By denominating accounts in SDRs, a diversification effect is created.

Prior to January 1981, the SDR was based on a weighted average of the currencies of the 16 largest trading countries (those whose share in world exports exceeded 1 percent of the total). In January 1981, the new 5-currency SDR was created. The move to a 5-currency weighted average has made the SDR much more attractive as a unit of account in the private sector, because it is much easier to compute and comprehend the expected changes in the value of 5 major world currencies than it is 16 currencies (which included some not so widely traded currencies). Although the SDR has grown in popularity, it must be made clear that the volume of business denominated in SDRs is dwarfed by the volume denominated in single currencies, such as the U.S. dollar. As for the official use of the SDR as a reserve currency, it is generally true that countries prefer to receive reserve inflows in freely convertible currencies, such as the dollar or pound, instead of SDRs.

MULTIPLE EXCHANGE RATES

Most countries conduct all varieties of foreign-exchange transactions in terms of a single exchange rate. But some countries (13 as of 1999) maintain multiple exchange rates. A typical arrangement is a dual exchange rate system with a free-market-determined floating exchange rate for capital account transactions and a fixed exchange rate, overvaluing the domestic currency, for current account transactions. Some countries have much more complex arrangements involving three or more exchange rates applied to various transactions.

The IMF has generally sought to unify exchange rates in those countries where multiple rates exist. The argument is that multiple exchange rates harm both the countries that impose them and other countries. With different exchange rates for different types of transactions, domestic relative prices of internationally traded goods tend to differ from international relative prices. This results in distorted decision making in consumption, production, and investment as domestic residents respond to artificial relative prices rather than the true prices set on world markets. Multiple exchange rates are also costly in that people devote resources to finding ways to profit from the tiered exchange rates (e.g., having transactions classified to the most favorable exchange rate category). Finally, the maintenance of a multiple exchange rate system requires a costly administrative structure.

Research has generally found that multiple exchange rates function as a form of protectionism, originally introduced to improve a country's balance of payments.*

---

*Interesting articles on multiple exchange rates include Charles Adams and Jeremy Greenwood, "Dual Exchange Rates and Capital Controls: An Investigation," *Journal of International Economics* (February 1985); Rudiger Dornbusch, "Special Exchange Rates for Capital Account Transactions," *World Bank Economic Review* (September 1986); Robert P. Flood, "Exchange Rate Expectations in Dual Exchange Markets," *Journal of International Economics* (February 1978); J. Saul Lizondo, "Exchange Rate Differential and Balance of Payments Under Dual Exchange Markets," *Journal of Development Economics* (June 1986); Nancy P. Marion, "Insulation Properties of a Two-Tier Exchange Market in a Portfolio Balance Model," *Economica* (February 1981); and Michael J. Moore, "Dual Exchange Rates, Capital Controls, and Sticky Prices," *Journal of International Money and Finance* (December 1989).

The elimination of a multiple exchange rate system could simply involve allowing all transactions to occur at the market-determined rate. If a unified fixed exchange rate is desired, the floating rate will suggest an appropriate level for the new fixed rate. Of course, after the fixed rate is established, monetary and fiscal policy must be consistent with the maintenance of the new exchange rate.

SUMMARY

1. Under a gold standard, currencies are convertible into gold at fixed exchange rates.

2. The IMF and a system of fixed exchange rates were created at the Bretton Woods Conference in 1944.

3. In March 1973, the major developed countries began floating exchange rates.

4. Countries with floating exchange rates tend to be large and closed, with inflation rates that differ from those of their trading partners and trade that is diversified across many countries.

5. The optimum currency area is characterized by mobile factors of production.

6. Target zones have maximum bands for exchange rate fluctuation.

7. A currency board exchanges domestic currency for foreign currency at a fixed rate of exchange.

8. A reserve currency serves as an international unit of account, medium of exchange, and store of value.

9. Composite-currency units have more stable values than individual currencies.

10. Multiple exchange rates are used to encourage exports and discourage imports.

EXERCISES

1. An international reserve currency serves several purposes including being (a) a unit of account, (b) a medium of exchange, and (c) a store of value. What determines which currency (or currencies) will serve these roles?

2. What is seigniorage, and how is it related to competition to become the key reserve currency?

3. Describe the international monetary system known as the Bretton Woods system, or the gold exchange standard, that existed from the mid-1940s to the early 1970s. How did the system work? Why did it eventually break down?

4. Table 19.2 lists the exchange rate practices of IMF members. Examining this table, consider the following questions:

   a. What is the common historical link among those countries that are listed under CFA franc zone (in column 5)? These countries all share a common currency, the Communaute Financiere Africaine franc (or FA franc) and generally peg the value of the CFA franc to the French franc.

   b. Some countries choose crawling pegs while others choose conventional fixed pegs. What is the difference and why do you suppose some countries have to choose a crawling peg instead of a fixed peg?

5. Why do you suppose that small countries tend to fix their exchange rate, whereas the largest countries float theirs?

6. In Table 19.2 we see that some countries do not have a unique domestic currency. Some European countries use the euro, some African countries use the CFA franc, and some Caribbean nations use the East Caribbean dollar. What advantage do these countries seek by the use of a common money?

7. Why might multiple exchange rates be undesirable?

8. If a country has a fixed exchange rate for current account transactions and a floating rate for capital account transactions, how can the country determine the correct exchange rate to establish a unified system with one fixed rate for all transactions?

9. List three factors relevant for a country's choice of an exchange rate system. Using the United States as an example, explain how these factors may have affected U.S. policy regarding floating exchange rates.

10. Suppose that the Indonesian rupiah is pegged to a weighted exchange rate index with its three major trading partners. One-fourth of its trade is with Australia, $1/4$ is with Japan, and $1/2$ is with the United States. If the rupiah appreciates 10 percent against the yen and depreciates 4 percent against the U.S. dollar, what is the percentage change in the exchange rate index for the rupiah?

11. Carefully explain how a target zone can help create a more stable exchange rate.

REFERENCES

Bordo, Michael David. "The Classical Gold Standard: Lessons from the Past." In *The International Monetary System: Choices for the Future*, edited by Michael B. Connolly. New York: Praeger, 1982.

de Vries, Margaret. "The IMF: 40 Years of Challenge and Change." *Finance and Development* (September 1985).

Edison, Hali J., and Michael Melvin. "The Determinants and Implications of the Choice of an Exchange Rate System." In *Monetary Policy for a Volatile Global Economy,* edited by William S. Haraf and Thomas D. Willett. Washington, D.C.: The AEI Press, 1990.

Enoch, Charles, and Anne-Marie Gulde. "Are Currency Boards a Cure for All Monetary Problems?" *Finance and Development* (December 1998).

Folkerts-Landau, David, and Takatoshi Ito, *International Capital Markets.* Washington, D.C.: International Monetary Fund, August 1995.

Humpage, Owen F., and Jean M. McIntire. "An Introduction to Currency Boards." *Economic Review,* 2, 1995.

INTERNET APPLICATIONS

Please visit our Web site at www.awl.com/husted_melvin for more exercises and readings.

CHAPTER 20

International Banking, Debt, and Risk

T he foreign-exchange market is a market in which monies are traded. Money serves as a means of paying for goods and services, and the foreign-exchange market exists to facilitate international payments. Just as there exists a need for international money payments, there is also a need for international credit, or deposits and loans, denominated in different currencies. The international deposit and loan market is often called the **Eurocurrency market**, and banks that accept deposits and make loans are often called *Eurobanks*.

Eurocurrency market
The deposit and loan market for foreign currencies.

The use of the prefix *Euro*, as in Eurocurrency or Eurobank, is misleading, because the activity described is related to offshore banking (providing foreign-currency borrowing and lending services) in general, and is in no way limited to Europe. For instance, the Eurodollar market originally referred to dollar banking outside the United States. The Euroyen market involves yen-demoninated bank deposits and loans outside Japan.

The distinguishing feature of the Eurocurrency market is that the currency used in the banking transaction generally differs from the domestic currency of the country in which the bank is located. This is not strictly true, as there may exist some international banking activity in domestic currency. Where such domestic-currency international banking occurs, it is segregated from other domestic-currency banking activities in regard to regulations applied to such transactions. As we learn in the next section, offshore banking activities have grown rapidly because of a lack of regulation that allows greater efficiency in providing banking services.

THE ORIGINS OF OFFSHORE BANKING

The Eurodollar market began in the late 1950s. During this period certain European banks began accepting deposits in U.S. dollars and promised the depositors the right to withdraw their deposits in the form of dollars. Why and how the market originated have been a subject of debate, but certain elements of the story are agreed upon. Given the reserve-currency status of the dollar, it was only reasonable that the first external money market to develop would be for dollars. Some argue that the Communist countries were the source of early dollar balances held in Europe; these countries needed dollars from time to time but did not want to hold their dollars in U.S. banks for fear of reprisal should hostilities flare up. Thus, the dollar deposits in U.K. and French banks owned by the Communists would represent the first Eurodollar deposits.

Aside from political considerations, the Eurobanks developed as a result of profit considerations. Banks make money by borrowing funds (from depositors) at one interest rate (the deposit rate) and lending these funds at a higher rate (the loan rate). The spread is the difference between the deposit and loan interest rates. Due to costly regulations imposed on U.S. banks, banks located outside the United States could offer higher interest rates on deposits and lower interest rates on loans than their U.S. competitors. For instance, U.S. banks are required to hold a fraction of their deposits in the form of non-interest-bearing reserves. Because Eurobanks are essentially unregulated and hold much smaller reserves than their U.S. counterparts, they can offer narrower spreads on dollars. Thus, deposits tended to move offshore, and so did potential loan customers. Besides reserve requirements, Eurobanks also benefit from no government-mandated interest rate controls, no deposit insurance, no government-mandated credit allocations, no restrictions on entry of new banks (thus encouraging greater competition and efficiency), and low taxes. This does not mean that the countries hosting the Eurobanks do not use such regulations. What we observe in these countries are two sets of banking rules: Various regulations and restrictions apply to banking in the domestic currency, whereas banking activities in foreign currencies go largely unregulated.

Figure 20.1 portrays the standard relationships between the U.S. domestic loan and deposit rates and the Euroloan and Eurodeposit rates. The figure illustrates that U.S. spreads exceed Eurobank spreads. Eurobanks are able to offer a lower rate on dollar loans and a higher rate on dollar deposits than their U.S. competitors. Without these differences, the Eurodollar market probably would not exist, because Eurodollar transactions are considered to be riskier to U.S. residents than domestic dollar transactions in the United States are. This means that, with respect to the supply of deposits to Eurobanks, the U.S. deposit rate provides an interest rate floor for the Eurodeposit rate, since the supply of deposits to Eurobanks is perfectly elastic at the U.S. deposit rate. (If the Eurodeposit rate fell below this rate, Eurobanks would have no dollar deposits.) With respect to the demand for loans from Eurobanks, U.S. loan rates provide a ceiling for Euroloan rates, because the demand for dollar loans from Eurobanks is perfectly elastic at the U.S. loan rate (any Eurobank charging more than this would find the demand for its loans falling to zero).

When making comparisons of actual loan and deposit interest rates in the United States with those in the Eurobank market, there is a problem of determining which interest rates to compare. In the Eurodollar market, loan interest rates are usually quoted as percentage points above **LIBOR**. LIBOR stands for **London interbank offer rate** and is the interest rate at which a group of large London banks would deposit or lend to each other each morning. The U.S. commercial paper rate is considered the most comparable domestic interest rate. The Eurodollar deposit rate is best compared with the large certificate of deposit (CD) rate in the United States.

London interbank offer rate (LIBOR) The key interest rate in the Eurocurrency market.

We have seen that the external interest rates on a particular currency will be constrained by the domestic spread. With capital controls, this may no longer be true.

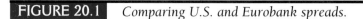

FIGURE 20.1 *Comparing U.S. and Eurobank spreads.*

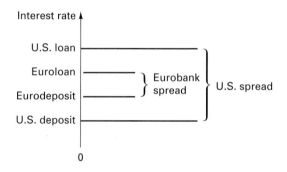

Controls on international capital flows could include quotas on foreign lending and deposits or taxes on international capital flows. For instance, if Switzerland were to limit inflows of foreign money, then we could have a situation where the domestic Swiss deposit interest rate exceeded the external rate on Swiss franc deposits in other nations. Although foreigners would prefer to have their Swiss franc deposits in Swiss banks to earn the higher interest, the legal restrictions on capital flows prohibit such a response.

It is also possible that a perceived threat to private property rights could lead to seemingly perverse interest rate relations. If the United States threatened to confiscate foreign deposits, funds would tend to leave the United States and shift to the external dollar market. This could result in the Eurodollar deposit rate falling below the U.S. deposit rate.

In general, risk contributes to the domestic spread exceeding the external spread. In domestic markets, government agencies help ensure the sound performance of domestic financial institutions, whereas the Eurocurrency markets are largely unregulated, with no central bank ready to come to the rescue. There is an additional risk in international transactions in that investment funds are subject to control by the country of currency denomination (when it is time for repayment) as well as the country of the deposit bank. For instance, if a U.S. firm has a U.S. dollar bank deposit in Hong Kong, when it wants to withdraw those dollars, say to pay a debt in Taiwan, the transaction is subject to two possible government interventions. First, Hong Kong may not let foreign exchange leave the country freely. Second, the United States may control outflows of dollars from the United States, so that the Hong Kong bank may have difficulty buying the dollars needed to fund the withdrawal. Item 20.1 provides

ITEM 20.1   Frozen Dollars in Manila

In 1981, the Philippine government banned foreign-exchange outflows from the country to hold on to the small stock of dollars remaining in the country. Following the government decree, Citibank froze the dollar deposits placed by international banks in its Manila branch. Even as the deposits matured and repayment was due, Citibank in Manila did not repay the dollars. Approximately 40 other banks and $550 million were trapped by the freeze.

Citibank claimed that it had no choice but to freeze the deposits because of the government decree. The creditor banks that could not obtain their dollars argued otherwise. It was asserted that Citibank had a moral obligation to repay the deposits and was violating standard banking practice. Even though dollars could not be taken out of the Philippines, they could be repaid by another branch of Citibank. In fact, Wells Fargo Bank filed a lawsuit in New York seeking repayment of the deposits in New York.

Since U.S. banking regulations do not guarantee the deposits placed in offshore banking offices, there is always a threat of blocked funds if capital controls are imposed. This is the extra risk inherent in the Eurocurrency market, which results in a narrower interest rate spread than exists in domestic markets.

an example of the problems that can arise with the imposition of foreign-exchange controls. It should be recognized that even though domestic and external deposit and loan rates differ due primarily to risk, all interest rates tend to move together. When the domestic dollar interest rate is rising, the external rate will also tend to rise.

The growth of the Eurodollar market is due to the narrower spreads offered by Eurobanks. We would expect the size of the market to grow as the total demand for dollar-denominated credit increases and as dollar banking moves from the United States to the external market. The shift of dollar intermediation would occur as the Eurodollar spread narrows relative to the domestic spread or as individual responsiveness to the spread differential changes.

Over time, important external markets have developed for the other major international currencies. But the value of activity in Eurodollars (which refers to offshore banking in U.S. dollars) dwarfs the rest.

Figure 20.2 illustrates the foreign assets held by banks of different nations. The major role of the United Kingdom and the United States in international banking is obvious. Note that the figure distinguishes between types of bank assets, including

---

FIGURE 20.2   *Deposit banks' foreign assets, by country*

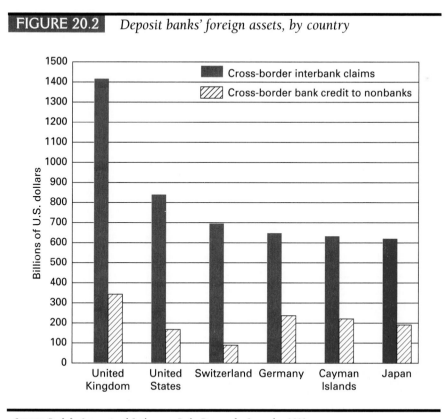

SOURCE: Bank for International Settlements, Basle. Data are for September 1999.
[http://www.bis.org/publ/index.htm].

interbank claims and credit extended to nonbanks. Interbank claims are deposits held in banks in other countries. If we want to know the actual amount of credit extended to nonbank borrowers, we must remove the interbank activity. Figure 20.2 illustrates the huge size of the interbank market in international finance. An example of interbank deposits versus credit extended to nonbanks is provided later in the chapter.

INTERNATIONAL BANKING FACILITIES

In December 1981, the Federal Reserve permitted U.S. banks to engage in Eurobank activity on U.S. soil. Prior to this time, U.S. banks that engaged in international banking processed their loans and deposits through their offshore branches. Many "shell" bank branches in places such as the Cayman Islands or the Bahamas really amounted to nothing more than a small office and a telephone. Yet by using these locations for booking loans and deposits, U.S. banks could avoid the reserve requirements and interest rate regulations that applied to normal U.S. banking.

International banking facilities (IBFs)
International banking divisions of onshore U.S. banks.

In December 1981, **international banking facilities**, or **IBFs**, were legalized.* IBFs did not involve any new physical presence on the part of a bank's offices in the United States. Instead, they simply required a different set of books for an existing bank office to record the deposits and loans permitted under the IBF proposal. IBFs are allowed to receive deposits from and make loans to nonresidents of the United States or other IBFs. These loans and deposits are kept separate from the rest of the bank's business because IBFs are not subject to reserve requirements, interest rate regulations, or Federal Deposit Insurance Corporation deposit insurance premiums that apply to normal U.S. banking.

The goal of the IBF plan was to allow banks in the United States to compete with offshore banks without having to use offshore banking offices. The location of IBFs reflects the location of banking activity in general. As the financial center of the country, it is not surprising that over 75 percent of IBF deposits are in New York State. Aside from New York, California and Illinois are the only other states with a significant IBF business. After IBFs were permitted, several states encouraged their formation by imposing low or no taxes on IBF business. The volume of IBF business that resulted mirrored the preexisiting volume of international banking activity, with New York dominating the level of activity found in other states. Of the $837 billion in cross-border interbank claims listed for U.S. banks in Figure 20.2, $279 billion is associated with IBFs.

---

*A description of the events and debate that led to the creation of IBFs is provided in K. Alec Chrystal, "International Banking Facilities," *Federal Reserve Bank of St. Louis Review* (April 1984); Sydney J. Key and Henry S. Terrell, "International Banking Facilities," in *International Banking and Financial Centers,* ed. Yoon S. Park and Musa Essayyad (New York: Kluwer, 1988); and Michael H. Moffett and Arthur Stonehill, "International Banking Facilities Revisited," *Journal of International Financial Management and Accounting* (Spring 1989).

OFFSHORE BANKING PRACTICES

The Eurocurrency market handles a tremendous volume of funds. Because of the importance of interbank transactions, the gross measure overstates the actual amount of activity regarding total intermediation of funds between nonbank savers and nonbank borrowers. To measure the amount of credit actually extended through the Eurobanks, we use the net size of the market—subtracting interbank activity from total deposits or total loans existing. To understand the difference between the gross and the net volume of Eurodollar activity, we consider the following example.

Let us suppose that a U.S. firm, company X, shifts $1 million from its U.S. bank to a Eurobank to receive a higher return on its deposits. Table 20.1 shows the T accounts recording this transaction. The U.S. bank now has a liability (recorded on the right-hand side of its balance sheet) of $1 million owed to Eurobank A, because the ownership of a $1 million deposit has shifted from company X to Eurobank A. Eurobank A records the transaction as a $1 million asset in the form of a deposit it owns in a U.S. bank, plus a $1 million liability from the deposit it has accepted from company X. Now, suppose that Eurobank A does not have a borrower waiting for $1 million (U.S.), but another Eurobank, Eurobank B, does have such a borrower. Eurobank A will deposit the $1 million with Eurobank B, earning a fraction of a percent more than it must pay company X for the $1 million. Table 20.2 shows that after Eurobank A deposits in B, the U.S. bank now owes the U.S. dollar deposit to B, which is shown as an asset of Eurobank B matched by the deposit liability of $1 million from B to A.

  Finally, in Table 20.3, Eurobank B makes a loan to company Y. Now, the U.S. bank has transferred the ownership of its deposit liability to company Y. (Note that whenever dollars are actually spent after a Eurodollar transaction, the actual dollars must come from the United States. Only the United States creates U.S. dollars; the Eurodollar markets simply act as intermediaries.) The gross size of the market is measured as total deposits in Eurobanks of $2 million ($1 million in Eurobank A

EXAMPLE

TABLE 20.1	*Company X Deposits $1 Million in Eurobank A*
Assets	Liabilities
	U.S. bank
	$1 million due Eurobank A
	Eurobank A
$1 million deposit in U.S. bank	$1 million Eurodollar deposit due company X

TABLE 20.2	Eurobank A Deposits $1 Million in Eurobank B	
Assets		**Liabilities**
	U.S. bank	
		$1 million due Eurobank B
	Eurobank A	
$1 million Eurodollar deposit in Eurobank B		$1 million Eurodollar deposit due company X
	Eurobank B	
$1 million deposit in U.S. bank		$1 million Eurodollar deposit due Eurobank A

TABLE 20.3	Eurobank B Lends $1 Million to Company Y	
Assets		**Liabilities**
	U.S. bank	
		$1 million due company Y
	Eurobank A	
$1 million Eurodollar deposit in Eurobank B		$1 million Eurodollar deposit due company X
	Eurobank B	
$1 million loan to company Y		$1 million Eurodollar deposit due Eurobank A
	Company Y	
$1 million deposit in U.S. bank		$1 million loan owed to Eurobank B

and $1 million in *B*). The net size of the market is found by subtracting interbank deposits and thus is a measure of the actual credit extended to nonbank users of dollars. In the example, Eurobank *A* deposited $1 million in Eurobank *B*. If we subtract this interbank deposit of $1 million from the total Eurobank deposits of $2 million, we find the net size of the market to be $1 million. This $1 million is the value of credit actually flowing from nonbank lenders to nonbank borrowers.

Since the Eurodollar market deals with such large magnitudes, it is understandable that economists and politicians are concerned about the effects the Eurodollar market can have on domestic markets. In the United States, Eurodollar deposits are counted in the M2 definition of the money supply. Measures of the U.S. money supply are used to evaluate the resources available to the public for spending. Eurodollars are not spendable money, but rather are money substitutes, such as time deposits in a domestic bank. Because Eurodollars do not serve as a means of payment, Eurobanks are not able to create money as banks can in a domestic setting.

Eurobanks are essentially intermediaries; they accept deposits and then lend out these deposits.

Even though Eurodollars do not provide a means of payment, they still may have implications for domestic monetary practice. For countries without efficient money markets, access to the very efficient and competitive Eurodollar market may reduce the demand for domestic money. Rather than hold domestic money balances, residents can shift funds to the Eurodollar market and earn a competitive, market-determined return.

The efficiency of the Eurodollar market may also have encouraged international capital flows and thus led to a greater need for sterilization on the part of central banks. In Chapter 18, we defined sterilization to be a change in the domestic component of base money aimed at offsetting a change in the foreign-reserve component. Thus, if international reserve flows are greater due to the international capital flows encouraged by Eurodollar market efficiency, then central banks must engage in large and more frequent sterilization operations to achieve a given domestic-money growth policy.

All banks are interested in maximizing the spread between their deposit and loan interest rates. In this regard, Eurobanks are no different from domestic banks. All banks are also concerned with managing risk, the risk associated with their assets and liabilities. Like all intermediaries, Eurobanks tend to borrow short-term and lend long-term. Thus, if the deposit liabilities were reduced greatly, we would see deposit interest rates rise very rapidly in the short run. The advantage of matching the term structures of deposits and loans is that deposits and loans are maturing at the same time, so that the bank is better able to respond to a change in demand for deposits or loans. Concerning risk management, we find interesting differences between Eurobanks and domestic banks. In the Eurodollar market, there was a period in the 1970s when the great bulk of deposits came from the Organization of Petroleum Exporting Countries (OPEC), the oil exporting nations (these deposits were known as petrodollar recycling). If one of these countries withdrew a large amount of funds from the market, there would be large costs for Eurobanks that did not have their assets and liabilities matched on a term basis.

Deposits in the Eurocurrency market are for fixed terms ranging from days to years, although most are for less than 6 months. Certificates of deposit are considered to be the closest domestic counterpart to a Eurocurrency deposit.

Loans in the Eurocurrency market can range up to 10 or more years. The interest rate on a Eurocurrency loan is usually stated as some spread over LIBOR. Recall that LIBOR is the London interbank offer rate, the interest rate established for interbank loans among the large London banks. For international loan pricing purposes, the British Bankers' Association announces the value of LIBOR each day at 11 A.M. London time. This value is taken by surveying several large banks. In January 2000 the following banks were used to set LIBOR: Abbey National, Bank of Tokyo–Mitsubishi, Bank of America, Barclays, Chase Manhattan, Citibank, Credit Suisse First Boston, Deutsche Bank, Fuji Bank, HSBC, Lloyds, Rabobank, Norinchukin Bank, Royal Bank of Scotland, National Westminster, and Westdeutsche Landesbank. Loans priced on LIBOR have the interest rate adjusted at fixed intervals, such as every 3 months. These adjustable interest rates serve to minimize the interest rate risk to the bank. Although LIBOR is the dominant pricing tool, the second most popular pricing mechanism is the U.S. prime rate, where the borrower pays according to the lower of the two rates at the time interest is due.

Large loans are generally made by syndicates of Eurobanks. The syndicate will be headed by a lead or managing bank, and then other banks wishing to participate in the loan will join the syndicate and help fund the loan. By allowing banks to reduce their level of participation in any one loan, the banks can participate in more loans, so that such diversification reduces their risk of loss.

Item 20.2 discusses a recent development in local banking syndicates—the rise of Islamic banking in the Mideast. It remains to be seen whether such profit-sharing

---

ITEM 20.2	**Islamic Banking**

According to the Muslim holy book, the Koran, Islamic law prohibits interest charges on loans. Banks that follow the Islamic law may still play the role of intermediary between borrowers and lenders, but rather than charge interest on loans and pay interest on deposits, the banks take a predetermined percentage of the borrowing firm's profits until the loan is repaid. These profit shares earned by the bank are then passed on to depositors.

Since the mid-1970s, over 100 so-called "Islamic banks" have opened that follow the Koranic guidelines. These banks are almost all located in Arab nations. Deposits in such banks grew rapidly as devout Muslims wished to avoid banking with traditional commercial banks. In fact, deposits grew much faster than did good loan opportunities, so that some Islamic banks refused new deposits until the bank's loan portfolio could grow to match the available deposits. One bank in Bahrain claimed that over 60 percent of deposits during the first two years of operation came from people who had never had a bank deposit before.

Aside from profit-sharing deposits, Islamic banks typically offer checking accounts, traveler's checks, and various trade-related services on a fee basis. The return on profit-sharing deposits has fluctuated with regional economic conditions.

Since the growth of deposits has usually far exceeded the growth of local investment opportunities, Islamic banks have been lending to traditional banks to fund investments that satisfy the moral and commercial needs of both. Such funds cannot be used for investing in interest-bearing securities, or in firms that deal in alcohol, pork, gambling, or arms. The growth of such mutually profitable investment opportunities suggests that Islamic banks offer a valuable service to Muslim depositors that meets both the dictates of their religious beliefs and the profitability requirements of modern banking.*

---

*Interesting reviews of Islamic banking are given in Rami Khouri, "The Spread of Banking for Believers," *Euromoney* (May 1987); and "Islamic Banking: First View of the Banks," *The Banker* (October 1996).

bankers can extend their reach to international banking, but the growth in Islamic bank funding of investment opportunities provided through traditional Western banks indicates that Islamic banking institutions may some day help in developing alternative financial instruments to interest-bearing interbank loans.

INTERNATIONAL DEBT

During the 1970s, banks were flush with **petrodollars**, when the OPEC nations deposited huge sums of dollars in the Eurobanks. The banks, in turn, lent these dollars, generated by the OPEC balance-of-payments surplus, mostly to developing country deficit nations (this pattern is often referred to as petrodollar recycling). At the time the loans were made, the developing country borrowers appeared to be reasonable credit risks. The prices of their export commodities were high, and no one forecast the global recession that occurred in the early 1980s. Creditor banks fully expected the loans to be repaid out of the borrowers' export earnings. As income and demand fell in the developed countries in the early 1980s, the debtor nations faced a falling demand for their products. At the same time, the interest payments on their debt increased due to a rising dollar interest rate. By 1982, many of these loans began to sour because the developing countries found themselves overextended. Table 20.4 presents estimates of the size of this external debt faced by major LDC (less developed countries) borrowers during the period of the debt crisis.

Petrodollars
Eurodollar deposits arising from OPEC trade surpluses.

TABLE 20.4   *External Debt/Export Ratios During International Debt Crisis Period*

(AVERAGE GROSS EXTERNAL DEBT AS A PERCENTAGE OF EXPORTS OF GOODS, SERVICES, AND PRIVATE TRANSFERS)

	Ratio (%)					Commercial Bank Claims Outstanding, Year End 1988 (billion $)
	1982	1984	1986	1989	1991	
Argentina	405	461	536	537	433	30.4
Brazil	339	322	425	302	325	67.6
Chile	333	402	402	188	154	11.0
Colombia	191	254	198	208	168	6.0
Ecuador	239	259	333	392	363	5.5
Mexico	299	292	413	264	224	63.4
Nigeria	84	158	300	390	257	6.7
Peru	269	356	497	432	484	5.3
Philippines	269	309	308	226	216	10.8
Venezuela	84	158	322	212	187	26.6

SOURCE: Data are drawn from *World Debt Tables, 1989–1990,* First Supplement (Washington, D.C.: World Bank), 1990, and *World Development Report, 1993* (New York: Oxford University Press, 1993).

Recalling that exports were counted on to provide the foreign-exchange earnings needed to repay the debt, we note, upon examining the columns of Table 20.4 on debt as a percentage of exports, the predicaments into which many of these countries fell. The only way that Argentina or Brazil could service its existing debt (meet its debt obligations) was to borrow more until their export earnings increased and/or interest rates fell, lowering its interest payments (remember, these are variable interest rate loans). In cases where the debt was simply too burdensome to repay, the debt was rescheduled. (It seems that no country defaults anymore; rather, it reschedules the repayment of the debt.) Rescheduling refers to renegotiating the terms of a loan—postponing and extending the repayment of principal and interest.

Paris Club
A gathering of creditor country governments to arrange debt rescheduling.

One of the most important arenas for debt rescheduling has been the **Paris Club**. The Paris Club is not an official organization with a continuous life. The Paris Club refers to irregular meetings of creditor governments (typically, the Western developed countries) with debtor nations. When a nation is in danger of default on existing debt, and creditor countries refuse to extend additional loans, the debtor may contact the French government and request a meeting with the debtor's official creditors. (There appears to be no special reason for holding such meetings in Paris beyond the tradition of meeting there due to the French willingness to host such activities.) The debtor must apply for a standby credit arrangement with the IMF before the meeting is held. The Paris Club meeting involves negotiations between the debtor and creditor governments for rescheduling repayment in terms of both timing and costs.

Aside from Paris Club reschedulings of debts owed to governments, debts owed to commercial banks have also been rescheduled. In these cases, commercial banks form committees to negotiate with the debtor. In addition to extending debt repayment and revising loan terms, commercial banks have also become involved in exchanging developing country debt for equity in commercial projects in these debtor countries. **Debt/equity swaps** involve an exchange of debt for the debtor's domestic currency, which is then used to purchase an ownership position in a debtor country business.

Debt/equity swap
An exchange of developing country debt for an ownership position in a developing country business.

The existence of debt/equity swaps has stimulated the growth of a secondary market where creditor commercial banks may sell their developing country debt. The buyers in this market can then trade this debt for an equity position in the debtor country. This market has remained quite small, accounting for as little as 1 or 2 percent of total developing country debt held by commercial banks. The "thinness" of the market can result in a single buyer or seller "moving the market." That is, with a relatively small market size, a single large order to buy debt could increase the price of the debt. According to one broker cited in *Euromoney*, Citibank once bought $62 million of Mexican debt for Nissan to swap for an auto manufacturing plant in Mexico. The purchase of this quantity of debt moved the market price of the debt more than 3 percent.

Debt/equity swaps rarely occur at the face value of the debt. The secondary market price of developing country debt is discounted from the face value. The prices reflect the risk of nonpayment. The higher the probability of the debt not being repaid, the lower the value of the debt.

IMF CONDITIONALITY

The IMF has been an important source of funding for debtor nations experiencing repayment problems. Earlier, we saw that debtors cannot approach a Paris Club rescheduling without a standby loan agreement with the IMF. The importance of an IMF loan is more than simply the IMF "bailing out" commercial bank and government creditors. The IMF requires borrowers to adjust their economic policies to reduce balance-of-payments deficits and improve the chance for debt repayment. Such IMF-required adjustment programs are known as IMF "conditionality."

Part of the process of developing a loan package includes a visit to the borrowing country by an IMF "mission." The mission comprises economists who review the causes of the country's economic problems and recommend solutions. Through negotiation with the borrower, a program of conditions attached to the loan is agreed to. The conditions usually involve targets for macroeconomic variables, such as money-supply growth or the government deficit. The loan is disbursed at intervals with a possible cutoff of new disbursements if the conditions have not been met.

The importance of IMF conditionality to creditors can now be understood. Loans to sovereign governments involve risk management from the lender's point of view just the same as do loans to private entities. Although countries cannot go out of business, they can have revolutions or political upheavals leading to a repudiation of the debts incurred by the previous regime. Even without such drastic political change, countries may not be able or willing to service their debt due to adverse economic conditions. International lending adds a new dimension to risk, since there is neither an international court of law to enforce contracts nor a loan collateral aside from assets that the borrowing country may have in the lending country. The IMF serves as an overseer that can offer debtors new loans if they agree to conditions. A sovereign government may be offended if a foreign creditor government or commercial bank suggests changes in the debtor's domestic policy, but the IMF is a multinational organization of over 180 countries. The members of the IMF mission to the debtor nation will be of many different nationalities, and their advice will be nonpolitical. However, the IMF is still criticized, at times, as being dominated by the interests of the advanced industrialized countries. In terms of voting power, this is true.

Votes in the IMF determine policy, and voting power is determined by a country's "quota." The quota is the financial contribution of a country to the IMF that entitles membership. At least 75 percent of the quota may be contributed in domestic currency, with less than 25 percent paid in reserve currencies or SDRs. Table 20.5 lists the quotas of countries. Each country receives 250 votes plus 1 additional vote for each SDR100,000 of its quota. Table 20.5 indicates that the United States has the most votes, as the U.S. quota accounts for almost 18 percent of the total fund. Then come Japan and Germany, with about 6.5 percent of the total, followed by the U.K. and France, with 5.2 percent. These five developed countries contribute more than 40 percent of the IMF quotas and dominate voting accordingly.

The IMF has been criticized for imposing conditions that restrict economic growth and lower living standards in borrowing countries. The typical conditionality involves reducing government spending, raising taxes, and restricting money

TABLE 20.5	IMF Quotas[1]

(MILLION SDRs)

Country	Quota	Country	Quota	Country	Quota
Afghanistan, Islamic State of	120.4	Ecuador	302.3	Macedonia, FYR	68.9
Albania	48.7	Egypt	943.7	Madagascar	122.2
Algeria	1,254.7	El Salvador	171.3	Malawi	69.4
Angola	286.3	Equatorial Guinea	32.6	Malaysia	1,486.6
Antigua and Barbuda	13.5	Eritrea	15.9	Maldives	8.2
Argentina	2,117.1	Estonia	46.5	Mali	93.3
Armenia	92.0	Ethiopia	133.7	Malta	102.0
Australia	3,236.4	Fiji	70.3	Marshall Islands	2.5
Austria	1,872.3	Finland	1,263.8	Mauritania	64.4
Azerbaijan	160.9	France	10,738.5	Mauritius	101.6
Bahamas, The	94.9	Gabon	154.3	Mexico	2,585.8
Bahrain	135.0	Gambia, The	31.1	Micronesia, Federated	
Bangladesh	533.3	Georgia	150.3	States of	3.5
Barbados	67.5	Germany	13,008.2	Moldova	123.2
Belarus	386.4	Ghana	369.0	Mongolia	51.1
Belgium	3,102.3	Greece	823.0	Morocco	588.2
Belize	18.8	Grenada	8.5	Mozambique	113.6
Benin	61.9	Guatemala	153.8	Myanmar	258.4
Bhutan	6.3	Guinea	107.1	Namibia	99.6
Bolivia	171.5	Guinea-Bissau	14.2	Nepal	71.3
Bosnia and Herzegovina	169.1	Guyana	90.9	Netherlands	5,162.4
Botswana	63.0	Haiti	60.7	New Zealand	894.6
Brazil	3,036.1	Honduras	129.5	Nicaragua	130.0
Brunei Darussalam	150.0	Hungary	1,038.4	Niger	65.8
Bulgaria	640.2	Iceland	117.6	Nigeria	1,753.2
Burkina Faso	60.2	India	4,158.2	Norway	1,671.7
Burundi	77.0	Indonesia	2,079.3	Oman	194.0
Cambodia	87.5	Iran, Islamic Republic of	1,497.2	Pakistan	1,033.7
Cameroon	185.7	Iraq	504.0	Palau	3.1
Canada	6,369.2	Ireland	838.4	Panama	206.6
Cape Verde	9.6	Israel	928.2	Papua New Guinea	131.6
Central African Republic	55.7	Italy	7,055.5	Paraguay	99.9
Chad	56.0	Jamaica	273.5	Peru	638.4
Chile	856.1	Japan	13,312.8	Philippines	879.9
China	4,687.2	Jordan	170.5	Poland	1,369.0
Colombia	774.0	Kazakhstan	365.7	Portugal	867.4
Comoros	8.9	Kenya	271.4	Qatar	190.5
Congo, Democratic		Kiribati	5.6	Romania	1,030.2
Republic of the	291.0	Korea	1,633.6	Russia	5,945.4
Congo, Republic of	84.6	Kuwait	1,381.1	Rwanda	80.1
Costa Rica	164.1	Kyrgyz Republic	88.8	Samoa	11.6
Côte d'Ivoire	325.2	Lao People's Dem. Rep.	39.1	San Marino	10.0
Croatia	365.1	Latvia	126.8	São Tomé and Principe	7.4
Cyprus	139.6	Lebanon	146.0	Saudi Arabia	6,985.5
Czech Republic	819.3	Lesotho	34.9	Senegal	161.8
Denmark	1,642.8	Liberia	71.3	Seychelles	8.8
Djibouti	15.9	Libya	1,123.7	Sierra Leone	103.7
Dominica	6.0	Lithuania	144.2	Singapore	862.5
Dominican Republic	218.9	Luxembourg	135.5	Slovak Republic	357.5

| TABLE 20.5 | *IMF Quotas[1] (Continued)* |

(MILLION SDRs)

Country	Quota	Country	Quota	Country	Quota
Slovenia	231.7	Sweden	2,395.5	Ukraine	1,372.0
Solomon Islands	10.4	Switzerland	3,458.5	United Arab Emirates	392.1
Somalia	44.2	Syrian Arab Republic	293.6	United Kingdom	10,738.5
South Africa	1,868.5	Tajikistan	87.0	United States	37,149.3
Spain	3,048.9	Tanzania	198.9	Uruguay	225.3
Sri Lanka	413.4	Thailand	1,081.9	Uzbekistan	275.6
St. Kitts and Nevis	8.9	Togo	73.4	Vanuatu	17.0
St. Lucia	15.3	Tonga	6.9	Venezuela	2,659.1
St. Vincent and		Trinidad and Tobago	335.6	Vietnam	329.1
the Grenadines	6.0	Tunisia	286.5	Yemen, Republic of	243.5
Sudan	169.7	Turkey	964.0	Zambia	489.1
Suriname	92.1	Turkmenistan	48.0	Zimbabwe	353.4
Swaziland	50.7	Uganda	180.5	Total	207,982.9

[1]Quotas are those in effect on April 30, .1999.

growth. For example, in July 1986, Mexico signed a $1.6 billion loan agreement with the IMF that included the following conditions: The budget deficit would fall by three percentage points over the next 18 months, monetary growth would be restricted to reduce capital flight, nominal interest rates would exceed the inflation rate, and the deductibility of business expenses would fall to increase the tax base.* Such policies may be interpreted as austerity imposed by the IMF, but the austerity is intended to help the borrowing government permit the productive private sector to play a larger role in the economy.

The view of the IMF is that adjustment programs are unavoidable in debtor countries that face payment difficulties. The adjustments required are those that promote long-run growth. While there may indeed be short-run costs of adjusting to a smaller role for government and fewer and smaller government subsidies, in the long run the required adjustments should stimulate growth to allow debt repayment.

COUNTRY-RISK ANALYSIS

International financial activity involves risks that are missing in domestic transactions. There are no international courts to enforce contracts, and a bank cannot repossess a nation's collateral, because typically no collateral is pledged. Problem loans to sovereign governments have received most of the "debt problem" publicity, but it is important to realize that loans to private firms can also become nonper-

---

*The Mexican loan deal is described in Art Pine, "Mexico–IMF Pact Is Seen Easing Cash Crunch, Altering Economy," *Wall Street Journal*, July 23, 1986, 25. A general review of IMF conditionality is provided in Susan Schadler, "How Successful Are IMF-Supported Adjustment Programs?" *Finance and Development* (June 1996).

ITEM 20.3   Blocked Funds

When a country blocks the transfer of funds from a domestic firm to its parent firm in another country, the firm stands to lose profits if the blocked funds are allowed to sit idly. Multinational corporations have responded in many ways to the challenge of blocking the conversion of local currency into reserve currencies for international transfer. One use of blocked funds is to finance films shot within the debtor country. Local funds that were blocked in Brazil, Argentina, Greece, Romania, Yugoslavia, India, the Philippines, and some African nations have been used to finance the filming of movies, such as *The Year of Living Dangerously*, *Transylvania 6–5000*, and *The Emerald Forest*. The multinational firm sells its local currency holdings to the film company for dollars or a percentage of the film's profit.

Typically, the multinational firm will use blocked funds to invest in financial assets or real estate. For instance, Volkswagen has purchased ranches in Brazil. Alternatively, the subsidiary of one firm may lend blocked funds to a subsidiary of another firm that has a use for the funds. The parent company of the borrowing subsidiary will lend a reserve currency to the parent company of the lending subsidiary in exchange. This is known as a parallel loan.

Yet another alternative is to receive tax benefits from the charitable use of the blocked funds. Universal Leaf Tobacco had millions of dollars blocked in Zimbabwe, so it took a U.S. tax deduction for local-currency donations to U.S. charities that had operations in East Africa.

Blocked funds can hurt a multinational firm in the short run, but in the long run, the biggest loser may turn out to be the debtor nations that impose them. Attracting new investors will be difficult once multinationals have been harmed by government policies. The suspension of private property rights to funds that have been legally earned in the host country makes for very bad international relations.*

_____
* An interesting discussion of these issues is found in Leo Welt, "Untying Those Blocked Funds," *Euromoney* (May 1987).

forming due to capital controls or exchange rate policies. In this regard, even operating subsidiary units in foreign countries may not be able to transfer funds to the parent multinational firm if foreign-exchange controls block the transfer of funds. Item 20.3 discusses the possible responses to dealing with blocked or frozen funds.

It is important for commercial banks and multinational firms to be able to assess the risks involved in international deals. Country-risk analysis has become an important part of international business. Country risk refers to the overall political and financial situation in a country and the extent to which these conditions may affect the ability of a country to repay its debts. In determining the degree of risk associated with a particular country, we should consider both qualitative and quantitative factors. The qualitative factors include the political stability of the country. Certain key features may indicate political uncertainty:

1. Splits between different language, ethnic, and religious groups that threaten to undermine stability.

2. Extreme nationalism and aversion to foreigners that may lead to preferential treatment of local interests and nationalization of foreign holdings.

3. Unfavorable social conditions, including the extremes of wealth.

4. Conflicts in society evidenced by the frequency of demonstrations, violence, and guerilla war.

5. The strength and organization of radical groups.

Besides the qualitative or political factors, we also want to consider the economic factors that allow an evaluation of a country's ability to repay its debts.* Country-risk analysts examine facts such as the following:

1. *External debt.* Specifically, this is the debt owed to foreigners as a fraction of GDP or foreign-exchange earnings. If a country's debts appear to be relatively large, then the country may have future repayment problems.

2. *International reserve holdings.* These holdings indicate the ability of a country to meet its short-term international trade needs should its export earnings fall. The ratio of international reserves to imports is used to rank countries according to their liquidity.

3. *Exports.* This factor is measured in terms of both the foreign exchange earned from exports and the diversity of the products exported. Countries that depend largely on one or two products to earn foreign exchange may be more susceptible to wide swings in export earnings than countries with a diversified group of export products.

4. *Economic growth.* This factor is measured by the growth of real GDP or real per capita GDP. It may serve as an indicator of general economic conditions within a country.

Although no method of assessing country risk is foolproof, by evaluating and comparing countries based on some structured approach, international lenders have a foundation on which they can build their subjective evaluations of whether or not to extend credit to a particular country.

Euromoney magazine surveys international bankers twice a year seeking their evaluation of country creditworthiness. In addition to the subjective evaluations regarding country risk, the *Euromoney* rankings also include an assessment of the following: economic growth, external debt and repayment record, and current credit terms available to a country. The possible points awarded total 100, so the closer to 100, the higher the ranking of a country across each of the dimensions. Table 20.6 provides the results from a recent survey. We should not pay too much attention to exact order of rankings, but should view the countries as falling into groups. All of

---

*There have been many studies in recent years analyzing the economic determinants of country risk. A small sample includes Sebastian Edwards, "LDC's Foreign Borrowing and Default Risk: An Empirical Investigation 1976–1980," *American Economic Review* (September 1984); Michael Melvin and Don Schlagenhauf, "Risk in International Lending: A Dynamic Factor Analysis Applied to France and Mexico," *Journal of International Money and Finance* (March 1986); R.A. Somerville and R.J. Taffler, "Banker Judgment versus Formal Forecasting Models: The Case of Country Risk Assessment," *Journal of Banking and Finance* (May 1995); and Richard Cantor and Frank Packer, "Sovereign Credit Ratings," *Current Issues in Economics and Finance* (June 1995).

TABLE 20.6   *Country-Risk Rankings*

Rank September 1999	Country	Total (weighting) 100	Rank September 1999	Country	Total (weighting) 100
1	Luxembourg	98.68	35	Saudi Arabia	66.56
2	Switzerland	97.79	36	Bahamas	65.84
3	United States	94.51	37	Bahrain	65.12
4	Norway	94.13	38	Chile	65.01
5	Germany	93.40	39	Hungary	64.27
6	Netherlands	92.41	40	South Korea	64.13
7	France	92.32	41	Oman	63.28
8	Denmark	92.30	42	Poland	62.55
9	Austria	91.80	43	Mauritius	61.99
10	United Kingdom	91.15	44	Brunei	61.62
11	Japan	90.87	45	Czech Republic	60.85
12	Finland	90.25	46	Malaysia	57.05
13	Ireland	90.00	47	Thailand	56.03
14	Sweden	89.81	48	Mexico	55.73
15	Belgium	89.53	49	Tunisia	55.30
16	Canada	88.76	50	China	55.09
17	Singapore	88.52	51	Philippines	54.38
18	Australia	88.10	52	Estonia	54.26
19	Italy	87.07	53	Uruguay	54.20
20	Spain	86.58	54	Argentina	53.77
21	New Zealand	85.37	55	South Africa	53.67
22	Iceland	84.44	56	Morocco	52.96
23	Portugal	82.84	57	Croatia	52.60
24	Taiwan	80.68	58	Egypt	52.28
25	Bermuda	77.95	59	India	51.80
26	Hong Kong	77.10	60	Botswana	51.10
27	Greece	76.82	61	Colombia	50.79
28	United Arab Emirates	75.01	62	Latvia	50.41
29	Cyprus	73.54	63	Trinidad & Tobago	49.37
30	Malta	71.10	64	Slovak Republic	49.04
31	Israel	70.97	65	Lithuania	48.74
32	Kuwait	70.01	66	Turkey	48.54
33	Slovenia	68.99	67	Panama	47.88
34	Qatar	68.81	68	Fiji	47.77

Continued

TABLE 20.6 *Country-Risk Rankings (Continued)*

Rank September 1999	Country	Total (weighting) 100	Rank September 1999	Country	Total (weighting) 100
69	Lebanon	47.30	103	Bangladesh	34.93
70	El Salvador	47.19	104	Dominica	34.86
71	Brazil	46.77	105	Senegal	34.47
72	Jordan	46.21	106	Uganda	34.46
73	Costa Rica	45.57	107	Swaziland	34.41
74	Peru	44.63	108	Nepal	34.33
75	Belize	43.21	109	Zimbabwe	33.93
76	Barbados	42.78	110	Macau	33.71
77	Sri Lanka	42.74	111	Honduras	33.46
78	Venezuela	41.33	112	Gabon	33.36
79	Jamaica	41.02	113	Azerbaijan	33.36
80	Tonga	40.62	114	Ecuador	32.90
81	St. Lucia	40.57	115	Kyrgyz Republic	32.79
82	Kazakhstan	40.30	116	Guyana	32.50
83	Dominican Republic	40.30	117	Algeria	32.32
84	Seychelles	40.08	118	Bhutan	32.23
85	Western Samoa	39.86	119	Lesotho	32.21
86	Bolivia	39.84	120	Mali	31.87
87	Papua New Guinea	39.74	121	Turkmenistan	31.81
88	Vanuatu	39.59	122	Burkina Faso	31.44
89	Bulgaria	39.33	123	Côte d'Ivoire	31.23
90	Guatemala	38.97	124	Gambia	31.18
91	St. Vincent & the Grenadines	38.86	125	Nigeria	31.17
92	Ghana	38.77	126	Cape Verde	31.09
93	Solomon Islands	38.34	127	Moldova	31.02
94	Paraguay	37.80	128	Mongolia	30.83
95	Romania	36.85	129	Ukraine	30.71
96	Maldives	36.76	130	Malawi	30.27
97	Vietnam	36.49	131	Pakistan	30.18
98	Indonesia	36.43	132	Benin	29.72
99	Iran	35.68	133	Togo	29.71
100	Kenya	35.59	134	Armenia	29.63
101	Grenada	35.04	135	Belarus	29.10
102	Syria	34.98	136	Uzbekistan	28.79

Continued

TABLE 20.6   *Country-Risk Rankings (Continued)*

Rank September 1999	Country	Total (weighting) 100	Rank September 1999	Country	Total (weighting) 100
137	Cameroon	28.13	159	Russia	23.02
138	Niger	27.99	160	FYR Macedonia	22.99
139	Equatorial Guinea	27.99	161	Madagascar	22.27
140	Mauritania	27.73	162	Rwanda	20.88
141	Laos	27.36	163	New Caledonia	20.24
142	Tajikistan	27.23	164	Democratic Republic of Congo	19.95
143	Cambodia	27.20	165	Sudan	19.03
144	Chad	27.17	166	Myanmar	18.70
145	Haiti	26.57	167	Albania	18.60
146	Djibouti	26.50	168	São Tomé e Principe	17.80
147	Tanzania	26.47	169	Sierra Leone	17.64
148	Zambia	26.39	170	Guinea-Bissau	17.43
149	Yemen	26.18	171	Antigua & Barbuda	16.63
150	Georgia	25.69	172	Libya	16.06
151	Guinea	25.68	173	Somalia	16.00
152	Central African Republic	25.57	174	Yugoslavia (Serbia/Montenegro)	14.83
153	Nicaragua	25.43	175	Liberia	14.37
154	Congo	24.97	176	Suriname	12.20
155	Mozambique	24.53	177	Cuba	7.39
156	Ethiopia	24.52	178	Afghanistan	5.06
157	Angola	24.44	179	Iraq	4.00
158	Namibia	23.33	180	North Korea	1.02

SOURCE: *Euromoney,* September 1999.

the countries at the top of the list are good risks where banks readily extend new credit. Countries in the middle of the table may have some limited access to borrowing. Those countries at the bottom would find new commercial bank lending impossible to attract. It is safe to say that bankers are not looking for new business in Iraq or North Korea.

SUMMARY

1. The international bank deposit and loan market is called the Eurocurrency market.

2. Eurobanking grew because of a lack of regulation that permits greater efficiency in providing banking services.

3. International banking facilities are departments of U.S. banks that are permitted to engage in Eurocurrency banking.

4. The net size of the Eurodollar market measures the amount of credit actually extended to nonbanks.

5. Large Eurocurrency loans are made by bank syndicates.

6. Sovereign loans are rescheduled with creditor governments in the Paris Club.

7. A secondary market in developing country debt has encouraged the development of debt/equity swaps in debtor countries.

8. IMF loans come with conditions requiring adjustments of the economy to increase the likelihood of repayment.

9. Country-risk analysis involves a consideration of both economic and political factors.

EXERCISES

1. Why are Eurobanks able to offer narrower spreads than domestic banks?

2. Create an example of $10 million being deposited in the Eurodollar market by a U.S. manufacturing firm, Motorola. Your example should include at least one interbank transaction before the dollars are borrowed by a French public utility firm, Paris Electric. How is the gross size of the Eurodollar market affected by your example? What about the net size?

3. Imagine yourself in a job interview for a position with a large international bank. The interviewer mentions that, recently, the bank has experienced some problem loans to foreign governments. The interviewer asks you what factors you think the bank should consider when evaluating a loan proposal involving a foreign governmental agency. How do you respond?

4. What are IBFs? Where did the initial growth of IBF business come from?

5. What kind of debt is rescheduled in a Paris Club arrangement? Why is an IMF standby loan agreement required before a Paris Club meeting?

6. Researchers typically look at Eurocurrency interest rates rather than country-specific bank quotations when they test for the validity of covered interest rate parity. What do you think is the rationale for this choice?

7. How might debt/equity swaps help solve the international debt problem? Point out the benefits and drawbacks from the viewpoint of the debtor country. Why do you think the debt/equity swap market has remained small over the years?

8. Pick five developing nations and create a country-risk index for them. Rank them ordinally in terms of factors that you can observe—GDP growth, exports, per capita GDP growth, and so on. How does your country-risk ranking compare with the latest *Euromoney* ranking?

REFERENCES

Bulow, Jeremy, and Kenneth Rogoff. "Cleaning Up Third World Debt without Getting Taken to the Cleaners." *Journal of Economic Perspectives* (Winter 1990).

Clark, Jack, and Eliot Kalter. "Recent Innovations in Debt Restructuring." *Finance and Development* (September 1992): 6–8.

"Daring to Hope, Fearing the Worst." *Euromoney* (September 1999): 250–254.

Sarver, Eugene. *The Eurocurrency Market Handbook*. New York: New York Institute of Finance, 1990.

Schadler, Susan, Adam Bennett, Maria Carkovic, Louis Dicks-Mireaux, Mauro Mecagni, James H.J. Morsink, and Miguel A. Savastano. *IMF Conditionality: Experience Under Stand-By and Extended Arrangements*. International Monetary Fund Occasional Paper 128 (September 1995).

INTERNET APPLICATIONS

Please visit our Web site at www.awl.com/husted_melvin for more exercises and readings.

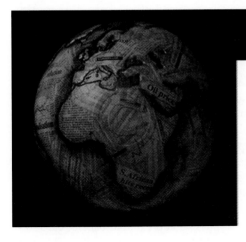

CHAPTER 21

Open-Economy Macroeconomic Policy and Adjustment

KEY WORDS

Internal balance
External balance
IS curve
LM curve
BP curve

Crowding out
Mundell–Fleming model
Locomotive effect
Open-economy multiplier

A n economy that is open to international trade and payments will face different problems from those of an economy that is closed to the rest of the world. The typical introductory economics presentation of macroeconomic equilibrium and policy is a closed-economy view. Discussions of economic adjustments required to combat unemployment or inflation do not consider the rest of the world. Clearly, this is no longer an acceptable approach in an increasingly integrated world.

Internal balance
A rate of domestic economic growth consistent with a low unemployment rate.

External balance
Achieving a desired trade or capital account balance.

In an open economy, we can summarize the desirable economic goals as being the attainment of internal and external balance. **Internal balance** means a steady growth of the domestic economy consistent with a low unemployment rate. **External balance** is the achievement of a desired trade balance or desired international capital flows. In Principles of Economics classes, the emphasis is on internal balance. By concentrating solely on internal goals, such as desirable levels of inflation, unemployment, and economic growth, simpler model economies may be used for analysis. A consideration of the joint pursuit of internal and external balance calls for a more detailed view of the economy. The slight increase in complexity yields a big payoff in terms of a more realistic view of the problems facing modern policy makers. It is no longer a question of changing policy to change unemployment or inflation at home. Now, the authorities must also consider the impact on the balance of trade, capital flows, and exchange rates.

INTERNAL AND EXTERNAL MACROECONOMIC EQUILIBRIUM

The major tools of macroeconomic policy are fiscal policy (government spending and taxation) and monetary policy (central-bank control of the money supply). These tools are used to achieve macroeconomic equilibrium. We assume that macroeconomic equilibrium requires equilibrium in three major sectors of the economy:

1. *Goods-market equilibrium*: The quantity of goods and services supplied is equal to the quantity demanded.

2. *Money-market equilibrium*: The quantity of money supplied is equal to the quantity demanded.

3. *Balance-of-payments equilibrium*: The current account deficit (surplus) is equal to the capital account surplus (deficit), so that the official settlements balance of payments equals zero.

We shall analyze the macroeconomic equilibrium with a curve that summarizes equilibrium in each market. The *IS* curve depicts goods-market equilibrium. The *LM* curve illustrates money-market equilibrium. Finally, the *BP* curve shows balance-of-payments equilibrium. These curves are then combined into one diagram, the *IS–LM–BP* diagram.* At the point where all three lines intersect, macroeconomic

---

*These labels are traditional in the macroeconomics literature. *IS* stands for investment and savings—important determinants of goods-marked equilibrium. *LM* stands for money demand (L) and money supply (M). *BP* represents the balance of payments.

FIGURE 21.1 *Equilibrium in the goods market* (IS), *money market* (LM), *and balance of payments* (BP).

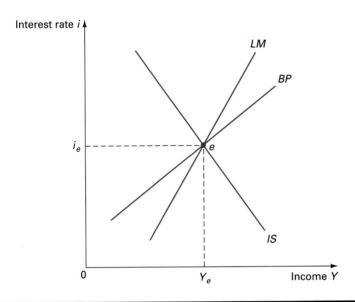

equilibrium is achieved. This occurs where the domestic interest rate i equals i_e, and domestic national income equals Y_e. We turn now to discuss how each of the equilibrium curves is derived. Figure 21.1 displays the *IS–LM–BP* diagram.

THE IS CURVE

First, let's look at the **IS curve**. This line represents combinations of i and Y that provide equilibrium in the goods market, holding everything else (e.g., the price level) constant. Equilibrium in the goods market occurs when the output of goods and services is equal to the quantity of goods and services demanded. In Principles of Economics classes, macroeconomic equilibrium is said to exist when the "leakages equal the injections" of spending in the economy. More precisely, domestic saving (S), taxes (T), and imports (IM) represent income received that is not spent on domestic goods and services—the leakages from spending. Injections of spending into the income stream include investment spending (I), government spending (G), and exports (X). Investment spending is the spending of business firms for new plants and equipment.

Equilibrium occurs when

$$S + T + IM = I + G + X \qquad (21.1)$$

IS curve
Combinations of i and Y that provide equilibrium in the goods market.

When the leakages from spending equal the injections, the value of income received from producing goods and services will be equal to total spending, or the quantity of output demanded. The *IS* curve in Figure 21.1 depicts the various combinations of *i* and *Y* that yield the equality in Equation 21.1. We now consider why the *IS* curve is downward sloping.

We assume that taxes (*T*) are set by governments independent of income, while the amounts people save (*S*) and spend on imports (*IM*) depend upon their income. The higher the domestic income, the more the domestic residents want to save, and the more they spend on imports. In the bottom of Figure 21.2, the *S* + *T* + *IM* line is upward sloping. This illustrates that the higher domestic income rises, the greater saving plus taxes plus imports is. Investment spending (*I*) is assumed to be determined by the domestic interest rate and does not change as current domestic income changes. This is because investment spending is paid for by borrowing funds. Exports are assumed to be determined by foreign income (they are foreign imports)

FIGURE 21.2   *Derivation of the IS curve.*

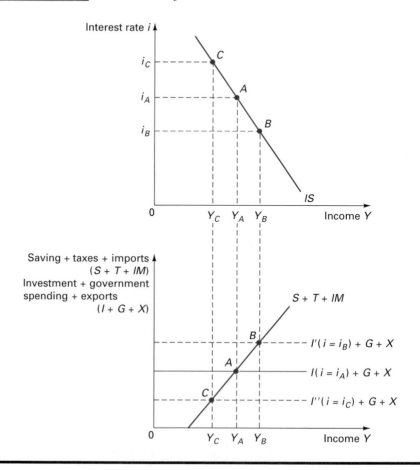

and don't change as domestic income changes. Finally, government spending is set independent of income. Since I, G, and X are independent of current domestic income, the $I + G + X$ line in the bottom of Figure 21.2 is drawn as a horizontal line.

Equation 21.1 indicated that equilibrium occurs at that income level where $S + T + IM = I + G + X$. In the bottom panel of Figure 21.2, point A represents an equilibrium point with an equilibrium level of income Y_A. In the upper panel of the figure, Y_A is shown to be consistent with point A on the IS curve. This point is also associated with a particular interest rate i_A.

To understand why the IS curve is downward sloping, consider what happens as the interest rate varies. Suppose the interest rate falls. At the lower interest rate, more potential investment projects become profitable (firms will not require as high a return on investment as the cost of borrowed funds falls), so investment increases, as illustrated in the move from $I + G + X$ to $I' + G + X$ in Figure 21.2. At this higher level of investment spending, equilibrium income increases to Y_B. Point B on the IS curve depicts this new goods-market equilibrium with a lower equilibrium interest rate i_B and higher equilibrium income Y_B.

Finally, consider what happens when the interest rate rises. Investment spending will fall, as fewer potential projects are profitable when the cost of borrowed funds rises. At the lower level of investment spending, the $I + G + X$ curve shifts down to $I'' + G + X$ in Figure 21.2. The new equilibrium point C is consistent with the level of income Y_C. In the IS diagram in the upper panel we see that point C is consistent with equilibrium income level Y_C and equilibrium interest rate i_C. The other points on the IS curve are consistent with alternative combinations of income and interest rate that yield equilibrium in the goods market.

We must remember that the IS curve is drawn holding the domestic price level (and the exchange rate) constant. A change in the domestic price level will change the price of domestic goods relative to foreign goods. If the domestic price level falls (holding the interest rate constant), investment, government spending, taxes, and saving do not change; but, because domestic goods are now cheaper relative to foreign goods, exports increase and imports fall. As a result, the $I + G + X$ curve will shift upward, and the $S + T + IM$ curve will shift downward to the right. Both adjustments will be consistent with a higher equilibrium income level. Since income increases with a constant interest rate, the IS curve shifts to the right. A rise in the domestic price level would cause the IS curve to shift to the left. A similar result would occur if the exchange rate were to appreciate while the price level remained constant.

THE LM CURVE

The **LM curve** in Figure 21.1 displays the alternative combinations of i and Y at which the demand for money equals the supply. Figure 21.3 provides a derivation of the LM curve. The left panel shows a money-demand curve labeled M^d and a money-supply curve labeled M^s. The horizontal axis measures the quantity of money, and the vertical axis measures the interest rate. Note that the M^s curve is vertical. This is because the central bank can choose any money supply it wants, inde-

LM curve
Combinations of i and Y that provide equilibrium in the money market.

FIGURE 21.3   *Derivation of the LM curve.*

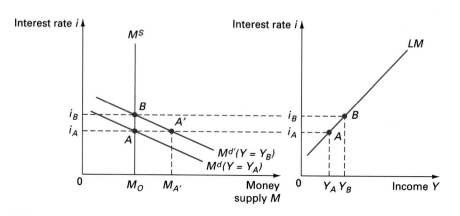

pendent of the interest rate. The actual value of the money supply chosen is M_O. The money-demand curve is downward sloping, indicating that the higher the interest rate, the lower the quantity of money demanded.

The inverse relationship between the interest rate and the quantity of money demanded is due to the role of interest as the opportunity cost of holding money. Since money earns no interest, the higher the interest rate, the more interest income people must give up to hold money instead of an interest-earning asset, so the less money people hold.

The initial money-market equilibrium occurs at point A with interest rate i_A. The initial money-demand curve M^d is drawn for a given level of income. If income increased, then the demand for money would increase, as in the shift from M^d to $M^{d'}$. Money demand at any given interest rate increases because at the higher level of income, people want to hold more money to support the increased spending on goods.

Now, let's consider why the *LM* curve has a positive slope. Suppose initially there is equilibrium at point A, with the interest rate at i_A and income at Y_A, as in Figure 21.3. If income increases from Y_A to Y_B, money demand increases from M^d to $M^{d'}$. If the interest rate remains at i_A, there will be an excess demand for money. This is shown in the left panel of Figure 21.3, as the quantity of money demanded is now $M_{A'}$. With the higher income, money demand is given by $M^{d'}$. At i_A, point A' on the money-demand curve is consistent with the higher quantity of money demanded, $M_{A'}$. If the money supply remains constant at M_O, there will be an excess demand for money, given by $M_A - M_O$. The attempt to hold more money than is in existence will cause the interest rate to rise until a new equilibrium is established at point B. This new equilibrium is consistent with a higher interest rate i_B and a higher income Y_B. Points A and B are both indicated on the *LM* curve in the right panel of Figure 21.3. The rest of the *LM* curve reflects similar combinations of equilibrium interest rates and income.

The *LM* curve is drawn for a specific money supply. If the supply of money increases, the quantity of money demanded will have to increase to restore equilibrium. This requires a lower i, so the *LM* curve will shift to the right. Similarly, a decrease in the money supply will tend to raise i, so the *LM* curve will shift to the left.

THE BP CURVE

The final curve portrayed in Figure 21.1 is the *BP* curve. The **BP curve** gives the combinations of i and Y that yield balance-of-payments equilibrium. The *BP* curve is drawn for a given domestic price level, a given exchange rate, and a given net foreign debt. Equilibrium occurs when the balance of payments equals 0. This can happen only when the current account surplus (deficit) is equal to the capital account deficit (surplus). Figure 21.4 illustrates the derivation of the *BP* curve. The lower

BP curve
Combinations of i and Y that provide equilibrium in the balance of payment.

| FIGURE 21.4 | *Derivation of the* BP *curve.* |

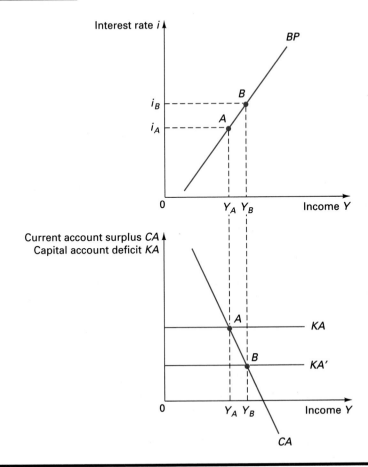

panel of the figure shows a *CA* line representing the current account surplus and a *KA* line representing the capital account deficit. The *CA* line is downward sloping because, as income increases, domestic imports increase and the current account surplus falls. The capital account is assumed to be determined by the interest rate, independent of income. Thus, the *KA* line is graphed as a horizontal line. Equilibrium occurs when the current account balance equals the capital account balance, so that the official settlements balance of payments is zero. Initially, equilibrium occurs at point *A*, with income level Y_A and interest rate i_A. If the interest rate increases, domestic financial assets are more attractive to foreign buyers, and the capital account deficit falls to *KA'*. At the old income level Y_A, the current account surplus will exceed the capital account deficit, so income must increase to Y_B to provide a new equilibrium at point *B*. Points *A* and *B* on the *BP* curve in Figure 21.4 illustrate that as *i* increases, *Y* must also increase to maintain equilibrium. Only an upward-sloping *BP* curve will provide combinations of *i* and *Y* consistent with equilibrium when *i* is allowed to vary.

EQUILIBRIUM

Equilibrium for the economy requires that all three markets—the goods market, the money market, and the balance of payments—be in equilibrium. This occurs when the *IS, LM,* and *BP* curves all intersect at a common (equilibrium) level of the interest rate and income. In Figure 21.1, point *e* is the equilibrium point, which occurs at the equilibrium interest rate i_e, and the equilibrium income level Y_e. Until some change occurs that shifts one of the curves, the *IS–LM–BP* equilibrium will be consistent with all goods produced being sold, money demand equal to money supply, and a current account surplus equal to a capital account deficit that yields a zero balance on the official settlements account.

MONETARY POLICY UNDER FIXED EXCHANGE RATES

In deriving the *BP* curve, we assumed that higher interest rates in the domestic economy would attract foreign investors and decrease the capital account deficit. With fixed exchange rates, the domestic central bank is not free to conduct monetary policy independent of the rest of the world. In the discussion of sterilization in Chapter 18, it was argued that, in the short run, the central bank could exercise some control over the money supply if domestic and foreign financial assets were imperfect substitutes. If assets are perfect substitutes, they must yield the same return to investors. With fixed exchange rates, this means that the domestic interest rate will equal the foreign interest rate. If capital is perfectly mobile, then any deviation of the domestic interest rate from the foreign rate would cause investors to hold only the high-return assets. Clearly, in this case there is no room for central banks to conduct an independent monetary policy under fixed exchange rates.

FIGURE 21.5 *Monetary expansion with fixed exchange rates and perfect capital mobility.*

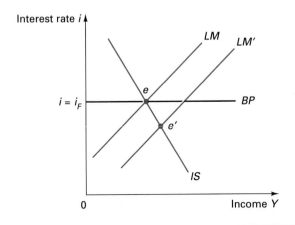

Figure 21.5 illustrates this situation. With perfect asset substitutability, the *BP* curve is a horizontal line at the domestic interest rate *i*, which equals the foreign interest rate i_F. Any rate higher than i_F results in large (infinite) capital inflows as the demand for foreign assets falls to zero, while any lower rate yields large capital outflows as the demand for domestic assets falls to zero. Only at i_F is the balance-of-payments equilibrium obtained.

Suppose the central bank increases the money supply so that the *LM* curve shifts from *LM* to *LM'*. The *IS–LM* equilibrium is now shifted from *e* to *e'*. While *e'* results in equilibrium in the money and goods markets, there will be a large capital outflow and a large official settlements balance deficit. This will lead to pressure for the domestic currency to depreciate on the foreign-exchange market. To maintain the fixed exchange rate, the central bank must intervene and sell foreign exchange to buy domestic currency. The foreign-exchange-market intervention will decrease the domestic money supply and shift the *LM* curve back to *LM* to restore the initial equilibrium at *e*. With perfect capital mobility, this would all happen instantaneously, so that no movement away from point *e* is ever observed. Any attempt to lower the money supply and shift the *LM* curve left would have just the reverse effect on the interest rate and intervention activity.

With less than perfect capital mobility, the central bank has some opportunity to vary the money supply in the short run. Still, the maintenance of the fixed exchange rate will require an ultimate reversal of policy in the face of a constant foreign interest rate. The process is essentially just drawn out over time rather than occurring instantly. For example, the movement from *e* to *e'* in Figure 21.5 can occur over an observable period of time (weeks or months). The consequent increase in the balance-of-payments deficit may also persist over several months. The fundamental reason for the slower speed of adjustment is the ability of the domestic interest rate to vary from the foreign rate in the short run.

FISCAL POLICY UNDER FIXED EXCHANGE RATES

A change in government spending or taxes will shift the *IS* curve. Suppose an expansionary policy is desired. Figure 21.6 illustrates the effects. With fixed exchange rates, perfect asset substitutability, and perfect capital mobility, the *BP* curve is a horizontal line at $i = i_F$. An increase in government spending shifts the *IS* curve right to *IS'*. The domestic equilibrium shifts from point *e* to *e'*, which would mean a higher equilibrium interest rate and income. Since point *e'* is above the *BP* curve, the official settlements balance of payments moves to a surplus due to increased foreign-capital inflows associated with the higher domestic interest rate. To stop the domestic currency from appreciating, the central bank must increase the money supply and buy foreign exchange with domestic money. The increase in the money supply shifts the *LM* curve to the right. When the money supply has increased enough to move the *LM* curve to *LM'* in Figure 21.6, equilibrium is restored at point *e''*. Note that point *e''* has the interest rate back at $i = i_F$, yet income has increased.

The latter result is a significant difference from the monetary policy expansion considered in the last section. With fixed exchange rates and perfect capital mobility, monetary policy was seen to be ineffective in changing the level of income. This was because there was no room for independent monetary policy with a fixed exchange rate. In contrast, fiscal policy will have a strong effect on income and can be used to stimulate the domestic economy.

FIGURE 21.6   *Fiscal expansion with fixed exchange rates and perfect capital mobility.*

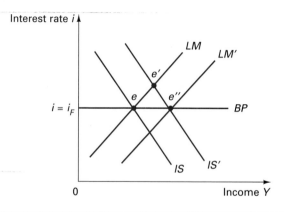

MONETARY POLICY UNDER FLOATING EXCHANGE RATES

We now consider a world of flexible exchange rates and perfect capital mobility. The notable difference between the analysis of this section compared with the fixed exchange rate stories of the last two sections is that, with floating rates, the central bank is not obliged to intervene in the foreign-exchange market to support a particular exchange rate. With no intervention, the current account surplus (deficit) will always equal the capital account deficit (surplus) so that the official settlements balance equals zero. In addition, since the central bank does not intervene to fix the exchange rate, the money supply can change to any level desired by the monetary authorities. This independence of monetary policy is one of the advantages of flexible exchange rates, according to proponents of a float.

The assumptions of perfect substitutability of assets and perfect capital mobility will result in $i = i_F$, as before. Once again, the *BP* curve will be a horizontal line at $i = i_F$. Only now, equilibrium in the balance of payments will require the exchange rate to change whenever economic conditions change.

Changes in the exchange rate will cause shifts in the *IS* curve. If we assume that domestic- and foreign-goods prices are fixed in the short run, depreciation of the domestic currency will make domestic goods relatively cheaper and will stimulate domestic net exports. Since net exports are part of total spending, the *IS* curve will shift to the right. A domestic-currency appreciation will decrease domestic net exports and cause the *IS* curve to shift to the left.

Figure 21.7 illustrates the effects of an expansionary monetary policy. The increase in the money supply shifts the *LM* curve to the right to *LM'*. The interest rate and income existing at point *e'* would yield equilibrium in the money and goods markets, but would cause a larger capital account deficit (and official settlements

FIGURE 21.7 *Monetary expansion with floating exchange rates and perfect capital mobility.*

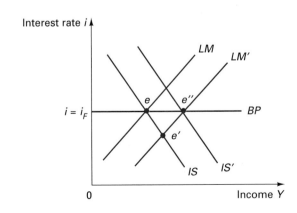

deficit) because the domestic interest rate would be less than i_F. Since this is a flexible exchange rate system, the official settlements deficit is avoided by the adjustment of the exchange rate to a level that restores equilibrium. Specifically, the pressure of the official settlements deficit will cause the domestic currency to depreciate. This depreciation is associated with a rightward shift of the *IS* curve as domestic net exports increase. When the *IS* curve shifts to *IS'*, the new equilibrium is obtained at e''. At e'', income has increased and the domestic interest rate equals the foreign rate.

Had there been a monetary contraction instead of an expansion, the story would have been reversed. A temporarily higher interest rate would decrease the capital account deficit, causing pressure for the domestic currency to appreciate. As domestic net exports are decreased, the *IS* curve would shift to the left until a new equilibrium is established at a lower level of income and the original $i = i_F$ is restored.

In contrast to the fixed exchange rate world, monetary policy can change the level of income with floating exchange rates. Since the exchange rate adjusts to maintain balance-of-payments equilibrium, the central bank can choose its monetary policy independent of the policies of other countries.

FISCAL POLICY UNDER FLOATING EXCHANGE RATES

An expansionary fiscal policy, such as a tax cut or increased government spending, will shift the *IS* curve to the right. Earlier it was shown that with fixed exchange rates, such a policy would result in a higher domestic income level. With flexible exchange rates we shall see that the story is much different.

In Figure 21.8, an expansionary policy shifts the *IS* curve to the right from *IS* to *IS'*. This shift would result in an intermediate equilibrium, at point e'. At e', the

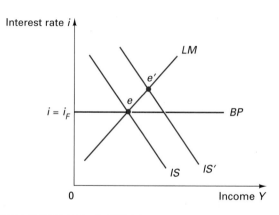

FIGURE 21.8   *Fiscal expansion with floating exchange rates and perfect capital mobility.*

goods market and money market will be in equilibrium, but there will be a tendency for an official settlements surplus to emerge due to the lower capital account deficit induced by the higher interest rate at e'. Since the exchange rate is free to adjust to eliminate the balance-of-payments surplus, the exchange rate will appreciate. This appreciation will reduce domestic exports and increase imports; as net exports fall, the *IS* curve shifts to the left. When the *IS* curve has returned to its initial position, equilibrium is restored in all markets. Note that the final equilibrium occurs at the initial level of i and Y. With floating exchange rates, fiscal policy is ineffective in shifting the level of income. When an expansionary fiscal policy has no effect on income, complete **crowding out** has occurred. This crowding out occurs because the currency appreciation induced by the expansionary fiscal policy reduces net exports to a level that just offsets the positive fiscal policy effects on income.

This world of flexible exchange rates and perfect capital mobility is often called the **Mundell-Fleming model** of the open economy.* The assumptions of a fixed price level and perfect capital mobility may be unreasonable as real-world propositions, but the popularity of the Mundell-Fleming model suggests that many researchers have found it to be a useful device for understanding macroeconomic policy under floating exchange rates.[†]

Crowding out
An increase in government spending is offset by a reduction in private spending, such as net exports.

Mundell-Fleming model
The IS–LM–BP model with flexible exchange rates and perfect capital mobility.

INTERNATIONAL POLICY COORDINATION

This chapter has so far demonstrated the effects of fiscal and monetary policy under fixed and floating exchange rates. From the early 1970s on, the major industrialized nations have generally operated with floating exchange rates. In this framework, fiscal and monetary policy can generate large swings in exchange rates. The high degree of capital mobility existing among the developed countries suggests that fiscal actions that lead to a divergence of the domestic interest rate from the given foreign interest rate will quickly be undone by the influence of exchange rate changes on net exports, as was illustrated in Figure 21.8. Many economists argue that the sharp reduction in U.S. net exports in the mid-1980s was due to the expansionary fiscal policy followed by the U.S. government.

How could such a reduction in net exports be minimized? If all nations coordinated their domestic policies and simultaneously stimulated their economies, the world interest rate would rise and the pressure for exchange rate change and net

---

*The model is named after two researchers who developed similar models in the 1960s: Robert A. Mundell, "Capital Mobility and Stabilization Policy Under Fixed and Flexible Exchange Rates," *Canadian Journal of Economics* (November 1963); and Marcus Fleming, "Domestic Financial Policies Under Fixed and Under Floating Exchange Rates," *IMF Staff Papers* (1962). There is a very large and growing body of literature in this tradition. A useful overview is provided in Jacob A. Frenkel and Michael L. Mussa, "Asset Markets, Exchange Rates, and the Balance of Payments," in *Handbook of International Economics*, ed. Ronald W. Jones and Peter B. Kenen, vol. 1 (Amsterdam: North-Holland, 1985).

[†]Obviously, prices are not fixed in the real world, so this is a convenient assumption. Perfect capital mobility is not as obvious a proposition, but research generally suggests that this may also be unrealistic.

export adjustment would fall. The problem illustrated in Figure 21.8 was that of a single country attempting to follow an expansionary policy while the rest of the world retained unchanged policies, so that i_F remained constant. If i_F increased at the same time that i increased, the *BP* curve would shift upward, so that the balance-of-payments equilibrium would be consistent with a higher interest rate.

Similarly, monetary-policy-induced changes in exchange rates and net exports can be lessened if central banks coordinate policy so that i_F shifts with i. There have been instances of coordinated foreign-exchange-market intervention when a group of central banks jointly followed policies aimed at a depreciation or appreciation of the dollar. Item 21.1 discusses a well-publicized example of a coordinated intervention. These coordinated interventions aimed at achieving a target value of the dollar also work to bring domestic monetary policies more in line with each other. If the United States follows an expansionary monetary policy relative to Japan and the euro-area countries, U.S. interest rates may fall relative to the other countries, so that a larger capital account deficit is induced and pressure for a dollar depreciation results. If the central banks decide to work together to stop the dollar depreciation, the Japanese and European central banks will buy dollars on the foreign-exchange market with their domestic currencies, while the Federal Reserve must sell foreign exchange to buy dollars. This will result in higher money supplies in Japan and Europe and a lower money supply in the United States. The coordinated intervention works toward a convergence of monetary policy in each country.

The basic argument in favor of international policy coordination is that such coordination would stabilize exchange rates. Whether or not exchange rate stability offers any substantial benefits over freely floating rates with independent policies is a matter of much debate. Some experts argue that coordinated monetary policy to achieve fixed exchange rates or to reduce exchange rate fluctuations to within narrow "target zones" would reduce the destabilizing aspects of international trade in goods and financial assets when currencies become "overvalued" or "undervalued."[*] This view emphasizes that in an increasingly integrated world economy, it seems desirable to conduct national economic policy in an international context rather than to simply focus on domestic policy goals without considering the international implications.

An alternative view is that most changes in exchange rates are due to real economic shocks, such as changes in tastes or technology, and should be considered permanent changes. In this view, there is no such thing as an overvalued or undervalued currency because exchange rates are always in equilibrium given current economic conditions.[†] Furthermore, governments cannot change the real relative prices of goods internationally by driving the nominal exchange rate to some particular level through foreign-exchange market intervention, because price levels will adjust to the new nominal exchange rate. This view, then, argues that government policy is best aimed at lower inflation and a stable domestic economy.

---

[*]An important and influential example is Ronald I. McKinnon, *An International Standard for Monetary Stabilization* (Washington D.C.: Institute for International Economics, 1984).
[†]A forceful presentation of this approach is found in Alan C. Stockman, "The Equilibrium Approach to Exchange Rates," *Federal Reserve Bank of Richmond Economic Review* (April 1987).

ITEM 21.1	The Plaza Agreement

On September 22, 1985, representatives of the United States, West Germany, Japan, the United Kingdom, and France emerged from a secret meeting at the Plaza Hotel in New York City to announce a plan to coordinate foreign-exchange-market intervention aimed at depreciating the dollar. The so-called Group of 5, or G-5, countries were responding to threats by the U.S. Congress to restrict U.S. imports with tariffs and quotas. The coordinated intervention was viewed as an alternative way to stimulate the U.S. trade balance through the effects of the dollar depreciation on international trade prices.

After appreciating through the early 1980s, the dollar began to depreciate early in 1985. In August and September, however, the dollar started to rise in value. The plan that was developed at the Plaza Hotel was designed to call attention to the view that the fundamental economic forces should have been contributing to a dollar depreciation. The finance ministers pointed to more moderate economic growth in the United States combined with stronger economic growth in the other countries. They felt that the market exchange rates did not reflect these forces for dollar depreciation, so they stated their intentions to follow macroeconomic policies and coordinated foreign-exchange-market policies to achieve a value for the dollar that seemed more in line with their desired value.

The Plaza announcement had a strong impact on the market. The announcement was unexpected due to very secretive dealings among the five countries. The announcement changed the way market participants formed expectations about future policies of the five governments. In particular, it seemed to signal a major shift in U.S. policy away from a free-market view—that is, a view that the exchange rate should move to whatever level traders brought about—to a belief that the U.S. government would help bring about a weaker dollar.

Because of the effect on traders' expectations, the dollar fell on the day after the announcement, before any official intervention occurred. Once the intervention began, it was often quite large.

Anytime the dollar tended to rise in the weeks following the announcement, the Federal Reserve sold dollars. Through the first week of October, the Federal Reserve sold $199 million for German marks and $262 million for Japanese yen. The goal was to firmly convince market participants that the five nations were committed to a lower dollar value.

The Plaza Agreement of September 22 is often referred to as a significant date in recent foreign-exchange-market history because of its effect on exchange rates as well as the public nature of the agreement. Central banks rarely hold press conferences to discuss their meetings and policy plans. The public announcement was considered a major change in the foreign-exchange policy of the previously free-market-oriented Reagan administration that signaled a new desire for international coordination of policy to achieve domestic political and economic goals.

Aside from exchange rate objectives, international policy coordination may involve other macroeconomic objectives that take into consideration the interdependent nature of the global economy. One example is the avoidance of so-called "beggar-thy-neighbor" policies where a country will devalue its currency to stimulate its exports and discourage imports. If other countries respond by devaluing their currencies, then the series of competitive devaluations will end with no one gaining at the expense of others, but all may face higher inflation associated with the deval-uations. Such competitive devaluations may be avoided through the international coordination of policies where it is made clear that individual countries will not find beggar-thy-neighbor policies successful. Policy coordination has, at times, been used to stimulate exports from certain countries to others. Large countries like Germany or the United States have stimulated their economies in order to increase their imports. The increased imports then stimulate economic growth in other countries. This is sometimes described as the **locomotive effect,** as the large economy pulls the rest of the world behind it as the locomotive pulls the rest of the train.

Locomotive effect
The stimulation of the large country economy aimed at increasing growth in the rest of the world.

The debate over the appropriate level and form of international policy coordi-nation was one of the livelier areas of international finance in the late 1980s.* Many leading economists have participated, but a problem at the practical level is that dif-ferent governments emphasize different goals and may view the current economic situation differently. This is a more complex world in which to formulate interna-tional policy agreements than in the typical scholarly debate, where it is presumed that governments agree on the current problems and on the way that alternative policies will have an impact on those problems.[†]

THE OPEN-ECONOMY MULTIPLIER

We can use the macroeconomic model developed in this chapter to analyze the effects of changes in spending on the equilibrium level of national income, assum-ing the interest rate is unchanged. We begin with the basic macroeconomic equilib-rium conditions seen in the bottom half of Figure 21.2:

$$S + T + IM = I + G + X \qquad (21.2)$$

In equilibrium, the planned level of saving plus taxes plus imports must equal the planned level of investment plus government spending plus exports. In order to find the equilibrium levels of national income (Y) and net exports ($X - IM$), we must make some assumptions regarding the variables in Equation 21.2. Specifically, we assume that saving and imports both depend on the level of national income. The greater the domestic income, the more people want to save, and the more they want to spend on imports. The fraction of any extra income that people want to save is called the marginal propensity to save, which we will denote as s. The fraction of any extra income that people want to spend on imports is called the marginal propen-

*An important collection of studies is found in Ralph Bryant, Dale Henderson, Gerald Haltham, Peter Hooper, and Steven Symansky, eds., *Empirical Macroeconomics for Interdependent Economies* (Washington, D.C.: Brookings Institution, 1988).
†Some studies have considered the importance and effects of individual government differences of opinion. These studies include Jeffrey A. Frankel and Katharine E. Rockett, "International Macroeconomic Policy Coordination When Policy-Makers Disagree on the Model," *American Economic Review* (June 1988); Atish Ghosh, "International Policy Coordination in an Uncertain World," *Economics Letters 3* (1986); and Gerald Haltham, "International Policy Coordination: How Much Consensus Is There?" *Brookings Discussion Papers in International Economics* (September 1986).

sity to import, which we will denote as m. So, $S = sY$ and $IM = mY$. The rest of the variables in Equation 21.2 ($T, I, G,$ and X) are assumed to be exogenously determined by factors other than domestic income.

With these assumptions, we can substitute the new specifications of S and IM and rewrite Equation 21.2 as

$$sY + T + mY = I + G + X \qquad (21.3)$$

Gathering our Y terms and subtracting T from each side of the equation, we have $(s + m)\, Y = I + G + X - T$. Solving for the equilibrium level of Y yields

$$Y = (I + G + X - T)/(s + m) \qquad (21.4)$$

If $I, G,$ or X increased by \$1, the equilibrium level of Y would increase by $1/(s + m)$ times \$1. An increase in T would cause Y to fall. The value of $1/(s + m)$ is known as the **open-economy multiplier**. This multiplier is equal to the reciprocal of the marginal propensity to save (s) plus the marginal propensity to import (m). Since s and m will both be some fraction less than 1, we expect this multiplier to exceed 1, so that an increase in $I, G,$ or X spending would cause the equilibrium level of national income to rise by more than the change in spending.

Let's consider an example of this multiplier effect. Suppose that we return to the model of Figure 21.2 as redrawn in Figure 21.9. In this model economy, the marginal propensity to save is .3, the marginal propensity to import is .2, taxes equal 20,

Open-economy multiplier
A multiplier equal to the reciprocal of the marginal propensity to save plus the marginal propensity to import.

FIGURE 21.9   *The effect of an increase in exports.*

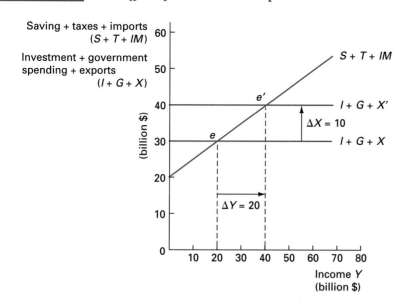

and investment, government spending, and exports each equal 10 (assume the units are billions of dollars). In this case, the macroeconomic model is given by

$$S + T + IM = .3Y + 20 + .2Y = .5Y + 20 \qquad (21.5)$$

and

$$I + G + X = 10 + 10 + 10 = 30 \qquad (21.6)$$

These two equations are drawn in Figure 21.9 as the $S + T + IM$ line and the $I + G + X$ line. The point of intersection occurs at e, where the equilibrium level of national income equals $20 billion.

The equilibrium level of income could have been found by using Equation 21.4 and substituting the values given for each variable:

$$Y = (I + G + X - T)/(s + m) = 10/.5 = 20 \qquad (21.7)$$

Whether we solve for the equilibrium level of Y algebraically or graphically, we find the value of $20 billion.

What would happen if exports increased? For instance, suppose exports increase from $10 to $20 billion. In Figure 21.9, the $I + G + X$ line shifts up by the amount of the increase in exports to $I + G + X'$. The two lines are parallel because they differ by a constant $10 billion, the increase in exports, at each level of income. The new equilibrium level of income is found by the new point of intersection e' at an income level of $40 billion. Note that exports increase by 10, yet income increases by 20, from the original equilibrium level of 20 to the new level of 40. Since the increase in equilibrium national income is twice the increase in exports, the open-economy multiplier must equal 2. Algebraically, the multiplier is $1/(s + m)$, which, in the example, is $1/(.3 + .2) = 1/.5 = 2$. An increase in I, G, or X would increase Y by twice the increase in spending in our example.

The intuition behind the multiplier effect is taught in Principles of Economics courses. If spending, such as export spending, rises in some industry, then there is an increase in the income of factors employed in that industry. These employed resource owners, such as laborers, will increase their spending on goods and services and further stimulate production, which further raises income and spending. This "multiplier effect" has a finite value because not all of the increased income is spent in the domestic economy. Some is saved and some is spent on imports. Saving and imports act as leakages from domestic spending that serve to limit the size of the multiplier. The larger the marginal propensity to save and the marginal propensity to import, the smaller the multiplier.

In the real world, such multiplier effects will be more complex due to the presence of taxes and feedback effects from the rest of the world. However, the essential point—that changes in spending may create much larger changes in the national income—remains. Stable growth of the economy requires stable growth of spending.

SUMMARY

1. Internal balance is a domestic rate of growth consistent with a low unemployment rate.

2. External balance is a desired level of trade or capital flows.

3. Macroeconomic equilibrium requires equilibrium in the goods market, money market, and balance of payments.

4. The *IS* curve presents combinations of *i* and *Y* that yield goods-market equilibrium.

5. The *LM* curve presents combinations of *i* and *Y* that yield money-market equilibrium.

6. The *BP* curve presents combinations of *i* and *Y* that yield balance-of-payments equilibrium.

7. With perfect asset substitutability and perfect capital mobility, the domestic interest rate is equal to the foreign interest rate.

8. With fixed exchange rates, a country cannot conduct an independent monetary policy to change domestic income.

9. Fiscal policy is effective in changing domestic income with fixed exchange rates.

10. With floating exchange rates, monetary policy is effective in changing domestic income.

11. With floating exchange rates, fiscal policy changes tend to be offset by the balance of payments, so that crowding out occurs and income is unaffected.

12. International policy coordination is viewed as a way to stabilize exchange rates.

13. The open-economy multiplier is equal to the reciprocal of the marginal propensity to save plus the marginal propensity to import.

EXERCISES

1. Define internal and external balance, and give an example of how the pursuit of one might cause a problem in achieving the other.

2. What are the major tools of macroeconomic policy? Explain and illustrate how each tool can shift the *IS* and/or *LM* curves.

3. Suppose that a nation has high unemployment and a deficit in its balance of payments. Use the *IS–LM–BP* analysis to explain how government policy may be used to increase income and restore balance-of-payments equilibrium.

4. Why will the effectiveness of monetary policy differ according to whether or not there are flexible exchange rates?

5. Derive the *IS, LM,* and *BP* curves from their respective market-equilibrium conditions. Explain why each curve has the slope it does.

6. Draw an *IS–LM–BP* equilibrium. Now, add a point labeled *A* at a higher income level and a lower interest rate than the initial equilibrium. Carefully explain the nature of the disequilibrium at point *A* (the situation in each individual market).

7. How does a coordinated intervention policy help bring about a convergence of macroeconomic policies?

8. Suppose that the U.S. Congress imposes an increase in taxes. Under a floating exchange rate regime, carefully illustrate and explain the process that will generate a new goods-market, money-market, and balance-of-payments equilibrium. What are the effects of such a policy on domestic income and employment?

9. If there is a large increase in the Mexican price level relative to the United States, what intervention policy would the Mexican central bank have to pursue to maintain a fixed exchange rate with the United States dollar? Use the *IS–LM–BP* diagram in your analysis.

10. Assume that the marginal propensity to save is .4 and the marginal propensity to import is .2. Calculate the change in the equilibrium level of national income if investment spending declines by $10 million. What is the size of the open-economy multiplier?

REFERENCES

"Complete International Policy Coordination Needed to Avoid Negative Policy Spillovers." *Economics Update.* Federal Reserve Bank of Atlanta (October–December 1993).

Dornbusch, Rudiger. *Open Economy Macroeconomics.* New York: Basic Books, 1980.

Obstfeld, Maurice, and Kenneth Rogoff. *Foundations of International Macroeconomics.* Cambridge, Mass.: MIT Press, 1996.

INTERNET APPLICATIONS

Please visit our Web site at www.awl.com/husted_melvin for more exercises and readings.

GLOSSARY

Absolute advantage   The ability of a country to produce a good using fewer productive inputs than is possible anywhere else in the world.

Absorption   Total domestic spending.

Adjustment mechanism   The process by which international disequilibria are eliminated.

Ad valorem tariff   A trade tax equal to a given percentage of selling price.

Antitrade biased growth   Growth that results in a reduction of trade relative to the size of the economy.

Appreciate   The value of one currency rises relative to another.

Autarky   A situation where a country does not take part in international trade.

Average tariff   A measure of the height of a country's tariff barriers.

Balance-of-payments deficit (surplus)   Balance-of-payments debit items exceed (are less than) the credit items in value.

Balance-of-payments equilibrium   Credits equal debits for a particular account.

Balance of trade   The value of merchandise exports minus imports.

Base money   Currency plus commercial bank reserves, which is also equal to international reserves plus domestic credit.

Basic balance   The current account plus long-term capital.

Black market   An illegal market in foreign exchange.

BP curve   Combinations of i and Y that provide equilibrium in the balance of payment.

Brain drain   The permanent relocation of skilled workers from one country to another.

"Buy American" acts   Laws that direct purchasing agents of U.S. federal, state, and local governments to purchase American products unless comparable foreign goods are substantially cheaper.

Call option   An option to buy currency.

Capital flight   Large capital outflows resulting from unfavorable investment conditions in a country.

Commercial policy   Actions taken by a government to influence the quantity and composition of that country's international trade.

Commodity money standard   The value of money is fixed relative to a commodity.

Community indifference curve (CIC)   A diagram that expresses the preferences of all the consumers of a country.

Comparative advantage   A country has comparative advantage in a good if the product has a lower pretrade relative price than is found elsewhere in the world.

Compound tariff   A trade tax that has both a specific and an ad valorem component.

Constant returns to scale   A technological relationship such that proportionate changes in inputs lead to proportionate changes in output.

Consumer surplus   The difference between the amount consumers are willing to pay to purchase a given quantity of goods and the amount they have to pay to purchase those goods.

Consumption possibility frontier   The various bundles of goods that a country can obtain by taking advantage of international trade.

Contagion effect   A crisis in one country spills over into other countries.

Council of the EU   One of two executive offices of the EU government; it has the power to make decisions about European Commission proposals and to issue directives and regulations to the member states.

Countervailing duty   A tariff imposed by an importing country designed to raise the price of an imported product to its fair market value.

Covariance   A measure of how two variables fluctuate about their means together.

Covered return   The domestic-currency value of a foreign investment when the foreign-currency proceeds are sold in the forward market.

Cross rate   The third exchange rate implied by any two exchange rates involving three currencies.

Crowding out   An increase in government spending is offset by a reduction in private spending, such as net exports.

Currency-contract period   The period immediately following a devaluation when contracts signed prior to the devaluation are settled.

Currency union   An agreement between countries to fix exchange rates and coordinate monetary policies.

Customs unions (CU)   An agreement among several countries to eliminate internal barriers to trade and to erect common barriers against nonmember countries.

Deadweight cost of the tariff   Value of wasted resources devoted to expanded domestic consumption and expenditures devoted to less desired substitutes brought about by a tariff.

Debt/equity swap   An exchange of developing country debt for an ownership position in a developing country business.

Depreciate   The value of one currency falls relative to another.

Destabilizing speculation   Speculators increase the variability of exchange rates.

Diminishing returns to labor   The fact that as workers are added to the production process, holding all other factors fixed, the marginal product of labor declines.

Diversified portfolios   Assets denominated in several currencies.

Domestic credit   The domestic component of base money.

Dumping   Selling a product in a foreign market at a price that is below fair market value.

Dumping margin   The difference between the market price of a product and its fair market value.

Dynamic gains from trade   Increases in economic well-being that accrue to an economy because trade expands the resources of a country or induces increases in the productivity of existing resources.

Economic development   The achievement of a quality of life for the average citizen of a country that is comparable to that enjoyed by the average citizen of a country with a modern economy.

Effective rate of protection (ERP)   The amount of protection provided to the domestic content of a product by the tariff structure of a country.

Effective return   The foreign interest rate plus the forward premium or discount.

Efficient market   A market where prices reflect all available information.

Elasticity   The responsiveness of quantity to changes in price.

Embargo   A complete ban on trade in a product or products.

Endogenous variable   A variable whose value is determined by some given factors.

Escape clause   A measure in U.S. trade law that allows for temporary protection against fairly traded foreign imports.

Eurocurrency market   The deposit and loan market for foreign currencies.

European Commission   One of two executive offices of the EU government; its chief responsibility is to draft and enforce EU laws.

European Court of Justice   Chief judiciary body of the EU that decides on the legality of council or commission actions.

European Parliament   Legislative branch of the EU government and the chief representative of the populace in the process of setting EU policy.

European Union (EU)   A CU among most of the nations of Western Europe.

Exchange rate   The price of one money in terms of another.

Exchange risk exposure   Translation, transaction, and economic exposure are three concepts of exposure to foreign-exchange risk.

Exogenous variable   A variable whose value is given to the economic system by an outside force, such as government or nature.

Exports   Goods sold by economic agents located in one country to economic agents located in another.

Export subsidy   A payment by a government to an industry that leads to an expansion of exports by that industry.

External balance   Achieving a desired trade or capital account balance.

Factor endowments   The quantities of factors of production (e.g., labor and machines) possessed by a country.

Factor price equalization (FPE)   Factor price equalization occurs if all individual factor prices (e.g., wages, rental payments) are identical when measured in the same currency.

Fisher equation   The nominal interest rate is equal to the real interest rate plus expected inflation.

Fixed exchange rates   Central banks peg exchange rates at desired levels.

Flexible exchange rates   Free-market supply and demand determines the value of currencies.

Foreign exchange swap   An agreement to trade currencies at one date and reverse the trade at a later date.

Forward discount   The forward exchange rate is less than the spot rate.

Forward exchange market   Where currencies may be bought and sold for delivery in a future period.

Forward premium   The forward exchange rate exceeds the spot rate.

Free-trade area (FTA)   An agreement among several countries to eliminate internal barriers to trade but to maintain existing barriers against nonmember countries.

General equilibrium   Simultaneous equilibrium in all the markets of an economy.

Generalized system of preferences (GSP)   A system where industrialized countries charge preferential lower tariff rates on goods from certain developing countries.

Gold standard   Currencies have fixed values in terms of gold.

Gross national product (GNP)   The value of final goods and services produced by domestic factors of production.

Gross domestic product (GDP)   The value of final goods and services produced within a country.

Guest workers   Foreign workers who are invited to temporarily relocate in a country to work in a certain sector of an economy.

Hedging   An activity to offset risk.

Home bias   Investors prefer domestic securities to foreign securities.

Immizerizing growth   Economic growth that results in a reduction in national economic welfare.

Importance of being unimportant   When small countries trade with big countries, the small are likely to enjoy most of the mutual gains from trade.

Imports   Goods purchased by economic agents located in one country from economic agents located in another.

Import-substitution development strategies   Policies that seek to promote rapid industrialization by erecting high barriers to foreign goods to encourage local production.

Incomplete specialization   A country is incompletely specialized in production if, after trade begins, it continues to produce some of the good it imports.

Increasing returns to scale   A technological situation in which proportionate increases in the use of productive inputs lead to greater than proportionate increases in output.

Index of openness   A measure of the importance of international trade to an economy, calculated as the ratio of exports over total domestic production.

Indifference curve   A diagram that expresses the consumption preferences of an individual consumer.

Infant industry argument   The argument holding that new industries may need temporary protection until they have mastered the production and marketing techniques necessary to be competitive in the world market.

Injury test   An investigation to determine whether an unfair foreign trade practice has caused or threatens to cause harm to a domestic industry.

Input-output table   A table that details the sales of each industry to all other industries in an economy.

Interest rate parity   The forward premium or discount is equal to the interest differential.

Internal balance   A rate of domestic economic growth consistent with a low unemployment rate.

International banking facilities (IBFs)   International banking divisions of onshore U.S. banks.

International division of labor   Specialization by nations in the production of only a few goods.

International price discrimination   Selling a product in two different countries at two different prices.

International reserves   The portion of base money used to settle international debts.

Intraindustry trade   The simultaneous import and export of similar types of products by a country.

IS **curve**   Combinations of i and Y that provide equilibrium in the goods market.

J **curve effects**   After a devaluation, the balance of trade falls for a while before increasing.

Labor (capital) abundant   A country is labor (capital) abundant relative to another country if it has more (less) workers per machine than the other country.

Labor (capital) intensive   A good is labor (capital) intensive relative to another good if its production requires more (less) labor per machine than the other good requires in its production.

Labor-saving (capital-saving) technical change   An innovation that results in a more than proportionate reduction in the use of labor (capital) relative to other factors in the production of one unit of output.

Law of one price   Similar goods sell for the same price worldwide.

Leontief paradox   The finding that U.S. exports tend to come from labor-intensive industries, while U.S. imports are produced using relatively capital-intensive techniques.

Linkage effects   Benefits to other industries or sectors of an economy that occur as one industry expands.

Liquidity balance   The basic balance plus short-term capital plus errors and omissions.

Locomotive effect   The stimulation of the large country economy aimed at increasing growth in the rest of the world.

Logrolling   The trading of votes by legislators to secure approval on issues of interest (e.g., tariffs) to each one.

London interbank offer rate (LIBOR)   The key interest rate in the Eurocurrency market.

Long position   Buying currency for future delivery.

LM **curve**   Combinations of i and Y that provide equilibrium in the money market.

Margin   A deposit with a broker required for trading in the futures market.

Marginal product of labor   The additional amount of output (in physical terms) that is produced because one more worker is added to the production process.

Mercantilism   A system of government policies and institutions aimed at increasing exports and decreasing imports.

Money illusion   A situation where individuals make decisions based on changes in some prices without taking into account changes in others.

Most favored nation (MFN) status   A country confers MFN status upon another country by agreeing not to charge tariffs on that country's goods that are any higher than those it imposes on the goods of any other country.

Multinational corporation (MNC)   A corporation that operates production or marketing facilities in more than one country.

Mundell-Fleming model   The IS–LM–BP model with flexible exchange rates and perfect capital mobility.

National demand   The amount of national consumption of a particular good at various relative prices.

National supply The amount of national output of a particular good at various relative prices for that good.

Neutral economic growth A proportionate increase in all factors and consumption so that trade expands proportionately to the growth of the economy.

Neutral technical change An innovation that results in an equiproportionate reduction in the use of all factors in the production of one unit of output.

News Unexpected information.

Nominal interest rate The rate actually observed in the market.

Nominal price A price expressed in terms of money.

Nominal value A value dependent on current price levels.

Nonsystematic risk The risk that can be eliminated with diversification.

Nontariff barriers A wide range of government policies other than tariffs designed to affect the volume or composition of a country's international trade.

Normative analysis Economic analysis that makes value judgments regarding what is or should be.

North American Free Trade Agreement (NAFTA) An FTA among Canada, Mexico, and the United States.

Official settlements balance The value of the change in short-term capital held by foreign monetary agencies and official reserve asset transactions.

Open-economy multiplier A multiplier equal to the reciprocal of the marginal propensity to save plus the marginal propensity to import.

Opportunity (or social) cost The amount of production of one type of good that must be sacrificed to produce one more unit of the other.

Optimal tariff The size of a tariff that raises the welfare of a tariff-imposing country by the greatest amount relative to free-trade welfare levels.

Outward-looking development strategies Government support for manufacturing sectors in which a country has potential comparative advantage.

Overvalued currency Currency worth more than PPP value.

Parallel market A free market allowed to coexist with the official market.

Paris Club A gathering of creditor country governments to arrange debt rescheduling.

Pass-through analysis The adjustment of domestic and foreign prices to devaluation.

Perfect capital mobility A situation in which there are no barriers to international capital flows.

Petrodollars Eurodollar deposits arising from OPEC trade surpluses.

Political gains from trade Increases in economic well-being that accrue to a country because expanded trade and economic interdependency may increase the likelihood of reduced international hostility.

Portfolio-balance approach A theory of exchange rate determination arguing that the exchange rate is a function of relative supplies of domestic and foreign bonds.

Positive analysis Analysis that studies economic behavior without making recommendations about what is or ought to be.

Predatory dumping Dumping in order to drive foreign competitors out of their market so that the market can be monopolized.

Pricing to market Adjusting export prices in response to exchange rate changes in order to limit changes in the prices paid by importers.

Primary-export-led development strategies Government programs designed to exploit natural comparative advantage by increasing production of a few export goods most closely related to a country's resource base.

Producer surplus The difference between the price paid in the market for a good and the minimum price required by an industry to produce and market that good.

Production possibility frontier (PPF) A diagram that shows the maximum amount of one type of good that can be produced in an economy, given the production of the other.

Product life cycle The process by which a product is invented and then over time becomes more standardized as consumers and producers gain familiarity with its features.

Protective effect   The amount by which domestic producers are able to expand their output because a tariff is in place.

Protrade biased growth   Growth that results in an expansion of trade that exceeds the rate of growth of GDP.

Put option   An option to sell currency.

Quota   A government-mandated limitation on either the quantity or value of trade in a product.

Quota rents   Profits that come about because a quota has artificially raised the price of imported products.

Random   Moving in an unpredictable manner.

Real interest rate   The nominal interest rate minus inflation.

Reciprocal demand   The process of international interaction of demand and supply necessary to produce an equilibrium international price.

Relative price   The ratio of two product prices.

Relative price change   The price of one good relative to another good changes.

Revenue effect   The amount of revenue accruing to a government from a tariff.

Risk aversion   The tendency of investors to prefer less risk.

Risk premium   The difference between the forward rate and the expected future spot rate.

Safeguards protection   A general name for measures such as the escape clause.

Section 301   A provision in U.S. trade law that requires the U.S. government to negotiate the elimination of foreign unfair trade practices and to retaliate against offending countries if negotiations fail.

Seigniorage   The difference between the exchange value of a money and its cost of production.

Shock   An unexpected change.

Short position   Selling currency for future delivery.

Single European Act   An act passed by the EU to remove various NTBs between the member countries.

Small, open economy   An economy that cannot affect the international price of goods or the foreign interest rate.

Specific tariff   A trade tax equal to a fixed amount of money per unit sold.

Spot market   Where currencies are traded for current delivery.

Spread   The difference between the buying and selling price of a currency.

Spurious relationship   Not a genuine relationship.

Static gains from trade   Increases in economic well-being, holding resources and technology constant, that accrue to a country engaging in international trade.

Sterilized intervention   A foreign exchange market intervention that leaves the domestic money supply unchanged.

Striking price (exercise price)   The price of currency stated in an option contract.

Subsidy   A government payment to an industry based upon the amount it engages in international trade.

Systematic risk   The risk common to all investments.

Tariff   A tax imposed by a government on either exports or imports.

Tariff escalation   Tariff rates that rise with stages of processing.

Tariff rate quotas (TRQs)   Policies that allow a certain quantity of a good into a country at low (often zero) tariff rates, but then apply higher tariffs to quantities that exceed the quota.

Terms of trade   The relative price at which trade occurs between countries.

Term structure of interest rates   The pattern of interest rates over different terms to maturity.

Trade adjustment assistance (TAA)   Payments made by the government to help factors retrain or retool after they have been displaced by foreign competition.

Trade creation   An expansion in world trade that results from the formation of a preferential trade arrangement.

Trade deficits and surpluses   A country has a trade deficit (surplus) if its imports (exports) exceed its exports (imports).

Trade diversion   A shift in the pattern of trade from low-cost world producers to higher-cost CU or FTA members.

Trade (or tariff) war A general reduction in world trade brought about by increases in trade barriers throughout the world.

Trade triangle A geometric device that tells us the amounts a country is willing to trade at a particular world price.

Unconditional most favored nation status The principle of nondiscrimination in international trade.

Uncovered interest parity The expected change in the exchange rate is equal to the interest differential.

Undervalued currency Currency worth less than PPP value.

Upstream subsidy A subsidy that lowers the cost of an input for a manufacture.

Value marginal product of labor The monetary value of the marginal product of labor.

Variance A measure of the dispersion of a variable about its mean value.

Voluntary export restraint (VER) An agreement reached between importing and exporting countries whereby the exporters agree to limit the amount they export.

Walras Law In a world with n markets, if $n-1$ are in equilibrium, so is the nth.

INDEX